FROZEN
MUSIC

W E S T E R N   I M P R I N T S
THE PRESS OF THE OREGON HISTORICAL SOCIETY

FROZEN MUSIC

A HISTORY OF PORTLAND ARCHITECTURE
gideon bosker & lena lencek

Frontis: Portland cityscape watercolor by Henk Pander.

This publication was designed and produced by Western Imprints, The Press of the Oregon Historical Society.

Library of Congress Cataloging in Publication Data

Bosker, Gideon.
    Frozen Music.

    Bibliography: p.
    Includes index.
    1. Architecture—Oregon—Portland.   2. Portland (Or.)—Buildings, structures, etc.   I. Lencek, Lena.
II. Title.
NA735.P55B6   1985   720'.9795'49   85-13911
ISBN 0-87595-164-3

The production of this volume was supported in part by funds provided by the Fred Meyer Charitable Trust, the Oregon Community Foundation's Swindells Fund and Bailey Fund, the estate of Janet M. Bailey, Oregon Arts Commission, Lloyd Corporation, Ltd., Zimmer Gunsul Frasca Partnership (who also supported in part the production of the dustjacket for this book), Cushman and Wakefield of Oregon, Coldwell Banker, and Fletcher, Finch, Farr and Ayotte.

Printed in the United States of America.

The description and concept of architecture
as
"Frozen Music"
is at least 150 years old.
On 23 March 1829,
the German author, Johann Wolfgang von Goethe
wrote to Herr Eckermann:

Ich die Baukunst eine erstarrte Musik nenne.
I call architecture frozen music.

Illustration Credits

Gideon Bosker
provided photographs taken expressly for
Frozen Music
These appear on the title page of each chapter
as well as the Foreword, Preface,
Introduction and Afterword,
and on pages: 25, 27, 29, 33, 35, 36, 43, 46, 50,
64, 69, 143, 144, 146, 147 (l&r), 148, 149,
150, 161, 162 (l&r), 163, 168, 169, 172,
176, 198, 199, 204, 292

Original illustrations from the following institutions
appear on the pages indicated:

Oregon Historical Society, Portland
   Regional Research Library
   Architectural Collections, 13, 17, 24, 49, 52, 60, 61,
   63, 65, 71, 73, 75, 82, 83, 84, 85, 201
   Photographs Library, 72, 117, 118, 119, 120, 122,
   127, 130, 136, 153 (Prentiss photo), 160, 186
Reed College, Portland, 6, 78

Syracuse University Library, Syracuse
   George Arents Collection, 8, 9, 89, 90, 93, 94, 95,
   98, 101, 102, 103, 104, 107, 110, 111
University of Oregon, Eugene
   Allied Arts and Architecture Library, 12, 14, 20, 21,
   22, 23, 32, 38, 74, 76, 80, 108 (all), 141, 142
   University Library, 5, 11, 53, 54, 55, 56, 57, 58, 139,
   155, 156, 157, 158, 164, 167

Original illustrations from the following architects,
architectural firms and associated businesses
appear on the pages indicated:

Allen, McMath and Hawkins, 189
Anshen and Allen Associates, 229
Pietro Belluschi, 15
Ray F. Becker Co., 137, 138 (Delano photo, 140
   (Delano photo)
Broome, Orindulph, O'Toole, Rudolf and Associates
   (BOOR/A), 272, 282, 283, 284
Michael Graves, 16, 247 (Bickford photo), 249
   (Bickford photo), 251 (Bickford photo)
Lawrence Halprin and Associates, 215
William J. Hawkins III, 188

Charles Luckman Associates, 233
Martin/Soderstrom/Matteson, 287, 289
Oregon Brass Works, 145, 151 (l&r), 152 (l&r), 171
Private collection, 159
Skidmore, Owening and Merrill (SOM), 213, 221, 225,
   227, 231, 235, 236, 241, 259, 303, 307
Hugh Stubbins and Associates, 299
Richard Sundeleaf, 165, 170, 174, 177
Robert L. Thompson, 296
Thompson and Vaivoda, 293, 294, 295
Morris H. Whitehouse and Associates, 48, 68
Zimmer Gunsul Frasca, 244, 268, 273, 276, 277, 298

Contents

FOREWORD: Pietro Belluschi   VIII
Photograph: Paramount (Portland) Theatre
Rapp and Rapp
1927

PREFACE   XII
Photograph: Mural
Geoff Clark
1982

INTRODUCTION   2
Photograph: Portland Armory
McCaw, Martin and White
1891

ORIGINS OF A MICROCOSM   18
Photograph: Elks Temple
Houghtaling and Dougan
1920

GETTING MODERN   86
Photograph: Federal Reserve Bank
Pietro Belluschi
1950

FILLING IN THE CRACKS   132
Photograph: Battery King
Architect unknown
1940

SPANNING HISTORY   180
Photograph: Powers Building
Architect unknown
1878

AFTER THE FALL   206
Photograph: 200 Market Building
Rudat/Boutwell and Partners
1973

POST-MODERN FACE-OFF   242
Photograph: The Portland Building
Michael Graves
1980

FASHION IN CONTEXT   260
Photograph: Justice Center
Zimmer Gunsul Frasca
1983

SEEING THE LIGHT   300
Photograph: U.S. Bancorp Tower
Skidmore, Owings and Merrill/
Pietro Belluschi (consulting)
1983

AFTERWORD: George McMath   312
Photograph: Signboard, North Portland
1984

BIBLIOGRAPHY   318

INDEX   323

FOREWORD

THIS BOOK is a most welcome addition to the architectural bibliography of our city. Based on thorough research of people, events and ideas, it is published at a time when widespread public interest in cities is most evident and when important decisions are about to be made affecting their future.

This book is important for yet another reason. An architect can never discover the value of his own work by looking at his own face in the mirror. Thus, it has been the challenge of these two authors as historians and cultural critics to uncover the character and motives of the architects who built the city on the basis of what they have done and thought.

The city is primarily a community of individuals, and each individual has a soul, so the city—and its architecture — must also have a soul. *Frozen Music* is an illuminating and provocative dissection of this soul. The reader will be stimulated to think of Portland as a living and loving community and to develop the kind of image of a city which can best meet his or her ideals of a good life. This includes not only the forms of buildings, the physical environment they create, the visual satisfaction they generate, but also the bounty of nature, its climate, the ease of movement within its boundaries, the continuity of its tradition, the congeniality of friends and the cultural fulfillment it has to offer. The book makes us feel that the city can be an unending source of pride, even a work of art, if it is free to express the life and the joys that animate it.

Often enough, we have been told that Portland is one of the most liveable cities on the continent; but the people who love it, in fact those who love it most, have some reservations. A young western city, Portland still shows the marks of its commercial beginnings and of fast industrial growth. As with all other cities, it has suffered from visual confusion, sprawl, obsolescence and congestion. Inevitably we have been tempted to compare its worst aspects with the best of the Old World's cities, where great monuments, parks, fountains and public squares were built. Undoubtedly, those elements produced a great and appealing sense of space and dignity, but those cities were the outcome of a social order which does not exist anymore, or at least does not exist in this country. The architecture of these cities represented the expression of social systems very different from our own.

Now we live in a different and much more difficult age; we still seek beauty, but we are forced to come to terms with change. We all know that the actual experience of urban living has been ambivalent at best. We love the social intercourse it affords, its choice of opportunities, the culture it can generate, the monuments and landmarks it can build; but we also hate its dark, dangerous sides, its mass disturbances, denial of nature and fostering of crime and alienation. If our attempts to imitate in America the externals of European cities have failed to give us a sense of order and convincing beauty it is because these attempts have been generally superficial. For we really have failed to solve the deep problems presented by a machine age; because it is not possible to create order by obsolete or confused thinking.

There is a strong drift in our time towards conserving the past. But I believe that our over-emphasis on preservation, so fashionable nowadays, springs from a deep sense of insecurity and of pessimism about our abilities to cope with the present. Indeed we are surrounded by many signs of incompetence, but I believe that lack of faith in the long run will annihilate our creative powers. This does not mean we should not preserve, and it is obvious that continuity gives a city its unique quality and adds to its texture, visual variety and richness. *Frozen Music* assembles these diverse architectural strands into a compelling fabric of verbal and visual images. At the same time, a city cannot be allowed to become a sterile museum. Renewal being a law of life, pride and much good sense must be our guides in keeping our city alive, beautiful and economically healthy. While the wisdom to achieve our ideals of a good life against self-serving motives, economic imperatives and the political jungle of decision-making processes has so far eluded us, this book gives us hope that we may yet be able to evolve credible symbols of our own humanity in a society grown too big and amorphous.

I am fully convinced that to foresee the future is an impossible task. If new colonies are eventually built in outer space, would we only then experience a true revolution in our image of cities and architecture? And what about contextualism and other newly coined buzzwords? Or what about the fat Doric columns that are the silly clichés of the Postmodern architects?

Changes are not produced by minor fashionable events but by strong forces—social, moral and economic—which the architect must recognize and accept, rather than control. We must hope that a new generation of architects will be concerned not so much with fashion but with the manner in which people act and live. Architecture, more than any other art, has always reflected our level of civilization, the aspirations of our citizens, and the passions and events filling the busy years of our history. I believe it should also reflect our sense of optimism in the progress of our institutions and that the future will be a better time for our children to live.

Some 37 years ago, together with Dean Sert of Harvard, I succeeded in establishing the MIT-Harvard Center for Urban Studies, the first such center in the country. Since then, it has been my privilege to have been involved as an advisor and as a participant in the planning problems of many cities. In this period, I have seen interest in cities grow to national importance, and its social implications—congestion, pollution, conservation, social stress—emerge as the central problems of our age. In the process, we have learned that beautiful architecture must spring from a deep conception of a more orderly social organization.

Beautiful architecture must include, also, the solution of all practical problems besetting and irritating us, from traffic congestion to smoke and noise, from ugly signs to car parking. Beauty, in cities as in persons, must emanate from a healthy and efficient body, not from cosmetics. The necessary work of utilizing the land, the goal of developing self-contained communities within the city, of providing schools in the proper places, decentralizing commercial centers with proper parking facilities, to providing infirmaries, amusement and play areas and all other amenities necessary for a fuller enjoyment of life, is a long and tremendous task that may seem visionary at present, but it is well to set our minds a little clearer on the direction we should follow, even if the immediate result be only that of avoiding mistakes.

While this book deals more specifically with the physical aspects of our city and with architecture as an art, I find it to be a document of great social and historic importance. It seems to me its special merit rests on the authors' decision to avoid developing their own special set of values, by which all architecture through the various periods of the city's history could be related and judged. Rather, they have chosen to explore in depth the various theories, comments, beliefs and motivations from as many sources as they could tap, in order to explain and give life to the very different and variegated aspects of the city from its birth to the present. Their decision to be responsive narrators rather than stern judges makes the reader accept, even appreciate, what at first may appear to be contradictions and ambiguities in the text; indeed, what emerges from their narrative is a civic microcosm of pervasive human interest.

In the end, the reader will discover that all buildings with a claim to architecture are in a profound sense genuine inventions, forever struggling between sky and earth, spirit and matter, logic and emotion, pure aesthetic and morality, in the end to be reminded of mother nature's own ecosystems with their marvelous underlying order where diversity becomes richness and innovation emerges as a green shoot of tradition.

Pietro Belluschi
Architect
Portland, Oregon

PREFACE

NSPIRATION for this book did not come from the blinding flash of light glancing off the internationally renowned Equitable Building, or the rosy columns of City Hall, or the exquisite cast-iron pilasters rimming the New Market Theatre. Rather, our involvement with the city's architectural landscape snuck up on us as we cruised Portland's Eastside, marveling at the neon signage, the luminous glass-block Mechano Deco shop fronts, the muscular warehouses, the stream-lined gas stations, their once modern, sleek lines jagged with rust and decay. To us—recent transplants to the Rose City—these seamy, commercial stretches of town still held a lingering flavor of the frontier, recalling that freewheeling time when the spirit of free enterprise, creative marketing, and ingenuous engineering had met the raw and savage beauty of the Pacific Northwest.

But this quintessentially American Portland marked only the first stage of an infatuation that lured us inward to the city's cosmopolitan core. Here, spanning the full gamut of historical styles, was Portland the Queen of Beaux-Arts architecture—in her cast-iron, brick, and terra cotta incarnations. Here too, was the experimental Mistress of the Contemporary, decked out in everything from the austere angularity of early modernism, to the exuberant pin-striping of the International Style, to the restrained ornamentation of Postmodernist historicism.

We discovered, in short, a city that could best be described as an intelligently curated architectural museum. In a little over a century, Portland had jelled into a magisterial modern metropolis, in which ancient spaces and futuristic skyscraper-sculptures were brought together on miniature, two hundred foot blocks. What we had first seen as a quietly exotic outpost of American civilization revealed itself as an exquisite architectural microcosm, an extraordinary tapestry in which relics of the past were fantastically interwoven with buildings that pointed the way toward the world of tomorrow.

Talking to the city's designers and planners, we caught the sense of excitement, pride and delight in Portland's complex architectural fabric. The city was in the grip of an architectural renaissance, taking the big leap into urban sophistication amid twentieth-century style. Our research began to take on a life of its own. The deeper we dug into Portland's neighborhoods and the more we spoke with the city's architects and planners, the more we pushed back the perimeter of our initial inquiry.

What, at first, seemed like isolated phenomena—the scorching controversy accompanying Michael Graves's Portland Building, for instance—eventually began to fit into a pattern, as distinctive of the city's history and temperament, as the whorls of its builders' thumbprints. A narrative began to emerge, bursting with plots, sub-plots, themes and motifs as gripping as those in any great novel. It was a story populated by ambitious and, some-times, world-class architects. Our job, it seemed, was to bring their ideas, work and ambitions back to life. The rest is *Frozen Music*.

Bringing this book to completion required the collab-oration and cooperation of many individuals and institu-tions. Our gratitude is due, first of all, to all the actors in the drama—especially the architects whose buildings grace the city's streets and whose written records, pho-tographs and renderings have found their way into vari-ous libraries throughout the country. Members of Port-land's architectural community—survivors of bygone eras and fresh young talents alike—have been most generous in discussing and enduring our questioning. Their lively perspectives and valuable insights continu-ously renewed our enthusiasm for exploring the rich collective imagination that has been at work shaping the architecture of the city.

Our special thanks go to Pietro Belluschi, Stanley Boles, Jared Carlin, Robert Frasca, William J. Haw-kins III, Bernard Heims, Wallace Kay Huntington III, Kenneth Lundgren, Millary Mackenzie, George A. McMath, David Pugh, Ronald J. Slusarenko and Richard Sundeleaf for helping shed light on past and present episodes of the city's architectural history. We should note that many of our sources have been unaware that they were adding pieces to our jigsaw puzzle and they certainly bear no responsibility for any weaknesses in judgment or interpretation in what follows.

A project of this magnitude could never have gotten under way without support from a number of different organizations and the people who administer them. Our warm appreciation goes to Carolyn Buan, managing di-rector of the Oregon Committee for the Humanities, for her enthusiasm and support through the early stages of the project, as well as to Wayne Mell and Helen Nelson for their encouragement. Kenneth Lundgren, past president of the American Institute of Architects, helped get the project off the ground and Delanne McGregor, executive secretary of the AIA, along with Julie Nelson, offered invaluable assistance in "network-ing." We are grateful to the Architecture Foundation Gallery for previewing the photographic work and for publicizing the project among the architectural com-munity. Without the financial assistance of the Oregon Arts Commission and the Oregon Community Founda-tion the project could not have been brought to com-pletion. For their part in generating the handsome poster accompanying the photographic exhibit at the Oregon Historical Center, we thank Byron Ferris of the Design Council for his striking design and the firm of Schultz/Wack/Weir, Inc. for donating printing services.

Architectural photography, we discovered, often pre-sents ticklish and unexpected problems that can require elaborate, and even hair-raising technical solutions. Getting a gargoyle's vantage point on buildings had us clambering on to fire escapes and rooftops until Coast Crane Company and McCoy Electric Company stepped in with a cherry picker and an operator to help us obtain unusual angles and perspectives on many of the city's finest landmarks. Young Kyle Austerman was our guide to the cavernous, dark and deserted ballrooms of the palatial Elks Temple, off limits to all but intrepid interlopers willing to steal into the locked building through a third-floor fire exit. Suggestions for likely photographic candidates came from nearly every Portlander who came in contact with our project. Our thanks go to them, to all our guides, formal and informal, to Lisa Marsh, James Greear, G. L. Selmeyhr, Bill Stanger and, for his research assistance, to Will Guthrey.

A research project relying so heavily on visual materials could not do without the assistance of various libraries and individuals who were kind enough to supply the renderings, photographs and sketches that have been reproduced in this book. Kenneth Duckett, director of Special Collections at the University of Oregon Library, Hilary Cummings, director of Manuscript Collections, and Jim Carmin of the Allied Arts and Architecture Library at the University of Oregon, deserve special mention for making available a large body of the renderings which appear in this volume. Layne Woolschlager and the staff of the Oregon Historical Society Research Library were unusually giving of their time and resources in obtaining rare renderings and archival materials relating to the city's architectural history, all housed in the Society's growing architecture collection.

Edward Lyon of the George Arents Research Library for Special Collections at Syracuse University graciously contributed considerable effort and expertise in making available to us materials pertaining to the work of Pietro Belluschi. For giving us access to the city's historic resource inventory, for his good humor and his readiness to track down the records of the oddly elusive designer, we thank John Neil of the Portland Planning Commission. For rounding up some extraordinary renderings, we acknowledge Becky Pollock of the Reed College Library. Special thanks also go to Arthur McArthur, director of Public Relations at Jantzen, Inc., to Lewis L. McArthur of the Ray F. Becker Company, and to Rob Driesner of the Oregon Brass Company, for sharing with us the archives of their respective companies. We are indebted to Harold Jacobs for locating a number of photographs of Art Deco storefronts built by the Oregon Brass Company. Our enthusiastic appreciation goes to Thelma Bengs, whose staggering collection of original picture postcards of Portland past and present furnished a number of fine nostalgia pieces.

We count the chance to use the splendid watercolor of Henk Pander on the cover of the book as a special privilege. Unfortunately, we have not always been able to uncover the authors of a number of admirable renderings. Since the work of these anonymous renderers has done much to amplify our thesis, we hope that these nameless artists will accept this laconic expression of our gratitude. Our special thanks also go to Robert Stark, assistant director, Museums, Oregon Historical Society and Greg Stevens for their help in setting up the "Frozen Music" exhibition in October, 1984.

We owe a particular debt to a number of architectural firms, based both in Portland and in other cities, which have taken a firm hold of the city's architectural rudder. For a great deal of assistance, ranging from providing us with original renderings of their work to offering generously of their time, we record our appreciation to the following firms and individuals: Zimmer Gunsul Frasca; Froome, Oringdulph, O'Toole and Rudolf and Associates; Allen, McMath and Hawkins; Robert Thompson; Gordon, Beard, Grimes; Skidmore, Owings and Merrill; Schuette and Wheeler; Anshen and Allen; Hugh Stubbins and Associates; Michael Graves, Architect; Lawrence Halprin; the Austin Company; Richard Sundeleaf; Willard Martin; Carter Case; Charles Luckman Associates; and Thomas Hacker.

To the architecture historians and the historians of the city who have piloted the way for our project we owe a special debt of inspiration, example and guidance. In particular, we should mention the pioneering studies of George A. McMath, Thomas Vaughan, William J. Hawkins III, Carl Abbott, E. Kimbark MacColl, Richard Marlitt and Richard Ritz who, each in his own vein, has contributed to a rich and engrossing profile of the city's political, cultural and architectural history. A similar expression of gratitude goes to Virginia Ferriday and Wallace Kay Huntington III—ground breakers in their respective areas of research—for their generous advice and encouragement.

Technical assistance was provided by: Elaine Parry, who typed the manuscript with dispatch; by Stu Levy, who offered sound advice on the use of photographic filters and film; and Miriam Seger, who printed many of the photographs which appear in the volume: and technical help was provided by the team at Pro Lab Northwest.

As is the case with every project, certain individuals provide seemingly tireless assiduity in hunting out facts, records and materials to illuminate the period under study. Certainly our enterprise could never have come to fruition without the generous help and tutelage of George A. McMath, who made himself available for almost daily consultation and direction for a period that extended more than two years. His knowledge of the city's architecture, its people, and its history, provided the foundations for much of what follows.

We owe a special debt of gratitude to Thomas Vaughan, executive director of the Oregon Historical Society, for realizing the need for this book and for his willingness to pursue a project of this scope with his characteristic intelligence and dynamism. This project would not have been possible without the scholarly contributions about architecture conceived, co-written and orchestrated by Mr. Vaughan during his illustrious tenure at the Oregon Historical Society. Along with Pietro Belluschi and George A. McMath, Mr. Vaughan read the manuscript and offered numer-

ous useful comments, suggestions and illuminating perspectives on the history of the city's architecture.

It is a special pleasure to acknowledge the contribution of Chet Orloff, assistant director, Development, Oregon Historical Society, whose catalytic interventions, genteel diplomacy and good humor nudged the project to completion. For their efficiency, care and sympathetic understanding, we are deeply grateful to the entire staff at Western Imprints, The Press of the Oregon Historical Society. Finally, for his encouragement, gentle prodding and wise guidance, our thanks to Bruce Taylor Hamilton, assistant director, Publications, at the Oregon Historical Society. Without Mr. Hamilton's editorial panache, conviction and stubborn faith, this book would not be what it is.

And—it should not go without saying—our resounding thanks to the city that inspired this labor of love.

INTRODUCTION

"Angels can do no more . . ."*

*Portland Architectural Club *Yearbook*, 1909

ARCHITECTURE has been called the beautiful necessity. "A work of architecture is made in the urging sounds of industry," declared Louis Kahn, "and when the dust settles, the pyramid, echoing Silence, gives the sun its shadow." More directly and in more dimensions than the written word or painted image, architecture travels with impunity to the heart and mind of the beast, collapsing the past and present into an intelligible, but untranslatable matrix of space and light. Buildings are the structural signposts with which culture registers its economic, aesthetic and technologic milestones. They are also power and conquest, impinging on us with more directness and force than nearly any other man-made object. While everyone is free to shut off the television set, to walk out of concerts, to boycott the latest Hollywood blockbuster, or to ignore a best-seller, no one can close his eyes to the works of architecture which define the stage of urban life.

As an art form, architecture has much that it holds in common with sculpture, but even more that it shares with music: a structure that intelligently apportions light through a three-dimensional space can radiate all the magic and passion of the perfect musical phrase. As Kahn put it, "it is the mind of the architect that is best suited to bring . . . a city into a symphonic character." Whether festooned with the fripperies of a bygone past or packaged in the stylistic containers of a more contemporary age, works of architecture are at once sculptures and monuments, stage sets and shelters, symbols and playthings. At their best, buildings can achieve a masterful synthesis of functional and spiritual imperatives. They encourage historians and critics to look at the entire range of visual and symbolic vocabularies, the sublime and banal all together, in an effort to reconstruct not only the dominant, culturally elite themes but the popular sensibilities of a period. Finally, architecture is time-pegged, circumscribed by history and rooted in fantasy and desire, which is why it moves us with such power.

In the *Architecture of Humanism*, the distinguished English critic Geoffrey Scott wrote that "space affects us and can control our spirit; and a large part of the pleasure we obtain from architecture—pleasure which seems unaccountable, or for which we do not trouble to account—springs in reality from space." To be sure, architectural compositions can stimulate the neuronal jungle, opening up one part of the brain to another, thereby unleashing a cascade of vivid memories and associations previously hidden beneath the threshold of consciousness. Spanked by the tepid breeze of a summer night, one can stand at the south rim of Portland's Pioneer Courthouse Square, and experience the vacant stillness of ancient temples—at Athens or Delphi—with their worn, mottled facades of dismembered stones and sun-bleached columns slicing into Mediterranean skies black as obsidian. A space that was once bursting with the bustle of a grand hotel, now stirs memories of semi-shambled buildings robed in the silence of advancing moss, unexhumed for centuries, left to decompose in a forgotten cove of Grecian space.

Reflecting on the theoretical relationship between form and meaning, Mies van der Rohe declared that, "Architecture is the will of an epoch translated into space." In this respect, a city's architectural output can be seen as a collection of man-made symbols that self-consciously address issues of culture and history through the seemingly abstract vehicles of space, structure and light. But architecture has to do with more than fixed silences—the juxtaposition of surface and volume against color and texture—or, what Le Corbusier called the ineffable "play of forms under light." While, to some degree, architecture encompasses all of these, it is also a cultural narrative in which forms, fragments and fabricated spaces activate personal and collective histories. This can be seen as a form of nostalgia, but it is not the easily packaged memory of whim or fashion—which tends to leave behind a ravaged field of empty gestures—but a serious commitment to defining the internal rhythm or spirit of an age. Architecture, then, represents the ongoing dialogue between traditional values and present circumstances. It is a way of keeping pace with time, reflecting it and, in the case of a "timeless" building, even overcoming it.

Experiencing architecture requires no formal training, no admission tickets, no special knowledge, no trips to art galleries. It is a source of fascination for the uninitiated and the cognoscenti alike, the one historic art form that is not only public, but a continuous work-in-progress, open 24 hours a day, 365 days a year. Providing us with symbols of permanence and a source of stability, architecture must take into account the full range of human experiences if it hopes to inspire the perceptual machinery of its users and spectators. Architects, after all, do not design their buildings in a void. The psycho-physics of human responses to architectural spaces—the feelings evoked by inflections of light, color, shadow and geometric arrangements—have been well researched and documented. "But what cannot be so readily documented," wrote Hugh Stubbins, architect for Portland's Pacwest Center, "is the overlaid emotional content of people's experience—their memories, their associations, the social or economic strata associated with different kinds of building materials, the prestige or vanity factor and the fads and fashions of the time."

The architecture of a city strives to reach a mythical point where the world that is completely fabricated by man coincides with the desires of its inhabitants. The evolution of Portland architecture, understood in its fullest sense, is the history of myriad factors which have informed its buildings over time and which have embraced nearly the entire gamut of human activities. Every building erected in the city has been the result of a

PROPOSAL FOR SCOTTISH RITE TEMPLE
Sutton and Whitney
1930

program based on economic conditions of the time, the individuals who sponsored its construction, and the aesthetic vision of those who designed it. In this sense, Portland's architectural canvas is a continuing catalogue of the symbols and aspirations of its inhabitants—their dreams, their social myths, their religious faiths and their visions of the future. Moreover, it is a history of the progress of science and technology and its application to the building arts, particularly to construction techniques and the availability of new materials. Finally, the built landscape reflects the plastic, intellectual and architectural vocabularies each generation has used as part of its expressive language.

"Architecture is the manifestation in form of the order of our experience," wrote architectural historian John Lobell. "It is a model of our consciousness, the fitting of ourselves between earth and sky, the patterns in which we relate to one another, and the physical presence of our institutions." In Portland, architecture has re-

sponded to such a variety of concerns—from philosophical to economic to purely functional—that to adequately characterize its evolution would mean writing a history of the city itself. It would mean recounting in exacting and excruciating detail, the multiplicity of political, economic and artistic forces that shaped the city's history, and showing how these factors, with the predominance first of one, then of another, have acted in concert to produce a three-dimensional urban sculpture in glass, steel and stone. It would require a critique and, perhaps, even a psychoanalysis of the creative personalities who, on the basis of a given conception of space or under the influence of a design movement, have produced acknowledged masterpieces, the formal elements of which would go on to become part of the city's permanent architectural vocabulary.

Modernistic or historicist, kitschy or lyrical, kinky or contextual, Portland's most celebrated buildings have reflected the work of architects who pursued with gusto

REED COLLEGE PLAN
Doyle, Patterson and Beach
1913

exhilarating causes and extravagant passions. Over the past century, the city's master builders—among them Justus Krumbein, Warren H. Williams, F. Manson White, Whidden and Lewis, Albert E. Doyle, Pietro Belluschi, Zimmer Gunsul Frasca, and Skidmore, Owings and Merrill—have guided Portland through a period of feverish, almost delirious expansion. Under their tutelage, Portland's urban fabric would change dramatically—not merely the hems and inseams—but its very fiber and tweed would be rewoven into one of the most impressive architectural garments any American city of its size had ever worn. These architects (or their firms) would satisfy the clamoring of the city's inhabitants for larger, more innovative buildings and a more cosmopolitan architecture.

The vigor, inventiveness, and very copiousness of their work still colors our lives today. During a visit to Portland in 1972, *New York Times* architecture critic Ada Louis Huxtable waxed poetic about a city "strong in natural beauty and turn-of-the-century civilization in the form of those fine classical buildings that come from Boston, the Athens of the East, and added Periclean splendor to the Athens of the West." In Huxtable's view, Portland "had scale, detail and a setting so breathtakingly lovely that it seemed nothing could disrupt the harmony between nature and man." To be sure, the city's finest buildings—the Portland Art Museum, the Equi-table Building and the Watzek house—were designed with the recognition that uses and symbols for buildings change over the decades, but that deeper parts of human nature remain immutable. The stage on which Portland's drama has been played out would be given special poignancy by the whirligig of time, which has led some observers to look back on this century not only with wonder and pride, but with regret for those parts of Portland's architectural heritage—particularly, its cast-iron buildings—which have been erased permanently by the wheels of "progress."

The city's tradition in urban architecture can be traced back to the smell of foundry fumes and the clang-jangle of iron ingots being stripped of their molds—in short, to the urging sounds of industry. Portland's "Venice by the Willamette," a clustering of cast-iron buildings bursting with exuberant ornamentation, sprang up along the riverfront between 1853 and 1889. After the San Francisco earthquake of 1906, which erased much of that city's cast-iron heritage, Portland would boast the largest collection of such structures west of New York City's SoHo District. Stylistically unified and packed like sardines along Front and First, the iron-fronted jewels of Justus Krumbein, Warren H. Williams and others cast a treasury of shadows along Portland's bustling, shop-lined streets. Ribbed with Roman Corinthian columns, and what might be called a muscular sense of member-ing, unbroken stretches of cast-iron buildings throbbed with the propulsive forces of a fifteenth century arcade along the city's commercial corridors.

Sadly, the directional rhythms and iron vestments of these structures would succumb to the demolition derby of the late 1940s and early 1950s, a period during which Portland architects and planners would become hostages to the automobile, and re-channel their focus from visual aesthetics to traffic engineering. In what must have seemed like an act of alchemy—or perhaps, black magic—the iron elements from many of Portland's most exquisite buildings, such as the Kamm and Ainsworth blocks, would be reincarnated as automobiles that whooshed along the city's pock-marked boulevards.

Keeping an eye on Portland's architectural development, Huxtable mused in the *New York Times* of 19 June 1970, that "some day, some American city will discover the Malthusian truth that the greater the number of automobiles, the less the city can accommodate them without destroying itself." And then, with some chagrin, added: "The remains [in Portland] are noticeable, gap-toothed with parking lots, often where other structures of the same vintage have been removed. Portland has some of the most beautifully detailed and dignified early 20th century classical revival buildings in the country, which add Roman richness to the decimated streets."

The New York critic was referring to the contributions of Portland's best and brightest designers who, by the end of the 1920s, had worked much of their magic. During the 1890s, Portland had been studded with massive, masculine Romanesque compositions by F. Manson White. His designs for the Plaza Imperial Hotel and Auditorium building combined the zestful sculptural features of Henry Hobson Richardson's Romanesque style (which helped greatly in liberating American architects from the indiscriminate aping of European revivals) with the structural cleanliness of Louis Sullivan's Chicago School. With its bold, rock-faced rustication and massive shaping, the Dekum Building would become one of the city's most elaborate examples of commercial architecture in the Richardsonian Romanesque tradition. Although direct and powerful, this style would forfeit its popularity by 1895, when Whidden and Lewis unveiled their dignified Italian Renaissance scheme for City Hall.

Between 1895 and 1928, all the prestigious European revival styles—from Italianate to Georgian to French Second Empire—were represented in the urban landscape. By 1930 the city could best be described, perhaps, as an intelligently curated architectural museum. Firms led by Doyle, Sutton and Whitney, Reid and Reid and others had colonized the city's increasingly muscular core with banks, department stores, office towers and warehouses packaged in regal fifteenth and seventeenth century envelopes. With sky-high loggias and Ionic colonnades advertising the imperial myths of ancient Rome, terra cotta palaces—such as the Yeon Building, the Public Service Building and Wells Fargo Bank Building—stood guard over the urban theater, announcing the city's architectural prowess and ambitions.

Although terra cotta would be used feverishly throughout the country by the early 1900s, it would enjoy an especially vigorous and extended lifespan in the history of Portland architecture. Modern, reflective and adaptable to utilitarian and ornamental uses, terra cotta was embraced because it was perfectly suited for maintaining architectural unity among the eclectic building designs fostered by the Beaux-Arts movement. Of equal importance, perhaps, was the ability of this glistening sheathing material to cut through the unrelieved grayness of Portland's lugubrious winter months. Glazed terra cotta was not only light and waterproof, but could be formed as desired, and, more importantly, was hospitable to virtually any pigment applied to it.

Not surprisingly, terra cotta would make a sparkling comeback. Taking his cue in 1983 from the city's architectural giants of the early twentieth century, Robert J. Frasca, chief designer for Zimmer Gunsul Frasca would look to Gladding, McBean and Company of Lincoln, California, Portland's principal supplier of terra cotta during the teens and twenties, and one of the last manufacturers of this product on the West Coast. Rediscovering the virtues of a sheathing material that had elevated some of the city's best buildings into works of art, Frasca's design team selected terra cotta as the exterior skin for the Institute for Advanced Biomedical Research (scheduled for completion in 1986). Writing in the spring 1984 issue of *Architectural Technology*, the architect explained that, "Terra cotta was chosen . . . because it has the unique quality of glowing in the typically overcast Portland light."

Claiming a sliver of the sun or, as was more often the case, getting light out of a cloud, would become de rigeur for any Portland architect who hoped to make a lasting imprint on the city's built landscape. When it came to the tonal range and inflection of the region's illumination, the city's most successful architects—from Doyle to Belluschi to Zimmer Gunsul Frasca—would always see the light, or, rather, the lack of it. Out of

PROPOSED HOTEL FOR PORTLAND
A. E. Doyle and Associate
1927

FRONT ELEVATION

OREGON STATE CAPITOL COMPETITION

OREGON STATE CAPITAL COMPETITION
A. E. Doyle and Associate
1931

necessity, their buldings were composed with the deepest respect for the city's parsimonious light content. Using marble and terra cotta, aluminum and precast concrete, these enlightened designers would be especially sensitive to the role played by the range and quality of the region's light in bringing their structures to completion. "Structure is the giver of light," Kahn once remarked. "The sun does not realize how wonderful it is until after a room is made. . . . Just think, that a man can claim a slice of the sun." In Portland, this was more easily said than done.

By 1928, the city's downtown was one massive terra cotta pavilion, in which the design genius of Portland's premier architects had shiningly materialized. As a consequence, the public had been introduced to a dazzling new architectural order that, to a great extent, attempted to mirror idealized European scenes characterized by palatial buildings, bridges, parks and open plazas.

Through technical wizardry and ornamental acrobatics, Portland's well-positioned retinue of cast-iron and "Beaux architects" had succeeded in carrying a stylistic movement, based on French decorative arts, to its fullest realization.

During the 1930s, however, the city's architecture would begin to move in an entirely new direction. Portland had limped through a blighted decade, but by the mid-1930s would begin to witness the results of economic recovery: Chrysler "Air Flow" automobiles cruising along its thoroughfares, Texaco filling stations designed by Walter Dorwin Teague, a burgeoning middle class, and a dizzying revolution in popular culture which could count "Flash Gordon" (1934) and "Superman" (1938) among its most revered icons. All this would disassemble the stable dominance of aristocratic taste which had provided a tried-and-true building vocabulary from the monumental edifice to the English cottage.

Suddenly, architecture demanded a whole new vocabulary, founded on something more relevant than the tenets of Vitruvius and Palladio.

With historic period architecture temporarily put out to pasture, the battle to establish a truly "modern" architecture in Portland could begin in earnest. Tossed in the tumult of history—or more precisely, the wreckage that was Wall Street—the city's young modernists, led by a triumvirate composed of Pietro Belluschi, John Yeon and Harry Wentz, discarded the dog-eared manuals of European "style architecture," which by this time seemed comically out-of-date. From the untidy vitality of their age, emerged a profusion of new images and spaces, some of which would seed a Northwest Regional Style in residential architecture.

Before the latent modernizing impulses of Belluschi and Yeon were given full expression, however, Art Deco and Moderne had become accepted architectural styles and were embraced by many of the country's most commercially successful architects. Ellis Lawrence, a practicing architect and dean of the University of Oregon School of Architecture, designed elaborate Art Deco storefronts and interiors for Gumbert Furriers and the Bohemian Restaurant, while architects from Atlanta, Georgia and Los Angeles, California introduced low-lying horizontal schemes for Portland's Coca-Cola and 7-Up bottling companies. As Paul Frankl noted in 1932: "The horizontal line, characteristic of our present day civilization has been taken over by the engineers. The conquest of space, will be symbolized in aesthetics through the horizontal line, the expression of speed and our time."

On streets west of Portland's Fifth Avenue terra cotta "cordillera," the scintillating zigzags and applied polychrome ornamentation of Art Deco architecture would be broadcast from apartment houses, store fronts, and fashionable office towers designed by Luther Lee Dougan, Harry Herzog, Elmer Feig and other local practitioners. In the Medical Dental Building, Jeanne Manor, and the Lafayette Apartments, applied motifs (many of them simplified versions of classical patterns) were coupled with triangles, double triangles, chevrons, fragmented circles and other geometric efflorescences. Regardless of the ornamental arrangement, the applied decoration hugged the surface of rectilinear exteriors, usually composed of brickwork arranged into tapestry patterns.

Writing in 1930, Aldous Huxley stated that, "the straight lines and jagged angles of a few years ago, have given place, wherever circumstances demand a less puritanical treatment, to undulations and curves." The evolution of Portland architecture during the 1930s confirmed Huxley's speculation. In the backwater industrial zones (such as Guild Lake, Northwest and Northeast Portland), a new stratum of Depression Modern architecture would be deposited shortly after Huxley's observation. Peppered with glass blocks and sensuous curves, the streamlined warehouses, auto showrooms and factories of Richard Sundeleaf, George Wolff and the John C. Austin Company of Cleveland, Ohio expressed the stripped-down, uncluttered ornamental programs of the machine aesthetic.

"The *Swing* is to functional design," noted an Austin Company advertisement in the October 1937 issue of *Fortune* magazine. In Portland, the pendulum had, indeed, swung in the direction of functionalism, and finally, by the late 1940s, would swing to the International Style and all its various progeny. Belluschi's Equitable Building—touted in the 1948 *Capital's Who's Who for Oregon* as an edifice that would "create for Portland one of the most modern and beautiful buildings in America"—and Yeon's Visitors Information Center were executed in the modernist vocabulary, and remain rarified and refined exemplars of the style.

In 1947, Belluschi had called himself "a compromiser . . . between the exciting ideas of new trends and the conservatism of the past." His design for the Equitable Building, a milestone in the city's architectural history, would be a triumph in technological expressionism. More exciting than conservative, it was the first building in the country to be completely sealed, the first to be air-conditioned, the first to use double-glazed windows, the first to utilize a traveling crane for window-washing, and the first to be sheathed in aluminum (which happened to be in large supply since the end of the war). Monuments in their own right, both the Equitable Building and the Visitors Information Center heralded the coming of a new age. Within two decades, however, their context-sensitive modernism would yield to the impoverished products of stylistic sterilization and architectural nudity championed by the towering giants of "Anywhere U.S.A." unistyle architecture. Beginning with the Standard Insurance Building in 1963, anonymous corporate boxes began propagating in Portland's urban renewal zones like an incurable skin disease.

Fortunately, that which would become vital by the late 1950s and 1960s—namely "Pop" and a growing infatuation with the commercial vernacular—would

PROPOSED BROADCASTING STATION FOR KGW

Hollis Johnston

1946

free architecture from the functional moralism of the International Style. As early as 1936, critic-historian Henry-Russell Hitchcock had bucked the tide by calling attention to the programmatic architecture of the 1930s. "The combination of strict functionalism and bold symbolism in the best roadside stands" wrote Hitchcock, "provides, perhaps, the most encouraging sign for the architecture of the mid-twentieth century." During the 1940s, Portland streets would be increasingly dotted with novel vernacular forms, from the bulbous Orange Blossom Jug Restaurant on Sandy Boulevard to the ennobling fluted towers of Associated Oil's "Flying A" filling stations.

America's love affair with the automobile would generate endless permutations of "symbol-architecture." Fast-food joints and filling stations became the pillars of the commercial mainstream, the shining stars of American entrepreneurship—with more converts coming each year. As ubiquitous as church spires piercing the sky, giant fluorescent ice cream cones, winged horses and illuminated sea shells became immutable fixtures of the built landscape. Like beacons, they charted our way through prototypical main drags across the land and told us where we could gather for time-tested grub and gasoline.

These were the architectural icons of the 1950s, beckoning us to stock up on food rations for growing, gawky, adolescent bodies and gasoline for "Bodies by Fisher." It was here that the spirit of mainstream America coagulated—the foothold of the rank-and-file, places where foreign enemy flags would have to fly before anyone could call the war over. Although thematic roadside compositions could not stand as "great" works of architecture, many were designed with flair and panache, and used evocative materials and symbolic forms that have since become a permanent part of our folk vernacular. As architectural historians David Gebhard and Harriette Von Breton emphasized, "The commercial vernacular of these decades has been made relevant today through its earlier transformation into contemporary sculpture and painting, and presently in its transformation into architecture."

By some quirk of fate, Portland would eventually jell into a magisterial metropolis. By 1985, the cityscape would be dotted with rare architectural specimens: a whimsical public square filled with copious historical illusions, a pink skyscraper that performed luminous metamorphoses against the region's cloud-mottled skies, and a deliciously painted polychrome building that looked like a cross between a Belgian truffle and a

NOTES: FRAMING 6×6 VERTICAL AND HORIZONTAL ⅞" V CUT SHEATHING 10" WIDE   3×4" ROOF RAFTERS ⅞" BOARDING - COVERED WITH SHINGLES

NOTES: FRAMING 4×4 - ⅞" HORIZONTAL SHEATHING LATTICE IN OPENINGS 1¼×⅞"   RAFTERS ¾" BOARDS AND SHINGLES   SEATS INSIDE

NOTES: POSTS 8"×8" WIPH BRACKETS   HORIZONTAL RAIL 3/8" V CUT SHEATHING ROOF SHINGLED ROUND CORNERS.

RUSTIC CONSTRUCTION WITH SHINGLES OR SHAKES STAINED BROWN.

SUGGESTIONS FOR A WAITING STATION
Doyle Patterson and Beach
1910

Wurlitzer jukebox. The skyline was peppered with lean and modernistic towers clad in aluminum skins, black boxes and sensuously sculpted historicist skyscrapers which recalled their Manhattan antecedents of the 1920s.

An extensive park system had blossomed within the city limits, fulfilling the expectations of John Olmsted who, in 1903, had cited Portland for being "most fortunate, in comparison with the majority of American cities, in possessing such varied . . . and interesting landscape features available to be utilized in its park system." Finally, the Skidmore/Old Town and Yamhill historic districts had been resuscitated, helping to remagnetize the urban fabric with the few works remaining from the city's grand era of cast-iron architecture.

Between 1963 and 1985, Portland had undergone a building boom that established a powerful and radically different scale to its downtown skyline. The completion of The Portland Building in 1982 helped distinguish the city as an architectural showpiece. Nabobs from around the world came to view this delectable building firsthand and, in the process of their peregrination, discovered that the city's architectural vein ran, in fact, much deeper than Graves's decorative masterpiece. Over time, Portland's own architects had become increasingly concerned about returning a spirit of cohesiveness, vitality and energy to the city's streets. In this respect, Portland's architecture had inched closer to satisfying the vision of Edward H. Bennett's Greater Portland Plan of 1912, which—although never adopted—had promoted the

"ideal [of an] *organic city* with its parts and activities closely related and well-defined but not conflicting; wisely and economically builded, not a cluster of villages, each with its own center, and with boundaries accidentally merged."

The result of all this architectural hubris was an eye-popping collage, in which ancient spaces and futuristic skyscraper-sculptures were knuckled together on miniature 200-foot blocks. In 1943, city planner Robert Moses arrived in the city, locked himself behind closed doors at the Multnomah Hotel, and emerged—$100,000 later—with a comprehensive plan, entitled "Portland Improvement." In the public edition of the "Moses Plan," published by the *Oregon Journal*, Moses pronounced that "the rectangle in the vicinity of City Hall, within which the major public buildings are found, is badly run down." But the city planner was somewhat consoling with his observation that "the buildings themselves are architecturally good and have a long and useful life before them, but the area should be cleared out and a park and genuine civic center be established there."

Portland planners and architects would make the best of Moses' prescription. By 1984, the civic center, a cluster of buildings that included the Justice Center, The Portland Building, Pacwest Center and City Hall, had the look of a handful of jewels dropped onto a cushion of gray velvet cloth. With relics of the past, such as Portland City Hall, fantastically interwoven with buildings that pointed the way toward the "World of Tomorrow,"

PROPOSAL FOR U.S. NATIONAL BANK
A. E. Doyle
1922

such as Pacwest Center, it became possible in Portland to assimilate the entire history of American architecture within the province of a short promenade and a diligent sweep of the retina. As early as 1930, John Logan had written in the *Oregonian*: "It is not generally known in our City of Portland—by all accounts the oldest and most individual city in the Northwest—that we have here in the morning's ramble or a leisurely survey from an automobile, a street drenched with pioneer associa-

tions which will please the eye and intrigue the memories of old days."

The first glimmer of Portland's future architectural prowess had come to light in 1881, when Henry Villard of the Pacific Terminal Company recruited America's most acclaimed architectural firm, McKim, Mead and White of New York City, to design and oversee construction of the Portland Hotel. Unwittingly, Villard had kindled a white-hot tradition of new architectural ideas that, over the next century, would enrich the city with buildings, parks, fountains and plazas reflecting the most enlightened architectural thinking of the times. Although subsequent Portland buildings were primarily the work of local architects (many of whom arrived and, then, remained in the city in order to advance their budding careers), Portland's architectural fabric was also significantly shaped by renowned outsiders such as Cass Gilbert, Benjamin Wistar Morris III, Lawrence Halprin, Michael Graves and Hugh Stubbins. As might be expected, colonization by foreigners produced its share of disasters.

Through a gradual accretion of architectural strata, the city would mature into a full-fledged architectural microcosm. Although these strata usually took the form of concrete additions (buildings, parks, et cetera) to the urban fabric, of equal importance were conceptual "blueprints," which exerted a powerful impact on the cityscape through design guidelines (and competitions), preservation ordinances, zoning laws and urban master plans.

To a great extent then, the built landscape crystallized under pressure from alternating cycles of selective *receptivity* and *resistance* to the contributions—direct and indirect—of outside architects. In fact, one of the city's most pivotal buildings would even bear the traces of a distant and invisible architect-critic of international stature. In 1931, the firm of A. E. Doyle and Associate, led by Belluschi, had been charged with the mission of designing the Ayer Wing of the Portland Art Museum.

Belluschi, who had "innocent dreams of a thoroughly functional building where spaces would be related in an organic way," met stiff resistance from the trustee in charge of the museum project, who expressed an irrepressible infatuation with the Georgian style that had been used for the Fogg Museum in Cambridge, Massachusetts. "Georgian was so beautiful—why not use it?" the client told the disbelieving architect. "Kicked between the fashion and dead tradition," as Belluschi put it,

PROPOSED ADDITION TO THE PORTLAND HOTEL
Doyle and Patterson
1914

he countered that "the Georgian style was beautiful only as a truthful expression of the habits, tastes, and knowledge of certain people at their particular age and place."

So on 2 July 1931, seeking support for his iconoclastic design—which in its final form had pared away the extraneous details from a Georgian facade—the renegade architect wrote to Frank Lloyd Wright, America's towering architectural genius. Including a sketch of the proposed museum in his communique, Belluschi praised

Wright in his letter for "sounding an intellectual awakening throughout the world," and added, perhaps somewhat frustrated by the tide of events in Portland, that "our great public needs to have the trumpets blown into their ears."

Although far removed from the controversy brewing over the design for the Ayer Wing, Wright returned Belluschi's sketch with a detailed critique penned in his own hand, and encouraged the architect's commitment

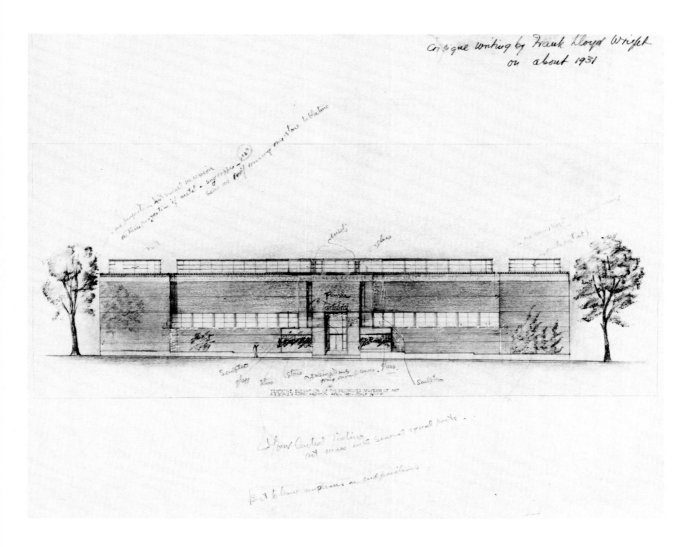

PORTLAND ART MUSEUM, AYER WING
A. E. Doyle and Associate, with critique by Frank Lloyd Wright

1931

to ease Portland out of its dependency on historical forms. "My dear Belluschi," wrote Wright. "Your client is making a serious mistake looking toward the future. Only a vanishing present looks upon a 'Georgian' outside as tolerable now." And then Wright added, in a tone every bit as powerful and persuasive as the notes that spewed out of Louis Armstrong's horn: "His Georgian design will only mark him as reactionary in an era when light was breaking all over the world. . . . I think your exterior would mark an advance in culture for Portland. Can't Doyle and Crowell stand up for Architecture?" Doyle, who had died three years earlier was in no condition to take a stand, but Belluschi's perseverance sufficed

to carry the contemporary scheme over the finish line. In 1940, Hitchcock would call the Portland Art Museum one of "the best works of semi-modern character in the country," adding that it had "no rival as regards its exterior."

Despite its sophisticated European sensibilities, its sublime regionalist aesthetic, and its scattering of brilliant imports, the city's architectural history was not without its dark chapters. In 1970, Huxtable would lament the "bomb-site look of downtown parking lots destroying the cohesive character of the city as decisively as a charge of dynamite." The critic went on to lambast Portland's "shiny scaleless, Chamber-of-Commerce im-

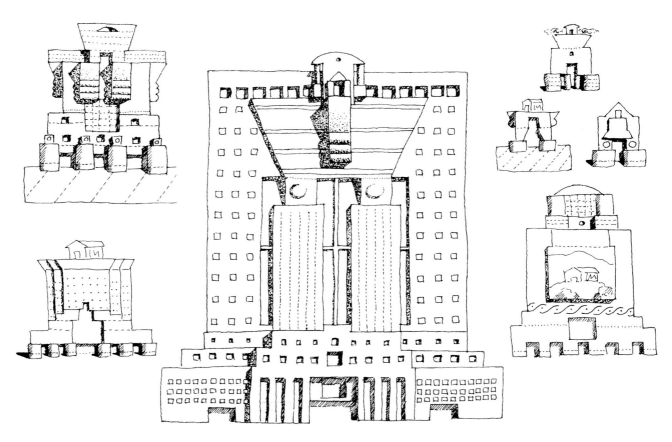

PRELIMINARY STUDIES FOR THE PORTLAND BUILDING
Michael Graves
1980

age, and [its] better-than-average assortment of Any-where, u.s.a., products of the large, national, big-city architectural firms, with their interchangeable towers and plazas multiplying a slick, redundant formula."

In retrospect, Huxtable's analysis was visionary. By the mid-1970s, the International style—with its uniform aesthetic of the pristine volumetric box skinned with ribbon windows—had lost much of its glamour. In short, architecture found itself in the midst of an identity crisis. With the Modern movement temporarily in-terred, the city's two mega-firms—Skidmore, Owings and Merrill and Zimmer Gunsul Frasca—scrambled for position. In Portland, and elsewhere, the schism-riddled profession was groping fitfully for new horizons, new formulae and a new direction.

In the early 1980s, the T square would shift dramati-cally and the city's architecture would be well on its way toward revitalization. Portland was on the rise, and a

new generation of local architects would come into their own. Among others, Robert J. Frasca, Stanley Boles and Willard T. Martin would infuse new life into the creative aspects of architectural design; an emphasis on "making place" in Portland's urban environment dominated their work. Through intensive questioning of the modern movement and its easily achieved debasement, this reti-nue attempted to steer an authentic course between the stringency of extraordinary concrete monoliths designed by Skidmore, Owings and Merrill, and the "confec-tionary" architecture—or what some had called, the "consolatory" kitsch—of certain architects of the Post-modern school. Naturally, there were growing pains. Engulfed by the eddying currents of opposing architec-tural ideologies, Portland would have been a logical loca-tion for shooting Michael Cimino's remake of *The Foun-tainhead*, a movie based on Ayn Rand's allegorical potboiler about an indefatigable architect who never

PROPOSED CITY, COUNTY AND STATE OFFICE
Tourtellotte and Hummel
1933

wavers in his unending struggle to erect an invincible citadel of modern architecture.

The Portland of 1970, according to Huxtable, "consisted largely of towers, bunkers and bomb sites," emerged little more than a decade later as the beneficiary of a movement based upon the "enlightened" repackaging of ancient forms, both in preservation projects and new structures. During a visit to Portland in 1979, *New York Times* architectural critic Paul Goldberger had opined that new edifices designed for the city's urban core "should be more consistent with what already is there." With praise for the city's terra cotta district, Goldberger recommended designs that "projected a hint of classicism," adding that "Meier and Frank and other [buildings] nearby are crucial to the city. They make for a white architecture that blends with the city." Consistency with the past was Goldberger's message.

With its unique stylistic, ornamental and spatial coordinates, Portland, perhaps more than any other American city, would be receptive to the latest theories being bandied about in fashionable academic circles. Historicism, contextualism, pluralism and what Charles Jencks had called, "Post-Modern Classicism," were stoking the imaginations of America's—and Portland's—architectural elite. "The principle of collage is the central principle of all art in the twentieth century in all media," an extremely confident Donald Barthelme told the *New York Times* in 1970. And in the 1980s, Portland buildings—awash in connotation and denotation—would give credence to the novelist's speculation. The city's best and brightest architects self-consciously would juxtapose elements from diverse genres and styles, and democratically affirm that—as long as the functional program encouraged it—anything could be spliced to anything else.

For Portland, the emergence of an architectural movement based on historicism and eclecticism could not have happened at a better time. Taken as an architectonic whole, the city's multi-layered foundation was ideally suited to furnish the design generators, the structural crystals and historical inspiration for a new, Portland-based architectural movement. The Justice Center, the Performing Arts Center, the Institute for Advanced Biomedical Research and other Portland edifices would be conceived more and more according to schemes that revealed a developing repertoire of spatial and ornamental strategies that, for contextural reasons, extended the city's existing language of classicism to current techniques, materials, functions and aesthetic sensibilities. Put another way, Portland's Postmodern vision was one that knew—and therefore, could renew—what Doyle called, "the old that was good."

ORIGINS OF A MICROCOSM

THE VITAL luminosity that has characterized Portland architecture during the past century can be traced to human sources at the end of the nineteenth century. Henry Villard of Northern Pacific Railroad Company sparked Portland's glowing architectural tradition in 1881, when he commissioned New York's most prestigious architectural firm, McKim, Mead and White, to design and oversee the construction of the Portland Hotel. The subsequent trajectory of Portland architecture in the twentieth century would be fueled by an inbred retinue of architectural luminaries, originating with William M. Whidden who had been dispatched to Portland by the McKim firm to preside over Villard's project. Almost without exception, Portland's finest

PROPOSAL FOR U.S. NATIONAL BANK TOWER
A. E. Doyle
1922

architects, at some point in their career, would cross paths with the earlier torchbearers of the city's rich architectural heritage which, in addition to Whidden and his partner Ion Lewis, would also include Albert E. Doyle, Frederick A. Fritsch and Pietro Belluschi. Fortunately, the sparkle and wicked intelligence of their vision continue to radiate from a number of "timeless" buildings still standing today, most notably, Portland City Hall (1895, Whidden and Lewis), the U.S. National Bank (1917, A. E. Doyle), the Masonic Temple (1924, Sutton, Whitney, Aandahl and Fritsch), and the Equitable (Commonwealth) Building (1948, Belluschi).

The roots of the ramose family tree that would bear some of Portland's most eminent "master builders" reach back some 3,000 miles east to the Massachusetts Institute of Technology (MIT) where Whidden and Lewis, college friends from the Boston area, received their architectural training in the late 1870s. Bright, enthusiastic and exceptionally talented, Whidden and Lewis were the first in Portland's distinguished legacy of architectural firms practicing in the Beaux-Arts tradition. With such buildings as Portland City Hall, the Hamilton Building (1893) and the Multnomah County Courthouse (1909–13), to mention only a few, their partnership would introduce lasting examples of the fashionable Renaissance revival styles that had emerged as distinctive signatures of "modern" East Coast metropolises in the late nineteenth century. Between 1889 and 1915, Whidden and Lewis would begin the process of transforming Portland's architectural landscape into a microcosmic replica of larger, cosmopolitan cities such as New York and Boston. There, the architectural landscape had already been colonized with the Romanesque and High Renaissance styles so enthusiastically promulgated by America's most acclaimed practitioners of the late nineteenth century.

The history of Portland architecture would convincingly demonstrate that Whidden, Lewis and, later, their apprentice Albert E. Doyle could compete most successfully with European architects in the fashionable revival styles. Trained in many cases, for reasons of American cultural snobbery, at the Beaux-Arts schools in Paris, American architects such as Whidden and Lewis would eclipse even their European masters in the inventiveness with which they decked out government buildings, office towers and hotels with Florentine Renaissance detail. Portland's best architects often accomplished these transformations with astonishing facility. Architectural critic, Ada Louise Huxtable, acknowl-

PORTLAND CITY HALL
Whidden and Lewis
1892

edged this exuberant local tradition in the *New York Times* on 19 June 1970, when she wrote: "Portland . . . has some of the most beautifully detailed and dignified early 20th century classical revival buildings in the country."

Schooled in the classical tradition of the Beaux-Arts, Whidden and Lewis launched their professional careers on the East Coast. After completing his training at the École des Beaux Arts in Paris, Whidden settled temporarily in New York, where he joined McKim, Mead and White, one of the country's most touted architectural firms. Lewis, one year Whidden's junior, would practice with the prominent Boston firm of Peabody and Stearns until 1882, when he formed a partnership with Henry Paston Clark. During their collaboration, Clark and Lewis developed a reputation as skilled practitioners in the influential Shingle style that had been pioneered by Henry Hobson Richardson and further elaborated by McKim, Mead and White.

Given the sterling professional alliances Whidden and Lewis had forged on the East Coast, it would have appeared unlikely that either architect would have left his budding career to launch a new practice in a city that, in the 1880s, offered little in the way of the urban sophistication and cultural amenities of fin de siècle New York or Boston. And, seen from the vantage point of their Portland contemporaries, it seemed even less likely that the new, increasingly cosmopolitan city of Portland would spring from the desolate eyesore in the center of town that, between 1883 and 1888, carried the unpromising name of "Villard's Ruins." Yet the story of Whidden and Lewis's arrival in Portland reads like a latter-day version of the ancient tale of the fortunate fall. The fall in question was the collapse of Henry Villard's financial empire.

Early in the 1880s, with completion of the Northern Pacific Railroad imminent, Portland's Henry Villard

21

PORTLAND HOTEL
Whidden and Lewis
1889

commissioned the firm of McKim, Mead and White to prepare designs for hotels and railroad stations in Portland and Tacoma. Charles Follen McKim arrived in Portland in 1882 to oversee the architectural development of these projects. McKim returned to New York leaving Whidden to supervise construction of the magisterial Queen Anne style Portland Hotel which, until its demolition in 1950, occupied the entire block that is now the site of Pioneer Courthouse Square. But no sooner had the hotel's stone foundations reached the first story, than Villard's fortunes plummeted. Construction finally ground to a complete halt in late 1883, and the young Whidden returned to Boston and formed a partnership of his own with William E. Chamberlin, another MIT

schoolmate and fellow draftsman at the McKim, Mead and White office.

The gray, basalt foundation stood abandoned for nearly five years before a group of Portland pillars, including Henry Corbett, William Ladd, Henry Failing and H. L. Pittock decided to resuscitate the project. Perhaps, the rescue was motivated not only by their interest in building a first-class hotel, but by the desire to put an end to the embarrassing and grisly events that had transpired on Villard's ill-fated building site. In 1888, the second of two murdered bodies was discovered on the vacant lot. The first had been a tramp whose mutilated corpse was found near the six-foot-high foundation. The second was a prostitute, whose throat had been slashed

PORTLAND PUBLIC LIBRARY
Whidden and Lewis
1891

from ear to ear. Clearly, the time had come to bring Villard's dream to fruition.

But Whidden's permanent return to the Pacific Northwest might never have transpired, had it not been for another fortunate coincidence signalled by the Villard setback. (For one, Whidden had married a granddaughter of Dr. John McLaughlin—former chief factor for the Hudson's Bay Company before returning east in 1883.) In 1888, the syndicate of Portland civic leaders who had purchased "Villard's Ruins" approached the McKim partnership to complete the Portland Hotel project. Not surprisingly, McKim's firm declined the offer, but prevailed on Whidden to bring the work to completion. Whidden, who under the auspices of McKim, Mead and White, had been with the project at its inception in 1882, accepted the commission, and returned to Portland in 1889.

That year, several months before the hotel's formal opening on 7 April 1890, Lewis visited his Portland

friend. Enchanted with what he found, he assented to Whidden's proposal that the two form a partnership. The firm of Whidden and Lewis was launched in 1889 and, in the process, the city acquired a design team that would dominate its architectural landscape for the succeeding two decades. During his collaboration with Clark, Lewis had gained proficiency in the Shingle style, but in partnership with Whidden, the architect would design primarily commercial and public buildings celebrating "Renaissance Revival" styles then in vogue. Interestingly, the Shingle style nearly disappeared from Lewis's repertoire of Portland commissions. The partnership nevertheless proved to be a cradle for subsequent Portland architects—most notable among them, Albert E. Doyle—who would refer to the Shingle style as their point of departure for developing an indigenous residential design tradition, which eventually crystallized as the Northwest Regional style.

A plethora of large public structures and private

23

BANK OF CALIFORNIA
A. E. Doyle
1924

buildings, representing the full gamut of "period styles," began to punctuate the city's downtown core. Their initial designs proved to be some of the most elegant the firm would produce, and reflected the distinct influence of McKim, Mead and White's Renaissance Revival style. Taking their cue from architectural trends in New York and Boston, Whidden and Lewis adopted the classical idiom for some of their earliest large-scale commissions—the Portland Public Library (1891), the Hamilton Building (1893) and City Hall (1895). Constructed on the site currently occupied by the Bank of California, the Portland Public Library (razed in 1913), was a particularly faithful rendition (on a very much smaller scale) of McKim, Mead and White's design for the Boston Public Library (1887).

One of the state's earliest steel-frame skeleton structures, Portland City Hall was a handsome, sparkling jewel adorned with understated and well-integrated ornamentation. More than any other structure completed during the Whidden and Lewis dynasty, the four-story building—with paired Tuscan columns, dentil moldings and keystones—reflected the architects' mastery over detail, proportion and mass. Writing in *A Century of Portland Architecture*, architectural historian and preservationist George A. McMath and executive director of the Oregon Historical Society Thomas Vaughan, captured the building's imposing elegance when they observed: "One sees in the detailing the influence of Italian mannerist architecture of the sixteenth century, particularly in the forceful rusticated columns embellishing the Fifth Avenue entrance. Several marble circular insets on the top story are as much mannerist as the beautiful cornices, balustrades, and finials are High Renaissance." The interior columns were sheathed with scagliola (imitation marble), while the lobby detailing included oak woodwork and marble floors.

As late as 1969, however, the splendid edifice still had not entirely come into its own. "This public building,

PORTLAND CITY HALL
Whidden and Lewis
1895

which in some ways was daring for its time," wrote McMath and Vaughan, "is of a superior, although currently unfashionable, style and design." But things changed dramatically over the next 15 years. The budding historicist impulse during the 1970s helped catapult the Whidden and Lewis magnum opus into a more fashionable light. The building's seductive pink and gray color scheme, its gently mannered inflections and geometric purity would be "in vogue" once again. And by 1984, additional "contextualizing" forces would be at work. The erection of a Bauhaus-inspired skyscraper—the Pacwest Center—on the block adjacent to City Hall virtually guaranteed that the superior qualities of the city's most prestigious public building would never again slip into obscurity. With Pacwest Center's shimmering black-and-silver skin as a backdrop, Whidden and Lewis's Renaissance Revival composition was cast into exquisitely sharp relief. Viewed from the graceful Fourth Avenue façade, the high-mannerism of City Hall and the high-tech of Pacwest played off each other, resulting in a dazzling juxtaposition of classical and ultra-modern morphologies.

Although the combination may have been one small step backward for stylistic "continuity," it was one giant leap forward for architectural counterpoint. That one of Portland's most cherished buildings could still be a source of inspiration after almost a century was confirmed by Boston architect Hugh Stubbins who, along with local supervising architects from the Portland office of Skidmore, Owings and Merrill (SOM), had seen the Pacwest Center to completion. As the building's principal designer, Stubbins molded the Fifth Avenue ground-level facade of Pacwest so it would respond to the Whidden and Lewis building in a very deliberate manner. At street level, two shallow "wings" of the Pacwest Center were connected by a sweeping, horseshoe-shaped facade of aluminum and glass crowned with six ornamental gablets. This solitary, two-toed "paw" gently embraced—and gave the impression of mirroring—the north and south wings of City Hall across the street. The final result was a glorious melding of the old with the new.

Although, in many respects, City Hall would become Whidden and Lewis's Portland showpiece, the Concord Building (1891) was their first significant commercial structure. Less bound to precedent and more innovative than other Portland buildings in its genre, the Concord Building emanated simplicity and strength, two hallmarks of the Romanesque style developed by Boston architect Henry Hobson Richardson and his assistant, Charles Follen McKim.

A pioneer of the multi-storied office block, Richardson designed in a style reminiscent of the Romanesque, without being imitative. He used massively modelled stone walling and semi-circular arcades to produce robust geometrical compositions whose sincerity did much to free American building from the trivialities of antiquarian fashions. "He was responsible for one building, the Marshall Field store in Chicago, completed in 1887," wrote the British critic J. M. Richards, "which served more than any other building of its time as a reminder that good architecture springs directly from honest construction."

And while the Concord Building was certainly not the Marshall Field store, it was, nevertheless, a progressive local departure from the ornate Victorian structures preceding it. With this bold building of variegated Japanese brick and buff sandstone trim, Whidden and Lewis demonstrated an experimental vision that would illuminate much of their later commercial work. The arches, pronounced rustication and plain surfaces emblematic of Richardson's Romanesque style seemed as if they had been married effortlessly to classical motifs that would spice the majority of later commissions.

Whidden and Lewis's bold departure from the canonical quality of the Richardsonian Romanesque style—which was, at the time, very fashionable for commercial structures—was for Portland an architectural milestone. And while their intermingling of Renaissance Revival and Romanesque elements was accomplished with the utmost subtlety and understatement, the effect was visionary. Except for a brief period following the construction of the Concord Building, Portland's commercial buildings would eventually break ranks with the prevailing taste in the Richardsonian Romanesque. Compared with the medieval solidity of the New Market Annex (1889), Oregon's first example of high Richardsonian Romanesque, the light Renaissance Revival touch of Whidden and Lewis's Hamilton Building offered the latest in contemporary design. The lucid simplicity of the rectilinear windows, the purity of the stone capitals and the smooth expanse of the brick facing projected a novel sense of forward-looking urbanity. Not surprisingly, the image-conscious business community was quick to embrace this style as the hallmark of a progressive commercial image. That the Concord Building had been ahead of its time was underscored by McMath and Vaughan who commented that, "In the late 1940s, when most of the original buildings were still standing on lower Stark Street, few people realized that the Concord Building at s.w. Second was only a few years younger than the 'Florentine Palaces' surrounding it. Its entirely different design and freshness of style gave it a much later appearance."

Whidden and Lewis's pioneering spirit in architectural design would come to the fore in the Hamilton Building (1893). Restored to its full splendor in 1977, the Hamilton Building was, in its time, the city's most "modern" and forward-looking office building. Its composition and structural design foreshadowed the dissemination of Louis Sullivan's Chicago-style to Portland over the next two decades. The building's rust-brown facade of pressed brick (made in Japan), Ionic capitals with

HAMILTON BUILDING
Whidden and Lewis
1903

freestanding columns of pink, gray and black granite at the ground floor, and window surrounds with lacy, unglazed terra cotta cable moldings were a tour de force, both stylistically and with respect to their execution.

Although the building's decorative elements were consistent with a Second Renaissance Revival style, the facade was composed of a number of layers, expressing a

skeletal construction new to the West Coast in 1893. "In appearance and general stylistic conception," wrote McMath and Vaughan, "the six-story brick-faced, cast-iron post structure was twenty years ahead of its time. One need only compare it to its northern neighbor completed two years earlier in the 'Romanesque' style— The Dekum."

To be sure, architects around the world, especially in fin de siècle Vienna, were in the process of liberating themselves from the shackles of futile ornamentation. In a number of Portland buildings, Whidden and Lewis—though educated in the Beaux-Arts tradition—championed this modernizing trend. Their design for the Hamilton Building, the first Failing Building (1900), and the retail office building at 804 s.w. Third Avenue (1911) that was once the site of Cordray's Musee and Theater, suggested that Whidden and Lewis were preparing the ground for a freer outlook. As with the "unknown" architect of the Olds and King store (now, the Exchange Building), completed in 1903 and purportedly the first steel-framed building in Portland, the visionary duo from Boston turned their attention to the establishment of new values based on, among other things, the discipline imposed by new structural techniques.

In their Corbett Building (1911), sandstone and tan brick sheathed a steel frame, and spacious Chicago-style windows occupied most of the facade, filling the space between brick-faced columns. Spare, but for the discreet historical detailing along the cornice, the Corbett Building represented Whidden and Lewis's compromise with the ornamented steel-frame functionalism of the Sullivanesque design trend. Beyond the reaches of this pragmatically generated domestic style, Whidden and Lewis's Beaux-Arts training would not permit them to venture.

As early as 1893, Whidden and Lewis had already shown their appreciation for the regular rhythm that properly belonged to frame buildings. And in 1895, their design for Portland's dignified City Hall would incorporate one of the state's earliest steel-frame skeleton structures. Their later commercial projects—the Stevens (1914), Corbett (1907), and Wilcox (1911) buildings—expressed their construction in a still more forthright manner, filling openings between the structural framework with large windows. Though masters of ornamental detailing, Whidden and Lewis shared the budding "modernistic" impulses revealed by F. Manson White in the Sherlock Building (1894) and D. C. Lewis in the Railway Exchange (Oregon Pioneer) Building (1910).

Few buildings erected in the early 1890s combined the decorative precision of the Second Renaissance Revival and the graceful arches of the Romanesque traditions with as much panache as the Gilbert (Jacobs) Building (1893). Sadly, credit for its exquisite design is, to this day, still shrouded in mystery; but on the basis of its detailings, delicate quoining, and the absence of stone capitals at the base, architectural historian Marion D. Ross has attributed this masterful composition to the Whidden and Lewis firm. The prominent Romanesque arches, however, are not entirely characteristic of Whidden and Lewis's work and, at least, suggest the possibility of yet another author—F. Manson White. The detailing of the Romanesque arches are strongly evocative of White's imposing designs for the Auditorium Building (1895) and the Plaza (Imperial) Hotel (1894), two of the city's sterling examples in the Richardsonian Romanesque tradition.

The Gilbert Building's yellow-brick facade was one of the city's most sensitively ornamented. The decorative brickwork at the arches and spandrels, the terra cotta parapet coping and window sills, and corbeled arcade cornice are the most prominent features of this elegantly synthesized, well-balanced structure. If the Gilbert Building was, indeed, the work of Whidden and Lewis, it would have represented, along with the Hamilton Building, an important transition design between the Concord Building of 1891 and the Second Renaissance flowering signified by Portland City Hall in 1895.

The Concord, Hamilton, and first Failing buildings, as well as City Hall, made clear that Whidden and Lewis had become the undisputed titans of Portland architecture. In each structure they revealed a vision that was original, experimental and expressive. Moreover, they introduced a body of innovative buildings that, much like Portland's crop of Postmodern edifices erected in the 1980s, reflected a penchant for *synthesizing* time-honored forms of the classical past with the structural capabilities of the time. In this respect, they had no peers among Portland architects practicing in the 1890s.

While Whidden and Lewis were "breaking down walls," other designers toed a more conservative line. During this period, a handful of outstanding buildings in the Richardsonian Romanesque style were built in the city, many of which, fortunately are still standing today. The Dekum Building (1892, McCaw, Martin and White) was, perhaps, the most indigenous contribution to Portland's remarkable collection of Richardsonian structures. Built for a cost of $300,000, "The Dekum" featured rough-cut Oregon sandstone on the first three floors, local pressed brick with floral terra cotta detailing on the top five floors, squat bulbous columns separating windows on the principal facades and a machiolated parapet. At Frank Dekum's request, the building was constructed exclusively with Oregon materials. In 1964 it underwent extensive restoration. Bold carvings on the sandstone reliefs, especially the leafy foliage motif on the Third

GILBERT BUILDING
Attributed to Whidden and Lewis
1893

Street entrance, were among the building's most distinctive features.

Portland's Romanesque flowering continued with the Haseltine Building (1893), the Plaza (Imperial) Hotel (1894, F. Manson White), the Ancient Order of United Workmen Temple (1892, Justus Krumbein), the Sherlock Building (1894, F. Manson White), the Auditorium Building (1895, F. Manson White) and the College (Goodnough) Building (1892, William R. Stokes). Between 1890 and 1895, Portland's commercial core was rapidly colonized with Romanesque structures, which varied considerably in the quality of their construction, ornamental detailing and composition.

Among designers who contributed to the Richardsonian tradition, perhaps none showed more finesse than F. Manson White. His design for the Auditorium Building—which combined Romanesque elements of the Richardson "school," with the compositional and structural elegance of Chicago's Sullivan style—featured a tightly knit, pressed red brick facade, carved stone capitals and terra cotta ornamentation on friezes below the roof cornice, spandrel panels and pilaster capitals. Emil Jorgenson, the original owner of the Auditorium and Music Hall, served as director of the Lewis and Clark Exposition in 1905.

With respect to lightness, quality of materials and execution, the Plaza (Imperial) Hotel, also designed by White, shared many features with the Auditorium Building. Another magisterial melding of the Sullivanesque and Richardsonian Romanesque styles, the Plaza Hotel featured richly pigmented red brick walls with a rock-faced ashlar line on the second floor corner bays. Decorative elements along the frieze and capitals suggested an increasing preoccupation with elaboration of ornamental detailing that characterized the Renaissance Revival styles introduced by Whidden and Lewis at the turn of the century.

Despite its popularity, the reign of Romanesque Revival in commercial design would be broken in 1895. While the style was not instantly abandoned, its application would shift from commercial to residential, religious and educational structures. The First Baptist Church (1892–94), designed by Minneapolis architect Warren G. Hayes, rounded out the repertoire of Richardsonian Romanesque structures in the downtown core. Along with West Hall at the University of Portland (1891, McCaw and Martin), the First Baptist Church offered considerable historical interest by introducing the "purest" local imitations of Richardson's designs. Using Rocky Butte stone at the basement and rock-faced ashlar stone from the Pittsburgh quarry in Washington, the First Baptist Church was a bold, impressive contribution to Portland's expanding list of Romanesque architecture. Hayes' design for the First Baptist Church—which included polished granite columns, leafy carved decoration, stepped-end gable walls and striking round arches with stone voussoirs—was based on Richardson's monumental Trinity Church in Boston.

West Hall was a modified version of Richardson's moody Sever Hall at Harvard University. An imposing, sensitively composed edifice with a bold-arched entrance, rounded bays topped with conical roofs and rough-cut stone foundation, West Hall lent considerable prestige to Portland's developing college campus. McCaw, Martin and White's talent for generating designs in the Richardsonian tradition was matched only by their unique talent for working with regional materials. Their First Presbyterian Church (1890), a high Victorian interpretation of English Gothic, featured magnificent bichrome exterior walls of black basalt (from Mt. St. Helens) and sandstone (from Bellingham Bay, Washington), which was rock-faced and laid with red mortar. The Armory Building (1891) continued the firm's uninterrupted line of massive structures. Its brick exterior was forced into submission by a thick coat of white paint in the 1970s, but the well-proportioned pentagonal tower, crenelated turrets arising from corbeled corners and compounded-arch entrance reflected the firm's commitment to compositional excellence.

That so many buildings designed by McCaw, Martin and White (the three collaborated on the Dekum Building before White formed his own firm) are still standing today, testifies to the richness and authenticity of their vision. Although these three architects generated Portland's most inspired body of work in the Romanesque tradition, their architectural influence declined precipitously after 1894. However successful and well-liked the designs for the Plaza (Imperial) Hotel and the Dekum, Sherlock and Auditorium buildings had been by 1895, the Richardsonian Romanesque style no longer held the appeal it once had for local businessmen. McCaw, Martin and White, the premier local practitioners in the Romanesque Revival vein, would have to defer to Whidden and Lewis's mounting popularity as the purveyors of the new "prestige" idiom for major public buildings.

Although the Romanesque style had gone out of vogue, Martin, who was much younger than the firm's senior partner, McCaw, would continue to generate fine designs in the Renaissance Revival style. Of curious interest was his design for the Masonic Temple (now Pythian Building) built in 1907, a Baroque-influenced structure which, perhaps, could be considered this architect's "swan song." The five-story building (presently occupied by the Knights of Pythias) was faced with tan brick and included quoins and voussoirs around the windows. Cast stone medallions, grilles and pedimented windowheads completed Martin's elaborate decorative scheme. A radical departure from his previous collaboration with McCaw and White, the Masonic Temple—while it could not compete with Whidden and Lewis's contributions in the Revival styles—represented an impressive and valiant attempt by the architect to keep pace with rapidly changing design sensibilities within architectural circles.

Impressed by the freshness of Whidden and Lewis's style and the connotation of "modernity" their prestigious Renaissance Revival style betokened, the leaders of Portland's business and social community—Ralph and Isaac Jacobs, Henry Corbett, and Henry Failing, among others—flocked to patronize the architectural "newcomers." The full measure of the city's esteem for the firm's work was expressed in 1903, when Ion Lewis was appointed director of architecture for the Lewis and Clark Centennial Exposition.

By this time Whidden and Lewis had already furnished ample evidence of their expertise in the full repertoire of Renaissance and Classical Revival designs. Among their most accomplished works in this vein were the Portland Library (1891), the Hamilton Building (1893), the old Arlington Club (1891, razed ca. 1909), the Portland Academy (1895) and the Meier and Frank store (1897–98, razed in 1915). Their free-ranging eclecticism had also yielded a number of noteworthy residential designs. The Scottish Baronial-cum-Revival-Romanesque scheme for the K. A. J. MacKenzie residence (1892) lent further support to the architects' qualifications to create an exuberantly symbolic and dramatic setting for the centennial exposition.

As the architectural planners of this momentous civic celebration, Whidden and Lewis were charged with defining the architectural theme and with designing no less than six of the "theme" structures. If, as Lenox R. Lohr, manager of Chicago's fabulous "A Century of Progress" fair of 1933 suggested, "the *architecture* of a fair should key the theme of the exposition," then Knox's choice of the "Spanish Renaissance" style was oddly out of register with the historical events it was meant to commemorate.

Planning for the Lewis and Clark Centennial Exposition began in earnest in 1902, at which time Portland's population stood at 161,000. Since the orchestration of an international fair was a formidable undertaking, it was not surprising that Lewis and the fair's directors chose to commission America's most celebrated landscape architect, Frederick Law Olmsted, to design an overarching plan for the exposition. Although Olmsted—who could count Central Park and the World's Columbian Exposition in Chicago among his aesthetic achieve-

ments—died in 1903, his firm would, nevertheless, execute the design for the Portland exposition in an admirable fashion. In 1903, one of his sons, John C. Olmsted, arrived in the city for a dual mission to inspect the Guild Lake site and to discuss a park program for the city. "The plan for the Lewis and Clark Exposition was patterned after the Columbian Exposition," wrote Portland landscape architect and historian, Wallace K. Huntington in *Space, Style and Structure*, "and considering the Mediterranean style of architecture that had been selected as the official mode of building, much of the pretentiousness of the Chicago fair would be repeated on a smaller scale in Portland."

With the notable exception of the Forestry Building, which drew acclaim as "the Parthenon of Oregon," and the "world's largest log cabin," the Spanish theme did not produce examples of architecture that signaled the full extent of Portland's transformation into an urban architectural microcosm. "Perhaps sensing the potential weaknesses of the eclectic architecture," continued Huntington, "the landscape architects avoided using any of the structures as the terminus of an axis. Passing from the enclosed spaces of the formal core of the exposition to the suddenly expanding panoramic view over the lake (originally intended to have 'decorative' islands), the natural beauty of the site was featured at the expense of possible grandiose architectural effects."

The Forestry Building, was the exposition's only bona fide "regional" contribution. Completed under the supervision of Whidden and Lewis, the drawings and, perhaps, the design were the work of none other than Albert E. Doyle, a quickly rising Oregon talent who was completing a 12-year apprenticeship with the Whidden and Lewis firm. Despite its oxymoronic, Greco-lumber splendor, the Forestry Building gave a glimpse of the intriguing possibilities lurking in Doyle's creative imagination. The wood Parthenon expressed an unholy, but provocative, alliance between materials of the region and classical Greek architecture. As a concept, the structure was bold and visionary—in short, a taste of things to come architecturally, both for Doyle and the city of Portland. Later in his career, Doyle would perhaps be spurred by a somewhat less iconoclastic impulse than that which produced the Forestry Building. Yet he continued to explore and would achieve brilliant effects from the marriage between regional materials and classical architectural forms. By 1917 Doyle's romance with Greco-Roman architecture would blossom into an ex-

FORESTRY BUILDING, LEWIS AND CLARK EXPOSITION
A. E. Doyle/Whidden and Lewis
1905

quisitely designed terra cotta palace also known as the U.S. National Bank Building.

Although Doyle had been the inspiration for the fair's most "regional" and provocative contribution, but the "extravaganza" clearly belonged to Whidden, Lewis and other prominent participating architects: James Knox Taylor, David C. Lewis, Emil Schacht and Edgar M. Lazarus. And while the exposition's "quirky" theme may not have encouraged structures that were representative of the city's growing architectural sophistication, it did spur a lively pastiche of buildings that expressed the spirit of the times and the nascent cosmopolitan aspirations of the region's commercial capital.

The United States Government Building, designed in the office of James Knox Taylor, architect of the Treasury, set the theme for what may have been the largest collection of "wedding cake" architecture in history. More than 1,000-feet long, the building's grandiose main facade consisted of a massive colonnade in the Corinthian order, separating two large towers mannered in the Spanish style. The ostentatious structure cost more to erect than all eight buildings commissioned by the state.

Taylor's reputation as a fine architect was, of course, already well-known within Portland architectural circles. Six years before the exposition, his office had been commissioned to design the United States Customs House (1901) for the city of Portland (Taylor also worked on the west wings to the Pioneer Courthouse between 1903 and 1905). A handsome and well-composed building, still standing today, the Customs House was one of Portland's first and finest buildings in the Italian Renaissance style. Featuring a granite colonnade opening into an expansive courtyard, extensive rustication and ornamented window pediments, the Customs House was a far cry from the voluminous and sumptuous Mediterranean monument designed by Taylor to grace the north side of the exposition lagoon.

Edgar M. Lazarus, the "local" supervising architect for the Customs House, was invited by Lewis to design the exposition's Agriculture Building. Described at the time as a "composite study of Spanish Renaissance and Mission Architecture." The unrestrained composition featured a massive "Golden Dome" and profusely ornamented corner pavilions. Another Portland architect, Emil Schacht, was asked to design the Oriental Building.

UNITED STATES CUSTOMS HOUSE
James Knox Taylor
1901

An imposing structure with eight corner towers and a Corinthian arch gracing the entrance, Schacht's entry, despite the exposition's theme, was curiously devoid of Spanish detailing.

After the exposition, both Lazarus and Schacht would go on to design a number of buildings in the city, but neither would be able to exercise the architectural muscles each had flexed for their bombastic temporary plaster buildings of 1905. After his flamboyant "Golden Dome" of green "weathered copper," and his important adjunct role in the Customs House, the aging Lazarus, for the most part, would have to settle for lesser commissions, among them the four-story Hotel Ramapo (presently the Taft Home for the Aged). But the architect also would have the opportunity to design one last "domed" building which, interestingly, would eventually be topped with copper. With the completion of the Vista House (1918) on the Columbia River Highway, Lazarus introduced Oregon's first example of Art Nouveau architecture. John B. Yeon supervised the construction of the domed octagon, which was faced with rough ashlar sandstone and expansive arched windows.

Schacht would be involved in a smattering of odd commissions, including the Ideal (Bluebird) Theater (1912) at 2403 N.W. Thurman, a barrel-vault structure, best described as "brutal Romanesque." His Classical Revival design for the Bullier Building (1906) was one of his finest. He would complete the Maegly-Tichner (1911), Mayer (1927, Schacht and Bergen) and the 1907 Swetland (Aus) buildings during the two decades following the Lewis and Clark Exposition.

Henry J. Hefty, who had received his architectural training in Munich before coming to Portland in 1881, was responsible for the Exposition's entrance peristyle, an expansive, gently curved 30-column colonnade inscribed with the following greeting: "Westward The Course of Empire Takes Its Way." Several years earlier the Swiss-born architect had designed the First Congregational Church (1890), a High Victorian Gothic adaptation, with walls of basaltic rock, broken ashlar and Tenino sandstone trim. Little did Hefty know that nearly a century later, both the formal elements of his design and the materials he selected would serve as "crystals" or, put another way, design generators, for the Performing Arts Center (Broome, Oringdulph, O'Toole and Rudolph; ELS Design Group). The Performing Arts Center scheme (whose two smaller theaters would wrap around the First Congregational Church) responded to the architectonic features of Hefty's edifice and transposed them into a modern idiom.

Without question, among those Portland architects whose work appeared in the Lewis and Clark Exposition, Whidden, Lewis and Doyle would eventually garner the city's most prestigious commissions. But David C. Lewis, designer of the exposition's European Building, would also go on to produce a number of respectable buildings, most of them in the Sullivan vein. Within a few months after the fair's closing, 15 October 1905, all of the exposition's structures, with the exception of the Forestry Building, were either demolished or moved from their site.

In retrospect, there is no doubt that the Lewis and Clark Exposition was more successful in illustrating an ideal in planning, than it was in masterminding Portland's architectural microcosm of the future. Not surprisingly, the seeds for a rich tradition in landscape architecture—that eventually would include such notable designers as E. T. Mische, Lawrence Halprin, Arthur Erfeldt and Wallace K. Huntington—were already being disseminated to the general public at the exposition, in the form of illustrated souvenir pamphlets bearing the following notation: "The sunken gardens, simple and beautiful, are an object lesson. Why should not every new American town and city have such in its center?" As Huntington suggested, "With the exception of the Forestry Building, the architecture of the fair seems bland to 20th century critics, but the photographs [of the exposition] testify to some of the excitement the fair generated. The view across the sunken garden was impressive . . . it was a totally manipulated view that incorporated all the 'Arts' in a grandiose assemblage of sculpture, architecture and planting . . . . Oregon's answer to the White City was a rather splendid statement of Western pride and optimism."

Whidden and Lewis had fulfilled the inspiring charge of Daniel H. Burnham, builder of the World's Columbian Exposition of 1893. Carved in stone over the massive fireplace in the studio atop Chicago's Burnham Building were words that informed the spirit of Whidden and Lewis's enterprise:

Make no little plans—They have no magic to stir men's blood and probably themselves will not be realized—Make big plans—Aim high in hope and work remembering that a noble-logical diagram once recorded will never die—but asserting itself with ever growing insistency—Remember that our sons and grandsons are going to do things that would stagger us—Let your watchword be order and your beacon beauty.

Within their own life spans, Whidden and Lewis would witness the results of architectural precedents they themselves had set. In the decade following the fair, the firm continued to attract some of the city's choicest commissions. Twentieth-century classical styles predominated in their commercial designs for the Farwest Assurance (Stevens) Building (1914), the Corbett Building (1907), the Gevurtz (Failing) Building (1907, 1913), the Imperial Hotel (1909) and the Wilcox Building (1911).

Almost without exception, these structures reflected the architects' finely tuned talent for combining classical ornamentation and glazed terra cotta facework with the structural tectonics of Sullivan's early Chicago skyscrapers.

The exposition was a catalytic event in the history of Portland architecture, helping not only to focus attention on the architectural talents of Whidden, Lewis and, of course, Albert E. Doyle, but also paving the way for a new epoch of architectural growth. Unlike the Chicago Exhibition of 1893, which had selected a grandiose Roman Renaissance architectural scheme as its theme, the fanciful plaster buildings erected for the 1905 Lewis and Clark Exposition would not change the fabric of the cityscape directly. Nor would the fair break new architectural ground, stylistically or conceptually, although E. T. Mische, the talented landscape architect recommended by the Olmsted Brothers for the position of park superintendent would, indeed, play a pivotal role in the designs for Peninsula Park, Laurelhurst Park and Terwilliger Boulevard.

But over time, the exposition paid dividends that the city's financial and social pillars would use for an architectural facelift of Portland's burgeoning downtown core. The fair ushered in a welcome period of economic expansion that continued virtually unabated until World War I. As a result, the city began to bulge with edifices decorated with loggias, Tuscan columns and boldly rusticated facades. Financial institutions from other cities, including the Wells Fargo Bank and Bank of California, flocked to Portland and colonized its core with sparkling new edifices, each boasting a distinctive terra cotta shell. State banks and local commercial enterprises followed suit, erecting their own crop of classically ornamented skyscrapers sheathed in glistening white skins.

The post-exposition years were fast and furious, not only in Portland, but for the world at large. Late in 1905, the year of the Lewis and Clark Exposition, Albert E. Doyle was already in New York City attending design classes at Columbia University and working in the office of Henry Bacon, who would be acclaimed for his design of the Lincoln Memorial. The same year, Albert Einstein would introduce his "special theory of relativity." In 1906, Cezanne and Ibsen died, and architect Stanford White—who along with McKim and Mead had been involved in the first design for the Portland Hotel—was murdered in New York City by Harry K. Thaw. This same year A. E. Doyle was sailing to Europe on his way to study the ancient ruins of Greece and Rome.

SCOTTISH RITE TEMPLE, MURALS
artist unknown
1906

In 1907 the Plaza Hotel opened in New York, Frank Lloyd Wright's Robie House was standing, and Doyle returned to Portland to open his own architectural firm (just how high the young architect was setting his sights was evident from his rendering of the tower for Madison Square Garden, which appeared in the 1906–1907 *Yearbook* for the Portland Architectural Club). The following year, 1908, the known past and the emergent future would meet in the vibrant hum of Doyle's drafting studio, where the seed for Portland's terra cotta future would be planted in the form of final revisions of the working drawings for the Meier and Frank department store. In the same year, New York's Singer Building, 47 stories of ornate brick and terra cotta, was completed, and proved in no uncertain terms that architects could design buildings that would "scrape the sky." In 1908, architect Adolf Loos wrote a famous essay in which he equated architectural ornament with crime, the Model T Ford was introduced, and Adolf Hitler was an art student in Vienna. At the same time, in 1909, Doyle's Meier and Frank store was completed in Portland, Bakelite (the precursor of plastic) was first produced, and Admiral Perry reached the North Pole.

Meanwhile, Portland architecture was on the rise. The economic upswing that followed the 1905 exposition had started to fuel construction of a new generation of buildings in the downtown business district. The combination of local architectural talent, the exposition and unbridled entrepreneurship were responsible for Portland's rising prestige within architectural circles. Between 1905 and 1915 the city would be peppered not only with the work of such Portland architects as Whidden and Lewis, A. E. Doyle and David C. Lewis, but also with much-publicized buildings designed by architects from other cities.

In 1910, Herbert Croly, a leading progressive intellectual and editor of the *Architectural Record* from 1900 to 1906, arrived in Portland and described what he saw:

> Portland, moreover, unlike any other city on the Pacific Coast, San Francisco excepted, has an architectural history. It has been erecting comparatively large business buildings ever since the essentially modern movement in American architecture began late in the eighties. The different phases of that movement can be studied to better advantage in Portland than in many middle western cities of larger population. Many of its earlier buildings were, indeed, designed by eastern or middle western architects, and at the present time an unusually large proportion of them are still so designed. Some of its earlier buildings are of exceptional interest and merit, and deserve a place of their own in any complete account of the development of American business architecture.

Things were moving so fast that, by the late 1920s, the city's business district was one sprawling terra cotta palace, consisting of several pavilions in which the architectural prowess of Portland's (and some of the nation's) finest designers had shiningly materialized. In fact, during this period of fertile expansion, the city evolved into something of a West Coast architectural showpiece, as it would again, in the 1980s. Its improving status was due, in large part, to the depth of local architectural talent. But, its rising reputation was also linked to the vision of Portland's most influential business leaders, who were anxious to absorb into the city's fabricated landscape the most innovative architectural talents and developments of the time.

Among these talents, none would vitalize the city more than Doyle, whose buildings, wrote Charles H. Cheney in the July 1919 issue of *Architect and Engineer*, "are so distinctly above the ordinary as to be considered of national artistic importance." The son of a building

PORTLAND UNION STOCKYARDS
architect unknown
1913

contractor, Doyle launched his remarkable career at an early age. Directly upon graduating from grade school at the age of 14, he embarked on a 12-year apprenticeship with Whidden and Lewis, who absorbed the young man's fledgling talents in a number of projects. Late in 1903, after completing the drawings for the Forestry Building, Doyle, like all ambitious young men of his day, went East, where he refined his skills in the Bacon office. Doyle's entré into this highly touted New York firm was most likely made easier by Whidden, under whom Bacon had worked in 1885, in the Boston firm of Whidden and Chamberlin.

Doyle sailed to Europe in the spring of 1906, on a scholarship to the American School of Archeology in Athens. Accepted early in his career into the prestigious architectural circles of New York and Portland, and now "finished," by the requisite exposure to the ruins of ancient Greece and Rome and the Renaissance sites of Italy, Doyle returned to Portland and opened his own office in 1907.

His timing, it turned out, was perfect. Portland was in the midst of an unprecedented business boom, spurred in large measure by the strong dose of civic confidence the Lewis and Clark Exposition had administered to the city. The national attention garnered by this centennial celebration had not only attracted an influx of commercial interests, but also a veritable flood of newcomers ready to invest in the city's future. Thus Portland's population in 1910 stood at 207,214, following a demographic swell that created a demand for an entirely new class of structures. The tide of development shifted the city's commercial center westward from the river, sweeping away the Victorian mansions, churches and shops along Fifth and Sixth avenues to deposit a new stratum of large stores, banks and office buildings. And Doyle, who in 1908 took on a partner, construction supervisor William B. Patterson, was ready to respond to the flurry of commissions that came to his new offices.

Although Doyle would design a number of residential buildings, he concentrated his energy on the city's urban core. From 1909 until the late 1920s, he would orchestrate some of the largest and tallest edifices in the city—much as the firm of Skidmore, Owings and Merrill would do in the 1960s and early 1970s. Through his extensive involvement in Portland's early city planning, Doyle would set a precedent for the downtown planning and renewal schemes which SOM would mastermind in the decades following World War II. During his most active years, Doyle served on the advisory committee appointed by the city council to review and help implement the 1912 Bennett Plan. Seven years later, when the first City Planning Commission was formed, Doyle became an active member.

"Mr. Doyle's clients say of him that they admired his ability as an architect first," wrote Cheney in *Architect and Engineer*, "and were surprised later to discover his great ability as a good businessman, careful of his clients' interests and appreciative of the necessity for respecting the limits of money available for the work in hand." Civic minded and interested in the arts, Doyle was responsible for much of the enthusiasm of the Portland Art Association and was a "useful" member of the chamber of commerce. "On the whole," continued Cheney, "Mr. Doyle is a man of whom both the community and the profession have good reasons to be proud."

Portland was growing and prospering. In Doyle's view the more the city's role as commercial center could be expressed through large buildings, the stronger would be its position. In many respects, he was a linchpin between regional, national and, even, international trends in architecture, and the slowly evolving needs of Portland as a commercial and trade center. Eventually his vision would be translated into a number of buildings

that spoke, in a variety of forms, to the notion of "place" and the gathering of human activity.

Eclectic in his command of period styles, Doyle applied the classical design principle of *matching* form with function that had formed the cornerstone of the Beaux-Arts doctrine. His erudition and keen sense of the "appropriate" invariably led him to select styles that, over the centuries (or even in the recent past) became the sanctioned "envelopes" for various building types. For Doyle, style was not meant to disguise the building's function, but rather to serve as an instantly recognizable "billboard" announcing the character of the activities taking place within the structure. "Bank directors, in selecting the design for a new building, want not only an effectively arranged banking room," wrote Cheney in 1919, "but an exterior that will attractively advertise the wealth and business of the institution as far as the building can be seen. This purpose Mr. Doyle has carried out very well in the United States National Bank."

More than any Portland architect before and after his time, Doyle made available to the general public a set of architectural experiences that transcended the specificity of Portland, and which linked the city with the great urban centers of Europe and America. In Doyle's hands, this "microcosmic" approach to design yielded a comprehensive inventory of building types—department stores, banks, libraries, schools—devoted to commerce, culture and enlightenment. Some of the architect's most successful projects resulted from the first rash of commissions his firm undertook in the teens and early 1920s. With the Meier and Frank and the Lipman, Wolfe department stores, Doyle began to wrest control from the hands of his predecessors, Whidden and Lewis.

The first of his major commissions, a ten-story addition to the Meier and Frank store, demonstrated his ability to combine modern structural methods with the historicist sensibility of the Beaux-Arts. It also announced the twilight of Whidden and Lewis's reign and the dawning of the "Doyle decades."

Whidden and Lewis, who had designed the original Meier and Frank department store (1897–98), might have expected the store's president, Sigmund Frank to select their firm to mastermind the expansion. But instead, Frank turned to the fresher talents of Doyle who, it has been surmised, may have worked on the original plans for the structure during his apprenticeship years. In a sense, history would repeat itself. Just as Whidden and Lewis had picked up where their parent firm,

BVILDING FOR MEIER & FRANK CO.
FIFTH, MORRISON, ALDER AND SIXTH STREETS.
DOYLE AND PATTERSON, ARCHITECTS, PORTLAND.

DEC 10 1909

MEIER AND FRANK DEPARTMENT STORE
Doyle and Patterson
1909

McKim, Mead and White, had left off on the Portland Hotel, so Doyle, too, picked up where his mentors, Whidden and Lewis, had left off on the Meier and Frank department store.

Doyle's final design for the project took considerable liberties with the stylistic orientation set by Whidden and Lewis in the original structure. Initially, Doyle had intended to match the facade of his addition with the yellow brick and stucco detailing of the original building. But, after traveling east with Frank to inspect the most contemporary examples of department store architecture, he deferred to his client's infatuation with terra cotta tile and "Chicago" windows of Louis H. Sullivan's Carson, Pirie and Scott department store (1901–1904). While the Italian Renaissance facade of Doyle's composition retained its allegiance to the Beaux-Arts taste for classical detailing, the fenestration and the sparkling white terra cotta sheathing carried the stamp of the "contemporary" that fashion-conscious Frank found so appealing. "The Meier & Frank Department Store is a 12-story building of white terra cotta covering three-quarters of a block," wrote Cheney, "it has all the labor-saving utilities that go with the modern department store, including 19 elevators, 7 escalators, 6 spiral chutes and thousands of feet of mechanical belt conveyors." Despite its obvious virtues, Doyle never seemed entirely pleased with the building. In later years he was quoted as saying: "It is a big dry goods box punched full of holes for light and looks like it."

Doyle would rapidly come to share Frank's penchant for terra cotta facing. Not only was the material accessible at a reasonable price, but it projected a "modern" image. More importantly, its reflective surface responded to the unique atmospheric conditions of the city. For years to come, terra cotta would appear in Doyle's major projects, dominating the facades of the Olds, Wortman and King department store (1910), Lipman, Wolfe and Company store (1911), Mead Building (1912) and subsequent additions to the Meier and Frank complex which, by the early 1930s, would cover an entire block on Fifth Avenue. Terra cotta would play an integral, but less pervasive, role in the Selling Building (1910), the Northwestern National (American) Bank (1913–14), the Pittock Block (1914) and the Oregon (Benson) Hotel (1913). Doyle's magic with terra cotta sparked a trend. His competitors rushed to contribute their own tile palaces, which included Francis C. Brendt's Henry Building (1909), and idiosyncratic entries such as William C. Knighton's Seward (Governor) Hotel (1909), whose Aztec-inspired terra cotta medallions would bear an uncanny resemblance to Michael Graves's preliminary sketches for the Portland Building completed in 1982.

Until the late 1920s, glazed terra cotta was without peer in its capacity for illuminating the geometric, floral and anthropomorphic subtleties of classical ornamentation. Terra cotta blocks were similar in size and configuration to concrete blocks but had decorative glazed faces, which were made by pressing fine clay into plaster molds. The clay blocks were then glazed, dried and fired. The use of terra cotta, by such a wide range of practitioners during this period of rapid growth, reflected its suitability as an exterior sheathing material, its relatively low cost and its responsiveness to the variable conditions of local light. But to some degree its omnipresence along Portland's Fifth Avenue was, almost certainly, the result of "peer pressure." Manufactured primarily by the California-based Gladding, McBean and Company and the Denny-Renton Clay and Coal Company of Seattle, glazed terra cotta became an effective and conspicuous device for establishing "material" continuity within Portland's downtown core, which by 1915 was bristling with terra cotta edifices in every shape, shade and form.

Glazed architectural terra cotta, or "ceramic veneer," a term coined by Peter McGill McBean, was first manufactured after 1875, the year Gladding, McBean and Company was founded in Lincoln, California. By 1890, rail connections to the East Coast, technological innovations in structural design and the introduction of terra cotta to the West Coast began to change the face of Portland architecture. Although local factors were certainly at work, much of what stimulated the vast rearrangment in Portland's architectural landscape can be linked to what might be called, the "Chicago experience." The Chicago fire of 1871 brought terra cotta to the fore as a fireproofing agent, although its popularization as a building material on the West Coast has been credited to the Chicago firm of Burnham and Root, which used terra cotta extensively in its San Francisco Mills Building of 1890.

The Portland-Chicago connection solidified in the early 1900s, when Meier and Frank president Sigmund Frank, upon returning from a business trip to the Windy City with glowing reports about the stream-lined terra cotta facade of Sullivan's Carson, Pirie and Scott store (1901–1904), recommended to A. E. Doyle that this material be used for his own enterprise.

Long before terra cotta became the vogue, however, it should be noted that it was a Chicagoan who, some 35 years before the Meier and Frank store was completed, recognized the potential in Lincoln (California) clay. Charles A. Gladding, while visiting California, read of the discovery of coal and clay near Lincoln. He tested samples, found them excellent and, on 1 May 1875, Gladding, McBean and George Chambers founded Gladding, McBean and Company.

The ubiquity of glazed terra cotta facework in Portland architecture during the early 1900s is perhaps best explained by its unique functional and aesthetic properties. In the early part of the century, Gladding, McBean and Company developed "granitex," a glaze simulating granite that was used on a number of Portland buildings.

But the complexity and variability of ornamentation permitted by the material was its tour de force. Terra cotta belt courses, cluster-column capitals and spandrels choking with foliate extravagance offered Portland buildings a richness and variegation not easily achieved—at an equivalent cost—with other materials available at the time. Terra cotta would be used, for example, in the ornate polychrome facades of the Wells Fargo Building (1907, Benjamin Wistar Morris III) and the Charles F. Berg Building (1930, Grand Rapids Design Service); for the secessionist-inspired, geometric ornamentation of William C. Knighton's Governor Hotel (1909), and for the Italianate, rusticated walls of the Bank of California (1924, A. E. Doyle). In every instance terra cotta permitted each stylistic idiom full expression.

Terra cotta was finely tuned to the needs of Portland's Beaux-Arts practitioners. It could take on a distinguished, lavish and, even, futuristic appearance without casting off entirely the moorings of the past. And it could claim other, equally significant, advantages. An article in *Architect and Engineer* in April 1917 extolled the virtues of using the material. It was the lightest veneer available, and had an attractive manufacturing time—six to eight weeks from order to delivery. Moreover, because of its lightness and easy anchorage to a steel frame, it was better able to withstand shock (as the 1906 San Francisco earthquake had verified). Its average four-inch thickness permitted thinner walls than before and more room for interior space. Finally, terra cotta offered a wide range of polychrome, textures and ornamental styles.

Although terra cotta would be used feverishly throughout the country by the early 1900s, this building material would enjoy an especially vigorous and extended lifespan in the history of Portland architecture. Modern, reflective and adaptable to utilitarian and ornamental uses, terra cotta was embraced, at least in part, because it was ideally suited for maintaining architectural unity among the eclectic building designs fostered by the Beaux-Arts movement.

Although many reasons accounted for its entrenchment in the material fabric of the city's built landscape, one thing seemed clear: The Portland-terra cotta "symbiosis" was nourished, to a great extent, by the region's climate. The material was not only lightweight and fireproof, but, more importantly, *waterproof*, and therefore well-adapted to the region's moisture-laden climate.

As Portland's built landscape congealed, absorbing buildings of more imposing mass and height into its downtown fabric, it became more necessary to provide "eye relief" for the city's increasingly dense, light-poor urban zones. With its hardy sheen, terra cotta was able to resist the dulling effects of constant rain. As the shimmering terra cotta facades of Portland's urban labyrinth were put into place—beginning with the Meier and Frank store in 1909—it became clear that this new and fashionable material had a special capacity for brightening up the city's overall tone. In fact, when A. E. Doyle, the maestro of terra cotta, turned to brick for the refined Italian Renaissance style of the Public Service Building (1928), even McMath, Doyle's grandson, would be forced to comment: "It suffers from the cool gray color which is somewhat oppressive during the long gray months of Portland winters." Portland architects, including A. E. Doyle, Whidden and Lewis and William C. Knighton, adopted terra cotta, as much for its purely ornamental virtues as for its ability to cut through the unrelieved grayness of Portland's doleful, rain-filled winter months.

To be sure, the availability of terra cotta had been a great boon to Portland architecture at the beginning of the twentieth century. Both before and after the heyday of terra cotta, however, a deep respect for the parsimonious light content of the region influenced the design strategies of Portland's leading architects and planners. As early as the mid-nineteenth century, two of Portland's first "urban planners," Asa Lovejoy and Francis Pettygrove, plotted 200-by-200 foot blocks in a way that maximized the effect of ambient sunlight on the city's architectural spine. By allowing for an unusually high ratio of *open* to *built* space and adopting expansive north-south avenues, the Lovejoy-Pettygrove program was, in every respect, a solar-sensitive urban plan. Stated simply, Portland architects would always be concerned with getting light out of a cloud—their "Mission Impossible." Eye relief, or, put another way, darkness relief, would always be an issue. In the 1940s, for example, Pietro Belluschi would provide eye relief in the form of light-colored marble and aluminum-skinned buildings. Later, in the 1960s, Skidmore, Owings and Merrill would attempt to soothe the eye with expansive panels of reflective glass. In the 1980s, a number of firms, most notably, Zimmer, Gunsul, Frasca, would light the city up with designs that called for bone-white, precast concrete facades.

But for the first three decades of this century, terra cotta, alone, was king. In fact, a look at Portland's thriving urban metropolis of 1928 would have suggested that the exposition of 1905 had been transplanted to the city's downtown core, and extended for 20 years or so under the aegis of a new theme—"terra cotta chic." Indeed, glazed terra cotta was to Portland architecture during the first two decades of the century, what high-gloss enamel paint would be to kitchen cabinets of the 1950s—the ubiquitous and indelible stamp of modernity. As an exterior sheathing material, terra cotta was the great equalizer, sprucing up a 5,000-year-old look, recasting forms of centuries past into a "brand spanking new" architectural envelope. If, as McMath suggested, the "ingeniousness" of Portland's Beaux-Arts practitioner "was measured by his ability to stuff a 20th century function into a first or 15th or 17th century package," then his ultimate success would be registered by his obsession for sealing that package in a terra cotta wrapper.

Although terra cotta had been very good—architecturally and financially—to Sigmund Frank and A. E. Doyle in 1909, this sheathing material was not everyone's cup of tea. In fact, by 1913 there would be hints of a minor, albeit impotent, backlash against "terra cotta chic." The 1913 *Yearbook* for the Portland Architectural Club included an advertisement by the McCann Stone Company, which featured a photograph of A. E. Doyle's Eliot Hall at Reed College, accompanied by the following inscription: "We do not deal in concrete, terra cotta or other *imitations*."

Cast stone (concrete) ornament, developed in the late 1920s, was even less expensive than terra cotta and eventually gained popularity over its glistening predecessor. But the downfall of terra cotta would take a more concrete form in the 1930s. "Following the fall of a lion's head from the Lipman, Wolfe cornice," wrote McMath in *Space, Style and Structure*, "city building inspectors examined all the cornices in the downtown area and directed owners to repair or remove those that were found unsafe." Lamented McMath, "unfortunately, it was usually cheaper to remove than repair."

A constellation of factors—architectural, financial and social—had signaled to designers in other cities that, with respect to architecture, Portland had come out of the "dark ages." Only two years after the exposition, the city received its first "skyscraper," the Wells Fargo Building (1907), designed by Benjamin Wistar Morris III. Morris, a native Portlander transplanted to New York, would become consulting architect for the Metropolitan Opera Company. Twenty years after Wells Fargo, along with the firm of Reinhard and Hofmeister, Morris would conceive the basic scheme for Rockefeller Center, which called for a tall central tower surrounded by lower buildings with an open plaza in the center.

Although his Portland contribution would never be a match for the stepped-back centerpiece of Rockefeller Center, Morris's Wells Fargo Building was an enormously graceful addition to Portland's built landscape. Along with the influx of other buildings designed by prestigious out-of-town architects, the handsome structure may have contributed to the erosion of Whidden and Lewis's unchallenged monopoly over the city's architectural landscape. According to a newspaper article that appeared in the *Oregonian* on 1 January 1908, it was through the influence of Colonel Dudley Evans, then president of Wells Fargo, that "the Wells Fargo skyscraper was erected" in Portland. Evans had been the company's agent at one time and, as a result, was "well posted on [the city's] present and prospective needs."

The building's facade was, in many respects, much more elaborate than those designed by Whidden and Lewis for commercial buildings of the same period. Melding the richness of Victorian architecture with classical forms characteristic of the Renaissance Revival styles, the Wells Fargo Building suggested new options for combining local materials. It was one of a handful of buildings in Portland with polychrome terra cotta and one of two in the downtown area not glazed in a neutral shade. At the time, the doorstep at the main entrance was said to require the largest piece of granite ever brought to Portland. The smooth-faced, buff-colored brick laid in snappy diamond and cross patterns and decorative terra cotta motifs—including the green keystones, wreaths and letters "Wells Fargo" above the top story windows—were a vibrant counterpoint to the gray granite plinth and limestone sheathing of the first two floors. Morris's ornamental bursts offered just the right degree of counterpoint to the sleekness and verticality of the major facade. On the whole, this building was well received and heralded the coming of a new, skyward-looking phase in Portland architecture.

By 1910 the city could already claim a large stable of fine architects. Firms led by Whidden and Lewis, A. E. Doyle and Morris H. Whitehouse were alive and flourishing. Despite this local crop of high-powered design talent, lumber magnate John B. Yeon commissioned the services of San Francisco architects, James William Reid and Merrit Reid, to embellish the Portland cityscape. Reid and Reid returned to Portland with impeccable credentials, having designed the Oregonian Building, completed in 1891 (and subsequently razed), as well as the lavish Fairmont Hotel and the Hotel de Coronado in San Francisco and San Diego, respectively. Yeon's precise reasons for passing up Portland's architectural heavyweights for the building that would bear his name are not entirely clear. But his decision to draw upon "foreign blood" to infuse new life into the city's built landscape supported a strategic, long-lived tradition of *architectural insemination* with out-of-town designers that originated with the selection of McKim, Mead and White for the Portland Hotel in 1882.

Completed in 1911, the Yeon Building was a gleaming edifice that featured off-white, glazed terra cotta, Ionic colonnades on the upper three floors and bold rustication at the second story. Sleek, symmetrical and rational, the Yeon Building sparkled with all the glory of the past, along with the promise of modernity.

The Journal Building (1912), later restored as the Jackson Tower, was also designed by Reid and Reid. Though smaller than the Yeon Building, it was, nevertheless, exceedingly elegant. Except for its square tower, the building bore a strong resemblance to the Spreckles Building in San Francisco designed by Reid and Reid more than a decade earlier. Faced with off-white brick, the terra cotta ornamentation of the Journal Building included the rusticated base, Doric columns and roof balustrade. A novel illumination scheme was one of the building's most unusual features. The current Jackson Tower "light show" came to life from the first, with bulbs that screwed directly into terra cotta blocks at the upper stories and tower. As much a theatrical device as an architectural embellishment, the lighting arrangement turned the building into a year-around "Christmas ornament." Writing in *Architectural Forum* in 1930, Harvey Wiley Corbett would reinforce the call for nocturnal illumination when he suggested "a wider use of color and proposed that buildings be flooded with harmonizing hues at night."

Working between 1905 and World War I, a number of other architects practicing in the Beaux-Arts manner fertilized the city's increasingly muscular urban core. In 1911 Cass Gilbert, of New York City, designed the Spalding Building (Oregon Bank Building), which, according to Herbert Croly in *Architectural Record* of June 1912, was the best of Portland's new commercial structures. Most of the large office buildings erected in Portland during this period were characterized by a tripartite system of composition, corresponding to the parts of a classic column with its base, shaft and capital.

Reminiscent of Gilbert's Broadway-Chambers Building (1900) in New York, the Spalding Building exemplified this compositional scheme. Its simple eight-story shaft offered an effective foil for the ornamental detailing above and below. It is of historical interest that, while working on the Spalding Building, Gilbert had also taken on the assignment of designing the world's tallest building, the Woolworth in New York. Completed in 1913, the Gothic behemoth rose 792 feet and according to architecture critic Paul Goldberger, "was one of the most remarkable skyscrapers ever built."

By 1915, major sections of Portland—the "financial district" budding at the north end of the retail core, the commercial spine spanning Fifth Avenue and the area in the vicinity of Pioneer Courthouse and the Portland Hotel—were already studded with lavish buildings that would become part of the city's ambitious program in the Beaux-Arts tradition. By the late 1920s, however, this tradition would come to be criticized as an ingrown Francophile system which considered the handling of India ink on stretched paper more important than building, and had its students designing "useless monuments" of the ancient past. Writing in *Skyscraper Style*, architectural historian Cervin Robinson would point out that "however monumental . . . these projects were, the buildings involved were meant as public amenities; their grandeur was intended to be both accessible to the general public and comprehensible to it."

Several Portland buildings erected between 1910 and 1930 could claim these virtues and the First National Bank of Oregon (Oregon Pioneer Savings and Loan Building), completed in 1916, was one of the city's most impressive achievements in the Neo-Classical idiom. Designed by the Boston architectural firm of Coolidge and Shattuck and built at a cost of $400,000, the bank was instantly readable with its chic exterior of Colorado marble and a pedimented portico braced with fluted Doric columns. Bursting with strong, highly stylized details, the attic story was festooned with swags, while the entablature and cornice were adorned with anthemion, lion masks and a frieze of fretwork, triglyphs and decorated metopes. "The same grand treatment was used by Coolidge and Shattuck in the interior," wrote McMath and Vaughan, "particularly on the upper level,

JACKSON TOWER (JOURNAL BUILDING)
Reid and Reid
1912

originally the main banking floor." Except for the splendid interior of Doyle's u.s. National Bank, completed a year later, the efflorescence of ornament and color that graced this bank's inner sanctum was without peer. The "heroic space"—flanked by Ionic columns of scagliola, a

Bottocini marble floor, and a broad, glass roof—was certainly one of the most dignified public rooms on the West Coast.

Between 1905 and 1915 the power base within Portland's architectural community would begin to change—

significantly and permanently—away from Whidden and Lewis, to the firm established by A. E. Doyle. Despite their undisputed reign during the first decade of the century, Whidden and Lewis produced few buildings after 1910 that expressed the compositional brilliance of City Hall or the Hamilton Building.

In all likelihood their swan song was the Multnomah County Courthouse (1914), an ungainly, obese building with a riveted structural steel frame and concrete fireproofing that was technologically up-to-date. The limestone facing, large Ionic orders on the east and west facades, glazed terra cotta roof cornice and bronze lanterns at the entrance, were part of the most ornamental program Whidden and Lewis had employed since their design for City Hall. The Courthouse was a definitive (although, perhaps, somewhat overwrought) contribution to Portland's catalog of twentieth-century classical buildings. However imposing, by 1917, it would be upstaged by Doyle's more extravagant, classical composition for the u.s. National Bank.

To this day, the decline of Whidden and Lewis's architectural influence has not been adequately explained, but, clearly, challenges to their hegemony were already being mounted, both in drafting studios and in the form of buildings erected in Portland's downtown core. Without question, Doyle's rising stature in the community was a significant factor. But there were other, Darwinian, forces at work. A fresh crop of design talents—D. C. Lewis, Morris H. Whitehouse, Fred Fritsch (along with his partners Sutton, Whitney and Aandahl), William G. Purcell and the redoubtable A. E. Doyle heading the list—began vying for commissions that would result in some of the city's most memorable buildings. A mixture of native Portlanders or recent newcomers, these "young bucks" strained to surpass the achievements of Whidden and Lewis, turning lots into buildings that mirrored the latest trends in national and international urban design. For the most part, their contributions remained within the decorous bounds of the Beaux-Arts school.

While the Whidden and Lewis firm might have reached its zenith at the cusp of the first decade, the historicist sensibility it represented had not yet exhausted its appeal. On the contrary, historicism in all its canonical forms was taking the profession by storm. The design neophytes boldly allied themselves with a newly emerging professional establishment that worked to disseminate the doctrine of the Beaux-Arts to both its members as well as the general public.

In 1908 a number of Portland designers had given the first sign of a growing esprit de corps by mounting an exhibition at the Portland Art Museum, featuring the work of local and nationally acclaimed architects. Shortly thereafter they joined with their fellow professionals across the country by forming the Portland Architectural Club, on the model established by the Philadelphia T Square Club in 1883. The cream of Portland society, as well as entrepreneurs in the building trades, were quick to lend their support to this new sophistication and self-consciousness on the part of the local architectural profession. They funded—in part through advertisements—a series of stunning exhibit catalogues that the Architectural Club published between 1908 and 1913.

The driving force behind this professionalization was Ellis F. Lawrence, principal in the firm of Lawrence and Holford and soon to become the founder and, eventually, dean of the University of Oregon School of Architecture. It was under Lawrence's firm guidance that the Pacific Architectural League would be launched in 1909. Two years later, the Oregon Chapter of the American Institute of Architects would join the regional and national architectural network.

More importantly, perhaps, it was largely on Lawrence's initiative that Portland acquired its first—and only—Beaux-Arts "atelier." Set up in 1909 under Lawrence's patronage and affiliated with the Society of Beaux-Arts Architects in New York, the Portland Atelier would become a local outpost for architectural scholarship and craftsmanship. Between 1911 and 1915, the last four years of the Atelier's existence, the city's finest young architects and designers gathered in a studio atop the "Old Sweeney Building" (now the Bishop's House) in downtown Portland. Here they honed their design skills under the critical supervision of recent Whidden and Lewis veterans, A. E. Doyle and Morris H. Whitehouse, who, like Doyle, had returned from a year's sojourn in Europe shortly before the Atelier's founding. These young designers would inject an even stronger dose of cosmopolitanism into the city than Whidden and Lewis had succeeded in doing during the heyday of their firm's domination.

This was an exuberant period in the history of Portland architecture. Most building designs reflected the Beaux-Arts-influenced classicism, which had become the trademark of the McKim firm in New York. While the city's most powerful architects—Whidden and Lewis, A. E. Doyle, Lazarus, Harrison Whitney and Morris

Whitehouse—were designing structures decked in the excessive ornamental manner of Beaux-Arts eclecticism, another Portland architect, William C. Knighton, would point the way to a different mode of architectural expression. As with the Viennese architects of the Secessionist period (1897–1918), Knighton would beat the bushes of historical revival for a new vocabulary of surface manipulation characteristic of Viennese Early Modern Design.

Born in Indianapolis in 1866, Knighton trained in Birmingham, Alabama and Chicago before moving to Salem in 1893, where he was an architect for the state of Oregon until 1896. He returned to Birmingham for several years before arriving in Portland in 1902. There is little doubt that Knighton, whose work was considered "far out" at the time, was the city's most iconoclastic practitioner in the early 1900s. His dismissal of the prevailing historicism in architectural design was aligned closely to the Secession manifestoes of Vienna and their rejection of nineteenth-century certainties. Taking his cue from Viennese architect Otto Wagner, Knighton supplanted the floral motifs and delicate swirling curves of Beaux-Arts classicism with the geometrical emphasis of the Vienna movement. In 1910 Knighton's orientation represented a radical departure for Portland architecture—the city was rapidly filling up with the glazed, ornate jewels of Doyle, Reid and Reid, and Whidden and Lewis—but his buildings, nevertheless, displayed a timeless element and indicated the path of future development.

His design for the Seward (now, Governor) Hotel (1909) reflected a unique formula of unrestrained, primarily geometric, ornament, which had found its fullest expression during this period in the carefully, elegantly composed pages of the Vienna Secession periodical *Ver Sacrum*. Knighton's hotel was decorated with flamboyant bursts of terra cotta, consisting of shield shapes, squares and large beads. "Spaceman" motifs—fashioned from bold, geometric styled components of glazed terra cotta—punctuated the cornice; the two "spacemen" protruding from the roof corner at right angles were the quintessential embodiment of Knighton's blazing audacity in the manipulation of applied ornament. The entire cluster, which crowned the building like an opulent diadem, confirmed the architect's infatuation with a vocabulary of ornament that was independent of all the prevailing revival styles.

A box-like, functional structure encrusted with ornament, the Govenor Hotel expressed the two sides of modern man as Otto Wagner and the Secessionists had seen him: the man of business and the man of taste. As with Wagner's highly praised Hofpavilion for the Vienna Railway (1898), Knighton's hotel carried this duality to a peak of intensity, with the decorative Aztec-like motifs protruding assertively from an otherwise prosaic and rational building design. Provocatively counter-balanced in the Governor Hotel—as well as in his functionalist designs for commercial warehouses (121 N.W. Burnside, 1910; 1231 N.W. Hoyt, 1906)—was the twentieth-century penchant for applied ornament (though in Knighton's work it eschewed classical styles) and a new, clear, cubic structural concept. A more restrained example of the architect's insistence on "the concept of unity of construction in a time of increasingly superficial decoration," was the hotel he designed in 1911, which now houses Jake's Crawfish Restaurant.

Otto Wagner, who towered over the whole development of architecture during the Secession Movement, "had declared war on the training of the memory, the faculty favored by historcism." In this vein, he condemned the Italian journey, classic capstone of a Beaux-Arts architectural education. Except for the imprint left by Knighton's work, the architectural innovations and spirit of fin de siècle Vienna—which, in retrospect, were startling harbingers of modern functionalism—did not leave their mark on Portland in any significant manner. Unable to devise an architectural style to express the outlook and needs of modern man, Portland practitioners continued dredging up *all* the historical styles to fill the void. Put simply, between 1907 and 1928 many of Portland's finest buildings were reduced to products of archeological study, an exercise, it should be pointed out, that was perfectly suited to the city's development during these architecturally formative years. Excluding his twentieth century classical design for Grant High School (1923), Knighton steered clear of the eclectic "style architecture" which had become synonomous in Portland with prestige, power and good taste.

In its place, Knighton referred to a "superb new ornamental vocabulary that was purely Viennese: spare, compartmentalized, geometric and bending the serpentine art nouveau line into Secessionist right angles." In the boldly geometric fireplace of tapestry brick that he designed for the Grout house in 1910, the architect revealed his penchant for the abstract, cubic forms of Viennese designers Josef Maria Olbrich and Kolo Moser. Again, combining concrete and picturesque appeal, Knighton's apartment building at 117 N.W. Trinity Place

GOVERNOR HOTEL
William C. Knighton
1911

(1910) boasted polygonal bay windows, stepped gables and a decorative frieze peppered with geometric ornamentation. In nearly all of his buildings, including the residence for Jesse R. Sharpe (1912, Knighton and Root) and the Tilford (Fine Arts) Building (1906), Knighton declared his commitment to a functionalist aesthetic.

Indeed, the architect's reverence for the modern would erupt with full force at the end of his career in his design for the Greyhound Bus Depot (Stage Terminal Building) (1939, Pengh, Knighton and Howell).

With its reinforced concrete and steel-frame structure, metal entrance marquee and glass block, the build-

46

ing was clearly informed by the spirit of streamlined modernity. A child of contemporary constructional methods, the Bus Depot was Knighton's permanent tribute to the primacy of the functional aesthetic. As with the Governor Hotel, it was extremely progressive in character, but by 1939 the influence of the Bauhaus School on Knighton's work was unmistakable. The emphasis on reduction of ornament, on flat surface and, above all, a severely rectilinear geometry, related it to the International Style that was taking architecture into a new era.

According to Fred Baker, a Portland lighting designer working during Knighton's time, the Governor Hotel, in its time, had been considered "far out." And yet, 30 years later, the Streamline Moderne of Knighton's Greyhound Depot—which was enlivened by a sensuously Deco blue-and-white sign added several years later—would be a convincing dress rehearsal for a technological future, which even the Great Depression would not completely dampen.

Knighton was not the only architect in the city who strayed off the beaten path during a period characterized by surging interest in classicism. Architect Robert F. Tegan, designer of Portland's Cotillion Hall (now, Crystal Ballroom), would also be up to his own devices. And the device in question was a ball bearing dance floor. In 1914 the tango, a new dance craze, had erupted in America, and a prominent Portlander would respond by erecting a building designed primarily as a public dance hall. With all their talent, there were some things that even Portland's best and brightest architects could not do, and designing a ball bearing dance floor was one of them. On 28 July 1913, a building permit was issued for the construction of a "Dance Pavillion and Garage" at the corner of s.w. 14th and Burnside. Completed in 1914 and named "Ringler's Cotillion Hall," the building featured an ingenuously designed "ball bearing floor" or "floating floor." The floor was designed to provide a resilient dance surface that could be "tuned" to accomodate various loads, rhythms and dance steps.

It has been said that Cotillion Hall houses the only remaining ball bearing dance floor built west of the Mississippi. McMath, who prepared a statement on the building for the National Register of Historic Places, has traced the intriguing history behind the structure which, although still standing, was put to rest as an entertainment facility after a Grateful Dead concert in the late 1960s. According to the Portland architectural historian,

Cotillion Hall was built and first owned by a prominent insurance agent, Paul van Fridagh and his widowed sister, Hortense van F. Taylor. But the real beacon behind-the-scenes appears to have been Portland's premier dance master of the era, M. Ringler.

After a stint which he held until 1903 as the physical director of the Portland YMCA, Ringler opened his own "physical culture studio" on Alder Street. Listed in the 1904 *City Directory* as "Physical Culture and Dancing," the enterprise, which soon became known as the Ringler Dancing Academy, moved into the Mulkey Building on Morrison Street. According to reports obtained by McMath, the heavy streetcar traffic on Morrison Street caused the rickety floor to tremble, which provoked the dance maestro to seek a financial backer for a new "up-to-date" facility. Apparently, Ringler solicited the services of a German-born architect, Robert F. Tegan, who had designed ball bearing dance floors in Chicago and Los Angeles. Tegan opened his Portland architectural office in 1910, and left in 1917 or 1918 for unknown reasons. The Cotillion Hall was inaugurated with a formal dress ball in 1914, and from all accounts, was a smashing success from its inception.

Exhibiting a strong Renaissance influence, the building's main facade was composed of seven arched bays, features whose spandrels were filled with 9″x9″ red and buff tiles laid in checkerboard pattern. Although private dance clubs had to lease the space for a year at a time, Wednesday and Saturday nights were reserved for public dance. Cotillion Hall, according to McMath, was "where young Portlanders were taught the rudiments of ballroom dancing, and with their elders, the stylish steps of the period—the tango, hesitation waltz, Charleston, fox trot, shag, varsity drag and many others."

Ringler continued his base of operations at Cotillion Hall until 1921, after which time the building was controlled by a succession of dancing instructors, under whose auspices it met with little financial success. The hall was closed from 1931 until 1935, when it was purchased by Ralph E. Farrier, who was also associated with the Oregon Casket Company. Despite its name change to "Crystal Ballroom" in 1951, the dance hall was a money loser and Farrier was forced to shut down operations.

In a 1961 interview in the *Oregon Journal*, Farrier commented on the building's architectural tour de force. "The floor of the Crystal 'gives', something like a mattress, as one walks or dances on it. It's called a ball

SIXTH CHURCH OF CHRIST SCIENTIST
Morris H. Whitehouse and Associates
1931

bearing because each of the scores of rockers supporting it has ball bearings." And the floor had some features even Tegan would have never anticipated: "You never get a Charley horse dancing on this," commented Farrier, "because the floor keeps time with the music. You can't get out of step . . . with 800 people out there the floor goes down when *their* feet go down. So if you try to go down at the wrong time, you find the floor coming up at you." As late as 1983, the curious ball bearing dance floor—believed to have been fabricated by a sash and door firm, the H. D. Carter and Company—had found a new raison d'etre. Using soda pop bottles as markers, several young disciples of "physical culture" had converted the springy floor of tango and shag fame into a

challenging slalom course for skate-boarders on their own ball bearing wheels. As might be expected, the reincarnation of Cotillion Hall into a "Skateboard Palace" was entirely unofficial.

By 1915, Portland's expanding population would require a greater diversity of downtown structures to accomodate a social and commercial life that began to show all the complexity and specialization of a maturing metropolis. Whitehouse, Fritsch and Doyle, while overlapping in many of their design projects, ultimately carved out reputations as architectural specialists. Of the three, Doyle provided the most encyclopedic range of building typologies, and would emerge as "*the* man" for banking and financial institutions, while Whitehouse's

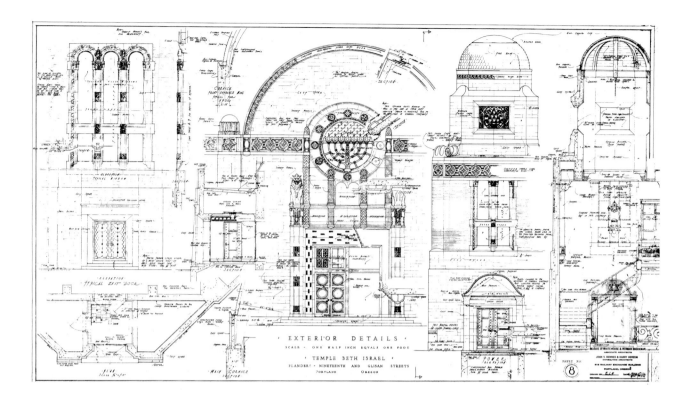

TEMPLE BETH ISRAEL
Whitehouse and Church/with Herman Brookman, John V. Bennes and Harry Herzog
1927

name would become synonymous with club design, and Fritsch's with "service" associations.

Ten years Doyle's senior, Whitehouse launched a practice in 1908 that would have the singular distinction of continuing, uninterrupted but for a changing cast of partners, through the present firm that bears the name Schuette and Wheeler. Trained at the Massachusetts Institute of Technology where he won the first Guy Lowell traveling fellowship for outstanding design work, Whitehouse spent the year following his 1906 graduation at the American Academy in Rome. His sojourn in Italy sharpened his eye for forms that would be peculiarly responsive to the light and moody rhythms of Oregon's atmospheric conditions.

By far the strongest expression of Whitehouse's immersion in Italian architecture would come forth in his design for the Columbia Gorge Hotel (1921). Set in a spectacular site west of Hood River on a high bluff overlooking the Columbia River, the hotel was executed in the white stucco and red tile of beachside Italian hostelries. These features theatrically transplanted the

Mediterranean resort idiom to the Pacific Northwest. That the commission for this swank hotel should have gone to "Molly" Whitehouse was, in retrospect, logical. Backed by Simon Benson, the promoter of the Columbia River Highway and former chairman of the Oregon State Highway Commission, the Columbia Gorge Hotel was to provide well-heeled Portlanders with an attractive destination for the sightseeing motor parties that were just coming into fashion. By the late teens Whitehouse had made a name for himself as the designer of Portland's most exclusive clubhouses.

Portland's upper crust had already been meeting for some years in the stately rooms of Whitehouse's Multnomah Amateur Athletic (1910) and University (1913) clubs, and passionate golfers traded—and would trade—notes in the clubhouses this architect designed for the Waverley (1912), Oswego (1923) and, eventually, Eastmoreland golf courses. Future members of the cigar-and-golf set would prep for college in the classrooms of Whitehouse's old Lincoln (1912) and Jefferson high schools, while the city's gilded and jaded youth would

49

TEMPLE BETH ISRAEL

Whitehouse and Church/with Herman Brookman, John V. Bennes and Harry Herzog

1927

turn out en masse at the Multnomah Stadium (1926), a collaborative venture between Doyle and Whitehouse.

For the Christian Scientist and Jewish congregations of the city, the firm led by Whitehouse designed the monumental and finely detailed Sixth Church of Christ Scientist (1931) and the Temple Beth Israel (1927). (The primary designer of Beth Israel was Herman Brookman; the Whitehouse office did the construction drawings.) An architectural triumph in a difficult-to-execute and distinctive Byzantine style, Temple Beth Israel drew its architectural inspiration, and much of its detailing, from the design of what was once the main synagogue in Essen, Germany (the synagogue is still standing today, but has been converted into a museum). The facework of Temple Beth Israel, with its delicately articulated Willamina brick, is among the city's finest. The Sixth Church of Christ Scientist, which R. W. Sexton called "a religious edifice designed along modern lines," also reflected Whitehouse's talent for brick ornamentation. Vaguely Aztec geometric forms appeared on the compounded main entrance portal and were continued throughout the stepped-back roof line.

Two major civic projects, both dating from the 1930s, evidenced Whitehouse's fluency with the Art Deco style that was rapidly making inroads into the designs for America's public buildings. Whitehouse's first venture in this new idiom was the Federal Courthouse commissioned in 1930. Into a time-hallowed Greco-Roman envelope, Whitehouse inserted Portland's most lavish Art Deco lobby. And he gave even freer expression to the precepts of "Moderne" design under the guiding hand of the New York architects who were totally responsible for design, Keally, Trowbridge and Livingston, with whom he collaborated in drawing up plans for the Oregon State Capitol Building (1938) in Salem. However, even here, the "Moderne" elements were discreetly underplayed to emphasize the proportions and the stripped down geometric composition so markedly derivative of classical morphologies.

The state capitol project exemplified the modus operandi which accounted, to some extent, for Whitehouse's success. In the Temple Beth Israel project, for example, no fewer than three designers—Herman Brookman and Harry Herzog rounded out the team—had reworked the plans a staggering 14 times before arriving at the final, richly symbolic and ornamented structure. Whitehouse's reputation, then, as a "correct" interpreter of period styles was explained, at least in part, by his knack for assembling crackerjack design teams.

The most notable among Whitehouse's collaborators were Frederick A. Fritsch and the French engineer, J. Andre Fouilhoux, both of whom worked on the University Club (1912), nationally acclaimed as an excellent and rare Oregon example of the Jacobean Revival style. Not the only European to seek and make his fortunes in the Great Pacific Northwest, Fouilhoux was one of those rare imported local talents—Pietro Belluschi was the

other—who would use their Portland experience as a springboard for world-class projects. Before forming a ten-year partnership with Whitehouse, Fouilhoux had put in a five-year stint in the Detroit office of world-acclaimed industrial designer, Albert Kahn.

After leaving Portland for combat duty in France, Fouilhoux joined Raymond Hood's New York architectural firm, which was awarded first prize in the international competition for the Chicago Tribune Building. Subsequently, as a partner in the office of Wallace K. Harrison and Max Abramovitz, Fouilhoux would be involved in the design for New York City's Rockefeller Center.

In Portland, there was meager opportunity for Fouilhoux to exercise the prodigious engineering inventiveness that went into plotting the soaring Chicago Tribune Building or Rockefeller Center. In the 1920s, after all, Portland architecture did not demand the engineering skills necessary to erect a true skyscraper. With the restrained exception of the Terminal Sales Building of 1926, designed by Frank Higgins of Doyle's firm, Portland's architectural illuminati showed little interest in the fashionable Gothic skyscrapers, such as the American Radiator Building (1924, Raymond Hood) and the Chicago Tribune Tower (1925, Hood and Howells), which had become the rage in Chicago and New York. The handsomely massed Terminal Sales Building was, nevertheless, a quirky, miniaturized "cloudscraper" worthy of note. Bearing a strong resemblance to Howell's Panhellenic Hotel (1928) in New York City, the Terminal Sales Building expressed the firm's latent modernistic impulses, and more than any other building in its time, pointed the way toward the crisp lines of the 1930s.

While practicing in Portland, Fouilhoux had more than ample opportunity to engineer the technologically advanced skeletons that Whitehouse fleshed out in "period" skins. In partnership with Whitehouse from 1911 to 1917, Fouilhoux would collaborate with Frederick Fritsch, a man described by his contemporaries as a "happy combination of an artist and a practical man . . . who had a clear understanding of engineering principles and respected them."

A "graduate" of the Whidden and Lewis' firm, which he had joined immediately upon graduation from high school, Fritsch came to be regarded as one of Oregon's most important and influential architects of the 1920s. He was one of the city's most skillful renderers, and had he lived beyond the age of 43, Fritsch likely would have

UNIVERSITY CLUB
Whitehouse and Fouilhoux
1912

seasoned into one of the undisputed giants of the region. His impact would have extended far beyond the buildings he designed and the students he taught at the University of Oregon Architectural School (1917–18) and its Extension Division in Portland (1924).

Like Doyle, the acknowledged grand master of encyclopedic historicism, Fritsch made the Beaux-Arts idioms of his buildings speak with a singular intonation. In the interest of expressing a personal style, Fritsch challenged the sacrosanct Beaux-Arts doctrine, which equated excellence with mere replication of a sanctioned stylistic model. While the Beaux-Arts-oriented architect enjoyed some freedom of choice in the catalogue of revival styles prescribed as appropriate to specific building functions, still, he was trained—and expected—to subordinate personal whimsy and taste to the ideal of fidelity to the classical model. Fritsch's design philosophy, to some extent, would violate the central premise of this approach.

As a card-carrying member of the Portland Architec-

PROPOSED ROOM FOR GOOD SAMARITAN HOSPITAL
Sutton Whitney and Aandahl
1946

tural Club, Fritsch invested six very active years in the Beaux-Arts Atelier (1912–17). He designed buildings whose exteriors seemingly invited easy identification with the Classical, Georgian or Colonial styles. In this respect, his early projects for the office of Whitehouse and Fouilhoux offered little in the way of idiosyncratic departures from the norm. As the firm's chief draftsman until 1917, Fritsch left the imprint of his architectural sophistication in the form of historically "correct" designs for the Multnomah Athletic Club (1910), the University Club (1912), and the clean, Sullivanesque lines of the little known C. S. Jackson residence (1916).

Only in projects completed during the decade of his association with the firm of Sutton, Whitney, Aandahl and Fritsch (1919–29), did Fritsch's mandarin underface came to the fore. A fluid repertoire of styles surfaced in the firm's designs for building types ranging from the commercial (Meier and Frank Warehouse and Delivery Depot, J. K. Gill Building, and Bates Motoramp Garage) to the bureaucratic (Roebling Cable and Wire Company and Weatherly Office buildings) to an assortment of hospital designs (Multnomah County, Shriner's, and Emanuel hospitals).

Fritsch's commitment to enriching the city's range of visual delights did not discriminate between the most utilitarian and the most august of structures. His design for the Public Comfort Station in Ankeny Park, for example, lacked none of the concern for dignified historicism that went into the palatial, gargoyle-studded facade of the Neighbors of Woodcraft Building (1929). But it was in the Masonic Temple (1924–25) and the Fruit and Flower Day Nursery (1928)—still considered the best examples of the "Fritsch" style—that historicism was most felicitously rendered in a *personal* vein.

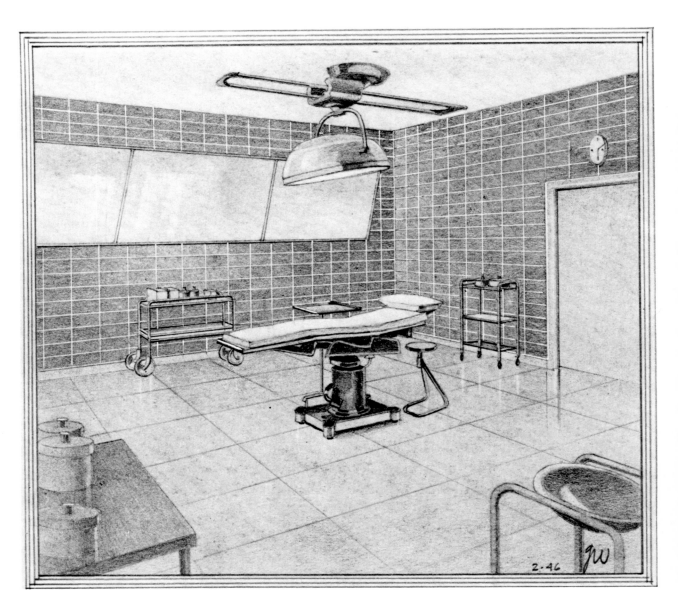

2·46

PROPOSED SURGERY SUITE FOR GOOD SAMARITAN HOSPITAL
Sutton Whitney and Aandahl
1946

Juxtaposing richly stylized Greek motifs with the loggia of Tuscan columns, the august Masonic Temple projected a sense of immovable solidity faintly reminiscent of the fabled Mausoleum of Halicarnassus (355-350 B.C.), one of the Seven Wonders of the World.

The eclectic detailing suggested not single, but rather, multiple historical associations. Fritsch's penchant for idiosyncratic and flamboyant designs would surface with numerous proposals for richly ornamented and sculpted towers that expanded on the Art Deco-leaning scheme

for the Neighbors of Woodcraft Building. Perhaps, only Tourtollette and Hummel's design for a sumptuously ornamented Art Deco tower slated, but never completed, for the present site of the Portland Building, could compete with the twisted and wickedly intelligent schemes that Fritsch produced during his relatively short career.

If the Masonic Temple conveyed the Fritsch "personal touch" with a mixed bag of historical tricks, the Fruit and Flower Day Nursery and the Waverly Baby

54

SHRINERS HOSPITAL FOR CRIPPLED CHILDREN
Sutton and Whitney
1925

Home bore the author's signature in a host of *original* details. Although wonderfully harmonized with the overarching Georgian or English Renaissance flavor, the dentilated cornice, the fenestration proportions and the architrave of the nursery originated in Fritsch's own imagination.

These designs, and particularly, Fritsch's exquisite drafting style, made a powerful impression on contemporary Portland architects. His superb handling of Willamina brick surfaces, which appeared in a number of his buildings, came to be considered something of a model. Among architects of the next generation, Pietro Belluschi greatly admired the fine brick work of Fritsch's buildings and in several of his own commissions, most notably the Portland Art Museum, would use it as a pattern.

Ill health prevented Fritsch from continuing his campaign to liberate the Beaux-Arts designer from a strict dependence on academic models. While undergoing medical treatment in Philadelphia, Fritsch sought to expand his own design skills and architectural vocabulary by studying the design and draftsmanship of Philadelphia architect William Howe. Along with William Lescaze, Howe would design the Philadelphia Savings Fund Building (1932)—acclaimed as one of the first skyscrapers in the International Modern style. However, in Fritsch's few remaining projects, some done in collaboration with his wife, architect Margaret Goodin Fritsch, no traces of this exposure to the revolutionary current of the International Style would emerge. It would be up to the new generation of architects—which included Pietro Belluschi and John Yeon—to effect the transition

PORTLAND MASONIC TEMPLE
Sutton and Whitney
1924

from the classical "academic exercise" school of the Beaux-Arts to the sublime "form follows function" aesthetic of the new modernism. Equally so, it would be up to these young mavericks to take Fritsch's individualistic ethic to its full elaboration in the personal Regional style.

However idiosyncratic his approach to academic design, Fritsch was not Portland's sole purveyor of innovative departures from the Beaux-Arts aesthetic. Before emigrating to Seattle, where he established a thriving practice, Floyd A. Narramore would earn himself the reputation of architect par excellence for the city's secondary schools. In 1919, Narramore's Franklin High School was voted one of the ten most notable examples of Portland architecture. In an article titled "The Most Notable Buildings of a City—What Are They?" Frederick Jennings described the school as "a large building, on the group plan, in Maryland Colonial style, which is eminently worthy of its purpose—the instilling of high

ideals in the youth of Portland." In his designs for such educational institutions as Franklin High School, Kennedy School, Couch School, and Benson Polytechnic School (the last two received Honorable Mention as Notable Examples of Portland Architecture in 1919), Narramore combined dignity, simplicity and charm with a number of twentieth-century classical styles. "When reviewing the structure from various angles and distances it has a most restful and pleasing appearance," wrote Jennings in *Architect and Engineer*, "and on closer inspection one finds that the simplicity of its well-studied detail is just as charming. The color of the brickwork and central cupola are exquisite . . . few cities of the country possess as successful an example of school architecture as is found in Franklin High School."

Portland's most elegant apartment houses, built during the early 1920s, were designed by Carl Linde, a talented architect who passed through the Doyle and Patterson office in 1911. Linde's Georgian-inspired de-

NEIGHBORS OF WOODCRAFT BUILDING
Sutton and Whitney
1929

sign for the Sovereign Hotel (1922) featured red tapestry brick juxtaposed with peach-colored glazed terra cotta facework. Richly ornamented, the Sovereign sat on a heavily rusticated base crowned at the second floor with a series of segmental-arched pediments, Doric pilasters and balustrades. Columns of bracketed balconettes with wrought-iron railings graced the Madison and Broadway Avenue facade, topped at the upper floor with a prominent round-arched broken pediment with Ionic pil-

asters, cartouche and round-arched opening. Designed in the Jacobean style, the Ambassador Apartments (1922) were also faced with red brick, but Boise sandstone, rather than terra cotta, provided most of the decorative embellishments. The reinforced concrete, H-plan structure featured bay windows with beveled glass, quoining and belt courses and symmetrically placed frontispieces with pediments, finials, pilasters and segmental arches.

Regardless of the style, Linde's apartment houses

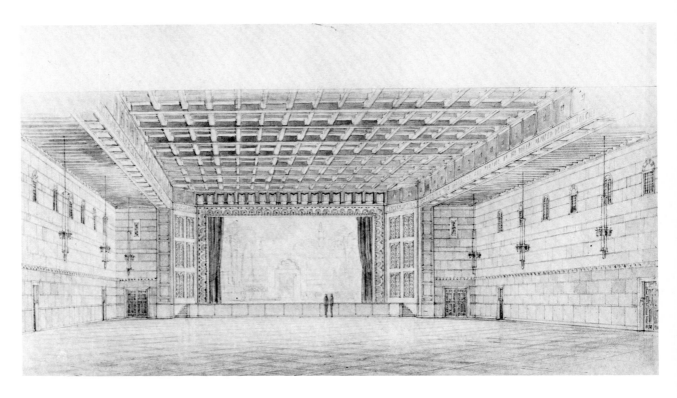

SHRINE HALL, PORTLAND MASONIC TEMPLE
Sutton and Whitney
1924

were a class act. His Envoy Apartments (1929) brought a touch of old-time Havana to its precipitously sloping southwest Portland hillside. Towering over a neighborhood of smallish apartment houses, the stucco Mediterranean-style behemoth looked like it could easily have been a transplant from the Lewis and Clark Exposition of 1905. Like Doyle, who had been his mentor for a brief period, Linde had a talent for fingering a broad range of revival styles. With the Embassy (1924), located only a short distance from the Envoy, he graced the Northwest residential area with Portland's first and only "Manhattan-style" apartment house. Lavishly ornamented with cast stone quoining and rustication, the Embassy was a powerful composition that melded features from the Georgian and Second Empire Renaissance Revival styles.

Clearly, Linde's architectural vision was rooted somewhere in the sixteenth or seventeenth century. When things took a turn toward the modern in the late 1920s, Linde's architecture took, well, a nose-dive. His "dime-store Deco" apartment house at 1736 S.E. Hawthorne (1929), would be eclipsed by more inspired apartment

houses in the Deco idiom designed by Harry Herzog, John V. Bennes and Elmer E. Feig in the early 1930s. And his mutant composition for the Ongford Apartments (1938) reflected little more than the architect's half-hearted attempt to keep pace with the modernistic spirit that had gripped Portland architectural circles by the late 1930s. A radical departure from the refined and elegant apartment buildings Linde had designed in the early and mid-1920s, the Ongford Apartments featured a prominent bull-nosed copper-clad canopy at the entrance, attached to a neon sign which beamed the building's name.

Historicism and its by-product, "style architecture," would dominate the building arts during the 1920s. But as early as 1891—beginning with Whidden and Lewis's Concord Building—an inchoate "modernist" sensibility had already begun to creep into the designs for a number of Portland buildings. Gradually, office buildings would be stamped in Louis H. Sullivan's "form follows function" mold. Built in 1894, only a few years after the Chicago Auditorium Building (1889, Sullivan), Portland's Sherlock Building imitated Sullivan's ground-breaking composition, which married elements of the Richardsonian Romanesque style with Sullivan's emphatically vertical composition. In 1894, F. Manson White would apply Sullivan's distinctive feathery vegetal ornamentation to his design for the Auditorium and Music Hall.

A decade later, David C. Lewis's European or, "Foreign Exhibit" Building (1905), at the Lewis and Clark Exposition would gain inspiration from yet another of Sullivan's pivotal models, the Transportation Building designed for the Chicago Exhibition of 1893. D. C. Lewis's treatment of the large arched opening at the center of his Foreign Exhibit pavilion dramatically recalled Sullivan's giant entrance arch, hyperbolically dubbed the "Golden Doorway."

Though D. C. Lewis may have been overly zealous in patterning his exhibition building on Sullivan's model, in three later Portland projects he found more appropriate vehicles for exploring the commercial style pioneered by Sullivan's Chicago School. The Lewis Building (1909), the Board of Trade Building (1907) and the Railway Exchange Building (1910, now the Oregon Pioneer Building) would complement the Sullivanesque lines of Whidden and Lewis's Corbett Building (1908). With its multitiered bay windows topped by wrought-iron balcony railings, the Lewis Building was reminiscent of the 1894 Chicago Stock Exchange Building designed by Adler and Sullivan.

In a period when many Portland architects were still fixated on the classical morphologies of Greek and Roman architecture, D. C. Lewis threw Beaux-Arts canons to the winds, and gave free reign to the Sullivanesque composition derived from the tripartite structure of the classical column. Except for the fussy ornamentation, the rational design and expansive windows of the Pioneer Building remained true to the precepts of Chicago School functionalism. Huber's, today Portland's oldest restaurant, founded in 1879, relocated to the building in 1910. Designed by Lewis and Beckwith, the dramatic interior featured Honduran mahogany panels, a marble floor and a vaulted ceiling with three stained glass skylights. Unfortunately, the exuberant Victorian color scheme applied to the Pioneer Building in the 1970s obscured, rather than highlighted, D. C. Lewis's attempt to "modernize" the face of Portland's commercial structures in the wake of the Lewis and Clark Exposition.

The Sullivan legacy would be best represented in Portland in a single work by William Gray Purcell. A relative late-comer to the city, Purcell settled in Portland in 1920, when he established the Pacific States Engineering Corporation. Bringing Sullivan's design precepts in their most pristine form, Purcell had worked briefly with the Chicago master before spending 11 years in the Midwest collaborating with George B. Elmslie, Sullivan's chief designer for more than 20 years. Key the dissemination of the Sullivanesque style, Purcell and Elmslie received national acclaim for the George C. Bradley house (1912) they had designed for a seaside perch in Woods Hole, Massachusetts. Splendidly sited and bursting with energy, the Bradley house was featured in the "Rise of American Architecture Exhibition" at the Metropolitan Museum of Modern Art in May, 1970. Although he designed a few nondescript private residences in the city, Purcell's principal Portland contribution was limited to the Third Church of Christ Scientist (1926), a crisp, modernistic edifice featuring an expansive, rhythmic fenestration scheme. Lacking historical and religious ornamentation, his Portland church expressed the strong lines and horizontal spatial oneness that characterized the Prairie School architects.

When it came to residential design, however, John V. Bennes was Portland's principal exponent of the Prairie School. Trained in Illinois and a great admirer of Frank Lloyd Wright, Bennes fashioned the Marcus J. DeLahunt house (1909), the Aaron H. Maegly house (1917), as well as his own residence, the John Bennes house (1911), in the Prairie idiom. The Bennes house, which in many respects, was a precursor for the more ostentatious Maegly home, revealed the architect's desire for order and abstracted shapes. With its low-pitched porch, tile roof, and band of ribbon windows streaming across the facade, Bennes' interpretation was not only bounded and clean, but exuded luminosity and permanence. In fact, at a time when his Portland contemporaries were beginning to turn toward the order of precedent, Bennes seemed interested in exhausting all at once the eclectic choices that had been exercised by the century that had just come to a close. In the Maegly house he floated the low-pitched roof as if it were an ornament, to cast it free from the flat, sharply windowed planes of the first and second floors. Melding the richness of the Italian "Renaissance Villa" with the stark horizontality of the Japanese teahouse, Bennes' lavish, earth-hugging home bore all the hallmarks of the Wrightian Prairie School: cantilevered bays, broad overhangs and narrowed window mullions. The interior was beautifully appointed with Honduras mahogany woodwork.

Although the Bennes and Maegly homes would become sparkling testimonials to the Prairie style sweeping

ELKS TEMPLE, LIGHTING FIXTURE
Fred Baker
1920

across the Midwest, the architect's later designs would cover the entire stylistic gamut from classical revival to Spanish colonial to Zigzag Moderne and, Art Deco. Each rearrangement in Bennes's vision was usually precipitated by the formation of a new architectural partnership. The Lowengart and Company Building (1910, Bennes and Hendricks), a seven-story building of reinforced concrete, would be one of Bennes's more unusual contributions to the city's expanding architectural museum. A slender, vaguely flatiron-shaped edifice, the Lowengart store popped out of its triangular plot between Burnside and Broadway like an eager weed. Except for being Portland's answer to Daniel Burnham's Flatiron Building (1903) in New York, the oddly shaped Portland curiosity had few redeeming features.

A versatile and hard-to-pin down stylist, Bennes shifted gears again with his designs for the Arthur Hotel

(1912, Bennes and Hendricks), the Hamilton Hotel (1913, Bennes and Hendricks), and Kidder Hall (1917, Bennes) at Oregon State University in Corvallis. Exhibiting classical symmetry, pilasters and anthemion embellishment at the cornice line, Kidder Hall reflected Bennes's skill with revival styles. His Portland hotels also reflected a classicizing bent. With Tuscan columns flanking the entrance, crisp yellow brickwork and terra cotta panels decorated with wreaths, cartouches, and pineapple motifs, the Arthur Hotel was a restrained, carefully embellished addition to the city's growing collection of buildings designed in a diluted classical style.

Only bare traces of the Chicago style would appear in the work of Portland architect Luther Lee Dougan who, after running away from home, obtained an architectural education at the Armour Institute of Technology in Chicago and Kansas State University. Ambitious and resourceful, Dougan supported himself during his training years by working as an office boy for Frank Lloyd Wright and, later, Louis Sullivan. The fledgling architect moved to Portland in 1903, and after a brief stint with Aaron Gould and A. E. Doyle in 1911, opened his own office in 1914. A year later, he entered into partnership with Chester A. Houghtaling to form Houghtaling and Dougan, a firm held in high esteem until its dissolution in 1925. Dougan practiced on his own, beginning in 1925, before forming a new partnership with Bernard A. Heims and Morton Caine (Dougan, Heims and Caine) in 1946.

With a string of collaborators, Dougan would embellish the cityscape with several precious, idiosyncratic edifices that reflected a broad stylistic palate. His best known contribution was the Elks Temple (1920, Houghtaling and Dougan), an ordered and exceedingly rational building whose uncluttered design was based on the Farnese Palace in Rome. Dougan's faithful fortress-like version of the Italian Renaissance classic was faced entirely with peachy-gray terra cotta and richly ornamented with Doric columns, a balustraded balconette, and segmental-arched window pediments. A stunning presence on its Eleventh Avenue site, the softly shimmering temple was the fourth home for this Elks Lodge, which had been organized in 1889. The declining membership which accompanied the Great Depression forced the Lodge into bankruptcy in 1932, at which time it lost possession of the building.

The interior of Houghtaling and Dougan's piece de resistance was a sybarite's dream. Banquet rooms and hallways were dominated by marbelized finishes and

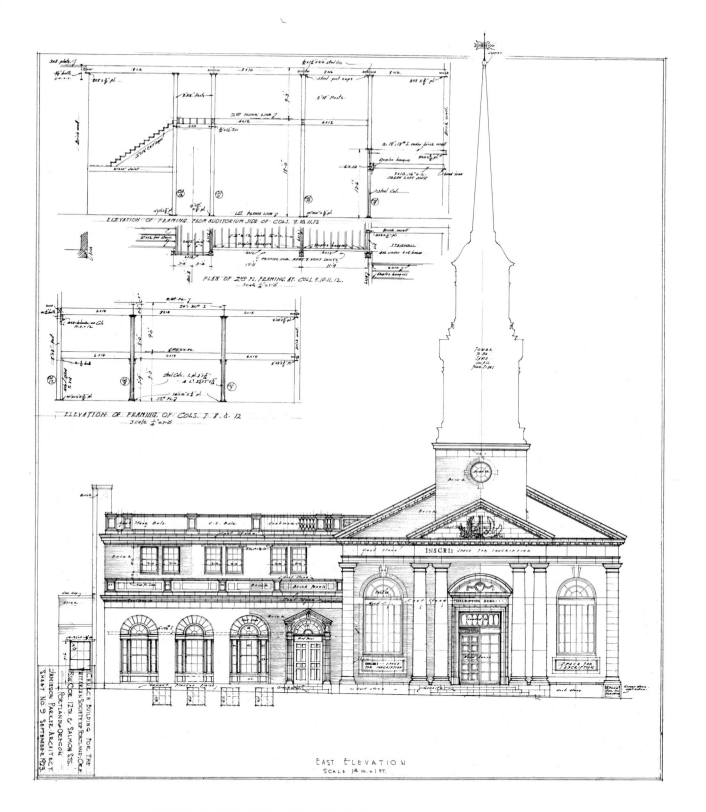

EAST ELEVATION
SCALE 1/4 IN. = 1 FT.

CHURCH BUILDING FOR UNITARIAN SOCIETY OF PORTLAND
Jamieson Parker

1923

garishly painted ceilings, while the library, paneled in black walnut, featured a marble fireplace and coffered plaster ceiling. The mammoth ballroom was decorated with elaborate cast plaster, Doric columns and lighting fixtures which, by 1984, had been converted into nesting sites for "stray" pigeons. The porcelain-tiled swimming pool in the basement provided still one more indulgence for Portland's short-lived pleasure palace.

The lavish Elks Temple would be followed by Houghtaling and Dougan's one-of-a-kind design for the Hunt Transfer Company Warehouse (1925). Although the foreboding, virtually windowless structure looked more like a military garrison in a politically troubled South American country than a storage warehouse, it, nevertheless, managed to revive the Spanish Renaissance theme of the Lewis and Clark Exposition of 1905. It was painted in a bold Post-modern color scheme in 1984.

After the Elks Temple (renovated and "postmodernized" as the Princeton Building in 1985) and the Hunt Transfer Warehouse, Dougan would devote his architectural talents to designing some of the classier medical and dental office buildings built in the city before the Depression. The Medical Arts Building (1926, Houghtaling and Dougan), an eight-story reinforced concrete tower faced with gray pressed brick, featured cast-stone quoining at the corner terminating in cast relief panels with human figures beneath the cornice. The colossal portico accenting the main entrance was the most dramatic element in the Houghtaling and Dougan scheme. Here, Tuscan columns and a round arch flanked by porthole windows conspired with profusive terra cotta ornamentation *within* the portico—garlands, fretwork, caduceus of Mercury, and a bust of Hippocrates—to make a powerful statement at the street level.

The Studio Building (1927) with its adjoining two-story Guild Theater was Dougan's first major project as a solo practitioner, and reflected his exploration of "off-beat" stylistic combinations. The building's mansard roof, with gable-roofed dormers, was juxtaposed with a brick facade that paid tribute to the Zigzag Moderne style Dougan used for his next medical tower. In the Studio Building, the architect again expressed his infatuation with decorative terra cotta elements. Busts of composers set in niches, panels with composer's names, and intricate medallions graced the exterior, while at the mezzanine level, the storefronts were arcaded with twisted columns and rounded arches. The grafting of an office building to a movie theater marked an intriguing exercise in contrasting functions.

Most of Dougan's work in the late 1920s expressed the kind of style and restrained elegance characteristic of modern architecture. If the Studio Building was imprecise and somewhat gawky in its melding of the Baroque and the modernistic, the Medical Dental Building would exhibit a number of characteristics of Art Deco architecture that would play an increasingly prominent role in Dougan's work. A ten-story steel-frame structure faced with brick and boasting a brightly decorated roofline, the Medical Dental Building (1928) had the quality of being a stage set, carefully related to the street on which the building faced. Dougan's penchant for sumptuous ornamentation was expressed both in the lobby's bronze molding bursting with chevrons and, on the facade, which featured cast stone motifs and medallions with busts in relief of historic physicians. The mausoleum-like marble entrance was flanked by two of the city's most elegant bronze light fixtures in the Art Deco style. Exuding the spirit of modernity, Dougan's building was a pastiche of lush textures and colors. The polychrome combination of brick, cast stone and marble showed Dougan to be moving clearly in the direction of Art Deco.

Between 1928 and 1930, one could see the emergence of tallish office buildings and apartment houses on the Portland skyline, but there was still a clear tendency to follow tried and proven architectural paths. Many of Dougan's compositions—including the Medical Dental and Studio buildings—derived their visual strength from the repetition of structural members and uniform steel-sash windows along tall rectangular facades. These restrained, modernistically inclined exteriors, however, were almost always broken by an interesting mix of humanoid and geometric details. The Lafayette Apartments (1930, Dougan), one of Portland's most unusual residential towers, boldly advertised Dougan's penchant for localizing ornamentation and sculpted panels at the upper stories—usually atop vertical piers—and at the entrance of his buildings. The flattened, incised designs included medallions, Ionic dentils and shields. But these geometric motifs would take second billing to the eight gargoyles—at the sixth story—broadcasting tragic, angst-ridden faces to theater patrons in the streets below. A two-story penthouse—with sculpted human figures at the cornice—continued the vertical thrust established by the piers on the main facade and, in the process, gave the building a stepped-back appearance.

In part due to his 100-year life span, Dougan produced works which illustrated a graceful transition from

ST. MARK'S EPISCOPAL CHURCH
Jamieson Parker
1926

historicism to modernism. Like Belluschi's work, Dougan's buildings of the early 1930s reflected a novel amalgam of traditional and modern ornamentation. Dougan, after all, was no stranger to style architecture. His devotion to the historicist bent of the Beaux-Arts education would come to life in the "Atelier Dougan," a thriving Beaux-Arts "revival" studio whose collaborating architects would garner several national awards in the period of its existence between 1930 and 1933.

That Dougan had become interested in the ascetic expression of the International Style was apparent in his remodeling scheme for Zell Brothers Jewelers (1949). Designed in 1917 by John V. Bennes, the three-story building originally featured an exterior finish of glazed terra cotta. The Dougan, Heims and Caine design called for replacement of the original exterior with polished limestone and steel-sash windows set flush with the facade. The crisp lines of the Zell's corner marquee—

with its finely hewn aluminum letters and crystalline composition—projected the strident geometrics and harsh angular forms that were also familiar in Art Deco crafts. By the early and mid 1950s, however, Dougan's firm would capitulate to the monotonous fenestration and boxy forms of the International Style which dominated the design plan for the State Office Building (1951) and the Park Plaza Apartments completed in the same year.

A number of other architects practicing during this period also filled in the fabric with notable buildings. The Jacobberger and Smith partnership designed additions for Marylhurst College completed in 1929, which included a swimming pool covered with a crystal palace-like dome, which is still standing (The original building was a convent designed by Doyle in 1911.). Their design for the Knights of Columbus Club (now Aero Club of Oregon) built in 1920 drew heavily on Byzantine influences (as did their Hibernian Hall, 1914) and featured a handsome loggia—since filled in—on the third story. The 1949 addition to the Aero Club (Whitehouse, Church, Newberry and Roehr) departed stylistically from the original structure, emphasizing instead the glass block aesthetic and clean, crisp format that was popularized by the International Style. Heirs to the oldest continuously running firm in the city, the Church, Newberry, Roehr partnership would produce a noteworthy Bauhaus-inspired design for the California Ink Company Building built in 1957.

For the most part, the Beaux-Arts tradition in Portland was still alive and well into the 1920s. Dripping with bulky terra cotta elements, Ernst Kroner's Odd Fellows building (1925) was one of the last designed in the Gothic style. Although by the early 1930s, Portland would witness the climax of these academic tendencies, toward the end of the 1920s most public and semi-official structures were still being clothed in period attire. Of those buildings still inspired by historicizing impulses, many would tend to be less archeological. While they retained a formal basis of composition, they often incorporated original twists. "When the taste of the designer was sure," wrote architectural historian Marion D. Ross, "this eclectic architecture was often very beautiful. The Masonic Temple in Portland designed by F. A. Fritsch (Sutton, Whitney and Anandahl, architects) and the Art Museum at the University of Oregon, Eugene, 1930, by Lawrence and Holford, well illustrated this trend."

The "artistic hangover" inflicting Portland's eclectic practitioners of "style architecture" was not easily palli-

ZELL BROTHERS JEWELERS (remodeling)
Dougan, Heims and Caine
1949

ated. The city's most established and influential firms—those led by Doyle, Sutton and Whitney, and Whitehouse—were still content, for the most part, with "personalizing" their designs within the constraints of what European architects, especially, saw as an increasingly suppressive Beaux-Arts tradition. The work of other talented local designers, however, would not be contained by historical prejudice. Such architects as Bennes, Harry A. Herzog, Luther L. Dougan and Elmer E. Feig would plunge headlong into the fiery furnace of a new architectural movement. But even among those architects hankering to rebel against traditional ideologies,

ODD FELLOWS BUILDING
Ernst Kroner

1925

most were not yet interested in an overtly revolutionary style or complete severance with the past but more in rephrasing the existing modes. In retrospect, Art Deco architecture provided a crucial link between nineteenth-century historicism and the exotic and dynamic influence which culminated in Europe during the first two decades of the twentieth century. "One could call the Art Deco architect an avant garde traditionalist," sug-

gested Rosemarie Haag Bletter in *Skyscraper Style*, "[who] provided rich textures, architectural ornament, and polychrome effects a clear bridge to the architecture of the past."

In Portland, and elsewhere, the 1920s marked a period of buoyant optimism butting against the dour realities from which Americans struggled fitfully to recover after World War I. However agonizing the effects of the war, the military campaign was instrumental in importing the most contemporary European developments in art, architecture and design into the American mainstream. But perhaps nothing heralded the shape of things to come more than the "Exposition Internationale des Arts Decoratifs et Industriels Modernes," held in Paris in 1925. The first international exhibition organized solely for the applied arts in more than a century, the Parisian design fair included displays of ceramics, textiles, wrought iron and covered every branch of the decorative arts from architectural interiors to children's toys.

"Upon being invited to exhibit at the Paris Exposition," noted Laura Cerwinske in *Tropical Deco*, "American designers realized they had nothing to submit that was representative of the U.S. character. American arts were still highly derivative, fixed upon such . . . period styles as American Colonial, Spanish and Italian Renaissance, Tudor and eighteenth century French and English." This startling recognition, suggested Cerwinske, "initiated an important period of self-examination" that culminated in architectural "expressions of amazing power and scope from which evolved many of the classic designs we consistently employ today."

Shortly after being hatched at the 1925 exposition, Art Deco would come to Portland. The patterning, color and geometry of Egyptian and Aztec cultures, the embellished and articulated doorways and tapestry-like brickwork celebrated by American Deco would gradually trickle into the schemes of such Portland architects as Bennes, Herzog and Elmer Feig. Smitten with the most up-to-date architectural fashions, these architects would infuse the decorative energy of Art Deco into apartment houses that began to sprout up along Park Avenue and N.W. Everett Street during the mid 1920s.

Bennes, whose work in the late teens was still heavily tainted by the Beaux-Arts tradition, would undergo one more architectonic shift. Under the spell of a partnership he formed in 1924 with Portland's "Deco King," Harry A. Herzog, Bennes's architectural focus was permanently deflected from the Prairie style of the Maegly house and the "diet classicism" of the Arthur Hotel, to the sculpted facades of Art Deco apartment buildings. The Bennes and Herzog firm rapidly gained a reputation for architectural renovations (Bullier Building, 1924, Bennes and Herzog), apartment houses (Jeanne Manor and Parkway Manor, 1931, Bennes and Herzog) and movie theaters (Hollywood Movie Theater, 1925, Bennes and Herzog) executed in the Art Deco and Streamlined Moderne idiom.

The visual energy of the Jeanne and Parkway manors rested on the dynamic interplay between the tapestry brickwork of their facades and a theatricalized doorway. Jeanne Manor was highlighted by cast stone ornamentation, geometric motifs and zigzag patterns. True to its Art Deco origins, the facade was punctuated by casement windows with metal sashes separated by brick piers which rose uninterruptedly from the ground floor to the roofline. In both the Jeanne and Parkway manors, there was a concentration of dynamic ornamentation in the compound segmental arch entrances and in the elaborate brick diaperwork between piers. Although sedate by New York or Miami standards, the apartment houses by Bennes and Herzog succeeded in bringing the rudiments of Art Deco design before the Portland public.

Perhaps the zenith of Herzog's contribution to Portland Deco would become manifest in his design for the Regent apartment house (Herzog, 1937), located at 1975 N.W. Everett Street. The decorative treatment of the doorway was markedly restrained compared to the mausoleum-like passageways he had concocted with Bennes for the Jeanne Manor at the beginning of the decade. But this understatement aside, the building was quintessential Deco. The progressive tensions and reliefs accomplished by the colorful tapestry arrangement that dominated the brick facework reflected the vision of an architect who composed his buildings with geometric deliberation. Attuned to the subtleties of the Art Deco style, Herzog carried this theme through to the smallest details. A radical transformation in typography had been accomplished during the Deco decades and Herzog was able to incorporate these changes into his plans for the building's signage. In the streamlined lettering scheme selected for the Regent, he made every attempt to integrate the clean angularity of the fashionable Futura typeface (1927) with the entire structural composition. And there were still other fine strokes. The recessed light fixtures embellishing the doorway featured fluted, frosted glass shades. Running horizontally at the center of each fixture, the word "REGENT" was beamed to passersby through turquoise-colored glass. Studded with graceful details, Herzog's designs were characterized by formal stylistic balance and, unlike other Portland buildings of the time, they capitalized on ornament, color and geometry to call attention to themselves and project with panache their Art Deco theme.

Working in the same idiom, architect Elmer E. Feig designed apartment houses that were even more flamboyant and self-promoting in character. Melding the

Egyptian revival style with Art Deco, Feig's Manhattan (1930) and Morland apartments (1931) were peppered with Egyptian motifs and decorative geometric elements. The symbols and imagery used by Feig had become popular after the discovery of King Tutankhamen's tomb in 1921. This archaeological milestone strongly influenced European and American adaptations of the Deco style, which eagerly assimilated the color, geometry and unfathomable richness of ancient Egyptian art. The Morland Apartments at 1530 N.E. Tenth Avenue featured terra cotta reliefs of sarcophagus designs and Babylonian motifs, while the Manhattan Apartments publicized itself with cast stone reliefs of King Tut flanking the entrance and sprouting atop vertical piers. The sculptural references to ancient Egypt imbued the buildings with elements of fantasy and surrealism rarely seen in other buildings of the period.

Though seldom celebrated in books or commentaries devoted to the history of Portland architecture, Feig was certainly one of the city's most colorful and capable designers. In addition to the Deco-cum-Egyptian Revival scheme of which he seemed so fond, the architect would also resuscitate the Spanish Renaissance theme of the Lewis and Clark Exposition in the form of several Mediterranean style apartment buildings he designed for northwest Portland. The Irving Manor (1929) featured stucco foliate reliefs and lacey spiral columns at the portico. With only slight variation, the sedate design was repeated for his Teshnor Manor completed the same year. His Deco style apartment house at 1938 N.W. Flanders, featured cast stone finials that sprouted gracefully just above the roofline.

Assertive, but never overwhelming, the architecture of Feig and Herzog reflected that part of the American character enthralled by esoteric cultures, the probing density of Cubism, the rhythms of the jazz age, and the fictional realms opened up by Hollywood movies such as *The White Sheik*. Attempting to put these new-age dreams into perspective, Cerwinske cautioned that "along with the idealism and drama of the new American style [Deco], there existed a line of divine caution, for just over that line lay decadence, mediocre indulgence and crassness." Fortunately, this was a line that Portland's Deco designers seldom dared to cross.

As Portland groped and shimmied through the 1920s, it became evident that the cityscape would derive a healthy dose of inspiration from the Art Deco rage sweeping across America. Apartments by Herzog, Bennes and Feig, as well as office towers by Dougan, combined the compostional cleanness intrinsic to the Bauhaus School with either the exotic ornamentation of esoteric cultures or the geometric dynamism of the machine age. "In a number of ways Art Deco had the characteristic of being an architecture of 'both-and'," wrote Cervin Robinson in *Skyscraper Style*. The Egyptian Revival style popularized by Feig in the Manhattan Apartments and the Aztec geometries used by Herzog in the Regent supported Robinson's suggestion that buildings designed in the Deco style relied on decorative forms that "might be both primitive and modern, or both traditional and exotic . . . [which made] the architecture . . . either richer in meaning, or . . . more imprecise in intention."

On the whole, Portland buildings flavored with Art Deco ornamentation projected a softer, more restrained image than "New York" or "Big City" Deco. In the nation's most formidable metropolises, emphatic skyscrapers and apartment towers in the Art Deco tradition celebrated, above all, man's control of his destiny and his domination over nature via the machine. Put simply, Deco in the Big Apple was powerful stuff. Portland buildings could hardly have been expected to compete with the Brobdignagian brick tapestries hung from the sky, designed by such architectural heavyweights as Ely Jacques Kahn, William Van Alen and Raymond Hood. Yet despite the paucity of structures in the city that could qualify as "Big City" Deco, Portland's architectural museum would, nevertheless, receive at least two stunning contributions in the "uptown style": The United States Courthouse (1931, Whitehouse and Church), and the Charles F. Berg Building (1930, Grand Rapids Design Service).

Publicizing itself with jagged points, chevrons, triangles, elaborate friezes and dense ornamental fields made from cast bronze, the lobby of the U.S. Courthouse gained a reputation as Portland's Art Deco jewel box. The exuberant detailing which adorned the grillwork, moldings, mail boxes and writing tables in the bronze and marble Art Deco lobby represented the finest Art Deco craftmanship in the state of Oregon. Easily up to New York standards, the lobby's crystalline design was one of the best produced by the Whitehouse and Church partnership. According to Earl Newberry—who traveled to Washington D.C. in 1930 to negotiate details for the Courthouse project (on the firm's behalf)—James Smith, one of the firm's architects, was responsible for the working drawings, which developed out of a collaboration with Walter Church and Roi Morin, as well as Newberry. By 1984, an enlightened restoration of the Art Deco lobby would be in

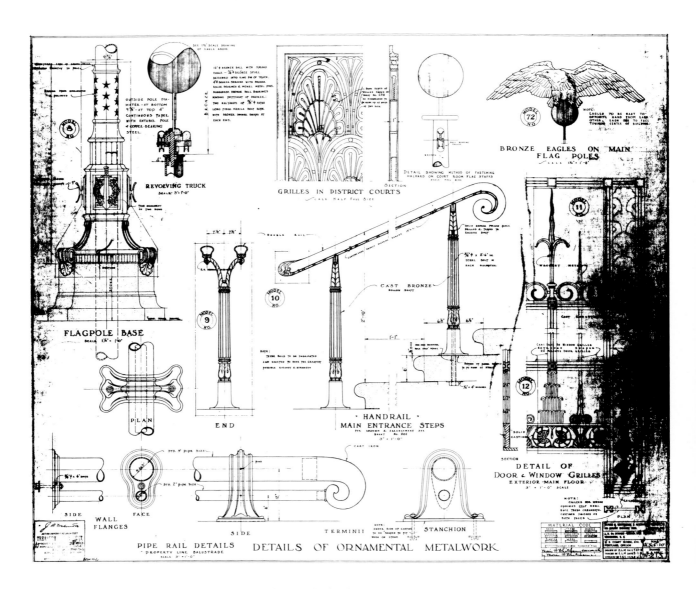

UNITED STATES COURTHOUSE
Morris H. Whitehouse and Associates
1931

progress under the design direction of Allen, McMath and Hawkins, acting as consultants to Zimmer Gunsul Frasca, the project architects.

New York style Art Deco architecture would also come to Portland in the form of the Charles F. Berg Building. Completed in 1930, this architectural "stage set" in glazed terra cotta consisted of an elaborate facade that had been applied to the structural frame of a pre-1930 building. Without question, Oregon's jazziest and most spirited entry to the Deco idiom, the design for the Berg Building was imbued with the drama and fantasy of Fritz Lang's *Metropolis* (1926). It combined the geometry of Aztec ruins with the refinement of Oriental

art and exhibited a love for luxurious textures and exquisitely applied ornament. Indulging in the use of rare and expensive materials, the "cinema-style" facade was a pastiche of rich surfaces that capitalized on images of exotic animals and organic motifs. Bursting with polychrome glazed terra cotta in black, cream, aquamarine and 18-karat gold, the building's exquisite face filled the retina with decorative motifs that included chevrons, sunbursts, rain clouds and peacocks. The visual impact of panels densely packed with ornament and color was further heightened by window mullions and pilasters sheathed in black terra cotta.

With its polychrome flashiness, theatrical overtones

CHARLES F. BERG BUILDING
Grand Rapids Design Service
1930

and explosive geometric forms, the Charles F. Berg Building projected the kind of style and elegance the Portland public was more likely to encounter in an Eric Von Stroheim film than in real life. This was Art Deco architecture at its finest, bristling with the razzle-dazzle of a fantasy period piece and screaming the ta-ra-ra-boom-de-ay of a gilded age. And something more. As

architectural historian Rosemarie Haag Bletter pointed out in *Skyscraper Style*, "Art Deco architecture, at least in New York, was created mostly for big business, and the result . . . was not an austere corporate imagery, but an architecture that was good advertising, meant to *entertain* and draw in the public." Portland's Deco master-piece satisfied these criteria. It was a retail outlet for women's clothing with which the passerby could instantly emphathize, as if it were some obvious theatrical gesture. "Such buildings are enticing on a common level," emphasized Bletter, "like the ruddy cheeks of a Rubens Madonna."

It can be safely assumed that during the 1930s, the powder room of the Charles F. Berg Building was teeming with the ruddiest cheeks in Portland. For the women's lounge, interior decorator George A. Mansfield applied an aquamarine color scheme he had seen in the submarine gardens of Catalina Island. Lavish sensuality and primping behavior must have certainly flourished in Mansfield's blue-walled room, handsomely appointed with mauve velvet divans, furniture finished in coral and silver, and a transluscent hand-colored mural depicting an underwater scene filled with irridescent rock bonitas and black-laced angelfish. According to an article appearing in the *Oregonian* on 31 January 1930, the store's original interior also included doors finished in silver-stippled lacquer with black enameled columns, draperies laced with silver threads, bronze or satin silver light fixtures with frosted glass and an elevator cab with chrome-plated fixtures designed by Tiffany of New York.

Brightly ornamented and lavishly furnished, the Charles F. Berg Building was a precious, one-of-a-kind addition to Portland's architectural microcosm. Purportedly designed by Kem Weber for the Grand Rapids (Michigan) Design Service, Berg's retail palace was built for the age of prosperity, hot jazz and the ball bearing. In front of Berg's gold-gilded facade gleaming like obsidian, sleek Packard limousines would disgorge Portland's demure and well-heeled matrons, who adjusted their boas, while flashing neon lights on Broadway reflected on slanted rear windows.

When the Charles F. Berg facade was installed in 1930, there were only two other buildings in the country with 18-karat gold decoration: the American Radiator skyscraper in New York and the 12-story Richfield Oil Company Building in Los Angeles. Referring to the gilding used on Raymond Hood's American Radiator Building (1924), Herbert Croly wrote the following in the January 1925 issue of *Architectural Record*: "The gilding of these stories suggests . . . bewildering possibilities as to the future use of surfaces with colors, glows, and lights in order to convert . . . places . . . into a wonderland of elaborate, fanciful and vivid masses and patterns." Less than a year after the Charles F. Berg Building was completed, the stock market crashed, casting the architectural nugget into a rather anachronistic light. Although

its design was conceived at the zenith of the glorious and prosperous decade, the building would spend its youth in an age characterized by the distant wail of saxophones and the nagged drone of "Brother, can you spare a dime."

If the Whitehouse and Church partnership and Grand Rapids Design Service looked to the flash and dazzle of New York for their inspiration, then Portland architect Ernst Kroner would find his in the small Deco apartments of balmy, sun-drenched Miami Beach. Kroner's design for the Rasmussen Village (1928) communicated the daintier side of Art Deco architecture, perhaps best described as Tropical Deco. An apartment complex of stucco buildings boasting gracefully streamlined interiors, the Rasmussen Village emanated the open-air, sociable tone of a Miami Beach ocean-front neighborhood. Each building in the development announced itself with a frontispiece decorated with rib mullions and planes of glass block. Bold horizontal "eyebrows" shading the doorway were reminiscent of the casual frivolities that tickled the white facades of small hotels and apartments in what is now designated as Miami's Tropical Deco Historic District.

Most other Portland buildings built in the Deco idiom during the 1920s and 1930s were only of modest quality, and could not compare with the elaborate jewels that studded New York and Hollywood. The four-story, reinforced concrete Commodore Hotel (1927, Herman Brookman), was typical of Portland buildings designed in the "dime store" or "low" Deco style. An important gathering place in the 1920s for the city's burgeoning "auto row," the Commodore was one of the few commercial buildings designed by Brookman and the only Portland hotel built in the Art Deco style. Sculpted pelicans and eagles and decorative balls adorned its pilasters, while diamond-shaped patterns of flowers graced friezes just below the building's roofline. Brookman, born in New York in 1891, came to Portland in 1923 at the request of businessman Lloyd Frank, who wanted him to design his own home (the Frank Estate has since become part of the Lewis and Clark College Campus and is in the National Register of Historic Places). In addition to his collaborative role in the Secession-influenced scheme for Temple Beth Israel, Brookman designed residences for Julius Meier, Martin Zell, Lee S. Eliot and Harry Green.

A number of minor luminaries (among others, Bennes, Herzog, Narramore, Parker, Houghtaling) contributed significantly to Portland's architectural museum. Work-

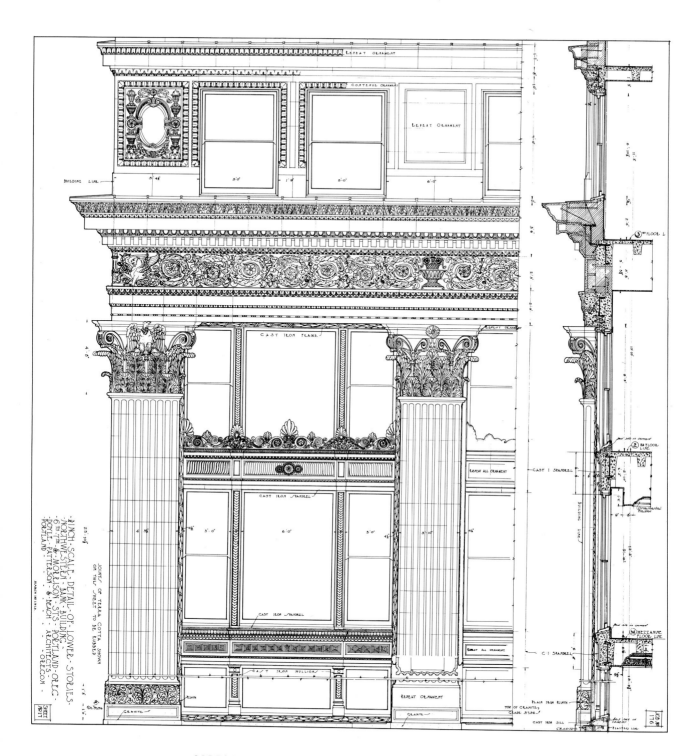

NORTHWESTERN NATIONAL BANK BUILDING

Doyle, Patterson and Beach

1913

U.S. NATIONAL BANK, DOORS
Avard Fairbanks
1931

ing usually within the framework of one or two styles, these designers embellished the cityscape with architectural nuggets that expanded the stylistic range and enlivened the texture of Portland's built landscape.

But none of these firms could compete with the phenomenal range and versatility of A. E. Doyle. The *Architectural Review* for June 1919 pointed out that "there is a popular idea, which like many other popular ideas is based upon the modern fetich [*sic*] of specialization, that architects are best in some one style or type of work. The actual fact is that an able architect deals ably with any type of work he undertakes. Mr. Doyle is an example."

In the best sense of the word, Doyle's contribution to the city's architectural landscape was pluralistic. He tapped a broad number of historical periods for the vocabulary of individual buildings. "Greece is the place for an architect," Doyle wrote to Donald J. Stewart in Rome on 12 December 1925. And then added: "And in these days when so many are running after false gods, there is a need for scholars trained in the Classical traditions." By 1927, a formidable body of work would have emerged from the drafting pencils of Doyle and his colleagues. His firm would be able to claim a long and distinguished catalogue of completed residential, commercial and educational projects. Doyle worked in a number of academic styles, and with the Neahkahnie cottages built between 1912 and 1916, he would even set the stage for a regional residential idiom with strong modernistic leanings.

Although his buildings encompassed a variety of styles, it was in his designs for banks and office buildings, which constituted the bulk of Doyle's commissions within the downtown core, that this versatile architect was at his inventive best. Here he skipped and jumped among a variety of Classical and Italian Renaissance palatial styles (Selling Building, 1910; Bank of California, 1924; Pacific Building, 1926), giving each of his clients a distinctive structure that would relay the unique message of status and prestige each required. In the Northwestern National Bank (1913, now the American Bank Building), Doyle expressed the "academic" sensibilities of McKim, Mead and White, which had been imparted to him during his apprenticeship with Whidden and Lewis, and, later, Henry Bacon. "The exterior ornament, cornices and detail are of good classic design," wrote Cheney, about the Northwestern Bank, "though perhaps not so interesting or restrained as in some other of Mr. Doyle's work."

NORTHWESTERN NATIONAL BANK BUILDING
Doyle, Patterson and Beach
1913

U.S. NATIONAL BANK
A. E. Doyle
1917

The late Roman Empire came to life for Portland in 1917 with Doyle's design for the U.S. National Bank Building. Modeled on McKim, Mead and White's Knickerbocker Trust Building in New York (now demolished), the U.S. National Bank Building also bore a resemblance to the Bank of California (1907, Bliss and Faville) in San Francisco, another Knickerbocker "knock-off." The light pinkish gray matte glaze for the exterior of Doyle's building was developed especially for the project by Gladding, McBean and Company. With its 49-foot colonnade and richly ornamented Roman frieze, cornice and balustrade, the building summarized Doyle's unwavering commitment to classical foundations. The bronze main entrance doors were designed by Avard T. Fairbanks, a professor of sculpture at the University of Oregon. Patterned upon Ghiberti's fifteenth-century *Gates of Paradise* doors to the Baptistry in Florence, Italy, the exquisitely carved panels of the western doors depicted scenes following the theme, "The Development of Oregon Country." The entire edifice, inside

and out, was rich, but tastefully, ornamented with the finest materials and appointments available at the time. The 30-foot high main banking space was dominated by a cast plaster coffered ceiling and tile floor of Italian and Hungarian marble. Cast plaster eagles which studded the column capitals, teller enclosures of Hauteville marble and bronze lighting fixtures designed by Fred C. Baker completed what, to this day, is still one of the most dignified interior spaces in the city.

Along with three other buildings designed by Doyle—the Central Public Library (1912), Reed College (1912) and F. J. Cobbs residence (1918)—the U.S. National Bank was recognized by an AIA jury in 1919 as one of the "ten most notable examples of architecture . . . within ten miles of Portland City Hall." In a comprehensive article (*Architect and Engineer*, July 1919) summarizing Doyle's finest work, architect Charles H. Cheney, one of the jury members, waxed poetically about the virtues of Doyle's Roman masterpiece. "Just enough color has been used on walls and ceiling to give a relief from

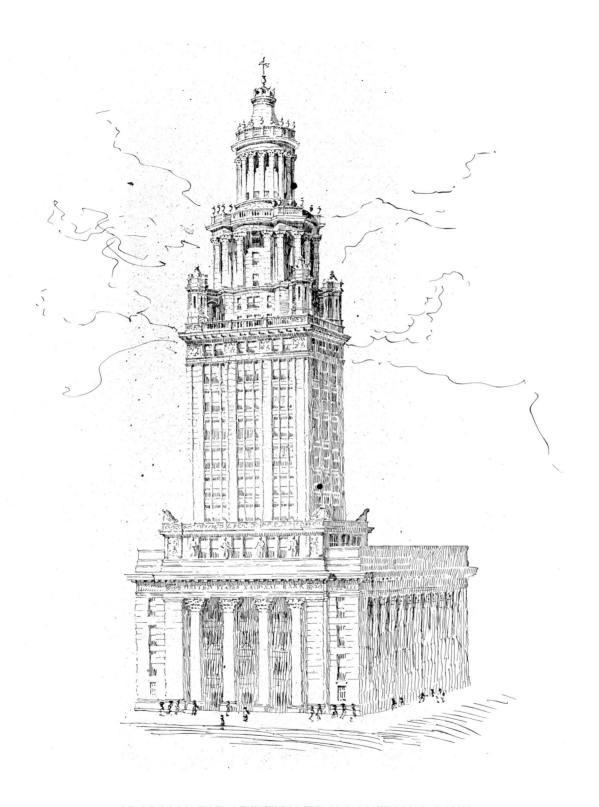

PROPOSAL FOR ADDITION TO U.S. NATIONAL BANK
A. E. Doyle
1922

MULTNOMAH COUNTY PUBLIC LIBRARY
Doyle, Patterson and Beach
1913

monotony, [while] the warm yellow tone of the marble floors and banking screen create an inviting atmosphere." But equally attractive in Cheney's mind were the "functional" features built into the banking complex: "A stimulating feature of this bank," wrote the architect, "is the large space devoted to gymnasium, recreation and rest rooms for both men and women in the basement and mezzanine floors. The good ventilation . . . is another noticeable fact, showing that the health and efficiency of the employees are well taken care of. No dull or nodding bookkeepers or stenographers are noticeable in this building."

Despite Cheney's glowing analysis in July, 1919, the jury's full report published in the March 1919 issue of *Architect and Engineer of California*, reflected a slightly different point of view. The u.s. National Bank Building was "an interesting business structure in a modern adaptation of the Roman style, selected largely because of its excellent plan and charming interior detail and color-

ing," wrote Frederick Jennings. And then he added, somewhat derisively: "It is not so striking in appearance as another Portland bank building [First National Bank, 1916, Coolidge and Shattuck], yet is devoid of the ponderousness and flaws of plan and design of the latter. The exterior is florid, lacks somewhat in originality of motive, and its three story colonnade may be criticized as not truly expressing the one-story banking room with two stories of offices above the interior." Even with its faults, "this fine banking room is so beautiful and appropriate," confessed Jennings, "that the jury felt the building was entitled to a place in this list."

When asked to design the Multnomah County Public Library (1913), Doyle again consulted the roster of period idioms in use for public libraries, and took his inspiration from a number of elements (especially the fenestration) in McKim, Mead and White's Boston Public Library (1888–92). But foregoing a slavish imitation of McKim's Italian Renaissance structure, Doyle turned to the English Renaissance or, as he called it, "Georgian" style. The result was a suavely understated structure that, in the architect's own words, conveyed a "certain refined dignity befitting a library building." And the critics agreed. "There is great beauty of detail in many parts of both exterior and interior," wrote Jennings in the official AIA jury report, "although the building quite plainly shows a limited purse at the disposal of the architect."

The same concern for working within an architectural convention had led him, a year earlier, to render Reed College's Eliot Hall (1912) in the crisp Tudor or "Collegiate Gothic" vein that formed a visual link between this educational institution and its Ivy League counterparts on the East Coast. As Cheney pointed out in *Architect and Engineer* of July 1919, Doyle "has contrived exceedingly well to get the spirit of the Old English Collegiate Gothic while adapting his style to present-day conditions." Despite his use of classical revival styles, Doyle would almost always attempt to link his buildings and ornamentation to the region, as he had done with his design for the Forestry Center in 1905 and then, again, with the door detailing on the U.S. National Bank in 1917. "In viewing these Reed College Buildings one finds there are many interesting subtleties in design and detail that are not apparent at first," wrote Cheney. "While taking the best of this fine old [English] style, Mr. Doyle has not let himself be intrigued into copying details appropriate to the Old Country only. Instead of the English Lion and Unicorn as finials, conventionalized typical Oregon animals have been used in the most interesting way."

For the Benson Hotel (1913), Doyle chose the French Baroque style popularized by Chicago's famous Blackstone Hotel completed a few years earlier. In this exceedingly attractive 13-story hotel building, Doyle featured an exterior of red brick, trimmed with white terra cotta, and a green mansard roof. The architect also received kudos for the ornate lobby, glowing with Circassian walnut imported from Russia. As Cheney emphasized, "The architect was engaged to select all furnishings and the rooms and lounges therefore present a most harmonious and restful view. Would that more hotels were inspired to employ a man of the good taste of Mr. Doyle in selecting their furnishings!"

The Terminal Sales Building, Portland's first version of the "Gothic" skyscrapers that were sprouting along the skylines of Manhattan and Chicago, was of an unabashedly modernistic design that massed rectilinear slabs like the vertical striations of a basalt formation. At street level, the modernistic tower was punctuated by the unexpected addition of a filling station, also designed by Doyle's office, that featured a conical gas-pump shelter reminiscent of a Japanese parasol, ingeniously doubling as a logogram advertising General Petroleum Gasoline. This daring excursion into the stripped-down geometries of the new modernism, however, remained only an isolated episode in Doyle's career as Portland's "master builder."

The years between 1921 and 1928 marked a transitional period in the Doyle firm. As the economic pace accelerated during the mid-1920s, the city's pillars began to take an interest in expanding the city upward. The building boom flooded Doyle's office with a number of large and prestigious projects including the Pacific Building (1926), the Public Service Building (1928), the Bank of California (1924) and the Terminal Sales Building (1926). Doyle's health was failing due to Bright's disease, and in 1927, anticipating his death, he sold the firm to three of his employees—Dave M. Jack, William H. Crowell and Sid Lister, who would continue his work under the name A. E. Doyle and Associate. Pietro Belluschi, who brought a fresh perspective to the firm with his arrival in 1925, became chief designer in 1926, and would eventually gain complete ownership of the firm by 1943.

Although Doyle certainly played an instrumental supervisory role in all the designs that issued from his studio, Charles K. Greene, the firm's chief designer at the time, was entrusted with the initial designs for the Bank of California as well as the Pacific and Public Service buildings. On the basis of research conducted under the auspices of the University of Oregon and the Oregon Historical Society, Felicity Musick advanced a thesis in 1976 that credited the design for these three Italianate gems to Greene, who had been with the Doyle office since 1909. Continuing an "educational" tradition established in the firm, Greene had been sent to Europe sometime between 1919 and 1922, partially at Doyle's expense, to gain first-hand knowledge of classical Greek and Roman architecture. Returning from this sojourn with an especially keen interest in Italian architecture, Greene would draw heavily upon Roman morphologies, composition schemes and detailing for the buildings that would subsequently come to life on his drafting table.

In 1921, the three sons of the late Henry J. Corbett enlisted the services of Doyle to design the Pacific Building on a site then occupied by the Corbett family home.

REED COLLEGE
Doyle, Patterson and Beach
1912

Under Doyle's supervision, Greene began the design in October 1922. His early drawings for the project showed a rather static, uninspired design that shared many features with the Lipman, Wolfe department store. The architect's initial drawing included a decorative cornice, but the tile roof and continuous fenestration that would give the Pacific Building its crisp, yet fluid, Italianate feel, were notably absent. According to Musick, "it was only *after* the designs for the Bank of California were completed, that the Pacific Building began to take shape." The final design for the Pacific Building was magisterial. The cream-colored, glazed terra cotta rustication at the lower three floors, decorated roof cornice and red clay tile roof were essentially an amplification of the palatial formula adopted for the Bank of California. The Italian theme was carried through into the interior, with the lavish use of marble, intricate metalwork and ornamented grills and light fixtures in the main lobby.

The Pacific Building forcibly asserted Doyle's ambition to build the city upward. The penthouse studios he designed for his firm and for Mrs. Henry Corbett offered magnificent views of the skyline. The functions of his own office were distributed on two levels, the first consisting of a business office and library with the second taken up by drafting rooms in the attic. Expansive windows allowed for uniform illumination in the drafting area, and the library was handsomely paneled in walnut and included a marble fireplace.

The Pacific Building opened in 1926 with a gala celebration. By this time plans were already underway for an even more formidable "skyscraper," the Public Service Building. Inspired to some extent by the design for San Francisco's Gas and Electric Building, Greene's early scheme called for a building with a forecourt, flanked by two wings, and a tower with a colonnade spanning the two uppermost stories. Constructed on the site of the Henry Failing home, the half-block, 16-story edifice was, in 1928, Oregon's tallest building. The two original occupants of the building, the Pacific Light and Power Company and the Portland Gas and Coke Company, had intended the building to be a tower that "would project above the skyline as far as possible." The terra cotta tile roof was crowned with a story-high neon sign beaming "GAS, POWER, HEAT, AND LIGHT" toward each coordinate of the compass. Due to shrinking economic horizons, however, the east and west wings were limited to a mere two stories—the lobby and mezzanine levels. They were eventually increased from two to five stories in 1947–48, and to the present 12-story height in 1957.

Unfortunately, Greene was never able to complete his final scheme for the Public Service Building. "Although [Greene was] an extremely talented architect," wrote Musick, "his personal life began to conflict" with his professional activities. In an interview with Musick on 21 May 1976, Belluschi, who some 50 years earlier had been a designer in Doyle's firm, moved to the heart of the problem when he said: "He [Greene] was a homosexual who made no bones about it, and he got into trouble because people were not ready to accept him." According to Musick's thesis—which was based upon interviews with McMath and Belluschi—Greene's "practice of throwing wild parties for the high school students of Northeast Portland was not looked kindly upon by the school board at the time. They finally took action and he was given forty-eight hours to *get out of town.*"

This "High Noon" intrigue temporarily sent shock waves through Portland's premier architectural firm. Doyle, who had been in Europe during the summer of 1926 consulting physicians about his illness (Bright's disease), was forced to return home and reorganize his design staff. Pietro Belluschi was appointed new chief designer and charged with continuing where Greene left off on the Public Service Building. In the shuffle, Greene relocated to Los Angeles, whence he communicated sporadically, claiming an "excellent job and good life." In reality, "he died alone of starvation several years later."

The original lobby, which has since been drastically changed and remodeled (by SOM), was the work of Belluschi alone. In the *Oregon Journal* of 1 January 1928, its Art Deco-like interior was described as "especially attractive with bronze work on the elevator shaft doors, large pendant lamps, golden brown marble and the vivid coloring of the ceiling." The Public Service Building opened on 3 January 1928 with much celebration including guided tours and the release of carrier pigeons. Described as "the latest word in efficiency," the building featured an elevator, which could travel 500 feet per minute, and thermostatically controlled heat and ventilation.

Of all his projects during this period, however, perhaps, the most unexpected to have issued from Doyle's office—with Belluschi's collaboration—was the Broadway Theater (originally Hippodrome, 1927). A flashy amalgam of vernacular and academic styles best described as "Beau Neon," the Broadway Theater was a three-dimensional calligraphic explosion crackling with the glitzy excitement of Hollywood "Mediterranean"

BENSON HOTEL
Doyle, Patterson and Beach
1913

come to Portland. Unprecedented though it may have been in Doyle's extensive portfolio, the Broadway Theater nonetheless obeyed the imperative to wed style with function, which was the hallmark of his architectural vision.

Throughout his career, Doyle's all-consuming ambition was to invent and build a Portland architectural microcosm commensurate with the demands and potential glories of a young West Coast metropolis on the rise. Shrewd, fiercely independent, and well-positioned in social circles, Doyle was Portland's master builder of the early twentieth century. His firm reigned over the city in much the same way that McKim, Mead and White had dominated the architectural landscape of New York and Boston.

Building by building, his firm enriched the fabricated landscape with layers that reflected a multitude of historical periods. In the process, Portland's architectural microcosm began to fill out. To an even greater degree than his mentors, Whidden and Lewis, Doyle recapitulated in Portland the course of Western history in architectural forms. To be sure, much of what happened in Portland architecture after 1909—with respect to scholarship, vision and design standards—can be traced through a lineage that had its origins in the Doyle firm. "Doyle set the tone of downtown," McMath explained in 1983. "He worked with first-class clients. And other architects envied him because he was able to convince his clients to spend money on quality materials. The true testament to Doyle's work is the fact that, with one exception, his buildings are still standing and serving the function for which they were intended."

In January 1928, three weeks after the gala opening for the Public Service Building, Doyle died of Bright's disease. On his deathbed, he wrote the following words to his colleague Sid Lister: "Wanting something is the first process in getting it. Sooner or later we all put concrete foundations under our air castles." But Doyle had done much more. He had escorted the city through an epoch of intense, almost delirious growth. He designed structures that gratified the public's demand for bigger buildings and a more cosmopolitan architecture. In the process, Doyle's firm—along with those led by Whidden and Lewis, Whitehouse, Jacobberger and Smith, Sutton and Whitney, Bennes and Hendricks, Lazarus, Schacht and others—nourished the development of Portland's architectural microcosm. It was one that could be seen as having taken form, in part, under the direction of Portland's own coterie of master architects, in part under the influence of architects based in other cities.

When Henry Villard selected McKim, Mead and White to design the Portland Hotel, he had planted a seed that would take more than a century to fully ripen. Unwittingly, the railroad baron set into motion a robust tradition of architectural infusion that, over the span of a century, would deliver the city into architectural maturity. Along the way, a number of significant, though not always stellar architectural projects would be introduced into the cityscape by "foreign" architects. These included: the landscape plan for the Lewis and Clark Exposition (1902, Olmsted Brothers); the Wells Fargo Building (1907, Benjamin Wistar Morris III); the Yeon Building (1911, Reid and Reid); the Spalding Building (1911, Cass Gilbert); Charles F. Berg Building (1930, Grand Rapids Design Service); Chase Bag Company (1944, Austin Company); the Harbor Drive Plan (now demolished, 1950, Robert Moses); the First Interstate Tower (1972, Charles Luckman and Associates); 200 Market Building (1973, Rudat, Boutwell and Partners); the Portland Public Service Building (1982, Michael Graves); and the Pacwest Center (1984, Hugh Stubbins and Associates/SOM), and the Opthalmological Clinic and Research Center (1987, Richard Meier).

Although designed and orchestrated primarily by local architects, the city's architectural fabric took shape under alternating cycles of selective *receptivity* and *resistance* to the contribution of outsiders. Even when a "foreign" building or design was poorly received, the city's architectural cognoscenti—short of eradicating the offender—would find a way of making the best of a blunder.

In the 1970s, the "error in judgement" that permitted the First Interstate Center to become part of the cityscape generated public outcry in both the scholarly and popular literature. "Los Angeles architects Charles Luckman and Associates, with apparent disdain for Portland's urbanity," wrote McMath, in *Space, Style and Structure*, "have ably expressed the essence of corporate power and arrogance in the marble sheathed tower with fake fins reminiscent of Detroit auto design in the Fifties." Even the distinguished architectural critic Ada Louise Huxtable, who has always kept her eyes sharply focused on the Portland building scene, would come to the city's defense. Writing in the *New York Times* on 19 June 1970, Huxtable quoted a publicist for the Luckman firm, which touted the design as "40 stories into the air, a towering challenge to Mt. Hood.' And then, in response, the critic continued: "Against the Suave Schlock of Portland's current California imports, Mt. Hood doesn't stand a chance."

OREGONIAN BUILDING
Reid and Reid
1891

JACKSON TOWER
Reid and Reid
1912

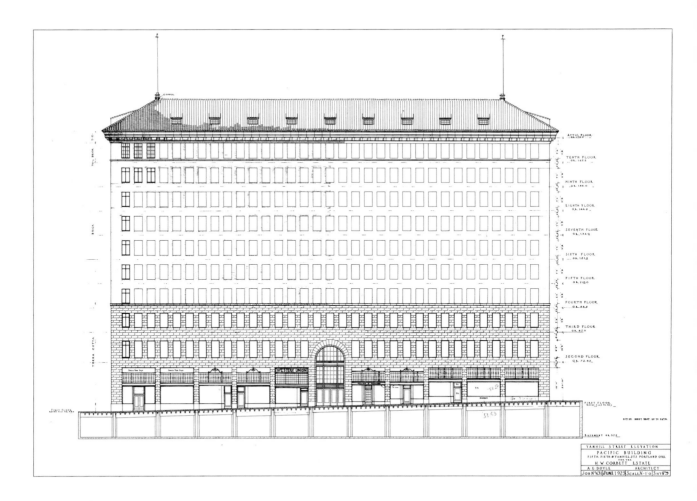

PACIFIC BUILDING
A. E. Doyle
1925

The Luckman gaffe produced an eruption of xenophobia in Portland, spoiling chances for outside architects with similar ideas from making their mark on the city. Even "naughty" additions such as The Portland Building by Michael Graves, would raise the red flag for architects and developers contemplating unrestrained, Postmodernist imports. In the wake of a backlash, local architectural firms with context-sensitive schemes, such as those for the Pioneer Square and the Performing Arts Center, would, in most cases, emerge victorious. On the other hand, well-behaved entries from the outside that "knew their place,"—the Yeon Building (1911), the Portland Hotel (1890), Auditorium Forecourt (Lawrence Halprin & Associates, 1972), and the Spalding Building (Cass Gilbert, 1911)—would not only stimulate the influx of foreign blood, but would give local architects a shot in their drawing arms.

In a letter written in 1925 to architect Donald J. Stewart, A. E. Doyle wrote: "I believe with him [Henry Bacon] that there is not much new that is good that is not in some way based on something old that is good." Although Doyle probably did not know it at the time, these words would characterize the architectural evolution of the city in which he had played such an important role. By the 1980s, the city's best building projects— whether new or restored—would respond, in one way or another, to Portland's rich architectural landscape. Portland's unique architecture "personality" would develop through a gradual accretion of architectural strata, which most often took the form of *concrete* additions— buildings, parks and public squares. But, these strata also took the form of *conceptual* blueprints that would make an impact on the city's architecture through design guidelines and competitions, urban master plans and

ST. VINCENT'S HOSPITAL
Justus Krumbein
1890

preservation policies. For the most part, the addition of new layers to the Portland cityscape was carefully conceived, carefully censored and carefully constructed. Although late in coming, with the introduction of historic preservation ordinances in 1968, even the subtraction of a layer would be carefully regulated.

These strata would achieve a "critical depth" approximately a century after Whidden had arrived in the city to supervise construction of the Portland Hotel. Taken as an *architectonic* whole, by the early 1980s this multi-layered foundation would furnish both the design and the historical inspiration for a new, Portland-based architectural vision.

In 1984, Willard Martin's ultra-historicist Pioneer Courthouse Square (a.k.a. "Willard's Ruins")—occupy-

ing the site of "Villard's Ruins"—suggested that Portland's architectural vision was one that knew its roots and, therefore, as Doyle had hoped, could renew "the old that was good."

The best buildings erected in Portland during the first three decades of the twentieth century had sprung from the recognition that uses for buildings change over the decades, but that deep parts of human beings do not change. Whidden, Lewis, Doyle and many others knew that great architecture must tell the meaning of their age to those who *first* experience the architecture. And to those who would experience it in the future, it would have to tell the stories of its past. "The test of a Classic," Doyle wrote in 1925, "is something so well done that it is impossible to tire of it!"

GETTING MODERN

THROUGH TECHNICAL acrobatics and decorative ecstasies, Portland's well-positioned retinue of "Beaux Architects" succeeded in carrying a stylistic movement based on French decorative arts to its fullest realization. Between 1890 and 1928, they left the city a lasting, singular, and respectable architectural tradition. Although the next generation of architects would produce work of equally impressive stature, their monuments would carry the signature of a new, entirely fresh aesthetic and social vision.

Following the death of Albert E. Doyle in January of 1928, Italian-born architect Pietro Belluschi, who had been a designer with the firm since 1925, quickly became the principal actor in the enterprise, which was renamed A. E. Doyle and Associate in 1927. Along with the firm's engineer William Kemery, Belluschi became a partner in 1933, and would purchase the firm's remaining shares a decade later. The talented architect, who had become increasingly enamored with the new "modernist" sensibilities in the air, would tap an altogether different architectural vein than that which had fed Portland's generation of "Beaux Architects" between 1895 and 1928. And while Belluschi's generation would resist the stylistic orientation of its predecessors, Doyle's spirit for architectural innovation, meticulous scholarship and insistence on high standards would be propagated by the Belluschi-controlled enterprise. Like the old firm under Doyle's tutelage, Belluschi's firm, too, would become the launch pad for a distinguished retinue of master builders and planners who would have a profound impact on the city's urban fabric and skyline in the following generation.

Although Belluschi would become the most celebrated architect to work in Doyle's stable, there would be other luminaries, among them Richard Sundeleaf, who spent several months in the firm between 1923 and 1924, and would design Jantzen Mills, the Woodbury and Company Warehouse and retain other prominent industrial commissions.

The lines of descent between Belluschi's firm and Portland's next generation of architects were solid in some cases and dotted in others. Architect, historian, and preservationist George A. McMath, whose firm Allen, McMath and Hawkins, would become the city's premier restoration firm during the 1970s and 1980s, spent the summer months of 1945 in Belluschi's office. McMath, who was 14 years old at the time, assisted in the lettering design for Waddle's Restaurant at Jantzen Beach. The line between Belluschi and the architectural movers and ground breakers of the 1960s and 1970s, solidified permanently in 1950 when Belluschi sold the firm to Skidmore, Owings, and Merrill (SOM) to form the entity Belluschi, Skidmore, Owings and Merrill (BSOM). According to the original agreement with SOM, Belluschi's name was dropped from the firm in 1955. And in the early 1950s, Robert Frasca, subsequently chief designer for Zimmer Gunsul Frasca, studied at MIT, under Belluschi, who was then dean of the School of Architecture.

As McMath pointed out in *Space, Style, and Structure*, "No other city has experienced such a succession of inter-related architectural firms as the Whidden and Lewis—Doyle—Belluschi triumvirate, each dominating a successive 20-year period from 1890 to 1950." In the course of 60 years, each of these master builders would draw deeply from his architectural imagination to shape the pieces out of which Portland's three-dimensional jigsaw puzzle would emerge. The city confronting each of them was a vital, living organism, undergoing constant, economic, demographic and cultural expansion, challenging each generation with architectural needs peculiar to its own time. Although lush, exquisite examples of the Queen Anne (Knapp house, 1882), High Victorian Renaissance (New Market Theater, 1871), Italianate (Pfunder house, 1883) and Richardsonian Romanesque (Leadbetter house, 1894) styles peppered the city's landscape in the late nineteenth century, Portland had only the bare beginnings of a significant tradition in urban structures.

Whidden and Lewis built on these beginnings. Their elegant Revival Style hotels, office buildings, banks and civic structures took the provincial city out of its architectural backwater and brought it into the orbit of sophisticated urban centers. Doyle expanded on the Beaux-Arts-inspired project of his tutors and brought it to completion. Pluralistic in his approach to styles, he created a new stratum of buildings synthesizing the historicist aesthetic with modern modes of construction. He had championed a campaign to tame the city by colonizing it with an encyclopedic range of place-making structures. But if by the end of the 1930s the city had blossomed into a vigorous and robust urban "place," it had sprung from the same architectural sensibilities that built European and East Coast cities of its day. In his choice of historicist styles, Doyle had made the architectural past of Western civilization come alive in the specific present of Portland.

Yet something seemed out of joint. In the world of architecture, there was a need to select and stress the details that conformed to the notion of an age coming into its own—the age of Hupmobiles and Packards, zoot suits and flappers, cubism and the clipped rhythms of Cole Porter; the age of the vogue for things elegantly understated, elegantly unornamented, for things modern. When it came his turn to take the helm, it was as if Belluschi heeded the advice a Persian general had passed along to his emperor in the fifth century, B.C.: "We should be more efficient, Sir, if less decorated."

Belluschi broke the tyranny of the exhausted past, and helped the city's architecture express the full complexity of modern sensibilities. Unlike Whidden, Lewis and Doyle, whose taste for fifteenth- and sixteenth-

PROPOSAL FOR COMMONWEALTH BUILDING
A. E. Doyle and Associate
1930

century architectural models had made them men of the Renaissance, Belluschi and a loosely styled fraternity of like-minded architects—John Yeon, Van Evera Bailey and Richard Sundeleaf—strove with varying degrees of success to be Renaissance men in the full sense of the word. Trained in the same Beaux-Arts tradition that had shaped his forerunners, Belluschi steered Portland architecture out of its dependence on time-sanctioned precedents and guided it into the virgin territory of a new critical regionalism that bridged the gap between local culture and architectural modernism. For Doyle and his

retinue of "Beaux Architects," architecture had been primarily an exercise in ornament, stylistic pluralism, city-building and scholarship. For Belluschi, architecture would become an aesthetic and even spiritual discipline that would question received ideas in the hope of creating an authentic modern architecture for the region.

Pluralism led Doyle to experiment with the full gamut of accepted period styles. It led Belluschi's generation beyond the architectural academe into the raw experience of life, space and light. In this respect, the Beaux-Arts language would bear no direct heirs in Belluschi's generation, though its line would again come to life in the new historicists—most notable among them, the firm of Zimmer Gunsul Frasca—that would surface in the late 1970s and early 1980s. The "lesser" legacy of vernacular architecture, with which Doyle's generation had experimented, would not go unclaimed. To the extent that Doyle himself had pioneered a regional vernacular with his Neahkahnie cottages (1912–16), the uninterrupted continuity of his influence would be assured by the fervor with which Belluschi and his colleagues adopted regionalism as the cornerstone of their design philosophy.

In the early 1900s, a number of nearly anonymous local builders as well as professional architects, most notable among them, Ellis F. Lawrence and Morris H. Whitehouse, would colonize the region with "Shingle style" residences. The main forces in innovation, however, would rest in the hands of architects whose professional lineage would be traced in a direct line to Whidden and Lewis' office. A. E. Doyle, credited with being the first outstanding figure in the "regional movement" in residential design, apprenticed under Whidden and Lewis, and broke new ground with his Neahkahnie designs.

Later, architects Pietro Belluschi and John Yeon would help give full expression to the new "regional" ideas burgeoning beneath the shingle facades of Doyle's cabins. Lean on commercial architectural commissions, the Depression decade produced a number of groundbreaking projects that expanded on the regional "seed" Doyle had planted in Neahkahnie.

Belluschi's first residence on Council Crest (1936), and later, the Kerr house (1941) as well as John Yeon's Aubrey Watzek (1937) and Kenneth Swan (1950) houses, made clear that a unique regional design idiom had emerged. Cross-pollinated with the new "International Style" of the early 1930s, Belluschi's and Yeon's residential "regionalism" would subsequently be cultivated by out-

89

standing talents such as John Storrs, Van Evera Bailey and Saul Zaik in the 1950s, and, in the 1960s by Richard Campbell and William Hawkins III.

With a few exceptions, the regional stamp introduced by Belluschi and Yeon in the early 1930s would remain limited to residential structures. "Regionalism," of course, was not an entirely novel concept in architecture. Architectural critics Alex Tzonis and Liliane Lefaivre pointed out in their essay "The Grid and the Pathway": "Regionalism has dominated architecture in almost all countries at some time during the past two centuries. By way of general definition we can say that it upholds the individual and local architectonic features against more universal and abstract ones."

By-and-large, Oregon's regional architecture was limited to log houses, wooden barns and covered bridges built by the early settlers of the 1840s and 1850s. These structures, however, rarely showed traits that might be considered distinctive of the region; they were not unlike those found in other areas with similar natural resources and colonization patterns. As Belluschi recognized, "A dominant industry always produces a corresponding architecture. And in Oregon, there was wood. When you go to Norway, or Russia, or, especially, Japan where wood is the natural material, you can recognize the development of a regional architecture."

While a dominant material may have been an essential factor in the evolution of a local style, it could not serve as the sole generator of a distinctive architectural idiom. Throughout the nineteenth century, settlers to Oregon built wooden structures that recreated architectural forms long familiar in the East and other parts of the country. Thus, for example, the late-Victorian houses and churches that appeared in Portland and its environs in the last decades of the nineteenth century were nearly indistinguishable from those sprouting in cities and towns across the country. Often their only claim to "regionalism" would be based on the use of indigenous materials. By skillfully working wood to imitate masonry, William W. Piper (Jacob Kamm house, 1872), Warren H. Williams (Corbett house, 1875; and Calvary Presbyterian Church, 1882), translated a gamut of popular Victorian styles into local materials. At best, the nineteenth century-residential Victorian architecture of Piper and Williams offered exquisite replicas of "alien" building styles originating in England (Queen Anne), France (French Second Empire), and Italy (the Italianate style). At worst, in the hands of lesser architects and builders, they were clumsy pastiches that did not reflect

PROPOSAL FOR COMMONWEALTH BUILDING
A. E. Doyle and Associate
1930

the peculiarities of the region. In short, authentic regional architecture had not yet emerged.

In this respect, until the tradition established by Doyle, Wentz, Belluschi, Yeon and others, "regionalism" was understood as little more than the realization of established designs adapted to indigenous materials. For the ambitious architects who surrounded Wentz, Belluschi and Yeon—as well as those that followed—a regional style depended upon the high level of place- and self-consciousness demanded by the regionalist philosophy of painter and philosopher Harry Wentz.

According to McMath, the Wentz philosophy espoused "the idea of a simple, organic, informal architecture using native materials and showing a respect for the site and the Oregon countryside." During the years 1912 to 1916, Doyle, Wentz's lifelong friend, designed four cottages at Neakhahnie, including his own and one for Wentz, considered the clearest expressions of the painter's regionalist ideas. "There were undoubtedly many influences on both Wentz and Doyle as no style blooms suddenly without relation to the past," McMath noted. "The wooden architecture of H. H. Richardson and McKim, Mead and White on the Atlantic Coast, the contemporary work of Greene and Greene, and Bernard Maybeck in California, the indigenous Oregon farm buildings and, being an eclectic age, possibly the traditional rural architecture of northern Europe, all contributed in some way to these early cottages."

In the late 1930s and early 1940s, Belluschi, Yeon and Bailey expanded Wentz's philosophy and Doyle's example into an autonomous Northwest wood tradition. Theirs would be a regionalism that found its governing inspiration in the age, in the range and quality of the local light, in the topography of a given site and in a structural poetic that precipitated—naturally, it seems in retrospect—from the combination of local materials, vegetation and construction methods.

Working primarily in residential design, these architects were committed to the ideal that authenticity precipitates under a constellation of factors specific to the environment, user and function. The results—Yeon's Watzek house (1937), John Storrs's Portland Garden Club (1954), Saul Zaik's Philip Feldman house (1957) among others—addressed a host of "intangibles" ranging from the psychological to the emotional to the aesthetic. When Belluschi set out to design his first house on Council Crest in 1936, he said he wanted it to be "clean and simple but not modernistic—above all, that it be in harmony with the hills and Oregon first."

Within this new group of regionalists, Belluschi would be especially successful in mediating between the individual and universal elements of a timeless architectural ideal. The most celebrated member of his generation, Belluschi promoted an "organic" approach to architecture that was directed not only to the aesthetic and intellectual, the cultural and emotional, but to the whole, integrated human being participating in architecture as space. "To view architecture from the standpoint of space is a good guiding principle," Belluschi said in a recent interview. Without question, for the designer of some of Portland's most elevating buildings, space was where spiritual ideals and social responsibility merged with function and beauty.

Bruno Zevi, an Italian architect living in Rome and one of the world's foremost architectural critics, distilled the essence of this position in *Architecture As Space*, when he wrote: "Like another sense, we shall acquire a feeling for space, a love of space, and a need for freedom in space. For space, though it cannot determine our judgement of lyrical values, expresses all the values of architecture—the sentimental, moral, social and intellectual . . . space is to architecture-as-art as literature is to poetry; it is the prose of architecture and characterizes each of its works." In the dignified and functional spatial arrangements of the Portland Art Museum and the Burke house, Belluschi made it clear that architectural space was not merely a cavity, a void or "negation of solidity." It was alive and positive. And for Belluschi, space was more than a showcase for style, more than a pretext for displaying erudition and power.

For this Italian-born architect, historical allegiances, architectural themes, design and trends, in themselves, could never produce a valid architecture. Unencumbered by stylistic constraints or architectural fashion, this prolific designer believed that what distinguished authentic (timeless) from non-authentic (transitory) architecture was a *process*, in which the social, material and sensory aspects of architecture were successfully combined and translated into space and light. "Architecture is not a pure art. It cannot lend itself, like sculpture, painting or music, to a complete arrangement of forms for the sake of giving pleasure to the eye or to the ears," Belluschi noted. "Architecture is a *social* art, and succeeds only if you can solve the problems to the satisfaction of human nature—which means that you give pleasure to the needs *and* senses of the person using it, whether it is an office building, a house, or a church."

Although Belluschi's contribution to Portland architecture included some of the most "artistic" structures in the region, he emphasized that, "The human spirit always adds something to a work of architecture. If you rely on it, you never come out flat footed. If you're flat footed and solve all the practical problems, you don't have architecture—you have a building. But between a building and art there is that relationship." And he cautioned, "The mistake is to think that architecture is merely a visual art. It's much more. But if you take it just as a visual art, you get the Michael Graves, or the Philip Johnson: the intent of having something to shock, of making something different simply because that's the movement of art."

Belluschi's interest in the social dimension had been translated into designs for a number of churches, including the Central Lutheran Church of Portland and the First Presbyterian Church of Cottage Grove. In both structures, light, space and proportion hang in meticulous balance. For Belluschi, good architecture was predicated on an understanding of life, a hierarchy of values, a metaphysic. Because it was not bound to any particular style, his program could always be realized and take form, despite any number of practical variables that had to be respected in each building. And what grew out of the practical program were solutions that carried the signature of his vision and understanding.

The Portland Art Museum (1932, 1938), the Sutor house (1938), the Equitable (now Commonwealth) Building (1948), to name just a few in the region designed by Belluschi, fulfilled not only visual and social needs, but, to use his own term, "spiritual" criteria as well. "The spiritual needs of a building are met only after a *synthesis of the entire problem is achieved*," noted Belluschi. "In the case of the Cottage Grove church, the clients had so much money, they wanted so many seats, they had a particular location, and there was a particular tree that had to be used. My intuition gave me suggestions which I interpreted in light of the practical elements—cost, number of seats, and place. The final structure was the culmination of a series of things and the creativity came only after these practical problems were solved. Then, I could begin to address which of the possible solutions best met the spiritual needs required by the church."

Whether the human "enterprise" was death (1937, Finley's Mortuary), prayer (1939, St. Thomas More Church), or taxes (1950, Federal Reserve Bank), Belluschi eschewed labels, classifications and categories. "It's not valuable to say 'This is modern', or 'This is not modern'," emphasized the master synthesizer. "My philosophy has always been, to analyze *all* the elements of an architectural problem. And you don't take it lightly, because the problems always are serious. And when it comes to generating a design, it is in the act of *synthesizing* that your sense of poetry or sense of creativity comes in."

Although Belluschi had served as a consultant-designer on many large commercial projects, including the Pan Am Building, Bank of America and additions to the Julliard School of Music in New York City, more

than half of his Oregon commissions would be devoted to spaces celebrating spirituality, private meditation or art. Unlike A. E. Doyle, the Zimmer Gunsul Frasca Partnership, and Skidmore, Owings and Merrill—firms whose reputations were built on architecture devoted to finance, commerce and government—Belluschi maintained a special interest in designing spaces which communicated ideals that were "inwardly compelling."

A number of his buildings became part of the spiritual life of the city. The Zion Lutheran Church (1951) boasted free-standing arches, warm interior colors and contrasting textures of brick, copper, glass and wood. The Jennings Sutor house (1938), a monument to the harmonious melding of landscape with edifice, and the St. Thomas More Chapel (1941), a rustic structure, reflected the architect's early visual encounters. "Fragments of the past—memory—always impinge when you are trying to translate your synthesis of a building into a form," commented Belluschi. "I saw farmhouses, columns, porticos built to beautiful scale. These are the things that stay with you. Not as an architect, but simply as a child, as a human being."

This sensitivity to the unique responses and needs of the individual explained both his repudiation of stylistic labels as well as his unwillingness to endorse the anonymous corporate architecture of the 1960s and 1970s. "The Modern movement . . . was a faith that was wholly incapable of organizing the human personality to produce 'the necessary corporate identities,'" wrote architecture historian Norris Kelly Smith. "Is there any way then that architects can communicate ideals that remain inwardly compelling? Probably not, since the institutions and corporations that commission the erection of buildings seem unable to do so."

For Belluschi, architecture had always been an enterprise where issues of spirituality and morality met questions of function and aesthetics. To be sure, there was poetry, creativity and the formation of abstract, ideal spaces. But, also, "There is a morality that should inspire architects," he said. In his view, architects could not be superficial, but rather, had to delve deeply into problems and exercise all their mental abilities in order to arrive at a solution. "Their work is a serious business," he cautioned. "That seriousness is derived from the fact that the product of the architect's labor and thought is something which is social, which exists in time, affects people in a particular way, and has the power to move people or to place them into a spiritual state which might be productive or destructive."

OFFICE BUILDING FOR THE UNION PACIFIC SYSTEM
A. E. Doyle and Associate
1937

Two passionate forces—one historical and one bio-graphical—were at work molding Belluschi's keen awareness of the architect's duties. A lifetime of experiencing and studying the architecture of the Old and the New worlds bred his enduring respect for the *genius loci* of each region and its people. Born in the small Adriatic town of Ancona, Belluschi grew to adolescence among the architectural splendors of Rome where, after World War I, he completed his training in architecture and engineering. A scholarship from the Italian-American Society of New York enabled him to round-out his post-doctoral studies at Cornell University. Following the advice of the Italian ambassador, he went West, to the mines of Idaho, where he acquired a taste for the rugged beauty of the great American hinterlands.

When Belluschi arrived in Portland in 1925, he would be just one of many "outsiders" to make a contribution to the city's architecture. Few of Belluschi's architectural predecessors—William F. McCaw, William W. Piper, Justus Krumbein, Warren H. Williams, E. M. Burton,

F. Manson White, William M. Whidden, Ion Lewis, William G. Purcell—were born in Portland or trained in the region. Most of them came from the East, settled in the city and perpetuated their own ready-made images of what Portland's architecture should be. Others, such as Cass Gilbert, Benjamin Wistar Morris, Reid and Reid, and more recently, Aalvar Alto, Michael Graves, Richard Meier and Hugh Stubbins, made up a fraternity of designers that responded almost exclusively to one or two commissions. These architects made their mark in Portland primarily by leaving a representative sample of their distinctive styles. But it took Belluschi's "alienated" perspective, nurtured on the domesticated landscape of northern and central Italy, to register the monumental beauty of the Pacific Northwest and assimilate it as the inspiration for a lasting tradition in both urban and rural architecture.

In April 1925, Belluschi joined the firm of A. E. Doyle. Though ailing, Doyle still actively presided over a bustling practice. Not surprisingly, Belluschi's early assign-

93

PROPOSED MARION COUNTY COURTHOUSE
Pietro Belluschi
1949

ments gave him little opportunity to test his modernist ideas. "In those years," Belluschi recalled, "I was exposed to a potpourri of architecture—big buildings, buildings in the Beaux-Arts style, commercial buildings, as well as some houses we were doing for private clients." These included the Broadway Theater (1927), the Hamilton Corbett residence (1928), and two of the city's most memorable office buildings—the Pacific (1926) and the Public Services (1928). By the early 1930s, Belluschi had grown used to the charms of Beaux-Arts ornamentalism, finding it particularly staid and pale by comparison with the city's august natural setting. Even Houghtaling and Dougan's old Elks Temple built in 1920, a masterful copy of Rome's Farnese Palace, at that time failed to spark his enthusiasm. To Belluschi, the Elks Temple dramatized the incongruity of replicating old architectural models in a new setting.

At the beginning of the century, decoration was exploited by Whidden and Lewis and Doyle in the Renaissance revival styles they transplanted to Portland. It was against these neo-classical jewels that Belluschi would direct his barbs. As Zevi emphasized, "applied decoration, however lifeless and academic in the hands of its imitators, corresponded in the 15th century to the spatial theme of its time . . . decoration in the Renaissance was an act of profound coherency and so of integral, cultural and artistic validity." As a young designer, Belluschi was not alone in his distrust for the glibly decorative forms of historical styles. In Portland, he found a growing circle of young colleagues who also saw the Beaux-Arts revival as a tendency to regress into a nostalgic historicism. It is interesting, however, that in 1984, once sufficiently distanced from the anti-Beaux-Arts polemic of the 1930s, Belluschi finally came to appreciate the exquisite proportions and refined craftsmanship of the Houghtaling and Dougan Elks Temple.

The inspiration for Belluschi's new ideas came, in large measure, from the region, the landscape, its people and their needs. "I remember going to the Oregon coast, where I traveled and walked, and was completely awed by this new landscape," Belluschi explained. "I was struck by the fact that one had the opportunity to design things here which could not be too expensive, and which had to meet both the emotional and the practical needs of the family. Little by little, I had fun doing that and, as a result, I designed a number of private residences."

A series of events—local and national—placed Belluschi in a position to put his architectural ideas to the

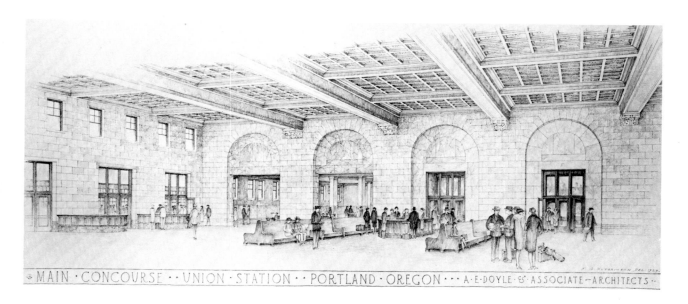

· MAIN · CONCOURSE · · UNION · STATION · · PORTLAND · OREGON · · · A · E · DOYLE · & · ASSOCIATE — ARCHITECTS ·

UNION STATION ALTERATION
A. E. Doyle and Associate
1929

test. Following Doyle's death in 1928, the architect quickly became a principal actor in the firm, which had been renamed A. E. Doyle and Associate. The stock market crash of the following year introduced a lean decade for designers of large commercial structures. In Portland only one significant public building was built in the immediate wake of the financial disaster. This was the u.s. Courthouse, designed by the office of Morris H. Whitehouse and Associates and built in 1931. When the flow of large-scale commissions stopped, Doyle and Associate nimbly retooled operations and turned to designing private homes.

For all their attendant hardships, the Depression years would have a positive impact on the evolution of Portland architecture. The u.s. Federal Courthouse would be the city's last major example of the Beaux-Arts academic tradition. In Portland, as in cities across the country, the stock of the Beaux-Arts School plummeted with the market. The historicist fashion had fallen out of favor with corporate and financial clients, discredited, perhaps, by its association with an economic fabric which ripped under the pressure of too rapid expansion and an equally precipitous contraction.

Across the country, reaction against period styles set in among designers, accompanied by widespread endorsement of the modernist International Style. At least since the turn of the century, American and Continental

architects had been formulating and applying a new architectural philosophy to replace the eclectic historicism of the Beaux-Arts. Caught up by the spectacle of new times that required unique architectural accommodations, architects on both continents feverishly questioned the relevance of doctrines inherited from the past.

While the Viennese Seccessionists sought a graceful transition from the Beaux-Arts ornament-fetish to their own brand of abstract purism, and the Bauhaus school pursued the ideal of functionalism, American designers such as Frank Lloyd Wright, Charles and Henry Green, and Bernard Maybeck looked for inspiration in nature and vernacular forms. The triumphs of science, technology and industry that came in the aftermath of World War I appeared to augur a universal, liberating era of modernization and cultural revitalization. In this respect, the universal solutions of the past appeared to threaten, rather than foster, the promise of the modern project.

For new solutions, modernists consulted mathematical principles, "timeless" forms, and concrete human activities generated by the technological advances of the new century. Engaged in a no-holds-barred polemic with the notion of style as an end in itself, Frank Lloyd Wright advanced the ideal of an "organic architecture," which he defined in 1910 as "an art of building where aesthetic and construction not only approve but prove each other." The same ideal was preached by Walter

95

Gropius, the master of the Bauhaus during its most fertile years in the 1920s. Committed to overthrowing the moribund design-by-precedent of the Beaux-Arts school, Gropius directed his early buildings and statements against the divorce between function and form. "We want," he announced in 1923, "a clear, organic architecture, whose inner logic will be radiant and naked, unencumbered by lying facades and trickeries; we want an architecture adapted to our world of machines, radios and fast motor cars, an architecture whose function is clearly recognizable in the relation to its form." At issue, then, was not the possibilty of revitalizing the architectural expression of an enervated society, but rather the necessity of creating an entirely new architecture that would capture the spirit of an emergent civilization and nurture its formation.

In Portland, too, architects began to resonate with this international sense of crisis in the field of design. Infected with the questioning virus of modernity, such young Portland designers as Yeon, Bailey and Sundeleaf paid increasing attention to the latest developments in the evolution of the International Style. "When I came here in 1925, there was already strong evidence of the 'International style,'" Belluschi recalled. "We may have been living at the other end of the universe from the Bauhaus, but we never lived in solitude. We were always receiving messages about what was happening on the 'outside' in national and architectural circles. Among us too, a growing reaction set in against the Beaux-Arts historicism which, some claimed, was not fitting for the commercial and industrial needs of the modern American metropolis, and to the specific needs of Portland, Oregon."

In Oregon, the first major institutional challenge to fin de siècle historical eclecticism was launched by Ellis F. Lawrence who, in the early teens, had been instrumental in organizing Oregon architects into a professional cadre. This break with tradition was a testament to Lawrence's enduring intellectual vitality and sense of professional responsibility (although he would eventually be suspended from the Oregon Chapter of the AIA for his willingness to design a commercial project on the site of the historic Pioneer Courthouse). As in the pre-Depression decade—when he had overseen the Beaux-Arts training of local architects under the aegis of the Portland Atelier—so, in the 1920s, he would inaugurate a new system of instruction tethered to regional and contemporary demands.

Founder and dean of the University of Oregon School of Architecture, Lawrence made the crucial decision to recruit Walter R. B. Willcox to head the Department of Architecture in 1922. An inspired follower of Louis H. Sullivan, Willcox would place the University of Oregon in the vanguard of architectural education by reshaping the program to reflect his belief that architecture should express the cultural system and values of its own time and place. Among his earliest students was Richard Sundeleaf, who would go on to apply Willcox's lessons with great success in the functional architecture of warehouses and industrial buildings.

In a less formal, though no less intense, arena, this spirit of exploration was continued by a circle of architects and artists brought together by the bonds of friendship and the excitement of philosophical inquiry. Belluschi, Yeon and other young designers who identified themselves with the process of modernization, coalesced into an informal West Coast version of the Bauhaus. Meeting frequently during the Depression decade of the 1930s, they cultivated a resistant, identity-giving architectural method, based on the concept of architecture as a synthetic art form that stood at the intersection of humanism, pragmatism and technology.

The guiding inspiration and spiritual center of this small group was Harry Wentz, painter, regional philosopher and founder-director of the Portland Museum Art School. Wentz's own interest in architecture had been nourished on a lifelong friendship with Doyle, to whom he was bound by close personal, social and professional ties. For many years, Wentz's Portland studio had neighbored on Doyle's office in the Worcester Block. When it came time for "Uncle Harry" to set up a studio and residence in Neakhahnie, the two worked closely on a design that fused Doyle's academic historicism with Wentz's sensitivity to the genius loci.

It is of historic interest that while Belluschi (along with local architects John Yeon, Van Evera Bailey and others) is usually credited with pioneering the sublime Northwest Regional style, it was Doyle himself, the eclectic high guru of the Beaux-Arts, who laid the foundation for this movement. Belluschi recalled that when he arrived in Portland in 1925, things were already beginning to move in this direction. "The regionalist sensibility," he explained, "took some time to catch on in this area. The main settlers of this region spilled over from the California Gold Rush or came from the Northeast, bringing their own local traditions and culture. It took a little time to catch fire, but finally, Whidden & Lewis and Doyle brought the potential for a local regional architecture."

Doyle's four Neakhahnie cottages—Library cottage (1912), A. E. Doyle cottage (1915), Crocker cottage (1916), Wentz studio-bungalow (1916)—most clearly laid the seeds for the regional residential vernacular championed by Belluschi and Yeon during the lean 1930s. With its elegant simplicity, respect for topography and climate, and structural gracefulness, the Wentz studio-bungalow elicited this response from Belluschi in 1953: "It has function, appropriateness, harmony, materials, setting, orientation; it is modern, emotional, beautiful." In the late 1920s, the artist's seaside retreat would become the concrete inspiration for the group of young architects.

The intensity and breadth of Wentz's interests drew these young designers like a magnet, helping them order their own thoughts about the relationship between "high" and "vernacular" architecture, the natural and man-made environment, the aesthetics and ethics of design. For Belluschi, Yeon and Wentz, the feature distinguishing architecture from all other art forms consisted in its working with a three-dimensional vocabulary which *included* man. Painting functioned in two dimensions, even if it could suggest three or four. And sculpture worked in three dimensions, but relegated man to the position of an inert spectator, remaining apart from the work, and looking at it from the outside. Architecture, however, was like a great hollowed-out sculpture which man entered and comprehended by moving about within it.

In his lifelong efforts to design structures with dignified interior spaces, Belluschi experimented with various devices, many of them first tested and refined in his designs for private residences. Building on the functional open plan derived from the American Shingle style, Belluschi strove to make each house into a space which would, in his own words, "invite and inspire its owner to live in awareness and communion with his surroundings, that will make him a wiser human being and better neighbor."

In the interest of promoting this awareness, Belluschi paid particular attention to zones that mediated between exterior and interior. The generous use of large windows and the position of the house on the site allowed for maximal points of orientation to the exterior and for the unimpeded play of light through interior space. In the case of Mies van der Rohe's Farnsworth house or Philip Johnson's "totally see-through" Glass House, this principle of openness to the environment produced an ambiguity between inside and outside. In Pietro Belluschi's houses, however, this ambiguity was to a great extent avoided.

For the Portland architect, the house had to communicate its function as shelter, extending itself outward to embrace the dweller and draw him into its inner haven. To this end, roofs and entrances played a prominent role. The broad, sheltering pitched roof extending far beyond the retaining walls of his houses became a recurrent motif in designs which included the original Belluschi house on Council Crest (1936) and the Moore residence (1949). The motif was modified in the Burke house (1949) (the roof was flattened, but still extended beyond the retaining walls), which has been called Belluschi's "closest brush with the International Style."

The accentuated porches, and verandas suggested not only an affinity with the American Shingle style, but also with the Japanese-inspired residences designed by Greene and Greene in California. The equation of influences which yielded these semi-enclosed exterior spaces also included verandas and balconies, ubiquitous features of Italian villas, farmhouses and town houses among which Belluschi had grown up. "A child is exquisitely sensitive to his environment," the architect explained in 1984. "He is a dreamer, a poet, without even realizing it. When I was a child, I used to spend summers in Tuscany. I would see the farmhouses with their porticos. And I was terribly impressed with them, with the beautiful scale, with the columns. It was raining outside and here you could sit in the portico without getting wet."

By far the most crystalline expression of the emotional and symbolic value Belluschi attached to the interior space was found in the fully or semi-enclosed gardens which graced nearly all his houses. Even though his clients' sites afforded spectacular views of nature— the Jennings Sutor house (1938), the Kerr house in Gearhart (1941), the Platt house in an apple orchard (1941), the Joss house (1941) overlooking the Tualatin Valley and the Cascade Range, and the Burke house (1949), with its constantly changing views of downtown Portland and Mt. Hood—Belluschi tried, whenever possible, to wrap his plan around a garden. Writing in an essay titled "An Eastern Critic Looks at Western Architecture," Henry-Russell Hitchcock described the Sutor House as follows:

MAIN BUILDING LOBBY ~ OFFICE BUILDING FOR THE UNION PACIFIC SYSTEM
A·E·DOYLE AND ASSOCIATE, ARCHITECTS ~ PORTLAND OREGON ~ SEPTEMBER 1937

OFFICE BUILDING FOR THE UNION PACIFIC SYSTEM
A. E. Doyle and Associate

1937

Of Belluschi's houses, that for the Sutor's must easily stand among the very finest in this country. The woods of the Northwest are used with greater simplicity and style than by Bailey; the oxide treatment of the wood sheathing produces immediately an agreeable and apparently natural grey comparable to wood which has been exposed for some time without treatment in this climate. . . . The plan of the Sutor house is remarkably straightforward and clear; the adaptation to the site superb, with the great sweep of the view on one side and the more intimate garden among the woods on the other. Possibly the exotic veneer in the living room was a mistake, though it is very skillfully handled as a sort of screen against two walls; and doubtless the supports of the rear porch could have been arranged more consistently with those at the front. But these are very minor details in a remarkably original and refined design.

Reflecting on the garden inserted in the Burke house which, since 1973 has been the architect's home, Belluschi explained how it had come to be such an important element in the overall conception of his houses. "The garden is so much an integral part of your experience that you don't want to miss it. It is intimate, and it means much more than the dramatic view from the living room windows. You look out of them and see Mt. Hood. It is beautiful, but somehow it is like flying over the forest versus walking in the woods. These are different views of nature. Perhaps you may want both of them, but the garden takes precedence, because it's an inward experience."

As with the enclosed Japanese garden, which the one in Burke house recalled, Belluschi's interior niches of cultivated nature were "tuned" to enhance the serenity and harmony of the home. Mitigating the contrast between the untamed, commanding beauty of the landscape and the humanly scaled delights of an acculturated nature, Belluschi's interior gardens provided quiet, meditative zones for recovering from the stresses of modernity and pondering on the meaning of the line where nature and culture met.

While acknowledging the essence of interior space, throughout his career, Belluschi continued to emphasize that the authenticity of an architectural work did not rest *entirely* in its spatial values. Rather, every building could be characterized by a plurality of values: economic, social, aesthetic, functional, technical, spatial and decorative. A valid architecture could not omit any of them.

Belluschi took particular issue with the compartmentalization of architectural priorities in which certain of the great masters of the International Style had engaged. Frank Lloyd Wright, Le Corbusier and Mies van der Rohe—whose ideas and work Belluschi admired—had fallen short of the syncretic ideal. Each, in his own way, had regarded one architectural value over the others: the "romantic" Wright with his intolerance for the age and its human problems, had placed art over life; the "formalist" Le Corbusier had sacrificed function to form; and the "functionalist" Mies van der Rohe had dehumanized space by idealizing the machine aesthetic. When Belluschi commented that, "architecture is a *social* art and succeeds only if you could solve the problems to the satisfaction of human nature," he echoed the pluralistic position of the distinguished Italian architect Zevi, who wrote: "Architecture is not art alone, it is not merely a reflection of life or the portrait of systems of living. Architecture is an environment, the stage on which our lives unfold."

Given their well-reasoned and deeply-felt humanistic position, it is little wonder that Wentz, Yeon and Belluschi—and later, Bailey, Storrs and Zaik—were devoted to interior spaces that created an interchange between inhabitant-participant and the architectural function. Their structures gave a special, human relationship in which interior spaces, once occupied, crackled with spiritual values, vitality, and, met the needs of modern man. In this sense, Bailey, Storrs and Zaik were committed to the ideals promulgated by designer Norman Bel Geddes who, in 1932, had diagnosed the shortcomings of American residential architecture. Writing in *Horizons*, Bel Geddes commented:

Owing to the fact that many American architects have been educated abroad, especially in France, we have had the influence of the chateau and other European styles. Tucked away in their original settings, the charm of these houses is undeniable. So, back they have come to the United States. The more closely the architect kept to the proportions and characteristics of the originals, the better job he believed he had done. But the world has progressed since the day when the originals of these houses were built. Useless rooms such as attic and large cellar add to the expense of construction and upkeep. Little-used rooms such as the dining room and sleeping porches are uneconomical. There is frequently the additional expense of exterior and interior ornament of old styles, Colonial, Tudor, Norman or Spanish, applied over modern construction. Houses are too often planned from the exterior. Rooms are fitted into a Cotswold cottage or a French chateau, with cramming and inconvenience in consequence. Porches cut off light from adjacent rooms. Heating and ventilation facilities are not thorough. Valuable garden space is given over to the unsightly garage.

Belluschi's architecture was centered around the living reality of interior space. He aspired to give his houses spatial continuity, in which an inner sanctum or central nucleus would project in all directions, and take on an expansive vitality. The final result, whether in the Burke house or the First Presbyterian Church was a spatial conquest that showed a desire to move away from the self-flagellating severity of early Bauhaus rationalism. For Belluschi, space was molded by the architect to correspond to his client's material, spiritual and psychological requirements, integrally considered.

Especially in his Oregon work, Belluschi pushed for an architecture that would give a sense of satisfaction derived from the interplay of space and the natural physiology of the human being which, to use his words, "could recognize intuitively, when the fabricated environment was sympathetic with its own make-up." Social content, psychological effects and formal values in the architecture of Belluschi all took shape in space. Any path to architecture that did not include, as part of its equation, the movement of the individual through *space* over *time*, was destined to miss the qualities which are unique to his architecture. Among his non-residential buildings, the Ayer Wing of the Portland Art Museum and the "lofty and dignified" Morninglight Chapel of the J. P. Finley and Son Mortuary, were, perhaps best able to evoke the ecstasy made possible to the eye as it traversed fabricated space. Indeed, there is a physical and dynamic element in grasping the fourth dimension as one moves through these, and other, Belluschi "spaces."

In *Architecture as Space*, Zevi elucidated the charged relationship between the human organism and architecture in a manner sympathetic to Belluschi's own position: "Whenever a complete experience of space is to be realized, *we* must be included, *we* must feel ourselves part and measure of the architectural organism. . . . *We* must ourselves experience the sensation of standing among the *pilotis* of a Le Corbusier house . . . of being suspended in air on a terrace designed by Wright or of

responding to the thousand visual echoes in a Borromini church."

"Visual echoes" provided the rhythmic spine for many of Belluschi's public works. The eurythmic *spaces* were always there, only the materials changed. In the Oregonian Building (1948), broad masses of pale limestone were interrupted by red granite and green glass, while in the exterior of the Tucker-Maxon Oral School (designed in conjunction with SOM), the visual pulse was expressed with a graceful sequence of wood beams. And while the U.S. Bancorp Tower, completed in 1983 (in which he played a consultative role for SOM), would draw the eye upward toward the infinite spaces of the sky, Belluschi's Central Lutheran Church and earlier commercial buildings such as the Federal Reserve Bank (1950), with its streamlined corner, would set the tempo for man's path *around* his buildings. Even when his designs were based on mathematical laws of composition, they always propelled the spectator through a continuous vibration of lines of force that took the form of repeating windows, slabs of marble, slender wooden members, and the eurythmic spaces created by alternating bands of light and shadow. One had the feeling that his buildings had been tailored to the itinerary that the spectator would follow. The viewer was an integral interpreter of the exterior spaces created by Belluschi's buildings, which came to life only as a result of the spectator's presence and movement around them.

This concern with the interactive dimension of architecture came to the fore with particular clarity in Belluschi's designs for six churches that were built in Oregon between 1939 and 1952. During this period, which was punctuated by the reorganization of A. E. Doyle and Associate into Belluschi's own firm in 1943, the architect was struck by the urgency of defining the spiritual and ethical role of architecture in a secular society.

In a recent interview, he recalled the issues that had then preoccupied him: "Architecture, like other art forms, must weather the problematics of a secular age. The monumental architecture of the tenth through the twelfth centuries was derived from a religious impulse—an *authentic* impulse—which governed every area of life. What is to feed an authentic architecture, an authentic *spiritual* architecture in a secular age? How, in other words, is the architect to proceed in an age which has replaced ethics with aesthetics?" Writing in the *Architectural Forum* of 1949, he succinctly summarized the problem: "Our heaven is now on earth; it takes the shape

CENTRAL LUTHERAN CHURCH
Pietro Belluschi
1948

of social security, the thirty-hour week, and restless and uncreative leisure—a heaven of course that gives neither serenity nor spiritual nourishment. Then what is to be done about church architecture if we cannot find refuge in a sterile copying of the past? The answer does not rest in the mind of the few of us, but in the very fabric of our society."

To address this dilemma, Belluschi drew on many of the lessons he had learned from his residential designs. But unlike domestic architecture, which tended to express individual tastes and meanings, ecclesiastical architecture demanded a universally recognizable symbolic vocabulary capable of transmitting a sense of collective history, identity and values. Historically, in order to give formal validity to the idea of a church, architects had used a vocabulary that included symbolic elements which had become emblems of religiosity. Yet by using historically sanctioned forms—the spire, the stained-glass rose window, the cross—architects ran the risk of producing sterile copies that no longer corresponded to the character of faith in a secular age. If the architect was to avoid making churches which were nostalgic retreats, he could only do so by *refiguring* the symbols of the past so

they would speak to the character and spirit of its own age and place.

Prior to Belluschi's contributions, Portland church architecture tended to fall into one of two molds: masonry structures in the traditional Gothic and Romanesque styles; and wood structures based on the steeple-centered design of rural New England churches. Jacobberger and Stanton's designs for Madeliene Church (1949) and Holy Trinity Church (1944) were characteristic of religious architecture during this period. Belluschi broke with these precedents and designed churches in the image of his own regional aesthetic. In the process, he created an iconoclastic, ecclesiastical vernacular, for which he would eventually win international recognition. Belluschi's religious structures announced themselves as churches, but they did so in their own words.

As in the case of his residences, Belluschi's inspiration initially came from the region: from its materials, its architecture and its people. In designs for the St. Thomas More Chapel (1941) and the Zion Lutheran Church (1951), Belluschi used the rural wooden church as his model. But while certain elements—the deep sheltering porches, pitched roofs and chiseled geometrical

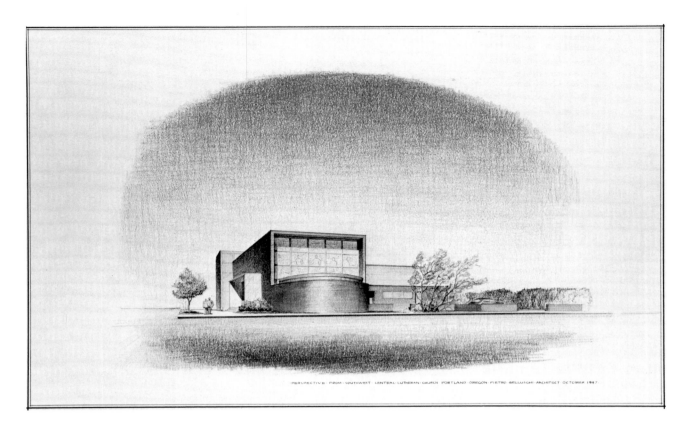

PROPOSED CENTRAL LUTHERAN CHURCH
Pietro Belluschi

1948

spires—might have recalled New England prototypes, their arrangements were idiosyncratic.

By shifting the spire to an unconventional position in the St. Thomas More Chapel, or giving it an unorthodox shape in the Central Lutheran Church, or even eliminating it altogether in the First Presbyterian Church, Belluschi altered the familiar profile of ecclesiastical structures. At the same time, he exaggerated certain features to make them coincide with this private understanding of the symbolic value of space. Belluschi always extended the sanctuarial space into the community. Details at the entrances—the bench at the entry porch to the St. Thomas More Chapel, the columned portico of the Zion Lutheran Church, the low brick wall at the entrance of the Central Lutheran Church or the covered gateway of the First Presbyterian Church—announced the social, congregational theme of the buildings.

While keeping to the unadorned simplicity of the rural church, Belluschi's interior spaces conveyed an exuberant, Mediterranean notion of spirituality. Here, the appeal to the senses was not muted or denied, but amplified. The sensuous play of chiaroscuro against the natural wood walls, pews and chancel suggested that Belluschi was substituting light for the conventional iconographic and ornamental references which, in nearly 20 centuries of Christian ecclesiastical design keyed the devotional experience. Many elements of the interior plan were ordered to draw the worshipper into a dynamic interaction with the spatial environment. Belluschi shifted the entrance to the *secondary* side of the building in the St. Thomas More Chapel, the Central Lutheran Church and the First Presbyterian Church at Cottage Grove. In so doing, he dramatized the rite of passage into the inner sanctum. His L-shaped plan required the worshipper to make a 90 degree turn at the threshold, thus orienting him to the longitudinal axis of the sanctuary and establishing his path inside the church as integral to the architectural space. Accompanied by the rhythm of arches and pews, one moved through the space, experiencing the dialectic of light and shadow. Thus, the observer became an organic part of the structure and an active participant in creating its meaning.

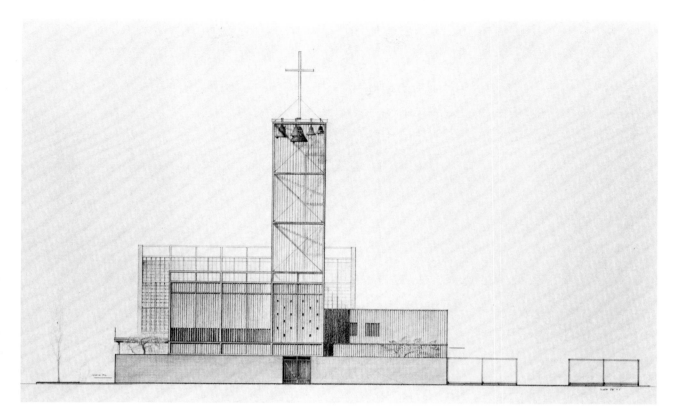

PROPOSED CENTRAL LUTHERAN CHURCH
Pietro Belluschi
1947

In this respect, Belluschi showed himself to have mastered the lessons of the early builders of Christian churches—such as the church of Santa Sabina in Rome. He had drawn on traditional Christian architecture, not for elements of decoration, but for the articulation of space which, in the fifth century, had marked a revolutionary departure from the static, monumental and passive spaces of classical Roman architecture. Belluschi's churches expressed the spatial revolution in Christian space which, according to Zevi, consisted in ordering all elements in terms of man's path inside the church. Zevi has written that for the fifth century Christian architect, "the entire planimetric and spatial conception, and in consequence all decoration, had only one dynamic measure: the observer's trajectory through the building."

At least in part, Belluschi's churches owed their inspiration to history. They also represented a synthesis of regional and universal sensibilities that served as the groundwork for a spirituality appropriate to the secular age. In this respect, the St. Thomas More Chapel, the Zion Lutheran Church and the Central Lutheran Church were only rehearsals for the First Presbyterian

Church in Cottage Grove. Singled out by Hitchcock as the most notable of Belluschi's religious structures, the First Presbyterian Church illustrated the architect's success at integrating "universal" forms with regional culture and giving them an idiosyncratic twist.

With its low profile, fenced courtyard and board-and-batten siding, the First Presbyterian shared many formal and technical features with its neighboring buildings. But while certain of its elements paid homage to regional culture, others had no precedents in local architecture. The dramatically stepped roof was entirely original. It bore a much closer resemblance to the profile of a mountain range than to conventional church roof lines. The interior courtyard, a usual feature of monastic architecture, was given an unorthodox Oriental interpretation that carried its own set of symbolic associations. Surrounded by a deep, covered walkway, the courtyard of the First Presbyterian featured an inscribed stone at the entrance gate and an assortment of carefully placed rocks reminiscent of the sand gardens of the Ryuanji Temple in Japan.

Belluschi set a precedent for this allusion to tradi-

ZION LUTHERAN CHURCH
Pietro Belluschi
1948

tional Japanese architecture in the ornamental timber framing at the side entry of the Central Lutheran Church. In the First Presbyterian, the Oriental idiom became the governing element of the design. This exotic touch was even more pronounced by virtue of the fact that Belluschi had moved the belltower—the universal Western symbol of the church—from its traditionally prominent position. The architect detached the belltower from the building, reduced its size and transposed it, in the form of a sculpture, into the interior of the courtyard. By transplanting the Christian belltower to a setting that signified an Eastern sacred context, Belluschi manipulated the associative capacities of two culturally distinct signs of the sacred space. The belltower and the garden each announced its religious nature. But, taken together, they did this in a way that precluded an exclusively Occidental or Oriental reading of the elements.

By means of this cross-cultural expression, Belluschi overcame the usual set of automatic responses to traditional religious references and activated a new experience of the sacred. In a highly secular age, where any symbolic allusion to the ecclesiastic usually degenerated into kitsch, Belluschi's blend of regional, historical and universal forms subtly reconstituted a viable, profoundly moving architectural expression of spirituality.

If Belluschi's churches proved the validity of passing a regionalist aesthetic through the filter of universal architectural symbols and forms, his designs for the Portland Art Museum—the Ayer Wing (1932), the Hirsch Wing (1938) and the 1967 addition (done in collaboration with Wolff, Zimmer, Gunsul and Frasca)—showed the success of the same procedure when applied to the secular religion of art. Represented among the AIA's "100 best Designs, 1920–1940" and winning accolades from such distinguished critics as Henry-Russell Hitchcock, Belluschi's Portland Art Museum brilliantly transposed the Italian monumental modernism of the 1930s into the scale and materials of Portland's urban context.

The Art Museum was Belluschi's first work to create national interest. The first sketches for the Ayer Wing revealed the forms of the Georgian revival style, but as the design matured, Belluschi gradually eliminated the historical fripperies of his first solution and arrived at a truly modern work. The morphological transformation from his original conception to the final result did not come painlessly. Charles Francis Adams, the Portland Art Association trustee in charge of the new addition, resisted Belluschi's attempts to break the shackles of style architecture, preferring instead the tried-and-tested Georgian formula that had been used for the Fogg Museum in Cambridge, Massachusetts. Undeterred by Adams, the young architect wrote Frank Lloyd Wright to seek support for his alternative and enclosed a sketch of his proposal. The architect's communique not only gave insight into the inner workings of Belluschi's mind, but illuminated the transitional state of American architecture during the early 1930s:

July 2, 1931

Mr. Frank Lloyd Wright, Architect
"Taliesin"
Spring Green, Wisconsin

Dear Mr. Wright:

A few months ago our firm was commissioned to design the first unit of a museum of art for the Portland Art Association. Aside from any argument as to the value of museums in regard to the artistic education of the people, the problem was a fascinating one considering that the small museum is a comparatively new idea and has definite new functions. Fortunately, the amount of money (between $100,000 and $150,000) was quite limited, thus automatically eliminating the possibility of marbles, colonnades, statues and other monumental mausoleum accessories.

Optimistically I set to work with innocent dreams of working a thoroughly functional building where spaces would be related in an organic way and where the most important problem of natural lighting would be solved as scientifically and economically as possible. It was inevitable that the exterior should reflect this solution of the problem. The first handicap imposed was the necessity of a symmetrical plan, but it wasn't an essential point in our case and the lot was cramped in all directions. After much experimenting with models I came to the conclusion that the high side light for the first floor and a sort of continuous monitor light for the top floor would be quite satisfactory and economical to build and to maintain.

Up to this point all was well with the trustee in charge and the man who donates the money, but when an exterior was tried to embody these ideas in a consistent way all was not so well. "Georgian was so beautiful—why not use it? We could put a little parapet in front of the top windows and then divide the other long windows into narrow ones, put a cornice here, moulding there, etc." When I explained that Georgian style was beautiful only as a truthful expression of the habits, tastes, and knowledge of certain people at their particular age and place, they partly agreed but still argued back that they were grown with it, loved it, and became sentimental about it, and what I had to offer was not beautiful because it disturbed them from their crystallized dreams, and there would be the necessity of apologizing continually to people in the future for having taken part in it. There is really no argument against a person's taste. The worst part was that they were so nice about it and so unmovable. I am writing this to you because that's what us young architects are pounding our heads against. It seems almost impossible to be spiritually alive in the right sense. In this country we are inevitably kicked between fashion and dead tradition.

You will say that a man, or rather an artist, has to be independent no matter what the outside circumstances, but the great majority of us would starve, and at all events be overpowered. In addition to this, in my particular case, I am a hired designer, and somehow it is difficult to assume a take it or leave it attitude.

I was born and educated in Rome, where the Renaissance is still heavily handicapping creative thought. I have been optimistic in hoping that in a new country so free from tradition as the Oregon country, a new attitude would be possible, but I have found out that in this country of pioneers, only culture is sought, and culture (here means admiration and blind imitation of the past) is the curse of civilization unless, as in Germany, there is an older intellectual consciousness back of it.

Just in the last two weeks we have been commissioned to prepare plans for a building to house the Oregon Historical Society and Museum of Natural History. It will be placed in a college campus surrounded by Tudor Gothic buildings so that the new building will have to be Gothic. Think of it, Oregon history, Indians, stuffed animals, etc., housed in a Gothic bulding. The situation would be comic if it weren't so serious and if fighting is necessary it requires a lot of courage. What could be done?

As things stand now I have my Georgian plans for the art museum ready and little hope for a change in the donor's attitude. Would a letter from you to him help?

You have sounded an intellectual awakening throughout the world, but our great public needs to have the trumpets blown into their ears.

I am enclosing a diagram plan of the art museum and two elevations, the honest one and the Georgian compromise. (Not even good Georgian was possible without too evident an insult to intelligent requirements.)

I am also enclosing a report I made at the beginning of my study, which has received the approval of the most competent museum directors in the country.

Yours sincerely,
Pietro Belluschi

Apparently, in Wright, the young aspiring Portland architect would find a set of sympathetic ears. Wright returned Belluschi's "modernist" sketch with a critique of the proposed Ayer Wing penned in his own hand and enclosed the following letter:

Mr. P. Belluschi
A. E. Doyle Ass.
Architects
1041 Pacific Bldg.
Portland, Oregon.

My Dear Belluschi:

Your client is making a serious mistake looking toward the future. Only a vanishing present looks upon a "Georgian" outside as tolerable, now. He is subscribing to a lost cause.

Your sensible modern exterior has everything to commend it and with the few alterations as to central feature (I've taken the liberty to suggest) it would make a building creditable to your "donor." His Georgian design will only mark him as reactionary in an era when light was breaking all over the world.

I cannot see how any man at this time could wish to go into the record as false to his own posterity in trying to be in fashion with his "past."

However, I know that "donors" will continue in the backwater a long time. I wish I might help. But taste is only personal idiosyncracy, cultivated, and so has no logic but fear, no sense but sentimentality.

I think your plan simple and sensible and the exterior would mark an advance in culture for Portland.

Can't Doyle and Crowell stand up for Architecture?

Sincerely yours,

Frank Lloyd Wright
Taliesin
Spring Green,
Wisconsin
July 6th 1931

Belluschi managed to gain approval for his modernistic scheme. It was the first building that expressed Belluschi's reverence for clarity, scale and light. Indeed, in the Ayer Wing there was a stamp of minimalism, a penchant for simplicity and a flair for arriving at the most austere solution, which would govern the design of his later buildings. The Portland Art Museum (Ayer Wing, 1932; Hirsch Wing, 1939), among others, reflected Belluschi's proclivity for simple, elegant solutions. Presenting a warm facade of Willimina brick interlaced with Travertine trim, the Ayer Wing relied on the rhythmical counterpoint of receding and protruding planes for its dynamic interest. Although its symmetrically grouped masses made no allusion to the neighboring Masonic Temple, the delicate brickwork of Belluschi's facade established a harmonious relationship with Fritsch's building. The Italian architect had long admired the fine craftsmanship of Fritsch's Willimina brick buildings. During construction of the Ayer Wing, he had even taken the bricklayers on a tour of Fritsch's Fruit and

PROPOSED CHAPEL FOR RIVERVIEW CEMETERY - A.E.DOYLE & ASSOC. ARCH'TS. PORTLAND ORE. 5.39

PROPOSED CHAPEL FOR RIVERVIEW CEMETERY
A. E. Doyle and Associate
1939

Flower Day Nursery so they could study the effect he wished them to duplicate.

Traditional in its arrangement of galleries, Belluschi's Ayer Wing marked a significant advance in museum design by shedding a regional light on world culture. In the 1930s, modern American curatorial practice favored the exclusive use of artificial light. Belluschi went against these received precepts and introduced a system of four-sided monitors cantilevered over the center of the galleries. In this manner, Belluschi was able to admit the play of local light across the surface of the paintings and sculptures. Whereas the practice of encapsulating an art work in an artificially lit environment tended to render art "placeless," Belluschi's use of carefully controlled monitors allowed for an interaction between culture and nature, between art and light. In this way, the museum

was transformed from a reliquary for inert artifacts into a vibrant forum where a universal culture was brought to life by the constant inflections of local light. Hitchcock praised Belluschi's composition when he wrote:

I will not speak of the earlier portions of the Portland Art Museum except to say that when it was executed some years ago it was one of the best works of semi-modern character in the country and that it has as yet, I believe, no rival as regards its exterior. In the newly opened portions of the museum, however, the development of the architect's (or more probably of the client's) taste is strikingly illustrated. The great skylight court is both ingenious and splendid, from the travertine slabs which flank the ground story supports to the

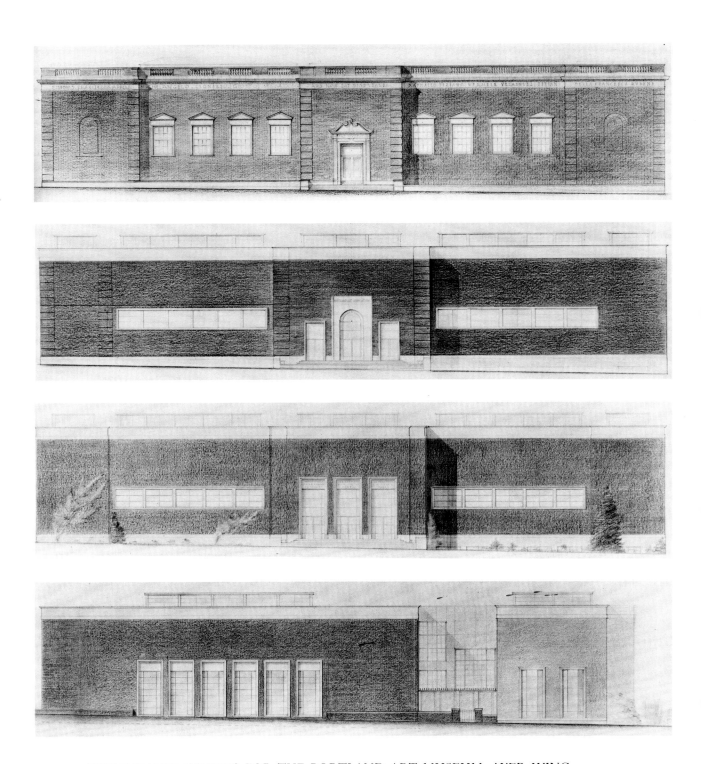

PRELIMINARY STUDIES FOR THE PORTLAND ART MUSEUM, AYER WING
A. E. Doyle and Associate
1932

skillful combination of symmetrical structure with a symmetrical lighting in the roof; while the little external court with its cantilevered travertine slab roof around the edge recalls the purity and richness of Mies van der Rohe's finest work. The actual galleries are more conventional but extremely effectively lit.

During the 1930s and 1940s, Belluschi would come to apply the same principles that governed his search for a critical regionalism in residential, church and museum design to a series of commissions in public buildings. But the wood vernacular that he had tapped for his residential and ecclesiastical aesthetic was less well adapted to serving as a template for an urban and commercial regionalism. The architecture of the city required a shift from an inward-looking to an outward-looking sensibility, from an idiosyncratic, meditative idiom to a more conventionally secular and functional vocabulary, and from the indigenous wood technology to the steel-and-cement techniques of modern construction.

The difficulties involved were immense, but, as McMath noted, Belluschi was up to the task. "I don't think it's possible to translate 'Northwest Regionalism' into an urban idiom without denaturing it," McMath explained. "It's a wood architecture. But if anyone came close to giving it a successful urban version, this man was Belluschi." Belluschi's commercial projects of this period—from storefronts (Northwest Airlines, 1945) and restaurants (Waddle's Restaurant, 1945), to office buildings (the Oregonian Building, 1948, the Equitable Building, 1948, the Federal Reserve Bank, 1950) and shopping malls (McLoughlin Heights, 1942)—extended the classical ideal of *utile et dulce* to a full range of urban structures. No matter how humble or grandiose the project, Belluschi rarely neglected the space- and place-making concerns of traditional urbanism.

Using many of the same devices that had integrated his residences and churches with their sites, Belluschi shaped his functional buildings to extend into the urban fabric. In the Boilermakers Union Building (1942), with its glass-block and opaque glass surfaces, Belluschi celebrated the transition from street to work space by gouging out a curvilinear entry way, sheathing it in marble, and overhanging it with a lozenge-shaped roof supported by a single column. With Waddle's Restaurant (1945), Belluschi's versatility in the drive-in restaurant idiom yielded a refined example of the building-as-sign.

Juxtaposing the horizontal axis of the covered pillared walkway with the massive vertical slab of the pylon sign, Belluschi provided a dramatic background for the "menu" lettering rendered by McMath. This latter project was the first for an adolescent who, twenty years later, would become Portland's premier restorer of historic buildings.

The concern for integrating the experiences of the urban observer and worker dictated the design of the Oregonian Building, completed in the following year. The huge pressroom windows on the building's lower side offered a fluid medium of communication between those working within and those passing without. Punched into the otherwise mortuarial skin of pale limestone and red granite, the green sweeps of glass did much to demystify the magic of mass communication in the age of mechanical reproduction. No such peeks into the secret machinations of high finance, however, were offered by the earthquake-resistant Federal Reserve Bank Building (1950). Sheathed in black and white marble and boasting an exquisitely detailed entry at its rounded corner, the bank was Belluschi's late, but refined response to the Streamline Moderne architecture of the 1930s.

When it came to office buildings, Belluschi again set an example that later architects would be hard pressed to rival. If there were ever an office building in Portland that could "sing," it was Belluschi's Equitable Building (1948). Critically acclaimed by Hitchcock as the "paradigmatic expression of the 'International style'," the light and airy tower was an exquisite realization of the "form follows function" imperative. Moreover, his aluminum and green glass monolith was, if not the first, then certainly the most "riveting" example of a Portland office building whose design generators were inspired as much by fashion as by pragmatic specifications. Belluschi recalled the evolution of his design. "They came to me and said, 'What are you going to do with all this aluminum? We don't know what to do with it.' So I began thinking—you can do windows, and they said 'Why not use it in the building?' I even used it for the structure instead of steel. The fire rules and fire marshals didn't approve because aluminum melts too low. But for a cover, it worked. This was an example where you start with a preconceived idea, but eventually change it for a better result. In the case of the aluminum, we had an opportunity to say, 'Let's see what we can do with it.'"

Without compromising the purity of the dialogue between form and function that made the Equitable

FEDERAL RESERVE BANK
Pietro Belluschi
1948

Building a self-referential aesthetic "object," Belluschi succeeded at the nearly contradictory task of integrating his structure into the architectural fabric and human texture of its setting. With its sensitive disposition of street-level retail stores, the skyscraper tempered the rationalist geometry of its upper stories by extending a "user friendly" image to the casual stroller. In one stroke, Belluschi managed to reinforce the specificity of the site and to relate to a generalized notion of urban "place." He did this principally by wedding a mathematically pristine structural scheme to materials selected for their regional expressivness: the locally produced aluminum and the reflective green-tinted glass, both extraordinarily responsive to the fluctuations in light and atmospheric conditions. The result was a building in which the expansiveness of the international vision was seamlessly melded with the specificity of an urban-cum-regional site. The Equitable Building catapulted Belluschi into national prominence. Photographers would settle on his buildings like flies, attempting to secure the architect's permission for publication rights.

After his series of architectural accomplishments, Belluschi would relinquish his position as Portland's leading practitioner of the critical regionalism he had largely pioneered. In 1950, he left Portland to become dean of the School of Architecture at the Massachusetts Institute of Technology, a post he retained until 1965. Although he exchanged the role of Portland's master builder for the position of teacher and consultant on world-class projects, Belluschi continued to exert a powerful influence on the shape of Portland's development. He did this, initially, within the framework of the

EQUITABLE BUILDING
Pietro Belluschi
1948

collaboration into which he entered with the firm of Skidmore, Owings and Merrill, to which he had sold his firm in 1950.

Between 1950 and 1954, a handful of buildings sprang from Belluschi's collaboration with SOM. "There was one good building that came out of that association," Belluschi recalled. "That was the Tucker-Maxon Oral School (1954) in southeast Portland." Integrating the regional wood tradition with internationalist modular technology, this school for deaf children—which was followed by a similar design for the Benington College Library (Belluschi with Carl Koch and Associate, 1959)— was an extraordinary exercise in modeling architectural syntax on acoustic phenomena. The vertical pattern of the double colonnade along the covered veranda formed a dynamic counterpoint to the horizontal striations of

the *brise de soleil* along the roofline. Indeed, the entire ensemble—its hide-and-seek of light and shadow glinting off the large planes of recessed windows—created a harmonious interplay that functioned as a visual analogue for the music the children would never hear.

For Belluschi, regionalism was the crutch on which he limped out of history into infinite time. Since coming to Portland in 1925, his goal has been to create an "authentic" and "timeless" architecture. He succeeded, and while the celebrated architect has always adamantly eschewed stylistic labels—"late-modernist" is the one most frequently invoked to describe his orientation— his designs have borne the indelible imprint of an aesthetic vision circumscribed by modern time. This leads to an apparent paradox, that is: his architecture had the quality of *timelessness*, yet his creations were formulated and designed on the basis of principles and materials that reflected a particular—unequivocably modern—historical moment.

To resolve this apparent paradox, Belluschi turned to nature and, specifically, to all her variations of *space* and *light*. In many respects, then, Belluschi's viewpoint was, like Ralph Waldo Emerson's, that of a Transcendentalist: to make anything useful or beautiful the individual must submit to the "universal soul," the "alone creator." For the Transcendentalists, nature was the omnipotent agent and representative of the universal mind and designers had to heed his wishes. As Emerson wrote in his essay, "Thoughts on Art," the "first lesson of the useful arts is, that nature tyrannizes over our works. They must be conformed to her law, or they will be *ground to powder by her omnipresent activity*." These were the principles Belluschi applied to a body of architectural work that spanned 60 years, that melded beauty, adaptation and teleological functionalism. With space, light and nature on his side, Belluschi did not have to worry much about time. It came with the territory. And so did timelessness.

Not surprisingly, the same impulse that fed Belluschi's search for timeless forms provided the driving energy for the regionalist architecture of John Yeon. The two designers, after all, had been associated since the early 1930s, both as colleagues in the office of A. E. Doyle and Associate and as informal disciples of regional philosopher and artist Harry Wentz. For Oregon-born Yeon, the regionalist inspiration of these early years would lead to an architecture of intimate spaces, aesthetic retreats and sublime gardens, reflecting a strong Oriental influence.

Building at a time which, according to Henry-Russell Hitchcock, had come to see the house as little more than "a box for housing machinery in," Yeon would design buildings that unfolded on Portland's landscape like the painted panels of a Japanese screen. The references to the exquisitely crafted "breeze walls" that graced traditional Japanese homes were always subtly integrated with a modernistic, International-Style inspired architecture.

In the Watzek house (1937), Victor Jorgenson house (1941), and the Van Buren house (1948), glass and wood facades were punctuated by a rhythmical succession of slim, vertical elements that organized the planes into a series of interconnected frames. With its Japanese-inspired hipped roof, the Shaw house (1950) carried the screen motif to its boldest realization. The house's horizontal spaciousness was emphasized by a rhythmic arrangement of columns, mullions and moldings. The effect was that of an airy pavilion which gave the appearance of having been assembled from the shimmering panels of countless screens. Ralph T. Coe, director of the Nelson Gallery in Kansas, observed that, "In this [the Shaw] house, what was tentative in the Watzek house has become codified and disciplined in design, without loss of sensibility."

In the Jorgenson house (1939), Yeon would use a modular system of construction to achieve a segmented facade. Against a background of articulated wood surfaces, the plants in the foreground of the structure appeared to have been painted by a Japanese master. Furnishing nearly all his houses with willowy pergolas and columned porticos, Yeon provided external passages that brought the ethereal naturescapes of Japanese screens to life.

At once functional and ornamental, the entrance to the Cottrell house (1950) offered a particularly striking example of screen architecture. The slim colonnade extending along the facade was filled in with plywood and glass to mark the transition from exterior to interior. By degrees, but without a change in scale, the columns were transformed into mullions framing the windows of the foyer. A carefully orchestrated planting of Japanese maples pressed against the wooden panels, at ground level, while at the second story, three glass panels reflected a composition of fir tops against a constantly changing sky. The architect's ingenious melding of landscaped foliage with the repetitive, panel-like elements of the exterior yielded an architectural analog to the Japanese screen.

The architect expressed his interest in Japanese screens more concretely in his design for the Crowell Wing of Kansas City's Nelson Gallery (1967). Praising Yeon for his sensitivity to Oriental spatial and pietorial values, Coe wrote: "The room he recently designed in our Crowell Wing for Japanese screens, manages to convey the visual quality that such screens have in Japanese homes when the observer is sitting on the floor in traditional Japanese fashion, and yet the viewer is able to stand in the American way. That is a subtle enactment of display connoisseurship in the manipulation of exhibition space, and it is truly one of the most beautiful rooms in any art gallery in North America."

The Visitors Information Center (1948), Yeon's only public building, would bring the Japanese screen motif to downtown Portland. In spaces defined by the columned pergola, Yeon framed a series of views—a panorama of screens from urban life—onto the Willamette River. Recalling the genre motifs of Japanese screen painting, fragments of the cityscape unfolded on the reflective glass panels placed on the north and south facades of the structure.

In the interiors of his buildings, Yeon arranged windows to offer a variety of strategically placed vantage points to the exterior, interrupting glass surfaces with subtle vertical members. But it was the views framed by his "picture windows" that brought the screen to life. A full range of landscape motifs traditionally found on Japanese screens were displayed on the glass panes of the Watzek house (1937). A spectacular panorama of Mt. Hood to the east, reminiscent of Hokusai's glowing renditions of Mt. Fuji, unfolded on the glass wall of the living room. By contrast, the dining room windows offered a lush view into a thicket of vine maples, fern fronds and trillium. The virginal vegetation, Portland landscpe architect Wallace Kay Huntington noted, is "so two-dimensionally displayed that the scene seems as unreal and as graphic as a landscape depicted on a Japanese screen."

While this riot of foliage gave the impression of an accidental collision between nature and architecture, its relationship to the structural elements had been calculated with great deliberation. Before allowing construction on the houses to begin, the architect had instructed the contractor to build a tall fence around the site, allowing a four-foot "construction channel" for workmen between the building and the natural landscape. Once the structure was completed, the fence was removed, and the untouched native flora was allowed to become an integral ornamental element of the design.

In many respects, the young designer's vision would be informed by the same conception of his vocation which Louis I. Kahn had advanced when he wrote that the architect "is the one who conveys the beauty of spaces, which is the very meaning of architecture. Think of meaningful space, and it can be your invention." For Yeon, the search for meaningful space would be carried on almost exclusively in the intimate scale of the home, the garden and the gallery. He would build more than a dozen residences, one public building, exhibition spaces for several museums and galleries (Nelson Gallery of the Atkins Museum, Kansas City, 1963, 1967; Helen Irwin Fagen Galleries, Legion of Honor Museum, San Francisco, 1972; Portland Art Museum, 1952, 1974), and

exquisite gardens, among them the King Street Garden (1934) designed for his mother.

Everything this native Oregonian built reflected the aesthete's superb sense of detailing and taste in design. Architect, connoisseur, scholar and conservationist, Yeon was an exemplary representative of the rare breed of Renaissance men which the modern age of specialization had rendered all but extinct. His would be a program that would owe little to formal education, and nearly all to lessons gleaned from long jaunts to the Oregon wilderness, from travel abroad, from practical familiarity with building materials and techniques, and from passionate study of Western and Oriental art.

Yeon's architectural biography, in fact, offered a convincing argument against the prevalent view that formal credentials spell professional success. The son of prominent Oregon lumberman John B. Yeon, the architect developed a lively interest in design while still a boy. At the age of 16, he was already getting his first taste of the profession working as office boy for Portland's leading architect of the time, A. E. Doyle. After one year at Stanford University, he abandoned formal schooling, preferring to acquire "hands on" experience as an apprentice in architectural offices in New York. Depression Manhattan, however, held little enduring appeal for the Portland lad. If anything, it only nurtured his nostalgia for the raw beauty of the Pacific Northwest and fueled his determination to preserve its natural landscape.

In 1930, fresh from a visit to Europe, the 20-year old Yeon returned to Portland, and to the office of A. E. Doyle and Associate. The years between 1930 and 1937, when he would make his professional debut with his design for the Watzek house (1937), marked a period of intense exploration. During his apprenticeship, the young designer would build the foundations for his subsequent tri-partite career as architect, landscape designer and conservationist. Much of his time in the early 1930s was taken up with a campaign to save Neakhahnie Mountain on the Oregon coast. This coastal landmark was in danger of being "mutiliated" by the construction of an expeditious, though ill-conceived stretch of the Oregon coastal highway.

Yeon's protests led to his being appointed to the State Park Commission, for which he prepared a detailed study of the endangered area. This comprehensive program—which he would later describe as "the first environmental impact statement"—included Yeon's own proposal for an alternative road design. The drawings he prepared showed a picturesque winding road hugging the contours of the mountain. The road was supported, at one spot, by an engaged aqueduct whose rusticated piers blended artfully into the rocky face. The design suggested a melding of Antonio Gaudi's surreal architecture with the colossal earthworks of such environmental artists of the 1960s as Robert Smithson. Only some of these ideas, however, were incorporated into the final plan.

Even though the Neakhahnie highway design was Yeon's only venture into monumental architectural forms, it would foreshadow his ambition to create structures informed by the deepest respect for nature. His next major project carried this ambition to fruition in the intimate scale of the garden he designed, in 1935, for his mother, Mrs. John B. Yeon. Exquisitely sited, Yeon's garden took shape under the dual inspiration of the Japanese garden and the architectonic sensibility of the early Frank Lloyd Wright. A circular lawn, defined by a series of low, broadly horizontal brick walls, provided the formal core of the composition. Bold outcroppings of rock contrasted with the skillfully worked grillwork of the Roman brick walls that punctuated a series of terraces descending to the central lawn. Along one side of the external perimeter, Yeon had designed a willowy arbor, which gave the garden the feel of an expansive room without walls.

According to Wallace Kay Huntington, this garden was an unprecedented achievement in the art of landscape design in the Northwest. "Unlike any previous Northwest garden," Huntington noted in *Space, Style and Structure*, "it can be evaluated as an independent art form; as such it would seem to be historically the first instance where the artist's major concern was in exploring original landscape forms." The architect would go on to cultivate his garden aesthetic in nearly all his residential designs, as also in the Visitors Information Center. Increasingly, however, his interest would focus on creating gardens that would draw almost exclusively from the native flora of the Pacific Northwest. In the Watzek house (1937) and in the Victor Jorgenson house (1939), the artist's subtle hand would frequently be discerned only in the careful "editing" of the indigenous vegetation surrounding the building or in the artful manipulation of growing branches into harmonious curves. For the Visitors Information Center (1948), Yeon would choose the native plants of the Northwest—the vine maple, madrone, salal and Oregon grape—for a boldly inno-vative garden which the Men's Garden Club soon replanted with the more conventional roses.

Perhaps no building designed by Yeon combined the architect's multiple interests quite as effectively and as boldly as did the Watzek house. Widely published and included in the Museum of Modern Art's tenth and fifteenth anniversary exhibitions, the Watzek house became a classic of Contemporary design. To promote its preservation, it was placed on the National Register, becoming one of the few modern houses to win this distinction. Exquisitely planned—the detail drawings alone ran 75 sheets, nearly as many as were required for the Public Services Building—the Watzek house was a refined compound of interconnected rooms wrapped around a serene reflecting pool. From the sensitive landscaping of the grounds, to the silver-gray siding and the harmonious arrangement of low-pitched roofs—which subtly echoed the distant view of Mt. Hood—the house paid homage to its magnificent natural setting. Writing of Yeon's pioneering design, landscape architect Wallace Kay Huntington observed that "the Watzek house is the ultimate 20th century anachronism."

In contrast to the "design-by-team" approach that increasingly characterized modern architectural practice, "the Watzek house was a Renaissance design with Yeon functioning as architect, landscape architect, interior designer and furniture designer even to the ultimate participation—personally helping to lay the stone masonry in the courtyard." But if the architect's intimate involvement in every aspect of the project made him a Renaissance architect, the resulting structure was a twentieth-century tribute to the humanist ideal of enlightened eclecticism. Encompassing a catholic range of architectural and cultural sensibilities, the Watzek house was an exercise in harmonious integration that invited comparison with the architectural model celebrated by Edgar Allan Poe in *Landor's Cottage*. "Everywhere was variety in uniformity," wrote the American Romantic. "It was a piece of 'composition,' in which the most fastidiously critical taste could scarcely have suggested an emendation."

The Watzek house expressed two "modes" which dominated much of his subsequent architectural work: the "barn style" and the "palace style." The tight cluster of wings, each with its low-pitched roof, and the rough-sawn fir siding established a direct reference to the "Oregon barn" vernacular. Beneath its rural wood-and-glass mask, however, the Watzek house was a modern descendant of the palatial Italian Baroque villa. As architectural historian Heinrich Wollflin pointed out, the typical suburban villa, such as Nanni Lippi's Villa Medici and Vasanzio's Villa Borghese, signaled its idyllic function by dramatically contrasting its street and garden facades. In the Watzek house, the severely restrained entrance was startlingly incongruent with the exuberant, columned lightness of the interior faces oriented toward Mt. Hood. Punctuated by a sedate rhythm of posts, the solid wall of the entry was a modern adaptation of the closed front, which the Italian model presented to the public thoroughfare. The garden and courtyard facades, however, bubbled over with sparkling expanses of glass, protruding wings and airy colonnades. The open courtyard at the core of the asymmetrical arrangement of rooms was, as Huntington noted, "an innovative introduction to the Northwest. Reminiscent of the Roman atrium, it provide a serene, self-contained, protected interior space."

But if history provided the distant inspiration for Yeon's gracious residences, modern architectural theory and practice gave him the tools for naturalizing the ethos of the Italian suburban villa and for rendering it in the spirit and materials of his time and place. His designs for the Watzek house, the nine "modular" houses commissioned by Burt Smith which included the Victor Jorgenson house (1939), the Visitors Informaton Center (1948) and such post-war private commissions as the E. W. Van Buren house (1949), the George Cottrell house (1950), the Lawrence Shaw house (1950), showed Yeon as the leading Northwest regional interpreter of the International Style. Nearly all of these residential designs expressed the modern conception of space which is based on the theory of the open plan.

Beginning with the Watzek house, Yeon's interiors recalled the spatial sensibilities of such modern exponents of the free and elastic plan as Mies van der Rohe, Le Corbusier and the American genius Frank Lloyd Wright. Closer to Mies van der Rohe's "rationalism" than to Wright's "organicism," Yeon's interior spaces were constructed according to simple mathematical relationships. The rectangle, the square and the triangle were the recurrent motifs in Yeon's orchestration of interior spaces and external planes. In the Watzek house, the columns, posts and wall surfaces were both structural supports and visual dividers, while glass surfaces were at once window, wall and reflective panes. Vertical expanses of the interior walls defined the series of fluidly interconnected zones, creating an uninterrupted flow through a succession of visual angles.

In subsequent projects, including the E. W. Van Buren house, the Kenneth Swan house and the highly "formalistic" Lawrence Shaw house, Yeon used variously proportioned modules to highlight the geometric patterning of space. This formal device, first applied in the design for the nine "plywood" houses, (1938–39) evolved out of purely functional considerations. Always responsive to indigenous building materials, Yeon was eager to experiment with a new exterior fir plywood that had been developed locally and became available in 1935. Manufactured in four– by eight–foot sheets, this material suggested the dimensions for the modular units of which the exterior and the interior of Yeon's plywood houses were composed. The Jorgenson house, the last and grandest of this series, was a particularly successful example of the architect's modular syntax in residential design. Using a two-foot module in the bedrooms and the service areas, and a four–foot module in the living-dining areas, Yeon established a clear formal code for differentiating functions. He then reiterated this syntax on the building's exterior by applying his signature dark blue-green—subsequently known as "Yeon blue"—to the battens at appropriate intervals.

While they were explicitly based on mathematical relationships, Yeon's houses avoided the obsessive dogmatism of Mies van der Rohe, whose spatial formulas inspired the Oregon architect's designs. Rich with movement, directional invitations and illusions of perspective, Yeon's interiors implied, rather than preached, the rational formulas that determined the pleasing proportions and spatial rhythms. When Yeon completed the Visitors Information Center in 1948, he proved he could sustain the same dynamic and visual excitement in a public structure that has been described as coming "as close to pure abstraction as a building can get."

Widely publicized and nationally acclaimed, the building was selected by Henry-Russell Hitchcock for the Museum of Modern Art's prestigious 1953 exhibit "Built in U.S.A.: Post-War Architecture." In the local history of symbolic public structures, the Visitors Information Center was Yeon's answer to the magisterial Forestry Building, which Doyle had designed for the Lewis and Clark Exhibition of 1905. As Doyle had chosen to celebrate the region's leading industry by designing a timber structure in the respected Beaux-Arts idiom of his day, so Yeon adapted the wood vernacular to the glamorous aesthetic of the International Style.

With its strongly articulated rhythm of rectilinear elements, the four-unit Visitors Information Center gave Portlanders a regional object lesson in the new architectural sensibility centering on the theory that "structure is its own best ornament." Using a three-foot module through the structure, Yeon boldly articulated the panel system by coding its elements in four consistently applied colors. In this respect, Yeon displayed a zeal for geometrical purism worthy of Mies van der Rohe. As architectural historian Charles Jencks noted, the Bauhaus master was not adverse to putting architectural space at the service of Platonic idealism. So drastically, according to Jencks, did Mies van der Rohe strip architectonic forms to their pure geometrical essence, that the entrances to his structures might well have borne the inscription that Plato put above the door of his academy: "Nobody Untrained in Geometry May Enter My House." The same could have been said for Yeon's riverside building.

Showing great sensitivity to the functional requirements and the symbolic charge of the structure he was commissioned to design, the architect chose to render his version of the International Style in a variety of woods culled from native forests. What resulted was a understated, but finely wrought building that performed its function as a billboard introducing the visitors to the city with a surprising range of inflections. Merely by scanning the polychrome wood skin of the building and noting the mathematical rhythms of its facade, the visitor could divine the many faces of Portland's civic and economic self image. The city's identity as a regional lumber capital was unambiguously beamed in the extravagant expanses of the wooden facade, while its progressive spirit was affirmed in the daringly futuristic forms of the International Style. From the perspective of the mid-1980s, this forward-looking architectonic arrangement concealed a visionary glimpse into the city's future. By highlighting the mathematical origin of his design, Yeon inadvertently predicted the shift in Portland's economic mainstay, which would take the city from the golden age of lumber to the silicon age of the computer.

Writing about the Visitors Information Center on 21 September 1977, Ralph T. Coe, director of the Nelson Gallery of Art in Kansas noted: "The Portland Information Bureau, in spite of the insults which have been done to it through misunderstandings of its original architectural integrity, is as appropriate a building to look at today—(providing it is properly restored) as it was when built and included in the Museum of Modern Art's 'Built in U.S.A.: Post-War Architecture' exhibition." And then, commenting on the Watzek house, Coe added: "Certainly the Watzek House was the pioneer example of what has become the modern indigenous style of Northwest domestic architecture, and having examined it recently at great length, I truly feel that as an individual house it surpasses anything that was done by Belluschi in housing, despite this architect's deserved eminence."

Yet for all his contributions, Yeon remained one of Portland's more mysterious figures. "Mildly eccentric, almost reclusive, brilliant," as his biographer Richard Brown described him, Yeon shunned publicity, preferring his works to speak for the man. But while his "minor career of avoiding public notice" successfully kept his name from becoming a household word, his major vocation won him the reputation of being an "architect's architect." According to Coe, "this designer's role in the history of twentieth-century American architecture has been somewhat obscured by the very quiet format in which he prefers to practice, as well as by the fact that some of his most important work was done quite a number of years ago."

Few Portland architects of the 1930s and 1940s could count more men of industry among their clients than Richard Sundeleaf in the heyday of his career. He gave them modernistic offices, amusement palaces, dignified warehouses, fashionable showrooms and built their houses in a dizzying array of period styles. But even Sundeleaf could not match the record of architect Van Evera Bailey for prestigious *residential* commissions between 1937 and the late 1950s. If Sundeleaf designed the offices, plants and warehouses for Portland's entrepreneurs on the rise, then Bailey designed the private retreats of their dreams. Put simply, Bailey was Portland's "architect to the stars" to real estate mogul William Naito, to techno-baron John Gray, and to men, like Lee Hoffman, whose companies would build the city beam by beam. By the early 1950s, Bailey's list of commissions would read like the "Who's Who" of Portland's corporate movers and shakers. His clients were men who worked quietly behind the scenes laying the foundations for a Portland that, by the mid-1970s, would be voted the nation's "most liveable" metropolis.

Bailey built for an America buoyed by postwar optimism and soothed by the quietude of the Eisenhower

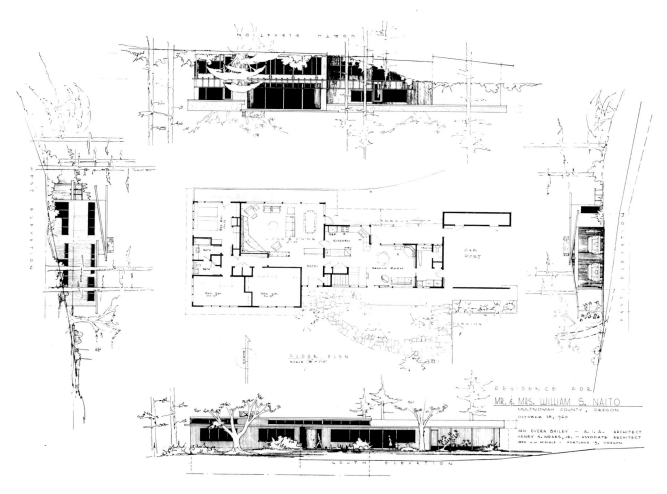

WILLIAM S. NAITO HOUSE
Van Evera Bailey
1960

years—for a country hypnotized by the marital bliss of Ozzie and Harriet, by large-finned automobiles and by a Marilyn Monroe who was taking America to steamy never-never land. Handsome, rugged and a tough-minded businessman, Bailey designed homes for the age of 5¢ Cokes, Burma Shaves and hard-working people addicted to the American Dream.

The Olympian vantage of his "stilt houses" with their ten-car parking decks, spacious laundries and big sunny kitchens (the Thomas Dixon house, 1951, the Van Evera Bailey house, 1958) suggested that Bailey had in mind the needs of an America that Thomas Wolfe, in *Of Time and The River*, had called "a fabulous country, the only fabulous country . . . the place where the Transcontinental

Limited is stroking eighty miles-an-hour across the continent . . . the place of the immense and pungent smell of breakfast, . . . the place of the huge stillness . . . the place of the child and laughter, where the young men . . . are drunk with the bite and sparkle of the air and mad with the solar energy, where they believe in love and victory and think that they can never die."

To be sure, children and laughter were an inextricable part of his architectural program. His designs addressed the whims of post-war babies, who had crawled out of their diapers and onto the seats of Schwinn tricycles. He designed for the needs of toddlers sitting on flagstone patios or cedar decks, munching Oreo cookies and slurping Kool-Aid as they listened to chirping red-

117

RADDITZ HOUSE
Van Evera Bailey
1951

winged blackbirds. In his award-winning design for the F. M. Radditz house (1951), chosen "House of the Month" by the *American Home* in June 1952, Bailey provided a number of features that catered to tots. Of special interest in his "House Designed for Children" was a tricycle course: "A boon in wet or windy weather," read the caption accompanying Bailey's floor plan. "It provides a protected route from front door to carport to bedrooms. Plan shows how a whole area was arranged so that youthful steam can be vented in an area built to 'take it'."

The architect's particular brand of hard-headed, warm-hearted acumen endeared him to his clients. "A native Oregonian, he [Bailey] thoroughly enjoys the informal indoor-outdoor life and his designs show it," read an article in *House and Home* in May 1952. Characterizing the house Bailey designed for Edwin Mittlestadt

in 1951 as "charm without schmaltz," the author of the article emphasized Bailey's unaffected handling of the rambling, low-slung Northwest idiom: "This particular house squeezes every advantage out of a handsome site. In the glass prow of their living room, the owners are virtually suspended over a triple-threat view: the river and city are 1,100 feet below and snow-capped mountains form a wall 40 miles away." Bailey was seen as having a rare talent for delighting the average customer and exciting his architectural cohorts at the same time. And, in this regard, according to *House and Home*, the Mittlestadt house was typical: "It has charm aplenty to beguile the laity, plus structural innovation that gives architects and builders something to think about."

Vibrant and gutsy, Bailey was the Gary Cooper of Portland architecture. It was not so much that the iconoclastic builder-designer personified the architect-hero

STEADMAN SHAW HOUSE
Van Evera Bailey
1952

Howard Roark, played by Cooper in the film version of *The Fountainhead* (1949). (Truth be told Bailey could not have cared less for Roark's struggle to erect an invincible citadel of modern architecture). Rather, Bailey personified Cooper, the *movie star*. "Van was a real man's man. He loved wine, women and all the good things," recalled Bill Naito, Portland real estate mogul who commissioned Bailey to design his own dreamhouse in the 1950s. "Van wasn't interested in building monuments like some of the other local architects. He'd sit back and laugh at those who did . . . he figured life was short so why bother." With great affection for "Van the Man," Naito continued: "But he had an ego . . . and a special way with women. When one of his clients wanted her

kitchen designed in a way that ran counter to Van's scheme, he'd just walk up to her, sling his big arms around her shoulders, and say, 'Now honey, you don't really want to do that to your kitchen, do you?'" Acquiescence to Bailey's position would inevitably follow moments later. Bristling with ferocious intensity, Bailey was recognized by his friends as a "big bear of a man," and according to Portland designer and long-time friend Douglas Lynch, he "did everything with intensity. He practiced architecture hard. He drove hard. He drank hard. All of his relationships were vital."

And so was his architecture. Although described by Lynch as "the mystical embodiment of Belluschi and Yeon . . . a real natural," Bailey did not always elicit

119

STEADMAN SHAW HOUSE
Van Evera Bailey
1952

praise from the city's architectural illuminati. Yeon, the gentleman aesthete with a keen eye for the understated and sublime, described Bailey's houses as "a little scratchy" for his tastes, and characterized his work as "architecture that should be appreciated without making architectural history." Yeon, who met Bailey when both were working in the office of Portland architect Herman Brookman during the 1920s—Yeon was an errand boy and Bailey a draftsman—confessed that he "just wouldn't be comfortable" in Bailey's houses because he liked "quieter forms and proportions." More kindly disposed toward Bailey's achievements, Belluschi remembered him as a designer "who may not have been terribly educated in doing the right things according to academic standards, but he could make up for it by being a very creative person." Perhaps Lynch put it best when he characterized the difference between Yeon's work and Bailey's as "the difference between a Zen temple and . . . a log cabin."

In the 1950s, America was a country sitting in the eye of a hurricane. Lulled by post-war quietude, even the

most astute cultural critics did not expect that razor-sharp tail fins on the '59 Caddy would metamorphose into bayonets of the 1960s. But this era was punctuated by more than flamboyant excrescences affixed to the rear ends of De Sotos and Fleetwoods. Hips spinning faster than a Waring Blender, Elvis Presley was effecting a vast rearrangement in the psyche of America's youth. Chuck Berry, in his blue suede shoes, was beating rudimentary chords out of an electric axe in a way that had never been done before.

And in Portland, architect Van Evera Bailey would add, in his own inimitable way, a little zing to the lassitude of the Eisenhower years. "Colorful. What other way is there to characterize this man who . . . left a generation of fine houses in Oregon and California as individualistic and distinctive as he was," wrote J. Kingston Pierce in an article titled, "Van Evera Bailey's Shaggy Legend." Describing the architect's white-hot joie de vivre, Pierce added: "he was colorful of deportment, colorful in personal relationships, colorful in his building style. This is the guy who scored highly among national design critics, yet would spend his weekends drunk as the proverbial skunk, shooting at floating lightbulbs in the Williamette River . . . and cruising through snowfalls in his big Buick convertible—top down, of course."

In many respects, Bailey represented a direct link to a major influence on the residential brand of modernism, Frank Lloyd Wright. His architecture addressed the Oregon "hillside" in the vivid, confident manner that Wright's homes in the Midwest had addressed the "prairie." The collision between nature and man-made platforms protruding from Portland's West Hills was a continuing theme in Bailey's work. In his own Neskowin Beach house (1952), as well as his private residence (1958), he introduced the bold, anti-gravity roofs, the sweeping lines, the strong connections to the earth, the flowing interior space as well as the futurist imagery of Wright to the regional idiom of the Northwest style.

Bailey's sympathy for the architectural imagination of Chicago's most eminent architect emerged with particular force in the design for the Neskowin Beach house. Built entirely of economical grades of local cedar, the beach house presented a sharp, triangular prow to the ocean. Cantilevered beyond the glass walls of the house, the roof was raised at a corner. The resulting composition, including the coarsely articulated "tweed" texture of the exterior and interior walls, anticipated the angular profile and surface treatment of Wright's Loveness Guest House in Stillwater, Minnesota (designed 1958, constructed 1976) with uncanny precision.

Although Bailey's residential architecture in Portland was certainly inspired by the region, his affinity with the modernistic design trends of Southern California (where he had a home) was declared strongly throughout his work. The opportunities of the postwar boom allowed architecture ranging from Belluschi's and Yeon's woodsy Northwest style to Richard Neutra's purism, full-rein in a new phase of modernism. There is little doubt that Bailey's "California Connection" instilled him with the sense that the 1950s had come to represent a new era, and that the long-promised future of benevolent technology and prosperity had at last arrived.

As much as anything, the designs for Bailey's dream homes reflected the times—in form, attitude, convenience and use of material. Glass walls, spatial arrangements and hillside sites were, for Bailey, a function of climate, lifestyle and topography, respectively. And his unique stilt system not only enhanced the closeness between environment and home, but was the architect's adaptation to Portland's shrinking number of buildable sites. "Desirable level building sites, in Portland, and elsewhere, are becoming hard to find, and expensive," he wrote to Herbert Smith of Architectural Record in 1960. "For a number of years I have been thinking about an inexpensive method of building on steep hillside ground. . . . I dislike to experiment on a client's money, so the need for my own house seemed to offer a wonderful opportunity . . . to build on stilts."

The architect's stilt system required light frame construction, consistent with hand labor and was based on diagonal bracing which stabilized the platform. But his interiors were conceived with convenience and comfort in mind. "The elimination of a lawn is one of the advantages of such a house on stilts," he continued in his letter to Smith. "My wife wanted the kitchen separate from the eating area, for the few times we might have outside help to serve for social occasions. Also, she wanted it off the kitchen work room, where she could leave the ironing board up. This has worked out nicely."

By 1950, more than a decade after Belluschi and Yeon had planted the seeds for modern residential design on the slopes of Council Crest, Portlanders did not find it difficult to embrace the clean, articulated structures of Van Evera Bailey. Modern ideas did not require an intellectual devotion or political position to be adopted. The Portland public had already associated technology with

the "good life." As architect Alan Hess pointed out, "Henry Ford saw to it that the machine, in the initial guise of the Model T, virtually became a member of the family, lifting burden and bestowing mobility. Electricity, radios, refrigerators, telephones, household appliances . . . and other gadgets constituted an education in modernism for the American middle class under the unknowing auspices of commercial capitalism." Reflecting the technological and structural wizardry of the times, Bailey's Dixon house (1952) was described in the Architectural Record of April, 1953, as "maybe not a 'machine for living,' but a building that would fit a better way of life."

Recognition came early in Bailey's career. Three years after he had begun his Portland practice, the architect was already winning accolades from distinguished architectural historian Henry-Russell Hitchcock. In the December, 1940 issue of California Arts and Architecture, Hitchcock commented that Bailey's "very considerable activities would make of him a better known and appreciated American modern architect than he has hitherto been." Bailey's claim to fame, according to Hitchcock, rested on his distinctive contribution to the development of the Northwest Regional style. In this respect, Bailey's name was linked with those of Belluschi and Yeon, all three of whom the East Coast critic cited as responsible for "some of the modern buildings on the [West] Coast." Bailey's small residences were praised for their "extremely ingenious and concise planning as well as admirable mastery of local wood materials and of the split tile masonry developed in Portland." To be sure, Bailey's work initially aroused Hitchcock's attention for his contribution to the Jan de Graaff house, a milestone in Portland architecture.

The de Graaff residence was designed by noted Los Angeles architect Richard Neutra whose forte was a brilliant sense for siting "glass" houses in the landscape and linking building with nature. While Bailey's official role in the project was limited to supervising construction, in reality he had a considerable hand in modifying Neutra's design to conform to local materials, building traditions and the client's specific needs. In a letter to Interiors Magazine dated 6 January 1945, Bailey described the elderly Dutch couple—"definitely left wing in all their thinking"—as requiring "simplicity in appearance," "quality in material things" and opposed to "any inclination to 'decorate' or to design for the sake of design." Bailey recommended making a number of changes, among them replacing Neutra's exterior stucco

GRACE SANDBURG HOUSE
Van Evera Bailey
1952

with cedar flooring boards, a contribution Hitchcock acknowledged. "Nor is it altogether invidious to suggest," the critic wrote, "that the de Graaff house, when completed, will probably owe some of its excellence to Bailey's command of local materials and local building methods." Hitchcock went on to observe that the Portland architect had gained "an increased clarity of expression" from his collaboration with California's leading residential designer. He was quick to add, however, that, "while stimulated by contact with Neutra's work, [Bailey's latest projects are] nevertheless not imitative."

Hitchcock should not have been surprised by Bailey's independence. The Neutra connection, after all, had crystallized after a series of earlier, maturing experiences

that had shaped Bailey's architectural vision. In the long run, perhaps, the most decisive collaborations dated from Bailey's acquaintance with William Gray Purcell. Purcell, who, along with Frank Lloyd Wright, apprenticed in the office of Louis Sullivan, gained international recognition as a key figure in the development of the "Chicago School."

Before coming to Portland in 1920, Purcell had been in practice with George Elmslie—Sullivan's long-time chief designer. Bailey met Purcell in 1925, when the 22-year-old designer was training in the offices of Otis J. Fitch, another Portland architect. In later years, Purcell recalled that Bailey was the "most capable and imaginative of the Purcell & Elmslie architectural family."

High praise indeed, coming from a man whose firm's best work, according to architectural historian Wayne Andrews, had "set standards that only Wright could equal and none surpassed." Impressed by Bailey's ability and passionate enthusiasm for design, the Chicago architect took a friendly interest in the young man's professional development. While working in the architectural offices of Purcell's friends, Bailey studied engineering and other subjects. But his real education occurred under the supervision of Purcell, with whom he spent much of his spare time.

By 1927, Purcell had gained enough confidence in his pupil's abilities to entrust him with a commission that he himself was unable to undertake. "As I was about to leave for Europe," Purcell wrote about the Harry S. Bastian project, "I recommended that they employ Otis J. Fitch, not that I had any high opinion of his work, but Van Evera Bailey, who had shown great promise and ability, was working for him." From this point on, the two men worked together on a number of residential designs, including the Sidney Bell, John W. Todd and W. H. Arnold houses. In 1946, Bailey would recall that Purcell was "a great experimenter and together we have tried many things in the building line."

Their Portland collaboration, however, was soon cut short by the Depression and Purcell's ill health, which prompted his move to California. While the older man was successfully recovering from tuberculosis, Bailey completed an independent commission for the George Rogers house (1929) in Lake Oswego. Described by Marion Ross as an early "modern" design that "freed the house from historical precedent," this two-story brick-and-stone structure was still a far cry from the sparse, crisp lines that would become Bailey's trademark. But aside from this commission, the young architect had little luck finding employment in Portland's arid construction market. Undaunted by meager prospects at home, however, Bailey took his career firmly in hand. In 1929 he packed himself off to Pearl Harbor where he became port architect. A year later, he was building miniature golf courses in New Zealand.

The venture could not have been lucrative, since Bailey was ready to sell his share of the practice to his partner "for the price of a ticket on the P & O Ship Line back to the States, via London." He had acted prematurely, however, if he counted on finding an improved job market at home. While still in Europe, the young itinerant received $159.00 and a wire from Purcell, telling him to "spend another month or two there; no jobs here." He followed the advice and stayed on to visit Germany, Scandinavia and the Netherlands, where he wrote back, he "saw more Frank Lloyd Wright (and Sullivan) design in Holland in two days walking than had been built in the USA." He would have done well, however, to prolong his travels. In 1931, even Purcell's glowing recommendations could not secure Bailey a job with New York firms. The best the tight market could offer was a summer stint in Minnesota. But that was not enough for a young man with Bailey's vision and drive. He pushed on to Southern California where Purcell had settled, and made Hollywood and the Palm Springs area his base of operations until 1937.

California, and Purcell, had been good to Bailey. In 1932, he became a registered architect, married and with Purcell's help, opened a small office in Hollywood. To spur business along, he began buying land and building homes, among them, a house built on speculation for Purcell in Palm Springs. This spare, compact residence, economical to build, but attractively comfortable, already announced Bailey's mature architectural manner. His respect for regional climate and the building traditions that had sprung up in response to it, was expressed in the low, concrete structure that was modeled on the adobe dwellings of native inhabitants. It had long windows to furnish adequate light, but there were overhanging grates that extended horizontally from the roofline to protect from the direct rays. In this, as in many of his California projects, Bailey adopted the use of a concrete wall form—the Van Guilder wall-builder—that he discovered while traveling in the Netherlands. What impressed him about this method of construction was its economy and the high quality of the product. When he returned to Portland in 1937, he brought with him both this method of construction and the sleek, curving lines of California's "Nautical Moderne" style.

Portland had just been introduced to modernism in residential design by Belluschi and Yeon. The Watzek house (1937), the Belluschi house (1936) and the Jennings Sutor house (1938) had broken ground for idiosyncratic interpretations of the clean-lined aesthetic promulgated by the Bauhaus School. Bailey's first Portland projects, however, took a different tack away from the wood vernacular championed by his Portland colleagues and moved toward the sleek concrete-glass block idiom of Streamline Moderne.

In the 1930s, some of the country's most elegant homes and apartment houses were being built in the curvilinear Moderne style. Architectural publications and popular magazines were full of praise for such spectacular aerodynamic palaces as the Earl Butler house in Des Moines, Iowa (1937, Kraetsch and Kraetsch), the Richard H. Mande house in Mt. Kisco, New York (1935, Edward Durell Stone and Donald Deskey), and the Herbert Bruning house in Wilmette, Illinois (1936, George Fred Keck). Portlanders in the know could point with pride to the exquisite streamlined residential work in which J. Andre Fouilhoux—former associate in the Portland office of Whitehouse and Fouilhoux—would be involved in New York. After leaving Portland for bigger and better opportunities on the East Coast, Fouilhoux would collaborate with New York architect Wallace K. Harrison on the design for the Rockefeller Apartments (1936). Described by Depression Modern historian Martin Greif as "New York's most beautiful apartment house of the 1930s," their building was a stunning composition of graceful curves and rectilinear planes, featuring silvery railings of tubular metal on the roofside terraces. Among architectural engineers who would practice in Portland, Fouilhoux would become the most distinguished alumnus in the streamline tradition.

In Portland, Fouilhoux based his reputation on the University Club (1913, Whitehouse and Fouilhoux), cited as Oregon's foremost example of the sixteenth-century Jacobean style. But, by 1939, along with Harrison, Fouilhoux would gain world acclaim in his "21st century" design for the Trylon and Perisphere, the symbol of the 1939 New York World's Fair. According to Greif, Harrison and Fouilhoux's spherical and pyramidal monuments represented a "streamlined phoenix emerging triumphant from the devastation of the Great Depression—the very essence of the Depression Modern style."

Portlanders, meanwhile, had only begun to acquire a taste for Streamline Moderne, primarily through Richard Sundeleaf's designs for commercial and industrial buildings. They had yet to encounter this style in local residential structures. Fresh from Europe and California, Bailey would introduce the streamlined residential style in a single, exemplary commission. In Europe he had certainly seen Walter Gropius's Bauhaus Faculty Residences in Dessau, whose right angles, straight planes, and curved nautical railings had inspired a host of imitations among European designers such as Robert Mallet-Stevens, Adolf Rading and Walter Reitz. More recently, in California, Bailey had been exposed to a distinctive

Southern California modernism that architectural historian Reyner Banham dubbed "Angeleno Modern." It was in Southern California, Banham noted, that such European exiles as Kem Weber, Rudolph Schindler and Richard Neutra produced an independent body of modern architecture contemporary with the rise of the International Style in Europe and fulfilled "some worthwhile possibilities of pre-1914 European architecture that were denied them in Europe." Schindler's acclaimed Lovell beach house (1926), Neutra's Lovell house in Griffith Park (1930) and his own residence by Silverlake (1933) were the work of "Californiated" European sensibilities—"European architecture going with the flow of the California dream."

Bailey brought this dream to Portland—more precisely, to Lake Oswego—when he completed the Thaddeus B. Bruno house in 1939. Perched on a hill overlooking Lake Oswego, the Bruno residence was described in the June 1939 issue of *Building News* as having been "planned to take full advantage of a magnificent view toward the snow-capped Cascade range of mountains." The house was placed as far back [i.e., toward the lake] on the plot as possible, primarily in order to develop a level front yard. But Bailey may have had another reason for pushing the house so close to the edge. Seen from the lake shore, the dazzling white curves and the silvery railings of the Bruno's dreamhouse might well have been taken for a dream *boat*.

Bailey's design took full advantage of the nautical metaphors that Californians so successfully combined with the Nautical Modern. To be sure, they had only applied and popularized a concept that Le Corbusier, among others, had formulated earlier in the century. In *Towards a New Architecture*, his architectural manifesto of 1923, Le Corbusier had cited the ocean liner as a model to architects stifled by the Beaux-Arts tradition of applied historical ornament. Describing ocean liners like the *Aquitania*, the *Lamoriciere* and the *France* as "an architecture pure, neat, clear, clean and healthy," Swiss modernist found the spirit of the age exemplified by "these formidable affairs that steamships are."

In the wake of the attention received by the *Normandie*, the *Nieuw Amsterdam* and other luxury liners, California's designers had lavished nautical details on a host of commercial and residential structures. Among the most dramatic examples of this sea-faring infatuation were the Aquatic Park Casino (1935–39, William Mooser, Jr.; now the Maritime Museum) in San Francisco, and the Coca-

Cola Bottling Company of Los Angeles (begun in 1937, Robert Derran). Built under the sponsorship of the Works Projects Administration, the Aquatic Park Casino was promoted in the Administration's press releases as "streamlined and modern to the last degree . . . . With rounded ends, set-back upper stories, porthole windows and ship rails, its resemblance to a luxurious ocean liner is indeed startling."

Bailey's Bruno house was equally startling in its woodsy setting. The architect spared no nautical motifs on the building, which was replete with decks, terraces, railings and even chimneys, that, in their strategic placement fore and aft, recalled the sleek stacks of an ocean liner. The flat roof lines, graduated in heights, enhanced the allusion to the tiered composition of the luxury liner's upper decks. The love of the curve was everywhere in evidence: from the graceful glass-block entrance bay to the swirling lines of the observation terraces. Inside, the foyer was a veritable paean to the Nautical Moderne style. Aglitter with glass block and tubular railing, the interior staircase descended to the living room in a cascade of organic contours. Yet for all its luxurious detailing, the house cost a mere $16,100— which by today's market would barely suffice for the price of a round-the-world cruise in a first-class stateroom on the QE II.

Shortly after completing the Bruno house, Bailey obtained his most challenging commission to date: planning and supervising construction of the Tongue Point Naval Air Station community near Astoria, Oregon. One of the earliest developments sponsored by the Federal Housing Authority, Bailey's riverside complex would be recognized as "an example of the advantages to be gained from planning a community as a pleasing and integrated unit." Working within the stringent financial limits set by the Federal wartime budget, Bailey showed considerable ingenuity in producing attractive, inexpensive wood structures in a variety of sizes and plans. So successful was his approach, that the editors of *Progressive Architecture* published the project "to help ward off the building of future slums which the huge small-house program could produce. We hope to be able to do this," George A. Sanderson, the magazine's feature editor, wrote to Bailey on 5 April 1946, "both by example [such as Astoria] and by urgings from top officials in Washington." Sanderson, unfortunately, had sadly overrated his magazine's influence in government circles. Only one of Bailey's design ideas would eventually be adopted among the "mini-

mum standards" established by the Federal Public Housing Authority.

But while the Astoria project did little to discourage the proliferation of shabbily designed and shoddily built public housing tracts during the 1940s, it did much to advance its designer's professional growth. He learned to outmaneuver economic log jams, bureaucratic controls, and to build houses on some of the trickiest terrain north of the San Bernardino Fault. As he commented in a letter to Sanderson, "I think you will agree that there has never been another housing project on a worse building site. I won my spurs from FPHA on this job, and later on I was always handed the projects (generally the smaller ones) which were to be built on rough ground." In the process, he also gave a generous clue as to what might have prompted Purcell to characterize his protegé in 1938 as "one of the most surprising characters—A person of contradictions . . . . He is lovable and exasperating. A grand companion and a damned nuisance."

In a letter to Sanderson, Bailey outlined the project's tangled tale. "Just after Pearl Harbor," he wrote on 12 April 1942, "contractor Lee H. Hoffman (local bigshot) was invited to PBA [Public Buildings Authority] in Washington to come East and figure a job of permanent housing for the Tongue Point Naval Air Station. Hoffman had had so many jobs thrown at him by the government that he arranged to have his son Lee and myself handle this relatively small job (then planned to be 100 units)." The young men traveled East and prepared a successful bid for the project. In the interim, however, the Federal Public Housing Authority had been formed and the project passed into its jurisdiction. Negotiations had to be resumed afresh. "This time," Bailey continued, "I went down to San Francisco alone, as Hoffman's interest was lagging." The original plans, designed to meet the minimum standards established by the PBA, had to be scrapped, since the new Housing Authority had not yet adopted them. Moreover, the "old PBA standards (full basements, central heating plants . . . concrete foundations, concrete streets, curbs and sidewalks) were beyond the war-time economies of housing."

To respect bureaucratic protocol, a completely new contract had to be negotiated in a byzantine procedure best described in Bailey's own words. "Inasmuch as I had seen the site (which was a corker) and was familiar with the local conditions, I was transferred to the next room. After verbally and literally disconnecting myself from the employ of L. H. Hoffman, a contract was drawn up with me to re-design the entire project." Collaborating with San Francisco architect F. J. McCarthy, he completed the design and drawings in an astounding ten days. The project was then passed back to the Hoffman Construction Company and Bailey was engaged as job superintendent.

Compared to the problems presented by the rugged site, the bureaucratic red tape had been mere child's play. "By the time the large trees were blasted out," the architect recalled, "the grades were found to be a terrific problem. Throughout construction of the project my entire time was taken up in site grading, re-establishing grades to fit the actual conditions which were at quite some variance with the original plan on account of the very bad site survey." At the same time, the architect had to re-think and re-design the post-and-beam underpinnings for each building, which in some cases, required 20-foot deep foundations. The experience, however arduous at the time, paid off grandly in the next round of Bailey's private commissions. On the devilishly tricky footing of the Astoria project the architect worked out the rudiments of the cone-shaped stilt foundations that were to support no less than ten of his houses during the next two decades.

Even before the Astoria project, Bailey had shown a knack for getting his name—and his projects—into print. His collaboration with Neutra on the Jan de Graaff house (1940) had brought him national attention not only from Henry-Russell Hitchcock, but also from the *Architectural Record* which wanted to publish the project. A shrewd diplomat, Bailey was anxious to preserve good relations with his colleagues. Particularly with the influential Neutra, he took pains to assure that he would not come off looking like a publicity hound. "I am writing Neutra," he informed the *Architectural Record* on 24 September 1942, "to allow him the opportunity of putting his stick in . . . . I do not want him to think I am trying to run off with the job." Professional courtesy was not the only motivating factor in this instance.

Portland was still buzzing with the misunderstandings that had exploded over the frequent misattribution of the Watzek house in popular and professional publications. Perhaps because Yeon had worked on this house while he was still affiliated with A. E. Doyle and Associate, credit for the design had sometimes gone to the firm, or to Belluschi, its chief designer. Even as late as 1947, in James M. Fitch's authoritative history of *American Building*, the Watzek house would be pictured with a caption reading, "To our domestic tradition in wood Pietro Belluschi has brought a sparse Italian elegance. His Portland houses are akin to Wright's, yet not derivative." It was to such gaffes that Bailey referred when he wrote, "We must avoid one of those Watzek episodes."

He was also eager to avoid antagonizing the numerous magazine editors who clamored for rights to publish his residential designs almost as soon as they came off his drafting table. As a rule, Bailey's considerable stores of discretion and tact sufficed to keep both editors and clients happy. On the rare occasions, however, when Bailey's preferences were at odds with his clients' wishes, the architect showed himself eminently up to the task of defending his interests. This happened, for example, in the great Hoffman house controversy of 1944. With no fewer than three publications competing to "scoop" the project and a client as headstrong as his architect, the situation verged on the explosive. "Hoffman, being a 'big-shot' constructor," Bailey wrote to *Pencil Points* (also known as *Progressive Architecture*) editor George Sanderson on 7 November 1944, "may have a choice or opinions in the matter. I will let you know what decision I get the minute I get it." He pointed out, however, that Condé Nast's *House and Garden* had already secured the client's permission, although "when the house was built before the war he [Hoffman] asked me not to publish it."

Architectural photographer Phyl Dearborn, who often photographed Bailey's projects for *Pencil Points* revealed another interesting twist in the conflicting interests. "Hope Hoffman is okay," he wrote to Bailey on 13 November 1944, "and that he approves publication of his house—he favored *Architectural Forum* he told me— that being before you had forbidden that magazine's entering the field. Hope his having had a row with you won't make any difference." It did not. Harmony was somehow restored, and the controversial house was published to the mutual satisfaction of client and architect alike.

The February 1945 issue of *Pencil Points* featured generous coverage of the residence, accompanied by Dearborn's crisp photographs. The review praised the sensitive siting of the house on the "beautiful, wooded ridge high above the city of Portland" and the "generous, almost luxurious" living accomodations within concrete, brick and cedar structure. "Certain details and elements echo historic tradition," the reviewer pointed out, "but in the main . . . the design reflects the aim of providing a good house rather than any textbook precedent." This

RADDITZ HOUSE
Van Evera Bailey
1951

characterization would apply to all of Bailey's architectural philosophy with astounding accuracy. "In a period when matters of identifiable architectural style are likely to produce violent partisanship," the reviewer noted, "the design approach to this Portland home—neither sentimental, on the one hand, nor iconoclastic, on the other—contributes light rather than heat to the argument."

It also contributed considerable interest to Bailey's architectural practice. Through the pages of the popular *House and Garden*, the Hoffman house reached a broad public and reaped a string of hidden benefits. Recognizing the popular appeal of Bailey's designs, manufacturers of construction materials began to approach the architect with requests for permission to use his residences in their publicity schemes. The Fuller and Smith and Ross

advertising agency, representing the Libbey, Owens, Ford Glass Company, offered Bailey "an architectural credit line" in exchange for rights to use the "intriguing photographs" of the Hoffman house in their advertising campaign.

But the real bonanza came from the demand for blueprints which the publications had created. Gearing up for postwar prosperity, Americans from Jackson, Michigan to Buffalo, New York wanted to live in their own versions of the pleasantly informal Hoffman house. And Bailey was ready to oblige them. In a letter to Walter and Mary Beiswenger, "Breeders of Fine Parakeets" and owners of "Beiswenger's Budgieland" in Jackson, Michigan, the architect proposed several options for his involvement in designing their Michigan home. "I could very well prepare your plans and specifications here," he wrote on VE Day (8 May 1945). "I have successfully handled jobs that way from a distance. Also, I could let you have a set of plans of the Hoffman house . . . . The cost of such a set of plans would be $50, and would probably be borne by the architect you chose there [to supervise the construction]."

Three years later, after thinking the matter over, the parakeet breeders decided that the world was once again safe for homes with lozenge-shaped living rooms. In their calculations, however, they had neglected to reckon with postwar inflation. "Here is the check for $100.00 for the . . . blueprints," Mary Beiswenger wrote to Bailey with some dismay on 11 March 1948. "Needless to say, we were certainly surprised to note that you had doubled the price you quoted us when we priced them before. . . . Do hope we don't meet with a doubling up on every price we have had quoted to us or we will never accomplish what you know we are trying so hard to do." The Michigan couple had fully expected that, "by this time, the cost would have lessened or remained constant." "Hope your latest quotation proves to be a mistake on your part," Mary Beiswenger wrote in her postscript, "so that part of this sum enclosed may be refunded."

However disagreeable this exchange might have been, it certainly was not typical of Bailey's way of doing things. Nor did it discourage him from actively cooperating with popular and professional publications, which continued to keep a close eye on his work. Over the next ten years, Bailey became something of a celebrity in architectural circles. Published widely in the *Architectural Record* and *Progressive Architecture*, as well as *Sunset*, the *American Home*, *Better Homes and Gardens* and the *Los Angeles Times*, his houses did much to bring the robust and outdoorsy Northwest tradition of residential design to all parts of the country.

They did even more to disseminate the rituals, attitudes and fashions of a new style of life. Bailey's stilt houses, beach homes and year-round residences were, above all, buildings designed for living. With a directness and an optimism that sprang from his own enthusiasm for the newly idealized middle-class family, his homes spoke to the multiple dimensions of his patrons' personalities and needs. "Framing our lives in our Oregon house," one of Bailey's satisfied clients reflected, "we are now quite sure that architecture affects one's daily life far more than we ever expected. Our home has given dignity to our days, pleasure to our senses, and scope to our thoughts." In this respect, Bailey followed the advice of

Frank Lloyd Wright, who had said that, "Every great architect is—necessarily—a great poet. He must be a great original interpreter of his time, his day, his age." Bailey's poetry moved in the realm of quiet domestic joys, creature comforts and the delights of the great outdoors. His houses were odes to the automobile, to the kitchen, to participatory democracy and to a domesticity in pursuit of the fashionable mind.

Captivated by Bailey's celebrations of the American Dream, glossy magazines from New York to Los Angeles played the "human interest" angle to the hilt, transforming building plans into exemplary tales. The July 1954 issue of *Better Homes and Gardens* brought the story behind the Eyre house (1952) to 3,800,000 American housewives. "Our House is the Way We Live," ran the headline of the article written by Cynthia Eyre. "We're not fancy, and we're not plain," she explained in her thumbnail "bio." "We have a 20-year plan on our house, plus two children to raise and educate." Half a child short of the national average, the Eyres wanted a home that would be distinctly their own—tailored to their needs, but still blending with the building traditions of their community. "We loved the bony structural rightness of our mountain cabins, with their massive stone fireplaces," wrote the wife of Portland newspaperman David Eyre. "That was our heritage—we hoped to make it our haven."

Bailey's wood-and-glass composition gave them this regional "structural rightness." But the crisp lines of his pitched roof, its deep overhang supported by willowy beams, did not draw its inspiration directly from the rude mountain cabin. Instead, it bore the unmistakable trace of Yeon's Watzek house—as would the columned porticos and pergolas of the Mittlestadt house (1951), the Radditz house (1951), and the Gray house (1949).

If Bailey called the shots in designing the exterior of the Eyre house, when it came to interior planning, he was architect, arbiter and psychiatrist rolled into one. "We entered into a period of nerve-wracking analysis and decisions," Eyre recalled of the preliminary planning sessions with the architect. "With the skill of a prosecuting attorney, our architect began the Big Quiz. What were our habits, our hobbies, our activities? What did we do every morning, noon, and night? Gradually, a pattern of life emerged. The Eyre pattern." From the laundry room that was Mrs. Eyre's "pride," to the "golden" room that combined bedroom, office and den, to the spacious kitchen that was the family's "most frequent gathering place"; every element of the house was designed to enshrine this distinctive—and yet typical—pattern. Down to picking out the last penny nail, the architect consulted with his client's wishes at every step of the project. But he was also not afraid to put in his "veto." When the clients wanted to add a study *and* a "lordly dining room" to their list of demands, Bailey "pointed out hoarsely that it was 1951, and prices were soaring almost as fast as materials were disappearing. He said our budget wouldn't stand for it." Mediating among the competing claims of the family members, balancing dream against budget, the architect gave the Eyre family a practical lesson in participatory democracy at work.

But, when necessary, he also knew how to make way for the rugged individualist who wanted the final say in the shape of the project. John Gray, future chairman of the board of Tektronix and Omark Industries, was a member of this rugged breed. To readers of the August, 1952 issue of *House and Garden*, however, this multi-millionaire-to-be was just a penny-pinching jack-of-all-trades who proved that a lot of elbow grease could buy a three-bedroom house for $11,500. "A young Oregon couple saved money by laying their terrace, building a barbecue, and painting their house inside and out," read the sidebar to the article entitled, "Stretch Your Building Dollar By Finishing Your House Yourself." The Gray saga, however, offered more than a set of step-by-step instructions for building up the dollar-stretching muscles. It provided, also, a hidden inspirational message that paid homage to the great American virtues of industry, patience and fortitude. "If your budget is the stumbling block between the house you dream of and the one you can afford," ran the opening remarks in reference to the Gray family's way of doing things, "one of the best things to do is roll up your sleeves—literally as well as figuratively—and go to work."

The helpful hints that followed this moralistic digression documented the small economies that led to the "substantial savings" on which the Gray's fortune was subsequently built. Among the various "cost-cutters" were movable, "space-saving storage cabinets" that replaced permanent partitions between the bedrooms. The rough-sawn Douglas fir siding that, once treated to an oil finish, required no further upkeep, removed another of the "stumbling blocks" between dream and reality.

Gray had such fun working with Bailey and finishing his "house-in-the-raw" that he would eventually branch out into building lush vacation retreats in Salishan, on the Oregon coast and at Sunriver. Recognizing the architect's talent for turning out homes that were as functional and beautiful as they were fun, the entrepreneur made sure Bailey would have ample opportunity to work some of his architectural magic at Salishan. While not within reach of every upwardly mobile Portland couple, Bailey's rusticated hideaways were a fitting reward for those prudent "self-helpers" who had learned the wisdom of Gray's dollar-stretching formulas.

Building in an era of gas-guzzlers, cheap gasoline, and flight to the suburbs, Bailey knew the importance of working the automobile into his residential designs. The car, after all, had become the latest member of the American family, and deserved a room of its very own. His homes gave as much attention to the spacious garage as they did to junior's bedroom—and they were just as sensitive to making the car feel a part of the family. Covered passageways connected the automobile's quarters with the family's rooms.

In Bailey's own house, this devotion to the king of the road could verge on fanaticism. "It might be mentioned somewhere," Bailey wrote to Elizabeth Thompson of *Architectural Record*, "that the driveway and deck provide parking for 10 cars. Actually, at a party, we had 14 cars parked without blocking the narrow street for two way traffic." Even after having made these generous provisions to keep the car in its place, Bailey could not manage to take a portrait of his house without getting the ubiquitous automobile in the foreground. "I think this house is jinxed as far as photography is concerned," the architect's wife wrote to an editor at the Meredith Publishing Company on 26 April 1961. "Something happens every time we take a picture." This time, a friend had parked his car in the driveway and left it, locked, to join the Baileys for a jaunt. In the meantime, the photographer "Carlos came to take the picture, no one was here, he couldn't move the car—so there we are with a dandy shot of a white Ford."

There were, however, few "dandy shots" of white Kelvinator refrigerators in the photographs of Bailey's kitchens. White was not a color the architect—or his clients—favored when it came to decorating the gastronomic hub of the home. As architectural historian James Martson Fitch pointed out in 1947, "The kitchen has been the object of more intelligent study than any other area of the house . . . . As a result, the kitchen is already the best-designed and best-equipped unit in the house."

So well equipped with the latest gadgetry were Bailey's kitchens, that something had to be done to distinguish

GRACE SANDBERG HOUSE
Van Evera Bailey
1952

them from home-economics classrooms and experimental laboratories. Never at a loss for an answer, the architect took his cue as much from his client's culinary habits as from their nostalgic fantasies. "Mrs. Steinberg is an enthusiastic—and gourmet cook," the architect wrote to *Better Homes and Gardens* editor Helen A. Dawson on 14 April 1966 "and much thought went into the planning of her department. The appliance center . . . is the best idea I've seen for handling modern electrical equipment. You may not approve of the row of herbs and spices lined up along the top of the kitchen cabinet, but it's a convenient arrangement, and gives rather a country air to that corner."

Playing off "high-tech" efficiency against the "soft touch" of regional materials, the architect created warm and functional spaces that celebrated the kitchen as the gathering place of the nuclear family. One of his most captivating designs that combined a "cozy fireplace" with a modern range, won high marks from Theresa Crowd, contributor to the 15 June 1952 issue of the *Sunday* [Portland] *Journal Magazine*. "Big, Roomy, Well-Equipped," Crowd announced in a sidebar, "This New Room Reflects Yesterday's Comfort." What particularly enchanted the local author was the owner's ingenuous contribution to carrying out the "country kitchen" theme. "Of interest to fugitives from the 'sterile white operating room kitchen'," Crowd wrote, "is the pink-brown color of the refrigerator and dishwasher. The owners took their equipment to an automobile paint shop and had auto enamel sprayed and baked on for permanent finish." Once again, it had been shown, that what was good for Detroit, was good for the country, or, in this instance, equally good for the kitchen of a Portland couple.

The charming housewives who appeared in photographs of Bailey's houses, however, could never be taken for automobile mechanics. Daintily sipping tea in silk shantung sheathes or petting the golden retrievers sprawling at their spike-heeled feet, the willowy ladies of Bailey's houses were the stuff of housewives' daydreams.

Unflappable, poised and elegant in their impeccable houses, they delivered photogenic lessons on the graceful arts of leisure domesticity. If, sometimes, they seemed too good to be true, this was because quite often they were *not* in fact real.

In the rosy glow of America's postwar fantasies, the brutal honesty of *cinema verité* held little appeal outside the art-film screening rooms. When, as sometimes happened, Bailey's clients looked a touch too rugged for the house, models—including labrador retrievers—were brought in for the photo sessions. Documentary photo-realism was sacrificed for that touch of glamor that Bailey's houses always promised and which his clients almost always delivered.

FILLING IN THE CRACKS

B Y 1940, Portland's built landscape was a rich pastiche of modernistic and ancient spatial
configurations and decorative manipulations. Teeming with buildings in myriad architectural styles, the city had coalesced into a mythical metropolis—a Brobdignagian urban
sculpture—fabricated from wood, glass, stone, terra cotta and cast-iron. While design
decisions in the city had always been motivated, to some extent, by a common vision of Portland as a
unique city, they were also faithfully cross-indexed with "fashionable" architectural developments in
other, more cosmopolitan, metropolises across the country, especially San Francisco and New York.

That Portland had developed pride in its architectural landscape was evident as early as 1867, when the *Portland Directory* had commented: "It is hoped that the work of improving the style of architecture in Oregon will not rest here, but will go on improving until Portland may be numbered among the architectural cities of the Union." Only five years later, in reference to the growing city's number of handsome cast-iron buildings, the *Oregonian* would praise Portland's architecture in words that would have the ring of truth in 1930 and, again, in 1985: "Another favorable indication that our people are progressive in their taste, as well as in matters of enterprise, exists in the fact that a very marked change is observable in the styles adopted in the construction of buildings. All the latest and most modern graces of architectural harmony, beauty and effect, are found combined in the useful and ornamental improvements of the city."

All the prestigious architectural models of the times (except for the skyscraper), had been installed in the city by 1930. Portland's version of "The White City" took the shape of terra cotta clad banks, department stores and government edifices occupying compact 200-foot blocks between Third and Sixth avenues. Sheathed in tried-and-true historical envelopes, the buildings of Whidden and Lewis, A. E. Doyle, Gilbert and others stood guard over the city skyline. In a show of optimism, strength and respect for the "old that was good," Portland's generation of Beaux Art architects had graced street-level facades and the uppermost reaches of Portland's mightiest and most elegant buildings—the Public Service Building and the Yeon Building—with columns, loggias and arcades recalling ancient Greece and Rome. Until the collapse of 1930, these revered symbols of antiquity symbolized progress and the hope of a better future.

Closer to the ground, however, Portland's budding microcosm was dominated by the largest collection of iron-fronted structures west of the Mississippi River. Interspersed among the most recent crop of skyward thrusting monuments to progress, were low-lying two-, three-, and four-story cast-iron jewels such as the Ladd and Tilton Bank (1868, John Nestor), the New Market Theater (1872, Piper and Burton) and the Blagen Block (1888, architect not known). The shadowy succession of Roman Corinthian columns along First Avenue and Front Street created an exhilirating rhythmic pulsation along the trajectory of man's path through Portland's shop-lined streets. From all accounts, it was a handsome and exciting city densely packed with snugly fitting—and, frequently, stylistically unified—ornate iron facades reflecting elegance, commitment to architec-

tural excellence and, as architect and cast-iron scholar William J. Hawkins III put it, "an air of permanence." By 1871, the *Oregonian* would be prompted to write: "Many of these buildings are costly and of handsome and imposing appearance. We doubt if any city on the Pacific Coast can show anything like a parallel."

By 1940, Portland's built landscape matured into a confluent—and singular—network of styles, vistas and antiquarian architectural spaces that came together like the pieces of a jigsaw puzzle. The result was a staggering architectural composite. Sculpted out of marble and plaster, the vast and dignified lobbies of the city's banking institutions and mortuaries recalled the static, monumental spaces that characterized the official buildings of ancient Rome. And on the streets, block after block of cast-iron pilasters—embellishing long slender urban cavities with a continuous row of iron "ribs"—projected the linear directives and dynamic forces of a fifteenth-century arcade.

At the western periphery of the commercial core, yet another architectural sensibility was in evidence. Combining the Art Deco themes of the 1920s with modern structural techniques and materials, Dougan and other Portland architects created rational, modernistic curtain walls, punctuated with Zigzag brick patterns and applied polychrome ornamentation. And by the end of the fourth decade, Belluschi and Yeon would send Portland's well-entrenched tradition in residential architecture into a new phase. Although outnumbered by the Georgian, Dutch Colonial and Italianate "replicas of replicas" which peppered the Northwest flats, the buildings of Yeon and Belluschi would be testimonials to new spatial arrangements that spoke both to the functional and psychological needs of a society in transition.

Portland's most significant architects designing between 1927 and 1945 recognized the need for the utilization of scientific and technological advances. In the stagnant economy of the 1930s decade, "getting things moving again" was a shared desire expressed vicariously in various modes of transportation which, as it turned out, had a profound effect on the architecture of the period. During the reconstructive years, a number of Portland practitioners—most notable among them, Richard Sundeleaf—began to specialize in industrial architecture. In the backwater industrial zones of Guild's Lake, the Hollywood District, as well as near Northeast and Southeast, a new stratum would be deposited where structures spotwelded to the industrial landscape, almost without exception, were bolder, rougher and less "decorated" than the "prestigious" edifices that had seeded the urban core. Often times, these buildings were the work of Portland's most inspired—and highly esteemed—practitioners, and were based on ornamental programs that looked to a new architectural symbolism based on the machine aesthetic and popular culture.

Recovery from the dark years of the Depression was characterized by industrial retooling, democratization, the rising power of labor unions and new consumer products and markets. In Portland, new buildings were erected that responded to these changes. The architectural cracks would be filled with streamlined gas stations and Art Deco style bottling companies, modern factories and automobile showrooms, pleasure palaces and mausoleums. Sadly, these contributions have largely gone unrecognized. Many of these Portland buildings were examples of a decent pluralistic architecture. Writing in the *Society of Architectural Historians Journal*, Forrest F. Lisle, in discussing Chicago's Century of Progress Exposition of 1933, examined the relationship between Art Deco architecture of the 1930s and the cultural climate of the times:

> Contrary to most historical and critical assessments of American architecture of the 1930's, Moderne architecture [his term for Art Deco] can be shown to have been the logical and, thus, perhaps, 'proper' stylistic choice, for America to have made in view of the nation's institutions, traditions, and ideals . . . it is demonstrable that basic to the development and acceptance of the Moderne was the existence of, and regard for, democratic, egalitarian, middle-class, commercial, free-enterprise, popular culture values and comprehensions.

Portland's architectural flowering between the recession of 1927 and World War II occurred against a background of economic upheaval, national disillusionment and confusion. It was a period that called for new, dramatic solutions in the political, economic and architectural arenas. Eventually, Franklin Delano Roosevelt, the New Deal and the dynamic functionalism introduced by industrial architects such as Albert Kahn would ease America out of an economically blighted decade. While in the darkest days of the Depression, a new breed of industrial architects had dreamed merely of orderly, hygienic cities. By 1939—at the New York World's Fair—they had gained enough confidence to set their sights on a streamlined "World of Tomorrow."

In *Horizons*, a visionary treatise on modern industrial construction published in 1932, Norman Bel Geddes predicted the following: "Just as surely as the artists of the fourteenth century are remembered by their cathedrals, so will those of the twentieth be remembered for their factories and the products of these factories." Bel Geddes was one of the most successful theoretical designers of his era, and his industrial work for Toledo Scales, Philco and the 1939 World's Fair in New York—for which he designed the sumptuously streamlined General Motors building—produced some of the most striking "Mechano Deco" achievements ever conceived.

His sympathy for the uncluttered forms of the machine aesthetic was uncompromising. "Due to its stark simplicity," Bel Geddes wrote, "one of the few memorials of the last century that will withstand changes in thought and time is the Washington Monument." Infatuated with the untapped potential for innovative ideas lurking in the industrial sphere, Bel Geddes promulgated the concept that modern factory architecture, above all, should be a product of engineering. "Architecture is an art. Building itself just a craft," wrote the designer in his magnum opus. "When Michelangelo, generally thought of as a sculptor or painter, conceived St. Peter's at Rome, he thought in terms of an engineer. But being an artist, the result was a work of architecture."

During the late nineteenth and early twentieth century, the architectural profession had shown little initiative or imagination in designs for industrial structures. At the beginning of the industrial age, ugliness, in varied forms, and poorly organized buildings were the rule. In fact, industrial architecture was the neglected stepchild of the design profession. Beaux-Arts architects may have been in their element doing mausoleums, government buildings and monuments, but they gave factories no architectural ranking. As Bel Geddes pointed out, "a factory had to be built economically; wasn't supposed to be seen by anybody except the workers; there was no reason why a factory should have aesthetic appeal as it was merely a place for machines and for people to work who used machines."

Only in the late 1920s was it recognized that light, cleanliness and agreeable surroundings were advantageous both to profits and the peace of mind of employees. Around this time, first in Germany and Holland, and then in America, sympathetic architects began to show a sense of appreciation for the significance of industrial architecture. But, in Bel Geddes's view, things were not changing fast enough. "As the dawn of modern

EASTSIDE TIRE SHOP AND SERVICE STATION
designer unknown
1929

factory architecture arrived," the designer hastened to add, "the dawn's early gleams escaped the attention of the architects themselves." Before architects such as Albert Kahn elevated industrial architecture to its revered status in the 1930s, most practitioners became involved in factory design because of the remuneration. Inevitably, these structures were like large cheap houses and the result was dark, depressing and inefficient. "And when they put forth a special effort," Bel Geddes noted in *Horizons*, "their contribution consisted primarily of adding something, such as pilasters, and cornices, or other decorations borrowed from antiquity to mask a structure that should have been approached as a new problem requiring new treatment."

This schism between exterior decoration and interior function was also apparent in Portland. For example, Fred Fritsch's design for the old Roebling Cable and Wire Company (1927, Sutton and Whitney), featured fluted stucco pilasters and a Romanesque entrance, both "applied" to the exterior of an otherwise purely functional building. Sutton and Whitney moved one step closer toward modern factory architecture with their crisp scheme for the Oregon Brass Works (1931) at 1127 S.E. 10th Street. A rational, rectilinear format was interrupted by a series of fluted pilasters gracing the building's main facade. The overall effect was that of a modernistic factory in the process of shedding its neo-

classical garments, which, of course, by 1932 were falling out of fashion.

In Portland, what was once known as "factory" or "mill" building between 1890 and 1925 would become "industrial architecture" by the late 1920s. That industrial and commercial structures built between 1925 and 1950 became recognized as feats of "modern architecture" was not only the result of a revolution in aesthetic standards, but also the outcome of fundamental changes that took place in the factory and the nature of production itself. Industrial warehouses and plants erected in Portland after 1928 would come, in fact, to represent a rich current in the city's architectural heritage.

Engineers, architects and industrial designers would form collaborations which adopted the machine aesthetic as the "proper inspiration for factory architecture." Although the cityscape was studded with internationally acclaimed industrial outposts such as the Jantzen Knitting Mills (1928, Richard Sundeleaf), and streamlined buildings—including the Chase Bag Company (1937, The Austin Company) and Canada Dry Ginger Ale Company (1946, Walter M. Cory)—designed and erected by America's premier "industrial" architectural firms, this fertile vein in the city's history, for the most part, has remained completely untapped. This, despite the fact that Depression Modern industrial architecture of the 1930s would have a profound, if not always direct,

ASSOCIATED OIL STATION
Constructed by Ray F. Becker Company
1932

influence on the body of modern work which followed.

Few industrial buildings built in Portland before World War I showed any architectural merit. As a rule, they were cheap, clumsy but necessary structures which housed production layouts in an inefficient manner. And most industrial structures, like the products made in them, continued to imitate, in one fashion or another, the gawky designs and muted styles of a bygone period.

After World War I, Portland's economic base expanded and shifted toward an industrial mode. The old mill and warehouse construction became less suitable for manufacturing; heavy timbers, short spans and dark interiors were inevitably forced out by lighter, more transparent and stronger structures. Indeed, it was the larger engineering works pressed into service by the demands of heavy industry and hydroelectric projects on the Co-

lumbia River—the dynamos, turbines and other equipment—that showed the path for a new architecture.

In fact, some of the country's most influential designers considered hydroelectric projects to be exemplary of the best architectural design of the age. Dedicated in 1935, Hoover Dam was a source of architectural inspiration for Walter Dorwin Teague, one of America's most celebrated designers of the 1930s. In his book, *Design this Day*, published in 1940, Teague included a photograph of the dam, and touted it as an example of "rightness of form." Featured were its four intake towers, polygonal and stairstepped in Deco fashion, and spillways on the Arizona and Nevada sides, which resembled aircraft wings with engines.

In rebelling against traditional ideologies that characterized Portland architecture in the late nineteenth and

TEXACO FILLING STATION
Constructed by Ray F. Becker Company
1937

early twentieth century, the industrial and commercial structures built during Oregon's Mechano Deco period constituted a unique body of work. The city's young architects—which included, among others, Richard Sundeleaf, Pietro Belluschi, George Wolff and Van Evera Bailey—groped for a new structural language and modern aesthetic to express the demands and perspectives of a mechanically inclined twentieth-century culture. For the most part, each would move toward an architecture that was functionally designed, dynamically balanced and harmoniously presented. "Whether you are sympathetic to the idea or not," Bel Geddes wrote in 1932, "industry is the driving force of the age."

And so it was. Prior to the 1920s, Oregon's economy centered heavily on timber and agriculture. Excluding the Depression years, the State's economy grew and

prospered between 1925 and 1950. These years were characterized by rapid industrial expansion and diversification: steel production, heavy and light machinery, dam and road construction. The architectural repercussions of this development would come to light emblematically in the Northwest, Northeast, and Southeast industrial sectors of the city. Not surprisingly, by 1945 commercial architecture in these areas would reflect the convergence of modernistic approaches in architectural design with newly available building materials—steel, concrete and glass—coaxed out by the demands of new technological imperatives and fresh consumer markets.

Recognizing Portland's commercial viability, a number of national industrial firms and merchandising giants opened or expanded regional branches in the city. The Ford Motor Company took the lead in 1914, erecting an

SIXTH AVENUE AND WASHINGTON BUILDING (PROPOSED IMPROVEMENTS)
Harry A. Herzog
1928

assembly plant (A. E. Doyle, architect) in Northeast Portland, which spurred the construction of myriad automobile-associated businesses, including foundries, tire and mechanical part dealerships, automobile showrooms and rubber manufacturing plants. The Montgomery Ward Company and the American Can Company, two of the nation's leading purveyors of consumer goods, rapidly followed suit with buildings in Portland's Northwest district. Thus, the local population's basic requirements for transportation, clothing and sustenance were readily satisfied.

In the 1930s and 1940s, the Guild's Lake area sprouted industrial complexes for processing raw materials and furnishing, among other things, the underpinnings for the city's industrial growth. East of the Willamette, the city diversified by catering primarily to the population's alimentary needs. Three beverage companies erected sparkling—and now, nationally acclaimed—examples of industrial Moderne architecture: Portland (7-Up)

Bottling Company (1941, Arthur Cramer); Canada Dry Ginger Ale (1946, Walter M. Cory); Coca-Cola Bottling Company (1941, Jesse M. Shelton); and Sunshine Dairy (1948, Claussen and Claussen).

While factors contributing to industrial expansion were complex, reflecting as much innovations in mass production, energy generation, demographic flux and new demands for consumer products, perhaps none assumed such a controlling importance as the automobile and the growing reliance on truck transport. As if to acknowledge its debt to the stylistic achievements which found their expression in the automobile, the new industrial architecture drew heavily on the accumulated influence of the machine environment.

To be sure, the automobile did more to shape Portland's architectural landscape of the 1930s than any single invention since the wheel. Wheels are what got America moving. Wheels are what got sex moving. And wheels are what got architecture of the 1930s moving. Writ-

GILMORE FILLING STATION
Constructed by Ray F. Becker Company
1936

ing in *The Streamlined Decade*, historian Donald J. Bush suggested that "when Walter Gropius, director of the Bauhaus, designed a series of elegant but boxy automobile bodies for the Adler Company of Germany during the late 1920s, he chose to ignore the trend toward aerodynamic design." Later, architecture critic Reyner Banham would interpret Gropius's design as disrupting the "visual link" between the International Style and advancing technology. Exalting the role of the automobile, Bush proposed that the "'whiplash' motif became a unifying device for the new environment. It was a fresh invention and nonhistorical movement that created a dynamic aesthetic and sought to apply it everywhere."

The contribution of the automobile aesthetic to the architecture of Portland's commercial and industrial buildings erected during the Mechano Deco period is

best seen in structures devoted to some aspect of the motor trade: gas stations, car showrooms and parts outlets. A variety of commercial enterprises capitalized on the streamlined aesthetic of the automobile to attract clientele. This architectural "auto-centrism" was evident in the form of buildings which were cut open to allow the passage of automobiles into an interior space. Large glass panels, sometimes beveled, and supported by steel sashing, were used to mediate between the building (a static monument) and the street (the medium of movement). By the early 1930s, wrote Bush, "the interpretation of functionalism had shifted from the static geometric forms promoted by the Bauhaus architects to the dynamic organic forms" of the sensuously shaped 1934 Airflow Chrysler.

During the heyday of Portland's Mechano Deco period, glass and steel provided the material basis for

PORTLAND CIVIC THEATER
Roi L. Morin
1950

architectural styles and concepts issuing, at once, from Germany, and exemplified by the Bauhaus movement of Walter Gropius and Mies van der Rohe; and from France, as represented by the work of Le Corbusier. This international code would be promulgated in the region by W. R. B. Willcox, who became chairman of the Department of Architecture at the University of Oregon in 1922, and set the tone for much of the industrial architecture which followed his tenure.

The character of Portland's industrial and commercial architecture was derived, in large part, from the technology of the times and from the new practice of directly incorporating utilitarian materials. Indeed, all of Portland's industrial and commercial buildings from the crudest to the most sophisticated, articulated an aesthetic derived, in large measure, from the physical properties of their materials: reinforced concrete, the load-bearing steel frame and glass.

These materials became readily available in the region by the mid-1920s, largely because local manufacturers such as Swigert, Hart and Yett and James A. C. Tait, re-tooled, upgraded or expanded their facilities to accommodate the building boom. The demand for a new architectural ornamentation supported a richly diversified group of craftsmen and artisans, ranging from glaziers, form builders and neon sign designers to graphic artists and sculptors such as Gabriel Lavare.

Glass, perhaps more than any other material, became the symbol of the modern American spirit, which came to life in the streamlined automobile with its panoramic windshielded view of wide open spaces. In the vernacular architecture built in Portland between 1925 and 1950, transparency became a favorite motif, rendered in

automobile showrooms, store windows and commerical office buildings, not only through large expanses of sheet glass, but also in the form of glass blocks.

Despite the importance of architectural magazines and the media in making available the new International and Depression Modern styles, many industrial and commercial buildings of this period were designed, not by professional architects, but by local engineers or contractors who, in some cases, were affiliated with the business itself. The Montgomery Ward Company warehouse and store, for example, were built in 1922 under the direction of company engineer W. H. McCaully, while the American Can Company of Portland used chief engineer, G. G. Preis of New York City, as its architect.

Viewed historically, the Mechano Deco aesthetic gravitated toward an ornamentation that was not only easy to read, but which projected functionalism and, at the same time, advertised the product being sold or the process by which products were manufactured. Despite their humble size, many structures built during Portland's Mechano Deco era were documents of a romance with technology, industry and modernism. They announced the aspiration to convert the place of trade into a space that reflected the new dynamism and fantasies of popular culture.

The crisp styling and streamlining which characterized commercial architecture of the 1930s was expressed most vividly in the hundreds of service stations that popped up like mushrooms after a rain shower on Portland thoroughfares. As a rule, the designs for these handsomely crafted Mechano Deco gas stations were generated by renowned architects commissioned by the country's major gasoline and oil companies. However, almost without exception, the sheet metal and, later, porcelain enamel components for these pump shelters were manufactured and assembled into structural units by the Ray F. Becker Company, a Portland "steel build fabricator," founded in 1925. Beginning with their first two-bay station built for Union Oil in 1930, the sheet metal firm—almost overnight—became Portland's undisputed titan of service station architecture. Working within a number of variants in the Moderne idiom, the Becker Company manufactured and erected the vast majority of stations built in Portland between 1930 and 1950.

Becker earned its reputation—and made its fortune—manufacturing and assembling "functional" filling stations that were smooth, clean and, like a machine, pared of superfluous parts. In the July 1926 issue of *Architectural Forum*, Alexander G. Guth had commented that, "good taste as well as the cost of building would seem to indicate that a simple, straight-forward style of architecture should be followed in the design of a filling and service station." And by the 1930s, the editors of the same publication would celebrate a new type of station that "was clean, unassuming, and has the inestimable virtue of looking like a filling station."

Efficiency and truth in packaging had been championed by the modern movement in architecture, and in 1932, the Museum of Modern Art (MOMA) would include a Standard Oil station as part of its "Modern Architecture" show. Designed by the American firm of Clauss and Daub in 1931, the station featured a continuous glass wall framed by a narrow red cornice of colored plates, under which the company's name appeared in bold red letters. At its zenith, gas station architecture would enlist the likes of Frank Lloyd Wright, Richard Neutra, William Lescaze and New York's Art Deco masters, Kahn and Jacobs. Streamlined Moderne prototypes would also come to life on the drafting tables of industrial designers Raymond Loewy, Walter Dorwin Teague and Norman Bel Geddes. And by the late 1970s, the filling station "preservation movement" would be in full swing, with several structures throughout the country having been listed in the National Register of Historic Places. In 1978, Edward Koren's *New Yorker* cartoon would illustrate the modishness of re-using gas stations by portraying a cocktail party guest commenting: "We live a few miles from here in an architecturally significant former gas station."

In large part due to the Ray F. Becker Company, Portland would become the repository of what, perhaps only in retrospect, one might call architecturally "significant" former filling stations. Celebrating the mix of Art Deco flashiness and the new technological expressionism, Portland's service stations exemplified two distinct variants of Moderne architecture: Zigzag and Streamlined.

Zigzag designs, found on the majority of stations built in the early 1930s, resulted in exciting and, sometimes, lyrical compositions. Associated Oil stations that sprouted up along Portland streets during the early 1930s were built at an average cost of $2,300, minus plumbing. They were exemplary of the best Zigzag Moderne architecture that could be built using simple materials. With their signature "Flying A" neon-illuminated logo sitting atop a fluted tower and expansive cantilevered canopies

PORTLAND CIVIC THEATER
Roi L. Morin
1950

the size of a DC-3 airplane wing, service stations bearing the Associated Oil imprint were among the most exuberant glass and steel concoctions built in this vernacular idiom.

In its most rudimentary form, a typical Associated Oil station amounted to little more than a glass-walled shed, crowned with a fluted tower bearing the Pegasus-inspired trademark. The company was bought by Phillips Petroleum in the 1940s but, fortunately, two of Portland's finest stations in the Associated Oil collection are still standing and well-preserved. Erected in 1940, the structure at 2311 N.E. Sandy has since been converted to a Battery King outlet, but still boasts the original cantilevered canopy and fluted crown. Sadly, the neon "Flying A" has been removed. Still serving its original function, the Mobile Jiffy Lube and Gas on 4212 N. Interstate has been immaculately restored.

With a virtual monopoly on the construction of filling stations in the city, the Becker Company could count Standard, Shell, Associated, Union, Signal, Texaco, Sinclair and Gilmore Oil companies among its steady clients during the 1930s and 1940s. Although less flamboyant than service stations in the Associated Oil stable, some of the finest Zigzag Moderne structures would come out of the design bin of the Gilmore Gasoline and Oil Company. These well-glassed structures were graced with cantilevered canopies and fluted sheet-metal pilasters that looked like modified Ionic columns. The belt course extending from the canopy to the building carried the signature three lines of Deco Moderne design. The result was a compact and crystalline service station embla-

CORNO AND SON GROCERIES, MURAL
Gary Crisp
1984

zoned with strong vertical and horizontal geometric ornamentation.

Surprisingly, many of the Standard Oil stations built during the period were clunky by comparison. Sometimes little more than boxy masses with thick-legged canopies, these early stations did not speak to their age. For reasons that are unclear, a handful of Portland station owners eschewed the "new" look altogether,

preferring instead to establish a link with a romanticized architecture of the past. The Spanish Colonial style was resurrected in a number of filling stations built during the 1930s. A fine example of this quirky contribution to "Fill 'er Up" architecture is still standing at 6901 N.E. Glisan.

By far the most attractive and numerous of the Art Moderne stations built by Becker were the Streamlined

RED STEER CAFE
architect unknown
1913

models of the late 1930s and early 1940s. Texaco favored smooth, sweeping curved forms that were compressed into light, but cohesive, packages. Although these streamlined stations often retained the blocky massing of their predecessors, they managed to project an impression of speed through the continuous slick metal sheathing that unified the entire structure. One of the best preserved stations in the Streamlined Moderne style is now an auto electric repair shop at 505 N.W. 14th Avenue. Built by Becker for Texaco in 1939, this "significant former gas station" is peppered with aerodynamic imagery that suggests futuristic transportation.

Many of Portland's Texaco stations, which featured a supported canopy crowned with two wing-like "sign cans," were based on a prototype model designed by Walter Darwin Teague in 1936. By the mid-1940s, Texaco would become America's most familiar service station. The streamlined crown—composed of three stark green bands encircling the building like a belt course, and bold red lettering on a white background—established Texaco's corporate identity for over two decades.

So successful was Teague at applying the concepts of packaging and streamlining to commercial architecture that his prototype Texaco station was presented in the February 1937 issue of *Architectural Forum*. The simple, practical design had an unmistakable look that many

architects attempted to replicate, usually without much success. Portland architect Harry A. Herzog who, in partnership with John V. Bennes, had produced some of the city's more respectable Deco apartment houses, tried his hand at filling station architecture in 1935. Still standing at 1005 S.W. Main Street, Herzog's sheet-metal shed with corner windows did not live up to the streamlined standard set by Teague's prototype. The same can be said for the clunky Signal Station (now J. A. Atwood Corp.) at 39 S.W. Third. One of the more enlightened filling station renovations can be seen at 8302 N. Lombard, where a two-island Union Station—still boasting its original tower—has been converted into a florist shop.

Not surprisingly, the automobile and its attendant architecture did not please advocates of urban beautification, who often singled out gas stations as examples of urban blight. This was especially true in Portland, where, by the late teens, a powerful City Beautiful Movement linked civic beauty to a variety of concerns, ranging from the quality of life to moral values. By the 1920s, Portland's downtown core had been studded with Beaux-Arts palaces reminiscent of ancient Rome and Renaissance Italy, as well as the cast-iron diadems of Justus Krumbein and Warren H. Williams. The City Beautiful Movement had worked wonders and, with the help of Whidden and Lewis, Doyle and others, the public had been introduced to a dazzling new architectural order that, to a great extent, attempted to mirror the idealized European urban scenes characterized by palatial buildings, bridges, plazas and parks.

But times were changing. Fueled by automobile mania, architects began to experiment boldly in the Streamlined Moderne style popular with commercial designers at the time. While in the mid and late 1920s, the tradition of historic eclecticism remained important in residential work (Lloyd Frank Estate, 1924, Herman Brookman), church architecture (St. Mark's Episcopal Church, 1925, Jamieson Parker; and the Central Presbyterian Church, 1924, F. Manson White) and banking institutions (First National Bank, Eastside Branch, 1928, P. T. Ainge), commercial architecture began to turn increasingly to bold geometric patterns and to the aerodynamic imagery of speed and movement.

Designs for gas stations drew on the basic streamlined motifs—bold horizontals, rounded corners, maximum glass area—which suggested speed and modernity when executed in stainless steel and porcelain enamel. The photographic archives of the Raymond F. Becker Company document the startling transformation of Port-

LIBERTY MOVIE THEATER
architect unknown

1931

land's architectural landscape during this period. In 1930, against the ornate cast-iron facade of the Portland Savings Bank (1885, Williams, razed 1951–52), a steely two-pump Union Station was erected on s.w. 2nd and Washington. Modernity, as it were, was beginning to wreak havoc on Portland's precious heritage of cast-iron architecture. A few years later, an Associated station, with its gleaming red-and-white sheet-metal frame and noble fluted tower was erected on the corner of s.w. Second and Burnside. The neon-illuminated "Flying A" provided a dramatic counterpoint to the classically sculpted facades of A. E. Doyle's reinforced concrete garage (1927) and the Wells Fargo Bank in the background.

In 1926, however, even Portland's master of classicism, A. E. Doyle, had seen the handwriting on the wall. He paid obeisance to the automobile culture with a very unusual design for a single island gas station located on a small lot adjacent to the Terminal Sales Building. Eschewing the snappy Zigzag and Streamlined designs promulgated by major oil concerns, Doyle's station featured an electrically-lighted conical roof on a stem. "No longer extant," wrote Elisabeth Walton in *Space, Style and Structure*, "it was curiously reminiscent of a Japanese umbrella, or perhaps a miniature Clatsop Beach Chautauqua pavillion."

Although gasoline stations were the first and most prolific architectural response to the automobile, a number of drive-in services and auto-related structures developed in Portland during the late 1920s and 1930s. In 1929, Charles Ertz designed an automotive garage at s.w. 12th and Burnside for the Henry Weinhard Company. The Zigzag Moderne style building was decked out with cast-stone shields, fluted pilasters and eagle motifs at the tops of piers. Stylistically, the Weinhard garage

LAURELHURST THEATER
architect unknown
1930

was a dress rehearsal for Ertz's continuing interest in Art Deco-style buildings. His design for Farmer's Insurance Building (now Salvation Army Building, 1947, Ertz and Burns) derived its power from the melding of classical proportions with imposing geometric shapes, which included rectangular piers and rounded concrete masses flanking the curved corner entrance.

During the 1920s and 1930s, Portland streets would slowly become engulfed with vernacular auto-centric architecture in every shape and form. Movie theaters boasting elaborate neon signs, drive-in restaurants and illuminated billboards (the White Stag sign, 1927, Ramsay Neon) proliferated wildly on the cityscape. Architects and designers would often dream up fanci-

MILLER PAINT COMPANY
Edmund Bidwell
1936

PENNY SAVER MARKET
architect unknown
1923

ful, dramatic buildings such as the Steigerwald Dairy (3705 N.E. Sandy Blvd., 1926, H. L. Camp and Company), the Orange Blossom Jug Restaurant (now Whiskey Jug, 7417 N.E. Sandy Blvd., 1929, architect unknown) and the since demolished mushroom-shaped Alcazar Service Station. Airplanes, boats, pyramids and pagodas were among the inspirations for drive-in architecture.

Movie theaters were fronted with marquees that flashed a quickly identifiable image to the speeding motorist. The Broadway Theater (1926, A. E. Doyle) announced itself with a flamboyant neon sign ablaze with color, zigzags and Art Nouveau-inspired serpentiginous bursts. Its neon-illuminated marquee—as well as that of the Paramount Theater (1928, Rapp and Rapp)—was made by the Electrical Products Company, a San Francisco-based neon firm that opened a Portland branch in 1927. The Broadway's peacock marquee—with its exuberant, fan-shaped coruscations—and the script lettering on the side of the building were added to the structure in 1931.

Exotic "theme" designs were de rigueur for commercial enterprises in the late 1920s and early 1930s. In a city where neoclassical designs were generally associated with diligent respectability, savvy movie house entrepreneurs understood the appeal of obscure and exotic styles to attract pleasure seekers. Moorish, Egyptian and

Mayan motifs appeared on the exterior of Portland movie theaters in wild profusion. The Broadway, for example, featured a "Roman" theme, with its painted frieze of foliate and urn motifs just below the clay tiled roof.

Designed by Rapp and Rapp—a nationally renowned firm that had gained notoriety for New York's Paramount Building of 1926—Portland's Paramount Theater was built in the finest tradition of the movie palace. The largely restrained exterior of light-colored brick with cast-stone trim was interrupted by large multi-paned windows enframed with decorative cast stone and topped with false pediments. The interior tossed restraint aside in a sumptuous display of ersatz ornamentation inspired by opulent Baroque examples. "Surprise," the life-size figure carved from cream-colored marble, was a late addition to this polychrome wonderland, which featured vaulted ceilings, marble and mirrored walls, and glittering chandeliers. The Paramount emulated all the features of a princely palace and, in a manner of speaking, was a theater-variant of the old Portland Hotel in its bigness and symbolic value to the aspiring city. In the Paramount restoration, completed in 1984, this visual exuberance was sterilized beneath a copious coat of neutral shades ranging from peach to gray.

Not quite as ostentatious, but almost as massive, was the Heilig (now, Fox) Theater (1911, E. W. Houghton).

RAVEN CREAMERY
architect unknown
1956?

Born in Pennsylvania in 1862, Calvin Heilig arrived in Washington in 1889, where he bought two theaters, one in Tacoma and one in Seattle, before entering the Portland scene as manager of the Marquam Grand. Specializing in resident and road show companies, Heilig's Portland Theater was considered one of the best in the West at the time it was built. The sparsely decorated twentieth-century Romanesque brick building received a facelift in 1953–54, when Dougan and Heims designed a dazzling marquee and neon sign for the front facade. But even

more enticing—or, at least, novel—was the part-Deco, part-Streamlined silver-colored ticket booth that theater owner Charles Skouras imported from Los Angeles and is still in use today.

Portland's smaller theaters also boasted eye-catching designs. The Nickel Star Theater (1912, David Lockheed Williams) featured a prominent arched brick parapet decorated with an ornamental harp at its center. By the 1920s, the Zigzag Moderne-influenced styles became increasingly popular. The Roseway (1925, Hubert

B. F. GOODRICH BUILDING
Goodrich-Silverton
1930

Williams), Laurelhurst, Aladdin (1928, Edward A. Miller) and Moreland (1926, Thomas and Thomas) theaters all paid homage to this new commercial idiom.

A sparkling tradition in neon signage developed in the city beginning in 1911 with the founding of the Ramsay Sign Company. In the years that followed, a number of top-of-the-line sign manufacturers—including Columbia Neon, Oregon Sign Company, H. L. Robinson Company and Electrical Products—would emblazon Portland streets with pulsating signs. The heyday of neon

illumination came in the 1930s and 1940s. With the introduction of plexiglass signs—which were less expensive to maintain—in the 1950s and ordinances restricting the size of commercial signs in the 1960s, the neon craze was gradually extinguished.

During the 1930s, Streamlined architecture was, for the most part, restricted to structures catering directly to the automobile culture. Other industrial and commercial buildings lagged slightly behind in adopting their style, gravitating instead toward the Zigzag patterns and

WILLIAMS AND COMPANY
F. M. Stokes
1936

bold geometrics of Art Deco. As Cervin Robinson noted in *Skyscraper Style*, Art Deco was "the overwhelmingly prevailing modernism." In fact, it was the first "populist" response to the abstraction of modernism, attempting to marry the mathematical purity of the International Style to the recognizable ornamental vocabulary that was the legacy of the Beaux-Arts. Crystalized in the chic

urbanity of Manhattan's Waldorf Astoria, the Chrysler and Rockefeller Center buildings, and, especially, the Empire State Building of *King Kong* fame, Art Deco rapidly established itself as the style of large cities.

From there it spread like wildfire to main streets large and small across the country. And to Portland, Oregon. One of the city's earliest and most intriguing examples of

GUARDIAN BUILDING, ENTRANCE
Oregon Brass Works
1937

MORGAN BUILDING, ENTRANCE
Oregon Brass Works
1938

Zigzag Moderne architecture came to life in a small neighborhood retail store located at 6643 S.E. Harold (1923, architect unknown). The strikingly bold horizontal banding that dominated the building's frontispiece and roofline was fashioned from wood slats. The curious one-story structure represented a marvelous—indeed, novel—melding of "big city" Art Deco geometrics with the regional wood tradition.

Portland's "concrete Deco" tradition would be championed by a number of buildings located in the Union Avenue industrial district. Edmund Bidwell's design for the Miller Paint Company Building (1936) on 317 S.E. Grand called for a low-lying one-story warehouse that terminated in a stunted corner tower heavily ornamented with zigzag panels separated by vertical piers. Always radiating a fresh coat of yellow-green paint, the Miller building brightened up an otherwise drab section of the city. Architect George Post adopted a similar zigzag motif for the Rex Lee Auto Service (now Lloyd Center Union) built in 1936, while fluted pilasters were chosen by architects Earl Cash and George Wolff (later to form Wolff, Zimmer, Gunsul) for the R.K.D. Brilliant Neon Co. (now Hollywood Auto Parts) built in 1930.

Slightly more streamlined was the Raven Creamery on 3303 N.E. Union. Looking as though its ornamentation might have been applied with a cake decorator, the building featured a continuous belt course composed of six creamy bands and a marquee affixed to the front by two pie-shaped supports that looked like airplane tailwings. Zigzag motifs on many buildings in the industrial area were also fashioned from other materials. For example, the sheet metal frontispiece on the B. F. Goodrich Building (1930, Goodrich-Silverton, architect) featured pleated steel panels, behind which sprouted thin metal members arranged in stepped-back fashion. The forceful verticality of the composition recalled a strikingly similar Art Deco arrangement atop the entrance of New York City's Fuller Building (1929, Walker and Gillette). Certainly, the most powerful—and fantastical—contribution to Portland's industrial Deco tradition must have

151

CORBETT BUILDING
Oregon Brass Works
1937

SELLING BUILDING ENTRANCE
Harry A. Herzog
1939

been the Williams and Company (once the city's leading potato chip manufacturer) Building on 2045 S.E. Union. Built in 1936, and designed by F. M. Stokes, the building offered a dramatic composition of vertical elements in its boldly sculpted entrance tower.

Although it was built on an out-of-the-way river bank site on Ankeny Street, the Portland sewage station building, completed in 1933, was a handsome addition to Portland's industrial Deco emporium. Planned as part of the seawall project in 1929, the Ankeny Station was designed by members of the Board of Consulting Engineers. Squat tank-shaped sewage pump stations built across the city as late as 1951–53 would also boast three vertical stripes that were the hallmark of Art Deco design. These streamlined, Deco-inspired jewels punctuated the cityscape. The design—which amounts to the vertical fluting—is attributed to Frank Kohler, who, at the time, was working with the engineering firm of Stevens and Koon.

If the Becker Company provided the ingredients for a gleaming tradition in filling station architecture, then Portland's Oregon Brass Works supplied the brass and bronze components for scores of exquisitely designed

Art Deco storefronts. During the 1930s, in collaboration with the craftsmen at Oregon Brass Works, the city's finest architects, among them Harry A. Herzog, McClelland and Jones, P. T. Ainge, Richard Sundeleaf and Lawrence and Holford deposited a sterling layer of Art Deco architecture in the form of small commercial structures, ranging from pharmacies to boutiques to candy stores. With a keen eye for typographic styles and harmonious proportions, Herzog designed crystalline storefronts for Wegert's Pharmacy (now Three Lions' Bakery, 1934), Wadhams and Company Inc. (1935), the Oregon City Woolen Mills (1937), the Guardian Building (1939) and the Oregon Art Tile Company (1939, Bennes and Herzog).

His bronze and brass facades for Wegert's and Oregon Art Tile were Portland's answer to the fashionable Art Deco storefronts introduced by Renee Herbst at the "Exposition Internationale des Arts Decoratifs et Industriels Modernes," held in Paris in 1925.

While Herzog may have been Portland's most prolific designer in the Art Deco idiom, Ellis F. Lawrence (principal in the architectural firm of Lawrence and Holford) had also been intrigued by the possibilities lurking in the

OREGON ART TILE COMPANY
Bennes and Herzog
1939

Art Deco style. Although Lawrence lived in Portland, where his practice thrived, he commuted for 30 years between the city and the Eugene campus, where he had established the school of architecture at the University of Oregon in 1916. Lawrence had an uncanny ability for matching a variety of revival styles—from Romanesque to Egyptian to Colonial—with diverse structures including his Art Deco-inspired Leaburg (Oregon) Power Station (1929), the Egyptian-influenced Hope Abbey Mausoleum (1939) and the part-Islam, part-Romanesque Museum of Art (1928–33) on the University of Oregon campus. As dean of the architecture school, Lawrence designed all the University buildings between 1916 and 1939. Applying a broad vocabulary to a diverse set of structures, the architect churned out schemes for McArthur Court (1926), Condon (1923), Straub (1928), Esslinger (1936) and Chapman (1939) halls, as well as for all the education buildings and hospitals at the University of Oregon Medical campus in Portland.

Eclectic and painterly in his approach, Lawrence believed in the integration of the arts and crafts in architecture—a purpose ably demonstrated in his elaborate Art Deco designs for Portland's Gumbert Furriers (1937) and the Bohemian Restaurant (1936). Like Herzog, Lawrence employed the services of Oregon Brass Works to give his stores a sparkling "uptown" finish. In the Leaburg Power Plant, Lawrence and Holford had used ordinary materials—concrete, industrial sash and paint—to lend an unusual flavor to a utilitarian structure. The same philosophy prevailed in Lawrence's design for the city's Public Market and the Holman Fuel Company (1938), a blue-and-white Deco-style warehouse, which is still standing in the industrial flats of Southeast Portland.

Although most of Portland's Art Deco fronts and interior lobbies have since been defaced or concealed beneath more "contemporary" architectural skins, a number of buildings from this period are worthy of mention. P. T. Ainge designed a light and lacy cast-bronze facade for the Prudential Savings and Loan Building in 1930, only two years after Belluschi had outfitted the interior lobby of the Public Service Building with elaborate bronze fixtures and walls of rich marble. The decorative zeal of the 1930s would give way, by the late 1940s and early 1950s, to the stripped-down format of modern design. Glenn Stanton's graphic composition for Caplan Sport Shop (1949) and Hollis Johnston's mock-up for the KGW Broadcasting station (1945) pointed the way toward a further dilution of the intricate curves and typefaces of Art Deco. F. Claude Butcher, one of Portland's premier delineators of the period, produced a striking design for the Claude Smith Building (1945). The expansive, uncluttered forms of the early 1950s—which, in many respects, recalled the Depression Modern industrial architecture of the 1930s—came to life in a number of Portland buildings, most notably in the Union Avenue Branch of the First National Bank (1953, Herzog), in Belluschi's design from the Federal Reserve Bank (1950) and Roi Morin's scheme for the Portland Civic Theater (1951).

Except for a smattering of apartment houses and office buildings by Feig, Bennes, Dougan and Herzog built between 1928 and 1931—and selected richer examples represented by the Charles F. Berg Company Store and the interior lobby of the U.S. Courthouse—Art Deco in Portland had become more or less synonomous with industrial and commercial architecture. Although the zigzags, geometric fields, and sculpted faces of Portland's buildings were rather bland by New York standards, they nonetheless enlivened what could otherwise have been a decidedly characterless industrial landscape.

By the mid-1930s, the flavor of industrial and commercial architecture in Portland would change. A generation of American industrial designers would be after an "authentic" ornamentation that would capture the "internal rhythm" or spirit of the age. Art Deco began its decline. Teague, one of the country's finest designers, wrote in 1939: "We achieve a high degree of simplicity because we are a primitive people . . . we have reverted again to a primitive state of human development. We are primitives in this new machine age. We have no developed history behind us to use on our artistic creations. We have no theories, no vocabulary of ornament, behind us to use in our work. That is why so much of our modern work today has a certain stark and simple quality that related very closely to the primitive work of Greece and Egypt."

Teague felt it was necessary to leave behind the luxury of decoration, "because we have no decoration today that is significant to us, that has a meaning." For a number of his colleagues, including Norman Bel Geddes, Raymond Loewy, Russell Wright and Lurelle Guild, who considered themselves to be, above all, industrial designers, the word decoration had become associated, pejoratively, with the effete luxuriousness of the pre-Depression past. As Martin Greif emphasized in *Depression Modern*, the new trend in 1930s architecture "was an art stripped bare of all ornamentation, an art in which the American home and office and factory—and everything in them—was built for just one purpose: to work, and to *look* as though they worked."

The clean and uncluttered forms of industrial architecture of the 1930s emphasized efficiency, economy and "right appearance." Streamlining, clean lines and sparse, disciplined ornamentation that often derived from industrial themes marked the "Mechano Deco" branch of the Depression Modern family of style.

The finest examples of Mechano Deco sprouted up along the city's main boulevards, but several jewels would be tucked away off the beaten track, in the industrial districts of Northwest, Northeast and Southeast Portland. For the most part, these streamlined buildings were the work of local architects, but a number of Portland-based industries would commission nationally recognized architectural firms such as the Austin Company of Cleveland, Ohio, to design their warehouses, stores and manufacturing plants. The Chase Bag Company Building (1937, Austin Company) on N.W. Nicolai and 26th Avenue was, perhaps, Portland's premier entry in the Mechano Deco idiom. Featuring crisp clean lines and a rounded corner highlighted by two stories of shimmering glass block, the Chase Bag Company Building expressed the purely functional and stark qualities that had been emphasized in the administration building of Federated Metals Company in Hammond, Indiana and the Church and Dwight factory (owned by Arm and Hammer Baking Soda), both designed by the Austin Company in the late 1930s.

Combining a design service and construction company into a single firm, the Austin Company was to American industrial architecture of the 1930s what McKim, Mead and White had been to the Beaux-Arts tradition at the beginning of the century, or what Michael Graves would be to the Postmodern movement in the 1980s. In short, they were top of the line, and Portland was fortunate to have one of their Mechano Deco gems

CAPLAN SPORT SHOP
Glenn Stanton
1949

set in its cityscape. Interestingly, before gaining a reputation for their streamlined architecture of the 1930s, the Austin Company designed a nondescript "dimestore Deco-style" garage complex, built in 1924, on 1906 West Burnside.

The firm came into its own in the post-Depression decade. "Among the most distinguished and extraordinary of American modern industrial buildings were those designed and constructed by the Austin Company of Cleveland, Ohio," wrote Greif, "whose stunning advertisements in *Fortune* magazine throughout the Great Depression stood out above all others in their stun-

ning—even startling modernity." The Chase Bag Company Building, like other Portland industrial structures in the same genre—Sunshine Dairy Building (801 N.E. 21st, 1947, Claussen and Claussen), McCall Oil Company Building (1935 S.E. Powell, 1946, Universal Plan Service), and Davis Business Center (originally Canada Dry Ginger Ale, Inc., 1946, Walter M. Cory)—remain to this day magnificent archetypes of the functional Depression Modern style. The trend toward simplicity and directness manifested by the Chase Bag Building was promulgated in a number of "classic" buildings designed by the Austin Company, most notably, its "Radio City Hall

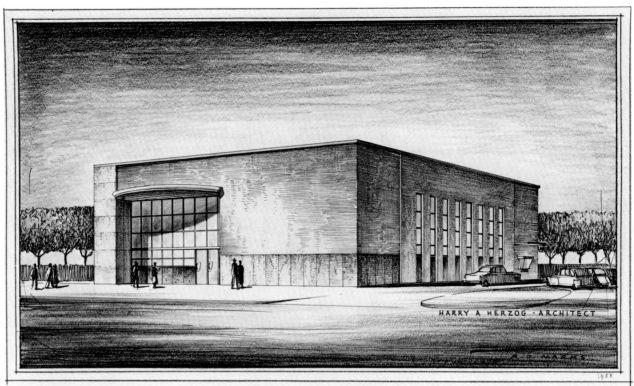

UNION BRANCH, FIRST NATIONAL BANK
Harry A. Herzog
1953

of the West," a Hollywood station designed in 1938 for NBC studios.

Flowing curves, stark horizontality and glass block would meet in the exquisite design for the Canada Dry Ginger Ale Company Building (now Davis Business Center, 4370 N.E. Halsey, 1946). A remarkably understated composition in which the only ornament was a pattern of fenestration with glass block—an arrangement dictated largely by function—the Canada Dry Building was designed by New York architect Walter M. Cory. Like the Austin Company, Cory was one of the nation's leading practitioners in the field of industrial architecture. His Johnson and Johnson Industrial Tape Building in New Brunswick, New Jersey was built in 1940, and clearly foreshadowed the sleek, streamlined contribution he would make to Portland's industrial landscape in 1946.

The vocabulary of architectural functionalism demanded new materials, most notable among them, glass block. Used in Europe (and especially in Holland) for many years glass block was not eagerly embraced by American architects until 1935. Then, however, it became the most obsessively used material for buildings in the Mechano Deco style. In Portland glass block was as integral to the architectural arsenal of the 1930s as terra cotta had been between 1909 and 1928. Unlike terra cotta, however, which lent itself readily to stylistic adaption, glass block demanded the structural purity of modern architecture. Glass block (or glass brick) was used for the walls and windows of many Portland buildings, including Gender Machine Works, Hay's Electric Company (1111 S.E. Sandy Blvd., now Chicago Style Fast Food, 1940, Clarence A. Hall Design), Kubli-Howell (600 N.W. 14th, 1945, Wolff and Phillips) and scores of others. Used extensively for interior partitions or decoration—especially for bars and soda fountains—glass block provided translucence without visibility, effective sound insulation, light with little heat transmission and low maintenance.

By the late 1930s, America's leading manufacturer of

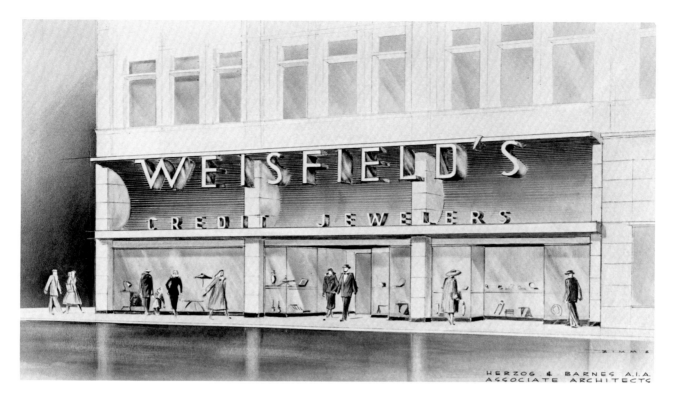

WEISFIELD'S
Herzog and Barnes
1950

glass block would publicize its product in trade magazines by building a glass playhouse for Shirley Temple. "In magazine advertisements that must have startled commercial architects," wrote Greif, "the dimpled moppet was shown, trowel in pudgy hand, building a towering glass-block structure, her smile of easy childish confidence antedating the Castro Convertible girl by at least a decade."

Although glass block was enormously popular in its day, it vanished from the scene about the same time as Shirley Temple. In the 1980s, however, spurred by a renewed national interest in Depression Modern architecture, Portland designers would revive glass block for architectural projects such as Macadam Place (1984, Thompson and Vaivoda), Father's Restaurant and Pink's. The interior of Father's Restaurant (1983, Karol Niemi) was lavishly appointed with ebonized bulwarks, pink marble tile and Josef Von Hoffman style chairs, and featured an expansive bar partition made from insulux glass blocks imported from Japan.

Built in 1946, the McCall Oil Building (1936 S.E. Powell) was one of the city's most elegant glass block

buildings designed in the Depression Modern idiom. While the white stucco exterior and *brise-de-soleil* shades recalled the new Bauhaus-inspired horizontality, the corner was broken by one flowing curve where a rounded glass block bay was introduced. Like many of the simple, but handsome one-story commercial buildings of the period, McCall Oil was not designed by a specific architect, but rather, was built according to "generic" plans obtained from the Universal Plan Service, located in the J. K. Gill Building.

Providing a full gamut of industrial and residential blueprints, the Universal Plan Service became a popular clearing house for architectural plans in the Depression Modern idiom. With its gently curved, faceted bay window and simple concrete exterior, the Phillips Electronics Building (originally, C-W-S Grinding and Machine Works, 1110 N.W. Flanders, 1946) was one of the finer examples of the understated elegance that could be achieved with designs available through this plan service.

Without question, one of Portland's most striking glass block facelifts was performed on the original Pacific Steel & Engineering Company Building (1910, Bennes

DAVID'S MENS SHOP
Harry A. Herzog
1946

and Hendricks) on 21st and N.W. Nicolai. In 1926, when the Fuller Company moved into the five-story red brick warehouse, Bennes and Herzog embellished the entry way with two bays and a massive doorhead made from glass brick. Presently illuminated at night, this architectural crystal is a "diamond in the rough" among its tawdry neighbors.

Glass block was so much in vogue that even Belluschi could not suppress the temptation to incorporate glass bricks in at least one of his modernistic commercial projects. His design for the Boilermakers Union Building (1942) called for no less than 1000 glass bricks to complement the building's colorful granite exterior and marble entrance way; and almost a decade later, the Zion Lutheran Church and Finley Mortuary would also be heavily peppered with glass bricks.

George Wolff and Truman Phillips also exploited the aesthetic and functional virtues of glass brick in their Depression Modern-inspired designs for the Shaw Sur-

gical Supply Company Building (1946) and the Kubli-Howell Company Building (1945) both located on N.W. 14th St. One of their most striking contributions to the industrial landscape was the Calbag Metals Company Building (1946, Wolff and Phillips). Although the architecture of the manufacturing space was undistinguished, the rounded streamlined face and prominent horizontal banding of the office was unadulterated Bauhaus.

With junk food and soda pop companies climbing up the Fortune 500 list by the late 1930s, it is not surprising that syrup giants such as Coca-Cola, Canada Dry and 7-Up were clamoring to introduce a few sparkling examples of "pop Deco" architecture into the city's industrial landscape. Touted for its strong geometric forms and smooth curved exterior, the Portland Bottling Company (now 7-Up Bottling Company, 1941, Arthur Cramer), was a fine application of the Art Moderne style to industrial architecture. The large faceted street-level windows not only created a streamlined effect, but al-

DAVIS BUSINESS CENTER
Walter M. Cory
1947

lowed pedestrians to observe workers and machines at work creating a sweeter tomorrow. When the Depression finally fizzled to a halt, the Coca-Cola Company commissioned Atlanta, Georgia architect Jesse M. Shelton (Robert and Company) in 1939 to design its syrup factory (completed in 1941) on N.E. 28th and Couch. The Bauhaus-influenced exterior was turned into an advertisement with its brightly painted reliefs of the company's logo and Coca-Cola bottles. But more than anything, this building was an impressive illustration of the understated elegance—and power—that could be achieved using little more than bold horizontal lines.

Industrial building was on the rise, and perhaps no name in Oregon was more frequently associated with industrial architecture than that of Richard Sundeleaf. If Belluschi was the architect of meditative spaces and Yeon the designer of rarified retreats, Sundeleaf was the premier architect of spaces devoted to business, commerce and industry. From buildings designed for ball

bearings, electrical supplies and cement to those made for cars, bathing suits and death, Sundeleaf wrapped the messy vitality of American life into the snappy forms of commercial vernacular design. Whatever the favorite idiom in corporate circles or the latest look in slick design magazines, Sundeleaf was ready to adapt them to his clients' needs. Writing his chapter in Portland architecture in glass, steel sash and concrete structures that ranged in style from "diet Classicism" to "automotive Bauhaus," Sundeleaf built up a practice that since 1927 executed over 2,000 commissions.

Several million dollars' worth of buildings carried the Sundeleaf imprint, and they were impressive both in terms of sheer bulk and the international acclaim they received. Equally imposing were the names of clients like General Electric, Hyster, Jantzen Knitting Mills, International Business Machines and Boise Cascade. So diversified was the catalogue of Sundeleaf's commissions, that a history of Portland's romance with technology and

JOLLY JOAN RESTAURANT
designer unknown
1938

modernism during the Roosevelt and Truman years could easily be written on the basis of his factories and mortuaries, automobile showrooms and ballrooms, bandstands and warehouses.

Armed with an arsenal of myriad architectural styles, Sundeleaf could respond with equal passion to both modernistic and traditional trends in architectural design. Few Portland architects of the 1930s would have a better understanding of their clients' needs and the times than did this regional interpreter of "magazine" styles. A dyed-in-the-wool populist, Sundeleaf championed the definition of architecture as a service profession. "People call me up," he explained in the *Oregonian* in 1982, "and if they can pronounce 'architect,' I won't say no. I've never turned down a job." With this versatility and technical know-how, Sundeleaf fit the mold of the jack-of-all-trades American architect.

In this respect, Sundeleaf modeled himself on Albert Kahn, the high priest of American industrial design, who taught that eclecticism was the path toward an architecture that reflected the spirit of its time. His buildings were not revolutionary in the sense of introducing un-

tried solutions to structural problems or reaching for radically new architectural idioms. Rather, Sundeleaf's work derived its distinctiveness from the melding of two sensibilities: the stylistic eclecticism of the Beaux-Arts with the functional honesty of Modernism. For Sundeleaf, as for Kahn, evolution was preferable to revolution, and the best architecture resulted from the re-use of well-tried forms.

Sundeleaf's career put Darwin's theory of the survival of the fittest into practice. Adaptable, dynamic and resourceful, he had the "right stuff" that, after the Depression, put America back on its feet and got it running to the whoosh of automobile tires. Born in Portland in 1900, the city's polygot of architectural styles trained at the University of Oregon School of Architecture at a time when Ellis Lawrence and W. R. B. Willcox were scrapping the traditional Beaux-Arts curriculum and replacing it with an innovative program based on the philosophies of Frank Lloyd Wright, the Bauhaus and the Arts and Crafts movement. Under the tutelage of Louis C. Rosenberg, who was then teaching at the school, Sundeleaf acquired a graceful, soft manner of architectural rendering that Portland practitioners recognized as the "Rosenberg" style. The teachings of Lawrence and Willcox helped the young designer straddle divergent approaches to architecture represented by Beaux-Arts historicism and International Style modernism. In the years to come, this ambidextrous training would enable him to apply a broad stylistic vocabulary to a diverse set of building needs.

If Sundeleaf subscribed to the Bauhaus promotion of function over form, he nonetheless acknowledged his Beaux-Arts education in his gravitation toward ornamentation. But while many of his teachers and early models would still draw their inspiration from the high culture of Greco-Roman models, Sundeleaf would increasingly tap the vernacular subculture of the machine, the automobile and the market place. In his architecture of the 1930s, the past, of course, would continue to receive some acknowledgement, but the present would not be subservient to it. His architecture would represent an extension of nineteenth-century individualism, but his industrial buildings would be increasingly clad in the austere geometric raiment of the 1930s and 1940s.

Were it not for his energetic and ambitious personality, Sundeleaf's architectural career might have ended with his first job. After obtaining his degree in 1923, the young graduate secured a position with the firm of A. E. Doyle, then at the height of its prestige. The experience

PHILLIPS ELECTRONICS
Universal Plan Service
1946

did not augur well for the young designer's future. During the 12 months of his employ at the Doyle firm, Sundeleaf recalled spending considerably more time out of the office, "on loan" to other, temporarily short-handed firms, than under the exacting supervision of Portland's reigning master builder. Proud to be affiliated with such a reputable firm, Sundeleaf at first did not question the arrangement. He soon learned, however, that he owed his migrant status to more than professional courtesy. When he asked "Mr. Doyle" for a raise, he received instead a chilling diagnosis of his architectural prowess. "Give up architecture," was Doyle's disheartening advice, adding: "You're not cut out for it."

Instead, in 1925, Sundeleaf gave up his position at the

McDONALD'S
architect unknown
1951

COCA COLA COMPANY
Jesse M. Shelton
1939

firm and joined the office of Doyle's top competitors, Sutton and Whitney. He stayed long enough to convince himself that he would really rather be working on his own. In 1927, he opened his own practice. His timing could not have been better. If his professional debut four years earlier had started off with a whimper, his independent practice took off with a bang. When the principals of Jantzen Knitting Mills approached him with a commission to design the company's new administration building in Portland, Sundeleaf knew his ship had come in. Jantzen, after all, was the country's original and oldest swimwear manufacturer. Since 1910, when it had been launched by Portlanders Carl Jantzen and Roy and John Zehntbauer, the company had grown by leaps and bounds.

In the 1920s, Americans were just beginning to shed the Victorian shackles that had encumbered their bodies since the nineteenth century. Capitalizing on the relaxation of morals during the Prohibition years, Jantzen had fanned the fashion for recreational bathing, creating a burgeoning market for its skimpy wares. By 1930, the firm had become the world's leading manufacturer of bathing suits. To keep up with the frenzied demand for its risqué products, it would open plants in Australia and England within the next two years. And while Jantzen was spinning out suits for millions, Sundeleaf would be

hard at work designing the firm's offices, factories, warehouses and pleasure palaces. The Administration Building in Portland would be the springboard for Sundeleaf's illustrious career as the firm's unofficial "in-house" architect.

In September 1928, when work on the new offices was nearing completion, *Jantzen Yarns* was already hailing the Administration Building as "one of the most beautiful industrial structures in the city." At a time when most utilitarian buildings showed little architectural flair, Sundeleaf's design was truly exceptional. Executed in fine Willamina brick and trimmed in terra cotta, the Romanesque structure might have been mistaken for an elegant seaside resort. A ceremonial staircase led up to a monumental, two-story portal that was trimmed in travertine and wrought-iron grillwork. On both sides of the entrance, symmetrical wings stepped back at the first-story level to create the impression of an airy, two-story structure. No hint of the utilitarian reinforced concrete construction would be given by the richly ornamented facade.

With considerable help from Gabriel Lavare, one of Portland's most accomplished architectural sculptors, Sundeleaf festooned the building with fanciful sea shells, mythical monsters and medallions featuring the gracefully arched red "Diving Girl" designed by Frank and

PORTLAND BOTTLING COMPANY
Arthur Cramer
1941

Florence Clark that would become Jantzen's trademark. The capitals of the engaged columns at the entrance effloresced in a swirl of aquatic plants that supported chimeric sea horses balancing stylized shells on the tips of their tails. All of these whimsical touches, however, were carefully understated so as not to compromise a respectable corporate image.

By judiciously melding fanciful ornament, modernistic detailing and the Romanesque "period" style, Sundeleaf hit on a design formula he would use in a number of subsequent commissions, including the Oregon Portland Cement Building (1929), the Jantzen Knitting Mills plant in London (1931), and the Wilson Chambers Mortuary (1932). The interior of the Jantzen building, how-

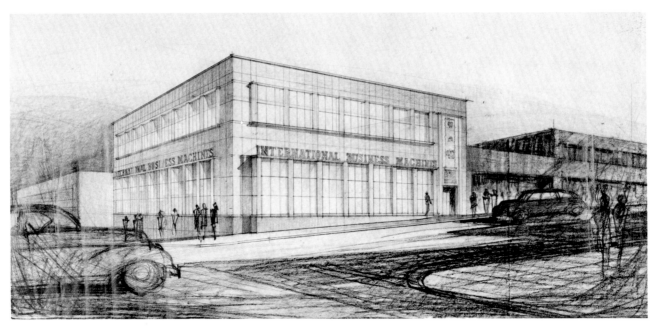

IBM BUILDING
Richard Sundeleaf
1950

ever, reflected a thoroughly modern, functional ap-proach, providing for "every comfort and convenience as well as beauty." The latest heating, lighting and ven-tilation systems will be used," announced *Jantzen Yarns*, and "the walls will contain a deadening felt to absorb as much of the noise as possible." And to insure that execu-tives could conduct their affairs in style, the private offices were finished in mahogany, "fitting with the beauty of the whole building."

Convincing department store buyers to stock a new line of "Shouldaire" swimsuits was one thing. Getting respectable ladies into them was another, particularly in Portland, where the dearth of safe bathing facilities of-fered little incentive to prospective bathing suit shop-pers. In the mid-1920s, the city still had no public pools. The best it could offer water enthusiasts was a bracing dip in the Willamette River. This was where Jantzen, and its outdoor amusement expert Paul H. Huedepohl, came into the picture. Huedepohl joined the firm's pro-motional arm in 1926. A visionary authority on water sports, he launched a program that would reshape Port-land's recreational and architectural fabric. According to the *Jantzen Yarns* of May 1928, Huedepohl "had a dream—to build the perfect swimming pool."

Before long, however, the idea for a perfect swim-ming pool, grew into a plan for a lively amusement park

that would become Portland's answer to New York's Coney Island. And to realize their dream, the company turned to Sundeleaf, who would design a place "where thousands came to ride the Big Dipper, swim in the pools, have a family picnic under the trees and then dance the night away, to the big band sound in the Golden Canopy Ballroom."

Jantzen's top brass put a lot of stock in dreams. Con-fident that they were on to the promotional idea of a lifetime, they went out looking for the perfect site, and came back with a new piece of real estate: Hayden Island on the Columbia River. It was the logical choice for the future "glorious wonderland of Portland." With uner-ring instinct, Huedepohl urged his firm to give "the public a clean, wholesome outdoor playground, some-thing," the September 1928 *Jantzen Yarns* clamored, "Port-land has longed for." Far enough from the center of town to give pleasure-seekers the thrill of an outing to the country, Hayden Island was still within easy reach by trolley, buggy and the Model-T. "Today, because a man dared," Carl Werner wrote in reference to Huedepohl's brilliant promotional scheme in the *Jantzen Yarns*, "and because an organization displayed confidence in him there stands on the edge of Portland's boundary line a monument to the aquatic world."

Werner, however, forgot to mention the other man in

OREGON MUSEUM OF SCIENCE AND INDUSTRY
Richard Sundeleaf
1955

whom the organization had shown faith. Without Sundeleaf, after all, Heudepohl's daring and Jantzen's confidence would have been put at the service of just another pipe dream. In commissioning the 26-year-old designer to create a "fun place for thousands," the company was putting its money on an architect who not only had few commissions to his name, but who two years earlier, had received something like the "kiss of death" from the city's reigning architect. Yet, by 1932, only eight years after Doyle had suggested that the young man look for another profession, Sundeleaf had scattered his architectural seed from Sydney to London, winning international acclaim and a bonanza of local commissions on the basis of buildings designed for Jantzen's administrative offices, factories and warehouses.

But if Jantzen gave Sundeleaf's career the boost it needed to get into orbit, Jantzen and Portland could

never have made the move into corporate and civic adulthood without the young architect's spunky melding of Beaux-Arts classicism, Modernism and technology. While Doyle, Belluschi, Whitehouse and Fritsch were clothing the west side of the city with dignified structures that catered to Portland's superego, Sundeleaf was gingerly groping toward an architecture of the id. His mind might have been under the sway of Beaux-Arts respectability, but his instincts were clearly on the side of popular fantasies. Even before he paid his dues to the profession and *earned* the right to design by whimsy, the young maverick burst the seams of sedate classical design with such exuberant touches as the canine gargoyles on the Oregon Portland Cement Building and the sea monsters and bathing beauties on the Jantzen Headquarters Building.

The Jantzen Beach complex gave Sundeleaf the opportunity to forge what would become his characteristic mix'n'match approach to the architecture of the id. Amusement parks, after all, had traditionally provided, what architectural historian Rem Koolhaas called, "a laughing-mirror-image of the seriousness with which the rest of the world is obsessed with Progress." Sundeleaf's ballroom, bathhouse and sports arena would show him attacking the problem of pleasure with the same technological means he would use in his later industrial designs. They would also show his knack for packaging pleasure in decorous styles that, to the general public, suggested class, money and the romance of far-away places. In this respect, the Golden Canopy Ballroom—acclaimed in the 12 April 1931 *Oregonian* as "one of the finest and most pretentious in the West"—would be exemplary.

The city's greatest dance emporium since Cotillion Hall (1914), the Golden Canopy Ballroom flashed as many faces as a Halloween crowd. Part palace, part warehouse and part mausoleum, the design melded Beaux-Arts gentility with industrial pragmatism. The result was a truly original alliance. With its Romanesque arches, engaged columns and ornamented cornices, the entryway was similar to that of Jantzen administration buildings in Portland and London. Four years later, Sundeleaf would continue this theme for the Wilson Chambers Mortuary (1932), suggesting that, at least for this designer of dance halls and death palaces, Eros and Thanotos really did go hand in hand.

In the case of the Golden Canopy Ballroom, classical allusions, however, stopped with the entrance facade. In its remaining faces, the Golden Canopy Ballroom was pure warehouse moderne. A stark succession of industrial steel-sash windows paraded around the exterior of the cavernous space that was covered by a bubble roof like that which would appear in the architect's General Electric Company Building (1943). Certainly, the public raised no objections to dancing and romancing under the crystal ball that hung from the center of the gold cloth-draped ceiling. In its heyday in the 1930s and 1940s, "as many as 4,000 dancers crowded nightly in the Jantzen Beach Golden Canopied [*sic*] Ballroom to hear the swing kings of the time. They danced to Tommy Dorsey, Stan Kenton, Benny Goodman, Dick Jurgens, and Woody Herman, gaining musical respite, from the cares of the Depression and war years."

To keep in shape for those long nights of "dancin' at Jantzen," Portland's fox-trotters spent their daytime hours pursuing the "secret of health . . . and beauty" in the crystal waters of the park's four swimming pools. "Health builds a likeable personality," ran the company's come-on, "and swimming in the great outdoors in clean safe-guarded pools is the ideal place to find it." Sundeleaf's Natatorium—as the bath house was called—and spectacular poolside fountain gave this healthful pursuit a delicious aesthetic dimension. A cascade of graduated streamlined plates, "over which a million gallons of pure crystal-like water will flow each day," was placed in the mammoth bathing pool. Behind it stood the architectural hub of the aquatic paradise—Sundeleaf's colossal bath house.

A two-story tribute to the architect's love affair with Deco Moderne, the Natatorium housed enough showers, lockers and dressing rooms to accomodate 2,500 bathers in various stages of undress. The building's entrance was flanked by symmetrical wings in a Romanesque style, but the overall inspiration was Art Deco. The rhythm of curving arches was replaced by the pristine geometry of protruding bays alternating with recessed fenestration. Vertical mullions boldly sliced the window areas into three dramatic lines that carried the signature composition of Deco designs. The Natatorium represented a design program to which Sundeleaf would return in future years. The architect's sensitivity to proportion and rhythm anticipated the "modular" system he would use in a number of buildings beginning with the Woodbury and Company Warehouse (1939). But more astonishing, perhaps, was the degree to which the Portland architect—with his pop-classical designs for the Jantzen Natatorium and Ballroom—had sown the seeds for the bombastic architecture that would come to fruition in the Portland Building (1982). In his own intuitive way, Sundeleaf had grafted classical elements onto modernistic structures creating something akin to the "figurative architecture" of Michael Graves. In this sense, Sundeleaf was a Post-modernist long before it would become fashionable.

Along with Ellis Lawrence, Sundeleaf would be among the first architects in the state to use the Deco Moderne style for industrial design. Lawrence's Leaburg Power Station was completed in 1929. A stunning synthesis of geometrical Deco motifs with classical detailing, this crystalline composition exemplified Lawrence's skill in combining modern and traditional elements in industrial structures. Sundeleaf, Lawrence's pupil, used a similar approach for the Jantzen Warehouse (1929). Finished in flesh-colored stucco, the Jant-

· LINCOLN · MEMORIAL · PARK · MAUSOLEUM ·
· PORTLAND ·   · OREGON ·
· JOS · W · HEILER ·   · ARCHITECT ·

LINCOLN MEMORIAL PARK MAUSOLEUM
Joseph W. Heiler
1947

zen building marked an interesting departure from the diluted historicism which had characterized the warehouses of A. E. Doyle and Associate (Meier and Frank Warehouse, 1914) and Sutton, Whitney, Aandahl and Fritsch (Meier and Frank Warehouse and Delivery Depot, 1926). The attached columns flanking the broad expanses of steel-sash windows of the Jantzen Warehouse were the only elements that referred to the Beaux-Arts-inspired warehouses built by his competitors. The zigzag banding at the cornice, the repeating "Jantzen Girl" medallions and the cresting wave motif framing the windows were pure Art Deco.

By 1930, the new wave in industrial architecture pioneered by Sundeleaf in Oregon received not only local accolades, but international recognition. That year, his buildings for Jantzen's overseas operations in Sydney and London were completed. Sundeleaf used fine, orange-tinted brick obtained from Messrs. Williamson, Cliff Ltd. of Stamford, England, for the Jantzen Knitting Mills he designed for the London branch of the company. The September 1931 issue of *Master Builder*, a prestigious English architectural magazine, devoted

three full pages and five photographs to the elegant structure and touted it, along with four other "modern factories" throughout the world. "We have had a great many compliments both as to the exterior and also in regard to the interior," A. J. Cormack, managing director of the London Jantzen plant, wrote to Sundeleaf. And there was still more international recognition for the Oregon designer. The editor of *Architecture Illustrated*, which devoted two full pages to the structure in its June 1931 issue, congratulated Sundeleaf for "his very fine building . . . and the color of the brick [which] was very remarkable and very pleasing." Explained Sundeleaf in the 1 November 1931 issue of the *Oregonian*, "As in the case of the plant here [in Portland] where color in brick was desired to make the building look pleasant in rainy weather, orange and brick limestone was used in England where similar weather conditions prevail." The Jantzen building in Portland, on which the London design was based, was selected in 1932 by the American Institute of Architects as the outstanding commercial building in Oregon.

All these kudos would net quite a bit of business from

LINCOLN MEMORIAL MAUSOLEUM
Joseph Heiler
1936

Portland's leaders of industry. During the early 1930s, when even such established firms as A. E. Doyle and Associate struggled to keep afloat, Sundeleaf's practice was flourishing. As a colleague would recall in later years, "Dick was just about the only architect in town who didn't feel the pinch of those lean years." While working on the Jantzen projects, he was busy turning out industrial buildings, including the Hood River Canning Company Plant (1930), the Enke Dye Works Addition (1930), and the Mail-Well Envelope Company (1931), which brought a touch of Deco glamor to utilitarian design. He even made room for humor in his architecture by using "pop" imagery, such as the envelope-shaped marquee that was built into the corner entrance of the Mail-Well Envelope Company Building. In 1931, when he gave a Zigzag Moderne face lift to the Fliedner Building in downtown Portland, he showed that a little paint and plasterwork could go a long way toward personalizing an otherwise bland exterior. The Fliedner featured zigzag motifs and decorative bas-relief panels below the parapet. Fluted pilasters terminated in stylized lotus capitals at the main entrance. But even with these decorative appliqués, Sundeleaf's "budget deco" was clearly a poor relative to the elegant opulence of Charles F. Berg's fashionable store a few blocks away on Broadway.

More than two decades later, when he would be given an even more challenging opportunity to modernize a downtown building, Sundeleaf would find inspiration in an acclaimed contemporary model. The assignment was to transform an eight-story terra cotta office building into the sixteen-story Portland Medical Center at Tenth and Washington. This time, the prototype was apparently Belluschi's sleek "aluminum building," as the Equitable (1948) had come to be known since its appearance on the Portland skyline. In 1957, after overcoming numerous engineering problems, the architect unveiled his own aluminum-and-glass-and-concrete monolith. Distinctive despite its evident kinship with Belluschi's tower several blocks to the east, the Portland Medical Center seemed to be an altogether fitting monument to the orthodontal arts practiced behind the building's metal and glass facade.

But while this building showed that the designer had lost nothing of his knack for tailoring an architectural style to fit his client's commercial image, it could not hold a candle to the quiet brilliance of the Oregon Portland Cement Building (1929). Unfortunately, since the construction of the elevated East-side access ramp to Hawthorne Bridge, this early gem has become one of Portland's best kept architectural secrets. With its cast-stone classical dentils and bulldog-faced gargoyles designed by Lavare, this creamy concrete structure projected a serene lyricism that celebrated the dignity of modern building materials. Similar in composition to the Jantzen Administration Building, the Romanesque design marked a sensitive transition from Beaux-Arts historicism to the simple, boxy forms of the Deco Moderne style. A small, formal garden nestled in the niche above the projecting entrance brought a little bit of nature to the otherwise arid warehouse district in Southeast Portland. In the interior, as well, every effort was made to demonstrate the versatility of the cement manufacturer's product. In this respect, the pre-cast beams that had been textured to resemble rough-hewn timbers were a triumph of trompe l'oeil detailing.

It was on the basis of designs such as this one that Sundeleaf proved himself worthy to execute commissions for the city's funeral industry. Portlanders, after all, had taken death seriously ever since the turn of the century when, as Wallace Kay Huntington noted in *Space, Style and Structure*, cemeteries had been held in "especial esteem by the Victorians." According to Huntington, "the cultivation of 'sweet melancholy' was con-

EASTSIDE MORTUARY
Thomas and Mercier
1930

sidered so enobling that no beauty was more poignantly expressive than that of a languid young woman expressing her grief for loved ones amidst the monuments and yews of the graveyard. . . . No less than parks, cemeteries gave status to a city and Lone Fir and Riverview

cemeteries are pictured in *West Shore* as legitimate objects of civic pride and as an appropriate place for a family outing."

The unrestrained manners of the roaring twenties might have driven the cult of "sweet melancholy" out

WILSON CHAMBERS MORTUARY
Richard Sundeleaf
1932

of fashion, but they did not appear to dampen Portland's fascination with dignified death palaces. Some of the region's finest architectural talents—among them Ellis Lawrence (Hope Abbey Mausoleum, Eugene, 1913, Riverview Cemetery, 1910), A. E. Doyle and Associate (Riverview Cemetery, 1928), Joseph Heiler (Lincoln Memorial Park Cemetery, 1926, 1937), Thomas and Mercier (Eastside Mortuary, 1930), Pietro Belluschi (J. P. Finley and Son Mortuary, 1937; Riverview Cemetery, 1945), Fred T. Webber (Portland Memorial Cemetery, 1933–39), George Wolff and Truman Phillips (Portland Memorial Cemetery, 1946–50) and William Fletcher (Riverview Cemetery, 1969, 1980)—would be sought out by the funeral profession. With their sophisticated designs they proved that, even in the death business, good appearance was a salable commodity.

Riverview Cemetery, one of the city's oldest, would be particularly discriminating in its choice of architects. The original board of directors boasted three of the city's founding fathers—Henry W. Corbett, William Ladd and Henry Failing—who had done so much to shape Portland into a sophisticated urban microcosm in the last decades of the nineteenth century. These visionary

entrepreneurs wanted to create a burial ground that would match, in every respect, the architectural splendors of their city. In 1910, the two-story Georgian brick caretaker's cottage capped with a "widow's walk" replaced the original Gothic Revival structure.

The 1910 building was apparently the work of Ellis Lawrence. The ceremonial portal fronting on River Road (1928), however, was the work of A. E. Doyle. While on his death bed, Doyle communicated his conception for the *inverted* Ionic columns—a symbol of death—to Pietro Belluschi who, at Doyle's bedside, sketched out the design according to Doyle's wish. Thus was the baton passed from the master builder of one generation to that of the next. In the following decades, the "Doyle tradition" at Riverview would be continued by the firm's inheritor, Belluschi, as well as by one of its "graduates," Sundeleaf, each of whom updated the facility with his own distinctive look.

Belluschi's design for the Riverview Chapel, Mausoleum and office, completed in 1945, would blend the intimate scale of his residential work in the regional style with the serene luminosity of his churches. Assembled under a series of low, gently pitched roofs, the complex also carried a faint allusion to traditional Japanese architecture. The most striking feature was certainly the semi-attached arbor connecting two of the three entry ways. The rhythmical pattern of the supporting beams, as well as the vertical window mullions interrupting the Willamina brick bore a marked resemblance to the fenestration of the Harry Wentz cottage, which had inspired many of Belluschi's residential designs.

The exterior, in fact, drew so richly from non-mortuarial sources, that one might easily have mistaken the structure for an elegant suburban clubhouse. Only the magnificent bronze door with its scattering of bas-relief figures suggested the building's somber function.

In the interior as well, Belluschi attempted to orchestrate an uplifting, life-affirming atmosphere. A series of monitors—similar to those he had used in the Ayer Wing of the Portland Art Museum—admitted a soft radiance into the marble-clad corridor of the mausoleum. An Art Deco flair was provided by the zigzag shaped aluminum baffles located beneath the monitors. The chapel, however, was clearly the building's center-piece. With its warm maple woodwork and boldly arched ceiling, this meditative space was a jewel of understated elegance. A circular stained-glass window and a series of bronze, tulip-shaped lamps flanking the chancel were the only ornamental touches. As in the architect's other religious structures, these ornamental devices were chosen as much for their sculptural impact, as for their contribution to the subtle lighting effects.

The three corridors that Sundeleaf added between 1957 and 1959 continued Belluschi's discreet vision along the interior. The exterior of this addition, however, was a radical departure from the delicate detailing and scale of the original structure. Executed in pale pink stucco and featuring steel-sash fenestration, Sundeleaf's section carried its designer's distinctly muscular and boxy proportions. William Fletcher, the architect for the Riverview's Hilltop Memorial (1969, 1980), would not face the problem of integrating his design with an existing structure. His free-standing, outdoor mausoleum brought a contemporary, almost neo-Brutalist version of the Parthenon to the hill overlooking the Willamette River. Combining travertine marble, brick and coarse-grained concrete, this graceful pavilion looked something like a scaled-down version of the Oregon Historical Center (Wolff, Zimmer, Gunsul and Frasca, in consultation with Belluschi, 1967) built two years earlier.

While an entire team of architects was helping Riverview Cemetery keep pace with the city's changing archi-

PORTLAND MEMORIAL CEMETERY
Fred T. Weber
1946

tectural tastes, Portland architect Joseph Heiler, almost singlehandedly, was building up the layers of Lincoln Memorial Cemetery's monolithic mausoleum. In this respect, Heiler might have been Portland's only "in-house" mortuary architect. To be sure, he had considerable help from the Milne Construction Company, the region's unsurpassed specialists in funerary construction, who were responsible for building scores of crypts, vaults and mausolea throughout the city and the Pacific Northwest.

Located at the far reaches of the city's eastern boundary, Heiler's forbidding installation reflected a succession of architectural fashions in a gloomy, stratified deposit of buildings. Stepping up the verdant hillside of the cemetery grounds, the mausoleum complex was as much a tribute to the architect's versatility as it would be to the memory of those buried within. Heiler began his climb to immortality in 1926 when the chapel and indoor mausoleum were completed. For his first installation, he chose the august Classical Revival style still favored by Beaux-Arts traditionalists. The ponderous portal, massive classical detailing and steely gray exterior were an appropriate prelude to the frigid symmetry of the interior, sheathed in black and white.

In the late 1930s, when a new bank of corridors was contemplated, Heiler produced an astonishingly bold Zigzag Moderne design. The far wall of the original chapel was removed to create an uninterrupted vista into a three-story octagonal rotunda. Flanked by two faceted, coffin-shaped niches holding sculpted angels of

PORTLAND MEMORIAL CEMETERY
Fred T. Weber
1946

death, a life-sized nude figure with wings sprouted from an eight-sided fountain. A skylight fashioned from creamy glass repeated the starburst design of the tiled floor, which sparkled in dusty tones of pink, mauve, green and blue. To complete the geometric exuberance, a cantilevered spiral staircase unfolded its faceted underside along the perimeter of the rotunda. (The geometric forms lining the staircase's underside were similar to those used in Ely Kahn's elevator lobby for New York's Film Center Building built in 1929.) The effect was nothing short of staggering—even for a city accustomed to seeing some of its finest Art Deco architecture in mortuaries.

By the time Heiler's new wing opened, Thomas and Mercier's crystalline Eastside Mortuary (1930, now the Volunteers of America Building) had already become something of a classic in Deco death palaces. In its day, this pristine example of the commercial Art Deco style must have produced quite a sensation. With its encrustations of swirling floral motifs, colorful windows and multi-hued brick, this faceted corner structure set the tone for a new, contemporary idiom in funeral facilities. The stepped-back mortuary—with its polychrome brick and cast-stone ornamentation—looked as if it had been chipped off New York City's Barbizon Plaza (1930, Murgatroyd and Ogden).

Fresh from his successes in modernizing classical styles for Jantzen, Sundeleaf seemed eager to experiment with a modified Deco look in the Wilson Chambers Mortuary (1932, now The Little Chapel of the Chimes Mortuary). At a time when the opening of a major new mortuary was covered in the local press with all due pomp and circumstance, Sundeleaf's design for this mortuary received more than its share of acclaim. Touted in the *Oregonian* as "a masterpiece of Italian Renaissance inspiration," the structure was hailed as "one of the most modern mortuaries on the Coast." While its style could more accurately be described as Romanesque, the building was indeed modernistic in spirit, featuring zigzag banding on the cornice, and touches of Art Deco ornamentation above its double Tuscan columns.

By blending the old with the new, Sundeleaf had hit on an architectural formula that held particular appeal for owners of the city's funerary facilities. His stylistic eclecticism would strike just the right balance between tradition and fashion to keep funeral directors knocking at his door with new commissions. During the next three decades, Sundeleaf would design facilities for the Mt. Crest Abbey Mausoleum and Crematorium (1969) in Salem, add several corridors to the mausoleum at Riverview Cemetery (1957–59), and join the fraternity of architects contributing to the fabulous Portland Memorial Cemetery (1944, 1953–54, 1961–64).

Touted as the largest indoor cemetery west of the Mississippi, Portland Memorial would become the city's answer to Los Angeles' Forest Lawn. By 1984, with over 57,000 "residents," including such Hollywood notables as actress Mayo Methot—Humphrey Bogart's first wife—among its clients, Portland Memorial would become the silent meeting ground for some of Portland's finest *living* architects. Over the decades, Richard Sundeleaf, Fred T. Webber, George Wolff and Truman Phillips, and the firm of Hagestead and Peace would turn this complex into a veritable museum of architectural styles. With its cheerful mix of Victorian, California Mission, Mediterranean Revival and Zigzag Moderne architecture, the elegant compound became a mirror-image of major architectural trends and styles that had shaped the city of the living.

Unfortunately, however, Portland Memorial would become neither a featured attraction on architectural walking tours nor would it rank among the city's tourist highlights. Despite the fact that the complex would not be difficult to spot, few Portlanders seemed eager to explore its hidden riches (perhaps the stark concrete walls jutting from a cliff above the lush east bank of the

Willamette River were too suggestive of conventional funerary installations). But one only had to approach the complex from its front to realize that this was no ordinary mausoleum. With its soothing, manicured grounds and bustling duck population, the necropolis presented the inviting face of a thriving resort hotel.

Inside, however, the mausoleum's spaces metamorphosed into a veritable jewelbox of period pieces and precious heirlooms. Hundreds of stained glass windows and skylights in delicate pastel tints created kaleidoscopic patterns along the walls and ceilings. Sweeping views of the Portland skyline alternated with Tiffany glass panels that had been worked into intricate floral patterns or picturesque views of the region's natural beauties. Water cascading into indoor pools provided a lulling background for the melancholy reveries that might spring to mind at the spectacle of marble angels supporting translucent basins gushing over with water.

Within the crypts and mourning chambers were enough treasures to stock a respectable provincial museum: statuary carved in Carrara marble that included replicas of Michelangelo's "Pieta" and Leonardo Da Vinci's "Last Supper," Art Deco busts, Ming vases and countless other curios. The corridors of the Portland Memorial Mausoleum boasted marble in more varieties and shades than any other building within the city's limits. The building's centerpiece, however, was Fred T. Webber's design for the spiral staircase—six stories of creamy marble rimmed with a metal handrail—boasting Art Deco patterns—rising to a large skylight at the top.

That Sundeleaf's watershed project—the Woodbury and Company Warehouse—was completed in 1939 was not a coincidence. It was, after all, the year of New York City's 1939 World's Fair, possibly the most ambitious ever. Ushering America out of the Depression and into a new period of economic stability, the fair was conceived as an actual model for the planned society of the future, whose avowed purpose was to "project the average man into the World of Tomorrow." The future, as the fair's planners saw it, had mainly to do with streamlined forms, fluorescent lighting, automobiles traveling on fantastic superhighways and all manner of new consumer items—a potent vision after ten years of economic retraction.

Sundeleaf's design for the Woodbury and Company Warehouse was a masterpiece of glass and concrete that marked a new epoch in the region's industrial architecture. If earlier warehouses, including Sundeleaf's own

Jantzen facilities, tended to mask function under a dainty veil of ornament borrowed from non-utilitarian structures, the Woodbury and Company Warehouse barred no holds in celebrating the rough, honest beauty of modern functionalism. "Although the interior . . . is strictly utilitarian in its layout and uses," the architect wrote in the *Architectural Record*, he modestly pointed out that, "its exterior is probably different from any other warehouse previously designed."

What distinguished this building was the architect's decision to steer a course between that of the Beaux-Arts exterior decorator who appliquéd a variety of stylish "period" motifs to the building's facade and the self-effacing designer who deferred his aesthetic vision to the client's budget. By the late 1930s, Sundeleaf had established an impressive record for winning over even the most penny-pinching client. In the case of the Woodbury projects, he talked the owners into a "limited expenditure in excess of the cost of plain flat walls cut with rectangular openings that characterize most warehouses."

Inspired by the example of Albert Kahn—whose books were always within reach of Sundeleaf's drafting table—and German architects Peter Behrens and Walter Gropius, the Portland architect concentrated on letting the building's function dictate the shape of the design. At the same time, however, he was not prepared to take functionalism to the minimalist extreme that marked the new industrialism of these early nineteenth-century architects. His Beaux-Arts training taught him, after all, that visual and technical excellence were not contradictory values.

The Woodbury and Company Warehouse would be Sundeleaf's parting tribute to the fanciful forms of La Belle Epoque. Abstracted into pristine, geometrical lines, the fussy legacy of Beaux-Arts ornamentation made its last stand at the entrance of Sundeleaf's building. Extending from ground to lintel, the entry way presented a sweeping expanse of glass block. Inserted into this sparkling grid was an exquisitely carved cast-stone door frame whose ornamental detailing was perfectly attuned to the bold, geometrical forms of the building. Designed by Lavare, the door frame—with its stepped-back jambs terminating in curlicues—echoed the building's vertical rhythms. The door head sported a circular medallion at its center and a cast-stone panel depicting heavy industrial machinery advertised the epic of modernism.

For the overall treatment, however, the architect used a new decorative vocabulary that would take the place of

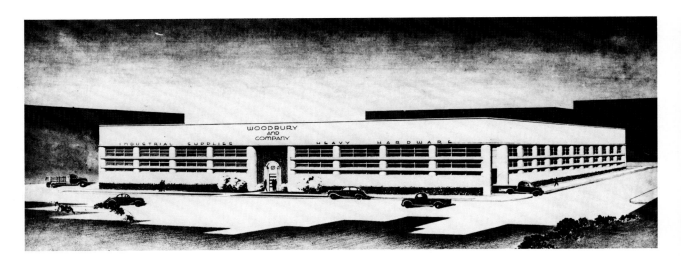

WOODBURY AND COMPANY
Richard Sundeleaf
1939

applied ornament. He found it in light, shadow and materials. "Without recourse to any decorative detail," Sundeleaf wrote, "but simply by accentuating structural and spatial features and by means of surface texture, a decorative pattern of strong light and shade was created." The dramatic building that resulted drew its strength from conventional industrial materials: board-formed concrete, standard glass and sash panels and glass block. From these, Sundeleaf created a ruggedly beautiful package of powerful bays banded at ground and cornice level by rough expanses of striated concrete. Somewhat in the manner of the New Brutalists, who in the late 1950s and early 1960s would spring from the *beton brut* ("concrete in the raw") aesthetic of Le Corbusier's late work, Sundeleaf exploited the expressive potential of concrete that still bore the traces of the board formwork. "The exterior," he explained, "was given a stucco dash finish, producing an interesting texture without disturbing the character of the board-formed surfaces."

While a far cry from the violently sculptured *beton brut* expressionism of Le Corbusier's Unite d'Habitation development at Marseille (1947–52), the massive forms and textured surfaces of Sundeleaf's pre-cast slabs and columns were groping toward a similar architectonic sensibility. His interest in exposing these expressive structural elements produced the region's first self-conscious flirtation with Brutalist forms. In this respect, the Woodbury and Company Building represented Sundeleaf's most original contribution to regional warehouse architecture.

With this building, he also began to experiment with an approach that anticipated the modular system which Le Corbusier developed in his later years and which he described in *Le Modulor* (1951). Whereas Le Corbusier would base his laws of composition on the male figure, Sundeleaf based his on the standard dimensions of *available construction materials*. The four-foot module, in particular, became the recurrent measure by which he achieved balance, rhythm and harmony. In an interview with the *Daily Journal of Commerce* on 20 November 1980, Sundeleaf explained the origin of his module system: "It first occurred to me when I realized that so many materials came in four-foot increments: plywood and fluorescent light tubes, for instance. Using the four-foot module can simplify the design process, and it allows me to draw almost as fast as I can think."

Sundeleaf applied the modular system to his design for the Director's Furniture Store (originally known as the Tarlow's Building of the Hollywood Furniture department store). Composed entirely according to the four-foot module scheme, the building's exterior was articulated by indented lines which crisscrossed to form a pattern of four-foot squares above a row of columns set on sixteen-foot centers.

When it opened to the public, this building won high marks for bringing the latest in retail display ideas to

Portland. Received with all the hoopla of the Pendleton Round-Up, the store celebrated its opening "by the play of night searchlights, souvenirs, and roses for all visitors," the *Oregonian* reported on 22 June 1947. According to the press release, "The three-story steel and concrete building, regarded as one of the finest of its kind in the Pacific Northwest, was designed by Richard Sundeleaf, who made a special nationwide tour studying furniture display problems. . . . A number of modern effects have been used. Highlighting the modern architectural styling marble entrances, bulkheads and columns, aluminum trim, marquees and inch-thick plate glass entrance doors. An innovation here will be the zorite-fluted letters used on the exterior, as well as the shaft of plate glass built in the corner that extends for the full height of the building."

For architects and designers, the interpretation of functionalism by the 1930s had shifted from the static geometric forms promoted by the Bauhaus architects to the dynamic forms of nature and of motorized objects moving through space. In 1934, an advertisement for the new Airflow Chrysler which appeared in *Fortune* magazine, included the following hype: "Old mother nature has always designed her creatures for the function they are to perform. She has streamlined her fastest fish . . . her swiftest birds . . . her fleetest animals that move on land. You have only to look at a dolphin, a gull, or a greyhound to appreciate the rightness of the tapering, flowing contour of the new Airflow Chrysler." By the 1940s, however, while Belluschi and Yeon had turned to the regional landscape and materials for the organic forms of their residences, Sundeleaf would bypass mother nature, Oregon-style, and take his cue directly from the streamlined shapes of new automobiles, buildings and appliances.

Since the late 1920s, a new breed of American industrial designer had been working to give the modern world a new shape. By the end of the 1930s the rounded, streamlined forms they pioneered were all the rage. The streamlining of man's environment was well-established by 1940. Rounded corners inspired by aerodynamics found their way into buildings of every description. Gas stations, skyscrapers and newsstands received the wind-swept treatment. After all, a public, long fed daily doses of Buck Rogers, Flash Gordon and Superman, began to see that space rockets, moon landings and space stations could be realities in its lifetime. As Marc Arceneaux noted in *Streamline*, "Steamlining represented an uncom-

plicated future world, no shadows unaccounted for, every step delineated. Americans looked toward tomorrow with unbridled optimism."

Infected by the national mania for aerodynamic styling and futuristic forms, Sundeleaf—more than any other local architect—was persuaded that the Streamline Moderne would be accepted as an "up-to-date" style by Portland corporations wishing to project a new image. He was not mistaken. Depression-weary Portlanders were itching to get things *moving* again—in buildings that *looked* like they could move through space.

In fact, elsewhere in America, people were interested in buildings that actually *did* move through space. Hyping the "Hurricane House" featured in *Popular Science* magazine in the 1940s, Carl Warden wrote: "When raging storms whip across the land, accompanied by violent gales that uproot trees, tear the roofs from houses, and turn a trim countryside into a scene of desolation, there could probably be no safer refuge than the interior of a novel hurricane house designed by Edwin A. Koch, New York City architect. Streamlined in the form of a mammoth tear-drop," continued the enraptured writer, "this amazing dwelling would revolve automatically to face into the oncoming storm, meeting it like the wing of an airplane and passing it smoothly around its curving sides toward its pointed tip." Using the latest in engineering wizardry, the "weather-vane" dwelling designed for both safety and comfort, would have rested on three circular tracks and featured a space-age control panel. "Merely by selecting the desired push button," the pilot/housewife could "point the rounded end [of the house] into the wind, defying gales of hurricane force." In ordinary weather, the entire house could be "rotated to face rooms toward or away from the sun or to point bedroom windows toward a cooling breeze."

In Portland, Sundeleaf was just the man to fashion such a streamlined look. Conversant with the entire spectrum of aerodynamic motifs, Portland's master of the sleek "magazine" styles was sought out by clients who appreciated the inventiveness with which he used popular imagery to give each building its own expressive edge. Three buildings in particular—the Bearing Service Company Building (1944), the General Electric Company Building (1945) and the Francis and Hopkins Motors Showroom (1949, now the University Station Post Office)—brought Portlanders a touch of the glamorous "World of Tomorrow" that New York World's Fair had promised them in 1939.

BEARING SERVICE COMPANY
Richard Sundeleaf
1944

The Bearing Service Company Building on N.W. Everett Street was a series of glass and concrete bays that stepped inward at the corner to emphasize a recessed, curved glass block entrance. Balancing its round cantilevered marquee on a single column, the building's entrance resembled a giant wheel axle turned on end. To boost the advertising impact of this architectural pun, Sundeleaf placed the entrance squarely in the center of the corner site, where it would be shown off to best advantage to passing motorists.

His design for the General Electric Company Building (now Dynagraphics, Inc.) owed a considerable debt to the streamlining genius of Raymond Loewy. Occupying half a block, the two-story production-cum-display center replicated the round-nosed column design which made its premiere in the Woodbury and Company

PORTLAND MEDICAL CENTER
Sundedleaf and Hagestad
1957

Warehouse. The entrance, however, threw the essentially boxy structure into an entirely new dimension. Reflecting the sleek curves of Loewy's design for the Sears Coldspot Refrigerator—combined, perhaps, with the contoured solidity of his Coca-Cola dispensers—the entry pavilion of General Electric thrust Sundeleaf's building into the cutting edge of aerodynamic chic. The windswept motif was carried through to the bubble roof whose bulging curves recalled the swelling dome atop Loewy's Lucky Stores Supermarkets (1945). The interior was styled to match the modern commercial image and provided an environment insulated from bad weather, production noise and other unpleasantries. Crammed full of state-of-the-art conveniences, the General Electric Building boasted "Day Bright Troffers with regulating Holophone Lenses" and "instant starting" fluorescent lights.

With the completion of Robert Moses's now defunct six-lane Harbor Drive in 1941, Portland, the "car city" came of age. Dazed by gasoline fumes and giddy with postwar prosperity, the public rushed to embrace the almighty automobile. In the process, some of the city's finest downtown buildings, including the Portland Hotel—and scores of cast-iron jewels—were razed to make room for parking lots and garages. Not surprisingly, the wreckers would spare A. E. Doyle's ponderous reinforced concrete garage at 630 S.W. Pine Street (1927), reputed to have been the first multi-level parking structure in the downtown area. They also left untouched the monumental Bates Motoramp Garage (1924, Sutton, Whitney, Aandahl and Fritsch).

These stately relics from the days when Ford's rectangular cars came in every color—as long as it was black—must have inspired downtown developers with reverential awe. With their arched corbel tables, denticulated bands and massive walls, these garages were built to stand the test of time and, apparently, fashion. Long after fleets of spanking new cars had stopped rolling off the assembly line of the Ford assembly plant designed by Doyle in 1914, these parking structures still provided a classy solution to the messy traffic problem. The "medieval fortress" look that Doyle and Fritsch had used for their garages was entirely appropriate for an age when cars were solid, stolid and built to last a lifetime.

But, by 1948, the times, and Detroit's masterminds, had changed. Today's ultimate chic was tomorrow's latest addition to the scrap pile of history. Sundeleaf, who in 1984 was still driving a 1957 Thunderbird, must have had a direct hotline to the corporate boardrooms of

Detroit. In short, what was good for General Motors was also good for the architecture of Sundeleaf. When it came to structures geared toward the automotive trade, the Francis and Hopkins Motors Showroom was his pièce de résistance. In 1949, when the building was headlined in the *Oregonian* as "The West's Most Modern Automotive Establishment," Francis and Hopkins was a stunning showcase for the smooth shells and sloping hoods of Detroit's latest gas guzzlers. Along with the Equitable Building, Sundeleaf's car dealership was one of the city's first glass boxes. A shimmering transparent membrane separated the window shopper from the display floor, where salesmen garbed in double-breasted suits and two-tone black-and-white shoes (popularized by Harry Truman) kicked whitewalls to punctuate their sales raps.

No one had to tell this Portland designer that, in the furious scramble to make planned obsolescence work, maximum exposure was the name of the game. Crossing the transparent angularity of Mies van der Rohe's Barcelona Pavilion with the functional honesty of Loewy's International Harvester Servicenter, Sundeleaf produced a design that pushed the automobile display window into the third dimension. Except for his signature rounded columns at the street elevation and the metal railing along the roof, every line of Francis and Hopkins Motors had been slicked down, smoothed over and modernized. Meeting crisply at the corners, continuous expanses of glass enclosed showcased cars, while at the rear, a graceful ramp invited buyers to take their dream-mobiles out for a test drive on the town. According to the architect, a 1982 renovation came dangerously close to being a "desecration," but the block-long structure still retains much of its former dash and elegance.

Not all of Sundeleaf's Streamline Moderne designs, however, made it past the drawing board. The Ford Tractor and Ferguson Implement Dealers Building, the Sagner Motor Company Showroom and the new Montgomery Ward Warehouse were among the best of the architect's "stillborn" projects of the period. Based on the modular, columned-bay system, each of these structures would have demonstrated Sundeleaf's originality in interpreting aerodynamic motifs and provided important "missing links" in the evolution of his distinctive industrial style. This absence was especially regrettable in the case of the new Montgomery Ward Warehouse. Had it been built, the building would have treated Portland to an ethereal expanse of low-slung curves and made the Woodbury Warehouse look pale by com-

FRANCIS AND HOPKINS MOTORS BUILDING
Richard Sundeleaf
1947

parison. It would also have bolstered Sundeleaf's reputation as one of the region's most original "middlemen" of progressive industrial design.

Important as architectural handbooks and publications were for Portland's "magazine regionalist," they were not the exclusive source of his inspiration. Sundeleaf also had occasion to contribute to local projects in which two of the nation's leading designers in the commercial Moderne style had been involved. In 1945 he added a sleek, low-lying warehouse to the Austin Company's Chase Bag Building (1939). In 1951, he collaborated with Russell W. Allen of New York, a leading retail designer and an associate of Raymond Loewy, in the design for the shop windows and retail display floor of the Weiner Store Building at 602 s.w. Washington.

Although, in retrospect, Streamline Moderne would prove to be Sundeleaf's favorite style—and the one that inspired his best designs—the architect produced a number of impressive buildings in the International and, even, Northwest Regional styles that were becoming popular during the 1950s and 1960s. His design for the Beverly Sundeleaf Mackenzie house (1956) was an outstanding example of the "stilt" structures which Portland architect Van Evera Bailey had popularized earlier in the decade.

It was only fitting that when Sundeleaf designed his own office building in 1965, he should have used the occasion to summarize the ideas that had shaped his protean vision. Based on the four-foot module, the two-story glass and gray, weathered cedar structure made a subtle allusion to the architect's infatuation with aerodynamic forms in the streamlined baffle that straddled the roofline. Below the parapet, the building's repeating mullions recalled the Japanese screen effect of Yeon's Visitors Information Center. It was as if Yeon's building had sent out runners and sprouted an additional wing two miles south an a hillside overlooking the Willamette River. Yet the overwhelming impression was not that of a replica, but rather of a hybrid design that could only be catalogued as "Streamlined Regionalism."

Straddling historical and contemporary styles, national fashions and regional sensibilities, Sundeleaf was, in some respects, Portland's master disseminator of "magazine" styles. And yet, he had a special talent. Particularly in his industrial buildings, he breathed new life into historical forms, and gave contemporary design trends the stamp of authenticity. Standing on the terrace of his office, Sundeleaf looked across the Willamette River to the "City View Park district" where he had been raised, and said: "Some people say that I live in the past. But I say, the past lives in me." Spoken like a true Postmodernist.

SPANNING HISTORY

BY THE early 1950s, Portland would become the "Car City" on the Willamette. During the Depression decade and prewar years, Richard Sundeleaf's streamlined architecture took the city's commercial and industrial buildings out of the tradition-bound Beaux Arts age and thrust it into the world of modernity. Van Evera Bailey's garage-centered residences of the postwar years officially acknowledged the arrival of the automobile as the most recent installation in the middle-class home. Drive-in restaurants (Waddle's Restaurant, 1945) and shopping centers (Bagle and Downs Shopping Center, 1942; McLoughlin Heights Shopping Center, 1942) had sprouted from the architectural imagination of such modernists as Pietro Belluschi. Gasoline stations shaped in the aerodynamic forms purveyed by national designers, embellished streetcorners throughout the city, serving as functional and ornamental reminders of the reign of the automobile.

By the mid-1940s, inflated with postwar optimism, Portland coasted into a new era of urban expansion and growth. Wartime mobilization transformed the city into a shipbuilding center, swelling its population by a staggering 32 percent, from 501,000 in 1940 to 661,000 in 1944. Workers from all parts of the country poured into the city to man the shipyards that, between 1940 and 1944, produced more than a thousand oceangoing vessels. Housing tracts, such as Kaiser's massive Vanport community (1942), sprang up almost overnight to shelter the influx. Public facilities, particularly the transit systems, were seriously strained. Businessmen, entrepreneurs and civic officials scrambled to keep pace with the booming wartime economy, and laid plans to continue the city's expansion and prosperity beyond the war years. Officials flooded the local press with inspirational messages boosting the city's confidence in its grandiose future.

Portland became a city that looked to the automobile for inspiration in urban architecture and planning. Indeed, as Carl Abbott remarked, "Portland planners were hostages to the automobile between 1920 and 1940, and the working definition of their job changed from urban design to traffic engineering." For Portlanders as for most Americans of the postwar years, the automobile would become the most accessible and ubiquitous symbol of progress, prosperity and upward mobility. With the same civic zeal that had fueled Portland's entrepreneurs of the railroad era, the business barons of the 1940s and 1950s would set about reshaping the city to suit the modern image of their times and their aspirations. Whereas Portland's nabobs of the mid- and late-nineteenth century had channeled their prosperity into an intense campaign of construction—that would produce a city of exquisite cast-iron buildings—their modern counterparts of the 1940s and 1950s, would funnel their investments into a program of architectural destruction. The target of their wrecking zeal—in most instances—would be the cast-iron stratum of the city's built landscape. Fashion, time and the automobile had turned the architectural assets of the past into liabilities.

Many of the grand old buildings—such as the Cooks' Building (1882, Warren H. Williams), the Allen and Lewis Block (1882, Williams), the Kamm Block (1884, Justus Krumbein), the Cosmopolitan Block (1878, Williams and Krumbein), the Ainsworth Block (1881, Clinton Day) and the St. Charles Hotel (1869, Elwood M. Burton)—which, in a bygone era, had been erected as monuments to the city's vitality and promise, came to be seen, at best, as charming, but useless relics of exhausted and outmoded ambitions. At worst, the public imagination had transformed them into sinister emblems of the city's obsolescence.

In this respect, destruction was licensed in the cause of progress. Both views were expressed in a tepidly nostalgic commentary published in the *Oregon Journal* of 11 May 1941, when large-scale demolition of the cast-iron heritage along the waterfront had gotten under way to accommodate the construction of Harbor Drive: "Portland's almost last link with the dusty past is about to go. The ornate facaded fronts of Front Avenue buildings will fall to the wrecker's zeal, and in their place will rise the austere severity of modern architecture. The cobblestones of the narrow streets will disappear under the paving of the new superhighway, and the last gas mantle lamp will metamorphize into neon. So look your last, Portland, as old Front Avenue goes glimmering. A new day is coming!"

The end was at hand for all but about 30 of Portland's 200 cast-iron beauties. Deposited between 1853 and 1889, this rich layer of Italianate, Second Empire, Gothic Revival and Baroque structures gave the city its first, truly urban character and legitimized its claim to architectural distinction. As architect, cast-iron historian and preservationist William J. Hawkins III noted in a recent interview: "Cast-iron was the predominant architectural style through the 1880s. Almost every downtown building used cast-iron in some aspect of the structure—in columns, pilasters, arches, or ornamentation. Cast-iron was the whole *look* of the city."

After San Francisco had lost its treasury of cast-iron buildings to a devastating earthquake and fire in 1906, Portland would boast the largest and finest collection of such buildings on the West Coast. "Seattle really developed in the 1890s," Hawkins explained. "And that was after the heyday of cast-iron. In the 1870s and 1880s, when Portland was growing into a major West Coast city, Seattle was just a little village." Throughout the first four decades of the twentieth century, the cast-iron facades along Portland's Front and First streets continued to lend an air of somewhat shabby, but still respectable cosmopolitan sophistication to a district that was once the civic, commercial and cultural hub of the city.

By the 1940s and 1950s, however, this sophistication would appear to have outlived its time and stood in the way of progress. Portlanders wanted buildings and streets that did not mingle the old with the new, but were boldly oriented to the future. In those decades, Postmodernism (with its historicizing impulses) and contextualism (with its plea for stylistic coherence), were not even a twinkle in the eyes of architectural theorists, critics or urban planners. Bewitched by visions of modernity, real estate developers and their architect accomplices were filled with fantasies of sparkling towers and expansive freeways. In the process of transforming their dreams into reality, they would destroy a good deal of the architecture that linked the city's past with its future. Like other American cities, Portland, swept up in the postwar mania for conformity, erased much of its distinctive architectural heritage.

If, as the French nineteenth-century historian Jules Michelet had written, "Chaque epoque rêve la suivante" (Each epoch dreams up its successor), the builders of Portland's iron age had certainly missed the mark with their fantasies. "In no preceding year have so many fine business blocks and handsome residences been erected in Portland," the *Oregonian* boasted on 1 January 1883, "and it is notable that they have almost without exception been built by our solid businessmen, not as speculators, but as permanent investments." It was these "permanent investments" that the founding fathers had hoped would put Portland on the architectural map. "The architectural beauty of many of these new buildings," the *Oregonian* again emphasized on 1 January 1884, "cannot be excelled by any city in the world, and credit is due to Portland's architects and builders for their beauty—to the former for their skill in designing the elegant structures that adorn our streets, and to the latter for the admirable manner in which they have carried out those designs."

The pride that resonated in these commentaries was amply justified. Just three decades earlier, the city had been a cluster of one-, two- and three-story wooden homes, warehouses and churches with the distinct flavor of a New England Greek Revival village. Thomas H. Pearne, an early settler and prominent citizen left a vivid sketch of the city's early appearance. "When I first saw [Portland]," he wrote in *Sixty One Years of Itinerant Christian Life in Church and State*, "it was a hamlet of perhaps five or six hundred people, in the midst of a dense fir forest. For years the only streets practicable for drays, on account of stumps of trees, were First and Second streets, running parallel with the river."

As the California Gold Rush and the Indian Wars of the 1850s brought trading ships to Portland in increasing numbers and stimulated a lively commercial life, the city's founding fathers—among them, William S. Ladd, Captain John C. Ainsworth, Jacob Kamm, Henry W. Corbett, Captain John H. Couch, Captain George H. Flanders, Simeon G. Reed, Robert R. Thompson, Cicero H. Lewis and Josiah Failing—set about the task of carving out their own financial empires. Encouraged by signs of mounting prosperity, they soon began to invest their profits in constructing commercial structures along the waterfront, creating, at once, a stunning architectural base for their budding enterprises and the foundations for a future urban microcosm on the banks of the Willamette.

The first bold step in this direction was taken by Ladd who, in 1853, commissioned A. B. Hallock to design and construct the city's first commercial brick structure, the Ladd Building, a one-story building on Front Street. The handsome Ladd Building, which served as a bridge between the wooden beginnings of the city and its efflorescence into one of the finest cast-iron metropolises on the West Coast, would survive until 1940, when it was demolished to make way for access ramps leading to the Morrison Bridge.

The new building sparked a healthy rivalry among the city's entrepreneurs, each of whom strove to surpass the other with stylish commercial structures. By the end of the Civil War, a bright new city had taken shape along the wharves and warehouses lining the riverfront. The muddy chaos along Front Street had been replaced by a sparkling cluster of nearly 60 one-, two-, and three-story Italianate commercial palaces, whose gracefully detailed arches, pilasters, columns and pediments announced the city's aspirations to European elegance.

Building fever was spreading during the 1850s and 1860s, time was at a premium and the formula for functional *and* elegant commercial structures required an instant architecture. The new cast-iron technology, which had been introduced to America in the 1840s by Daniel D. Badger, founder and owner of Boston's Architectural Iron Works and inventor-designer-engineer James Bogardus in New York, was just what the city needed.

Iron had come into its own as a principal ingredient in industrial and commercial structures during the great age of railway building in Europe in the 1830s and 1840s. As Walter Benjamin noted in his essay, "Paris, Capital of the Nineteenth Century," the decisive moment that spurred the use of iron as a building material occurred when "it emerged that the locomotive, with which experiments had been made since the end of the [eighteen] twenties could only be used on iron rails. The rail becomes the first prefabricated iron component, the forerunner of the girder. Iron is avoided in residential buildings and used in arcades, exhibition halls, stations—buildings serving transitory purposes." In the world of rapid urban expansion, iron would show itself to be the perfect material for what, in another context, Benjamin had called the age of mechanical reproduction.

Not surprisingly, it was in England that the earliest experiments with iron construction had been undertaken. Since the end of the eighteenth century, British engineers and builders tested the structural and aesthetic possibilities of iron in a wide range of building types, from bridges to greenhouses to railway stations. The cumulative experience of five decades of British engineering ingenuity would find its finest expression in the renowned Crystal Palace, designed and built in 1850–51 in London by Sir Joseph Paxton and his engineer associates Fox and Henderson. Erected in the incredibly short span of nine months to house the Great Exhibition, the Crystal Palace was a stunning architectural achievement and the first example of a completely prefabricated structure. As such, it became the model for numerous imitations in England, as well as on the Continent and in America. Moreover, it entered the literary and popular imagination as an ambiguous emblem of the benevolent and sinister promises of modernity.

But while Britain produced the most spectacular masterpieces of iron construction, America applied its trusty "Yankee ingenuity" to the task of disseminating the full potential of the material in commercial and industrial structures throughout the country. In America, the cast-iron craze was sparked by Badger's cast-iron storefront in Boston (1842) and Bogardus's iron-fronted drugstore in New York City (1848). Businessmen throughout the country were quick to appreciate the practical and aesthetic advantages of cast-iron technology. Entire facades could be cast in components, shipped to any part of the country and assembled in a fraction of the time it would have taken with conventional materials and construction techniques.

The broad range of architectural styles, which could be fashioned into arches, columns, pediments and cornices, held particular appeal for image-conscious entrepreneurs. As Margot Gayle and Edmund V. Gillon pointed out in *Cast-Iron Architecture in New York*, "Virtually every architectural style was within reach. None was too bold or too delicate to be reproduced in iron, no decoration too intricate. Any desired shape could be recreated so long as the initial patterns could be carved, and then pressed into damp sand to form sand molds into which molten metal could flow." Foundries sprang up throughout the country to meet the heavy demand for cast-iron ornamental and structural components, and cast-iron pattern books disseminated the latest—and most ancient—architectural models to towns and villages from Portland, Maine to Portland, Oregon.

If New York set the fashion for iron buildings in the nation as a whole, San Francisco provided the earliest inspiration—and supplied the first materials—for Portland's dawning iron age. By the mid-1850s, San Francisco's burgeoning, gold-rush shantytown had been transfigured into the cast-iron capital of the West Coast. Handsome Italian Renaissance buildings began to take over San Francisco's fashionable Montgomery Street. Their components had come from such local purveyors as the Pacific Foundry (a branch of Badger's New York Architectural Iron Works), the California Foundry and the Phoenix Iron Works, owned since 1856 by Jonathan Kittredge.

San Francisco's architectural supremacy would not go unchallenged on the West Coast. Hallock, Portland's first architect and official surveyor, was standing by, ready to help his city match—and even eclipse—San Francisco's architectural achievements. As official representative of the Phoenix Iron Works, Hallock became the local purveyor of San Francisco's architectural cast-iron. In his J. Kohn and Company Building of 1854, Hallock introduced the city's first cast-iron columns and arches at the first floor level. By 1860, no fewer than 18 brick buildings, at least half of them using Phoenix components, had originated in his office, among them the Penitentiary Building (1853), an imposing structure featuring a temple exterior and a central cupola, and the Italianate Patrick Raleigh Building (1860), a tour de force of elaborate columns, arches and ornamented cornices. Hallock's architectural practice flourished as he added to his list of commercial and residential clients some of the city's most prominent families—among them, the Ladds, Corbetts, Failings and Starks. Soon, however, architects would begin to arrive in Portland from other cities, bringing with them design schemes more sophisticated than those favored by Hallock.

Between 1854 and 1873, five new architects took up permanent residence in the city, coming at intervals that seemed calculated to give each newcomer enough time to firmly establish his local reputation and practice. E. M. Burton's arrival in 1854 was followed, in 1862, by W. W. Piper's, then by John Nestor's in 1864, and, in rapid succession, by Justus Krumbein's in 1871 and Warren H. Williams's in 1873. While each of these masters of the iron age infused a distinctive style into the city's architecture, each architect managed to maintain continuity with the tradition his predecessor had cultivated. The history of Portland's cast-iron architects was full of cross-affiliations through which the baton of Hallock's architectural preeminence was passed from hand to hand, sometimes in lines of direct—and sometimes oblique—descent.

Burton who, according to cast-iron historian Hawkins, "typified the rugged individualist who helped form the character of pioneer Portland," migrated to the city from the mid-west in 1854. His architectural bag of tricks was crammed with the latest Eastern fashions, from the Greek Revival and Gothic to the General Grant Baroque and the Second Empire styles. Shortly after his arrival in Portland, Burton began to embellish the city's landscape with an impressive array of new buildings, which included the Gothic-inspired Episcopal Church (Trinity Parish, 1854), a two-story firehouse for the Vigilance Hook and Ladder Company Number 1 (1854), and Central School (1857–58). In 1869, he would astound the city with his impressive design for the St. Charles Hotel—a three-story brick and iron extravaganza boasting a French-inspired Mansard roof—that became the center of Portland's social life for at least a decade. When completed, the St. Charles became an instant eye-grabber. "The top story is unlike anything ever built in Oregon," the 1869 *Portland Directory* reported, apparently ignoring the fact that in the same year, the San Francisco firm of Stephen Hedders Williams and Son had brought the first mansard roof to the clock tower atop the Odd Fellows Temple (1869).

Burton joined Hallock, his main competitor, in 1862. Over the next six years, their collaboration would yield the First Presbyterian Church (1864), the Harrison Street School, the Savier and Company Building, the Oregon Steam Navigation Company Building (1865), the Pearne Building (1865) and the Gilman Block (1868). His fascination with Italianate styles became apparent in both the First Presbyterian Church and the Oregon Steam Navigation Company Building. The design for the steeple of the First Presbyterian Church included a spectacular Venetian window, the first, according to Hawkins, gracing a Portland building and "conveying . . . images of European gothic architecture, and exotic suggestions of that Grand City of the Adriatic." After this series of joint ventures, however, Burton's and Hallock's careers would take divergent tracks. Sometimes working alone, but more often in association with a succession of young architects, Burton would fill in Portland's architectural fabric with a number of fine cast-iron buildings.

Hallock's architectural fortunes, however, would peak during his association with Burton. Taking an increasingly stronger interest in the production of iron architectural and structural components, Hallock joined with Portlanders John Nation and John L. Thomas in establishing the Willamette Iron Works in 1865. Their firm competed successfully with the Portland Foundry (which had been launched in 1853 by Captain James Turnbull, H. W. Davis and David Monastes) and with the Oregon Iron Works, founded in 1863. Nor would their venture suffer from the appearance of yet another local ironmonger, the Smith Brothers' Foundry and Iron Works (later, Smith and Watson) in the same year.

Portland's infatuation with cast-iron buildings had become so intense by the late 1860s that the 16 September 1868 *Oregonian* reported that "the iron foundry business seems likely to become the leading feature of Oregon enterprises. There are four foundries in the city and they are all kept busy, some of them running day and night."

The arrival of William W. Piper in 1863 must certainly have been welcomed by the proprietors of the city's foundries. Particularly in the early 1870s, the most prolific years of his Portland career, Piper would make considerable additions to the growing waterfront community, which propelled the city to new architectural heights. A native of New Hampshire, Piper was drawn to Portland by an advertisement soliciting proposals for the new courthouse which the Court of Multnomah County projected for the site currently occupied by Pioneer Courthouse. The possibility of securing the $200 award for the winning entry was sufficient to entice the architect from Idaho's Rocky Bar mining region.

As it happened, Burton had also set his sights on winning the competition, and the two architects joined forces. Their Italianate design was to the judges' taste.

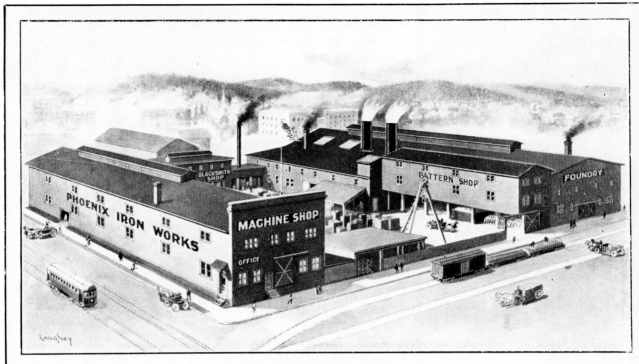

PHOENIX IRON WORKS
ENGINEERS, FOUNDERS AND MACHINISTS
BUILDING AND STRUCTURAL WORK

Office and Works:
Hawthorne Ave. and
E. Third St.

Telephone
East 29; Home B 1145
Portland, Oregon

PHOENIX IRON WORKS
architect unknown
date?

Cruciform in plan, and rising two grandiose stories, the stately building featured a 106-foot tall windowed dome at the center. From the balcony at the base of the dome, Portlanders gained a new perspective on their city's natural and artificial beauties. At the same time, they could draw favorable comparisons between the achievements of their urban microcosm and their chief rival to the south. "Here is a city of no insignificant proportions, out of debt," the editorial comments in the 7 August 1866 *Oregonian* pointed out. "And here is a most creditable building for the county of Multnomah, costing $80,000 and paid for when completed. As the *Bulletin* correspondent once remarked, an example of 'pay as you go' which he begged to commend to the debt-ridden and interest-paying communities of California, who sometimes sneer at Oregon slowness."

To be sure, neither Piper nor Burton provided any fodder for the State's ungenerous reputation. After a five-year absence from Portland, Piper returned to the city to challenge Burton's primacy. Garnering the lion's share of prestigious commissions during the late 1860s, the two architects were virtually mass-producing iron-fronted buildings along First and Front streets. More often than not, they would find themselves working in the close proximity, as they did in adjoining structures for the Ankeny Block (1869, Piper), the Thompson-Reed Building (1870–71) and Savier and Co. Building, or "filling in" each other's projects, as Piper did with his addition to Burton's Oregon Steam and Navigation Company Block (1865, Burton; 1870, Piper). A splendid Florentine structure with an impressive arcade of cast-iron columns, the Navigation Company Block was de-

186

molished in 1941 to make way for the Harbor Drive expansion.

Burton's and Piper's predilection for Italianate styles—often extending to the use of the same patterns—gave remarkable unity to the north end of the city. Their stylistic compatibility to some extent, persuaded them to join forces (officially) in 1871. Their partnership would be brief, but brilliant in its achievements. In a little over a year, the firm built a spate of splendid structures to accommodate the city's dandies and criminals, journalists and gastronomes and devotees of the theater and high culture. Their buildings signaled that Portland had left behind its makeshift adolescence and was entering into the first glow of young adulthood.

Dekum's Block (1871), which occupied the northwest corner of First and Washington streets, was one of the more substantial commercial structures in the city. With its Venetian arched windows and robust cast-iron parapet—punctuated, over the main doorway, by a broken pediment—the block offered a sweeping expanse of glass windows at street level. The sparkling display windows belonged to the drygoods house of S. Lipman and Company, forerunner of Lipman's Department Store. Much to the city's discredit, Dekum's Block was demolished in 1954.

The Portland City Jail (1872), the "forerunner" of Zimmer Gunsul Frasca's Justice Center (1984), was a somber two-story palace of stone, brick and cast-iron ornamentation. Its strictly symmetrical design, featuring no fewer than two broken pediments at the parapet, was, according to Portland historian Harvey W. Scott, "somewhat grim and stern in general appearance, but very well suited to its purpose." In 1912, the jail yielded its site to the present police headquarters building.

For the Masonic Hall (1871), the architects abandoned the Italianate style which both had favored for commercial structures, and chose, instead, a grandiose Second Empire style. Festooned with paired columns at the second and third stories, and topped with a mansard roof, the building resembled a four-tiered wedding cake. In the same year, they received the enviable commission to design the South Wing of the New Market Block.

Much of the detailing Burton and Piper had used for the Dekum's Block would make a reappearance in the two-story New Market Block, South Wing (1871) on the corner of First and Ash streets, where it has survived to the present. Featuring iron console brackets emblazoned with scrolls, leaves and grape clusters, the building was originally built to house the offices of the *Portland Bulletin*. The opening of the New Market Theater (1875) would anchor the city's cultural life firmly at the north end of First Street. One of Burton and Piper's finest efforts, the Theater building displayed huge iron columns, ornamented arches and exquisite Venetian windows. Within its ornamented walls, it offered Portlanders the combined delights of "bread and circus." The first floor housed a 200-foot arcade lined with marble produce stalls.

The combination of hygiene and beauty drew immediate plaudits from local commentators, such as the writer in the *West Shore* of May 1876, who noted that, "It is a matter of pride with our citizens, and especially the owner, Captain Ankeny, that they can truthfully say that even San Francisco, with its 160,000 inhabitants, can not show so neat, clean and well furnished a public market." And while San Francisco would still outstrip Portland's fine new theater, the lavish, 1,200 seat installation on the building's second and third floors would be touted as "*The* High-Class Theater" north of San Francisco. Between 1875 and 1887, the height of the theater's popularity and prestige, a curtain drop featuring a "Mediterranean View" would rise on such outstanding stars as Helene Modjeska, Annie Pixley, Fannie Davenport, Henry Ward Beecher and John H. Sullivan. Elegant patrons would also applaud such visiting dignitaries as General Ulysses S. Grant.

After the New Market Theater, Burton and Piper completed several other commissions. A series of awkward problems which arose during construction of the New Market Theater, however, led to the dissolution of their partnership. Burton, who had been keeping an eye on Warren H. Williams ever since the young architect had come to town to supervise construction of the Odd Fellows Temple (1869), formed a new partnership with the San Francisco architect one month after his arrival in Portland on 22 January 1873.

Piper, in the meantime, was doing his best to secure a stable position in the increasingly competitive architectural market. He affiliated with Sacramento bridge-builder, H. R. Leonard, and completed a series of projects until the recession of 1873, coupled with disastrous fires in December 1872 and August 1873, brought his practice to a virtual standstill. One of his memorable projects of this period was the Portland Central School (1872), whose mansard tower lent distinction to an otherwise ordinary three-story wooden structure.

SMITH AND WATSON BUILDING
Warren H. Williams
1883

In 1883, Piper's school would fall victim to the wrecker's ball. On its site, construction would begin on the Portland Hotel, whose appearance would ominously mark the demise of Portland's great iron age. Piper's two-story Smiths' Block (1872), however, would survive to the present. The half-block structure that once housed a bustling stock exchange, would become the only remaining example of Piper's "solo" commissions in cast-iron. Somewhat abbreviated to accommodate a parking lot in the 1950s, and solicitously restored in the early 1960s, this wonderfully detailed building would be all that remained of the refined Florentine Renaissance style Piper introduced to the city in his design for the Ankeny and Watson Building (1868). In its day, this cast-iron pattern graced no fewer than eight structures, along First and Front Streets and, in Hawkins' words, brought "to the streets of Portland an architectural unity rarely seen in any United States city at any time."

Deady Hall, at the University of Oregon, would be Piper's finest architectural achievement and, sadly, his last. An austerely elegant building terminating in a grace-

ful Mansard roof that sprouted twin dormered towers, Deady Hall signaled an ominous decline in Piper's fortunes. Hard hit by the 1873 recession and encountering innumerable delays in collecting his fee for the Deady Hall project, the Portland architect sold his practice to Justus Krumbein and W. G. Gilbert, two rising stars on the Portland architectural circuit.

For several years, Piper retired both from the city and from architecture. His brief "sabbatical," however, did nothing to improve his chances when he returned to practice in 1876. For eight years he valiantly, and vainly, tried to regain a foothold in the profession. Finally, in 1886, saddled with debts and demoralized by lawsuits, he set off by train to visit a sister in Ohio. According to John Michael O'Hara, Piper's biographer, the architect "never reached his destination. As the train was approaching Medicine Bow, Wyoming, Piper, apparently in a crazed state, jumped up from his seat and ran to door screaming, 'Help me, help me! Will no one save me?' At that point, witnesses said, he 'threw open the door and plunged wildly' to his death."

WALDO BLOCK
Restoration by Allen, McMath, Hawkins
1984

Thankfully, the stress and strain of cast-iron architecture would be a perilous undertaking only in Piper's case. While a dearth of business drove this talented designer out of the city, other architects would succeed fabulously in launching new careers. John Nestor, an accomplished San Francisco architect, brought his practice to Portland in 1864. Three of his notable buildings—the Carter Building (1868), the Hodge-Calef Building (1868) and the Ladd and Tilton Bank Building (1868)—introduced a continental glamor to the city's waterfront and fueled the fashion for commercial palaces in the Italianate style. A year before Nestor's Venetian design was constructed, Portlanders marveled at the Bank of British Columbia Building (1873, A. H. Jordan). Delicately worked into a small triangular site, this Palladian three-story structure was probably the city's first "flatiron" building. Painted—like the Carter Building—to resemble white marble, Nestor's bank was a worthy antecedent to the august bank structures that A. E. Doyle would subsequently bequeath to the city in the early decades of the twentieth century.

The Ladd and Tilton Bank sparked a trend among Portland bankers to solicit building designs from out-of-town architects. As a result, the city acquired two of its finest buildings, both designed by the acclaimed San Francisco architect Clinton Day. Described by Hawkins as "one of the best [cast-iron buildings] ever to be constructed in Portland," the Ainsworth Block (1881) rose three graceful stories to a splendid cornice capped with

pediments and finials. The corner entry, overhung by horizontal belt cornices that were cantilevered above the banking entrance, was defined by paired iron columns, which formed monumental portals on either side of the entrance. Behind the wood-and-glass door, the banking firm of Ainsworth and Company, composed of J. C. and George J. Ainsworth, L. Leander and William J. Hawkins, conducted business until 1902, when it merged with the United States National Bank.

Not to be outdone, the First National Bank also commissioned Day to design its new building in 1882. An even more grandiose structure, the First National Bank boasted three-foot thick walls of basaltic rock on the lower-wall floors and entry portals that seemed designed to defy the assault of time, recessions and bank robbers. When it opened, the First National moved a local commentator to remark that "It is the most permanent and enduring building in Portland, and was erected just in time to mark, as a monument, the opening of the era of the city's material greatness. It will stand as it is for a thousand years while fifty generations of merchants pass in and out of its portals." History would show that barely five generations would pass through the bombastic portals of this fine building. After surviving several economic disasters and numerous floods, the First National Bank Building would vanish in 1954.

By comparison with Day's architectural extravaganzas, the Ladd and Tilton Bank, was a delicate jewel.

Based on the sixteenth-century Venetian Libreria Vecchia (1536, J. Sansovino), Nestor's bank building seemed perfectly attuned to the modulations of Portland's misty light. The *Portland Directory* of 1868 drew attention to this feature when it praised the facade for being "so artistically arranged as to light and shade as to give the building a beautiful appearance." In 1954, when it was demolished, a Portland contractor salvaged the cast-iron front, which was eventually incorporated into the Ladd and Bush Bank (now the United States National Bank, Salem Branch) restored in 1967.

Nestor's sophisticated designs were held in high esteem, so much so that some local architects "borrowed" his design scheme for rusticated pilasters. The age, to be sure, did not place great value on original designs, but rather, on inventive combination of stylistic options culled from a variety of sources. In this respect, Portland's early architects—perhaps inadvertently—showed a lively respect for the existing architectural fabric and created a wonderfully integrated commercial core. Borrowing ornamental details and structural components from each other's structures, they were "contextualists" long before the concept would be "rediscovered" in the 1980s.

Buildings designed by outsiders were particularly valued for suggesting new stylistic directions. With his Ladd and Tilton Bank, Nestor ushered in the fad for Venetian palaces that had been popular on the East Coast since the early 1850s. (An almost identical double to his bank could be found in Brooklyn's Ironclad Bank, 1868.) One of the notable off-spring of this Venetian fever was E. M. Burton's splendid Central Block (1879). Burton, of course, had long nourished a fondness for the architecture of Venice, but in this structure he offered a specific reference for his Italianate detailing. The influence of Andrea Palladio, Italy's sixteenth-century architectural genius, was clearly stated in Burton's use of the tripartite "Palladian window" above the corner entrance. The foliated ornamentation intervening between the column capitals and the arches also derived from Venetian designs. As cast-iron historian Hawkins noted in *The Grand Era of Cast-Iron Architecture in Portland*, Burton's decorative motifs clearly alluded to such late fifteenth-century Venetian structures as the Scuola Di San Marco. This remarkable structure would dissappear from the cityscape in 1942.

The Bishop's House (1879), most likely designed by P. Heurn of San Francisco, sparked the fashion for modern Gothic buildings that would include such gems as Williams' Allen and Lewis Block (1882), and Krumbein's Ladd Block (1881), Green's Building (1882), Bickel Block (1883) and Kamm Block (1884).

Two picturesque fragments of distant cities appeared in Portland with the construction of the Esmond Hotel (1879), designed by J. A. Knapp, and the B. L. Stone Building (1883). While, by 1879, the city could offer its visitors dignified accommodations in the St. Charles Hotel (1869, Burton), it still had nothing to rival San Francisco's luxurious Palace Hotel (1874), designed by Brooklyn architect John P. Gaynor for the colorful millionaire banker William C. Ralston. The Esmond Hotel was a bold attempt to correct this imbalance. On the premise that what had worked for San Francisco was bound to work for Portland, Knapp scaled down the Palace hotel design and replicated it, bay for bay, ornament for ornament, including the opulent Mansard roof.

Parisian chic would come to the city with the erection of the B. L. Stone Building in 1883. Until 1968, when the structure was demolished to make way for improvements around Civic Auditorium, the Stone Building offered the city-bound traveler a glimpse of sixteenth century Renaissance France. Modeled on the famous Parisian Place Des Vosges, it played off brick against stone quoins, pediments and sills, and cast-iron pilasters that bore a faintly Gothic inspiration.

While it was customary for most cast-iron buildings to be assembled from components prefabricated either locally or on the West Coast, one of Portland's cast-iron palaces had the distinction of traversing half the globe before arriving in the city. Cast in the Baltimore foundry of Hayward and Bartlett, the Corbett Building (1870) was shipped to the city by way of Cape Horn. Something of a cause célèbre by virtue of this circuitous journey, the Corbett Building also had other unusual architectural attributes. The simplicity of its columned design, broken only by the dainty scrollwork at the roofline arch, was alien to the luxuriant ornamentation of most existing cast-iron structures. In this respect, the Corbett became an early harbinger of the honest, functionalist aesthetic that would produce the steel-beamed towers of the 1960s. In 1956, this dainty prototype of the glass-and-steel boxes was demolished to accommodate a parking lot between the new approaches to the Morrison Bridge. In this respect, it would continue—even in its absence—to bear out the remarks of Ferdinand C. Latrobe, who wrote in *Iron Men and Their Dogs*, that in 1868 "an east-coast manufactured cast-iron building could be shipped around the Horn to be erected in a

Pacific Coast city as fast as it was unloaded. The Corbett Building in Portland stands today as a reminder of this impetuous haste of the Golden West." A hundred years later, the same impetuosity would erase this edifice to permit Portlanders even greater speed of movement.

Portland's architectural flowering during the decades of the "Iron Age" did not progress unchecked by the forces of nature or financial disasters. Every decade's growth was nipped by successive floods which pushed the swollen waters of the Willamette against the cast-iron facades along Front and First streets. Photographers recording the disasters gave no indication of the psychological and financial trauma to which these floods must surely have subjected the citizenry. Instead, they offered a glimpse into a wonderfully exotic city of Italianate palaces rising out of murky water with all the splendor of an Americanized Venice.

During the record flood of June 1894, Portlanders cheerfully paddled about the watery streets as far west as N.W. Tenth and Glisan and s.w. Sixth and Washington. As Portland historian E. Kimbark MacColl noted in *The Shaping of A City*, "August Erickson, proprietor of the saloon boasting the longest bar in the world—684 feet long, horseshoe shaped—rented a houseboat and stocked it full of booze and other necessities for his thirsty customers. . . . Row boats, homemade crafts, catamarans and canoes brought customers to the floating saloon. . . . Some of the customers never left the floating saloon until the waters receded *and* they were broke." The frequent fires which swept through the business district left Portlanders equally unperturbed. Indeed, the fire of 1872, bemoaned one of the great disasters to have befallen the city since its founding, brought an unexpected benefit in the form of Warren H. Williams, who was to become Portland's brightest luminary of the cast-iron age.

The son of a famous San Francisco architect Stephen Hedders Williams, Williams settled in Portland in 1873. He had visited the city earlier, in 1869, to supervise construction of the new Odd Fellows Temple which the firm of Stephen H. Williams and Son had designed. The conflagration of 1872 persuaded him that his future lay in rebuilding Portland, a task to which he applied himself immediately upon arriving in the city, when Burton invited him to form a partnership. A still more devastating fire, which destroyed over 20 blocks of the city center in August of 1873, brought a bustling business in reconstructions and new commissions to the distinguished firm. During the duration of their partnership from 1873

to 1875, Burton and Williams would design a number of outstanding structures. After the firm dissolved, Williams joined Justus Krumbein, a German-born architect and recent newcomer, for a brief partnership lasting from 1876 to 1878.

Krumbein's considerable architectural erudition and European training offered an interesting counterpoint to Williams's Americanized Beaux-Arts training. During their collaboration, the two would display their stylistic ingenuity by striking a happy balance between the Italianate proclivities of Williams and the more flamboyant and eclectic tastes of Krumbein. Among the memorable fruits of their association would be the Cosmopolitan Block (1878), whose arched central cornice featured a sculpted alighting eagle, the sophisticated Alisky and Hegele Building (1878) and the Fechheimer and White Building (1885), which still adorns s.w. Front Avenue.

By 1878, however, the two architects decided to go their separate ways, so that each could give full expression to his distinctive vision. Staggeringly prolific, Williams would contribute a grand array of buildings to the tightening fabric of the city's commercial zone. He would also delight the city with a number of innovative designs that documented his impressive ability to keep pace with the changing world of fashion—and of technology. In 1880 Williams's Labbé Block would not only be the first *fully* four-storied commercial block in the city, but would also be the first building to feature a passenger elevator. Some of the smartest shops in town opened for business in this finely decorated building.

The Allen and Lewis Block of 1882, offered an imaginative blend of Italianate inspiration and Gothic Revival styling that showed the subtle influence of Krumbein. But the ornate brackets and medallions adorning the intervals between the windows along the second and third stories carried a discreet reference to the Austro-Hungarian aesthetic that would pervade the Cooks' Building, also completed in 1882. Applauded as "one of the neatest and most beautiful business blocks in Portland," Cooks' Building was embellished with iron-columned bays, Corinthian columns and heavily fluted pilasters resting on rusticated pedestals, bringing a touch of Central European urbanity to its stretch of Front Street. Riverfront "improvements" removed this civilized monument in 1942.

Williams's enthusiasm for high-rise structures was expressed again in 1885 with the Portland Savings Bank, which took its stand diagonally across the street from the Labbé Block. A corner structure with street-level columns and pilasters of gigantic proportions, the Portland Savings Bank sported an imaginative tower and a graceful Mansard roof. According to Hawkins, Williams's bank signaled the limit to which Italianate form could be stretched to accommodate ever taller structures. Hawkins noted that "four stories were about the maximum the design could accomplish well. . . . But clearly, if elevators were permitting taller structures, an entirely new architectural philosophy would be needed to accomplish this."

The Portland Savings Bank would be the last building in Portland to use cast-iron in its upper floors. A new structural and visual aesthetic was slowly beginning to percolate into the architectural subconscious of the city. By 1887, fresh architectural currents, structural principles and new tastes and aspirations would pour into the city on three recently completed railway lines. The Northern Pacific had arrived in 1883, followed, in 1885, by the Union Pacific, and, in 1887, by the Southern Pacific. Ironically, the dawning of Portland's railroad era would spell the demise of its cast-iron architecture.

Before vanishing from the repertoire of architectural modes, however, the cast-iron aesthetic would make an intensely glorious showing on Justus Krumbein's extraordinary Kamm Block, completed in 1884. Since venturing into his own architectural practice in 1872, Krumbein had been displaying his structural versatility by ornamenting the fashionable residential sectors of the city with splendid homes, such as the Captain Flanders house (1882), the C. E. Smith house (ca. 1882), the George V. James house (1882) and the astoundingly ornate R. B. Knapp house (1882), a fabulous amalgam of Queen Anne, Japanese and Stick Style elements.

At the same time, Krumbein continued in the cast-iron idiom. The Bickel Block (1883), owned by the confectioner Frederick Bickel, was a spun-sugar fantasy of Gothic geometric patterning. It was only a dress rehearsal, however, for Krumbein's crowning masterpiece, the Kamm Block of 1884. Commending the structure in the November 1885 *Northwest Illustrated Monthly Magazine*, Thomas B. Merry wrote, "Mr. Jacob Kamm, the owner, is justly praised for the liberality and enterprising spirit shown in the erection of such a magnificent structure in these dull times."

Times, indeed, were dull, since the national economic dip of 1883 had not spared Portland, and had toppled more than one financial empire, including that of Henry Villard. But Kamm, an enterprising Swiss who had come to make his fortune in the West, was not easily intimi-dated. He earmarked the fabulous sum of $125,000 for his new palace and Krumbein's design did full justice to the princely sum. The four-story structure, complete with a central tower in the "Modern Gothic" style, was a veritable encyclopedia of the historical styles, which made their appearance in the city during the previous three decades. Reminiscent in its overall design of a late Tuscan palace, the facade featured bold Gothic lines, large wood sculptures, Romanesque columns, pediments with flying eagles, rusticated pilasters, and two wooden female Hermes supporting a Baroque balcony. By demolishing this fantastical period piece in 1948, the city shortsightedly deprived its subsequent architectural historicists of an invaluable three-dimensional reference work for their own contextualizing constructions.

The Kamm Block, however, was not the last cast-iron building to be erected in the city. That distinction would belong to the Rodney Glisan Building (1889), still standing on its original site at the southeast corner of Second and Ash. As if symbolic of its terminal position at the juncture of two architectural epochs, the Glisan Building summarized some of the most characteristic traits of the great period of cast-iron buildings, while at the same time foreshadowing the new stylistic influences, which would soon be disseminated by such new architectural stars as the firm of McCaw and Martin in the Dekum Building (1892). The rhythmical fenestration of the second floor, marked by piers fashioned to resemble columns, and the iron components on the street level, reiterated the dominant forms of the cast-iron tradition. The detailing, however, described by Hawkins as "somewhat Art Nouveau, if not Celtic, in origin," looked ahead to the feathery and floral motifs so cherished by Art Nouveau and Sullivanesque designers. In this respect, this Janus-faced building furnished an exemplary pivot on which the age would turn.

Only two of Portland's five masters of the cast-iron age—Burton and Krumbein—would negotiate the transition to the new age of stone and brick commercial structures. In 1883, Burton, the grand old master of iron, allied himself with William F. McCaw, one of the city's earliest practitioners in the Richardsonian Romanesque style. Although he continued to practice on a sporadic basis, Burton would quietly fade into history. Indeed, the extent of his involvement with McCaw would remain, to this day, uncertain. Only the redoubtable Krumbein would show the requisite vitality to continue his work into the twentieth century. Appropriately, he would close his career by contributing one last—though short-lived—structure for the Lewis and Clark Exhibition of 1905.

The signal that the reign of cast-iron architecture had come to an end was given when Henry Villard commissioned the New York firm of McKim, Mead and White to design his fabulous new Portland Hotel on the block bounded by s.w. Sixth, Morrison, s.w. Seventh and Yamhill. While the city's center had already begun its gradual shift west, Villard's hotel provided a glamorous crystal around which the vital new core could develop. Stylistically and geographically, this imposing structure would make a leap into new cultural, economic and architectural sensibilities.

Significantly, the Portland Hotel would spell double trouble for Portland's grand old iron district. When completed in 1890, it put an end to the dissemination of the cast-iron aesthetic, and in 1951, its demolition would give the green light for the wholesale destruction of the city's cast-iron heritage. The iron buildings that had made Portland something of an "overnight sensation" during the second half of the nineteenth century, crumbled, one by one, many of them victims of overnight fires, daytime demolition derbies and scrap-iron scavengers. Withstanding countless floods, fires, financial doldrums and the shifting winds of fashion, Portland's cast-iron "Venice by the Willamette" vanished like the lost city of Atlantis.

Recalling those years, architectural historian and preservationist George A. McMath described the temper of the times that had so little respect for preserving the old that was good. "I think you have to understand the mentality of the immediate post-war years," he said. "During the 1930s, virtually nothing was being built. The worriers were holding on to their money—if they had any to hold on to." World War II pacified the worriers, and peace brought a new burst of prosperity to the city. Between 1945 and 1949, the city attracted a host of new businesses and major corporations, including Reynolds Metals, Alcoa, Nabisco and the Continental Can Company. Eager to resume the pleasures and responsibilities of civilian life, returning veterans put new life into the residential building market. Downtown office space was in great demand, short supply and rented at a premium. Downtown streets were choked with traffic, and parking was becoming a rampant problem. "Finally, by the late 1940s," McMath explained, "post-war money was becoming available. And, by then, people wanted everything to be new, new, new. Anything old, to their way of thinking, might as well go to hell."

But Portlanders seemingly forgot that their obsession with novelty was just another twist in the spiral of recurring fashion. Despite the fact that they had seen history repeat itself, both globally and locally, they enthusiastically embraced a myopic perspective that denied value to the past. Had they spared only 20 more cast-iron buildings in the Yamhill and Skidmore Fountain districts; in addition to those that narrowly escaped destruction, Portland could have boasted a coherent, though Lilliputian "European" city along its waterfront that would have rivaled the historical SoHo District in New York.

The architectural landscape of the city would have borne more than a handful of orphaned traces of its urban beginnings. A *cluster*, and not merely a scattering of solitary specimens, would have provided the rich historical context and stylistic continuity that distinguishes a great city from one that is just a cut above the average. As Robert Frasca pointed out in an interview, "Great cities such as Paris or Rome, are not the work of a single creative impulse, or a single generation. They are built up gradually, much like geological strata, by the deposits of several successive generations."

Particularly in an age of sweeping cultural and social change, an uninterrupted stretch of cast-iron buildings would have done much to maintain the sense of continuity so crucial to the city's collective, historical identity. In the 1940s and 1950s, however, concern with history was at an all time low. The same kind of anti-historicism that created the disruption in the Beaux-Arts tradition in architecture after the crash in the 1930s, emerged again in the 1950s. "During the entire first phase of urban renewal," McMath observed, "mass clearance, freeways and parking lots for automobiles were the priority. The importance of preserving the old was almost forgotten, even by some of the city's best architects. Even some of the remodeling jobs Belluschi did in the early post-war period totally ignored the context." Little did architects know, at the time, that the historicist movement was in the wings, waiting to pounce on the past to ransack it for its riches.

The insensitivity to Portland's architectural past, however, did not sit well with McMath and William J. Hawkins III. Emerging from their adolescence when Portland's modernization was getting under way, these two architects (and future preservationists) were attached to the city by roots that ran deep into its past.

Great-grandson of Jonathan Kittredge, pioneer San Francisco foundryman, and grandson of William J.

Hawkins, prominent Portland banker, Hawkins would develop a passionate attachment to the city's dwindling number of cast-iron buildings. By a satisfying turn of history, the Kittredge-Sargent-Hawkins family would play a crucial role in helping Portland's cast-iron microcosm retrace the fate of the mythical bird for which the San Francisco foundry had been named. It had been Kittredge's Phoenix Iron Works that had supplied the first cast-iron fronts for Portland. And it would be the young Hawkins who, along with Frank Allen and George A. McMath (principals in the firm Allen, McMath, Hawkins), would breathe new life into the few cast-iron relics that would survive into the 1960s and 1970s.

Since the 1950s, Hawkins followed with grim fascination the demolition of Portland's cast-iron gems, recording, with camera and sketch pencil, the dismal rubble heaps to which the grand old fronts had been reduced—sometimes overnight. Over time, he found little satisfaction in playing the role of silent witness to this devastation. Rallying other devotees of cast-iron around him, he looked for ways to preserve the buildings whose destruction he could not stop.

In many instances, he would succeed in rescuing the battered fragments of dismembered fronts, just in the nick of time. His store of anecdotes would be full of hair-raising escapades, all-night vigils to fend off scrap-iron scavengers, and frantic pursuits, which sometimes ended in a disappointing glimpse of the final vestige of some cast-iron beauty disappearing into a fiery furnace. Because there were no appropriate facilities for storing the fragments he did manage to rescue, Hawkins would haul columns, pediments, arches, finials, balconies and leonine masks to the farm of his wife's parents. There, the skeletal and rusting remains of a city would crowd a barn and cover an entire field, waiting until they would again be pressed into service.

Taking a curatorial, rather than proprietary, interest in his cast-iron hoard, Hawkins was eager to place his orphans in hospitable homes. Some of the ironwork found its way into modernistic lobbies or into renovated old structures. This was the case with the balcony from the demolished Abington Building (1886), which reappeared to ornament the interior of the new Yamhill Market. Other components, such as those belonging to buildings that once fronted on the historic Skidmore Fountain (1888)—the work of nationally acclaimed New York sculptor Olin Warner—were returned to their original site during the 1976 restoration of the Skidmore-

Old Town Historic District, where they would sketchily revive the memory of the grandeur that had once been Skidmore Square.

In 1973, Hawkins formed the Portland Friends of Cast-Iron Architecture, an organization that worked to educate the public in the value of preserving the city's nearly lost heritage of iron-fronted buildings. Established to "encourage and promote a permanent historic district for Portland," and to purchase, secure and find displays for preserved artifacts, the Portland Friends of Cast-Iron Architecture was instrumental in establishing the Skidmore/Old Town and Yamhill historic districts. It also revived the memory of Portland's great architects of the cast-iron era, publishing newsletters that featured scrupulously researched biographies of Burton, Piper, Williams and Krumbien. By 1983, the organization assembled a collection of 243 artifacts, some of which, it was hoped, would find a permanent home in a small museum projected for one of the historic districts.

Not surprisingly, the initiative for reclaiming the old city from the hands of "modernizing" developers would lie with local architects whose vision of the city had been shaped not by professional training, but, rather, by the experience of having grown up in the city at a time when its historical architectural strata were still intact. Hawkins's concern for preserving and restoring the city's architectural past would be shared by McMath. Unlike many of Portland's prominent architects of the postwar era, who had migrated to the city as fully formed professionals, Hawkins and McMath were children of the city. The innumerable impressions of urban life culled from childhood years were the stuff that fed their enthusiasm for architecture and bred their sensitivity to the genius loci of Portland.

"That's probably the source of much of my concern for preserving the old architectural fabric of the city," McMath explained. "I grew up in Portland. I used to take the streetcar from my house on 24th Street and Knott and went to the downtown theaters for a dime. I was very involved, as I think most kids my age were, especially in the downtown area. I remember Broadway, with its very real, very strong sense of richness. We used to go to the Oyster Bar, to Jake's." Grandson of Portland's premier Beaux-Arts architect A. E. Doyle, McMath developed an intimate, familial affection for the city's architecture. "My parents went out quite a bit and we were always taken along. Of course, they would always point out that that was one of grandfather's buildings. I never knew him, since he died before I was born. And although, at the time, I wasn't aware of it, these experiences made a profound impression on me."

The subliminal messages of those years, however, had less to do with architecture than they did with the peculiar energy and temperament of a city that, for McMath, was both stage and companion. The Portland of his boyhood and adolescence was not an abstract inventory of architectural theories and styles. It was an intricate, living fabric of impressions and memories of visits to the Portland Art Museum, rainy afternoons at the Broadway and the Paramount, and the ritual of meeting friends "under the clock" at the Meier and Frank department store. "In those years, as far as any teenager in Portland was concerned," McMath recalled, "that was where you went . . . the great clock by the elevator. I don't know what the equivalent would be today, although I'm sure there must be one, maybe the Metro Cafe. At least that's where they bring their orange hair."

But if Meier and Frank's clock was the center for the city's youthful subculture, the Portland Hotel, which stood on the site of the present Pioneer Courthouse Square, was the real and symbolic hub of the city. "This famous hostelry for years has been this city's guest house, occupying an entire block in the very heart of the city, yet it has an atmosphere of seclusion," ran the description published in the 1948–49 edition of *Capitol's Who's Who for Oregon*. "Notable is the hotel's open courtyard and its grassy plot and fragrant blossoms and vine-clad veranda. Every room is an outside room, handsomely furnished. From the upper windows may be seen the green heights above the city, the Cascades, the snow-clad peaks, the famous Mt. Hood. The Portland Hotel is in the center of everything, within a block of nearly all places of entertainment, across the street from the famed Meier and Frank Department Store, adjacent to a post office and bank and the principal office buildings and retail shops."

Many of McMath's childhood memories were linked with Sunday brunches at the Portland Hotel, particularly during the Depression years. In 1950, word went around that the stately hotel was to be demolished. "I remember having lunch with my mother there just before I went into the Army," McMath remembered, "I knew it would be the last time I would be in there."

The hotel came down in 1951, and with its demolition, much of the continuity and "street energy" that McMath remembered as such an integral part of his Portland experience began to dissipate. When he re-

turned in 1956, parking lots and garages had proliferated in the downtown core. Along the waterfront, urban planners and developers dismantled much of the cast-iron armature, leaving a messy tabula rasa to accommodate the smooth stretches of the expanded Harbor Drive. Huge gaps appeared in the intricate three-dimensional jigsaw puzzle of the built landscape, and the city's vital energy was slowly seeping out to the suburbs. By 1959, when McMath completed his architectural training, much of the city's fabric was frayed.

Describing the painful impressions which the spectacle of Portland's second adolescence produced in him, the architect recalled that, "Much of my [subsequent] activity was a response to all that mindless demolition of the 1950s." In this respect, his architectural training played an ancillary role in nurturing his commitment to preserving the city's architectural past. As he himself explained, his career goals were shaped by two distinct strains. "My education was 'classically' modernist and, aside from a few obligatory courses in architectural history, payed little attention to the deep past. Mies van der Rohe, Le Corbusier, and Frank Lloyd Wright were our heroes." On the other hand, his sentimental attachment to the city of his boyhood activated a genuine historical consciousness. "My concern for the Portland Hotel and the city's historical tradition is entirely separate from my intellectual development as an architect. It came out of a deep, visceral response, from the realization that parts of my past were being taken away from me, and would continue to be taken away unless something was done to stop the erosion."

In 1959, when he joined the firm of Stewart and Richardson, McMath would find a professional channel for expressing—and acting upon—his devotion to the city's historical riches. At the same time, an interesting twist was added to the fantastically interwoven history of Portland's architectural profession. The firm with which McMath began his career—and with which he would remain to the present—had been assembled in 1952 by Donald J. Stewart, a direct "alumnus" of A. E. Doyle's original firm.

Between 1922 and 1923, Stewart had been one of Doyle's star proteges. After touring Europe and working in a New York firm, he returned to the Pacific Northwest, opening his own office in Vancouver, Washington in 1931. Doyle's firm, in the meantime, passed into the hands of Dave M. Jack, William H. Crowell, Sid Lister and Pietro Belluschi, who, since 1943, had continued the practice under his own name. After Belluschi sold his practice to Skidmore, Owings and Merrill in 1951, two of his colleagues—chief designer Kenneth E. Richardson and chief draftsman Frank C. Allen—joined Stewart in a new partnership, swelling the firm's name to Stewart, Richardson, Allen, McMath. Early in 1963, Richardson left the firm to open his own practice in Seattle. The Stewart, Allen and McMath configuration lasted until 1967, when the addition of Hawkins—who had started his career as an office boy with Skidmore, Owings and Merrill—yielded the present office of Allen, McMath and Hawkins.

The principal players who would take part in some of the most exciting and excellent restoration projects of the next two decades were in place. Appropriately, the firm that reclaimed many of the finest buildings in Portland and would educate the public on its lost and restored architectural heritage, could trace its lineage through direct blood lines and oblique professional links to the office of Portland's master historicist, A. E. Doyle. Only public apathy and unenlightened legislation now stood in the way of the most exciting reclamation projects the city had ever undertaken.

By the mid-1960s, a new attitude toward the city's "modernization" began to manifest itself among many of its residents. As Carl Abbott pointed out in *Portland: Planning, Politics, and Growth in a Twentieth-Century City*, "Portland planning went through startling changes between 1966 and 1972, as the emergence of active and often angry neighborhood organizations made local residents the actors rather than the objects in neighborhood decisions." On the national front, as well, the tide was turning against the insensitive and often needless destruction of some of the country's most significant historic buildings and districts.

In 1966, a national framework for historic preservation on a broad scale was created with the passage of the National Historic Preservation Act, in which Congress declared that significant architectural achievements of the past must be preserved. To this statement of principle, it added the means for channeling and implementing preservationists' concern with the rescue of historic buildings. Matching grants-in-aid were authorized to state and local governments, and assistance was extended to private preservation organizations through the National Trust for Historic Preservation. The act also provided for expansion of the National Register of Historic Places, a growing list of properties worthy of preservation, and assured that these places would not be destroyed without due process. At the base of this legislation lay the belated recognition of the profound psychological effects of landmarks and of their crucial role in giving a sense of orientation to the American people.

This point was reiterated by James Biddle, president of the National Trust for Historic Preservation, and Thomas D. F. Hoving, director of the Metropolitan Museum of Art, in 1970 when New York's Metropolitan Museum celebrated its centenary anniversary with the important exhibition "The Rise of An American Architecture 1815–1915." "The historic landmarks that still surround us, many of them largely unnoticed, can greatly enrich our lives," Biddle and Hoving wrote in their foreword to the exhibition catalog. "This is not simply a nice thing. It is a crucial thing. In the midst of the dislocations of today's life, landmarks can help provide emotional security and sanity. America came of age and established an architectural identity in its nineteenth-century past. Today, in the twentieth century, it has attained an age when it must realize that its national past is an indispensable part of its present."

By the mid-1960s, Portland was beginning to attain this age of sober reflection. McMath recalled two events which were especially crucial in helping Portlanders reassess their relationship to the past—and the future—of their architectural environment. "In January of 1964, when the historic Pittock Mansion was slated for the hammer," the architect explained, "several of us decided it was time to get involved." A campaign, which was a partnership of public and private forces, was quickly organized, and the extravagant French Renaissance chateau designed by San Francisco architect Foulkes was rescued.

More significant and far-ranging, however, was the campaign which Lewis Crutcher, Walter Gordon, Dan McGoodwin (who led the effort) and a handful of other concerned architects and citizens initiated in 1965. In this instance, the fate of an entire district—the Skidmore Historic District—was at stake. Underfoot were plans to construct an elevated access ramp from Harbor Drive to Ash Street. "A lot of people coming into the city from Harbor Drive had to cross First Street to get into the downtown," McMath recalled. "This was felt to be inconvenient."

The Ash Street Ramp project, as it was known, would have eliminated the additional maneuver, as well as the integrity of one of the city's last remaining colonies of historic buildings. Metropolitan Planning Commissioner William Bowes, whom McMath described as a "man of the old Robert Moses school," had asked the highway people to design a ramp that would have gone over Front Avenue, wiping out the Smiths' Block. Still elevated, it would have continued along Ash Street before finally touching ground at Third Avenue.

"The Ash Street Ramp," McMath explained, "would have divided the district and isolated it from the rest of the downtown." Although the Skidmore District had been identified as a "historic" district in 1959 and had enjoyed some design review protection, the Ash Street project dramatically illustrated the need for instituting muscular preservation legislation. "In the old days of private government," McMath recalled, "these decisions were made without any public consultation. The construction contract came up before the City Council and by sheer chance someone caught it on the . . . agenda and managed to get it stopped."

The next major impetus to historic preservation came in 1965, when the Ladd Block was demolished "virtually overnight." In keeping with the Urban Renewal "area guide plan," the Portland Development Commission had strongly recommended the preservation of some picturesque buildings, including the iron-fronted Ladd Block on the northwest corner of s.w. Fourth Avenue and Columbia Street. A sketch of the proposed restoration appeared in the *Oregonian* in 1965, and within a week of its publication the owners, Boyd Coffee Company, opted to demolish the building in order to make room for a new warehouse.

The prospect that other historic buildings would fall prey to these "midnight" disappearing acts fueled formation of another citizens committee to insure continued protection for this stratum of Portland architecture. Working under the aegis of the Portland Art Commission, the ad hoc committee transformed the Ladd Block into a cause célèbre, and proceeded to draft an ordinance which would establish formal procedures for maintaining historic structures and areas in the city.

In September 1968, Portland officially adopted City Ordinance, Chapter 33.120, "Historical Districts, Buildings and Sites," which provided the regulatory controls and administrative protocol for preserving historical landmarks and districts. A further incentive to local proprietors and real estate developers came in 1975, when the Oregon Property Tax Assessment Freeze was passed. According to this legislation, buildings with historical status would be taxed for a period of 15 years at their assessed value prior to restoration.

For owners of landmark structures, the tax assessment freeze gave an opportunity to recover investments

that would go into improvements and did much to enhance the appeal of preservation efforts. The introduction of the Urban Conservation Fund in August 1976, cleared away additional financial obstacles. Jointly administered by the Portland Development Commission and the Portland Historical Landmarks Commission, the Urban Conservation Fund provided loans, grants and various other financial incentives to assist preservation and restoration of historic properties.

To assure sensitive urban development, in 1972, the Portland City Council adopted a series of guidelines, *Planning Guidelines: Portland Downtown Plan*, prepared by a Citizens Advisory Committee to assure sensitive urban development. Drafted to enhance the architectural integrity of the downtown core and to create distinctive districts within the city, the *Planning Guidelines* projected enlightened, context-sensitive objectives as the desired ends of the design review process. Additional aid to developers and preservationists was supplied in 1981, when ERTA Tax credits were introduced, giving 25 percent tax credits to proprietors of developed or improved historic landmarks.

While, to be sure, much of the cast-iron heritage had already been eliminated by the early 1960s, and irreversible damage had been done to many distinctive districts of the city, legislative efforts of the last two decades did much to insure that future generations of Portlanders would be able to read the past of their city on the faces of their buildings.

A number of conscientious citizens joined in the effort to stem the tide of deterioration, neglect and indifference to the handful of surviving cast-iron structures. Firms led by Norman and Stanich, Neil Farnham and Wolff, Zimmer, Gunsul and Frasca, as well as real estate developers extended the life-span of some remarkable cast-iron buildings.

Thanks to the sympathetic restoration work of Norman and Stanich, the Love Building (1878) and the Harker Building (1880), which had constituted a stylistically unified stretch of cast-iron structures along First Avenue, evoked the grandeur that had once been Portland's cast-iron thoroughfare. Their restoration of the Mikado Block (1880) preserved the memory of Portland's infatuation with Gilbert and Sullivan's delightful operetta *The Mikado*, in whose honor the richly detailed structure has been named.

In Portland's "Old Town," the Naito brothers revived three pivotal relics from Portland's cast-iron age— the Merchants' Hotel (1880, attributed to Warren H.

MILLER PAINT (CUILLY) BUILDING
architect unknown
1884

Williams), the Bickel Block (1883, Justus Krumbein) and the Simon Building of 1883. The Fechheimer and White Building, which had used Corinthian columns and arches similar to those chosen by Williams and Krumbein for the 1878 Cosmopolitan Block, was restored by owners Ralph Walstrom and Jeff Holbrook to stand as a fragmentary reminder of the sophisticated elegance of Portland's pre–automotive Front Street.

In refurbishing the Franz Building (1878) and the Failing Building (1886, Warren H. Williams), architect Neil Farnham and the firm of Wolff, Zimmer, Gunsul and Frasca revived the customary practice of Portland's cast-iron architects who set up their offices in buildings they had recently designed. According to Hawkins, when Wolff, Zimmer, Gunsul and Frasca took over the Failing Building in 1975 they did much to "bring some

MIKADO BLOCK
C. E. Smith
1880

stability to a group of buildings in the Skidmore Historic District that would otherwise have disappeared years ago."

In the endeavor to preserve and reconstruct the largely lost epic of Portland's historic heritage, however, the firm of Allen, McMath and Hawkins would take the lead. Working as principal architects or consultants on nearly 50 restoration projects within the city and the

state, members of the firm would become the city's leading experts on outmoded building techniques, materials and styles.

As McMath recalled, the firm's preeminence in this highly specialized vein of architectural design developed gradually. "When I started out with the firm," McMath explained, "I did several typically modernist buildings. In the early 1960s, when a few restoration projects came along, I was the member of the firm who took an interest in them. It wasn't really a matter of my *professional* preference for the 'old stuff'. Rather, what got me involved was the sense that these were buildings that *needed* to be saved."

McMath's first project—restoration of the "Parsonage," an early pioneer wood frame structure built in 1841 in Salem, Oregon—gave him the opportunity to discover that his true architectural passion lay in restoration work. "I enjoyed the historical research and the investigative aspect of the project. In so many ways," McMath explained, "the restorer is like a detective. He has to find the original elements in the structure. He has to look under the surface, he has to be able to recognize clues and know what to look for. For example, the saw cuts might tell you that a piece was not part of the original structure because that particular technique of sawing wood was not used in that period. Some of these things I had learned in school, but most of the information I needed just wasn't a part of our post–Beaux Arts education."

The pivotal project—both for the firm, and for the city's restoration activities—came in 1970, with the commission to restore Pioneer Courthouse. Built between 1869 and 1875, this stately Italianate structure, topped by an exquisite octagonal wood cupola, led a precarious existence since the early 1930s, when the completion of the new U.S. Courthouse had rendered it obsolete. At that time, the Federal Government placed the old courthouse on the surplus property list and offered it for sale to private developers. This spurred one of the more picturesque collisions between local merchants and architects, and even sowed discord among the members of the city's architectural profession.

Taking a firm stand against profit-hungry commercial developers, the Portland Chapter of the AIA adopted a strong resolution urging preservation of the landmark building. Its sentiments, however, were not shared by Ellis Lawrence, one of the city's and the state's most distinguished and influential architects since the early decades of the twentieth century. Breaking ranks with his organization, Lawrence prepared sketches for a new office building to replace the historic courthouse. By the time the smoke cleared, the building had been saved, but Lawrence's professional standing had been seriously shaken. For his perceived insensitivity to the historical heritage, Lawrence was suspended from the Portland Chapter.

Pioneer Courthouse nearly succumbed to the wrecker's zeal in the early 1940s. "At that time," McMath recalled, "the courthouse was coveted by Meier and Frank, but they got the Portland Hotel instead. Actually, they would have been happy with either block. Then World War II saved it, because the Federal Government needed all the space they could get their hands on." In the early 1960s, the building was again threatened when the General Services Administration planned to construct a new Federal Office Building on the site. Through the efforts of Congresswoman Edith Green and the Ninth Circuit Court judges, the G.S.A. was pursuaded to locate the new building farther south, in the newly emerging commercial core of the downtown.

"This was the first indication by the Federal Government, particularly in the West," McMath explained, "that it was willing to restore and maintain these old buildings. After all, the courtroom could easily have gone into the new Federal Building." For the firm of Allen, McMath and Hawkins, retained to restore the structure, the decision was crucial. "It was a very important job for us, because from that time on, we became *the* restoration architects. No one else was really getting into restoration on that scale at that time."

This ground-breaking project offered considerable challenges, particularly since the restoration ethic was still so young throughout the country that many techniques had yet to be developed and tested. Resources were few, and, among those that were available, some had been the brainchildren of ingenuous businessmen eager to fill the cracks in an untested market. McMath recalled one such "snake oil salesman" who had concocted a marvelous stone restoration product that could be applied to the surface and would match the color and texture of masonry. "It was called 'Dekosit,'" McMath explained, "and it was used in the Renwick Gallery in Washington, D.C. The building was suffering from severe stone deterioration. The National Park Service owned it at the time, and was putting it out for bids to replace the stone. But the expense was exorbitant, so when the 'Dekosit' manufacturer claimed it could do the job for half the price, he was awarded the contract. The results were marvelous, and got a lot of national publicity. Unfortunately, about ten years later, the Renwick "stone" started to come apart."

Allen, McMath and Hawkins tried to take a more conservative approach in their restoration work. "We take a little longer view of things," said McMath, "mainly

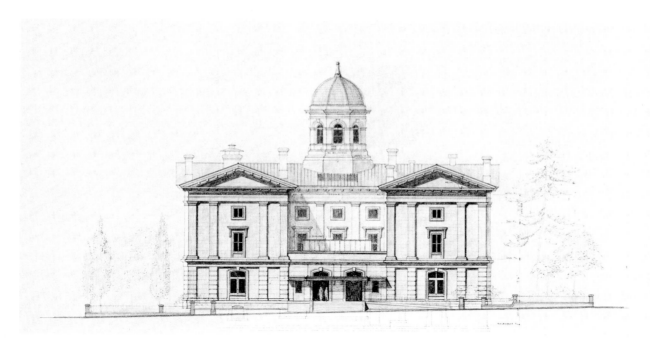

PIONEER COURTHOUSE
A. B. Mullet
1869

as a reaction to this one particular product." Much of the Pioneer Courthouse restoration involved integrating modern elements while preserving the original features. The architects restored the sparkle of the exquisite sandstone exterior, bringing new life to the rusticated pilasters, Doric pilasters and entablature which animated the building with classical elements. The interior, particularly the lobby and the magnificent two-story courtroom, presented a number of difficulties, since some of the original paneling as well as the marble and terrazzo flooring had been lost. In 1972, when the restoration was completed, the Court of Appeals took up its new quarters in the stately landmark building. With this superb restoration project, the firm had rescued a cherished building which, in the years to come, would inspire architects, developers and the general public with a new historical consciousness.

As the firm's tally of restoration projects mounted, so did its expertise in a broad variety of restoration techniques. At the same time, the architects invested considerable energy into educating the public on what they called the "restoration ethic." Rather than replacing components with contemporary elements, they often preferred to stabilize the old elements to prevent further

deterioration until a trustworthy product would become available. "One of our major tasks has always involved educating the client's sensitivity to the preservation aesthetic," McMath explained. "We often have to persuade a client to accept an old, beat-up newel-post, for example, instead of giving him a shiny new one."

A measure of the firm's far-ranging command of architectural styles and building techniques would become available in the expanding repertoire of projects executed during the last two decades. In their hands, the "Carpenter Gothic" of the Old Church (1883) would be as intelligently and sensitively restored as the "period" revival styles of later landmark buildings, such as the Italianate Mann Building (1884; in collaboration with Zimmer Gunsul Frasca) and Gilbert Building (1893), the Renaissance Revival St. Patrick's Church (1889) or Postal Building (1900), the Romanesque Revival Logus Block (1892), or the assortment of Georgian Revival structures that included the Neighborhood House (1910), the Albertina Kerr Nursery (1912) and the interior of the Portland Public Library (1913).

Some of the most challenging commissions, particularly those involving restoration of buildings completed before 1900, would lead into the intricate mazes of urban archeology. Plans for non-government buildings were seldom available for Portland's nineteenth-century structures. In such cases, the architects would have to conduct extensive scholarly research, piecing together slender clues culled from the most diverse sources, and consulting original renderings or photographs in the fortunate instances when these were available. The difficulties of restoring cast-iron elements were usually compounded by the fact that many of the original elements had been lost to fires or crude remodeling attempts.

Sometimes a prudent early owner of a structure had the foresight to store ornaments that had been removed when the building's original function had changed. This happened in the instance of the Bishop's House, whose airy Victorian Gothic patterns delighted Portlanders since 1879. When the building was built, most likely according to the design of San Francisco architect Prosper Huern, it was the first of two structures in the same style that belonged to the Catholic Church.

Immediately to the west of the "Bishop's House," which housed the diocesan library and offices, stood the Catholic Cathedral (1878). In 1894, when the new cathedral at Fifteenth and Davis streets was completed, the property passed into other hands and the old cathedral had been demolished. At the same time, the cast-iron finials and the cross that had graced the front of the lacy, arched central window on the third story had been removed. The subsequent owners and tenants of the structure—among them the Beaux-Arts Atelier and the Ramsay Sign Company, which was responsible for some of the city's finest commercial neon signage—saw no need to return the ecclesiastical emblems to the building's facade. In the interest of historical accuracy, Edmundsen and Kochendorfer restored the missing ornamental touches and brought the building back to the pristine condition. Ironically, however, the very excellence of the restoration drew attention to the sadly solitary position of this fine, final remnant of what must surely have been Portland's sublime Victorian Gothic enclave.

The relative ease with which the reconstruction of the Bishop's House had been accomplished was not typical, of most restoration projects undertaken by Allen, McMath and Hawkins. More often than not, an inventory of available "spare parts" failed to turn up the particular elements which an existing building had lost. The Willamette Block (1882), an elegant four-story masonry and cast-iron commercial building in the Italianate style, offered one of the more dramatic examples of the firm's reconstructive ingenuity. In collaboration with the Portland firm of BOOR/A, Allen, McMath and Hawkins were faced with reclaiming a structure which a disastrous remodeling had deprived of cast-iron pilasters on the main floor and upper-floor facades.

Since the cost of recreating the components in iron was prohibitive, the architects turned to the fiberglass technology so successfully implemented by automobile reconstructors. They prevailed on two local mechanics to put their fiberglass expertise to the service of architectural reconstruction. What had worked for damaged Corvettes proved applicable to battered cast-iron buildings. When reconstructed in 1981, the landmark Willamette Block boasted a lavishly ornamented facade of pilasters, arches and key-stones that had the solid look of authentic iron. Only a magnet or the tap of a knuckle would reveal that fiberglass underlay the sparkling coat of paint of the larger elements, and that some of the exquisite smaller ornaments had been fashioned of aluminum.

The reapplication of automobile technology would supply missing components for many cast-iron structures refurbished by Allen, McMath and Hawkins. At the same time, a flurry of local restorations spurred a minor revival in old building techniques and engendered new ventures into architectural reconstruction. Responding to an increased demand for modern replicas of cast-iron decorative and structural components, John Holloway would abandon the automotive trade to open—along with David Talbot—a bustling business in architectural reproductions. Beginning with the Powers Building, Talbot would go on to provide not only many of the fiberglass counterparts for major structural elements, such as pilasters, columns and arches, but also aluminum copies of the micro-ornamentation which had peppered many of the original cast-iron structures.

Scattered throughout the old commercial center of the city along Front and First avenues, cast-iron buildings reconstructed by Allen, McMath and Hawkins offered pristine examples of styles that had given the city a European flavor. The Blagen Block (1888), restored by the firm between 1980 and 1983, was, according to Hawkins, the "last remaining example of the rhythmic rows of columns and arches that once united hundreds of block fronts on Portland streets." In refurbishing the structure, the restorers stripped away layer upon layer of paint to determine the building's original color scheme. Their analysis yielded the deep blue and gray composition which lent dignity and harmony to the exuberant ornamented front. Scintillating with acanthus leaf decorations, stars, stripes, arrows, laurel leaves, bracketed scrolls and lions' heads, the 100-foot long facade of the Blagen Block became an eloquent monument to the days when commercial architecture had been calculated to delight the eye and tickle the imagination.

Several blocks to the south, the Poppleton Building (1867) presented a striking leap into Baroque sensibilities. Built in 1867, and acquiring a lush Mansard roof in the 1880s, the Poppleton packed an intense pattern of columns, pilasters, scrolls, satyrs, medallions and a serene Roman female head onto its slender exterior. According to Hawkins, the Poppleton provided a good lesson on the importance of color to the sensitive integration of a refurbished building into its immediate context. "We wanted to recapture some of the unity of the original cast-iron fronts along First Avenue," Hawkins explained, "particularly since it was situated between two landmark cast-iron buildings—the Pearne (1865) and the Harker (1880)." Taking their cue from the gold-and-beige composition of the flanking structures, the architects chose a color scheme that harmonized with the warm tones.

In 1981 the Glisan Building (1889) would be reintegrated into the city's architectural fabric. A hybrid of traditional cast-iron elements and floral ornamentation with a distinct Art Nouveau flavor, the Glisan could be seen as the missing link between the old stratum of Portland's cast-iron styles and the new layers of Richardsonian Romanesque structure that replaced them. It also recalled the hustle and bustle that had animated the old part of town in the heyday of cast-iron architecture. "Buildings like the Glisan," McMath remarked, "were at the hub of human activity in the 19th century. A lot of them housed light manufacturing. But few could surpass the New Market Block, especially the New Market Theater. That part of town was just bursting with vital energy."

In 1984, as consultants to Sheldon, Eggleston, Reddick, Anderuel, the firm brought back much of the lost excitement and vitality to the New Market, the core of the city's cultural life during the 1870s and 1880s. Three years short of a century after the New Market Theater had closed its doors, the splendidly refurbished South Wing of the New Market Block and the New Market Theater itself could reclaim their past charm and glory. Modeled on the luxurious Venetian Palazzo Vendromini (1481), the New Market Theater injected a powerful dose of culture and glamor into the city when it opened its theater doors to the public in 1875. On the sumptuous

second- and third-floor theater, festively costumed Portlanders delighted in lavish productions of such theatrical favorites as "The French Spy," "Our Country Cousin," "Faust," "Camille" and "Pygmalion." By day, a more sedate public streamed past the colossal entrance columns into the spacious 200-foot arcade to browse among the sparkling marble stalls of greengrocers. In 1984, a new generation of vendors were once again peddling their wares in the refurbished public market. But even though no theater crowds would linger by the entrances at dusk, the New Market Theater would come alive by night. Dramatically illuminated by spotlights that coaxed razor-sharp detail out of the deep shadows, the ornate facade of the Theater presented a silent spectacle of architecture at its theatrical best.

For years, the expense of restoring the New Market Theater and the South Wing of the New Market Block stood in the way of their regeneration. As McMath explained, the New Market Theater "is a long, narrow building, and the structural enhancements that were necessary were quite extensive relative to some of the other structures." The stately columns supporting the arcade along the first floor had survived the building's long reincarnation as a parking facility, but they had been so badly battered, that an entirely new facing was required. "The contractors came up with a very ingenious solution to that problem," Hawkins explained. "They concocted a sort of thick wall-papering material which they wrapped around the columns to give them that splendid surface." The exterior, however, had not fared quite as well. Many of the ornamental details—including the finials and the intricate acanthus leaf detailing— had been lost. Using photographs of the original structure and blowing them up countless times, the architects were able to reproduce the proportions and shapes of the original finials in fiberglass. A sculptor painstakingly fashioned the elaborate curves of the acroterium to match the splendor of the original "tiara" in every detail.

The architects' most ambitious reconstructive effort, however, centered on reinstalling a fragment of the New Market Block's North Wing, which had been demolished in 1956. Only the columns of this building, harmoniously reiterating the scale and design of those used in the New Market Theater, survived demolition. Using the original parts—some of which had unexpectedly materialized from an odd collection of cast-iron components stored by a couple on suburban Scholls Ferry Road—Allen, McMath and Hawkins reconstructed the first-floor facade of the missing building.

NEW MARKET BLOCK
Piper and Burton
1872

Once again, the graceful arches continued the sublime rhythm of the New Market Theater's facade, catching the slanting rays of the morning sun and glimmering through the lilac mist of rainy afternoons. Within a courtyard defined by the line of columns and arches, a collection of outstanding cast-iron relics would be put on display including splendid cast-iron ventilators, the second-floor keystone from the North Wing of the New Market Block and a solitary column. "In reconstructing this arcade," McMath explained, "we were not as concerned with how it might benefit the theater, as we were with beginning to redefine the space in which the fountain had once sat. Our great desire is to see that parking lot behind the arcade transformed into a building. The arcade is designed so that a two or three-story building—something like the original structure—can be slipped directly into the front."

This ambidextrous approach to restoration, which balances concern for the city's architectural heritage with an appreciation of the city's needs, had been the basis of the preservation ethic disseminated by the firm. "I quarrel with the view that restorers and preserva-tionists are primarily interested in transforming the city into a museum jewelbox," McMath explained. "If you can't make these buildings useful once again, then you shouldn't bother saving them. Few people involved in restoration would advocate keeping buildings around just as museum artifacts. The past has to be made to live again in the present. I think one of the main attractions for people is urban variety—a collection of historical periods tucked into pockets throughout the city. It's as simple as that. I love to walk in the center of the city, but I also like to walk along Sixth Avenue. And I like to walk here, past the New Market Theater."

AFTER
THE FALL

MODERNITY, MID-TWENTIETH century style, came to Portland in a swirl of gasoline fumes, the dull roar of dynamite and the syncopated thud of the wrecker's ball. With the construction of the St. Johns, Ross Island and Sellwood bridges in the 1930s, and the opening of Southwest and Southeast express highways, the vital current of downtown life had steadily begun to disperse into outlying areas.

Since the late 1940s, the city had been doggedly undoing the colorful architectural fabric that had been a century in the making. Postwar prosperity, followed by the creeping postwar recession of the 1950s, had transformed the once lively core into an inhospitable, threadbare zone of deteriorating office buildings, run-down theaters, desolate shops, and the proliferating bald spots of parking lots. Encircled with freeways, Portland appeared to be held in seige by the automobile. "The impact of the city used to be dramatic," Portland architect Lewis Crutcher noted about pre-expressway Portland in the 8 June 1965 *Sunday Oregonian*. "We have clobbered the effect with ramps . . . the effect from the south used to be magic. . . . Now we have tentacles. . . . I have studied the situation all over the world and I know how sick we have become. . . . American cities are built for cars. . . . In a few years we are going to have an L.A. here, unless we do something."

The spectacle was not unique to the City of Roses. "Currently the most popular and effective means of destroying a city," Louis Mumford wrote in 1961 in *The City in History*, "is the introduction of multiple-lane expressways, especially elevated ones, into the central core. . . . Thus the bombs that devastated the City of London in the Blitz did no more damage than the unrestricted planning of expressways and parking lots are now doing every day, abetted by a national highways program planned on the same assumptions of monotransportation from 'door to door'."

But while freeways and parking spaces made downtown Portland superbly accessible to drivers, they left little behind to make it attractive to the pedestrian, the pleasure-seeker, or the entrepreneur. Surrendering more than one-half of its downtown area to the automobile by 1972, Portland had begun to resemble a ghost town. "The automobile is the destroyer everywhere," Pulitzer Prize-winning architectural critic Ada Louise Huxtable commented after a 1970 visit to the city. Writing in the *Oregonian* of 12 July 1970, she noted that, "In Portland, the cohesive and intimately scaled core city is being decimated for parking lots and parking garages. The trend can only lead to total physical disintegration. But here, as elsewhere, there is no sign that anyone is willing to take to anything except his car, whatever the urban consequences may be."

The automobile was the undisputed villain in the postwar compulsion for modernization, but it was by no means the only pernicious intruder into the delicately balanced landscape of the city. With its ambitious new construction and redevelopment projects of the 1960s, Portland, like other cities across the country, was announcing that it too had fallen prey to what Huxtable called "the terrible pressures and critical changes that are destroying urban identities and values everywhere."

Faced with the ugliness and decrepitude of a maimed downtown, Portland's planners, developers and civic leaders had responded to the need for a radical urban transformation by drastically altering the face of the city. To Huxtable and other observers, these alterations appeared in a highly ambiguous light. "The near past has been destroyed or eclipsed by new skylines of massive scale giving new profiles to familiar names," Huxtable lamented. "Some cities might as well have new names."

In Portland, the new profile to which Huxtable alluded belonged to a new generation of no-nonsense International Style towers that popped up on stretches of pock-marked city streets: the Hilton Hotel (1963, Skidmore, Owings and Merrill), the Standard Plaza (1963, Skidmore, Owings and Merrill), the Pacific Northwest Bell Building (1969, WEGROUP), the Bank of California (1969, Anshen and Allen), the Boise Cascade Building (1968, Skidmore, Owings and Merrill), and, climbing to vertiginous completion at the time of Huxtable's visit to Portland, the Georgia Pacific Building (1971, Skidmore, Owings and Merrill), and the First National Bank Building (1972, Luckman and Associates).

Architects entrusted with the task of finding a new image for postwar Portland began by reacting against its architectural traditionalism. As if intending to demonstrate that in architecture, as in physics, every action leads to an equal and opposite reaction, the newest wave of firms including Skidmore, Owings and Merrill, Rudat/ Boutwell, Campbell, Yost, Grube, and Wolff, Zimmer Associates, turned their backs on styles used during the first century of the city's growth. Rather than borrowing styles from the past, they used the freedom the city's postwar identity crisis had given them to search for a new model, one that was part and parcel of fashionable utopian images. In the process, they jumped on the bandwagon of corporate architectural chic that threatened to make Portland into what Huxtable called an "instant international city in the universal corporate mold."

Whether Portland-based or imported from California, architects responsible for the most visible and dramatic new constructions eased the city into the twenty-first century with a generation of minimalist behemoths that mimicked the severe skyscraper design of corporate headquarters from New York to Los Angeles. "Certain firms of national reputation," Huxtable was quoted as saying in the 5 June 1970 *Oregon Journal*, "are making American cities monotonous by repetition." Uncluttered by historical allusion and pursuing the purist theory of form following function, Portland's new buildings lent the downtown skyline all the charm of a giant display of glass and metal rectangular coffins standing on end.

For developers, planners and architects who had put up the shimmering blockbusters, the glass-box minimalism of the International Style seemed to offer the most hopeful way out of Portland's mid-century identity crisis. But to Huxtable, the modernizing cure of Mies van der Rohe's "less is more" school of architectural philosophy was even more pernicious than the malady it had been designed to remedy. "The dramatic clutch of new Portland skyscrapers," the critic wrote, "is killing the life of the street with parking garages in 'podium' bases beloved by Establishment architects who successfully isolate their corporate totems from the urban fabric and the city's essential humanity."

To be sure, Huxtable cast her critical eye at Portland during the zenith of its urban necrosis. If she decried, and publicized, the city's fall from architectural grace, it was because she saw the formerly coherent and elegant city transformed into a modernist militant. The intrusion of gargantuan towers, however, was only the most strident sign that urban renewal was finally gaining momentum. Along the fringes of downtown, in the South Auditorium and Portland State University areas and along the waterfront, large-scale development projects were keeping pace with the vertical growth of the skyline.

Ironically, it was the automobile—the original catalyst for much of the wholesale destruction—that triggered concern for the future of the city's downtown and dramatized the need for a drastic and systematic reconstruction campaign. As Portlanders increasingly took their business and pleasure to the city's outskirts, the parking facilities for which so many stately old structures had been demolished went begging for customers. "Retail sales in the central business district actually declined in dollar value from 1948 to 1958," Carl Abbott pointed out in *Portland: Planning, Politics, and Growth in a Twentieth-Century City*, "and the recession of 1958–59 cut further into department store receipts . . . Over the slightly longer period from 1946 to 1960, the number of daily personal trips into the core business area fell from 118,500 to 105,000." Not only were fewer shoppers venturing downtown, but the number of pleasure-seekers showed an even more shocking decline. "The count of commuters . . . coming in for shopping fell by 2,000, for personal business by 3,000, and for recreation by 11,000."

When Skidmore, Owings and Merrill's general partner David Pugh, arrived in the city in the early 1950s, he found a downtown that had little to offer by way of the urban razzle-dazzle and magnetism that might stem the leak of urban energy into the outlying suburbs. "Nothing was happening downtown," Pugh recalled. "Certainly no major building." There was little in way of new construction to supplant the patchwork of cast-iron Italianate palaces, Renaissance Revival blocks, and terra cotta emporiums ripped apart to make way for a robustly modernized downtown. Once the dust of demolition cleared, the city's developers found themselves in the tragicomic position of hosts who had cleared their home for a party to which no one came. In short, as Carl Abbott noted, "Portland faced real dangers of downtown obsolescence."

The 1950s would be nearly at an end before planners, architects and civic leaders began the formidable task of rebuilding an infrastructure for Portland's unhealthy urban core. The incentive for action had come a decade earlier, when the 81st Congress established the urban redevelopment program with the Federal Housing Act of 1949. Oregon was quick to respond. Within a year, the Oregon State Legislature authorized the Housing Authority of Portland to act as the local planning agency charged with identifying potential renewal areas and administering the redevelopment.

In the spring of 1952, the housing authority staff drew up plans for the ill-fated "Vaughn Street Project", which would have transformed "Slabtown"—the 44-block area of mixed residential and industrial use in the Northwest industrial section of the city—into an enclave of light industry and warehousing. The plan did not sit well with Portland voters, who denied their approval in the 1952 general election. Shortly after the election, the state legislature removed the planning function from the housing authority and placed it in the hands of the city council. Bureaucratic and political entanglements, however, hampered planning efforts until 1957, when Santa Barbara planner John Kenward was engaged to head the newly formed Urban Renewal Section.

In the summer of 1958, a new agency, the Portland Development Commission, headed by Ira Keller with John Kenward as director, was established. With the political and administrative machinery for systematic planning finally in place, Portland was ready to respond to the urgings of various civic groups and organizations such as the City Club, which, in 1958, had issued a report stating that "if Portland is to keep step with the growth of the Pacific area, it must plan not only for industrial development, . . . but must also protect against deterioration and stagnation."

For its maiden project, the new agency concentrated its efforts on a 44-block section in South Portland bounded by s.w. Market Street, Harbor Drive, Arthur Street and Fourth Avenue. Targeted as a potential renewal zone as early as 1952 and designated the "South Auditorium Project," the area was officially approved for redevelopment in 1958. For years the neighborhood on the southern edge of Portland had sheltered many of the city's ethnic groups, craftsmen and quaint delicatessens in rundown hotels, apartments, commercial blocks and junkyards. To its inhabitants, South Portland was a tightly-knit, if shabby, island of ethnicity. To Kenward it was a "blighted and economically isolated neighborhood" deserving no better fate than eradication.

In the late 1950s and early 1960s, Portland's professional planners had not yet warmed to the idea of reweaving the urban fabric from the existing fraying strands. "They took for granted," Abbott explained, "that neighborhood decline is an inevitable process, 'the end product of a long slow process of erosion'." Like other planners throughout the country, they assumed that this was an irreversible erosion in which inner, residential neighborhoods "naturally give way to institutional and fringe commercial uses as the city grows and demands space for its central functions." By deciding to "clear" the South Auditorium Project area, planners produced a clean slate on which a new architectural and urban vision of the city would be inscribed.

The stage was set for Portland's most ambitious reclamation campaign of the postwar years. Throughout the Western world, from London to Paris to Montreal, schemes for central area redevelopment were reaching, in the words of architectural historian Bill Risebero, "an extravagant climax." In Portland, however, the Urban Renewal Agency produced an unworkable master plan for the South Auditorium Renewal area. Dogmatic and inflexible, the plan carved the zone into rigidly defined sectors of commercial, residential and service functions, liberally sprinkled with arid parking lots. By partitioning the area into three master "superblocks," the agency's plan not only ignored the existing utility infrastructure, but threatened to disrupt the visual integrity and spatial rhythms of the city's 200-foot square blocks. Finding no "buyers" for its white elephant, the planning commission scrapped the plan and turned the project over to a relative newcomer to the Pacific Northwest—the architectural firm of Skidmore, Owings and Merrill.

It was an inspired decision that launched the eminent firm on a brilliant career as the "roto-tiller" of the city's exhausted urban zones. With pioneering and award-winning planning schemes—for the South Auditorium Project (1961; 1966), the Portland State Urban Renewal Project (1965), the Portland Waterfront Renewal Plan (1975) and the Portland Transit Mall (1978)—Skidmore, Owings and Merrill would stem the leak of urban vitality by throwing up "dikes" of developed zones along the downtown perimeter and running an "aorta"—the Transit Mall—through its center.

As had so often happened in the history of Portland architecture, the firm which emerged to spearhead reconstruction efforts could trace its lines of descent to the established master-builders of the city. Skidmore, Owings and Merrill had been grafted to a genealogical tree that had borne a succession of firms from Whidden and Lewis to Doyle and eventually, Pietro Belluschi. In 1951, the firm had been imported to the city by Belluschi. Becoming increasingly committed to education, and opting for the role of consultant on world-class architectural projects, Belluschi accepted the position of dean of the School of Architecture and Planning at the Massachusetts Institute of Technology in 1950. Prior to leaving the Pacific Northwest, however, Belluschi offered to sell his practice to a group of local architects who had been senior employees of his firm: Kenneth E. Richardson, the chief designer, Frank C. Allen, Irving G. Smith and George Kotchik.

During their years with Belluschi, these designers had contributed much to developing the "regionalist" aesthetic for which the Portland office became renowned. Richardson, in particular, had shown great flair in the glass-and-wood idiom of the "Northwest Style," which he continued to cultivate throughout the 1950s as partner in the office of Stewart and Richardson. In subsequent projects, including the First Presbyterian Church in Vancouver (1956), the Midland Branch Library (1957), and the House of Religious History designed for the 1959 Oregon Centennial Exposition, Stewart and Richardson continued to experiment with melding the regional Northwest wood tradition with the geometric minimalism of such modernists as Le Corbusier, Walter Gropius and Ludwig Mies van der Rohe. It is interesting to speculate how the face of Portland's downtown would have developed had financial obstacles not prevented Belluschi from carrying out an "in-house" transfer of his firm's ownership.

As it happened, however, the baton of his architectural preeminence passed into the hands of designers and planners at Skidmore, Owings and Merrill. The firm, after all, had an established track record for creating, with great efficiency and competence, imposing structures that were in every sense international. For the most part, their buildings responded to the visual rhythms and proportions of no *particular* setting or place, and bore the unmistakable signature of the firm's pared-down, modernist aesthetic.

Destined to become the undisputed titans of the first concrete-and-glass period of Portland's reurbanization, the design team at SOM offered the most sterling credentials for occupying the position of architectural leadership vacated by Belluschi. In the late 1930s, the firm's originators—Louis Skidmore, Nathaniel Owings and John O. Merrill—had embraced the lofty architectural philosophy and aspirations of Ludwig Mies van der Rohe, high priest of the austere glass-and-steel box sect of architectural modernism. Director of the seminal Bauhaus school of design from 1930 until its closing in 1932, Mies van der Rohe had settled in Chicago after fleeing the Nazis in the late 1930s. His presence among young Chicago skyscraper designers lent their experiments the kind of authority and prestige that helped launch rectilinear glass-walled abstractions as the canonical forms of enlightened corporate design. Mies van der Rohe's rallying cry, "I don't want to be interesting, I want to be good," set the exacting standards for the precision of detail and pristine functional expressionism that became a trademark of the best SOM skyscrapers of the 1950s and 1960s. Such architects as Gordon Bunshaft, designer of the acclaimed Lever House (1952) in New York, shared Mies van der Rohe's central conviction that decoration plastered onto a facade or historical echoes gratuitously sounded were obstacles to the utopian conquest of the machine.

But if dogmatism had been alien to Mies van der Rohe's architectural experiments, among his followers it became, more often than not, the rule. With the notable exception of Lever House and the Inland Steel Building (1957) in Chicago, the firm processed Mies van der Rohe's idealistic functional purism into buildings that preached a doctrinaire sculptural vision. "Most of the architects of the 1950s," wrote Paul Goldberger, "eschewed any overt symbolism for their buildings, although in spite of this their structures still managed to convey a certain kind of message—a message of a rather faceless corporate bureaucracy housed in boxes that looked like other boxes." Based also in Chicago, New York and San Francisco, the mega-firm would bring to Portland a baker's dozen of what Henry-Russell Hitch-

cock dubbed "the most characteristic later examples of what . . . was not improperly called the International Style."

As the firm's contributions to the skyline's vertical expansion would suggest, the transfer of Belluschi's architectural practice to SOM was more legal and contractual than it was "spiritual." In Portland, Belluschi's residences, churches, museum spaces and commercial buildings had primarily addressed the emotional and spiritual needs of the *individual* and had spoken to the humanistic values of a vital urban organism. In their architectural projects, SOM would respond to the considerably more circumscribed ambitions of their institutional and corporate clientele.

With their turgid towers and glittering obelisks, a standardized urban environment would penetrate into the city. The designers at SOM seemed more concerned with bringing to the city universal, corporate emblems of modernity, than with giving their skyscraper idiom a local identity that would affirm the qualities of urban "place." Buildings such as the Standard Plaza (1963), the Hilton Hotel (1963), the Georgia Pacific Building (1971), the Federal Office Building (1975) and the Orbanco Headquarters Building (1980) reflected, with unadorned honesty, the hard-nosed pragmatism of their designers.

The legal transaction that placed Belluschi's firm in the hands of SOM would not be followed by the transfer of his intellectual and aesthetic legacy. That heritage would be passed along not in legal boardrooms, but in the classrooms and drafting studios of the Massachusetts Institute of Technology, where Belluschi met an aspiring designer, Robert J. Frasca. Eventually imported to Portland by his mentor, Frasca would subsequently join the firm of Wolff, Zimmer, Gunsul which would shape much of the city's skyline during the decade 1975–85. Belluschi marked this informal transfer of his baton when, in the late 1960s and early 1970s, he acted as consultant and designer on several projects undertaken by the firm, including the Equitable Center (1965), the Oregon Historical Center (1966), the addition to the Portland Art Museum and the pivotal Willamette Center (1975).

If in the decade 1975–85, firms such as Zimmer Gunsul Frasca could concentrate on creating buildings that interacted with their architectural environment, to a great extent, this was because SOM had done much of the preparatory work of laying the foundations for an urban "space" in the ruins of postwar Portland. Only on the basis of this preliminary work were subsequent architects freed to shape a finely tuned urban architecture in the spaces mapped out, cleared and colonized by SOM. In this respect, the firm continued the groundbreaking role of the city's past master builders, such as Burton, Whidden and Lewis and Doyle, whose buildings, in their time, had extended the frontiers of Portland's metropolitan core.

"Properly trained in the right attitudes," SOM's Pugh explained, "architects are the only really meaningful physical planners in our society. Unfortunately," he added, remembering the planning commission's original scheme for the South Auditorium Project, "planners as such too often limit their objectives to putting out the plan without going the critical next step of implementing their vision. Our objectives are more comprehensive. We are taught to take a global view. For that reason, I think that most of the meaningful planning in Portland has been the work of architects rather than planners."

In the case of the South Auditorium Renewal Project, taking a global view meant balancing a bewildering variety of conflicting interests. With its team approach to planning and design, the firm combined skills and expertise that, by the mid-twentieth century, could no longer be packaged in the skin of a solitary "Renaissance man." "We worked with economists, real estate people, city planners, neighborhood groups, and we pulled everybody together, because we knew we had to produce a plan that was uniquely tailored to Portland's size and economic position," Pugh explained. The scheme devised by SOM called for a harmonious mix of residential, commercial and recreational facilities that would be as "user" and "city"-friendly as it would be attractive to hard-nosed, "bottom-line" entrepreneurs.

Attempting to meld the city's traditional notions of "place" with modern, large-tract concepts current in professional planning circles, the firm modified the original superblock scheme to respect the scale and disposition of existing downtown streets. It retained the 200-foot square grid that defined the typical city block in downtown Portland, and merged the twenty-seven blocks into three superblocks. A series of streets, pedestrian ways and "green" islands were to form a coherent system of communication between the older core area and the new development. Now commonly accepted as sound renewal practice, this hybrid strategy was radically innovative in its time. "In the early 1960s," Pugh explained, "many urban planners thought of urban renewal areas as 'oases' in the middle of an urban grid, and tried to disassociate them from the surrounding city. We

did just the opposite. We kept all of the street right-of-ways and transformed them into pedestrian malls."

The solution was as context-sensitive as it was sound. "We were able to keep all of the basic utilities that were already in place under those streets, thereby minimizing the 'front-end' infrastructure costs." By preserving the 200-foot square grid pattern, the plan was sufficiently elastic to accommodate a variety of construction sizes. "The plan had to be attractive both to the major developers cropping up around the country," Pugh recalled, "and to the individual entrepreneur in Portland who wanted to buy a little piece of land in the urban renewal zone and develop it. We designed a lot of flexibility into the scheme so that people could move around in it without ruining it. The plan had 'flex'; but it also had sufficient backbone so that regardless of the kinds of buildings one would construct, the basic scheme would still work."

In 1963, construction on the award-winning South Auditorium Project got under way with SOM as principal architects. When the renewal area land was offered up for public sale under the new plan, the firm canceled its contract with the planning commission to become architects for a private organization—the Portland Center Development Company. "When it came around to competing for the commission to actually design the buildings," Pugh explained, "our firm was eager to continue into the next phase. We are architects, after all, and we still like to do buildings. We were involved in the project to improve our community, but of course we also wanted to build."

And build they did, covering nearly a third of the total development area with apartment towers, garages, retail and commercial buildings, and a scattering of corporate headquarters—including the eight-story Boise Cascade Building (1968), the seven-story Blue Cross Building (1969) and the two-part Harrison Square Complex (1972). In exchanging the planner's for the architect's hat, however, the firm did not hold a monopoly on the design process.

Before canceling its consultative role with the planning commission, SOM helped Kenward, its director, find an architectural consultant to oversee the implementation of the plan. Walter Gordon, who had just completed a two-year stint at the University of Oregon as dean of its School of Architecture, was engaged as resident design consultant to the planning commission. On Kenward's further initiative, a design advisory board was soon assembled, including as members Pietro Belluschi,

PORTLAND CENTER APARTMENTS
Skidmore Owings and Merrill
1966

Paul Hayden Kirk, George Rockrise, and later, San Francisco's Lawrence Halprin. Under the watchful eye of this distinguished group, a solid—if not always inspiring—body of architecture infiltrated the southern reaches of Portland's downtown.

By 1966, the renewal zone sported three high-rise apartment towers and three small colonies of two-story garden apartments—24 in all—equipped with garage, retail and commercial buildings. Stacked like the building blocks of a child's erector set, the bleached-bone towers offered few visual surprises to the observer accustomed to a clean, right-angled modernist aesthetic. Uniform bands of windows alternated with boxy balconies that ran along the four faces of the buildings like the exposed vertebrae of a museum dinosaur. Though the high-rises were decorated with panels of texturized

concrete that, in strong sunlight, broke into a pattern of dimpled shadows, the effect was rather bland—just another clutch of residential towers, which could have been part of any urban renewal program. It seemed the architects had wished to give tenants a vertical alternative to the architectural anonymity of suburban tract homes. They replicated the prefabricated "feel" of standardized housing units, even to the extent of providing balconies as substitute lawns for rugged individualists in need of personalizing touches.

The impact, however, was commendably pleasing at a time when high-density residential projects in other American cities teemed with dreary, pre-cast concrete tower blocks, which made living in them, or even seeing them, an undeserved punishment. To counter the impersonality of high-rise living, the SOM team threw in various amenities at ground level. For the residents of the Portland Center Apartments, as the complex was named, the transitional spaces leading into the lobbies offered numerous opportunities to cultivate "neighborliness" and touch ground with nature. Landscaped setbacks, gracefully curving benches, tree-lined walkways and three generous parks wove through and around the complex, linking it with the new corporate structures that began to crop up in the renewal area. The ground planning was primarily the work of Halprin, acting as a consultant to SOM.

The Boise Cascade Building (1968), Blue Cross Building (1969) and Harrison Square (1972) were all designed by SOM. Sinewy and symmetrical, these conservatively scaled office buildings were of one piece with the concrete-and-glass aesthetic of the apartment towers. What made them recognizable as business rather than residential structures was their emphasis on the horizontal instead of the vertical coordinates of their graph-paper inspired exteriors.

Considerably more striking was the 18-story "Black Box," the 200 Market Building designed by the firm of Rudat/Boutwell and Partners (1973). Uncompromisingly minimalist like a Mondrian abstraction, the 200 Market Building performed the extraordinary feat of making high drama out of the understated and potentially boring modernist glass box. The drama, in this instance, derived from the black glass skin that stretched unbroken over the surface of the tower. Polished to a gleaming reflectivity, the building's faces seemed to disappear, substituting for their architectural statement a continuous diorama of the city's changing moods. Whatever the weather, its dusky surfaces invariably reflected Portland's growing modernist accretions in a somber light. To observers such as George McMath, who commended the design in *Space, Style and Structure*, the 200 Market Building recalled the mysterious monolith in *2001: A Space Odyssey*.

At the time this black jewel took shape, it was clear that the South Auditorium area had little tolerance for new buildings in "traditional" idioms. When the Ramada Inn developers contemplated building on the southern end of the redevelopment area, a motel in their trademark pseudo-colonial style, the Development Commission was horrified. Equally so was Ada Louise Huxtable. The 5 June 1970 *Oregon Journal* reported that during a 1970 visit to Portland, "Mrs. Huxtable could hardly finish her dessert when we told her that something 'big and colonial' was under consideration for a block near the Auditorium forecourt." After protracted negotiations with the developers, the development commission finally convinced the owners to design a red brick complex more in tune with the surrounding architecture.

With residential, commercial and business facilities firmly in place, the South Auditorium Project was well on its way to bustling vitality by the early 1970s. It was also beginning to make a noticeable contribution to the urban experience of Portland. The graft, it seemed, had taken. On sunny afternoons, clusters of lunchtime sun worshipers gossiped on park benches, businessmen strolled along the pedestrian-ways while lovers lounged on grassy patches in the parks.

The novelty of modernist architecture was only part of the attraction. The real magnets were the ecologically sensitive Lovejoy Fountain (1966) and Pettygrove Park (1966) flanking the north and south ends of the apartment towers. Designed by the San Francisco office of Lawrence Halprin and Associates, the mini-parks were a tribute to the "quality of life" liberalism that gathered momentum during the "Flower Power" decade. While the muscular monoliths of SOM proclaimed the institutional values of the mainstream establishment, Halprin's "back to nature" parks spelled out the bucolic ideals of the "alternative" life-style.

There was nothing conventional about these designs, at least by Portland's conservative standards. Certainly none of the traditional monuments that normally formed the focal point of public parks found their way into the formal vocabulary of Halprin's "green" spaces. Instead, nature was both the protagonist and the stage set for his landscape extravaganzas. In Pettygrove Park, a miniaturized mountain landscape was nestled at the approach to the futuristic 200 Market Building. Shady groves sprouted from precipitously contoured mounds of turf, and curving paths snaked among the hillocks for the convenience of timorous strollers. Though the effect of full-sized trees against the dwarf hills was mildly incongruous, the combination yielded a pleasing sculptural composition.

All serenity and organic curves, Pettygrove Park was a striking antithesis to the concrete fantasies of Lovejoy Fountain. Clearly the idea here, as in Pettygrove Park, had been to offer a conciliatory gesture to nature. But Lovejoy Fountain attempted to bridge the gap between city and country with a devotion to each that verged on the obsessive. Perhaps, the design was inspired by the rocky massings of the Cascade Range and tumbling wa-

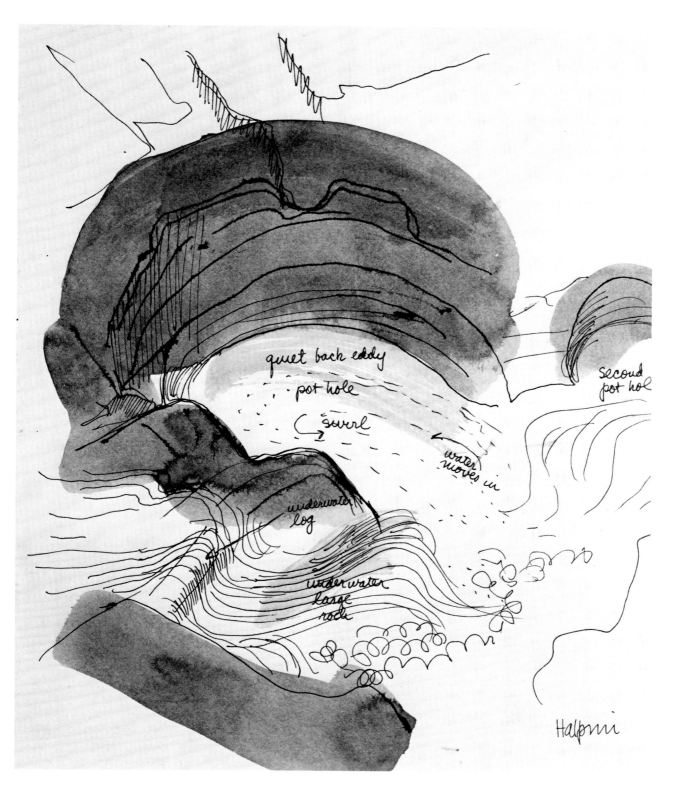

LOVEJOY FOUNTAIN
Lawrence Halprin and Associates
1966

ters of the Columbia River Gorge. In essence, Halprin domesticated and urbanized the powerful torrents, sending them rushing through the jagged, concrete walls of a scaled-down broken dam. A series of haphazardly overlapping tiers ascended the sloping site, leveling off at the head of the "waterfall" to provide a base for a squat pavillion. Its soaring trellised roof, rising and falling at angles, mimicked the serrated profile of a mountain range. All of this created a slice of the Columbia River Gorge.

It would have worked, too, if the designers had not introduced trees into the composition. Ironically, the scattering of trees along the periphery seemed oddly and messily out of place in this stylized landscape. Their unmanipulated vitality—somehow out of register with the overall scheme—suggested the painstakingly recreated natural habitat of enlightened zoo design. Particularly when filled with cavorting hippies, the Lovejoy Fountain seemed like the carefully contrived "eco-niche" where the last hardy survivors of an endangered species held out against urbanism.

The point, of course, had been to create a simulacrum of rugged rock formations, but without recourse to such naturalistic effects as actual boulders and rocks. A strictly reconstructive approach, after all, would have blunted the ideological thrust of a design intended to celebrate the harmonious merger of nature and technology. Something grand, chaotic and powerfully "natural" might have seemed an appropriate counterbalance to the controlled architectural forms of the city's newest enclave. At the same time, something unmistakably "man-made" was required if the natural forms were to relate to the surrounding architecture. The solution took the rawness out of nature and packaged it into concrete and the abstract geometries of modernist design.

In its execution, the Lovejoy scheme did nothing to disguise its architectonic inspiration—or to temper the artificiality of modern construction materials. It was not difficult to recognize, as Wallace Kay Huntington pointed out in *Space, Style and Structure*, "the arbitrary angular forms of the stepped terracing as being derived from cardboard models of contoured sites." In this impersonation of nature, the architectural model was the undisputed leader, with concrete playing a heavy and heavy-handed supporting role. Framing the free-form upper and lower pools, it covered the sloping site in an explosion of ragged, geometrical slabs that recalled the tortured stage sets of German Expressionist films. If the intent had been to replicate nature's effects, it was

most successful in bringing only the sound and fury of Oregon's waterfalls to the heart of the city.

Theatricality, pure and simple, was the dominant theme of yet another, though later, park design issuing from the office of Halprin and Associates. Several blocks to the north of the core South Auditorium Renewal area, Angela Danadjieva of Halprin's office devised an august public space on the motif of nature as urban spectacle; The crystalline Forecourt Fountain (1970), subsequently renamed the Ira C. Keller Fountain. Generously landscaped, the Forecourt Fountain struck a happy balance between the sharp, contrived angularity of the Lovejoy Fountain and the organic forms of Pettygrove Park. Recessed into a sloping site, the fountain sounded a naturalistic echo to the newly refurbished Civic Auditorium. Its inspiration was the classical amphitheatre—harmonizing, in spirit, with the "diet" Classicism of the Civic's design.

Whereas the Civic, all spindly columns and spidery mullions, was a timid imitation of classical temple design, the Forecourt Fountain was a boldly inventive reinterpretation of the ancient Greek amphitheater. Its boxy forms, clustered at the far end of the site, recreated the rugged topography of rocky massings. This was a stage set for the continuous sound-and-light show of cascading water that gushed and seeped along the glistening faces of the concrete forms. At the foot of the waterfalls, a basin filled with island-like concrete pads suggested a sweeping proscenium. A generous planting of indigenous trees established just the right counterpoint between natural forms and "high-tech" materials. The result, in short, was a delightful and functional compromise between tradition and modernity, nature and artifice.

Portlanders took to the Fountain with a passion. Ever since Halprin took the inaugural plunge in the fountain—flaunting the protectionism of the city government—crowds of weary shoppers and frustrated nature-lovers have dangled their feet in the eddying waters and thrilled to the "call of the wild" in the heart of downtown Portland. If Lovejoy Fountain had become the scene of outdoor theatrical performances, the Forecourt Fountain brought the principles of the experimental "Living Theater" to life. As Huntington noted, this stage-like park demanded "audience participation." In this respect, the Forecourt and the Lovejoy fountains in particular were scaled-down versions of the amusement park. Their appeal was pluralistic and hedonistic; their imagery, derived from natural forms, was primal, optimistic and spoke of a utopian vision of the city that was accessible and appealing to all.

But the Halprin designs also acknowledged that a public park, on some level, should convey a message. "In a public park, there's a civic responsibility to uplift and educate," Joshua Freiwald wrote in *Arts and Architecture Magazine*. "Its monuments need to refer to something, some source of civic pride or manifest destiny." By substituting nature for traditional monuments, Halprin's designers had provided a landscape architecture with a legible message that everyone could read. This message, profoundly symptomatic of the times, was that technology, properly attuned to nature, could provide a passage to paradise. Pettygrove Park, Lovejoy Fountain and the Forecourt Fountain celebrated the grandeur of nature, participatory democracy and self-determination. Surrounded by the strident shapes of new buildings, Halprin's work spelled relief from the tyranny of rational forms.

His parks brought the first glimmer of contextualism to a part of the city that threatened to succumb to the anonymity and placelessness of modern architecture. For all their incongruities, Halprin's parks worked because they brought the city back into the orbit of the region. With their pointed allusions to Portland's geographical setting, they established purely local points of reference for the international imagery of the new architecture. For the general public, they also signaled that the first serious steps had been taken to return the city to the people: to make it, once again, the domain of the pedestrian. In this respect, Halprin's designs did much to dramatize and publicize the success of the master plan for the South Auditorium Renewal area that had been plotted by SOM.

By the mid-1960s, it had become clear that the South Auditorium Renewal Project was not only the most innovative urban development scheme on paper in America, but that it was a practical success. "Simply stated, the project was successful," Pugh recalled in 1984, "because it was rapidly developed, it met city and federal stipulations for minimizing fire, crime, and sanitary hazards, and, once completed, yielded to the city a tenfold tax return on investment." The firm's multipronged approach to problem-solving and its ability to draw upon a large, diversified staff made the transformation of the South Auditorium blocks paradigmatic for future developments.

The first opportunity to apply the lessons of this seminal plan came as early as 1965, when the Portland City Council approved a 13-block extension of the urban renewal area at the north end of the original project. On the foundations of the original 200-foot grid, new buildings such as the prim Crown Plaza (1971) and the colorful Evans Products Building (1975), both by Wolff, Zimmer, Gunsul and Frasca, took their stand. Though strictly within the canons of International Style good taste, both attempted to give modernism a refreshing, if subtle, local inflection. Straddling two blocks, the Crown Plaza complex linked a seven-level parking structure with the eleven-story office building by means of a bridge. This futuristic accretion, while admirably convenient for the office workers, did little to enrich pedestrian vitality at street level. In this respect, the outdoor terraces also appeared to satisfy a cosmetic rather than functional need. While of little use to the stroller, they did provide a welcome visual digression from the arid repetitiveness of the rectilinear exterior.

As the South Auditorium Extension filled out to its new limits, development got under way on the 46-acre site of the Portland State University renewal project. In 1964, SOM prepared a master plan for the area in conjunction with their design for the new Portland State Science Building (1964). The master plan was required to demonstrate the logic of expanding the University west of the Park Blocks. The firm of Campbell and Yost followed up shortly with two additional planning schemes that affected the shape of the campus proper.

With the collaboration of San Francisco planners Livingston and Blayney and the internationally acclaimed landscape architects Sasaki, Walker and Associates, the southwestern fringe of downtown took on the firm character of a scholarly, metropolitan center. A shaded quadrangle—that inalienable attribute of American universities—was plotted into the core of the campus. Along this verdant corridor, SOM designed the new Portland State University Library (1967). Their "expandable" five-story building gave the library a Brutalist interpretation of the venerable ivory tower. The tower, in this instance, had been placed on its side, presenting a formidable brick, concrete and glass exterior built to withstand the assaults of radical student activists. Surrounded by a brick wall, it seemed capable of surviving countless sieges and offered school administrators a secure staging area for mounting counter-offensives of their own.

As the turbulent 1960s leveled off into the relatively quiet 1970s, SOM would assert its leadership in the reclamation of downtown Portland by applying new planning strategies. Major surgery in the South Auditorium and

Portland State University areas restored the southern fringes of downtown by replacing the diseased zones with healthy grafts of new architecture. The new planning campaigns, into the waterfront and, shortly afterward, into the core of the downtown, would mark an advance over the blast-and-level tactics of the first renewal thrust. The next phase would coax out of SOM's planning teams the skills of both the diagnostician and reconstructive surgeon.

The financial climate had changed considerably since the early 1960s. Large federal grants available during the first part of the decade would run out by the decade's end. This meant that new development programs would depend primarily upon private investment and public monies, whose availability, to a great extent, would hinge on public approval.

By the end of the 1960s, a new spirit of activism was beginning to assert itself. Groups of citizens began to insist on having a voice in the planning process. To a large extent, participatory design—the involvement of a team of public and client representatives in programming and early conceptual design phases—was a stepchild of the 1960s, a decade that gave birth to a strong wave of public activism and consumer protectionism. It became clear that Portlanders were getting anxious about the piecemeal approach to their city's reconstruction. "No one has asked what downtown should be doing and come up with a list of needed improvements," local architect Howard Glazer complained in the 6 June 1976 *Sunday Oregonian*. "We have failed to come to grips with a number of choices for downtown. . . . We're simply drifting and Portland is particularly cursed. . . . We need a 20-year scheme so that urban renewal and other projects can be fitted into something. What we need is a two-way dialogue between planners and 'people'."

By the mid-1970s, this dialogue had not only gotten under way but started to produce concrete results. In Portland, it led to the formation and proliferation of agencies, organizations—including the engineering firm of CH₂M-HILL and the Urban Studies Center of Portland State—and committees, such as the Portland Improvement Corporation and the Citizens Advisory Committee, which became involved in the design process to protect the public from arbitrary, insensitive architectural and planning decisions.

By the early 1970s, comprehensive plans were required for all cities and counties; and citizen participation on major planning projects became mandatory. Portland was ready to comply on both counts. In May 1971, a Citizens Advisory committee was established to assist the Portland Planning Commission in formulating a list of fundamental downtown goals. One year later, after holding numerous public meetings and studying extensive questionnaires, the committee presented the city council with a comprehensive document, the *Planning Guidelines/Portland Downtown Plan*. Adopted by the city council in December 1972, the document set goals for land use, transportation and the environment in the city's downtown, and recommended policies to guide the city toward achieving these goals. It also provided a frame of reference for more detailed plans and for the consideration of specific projects, both public and private.

Functional diversity, a balanced transportation system, a distinctive urban identity and context-sensitive development were the key objectives of downtown planners. "Variety" was the buzz-word of the day, and the plan identified no fewer than 21 districts within the core, each with its peculiar uses, opportunities for redevelopment and architectural character. The guidelines recognized the stylistic homogeneity of certain sectors of the city and recommended the preservation and enhancement of districts with special significance or unique qualities. At that time, the concept was to reinforce patterns that existed in areas such as the Park Blocks and the Broadway, Chinatown, and Skidmore/Old Town districts. Office tower development, projected for the core, was concentrated in a corridor between Fourth and Broadway, with high-intensity retail cutting across the office corridor.

Sounding the slogan of sensitivity to context, the guidelines also attempted to insure that new construction would respect the scale and geographical setting of the city. Scenic views to the mountains, airy streets flooded with light—amenities that the 200-foot grid of Portland's downtown streets and the "lulliputian" scale of its buildings had formerly made available—were recognized as resources worth protecting.

With the boom in new office development during the 1960s, many Portlanders had begun to feel that the city's scenic views and restrained skyline were being seriously threatened by what could become the "Manhattanization" of downtown. The guidelines called for the establishment of height and bulk limitations in the context of the existing environment, which would minimize the intrusion of tall buildings and make them compatible with the scale of existing lower buildings. Juxtaposition of tall and low structures throughout downtown, it was feared, would create excessive shadow on streets and public open spaces. In short, space and light were recognized as key components to the liveability of the city.

A happy truce between the competing claims of automobile and pedestrian traffic was also in the works. The guidelines recognized that the success of the planning scheme ultimately depended on developing a balanced transportation system that would reduce reliance on the automobile. The idea was to create an efficient mass transit service with a clearly defined transit mall as its highlight. A convenient shuttle system to distribute people throughout downtown was envisioned as a further incentive to bus riders.

To stimulate healthy circulation of pedestrian, automobile and transit traffic, downtown streets were to be segregated according to their dominant functions. If, as Glazer had noted in the 6 June 1976 *Sunday Oregonian*, "The real problem of Portland is returning it to the pedestrian," the planning guidelines tackled this problem with a set of viable and integrated solutions. In the process, the plan provided the closest thing to a coherent and beautiful vision of the city's self-image since the stillborn Bennett Plan of 1912.

The new plan had something for everyone. As Carl Abbott described it, "The vision of a lively, multipurpose downtown that tried to copy San Francisco attracted the young, affluent Portlanders who were also recolonizing stopover neighborhoods during the 1970s. The provision for a strengthened retail core and for larger concentrations of office buildings satisfied the entrepreneurial middle class. The promise to reestablish the waterfront as a magnet for public activity appealed to everyone."

Having overseen the revitalization of downtown along the southern limits, SOM was eager to become involved in the development of the waterfront. In 1971, the architectural firm of Wolff, Zimmer, Gunsul, Frasca had been engaged by the city to draw up a plan for a riverfront park. Three years later, the young mayor Neil Goldschmidt, who had swept into office in 1972 on a platform of neighborhood preservation and downtown revival, unleashed an army of jackhammers on Harbor Drive. At the same time, the riverfront and adjacent blocks were designated as the Downtown Waterfront Urban Renewal Area. The opportunity to reweave yet another fraying patch into the city's fabric knocked again on SOM's door, and the firm accepted the commission to mastermind the Waterfront Renewal Plan.

The *Urban Design Plan and Program: Waterfront Renewal Area*, completed in 1975, pooled the ideas and recommendations of a formidable team that, under the leadership of SOM, included San Francisco planners Livingston and Blayney, preservation specialists Allen, McMath and Hawkins, as well as economists, social planners and traffic engineers. Targeting a 130-block area that extended from Jefferson Street north to the Broadway Bridge and west from the Willamette River to Fifth Avenue, SOM's *Urban Design Plan and Program* took the Guidelines Plan of 1972 and put muscle on its skeletal recommendations. Conservation of historical buildings, development of a waterfront esplanade and construction of downtown housing were the themes of the master plan. The principal thrust was to redirect downtown toward the waterfront, which had recently been made accessible by the removal of Harbor Drive, the old-fashioned expressway along the river's edge. Sensitive to the spirit of participatory design, the project involved extensive community review.

The catchy, tabloid document circulated by SOM spelled out specific policies for economic development, parking and circulation, social welfare, historic preservation and development regulations. Replete with color-coded diagrams, charts, photographs and snappy drawings of downtown streets teeming with festive strollers and bursting with greenery, the plan made urban renewal look like the stuff of *National Geographic*. SOM's approach to planning was right up to Madison Avenue snuff. Recommendations centering on land-use and transportation concepts, projected a Portland that would have no problems selling its liveability to the rest of the world.

The "new" Portland, as SOM saw it, would be a close cousin to New York City, a metropolis with a hefty spine of glamorous skyscrapers, a generous scattering of pungent ethnic neighborhoods, historical pockets and fashionable residential enclaves, with a healthy circulation system and enviable public parks thrown into the package. As Pugh summarized this vision in 1984, Portland's development would have mirrored the evolution of Manhattan, at least in its broad contours. He saw the South Auditorium area, where Portland's renewal had begun in earnest, as occupying an analogous position to New York's Rockefeller Center. "Before Rockefeller started to build the Center in 1927, the vital core of the city was concentrated in lower Manhattan—reaching as far as 33rd or even 36th Street. Portland had a similar situation. We were very active in building up the southern development and then we worked our way back into the core." The *Urban Design Plan* supplied the blueprint for further "Manhattanization" that would spill from the waterfront into the central business area and then leap across West Burnside into the Union Station district.

A high-density corridor extending from West Burnside south to Jefferson and running along the projected Transit Mall on Fifth and Sixth avenues was to correspond to Manhattan's towering midtown. Maximum heights, set on the basis of consistency with "floor area ratios," were not to exceed 350 feet (27 stories at 13 feet per story) in this area. From this spine, buildings were to step down gradually in height, to 250 feet (19 stories) in the belt along Third and Second avenues, and leveling off at 130 feet (10 stories) along the waterfront. The intent was to preserve views of Mt. Hood and Mt. St. Helens from public points outside the downtown area, including the Rose Garden, Vista Bridge, and Terwilliger Boulevard, and to maintain the existing scale of buildings, public open spaces and the adjoining historic districts.

Major shopping facilities, offices and a hotel would be concentrated in the Morrison Bridgehead district. On either side of this strip, two historical sectors—the Skidmore/Oldtown and Yamhill districts—would make up Portland's version of New York's SoHo. All buildings within the historic district boundaries were to be under the jurisdiction of the Portland Historical Landmarks Commission, which would be advised on each alteration, demolition or development proposal by a district advisory committee made up of tenants and owners within the district. While new buildings would not have to emulate historical styles, they would have to be compatible with the character of the area. This meant that building height and bulk would be controlled to preserve the harmonious scale of the small landmark buildings.

As an incentive to developers, the plan provided for the transfer of an estimated million square feet of floor area ratios—the total building floor area divided by the site area—from landmarks to sites in the high- and medium-height corridors. To prevent further erosion of the old structures, the planners proposed a variety of tax incentives to restoration. They also recommended the creation of an Urban Conservation Fund, to be administered by a public and private non-profit corporation, that could buy and sell landmark properties and could make loans at below-market rates.

Making downtown a desirable place to live was a high priority in the SOM plan. "One of the strongest attributes of the South Auditorium project," Pugh explained in 1984, "was that it started a positive attitude toward living downtown. For a city where everyone lived in detached houses, downtown addresses were not very

popular. The Waterfront Renewal Plan tried to spur interest in the downtown residential market. We wanted to give people a place to work, to shop, to play—and to live." To this end, the planners recommended that 20 or 30 percent of new construction in the renewal area be given over to non-transient residential space. Much of this housing was slated for the Lownsdale Square/ Hawthorne Bridgehead district which, at the time, was an island of residential hotels for elderly pensioners surrounded by new office towers—including the Evans, Federal Building, Georgia Pacific and Portland General Electric Buildings.

The plan concept was to increase the supply of housing for middle-income families by combining new construction with rehabilitation in a superblock residential development. Creation of the superblocks assumed that several blocks along Main Street and Second Avenue could be cleared and freed of traffic. As the planners envisioned, "The ability to close streets to create a four-block superblock, the park blocks, the Waterfront Esplanade, and the prestige office buildings nearby are the elements that provide the opportunity for a successful residential development." The effect, as the architectural renderings suggested, would have been visionary. Apartment towers bristling with lush roof gardens and terraces, skyways and landscaped pedestrian-ways would have provided a solid modernist frontier to abut on the historical sections along the river's edge. And recreational boaters on the Willamette would have been treated to a colorful pageant of Portland's diverse architectural styles, all neatly related to the broad expanse of the Waterfront Esplanade.

The program of beautification did not, however, stop south of Burnside Avenue. In his 1943 *Portland Improvement* plan, New York planner Robert Moses made the point that "the appearance of the city of Portland, in spite of its magnificent surroundings and rather orderly development, is marred by the unnecessary ugliness of certain highly conspicuous places." The Union Station district, in his opinion, was among the most grievous offenders, being at once old and obsolete. "Access to trains is primitive and unworthy of the great railroads which use it, and of the impressive transcontinental service they have inaugurated," Moses wrote. "There have been suggestions that a high-level access to trains and other repairs and readjustments in the Union Station are all that is required. We believe that funds expended in this way would be wasted and that an entirely new station should be built by the terminal company. Railroad stations should be as modern as airports. As it

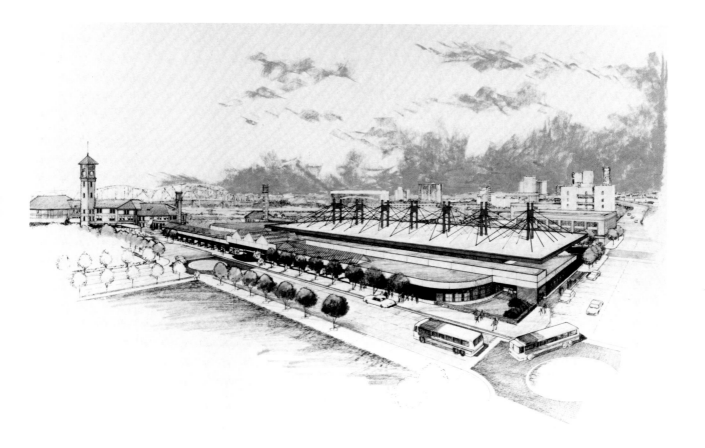

GREYHOUND BUS TERMINAL
Skidmore, Owings and Merrill
1985

is, the first and last impression of visitors on entering and leaving Portland by rail are bad."

Designers at SOM were just as sensitive to the power of first impressions, but they were all on the side of rehabilitation. According to their calculations, Union Station, with its 150-foot clock tower, was to remain, serving as the focus for revitalizing the under-used railroad district. The intent was to unify the area functionally, concentrating within it bus, passenger rail and marine services, and to transform it into the transportation hub for the city and the region. The central urban design feature called for a large public plaza which would serve as a forecourt to the station and as the terminus of the Transit Mall along Fifth and Sixth avenues.

By 1985, elements of this plan were already in place— most notably in the form of the SOM designed Greyhound Terminal, a low-lying brick structure whose subdued ornamentation timidly acknowledged the stylistic exuberance of Postmodernism. The planners also worked Portland's "Chinatown" and the shabby North Park

Blocks District into their overall scheme. An Oriental Community Center, proposed for the vacant block bounded by Fourth, Fifth, Couch and Davis, was projected as a magnet for attracting Oriental businesses into the district and providing the focal point for cultural and social activities.

In drawing up this ambitious shopping list for the city's development, SOM was particularly sensitive to the visual impact of new construction. The new city would not only be functional, but would be keyed to the pedestrian's experience of moving through an urban space. The plan made detailed recommendations that would maintain an enclosed urban feeling on street level by setting standards for maximum building dimensions and limiting blank walls at pedestrian level to avoid monotony. Rain protection, in the form of awnings, overhangs, marquees or arcades, was also recommended for new or remodeled buildings.

Most importantly, the plan tried to bring coherence into what threatened to become a chaotic expansion of downtown by anchoring it to the small scale of the city's distinctive grid. "The small Portland blocks (200 ft. by 200 ft.) and the ability to transfer development rights between them," the planners recognized in 1974, "began to promote a building type and development form which, if allowed to spread across downtown, would have destroyed much of the character and scale of Portland."

Like skilled prestidigitators, SOM put the "old that was good" in Portland into the black pouch of their planning strategies. They added the trappings of a modernist utopia—high-rises, super-blocks, skyways, pedestrian-ways and transportation malls—then shook up the incompatible elements, and pulled out a blueprint for "collage city." It was a model formula that won the approval of the U.S. Department of Housing and Urban Development which, in 1980, gave it the Special Mention Award for Urban Design Concepts.

As a result of the Urban Design Plan and Program of 1975, SOM was drawn into the next major renewal push in the city—the Transit Mall. The Transit Mall project developed out of the Mt. Hood Freeway study, undertaken during mayor Neil Goldschmidt's term to assess the desirability of constructing a freeway that would run directly from the Marquam Bridge to Mt. Hood, cutting a deep canyon through east Portland. Goldschmidt succeeded in dissuading local and federal governments from building the freeway and convinced them it would be more effective—and far less disruptive—to invest the same funds in light rail and bus transportation. "Along came Tri-Met wanting to improve their bus system," Pugh recalled, "so we eventually drafted a proposal and were commissioned to do the Transit Mall."

Winning a bonanza of awards and citations, SOM's plan became a reality early in 1978. On 11 parallel blocks of Fifth and Sixth avenues, the Transit Mall harmoniously combined circulation systems for buses, private vehicles and pedestrians. Set within the city's grid, the Mall was a mechanized, high-tech artery, pumping buses through downtown 12 to 15 minutes faster than they had moved before the one-way circulation corridors were built. The intent, however, was not only to improve efficiency of circulation, but to contribute in some tasteful and effective way to the substance and quality of the streets. This was accomplished with a hefty assist from Lawrence Halprin and Associates. The result was a success, even by the exacting standards of architectural critic Paul Goldberger. The Portland Mall—a tightly integrated design unified with surrounding buildings . . . stands in contrast to the 'lack of identity' elsewhere downtown."

Fifth and Sixth avenues were prettier, tidier and cleaner after this streamlining than they had been in decades. Refurbishing light fixtures, dating back to the 1920s, historic cast bronze drinking fountains, lozenge-shaped bus shelters with a faint flavor of Parisian Art Nouveau metro stations, sculptural benches and information kiosks added a certain charm and Old World quality not evident before the beautification. The new signaling system, using shape, color and texture to direct and orient the pedestrian along the circulation corridor to bus stops, contributed to the ambience, and lent the streets a sense of refinement, an image of wealth, commercial prosperity and substance. Red brick paving banded by light gray granite curbs and large granite circles at each intersection linked the streets to the building materials of the older buildings along the transit zone.

Remnants of the past—old graceful buildings faced with terra cotta and cut stone—took on an even more antiquated appearance when glimpsed from within the bus shelters. Equipped with a computerized information system that included closed-circuit television displays, back-lit maps and instructions, the shelters seemed to have been designed with space travel in mind. Trip planning kiosks in eight locations along the mall featured closed-circuit screens and keyboards that invited riders to punch in their route numbers and retrieve all the information they needed to plan a trip almost anywhere in the Portland metropolitan area. For Goldberger, the information kiosks, while fascinating, may have tried to get too much information across. "But then maybe the Portland bus system is more complicated than the entire routing system of United Airlines," the critic noted. For computer game buffs, these space-age amenities offered free warm-up sessions en route to video-game arcades.

Passengers with a less futuristic bent could find diversion in watching the drama of the street unfold. The broad, brick sidewalks were throbbing with people standing around doing nothing, people watching people or selling something from the vendors' booths and carts. An obliging, "ghetto-blaster"-carrying adolescent could always be counted on to disrupt conversations with the driving rhythms of a rock band. By night, when the organized mayhem of the day had quieted down, Portland's small band of "bag ladies" took over, camping out in the shelters, waiting for the bus that would never come to take them home.

In this respect, the Transit Mall was more than a two-way channel for fast circulation. Until the opening of Pioneer Square, it became Portland's liveliest public park. The Mall gave form to the plurality of the city. Past, present and future crossed paths in its blend of technology, history, "people energy" and even nature. The planners borrowed the local accent of the landscape to make the futuristic mall a horticultural enclave. Trees, tubs full of flowers and overhead banners marked the change of seasons—a must in Portland's rainy "uni-seasonal" climate—and introduced a natural order into the sophisticated transit corridor.

Their plan also carried a subtle nostalgia for the metropolitan glamor and grandeur of distant European capitals. The rows of London plane trees on each side of the street and 11 new sculptures by Northwest artists helped create the impression of a grand boulevard, in the manner of a Champs Elysees, but without the passion for heroic statuary or the drama of a royal concourse. Portland's Mall was as American as hot dogs and skateboards. Its sculptures—free-form abstractions, pop-art bibelots, and a restrained nude—were sidewalk diversions, casual pieces of street art that blended art, technology and nature.

SOM's master plans for the Transit Mall, the Waterfront, Portland State University, and the South Auditorium area, as well as their architectural spin-offs had much in common with the first modern land use scheme, devised by Baron Eugene Georges Haussmann in Paris for Emperor Napoleon III. Between 1853 and 1868, the Parisian core underwent a vast spatial rearrangement. Haussmann reshaped the imperial capital into a grand design of new routes and ceremonial public spaces. The city's reconstruction was, of course, part of a much bigger program of architectural enhancement in which Haussmann overhauled the local government planning system, provided a new water supply, laid out parks—including the Bois de Boulogne and the Bois de Vincennes—and built new bridges, fountains and public buildings.

Addressing many of the same concerns that had occupied Haussman, SOM's land use planners in Portland during the 1960s and 1970s laid down strict design rules for the buildings lining the streets, determining their height in relation to the street-width, and other architectural guidelines. Both the Haussmann plan of Paris and the succession of SOM-inspired plans, beginning with the South Auditorium Renewal and ending with the

Transit Mall, turned unruly cities into cohesive urban matrices. In Portland, the land-use planning system introduced by SOM was in step with the investment ethic that began to dominate the architectural scene in the 1960s. Development proceeded, but the plan also provided an invisible glue among urban districts. The new patterns were hospital to architectural *growth* and stylistic *experimentation*.

In Paris, the Place de l'Opera (1858–64) by de Fleury and Blondel, the Boulevard de Sebastopol (1860) and Mortier's Rue de Milan (1860) were typical of the variety that could meld within a standard dimensional framework. In Portland, heterogeneous styles also could thrive within the restrictions of land use plans. Historical preservation flourished and the urban core, waterfront and Old Town districts were slowly revitalized. With respect to architectural design, advances were made that went beyond "generic" urban expansion. The high-tech, ultra-modern 200 Market Building (1973, Rudat/Boutwell and Partners), the Postmodern-leaning Justice Center (1983, Zimmer Gunsul Frasca), the discreetly historicist Fifth and Oak Building (1984, Broome, Oringdulph, O'Toole, Rudolf & Associates) and the exquisitely restored New Market Theater (renovated 1983, SERA/Allen, McMath and Hawkins), were typical of the various styles that could coexist within urban-renewal zones. Accommodating a plurality of architectural sensibilities and functional needs within a coherent framework, SOM's planning schemes promoted a historically sensitive ideal of urbanism that ultimately respected and advanced the city's distinctive character.

Ironically, however, when it came to designing buildings, the firm's architectural ethic seemed oddly out of register with its pluralistic planning strategies. The vast majority of Skidmore, Owings and Merrill designs during the 1960s and 1970s showed a persistent attachment to the anonymous, uni-style aesthetic of corporate modernism, which paid little attention to the local context. In comparing the two areas of the firm's impact on Portland, it often seemed that its highly "visible" contributions in the form of high-rises and blockbusters were much less successful than its "invisible" planning concepts. By the mid-1980s, even members in the firm which had authored some of the city's highest structures were ready to acknowledge this discrepancy. When asked to identify the firm's best project in Portland, SOM's chief designer James Christensen pointed to a structure that was barely the height of a sidewalk. In fact, it was not even a building. It was a mall—the Portland Transit Mall.

But if the firm's strongest achievements did not include imaginative architectural design, stylistic innovation or integration of new structures into the urban fabric at the historical level, its buildings played an important role in Portland's urban evolution. To a greater extent than any other Portland firm, SOM could be credited with injecting the biggest dose of modernism—in its conservative, International Style variant—into Portland's atrophied architectural muscle. And though buildings such as Standard Plaza, the Hilton Hotel, the Georgia Pacific or the Federal Office Building could hardly be described as context-sensitive, they held the distinction—along with the Bank of California Building and the First National Center—of creating a new context for Portland.

SOM introduced a new look for downtown that was more in tune with corporate architectural trends reshaping the topography of American cities in the 1960s and 1970s, than with the constraints of Portland's architectural heritage. Throwing up a series of Miesian boxes, the firm gave the Portland skyscape the rudiments of the inflected, high-rise spine marking it as a "modern" city. In short, it established verticality as the new—if bland—coordinate for Portland's profile.

In part, of course, the stylistic uniformity of the firm's buildings derived from the tastes of its clients who tended to move in high corporate and financial circles. In Portland, as in most American cities, banks, insurance firms and corporations had traditionally been the purveyors of "prestige" architectural idioms. Ever since John Nestor, Warren Williams and Clinton Day displayed the fashionable Italianate style on the cast-iron faces of Portland's banking institutions, "prestige" architecture had gone hand-in-hand with money. The difference, however, was that whereas in the past, architects were free to pick from a wide range of historical styles, in the postwar decades, they were restricted to a narrow spectrum of variations within the single privileged idiom of the International Style.

SOM's avowed distaste for extremism and faddishness in design was not out of tune with corporate preferences. To be sure, buildings such as the U.S. National Motor Bank (1958), Orbanco headquarters (1980), or the Pacific First Federal (1983) reflected general architectural trends, materials and economic changes. But they did so with discretion and with a time-lag that allowed the shock waves of the new to subside. "Granted, we appeal to the more conservative client, whether this be an individual, a corporation, or a municipality," Pugh conceded. "But by and large, we do subscribe to the view that architecture keeps pace with history." He recognized, however, that his firm's slice of history was cut from a very specific cake. "Our architecture reflects the mentality, the interests, and the drive of a particular clientele at a particular time. This firm, for example, designed a lot of buildings out of glass and steel at a time when these materials and that aesthetic were prevalent choices among corporate clients."

By this reasoning, what was good for the client was not only good for the firm, but was also good for Portland. SOM, after all, had expressed a commitment to nursing the city back to economic and architectural health ever since it arrived on the scene in the early 1950s. "It seemed possible, even then, to make something happen to reverse the deterioration within one professional's lifetime," Pugh recalled in 1984. "In a city this size, no problem is so vast that one mind could not begin to work on it and, hopefully, see it solved." At the end of the 1950s there was an urgent need to attract sufficient commerical investment in downtown to preserve and promote a high-rise office core. SOM's architecture crystallized around the imperative of generating business for the core by creating buildings that would function, in some way, as outposts of commercial and urban vitality.

The idea, at that time, was that isolated development would provide a strong stimulus for urban growth by establishing "anchors" around which new businesses would eventually cluster. The opportunity to test this hypothesis came in the late 1950s, when two major clients—Hilton Hotels and the Standard Insurance Company—approached the firm with commissions to design new structures.

SOM had already made a step into a new zone—though not in downtown—in 1960, when their design for the new Portland Memorial Coliseum had been completed on the east side of the Willamette. Touted as the largest multi-purpose facility of its kind in the Pacific Northwest, the Coliseum was originally to have been built of wood. The use of this material in a structure earmarked for public gatherings and exhibitions would have made it a modernist analogue to the wooden Parthenon A. E. Doyle had designed for the Lewis and Clark Exposition at the start of the twentieth century. It would also have continued the spirit of Yeon's Portland Visitors Information Center (1948), which had melded regionalism with internationalism and had given abstract form a local inflection.

PORTLAND MEMORIAL COLISEUM
Skidmore Owings and Merrill
1960

Cost and safety factors, however, argued against using wood—the regional building material—for the new civic structure. Any allusion to the woodsy Northwest style was erased when the designers substituted steel for the primary structural material and ran a diaphanous gray-glass-and-anodized-aluminum curtain wall around the vast central concrete seating bowl. The result was a Miesien skyscraper laid on its side, with abstraction as its dominant theme. At the main entrance, a sculptural awning supported on four trapezoidal piers represented the architects' attempt to add a humanizing element to a structure that was fundamentally a cerebral object. Though the Coliseum did much to attract crowds to this underused part of town, it did little to enhance the urban character of the neighborhood. Rather, it did the op-posite. The Coliseum remained an island unto itself, set off from surrounding streets by acres of parkings lots.

The Standard Insurance and Hilton Hotel projects posed a similar reclamation challenge to the design team at SOM. Both buildings offered little in the way of dyna-mism. The new hotel, the first downtown facility of its kind since the New Heathman in the late 1920s, and the new corporate headquarters of the Standard Insurance Company, were pioneering projects that planted the seed for high-rise "row" along the downtown's median spine. Both completed in 1963, they set in motion an architectural process that changed the face of downtown Portland and determined the shape and direction of its development for years to come. The Hilton Hotel and Standard Plaza were one-block city plans that served as

225

templates for the architectural and siting schemes of the next two decades.

"The Standard Insurance Building was very important for expansion of the urban core southward," Pugh explained in 1984, "because it opened up the possibility of building large buildings in a part of town that had previously not been characterized by these kinds of structures. It was the first instance in which a firm was willing to step out of the 'inner circle' of Portland's retail core." For SOM, the project offered an opportunity to join an architectural design with a long-range planning concept for Portland's downtown. After considerable comparison shopping, which involved weighing the advantages and disadvantages of alternative sites, the client agreed to the daring move proposed by the architects. It was a significant step. In Pugh's opinion, the decision to build the Standard Plaza on its present site on Sixth Avenue was "just as important to Portland as the shift from downtown to midtown was to New York when Rockefeller Center was developed there in the 1930s."

The analogy to New York's Rockefeller Center applied not only to the long-range planning consequences, but to the architectural implications as well. Rockefeller Center, after all, was, as Goldberger noted, "the nation's first large-scale, privately financed, mixed-use urban renewal project." Commanding a three-block site in midtown Manhattan, Rockefeller Center introduced a coherent, and self-sufficient island of urban vitality, set off from the surrounding neighborhood by its tight architectural integration.

In architectural historian Rem Koolhaas' often irreverent account of New York's architectural evolution, Rockefeller Center was described as the culmination of its chief designer's private fantasy for New York. Raymond Hood, working in collaboration with Harvey Wiley Corbett and Wallace K. Harrison, was alleged to have concocted the Rockefeller Center design from elements of his private theory about the skyscraper. "In his [Hood's] vision the future Manhattan is a *City of Towers*, a subtly modified version of what already exists," Koolhaas wrote in *Delirious New York*, "instead of the ruthless extrusion of arbitrary individual plots, larger sites within a block will be assembled in new building operations. The space around the Towers within the blocks will be left unbuilt, so that the Tower can regain its integrity and a measure of isolation. Such pure skyscrapers can insinuate themselves strictly within the framework of the Grid and gradually take over the city without major disruptions. Hood's City of Towers will be a forest of freestanding, competing needles made accessible by the regular paths of the Grid."

To a great extent, SOM's designers shared Hood's consuming reverence for the sanctity of the tower as a free-standing object. In the Hilton Hotel, they had commandeered an entire city block for their 21-story tower, anchoring it on a one-story base which extended to the limits of the building site. Portlanders, by and large, were not amused by the formidable street-level podium. Despite the architects' earlier attempts to set the building back from the street lines in order to provide light, space and a public plaza, the final design capitulated to the pragmatic requirements for underground parking, ample convention facilities, as well as the usual complement of lobbies, restaurants and guestrooms. Portland's 200-foot square block, it seemed, was too small to accommodate both public amenities and the developer's private goals. The architects' solution was a compromise. The tower proper was set back on the base structure to create a central open plaza at the second level which contained what Wallace Kay Huntington described as a "romantically jumbled planting scheme." Unfortunately, however, only members of the Hilton's International Club could appreciate the delights of this airy space.

But while Portlanders railed against the "fortress walls" of the podium and the "anti-pedestrian" public plaza, they tended to be pleased by the tower's architectural achievement. The 21-story structure, after all, offered what was then the grandest example of "structural honesty" at work. The reinforced concrete frame sported projecting columns which tapered upward as the bearing loads decreased. At plaza level, concrete transfer girders expressed the shift of the total load to the base structure. A brush-hammered finish was applied to the concrete frame to expose the warm color of the stone aggregate. This finishing technique, according to architectural historian McMath, had not been used in Portland since Doyle's 1926 Motoramp Garage.

Though the modernist SOM tower was light-years away from Doyle's antiquating design, the rugged finish, particularly in the podium base, recreated the embattled spirit of Doyle's medieval fortress. But if the base of the Hilton was rooted in the Middle Ages, the tower was the unabashed offspring of International Style modernism. A spidery tracery of aluminum window mullions ran across the facade, at curious odds with the bold structural expressionism of the frame. This contradiction, in fact, appeared to provide the dominant visual interest in an architectural scheme that verged on the pedantic. It

HILTON HOTEL
Skidmore Owings and Merrill
1963

was not sufficient, however, to offset the intrusive impact of the large building.

In their scheme for the Standard Insurance Building, SOM made a deliberate effort to let the corporate client eat his cake—in the form of an imposing tower—and have it too. The idea here was to give the client the requisite high tower which, since the Middle Ages, had demonstrated the pride and prestige of its owner. At the same time, the architects wanted to make a civic, urbanistic gesture that would take into account the life of the city around the building.

Ever since Asa Lovejoy and Francis Pettygrove laid out the city's streets in the small 200-foot square grid in the mid-1840s, the size of building projects had gradually increased. Most early developments had been on 50-foot by 100-foot, or even quarter-block lots, the latter becoming standard for office construction throughout the business area. Between 1915 and 1950, the half-block—100 feet by 200 feet—became more common. In the late 1950s, when the Standard Insurance Company approached SOM to design its new headquarters, the client was prepared to follow this established precedent. The architects, however, wanted to push beyond the half-block size. Bigger, in their view, was better, especially when it came to the headquarters building of a national corporation. The argument was as old as the tradition of free economic enterprise. If, the reasoning went, control was exercised at the scale of the individual plot, then the bigger the plot, the stronger the architectural and symbolic statement. The client was persuaded, and a precedent for Portland's new corporate structures was established. The full-block became not only the rule, but the minimum basic site-unit for corporate behemoths.

SOM's solution for the Standard Insurance project was innovative—at least in Portland—for yet another reason. The Standard Insurance Building was not only Portland's first full-block office building, it was also the first *not* to be built to the property lines. Skidmore, Owings and Merrill scooped out the entire block site, but turned a good half of it over to an open public plaza. For the Standard Insurance Company, this was a splendid act of corporate philanthropy, emulating the examples set by the owners of New York's Lever House (1952) and Seagram Building (1958). In both instances, the corporate clients had been willing to surrender valuable real estate to public amenities. Gordon Bunshaft of SOM's New York office, designed Lever House to be much smaller than maximum zoning laws would have permitted, and gave the public a stunning pool and courtyard. In the Seagram Building, Mies van der Rohe provided for a deep plaza with green Italian marble rails as benches along its sides and two great fountains in its foreground. Portland's SOM was prepared to follow suit in the Standard Plaza project with a design chock-full of public attractions.

Inserted into the center of the sloping, one-block site, the Standard Building thrust a graph-paper face 17 stories into the sky. As with the Hilton Hotel, this building relied on structural expressionism for drama. The treatment of the exterior was deliberately calculated to reflect the distribution of stress points and loads of the supporting framework. One of the first buildings to use high-strength steel in the frame, the Standard also featured a central utility core of reinforced concrete, which eliminated the need for columns from the core to the outside walls. Along the exterior, slim vertical aluminum columns articulated the frame construction. The tapered form of the aluminum cladding on the lateral beams also expressed the form of the structural stresses on the members beneath. In the opinion of at least one observer, the result was a correct, if hardly imaginative rendition of the Meisian "form expresses function" doctrine. "By this time it had all been done," wrote McMath

in *Space, Style and Structure*, "the designer was hard put to create anything very original. The style had served its purpose through the Fifties and early Sixties and the Standard would be the last major building of its genre in Portland."

The street-level plaza, on the other hand, was only the precursor of things to come. As if to compensate for the humdrum minimalism of the tower, the designers concentrated a veritable bonanza of diversions at its base. A curving ramp and stairway led down to the sunken plaza from Sixth Avenue. Two entrances provided access to the building itself. One, opening directly from the lower level of the plaza, drew pedestrians across a miniature-scaled sunken garden that featured blue pools with circulating water. A bridge connecting the street with the building's upper level transformed this sunken landscaped fragment into a moat. In a gesture of corporate largesse, the Standard Insurance Company celebrated this ceremonial entrance by installing a sculpture by local artist Hilda Morris—the bronze "Ring of Time."

As a further invitation to pedestrian use, the architects eliminated sidewalks and parking along the sloping side streets. This would have guaranteed a heavy dose of street vitality in the set-back zone. The planners' hearts were in the right places, but local politicians frustrated good intentions. Bending to the wishes of downtown merchants, Commissioner of Public Works William Bowes insisted on having the sidewalks and parking reinstalled. Unfortunately, the granite sidewalls of the plaza allowed only for 42-inch sidewalks. Surprisingly, however, even though Portlanders were accustomed to the city's generous 12-foot and 15-foot sidewalks, they preferred these narrow passageways to crossing the spacious plaza.

Despite the designers' best wishes, this public space remained under-utilized. If anything, it served to dramatize the perils of using the block as a basic unit of urban construction. As long as building sites had taken up fractions of the entire block, a more or less homogeneous mixture of styles could thrive along the city's streets. In Portland's clearly defined grid system, the streets themselves often helped neutralize any stylistic conflicts and transformed the whole into a mosaic of complementary urban fragments. But as building sites began to coincide with the area of the entire block—as in the case of the Hilton and Standard Plaza—each block tended to turn into a self-contained enclave. For the owners of such corporate monoliths, the full-block schemes offered the advantage of a well-defined field for

BANK OF CALIFORNIA
Anshen and Allen Associates
1969

asserting corporate identity and ideology. For the city, however, they spelled a potentially sinister message. The towering blockbusters, after all, implied the potential for the essential isolation of the block and the break-down of an architecturally integrated urban matrix.

In 1969, two new buildings appeared at the north end of the downtown core that dramatized the unequal impact of quarter-block and full-block schemes. Pacific Northwest Bell's Capitol 2 Building, designed by H. Robert Wilmsen and Charles W. Endicott of WEGROUP, was an early attempt to harmonize the modernist aesthetic with the Beaux-Arts traditionalism of the Benson Hotel and the Broadway office of the Pacific Telephone and Telegraph Company. Commissioned to design an extension to the Italian palazzo-inspired headquarters of the Pacific Northwest Bell Telephone Company, WEGROUP architects attempted to respect the composition of the original terra cotta and brick structure (1913, E. V. Cobbey; addition, 1926, A. E. Doyle). In this respect, they were following the lead of Doyle, whose office had designed an addition to the building in 1926 that was indistinguishable from the original structure.

A Brutalist style, concrete equipment building, the annex was attached to the southern wall of the Broadway office. While stylistically competitive, the gray neutrality of the new building's quartz-faced concrete skin established an unobtrusive relationship with the Italianate structure. Both the horizontal and vertical rhythms of the original structure were replicated, though in greatly abstracted form, in the pre-cast members of the new structure. The result was a graceful transposition of the structural members underlying the Beaux-Arts structure into the muscular syntax of a modern form. At the same time, WEGROUP designers had shown that a stylistically incompatible building could take its stand in Portland's terra cotta enclave without introducing a morbid mutation into the delicately attuned urban topography.

The Bank of California Building, designed by the San Francisco firm of Anshen and Allen, made an entirely different impact. In designing their full-block structure, the architects followed the preference of the time in the massing. It was a boxy tower, rising straight for 15 stories, but it broke sharply from the prevailing SOM style in its form. The tower was given a roughly cruciform "footprint." A service core faced with dollar-bill gray-green slate intersected a vertically striated white concrete office slab. The overall effect was of two inter-connected boxes, with triangular columns of white concrete providing a strong vertical emphasis. The first banking floor was emphasized by four massive piers which gave the structure a classical flavor reminiscent of the Beaux-Arts temple designs which architects such as A. E. Doyle had once popularized for banking structures.

The building had great dignity to it—it would have been hard for anything with so much gray-green slate not to have—but it stood aloof from its surroundings. In anchoring their building to the site, Anshen and Allen had followed the lead of SOM's Hilton Hotel, which avoided any direct acknowledgement of the surrounding architectural context. The Bank of California stood back from the sidewalk on three of it sides. Its plaza was even set a few steps above street level to emphasize its disconnection. In forcing the bank's clients to climb a brief flight of stairs to the banking facilities, the architects might have wished to provide an elevating experience more appropriate to a church or a temple than to a financial institution. In the age of the almighty dollar, this stand-offishness might have worked hand-in-glove with the ideology of high finance. But it did not work urbanistically. Though enlivened with a formal landscaping scheme, the Bank of California plaza did little to relieve the massive encroachment of the new building.

The early 1970s brought a new round of high-rise construction that made the blockbusters of the 1960s—and their street level problems—seem lilliputian by comparison. With SOM's Georgia Pacific Building (1971) and Charles Luckman and Associates' First National Center (1973), building scale in Portland took a quantum leap upward. Spurred by the building boom and the infatuation for powerful architectural statements, architects launched a veritable "sky war" for control of the city's skyline. Zoning laws were not amenable to unchecked vertical expansion. But a way was found to circumvent maximum limits allowed by the zoning code. By assembling multi-block parcels, developers were able to take advantage of the so-called "grandfather clause" that permitted the transfer of unused "air-rights" between adjacent properties. The way was cleared for an unprecedented invasion of Portland's skyline that put the city on the map as owner of the "state's tallest" structures.

SOM took the lead in bringing this distinction to Portland. The firm was also responsible for introducing the first multi-block development into the downtown area. On adjacent sites, the firm designed an eight-level parking garage and a 30-story tower, the Georgia Pacific

GEORGIA-PACIFIC BUILDING
Skidmore Owings and Merrill
1971

Building, connecting the two with an underground tunnel. Battered granite walls maintained continuity between the garage structure and podium-based tower. Considerable care was taken to make both structures hospitable at street level. Shops with large expanses of glazing lined the garage and podium along Fourth Avenue, and a raised plaza marked the approach to the structure along Fifth.

The "humanizing" centerpiece of the granite-surfaced plaza was a rectangular fountain crowned by a 17-ton white marble sculpture entitled "The Quest." The work of Count Alexander Von Svoboda, the massive composition featured three nude figures in gravity-defying postures that suggested a frustrated impulse toward flight. Local wits preferred a more down-to-earth interpretation, calling the ensemble "Family Night at the Y" or "Three Groins in the Fountain." A counterbalance to this ungainly piece—which the sculptor had represented as "one of the last modern classical pieces ever done"—was Von Svoboda's tortured "Perpetuity" on the second-floor landscaped terrace. Taken as a commentary on the building's International Style aesthetic, this wood-and-bronze sculpture was the agonized counterpart to the ecstatic "Quest." Cast to resemble a massive, hollowed-out tree section transfixed with spikes, the sculpture vaguely alluded to the sinister underside of the lumber industry.

Georgia Pacific had wanted a top-of-the-line *modern* tower, and SOM's design fit the bill. At the time of its completion, Georgia Pacific was the tallest reinforced concrete structure in the country. It was also one of the safest and most energy-efficient buildings in Portland. Tectonic shifts, fires and high utility fees were no match for this earthquake-resistent high-tech tower. SOM design teams pioneered a flexible automatic sprinkling system—the first in a high-rise office structure—that did away with the need for conventional precautionary devices such as smoke towers and loop corridors. Coffered ceiling grids, each equipped with its own light and "heat recovery" air conditioning system, were also among the innovative firsts that appealed to energy-conscious tenants.

The attractions of this high-rise business address were spelled out with considerably greater restraint on the exterior. As in the Hilton and the Standard Plaza, function and structure were the principal design generators. The poured-in-place reinforced concrete frame formed deep-set window openings that clearly expressed the modular flexible office space within. An illusive tension was introduced into the building's grid-work cladding by tapering the structure as it rose to the sky. The effect was similar to the one that had been achieved in the Hilton Hotel, but was so subtly rendered in the Georgia Pacific as to be nearly imperceptible.

Nothing so understated would do for the developers of the First National Center. Hyped by the designers as the "New Symbol for Urban Portland's New Age," the First National took over the title of Portland's tallest building when it was completed in 1973. Thrusting 40 stories into the Northwest sky and covering two entire blocks of prime downtown real estate, the First National was more than two disproportionate buildings linked by a skyway. It was, in the words of architectural critic Ada Louise Huxtable, a "monument that tacitly advertised the values of insensitivity, unsuitability and flashy vulgarity."

In an imaginative reconstruction of the reasoning that produced this architectural and urban disaster, Huxtable pointed an accusing finger at the First National Bank of Oregon—the oldest and largest institution of its kind in the state. "First you decide to build a skyscraper for immediate status and identity value, making sure that it will do maximum violence to the skyline and setting, its architectural neighbors and the character of the city," she wrote in a *New York Times* review reprinted in the 2 July 1972 *Sunday Oregonian*.

If no local architect seems to qualify, go out-of-state, preferably to California, which has a reputation for a kind of genius for environmental malapropisms. Take a big, confident firm that will produce something jazzy and schlocky enough to batter all sensibilities.

To make sure, build a tower with tailfins flaring out at the bottom. Even Detroit abandoned these some years ago, so the effect will be both passé and outré. This doesn't have to be very convincing, because it's a phony detail anyway, buttressing nothing. Cover it all thinly with marble to give it class, detail it crudely. Color it corn.

However heavy with sarcasm, the description fit—as did the charge of architectural megalomania. The promotional material prepared by the firm made this as clear as the pink granite walls and Italian marble-clad columns of the First National's exterior. The brainchild of the Los Angeles office of Charles Luckman and Associates, the First National was designed to assuage Portland's inferiority complex—and to appeal to its ambition to rank among the "status cities" of the country.

FIRST NATIONAL BANK TOWER
Charles Luckman Associates
1972

In a slick marketing brochure, Luckman's publicists tried to sell the city on itself with their version of the "Portland Story." This was a city that "had developed through many stages, each with its characteristic symbol: The churning riverboat, the steam locomotive, the ocean-going freighter, the log raft, the shipways of the two World Wars." Curiously, not a single one of Portland's architectural monuments made it into this inventory of civic emblems. That role was reserved exclusively for the First National Bank Tower which was to embody a "city vigorous and growing, yet a growth [*sic*] in harmony with nature." As the firm's prospectus promised, the 40-story, block-square tower would be the "tallest manmade work between San Francisco and Seattle, one of the four largest buildings north of Los Angeles." This in itself was expected to make it the symbol of "a new, faster-paced, more modern Portland—a Portland rich in its past and eager for its future."

Tickling the tooth-and-claw nerve of prospective tenants, the brochure painted a gripping drama of Darwinian competition that guaranteed supreme survival to its brawny complex. "Presence of the five-story companion structure 'closes the square' of buildings around the monolithic tower," the brochure read. "This assures that no adjacent building can in the future rise to challenge the First National's preeminent height, nor compete for its air-space-light freedom."

The architectural fantasy went even farther. According to Luckman's vision of the city, the First National was to be the fixed center of Portland's universe, the measure of its grandeur and the pacesetter for future development. "The impression one gets of the expanded downtown area is one dominating influence" ran the firm's projection for the city, "the First National Bank tower—with other modern buildings radiating around it and from it. . . . Other new buildings and complexes will follow First National Center in construction." None, however, would usurp its position as the perfect symbol of "the new Portland and the new America." In the architects' minds, at least, the "upward reach of the tower epitomizes growth, its architecture states energy, salutes beauty."

For all its proclaimed respect for the city's "gem-like" architectural character, the First National was distinguished neither architecturally nor urbanistically. The same firm which had brought the watered-down automobile aesthetic of the First National to Portland had deposited, ten years earlier, the Prudential Center into the heart of stately Boston. Portland should have known better. As Paul Goldberger described it, the Prudential Center was a "collection of mediocre towers arranged around an austere and ugly mall, the aesthetic of a suburban shopping center thrust into an unwilling downtown." First National took the suburbanite's downtown-phobia a step further. With its forbidding granite podium and mammoth piers, the complex proclaimed the city street a battlefield—an uninhabitable no-man's land best reserved for speeding traffic.

Even with work on the tower still in progress, Portlanders began to register a vague sense that they had been hoodwinked by the developers' feigned reverence for the city's distinctive way of life. A chorus of local voices seconded Huxtable's outrage at the modernist "towering challenge to Mt. Hood." Some commentators, such as the *Oregonian*'s Paul Pintarich, bowed their heads in quiet resignation. "Granted, the First National Tower may be demonically monstrous, out of scale, or an 'environmental malapropism'," Pintarich wrote in the 2 July 1972 *Sunday Oregonian*, "yet, in lieu of a natural cataclysm, it will be here to stay for a long time."

But while the Luckman complex may have become a permanent installation, when it came to the city's architectural fashions, it proved that everything that goes up must come down. What came tumbling down within the decade was the uncritical acceptance of the modernist idiom that had spawned the uni-style glass boxes on Portland's horizon. The First National *was* an important building—but only in the sense that it was a hyperbolic expression of the worst in architectural modernism. In retrospect, it would become clear that it served as the modernist analogue to Michael Graves' Portland Building. But where Postmodern architects pointed the city toward a new, context-sensitive architecture, the First National suggested what Portland's planners and builders should rail against.

The minimalist aesthetic of the International Style died a slow death in Portland. Before the decade of the 1970s would come to an end, the city would acquire a generous crop of new variations on the theme of the glass-box. SOM followed up the Georgia Pacific with the modestly scaled 18-story Federal Office Building (1975), the hexagonal, 20-story One Main Place (1980) and the shimmering 23-story Orbanco Headquarters (1980). Reflective glass had become the favored sheathing material of the post–Luckman years.

In the case of the Portland Plaza Condominium (1973, DMJM), the skin's extreme reflectivity enhanced the

ONE MAIN PLACE
Skidmore, Owings and Merrill
1980

ORBANCO HEADQUARTERS
Skidmore Owings and Merrill
1980

graceful sculptural curves of the petal-shaped towers. On the exterior of the Orbanco Headquarters, however, the dark glazing tended to heighten the heavy dose of abstraction that the building's overall shape had given it. Faithfully reflecting its surroundings, the Orbanco Headquarters seemed not like a building at all, but like a great mirror stood up against the sky. Though the architects had provided a touch of local color at the building's base—in the form of a free-standing gazebo decorated with terra cotta arches salvaged from the former hotel on the site—the glass tower remained oddly aloof from its surroundings. In the opinion of Paul Goldberger, "the new mirrored-glass building does not blend well. It confirms the validity of white masonry as being in the character of this city." One Main Place met the specifications of Goldberger's monochromatic palette. Faced with finely textured off-white concrete, the complex acknowledged the creamy aesthetic of the city's terra cotta heritage.

In the early 1980s, SOM would shift its architectural aesthetic to bring it more in line with concerns for preserving Portland's visual continuity. Each in its own way, the Pacific First Federal Building (1983), the U.S. Bancorp Tower (1983) and the First Farwest Building (1983) responded to the stimuli of the city's new skyline. The most manifestly context-sensitive of the three, the First Farwest took its cue from the glass-and-aluminum composition of Belluschi's Equitable Building, its immediate neighbor across Sixth Avenue to the west.

Modernism had given the city a new profile. Unlike New York, however, which easily absorbed the minimalist glass boxes in the limited doses of its infill sites, Portland had borne the full explosive force of the shock of the new. The city had been so leveled during the immediate postwar decades, that it was an eager host to the foreign International Style invaders on a large scale. It became, in a sense, a model modernist city. By the late 1970s, a crisis of confidence set in among Portland's movers and shakers, which became emblematic of the growing international disillusionment with the promise of Modernism.

Reaction against the plethora of "glass boxes," which SOM architects had spot-welded to Portland's increasingly anonymous skyline, was brewing for more than a decade before Postmodernism (and its many variants, "pluralism," "historical eclecticism," or "Postmodern eclecticism") became part of the architectural lexicon. By the time designs for three major Portland projects—the Performing Arts Center, Pioneer Square and the

British Pacific Building—had surfaced, it became common to speak of a new epoch in Portland's architectural evolution—pluralism. It is a "moment in architecture when the eclectic impulse is paramount," Goldberger wrote in *The New York Times*, "a time, even, when we yearn to expand our aesthetic to take in all of history." In the eyes of many, Portland had launched this movement. "After all, if there are any buildings that seem to sum up the concerns of the moment," continued the New York critic, "they would have to be the Portland (Oregon) Building by Michael Graves, which is a brightly colored pile of reinterpreted classical decoration."

While Modernism was collapsing in its own backyard, Portlanders stood still—and watched. The essential dogma of Modernism in architecture on whose foundation SOM was built was the expression of technology as a force for change symbolizing the future, and a rejection of history. Early in the twentieth century, Modernists argued that architecture based on historical styles and decoration was somehow unclean, decadent—even immoral. The Modernist polemic reached its climax in Adolf Loos' essay in which he equated "ornament with crime." Modernists claimed that "abstraction offered architecture the formal vocabulary to represent the future as a visual rejection of the existing world," wrote Stuart Cohen, "and to represent symbolically a rupture in historical continuity between the old and the new. . . . This faith in technology [of the present], progress, and the future made the past irrelevant. History offered no insights, so architects believed."

Bristling with visions of utopia, the apostles of the Modern Movement were led by Mies van der Rohe, Walter Gropius and Le Corbusier. These early pioneers promulgated the notion (it was not the first time) that men could construct for themselves "a technological civilization that would render superfluous what was considered [until then] to be our civilizing heritage." At the same time, a fresh generation of designers began to work toward alternatives that would both realize their inchoate visions of a radically new architecture and that would appeal to the corporate and governmental clientele on which, they had learned, the "legitimization" and "prestige" of their innovations ultimately depended.

They found their most successful solutions in the new minimalism issuing (with increasing force since the late 1910s and 1920s) from the Bauhaus designers and from the swelling number of European and American innovators indiscriminately grouped under the label of the International Style. Uncluttered by historical allusions and realizing the Ludwig Mies van de Rohe slogan "less is more," the buildings designed by many of these Internationalists presented clean faces onto which corporations, cultural institutions and civic enterprises inscribed their own, fresh message of prosperity and power.

By 1952, the Modernist movement, with SOM at the designing table, would produce New York City's Lever House, hailed "as the vision of a new age." Over the next quarter century, thousands of Lever-like glass-box clones sprouted on America's skylines like mushrooms after a storm. But by the 1970s, it had become clear that the future world promised by the Modern movement had failed to materialize. As a result, it became all but impossible for contemporary architects to believe in the Bauhausian visions of Gropius and Mies von der Rohe, or in an architecture of idealized forms that would prefigure the new world it was to create. The Modern movement in architecture was discredited, not because of its cool aesthetic or the designs of its diaphanous skyscrapers, but because of its sweeping polemic that called for rearranging the fabric of culture through technology and the scientific method.

What happened is that the Modernists had forgotten history. "There can be no doubt . . . that in the early 1920s, Le Corbusier was genuinely committed to achieving a utopian urbanism that would combine the timelessness of scientific law with timelessness of Platonism," wrote architecture historian Norris Kelly Smith, "but his *ville moderne* was doomed to stillbirth for the same reason as Plato's republic: neither could be realized because both stood outside the *historical* world of human beings . . . a world occupied not by totally malleable nonpersons but by real people who were not about to turn their cities or personal destinies over to the tyrannizing totalitarianism of an Athenian philosopher or a Parisian architect."

In the misguided belief that men could forge a purely *technological* civilization that would promise not only the perfection of architecture but society itself, the disciples of Modernism turned their backs on architectural history. The "past is less" platform reached its zenith when the Modernists proclaimed that the perfection of architecture depended upon a repudiation rather than a celebration of history. Norris Kelly Smith exposed the philosophical bankruptcy of this position (and its disingenuousness) when he wrote: "Architecture of the Modern movement has been made for [Nietzsche's] lost men, has it not? Has it not been devoted to putting up a false front

of austere efficiency and economy in order to *disguise* the fact that the populace has been increasingly inclined, indeed, urged to identify goodness with profligate consumption, the good life with having fun and getting more and more for doing less and less."

This is hardly what the apostles of Modernism had in mind when they preached their "less is more" polemic. But the austere, self-denying glass boxes of Modernism were indeed a trompe l'oeil. Offering less a reflection of, than a contradiction of the acquisitive culture which produced it, this body of architecture, according to Smith, promoted the comforting thought that "ancestral standards of civility and decorum" were no longer relevant to modern lives; "that we had been liberated once and for all from the oppressive, *time-honored* notion that words like 'ultimate' and 'eternal' might really mean something after all."

As early as the seventeenth century, the British architect Sir Christopher Wren recognized that there was no inherent incompatibility between ancient and modern modes. He went so far as to claim that architecture should encompass the "attribute of eternal," and should be "the only thing uncapable of new fashions." The Modernists, however, had forged ahead toward a vision so absolute in its renunciation of the past, that it would eventually prove their undoing. Ironically, in its aspiration to transcend time and abolish the notion of architectural tradition, Modernism itself was devoured by history. It became outmoded.

The Modern movement, however, was more than a mere blemish on the face of history. It was a facelift that would change the complexion of architecture for the next 75 years. By exhausting itself ideologically and stylistically—Mies van der Rohe's "less is more" would become Robert Venturi's "less is a bore"—Modernism came to represent an important wall among walls. Indeed, the history of architecture would reap permanent benefits from the demise of Modernism. But first, it was necessary for the movement to run its course, to hit a wall, through which it would never pass without the aid of something entirely unexpected—the *past.*

The Modern movement repudiated the past and pushed austerity to its self-negating endpoint, in much the same way Classicism had extinguished itself in the profligate excess of ornamentation and symbolism. In the case of both Classicism and Modernism, the *absoluteness* of their visions had terminated less in a novel mode of expression, than in a lifeless scholasticism.

Modernism had stripped away all the symbols and ornaments that had accumulated over 6,000 years of architecture. Although architects were probably unaware of it at the time, this was a transitional step on the way to something important: to a perspective that could unify seemingly contradictory architectures of the past and present. As Wallace Stevens wrote in *Sunday Morning*: "Death is a mother to beauty." So it was in the world of architecture. The demise of Classicism in Bauhaus Germany at the turn of the century followed by the unexpected death of its stylistically polar opposite, Miesian Modernism, nearly 75 years later, suggested that "absolutes" in architecture, no matter what the form, were deadend walls.

Two stylistically divergent movements—Classicism and Modernism—terminated in a static equivalent of the other when each was taken to its extreme. This suggested a new set of equations for architecture—already well-established in the quirky world of physics—in which paradox, uncertainty and *unity* of space and time were the only reliable "absolutes." Lebbeus Woods, architect and author of *Architecture-Sculpture-Painting: Toward the Heroic*, proposed a universal theory:

> Monumental public architecture must affirm the highest aspirations of its time . . . a unity of spirit arising from . . . the most elemental and universal human myth. The outlines of this myth are emerging. . . . Relativity, quantum mechanics, analytical psychology and contemporary philosophies concerned with the dynamics of evolution and change confirm ancient wisdom about the cyclic forms of existence and the attainment of harmony through a creative interplay of opposites. The language of mythic symbols, interpreted in light of the most advanced knowledge, is the basis of a dialectical world view that will find expression in a new mythic art.

By the end of the 1970s in Portland, a number of designs on the drawing board at Zimmer Gunsul Frasca ranked as final admissions that the corporate, International Style of architecture no longer suited the needs of even the most conservative of clients. In Portland, as in New York, it was economics, and not aesthetics, which were deterring local firms, especially SOM, from designing more Miesian boxes. The modernist aesthetic, after all, had gained credibility in the corporate board rooms of the late 1950s, not in the Bauhaus design studios of

Europe in the 1920s. By the late 1970s and early 1980s, rumblings in those same board rooms, suggested that the Modernist revolution was more evanescent than anyone could have predicted.

With Zimmer Gunsul Frasca acquiring a lion's share of the commercial skyscraper market, even dyed-in-the-wool modernists like SOM began to have their doubts about the economic—and perhaps, even aesthetic—virtues of the stark Miesian model. In late 1980, the partners in the New York office of SOM invited what Goldberger called "a group of younger, so-called postmodern architects to present their work and engage in a dialogue" at a private symposium. "Skidmore consistently refused to permit the event to become a debate," noted Goldberger. "It ended up with the firm's partners showing designs that they believed to be different or more eccentric than their previous work, as if to prove they were no longer producing Miesian buildings by reflex." And indeed, in Portland, it was true that SOM's new work—like the Palladian-influenced addition to the Veterans Administration Hospital designed in collaboration (not surprisingly) with Zimmer Gunsul Frasca—was far from anything that the Bauhaus master who so inspired Skidmore could have imagined.

Change was one thing, good architecture another. Discarding the Miesian aesthetic in favor of something new, however, did not in itself resuscitate the International Style to which the Portland office of SOM had clung so tenaciously for two decades. Their "late modern" towers—for example, the Petroleum Headquarters in Bangkok and the Pacific First Federal Building, both designed by the Portland office—did not go far toward assuaging the boredom of the International Style. Sculpted for the sake of variety—with a setback here and a tuck there—these carved boxes demonstrated nowhere near the finesse or compositional acumen of Doyle's "cloudscrapers" of the 1920s.

While vibrant and glitzy, new buildings designed by the Portland SOM office suggested the firm might be willing merely to trade in its old glass box for a brand spanking new model. To be sure, the jazzy parallelograms, creases, nips, tucks and setbacks that appeared on their drawing boards in the early 1980s indicated that the glass box had been gently "spanked" into a unique, albeit, hauntingly familiar structure. "The architects of the new group of sculpted towers have not, ironically, expanded their interests as much beyond those of the International Style as they might wish the public to think," wrote Goldberger. "They are still largely preoccupied with the effects of manipulating form . . . this concern . . . often serves as an excuse for more sculpting of the box."

By the late 1970s, the International variant of modernism, which had been SOM's "brick and butter" for more than 25 years, was under siege. This was the case not only in New York and Houston, but in Portland where the City Council as well as private developers were amenable to exploring a new architectural idiom. In response to this new climate, the firm of Zimmer Gunsul Frasca (which during the decade had made steady progress in its bid for architectural supremacy in the city) cut loose from the chains of Miesian Modernism.

Zimmer Gunsul Frasca's move from the International Style (which characterized their early buildings) to the Postmodern eclecticism of the Justice Center and KOIN Center was motivated, at least in part, by competitive factors. With respect to large commercial projects, Portland had become somewhat of a two-firm town. Although stimulated partly by aesthetic and philosophical considerations, the firm's decision to embrace an architectural idiom that could marry Modernism with the richer languages of Classicism distinguished itself stylistically from its arch-competitor SOM.

A cause-and-effect relationship is difficult to prove, but Zimmer Gunsul Frasca's endorsement of a pluralistic, eclectic design strategy coincided with their consolidation of architectural influence in the city. This new direction seemed at once promising, both economically and stylistically. "The new Post–modern classicism is more liberated from convention and snobbery at once," wrote Jencks in *Late Entries to the Chicago Tribune Tower Competition*, "It is not as rule-bound or as smug as in the past, no doubt partly because the Modern movement has intervened to break these restrictions. We arrive back at where we started, with the Western tradition of Classicism, all its orders, moldings, and plans a possibility, but in new materials and with a possible freedom of application."

The new pluralism in architecture celebrated the eclectic impulse, and was well-received in Portland's architectural design-tanks by the early 1980s. Zimmer Gunsul Frasca, while not referring to any style by name, had clearly emerged as the city's reigning practitioners of Postmodern eclecticism. A number of their buildings, most notably the Justice Center (1984), the Biomedical Research Center (1986) and the KOIN Center (1984) were explicit in their basic intention to enrich Modernism with the expressive languages of the past. The hope, of course, was that Classicism could be used innovatively, in a freestyle manner. The move towards historical eclecticism would, by 1984, even appeal to the traditionally conservative design group of SOM. In 1983, the firm would bring designer Jared Carlin from San Francisco to revitalize their design team. There, it was hoped that Carlin's eclectic Postmodernist aesthetic would provide a welcome antidote to the well-worn Miesian formula that had dominated the firm's design program for more than three decades.

Unfortunately, despite attempts to revitalize the firm with a new design head, by 1985 commissions for major Portland buildings slowed to a trickle at SOM, once the city's most influential architectural firm with almost 100 people in its employ. "After the Fall," with its future role in Portland architecture uncertain, and with no sign of relief in sight, SOM decided, in May 1985, to move its now skeletal staff to more humble quarters. The rise and fall of Portland's SOM office paralleled the flowering and demise of the modern movement in the Rose City.

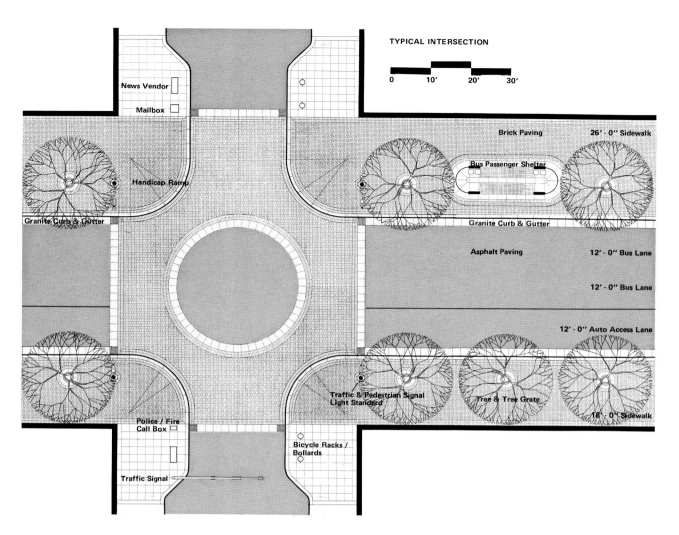

TYPICAL INTERSECTION

0   10'   20'   30'

News Vendor

Mailbox

Brick Paving   26' - 0" Sidewalk

Bus Passenger Shelter

Handicap Ramp

Granite Curb & Gutter   Granite Curb & Gutter

Asphalt Paving   12' - 0" Bus Lane

12' - 0" Bus Lane

12' - 0" Auto Access Lane

Traffic & Pedestrian Signal
Light Standard

Tree & Tree Grate

18' - 0" Sidewalk

Police / Fire
Call Box

Bicycle Racks /
Bollards

Traffic Signal

PORTLAND TRANSIT MALL, INTERSECTION DESIGN
Skidmore, Owings and Merrill
1978

241

POSTMODERN
FACE-OFF

N 1982, Portland would meet Postmodernism, the latest architectural rage, face to face. The erection of two buildings, the Justice Center and the Portland Public Services Building, within a one year span between 1982 and 1983, guaranteed that Portland would occupy a singular architectural niche among American cities. If a kind of free-form eclecticism—a merging of the forms of architectural history in an increasingly painterly and unpredictable fashion—could be considered the preoccupation of a new wave of architects coming to maturity in the 1980s, then the city of Portland, taken *as a whole*, could be seen as having jelled into a full-fledged Postmodern metropolis. Replete with striking edifices and historic districts that spanned the entire stylistic gamut—from the

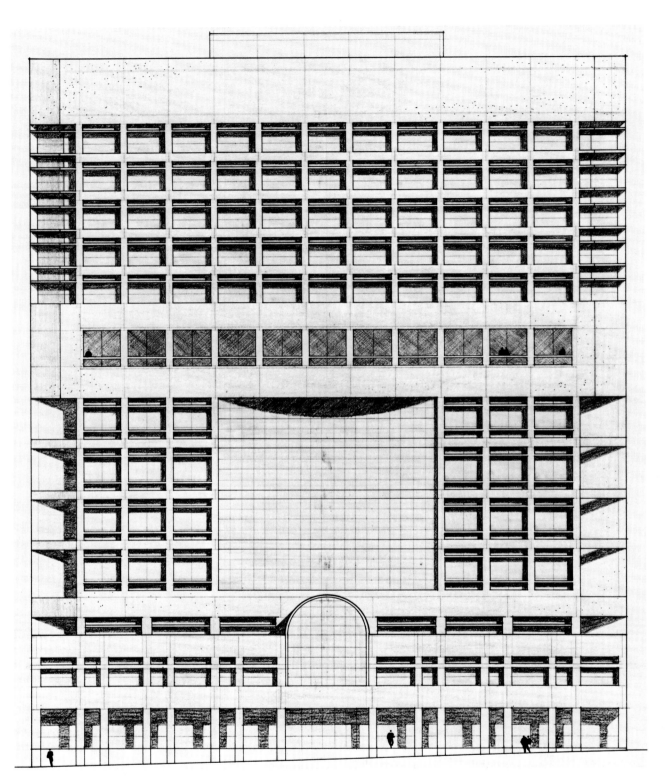

JUSTICE CENTER
Zimmer Gunsul Frasca
1983

Beaux-Arts-inspired buildings of A. E. Doyle to the International-leaning contributions of Pietro Belluschi to the Postmodern neoclassicism of Michael Graves—the Portland landscape made it possible to assimilate the history of American architecture within the context of a three block promenade and a diligent sweep of the eyes.

Portland's rich and eclectic architectural heritage made it an ideal proving ground for design trends—among them, Postmodernism, which was coming into fashion during the late 1970s. To feed this impulse, history was like a vast smorgasbord for Portland architects entering design competitions for large public projects and private commissions scheduled for completion by 1985. Myriad architectural styles—from classical to modern—were there to be ransacked, with visual pleasure the only criterion for choice. It seemed as if the spirit of architectural eclecticism, which had been spurned for the Modernist ethos during the 1970s, had emerged the real victor by the mid 1980s.

By 1980, the Skidmore/Old Town and Yamhill historic districts were well on their way to being revitalized, commercially and architecturally. A number of other areas more peripheral to the urban core had also coalesced. The city had become a more or less continuous showcase of architectural styles. While growth, restoration and integration of historic districts were proceeding on the local level, two complementary architectural movements—historicism and contextualism—had become the fashion in schools of architecture throughout the country.

By 1984, a number of architectural styles had either been introduced or meticulously preserved in the city. Portland's most important public projects, Pioneer Courthouse Square, The Portland Building and the Justice Center, reflected an increasing preoccupation with historical and contextual concerns. During this period a number of preservation projects were also in progress, including the New Market Theater (1871, William W. Piper) elegantly restored by Allen, McMath and Hawkins (1983) as restoration consultants to SERA. As consultants to Zimmer Gunsul Frasca, the same firm was also commissioned to restore the lobby of the Federal Courthouse (1931, Morris H. Whitehouse) to its original Art Deco splendor. In short, history seemed to be making a comeback.

After a hiatus of nearly 50 years, ornamental elements began again to animate the surfaces of Portland's newest buildings. Since the early 1960s Portland architecture had, for the most part, been wearing the regulation Mies van de Rohe minimalist wardrobe which had been em-

braced, to some degree, by the late-Modernist Pietro Belluschi and, more wholeheartedly by Skidmore, Owings and Merrill. While local revival of Beaux-Arts sensibilities reflected national, as well as international, trends in architecture, the fact that they were so readily adopted and encouraged by some of Portland's most influential architects could not be attributed to fashion alone. Rather, this revival signaled their desire to explore designs that would resonate with Portland's richly stratified architectural landscape. To be sure, by providing stylistic reference points from many historical periods, Portland would prove especially hospitable to the eclectic historicizing impulse that had become the architectural sign of the times.

Around the time Portland was reactivating its love affair with ornament and history, architectural historian Charles Jencks coined the term "Postmodernism" to describe a general trend he saw emerging in the late 1970s. Jencks recognized a trend characterized by less concern for the puritanical forms of the modern movement, and a greater interest in richness, ornament, expressionism, in the frivolous and bizarre. Princeton architect Michael Graves, whose designs merited inclusion in this new movement, reflected this penchant for Beaux-Arts formalism. In this respect, the trends in Portland architecture during the 1980s recapitulated stylistic and theoretical concerns that preoccupied McKim, Whidden and Lewis, and A. E. Doyle in Portland during the first 20 years of this century. Architecture critic Alan Colquhoun emphasized these similarities, when he commented that "Graves' work of the French tradition—its assimilation, initially through the example of Le Corbusier, of the Beaux-Arts discipline of the plan, has its origin in a purely American tradition going back to Richardson and McKim."

Portland's Postmodern era would be in full swing in 1983. By the end of that year, two examples of Postmodern architecture had been erected, and were locked in face-to-face combat in the downtown core. Both buildings—the Justice Center, a subtley ornamented edifice of precast concrete and sky-blue glass, and its style-mate, The Portland Building—had emerged out of a belief that the cool, unadorned forms of modern architecture were no longer a valid expression of the times.

Like a pair of "his" and "hers" bookends, the Justice Center, with its protruding arcade and The Portland Building, with its tunnel-like garage, seemed blissfully joined to one another over the fertile expanse of Lownsdale Square. In a show of mutual respect or, perhaps, in their attempt to spread the Postmodern gospel to passersby, each edifice cast an image of the other on its reflective surface. It was as if architects Graves and Frasca had wished their buildings to be engaged in a silent dialogue (maybe, a prayer) extolling the virtues of composition, decoration and historical styles. Though both were engendered by the Postmodern movement, the buildings had little else in common. If the Graves entry was the primitive progeny of an elite East Coast brain trust, then the Zimmer Gunsul Frasca structure was all Portland. It reactivated, in muted form, a rich tradition of Beaux-Arts architecture that had flourished, and served the city so well during the dynasty of A. E. Doyle.

The city's Postmodern face-off became not only national but, international news. In an article titled, "Design: Craftsmanship, Quality Reach New Heights," which appeared in the 1 December 1983 Paris edition of the *International Herald Tribune*, Carter B. Horsley called attention to Portland's dueling buildings. "Surprisingly, given all the attention of the Graves' project, directly across the park from the Graves' Building is another new major civic building, the equally striking Justice Center designed by Zimmer Gunsul Frasca Partnership," wrote the journalist. "Containing retail space, the headquarters of the police department, courtrooms and a jail, the building, which has a triangular tower, has a granite facade of unusual fenestration with a concave reflective-glass center portion over its skylight galleria entrance approached through its pink mosaic and Venetian ceiling loggia, which is framed by two stunning travertine marble modern sculptures by Walter Dusenberry." In Horsley's opinion, the Justice Center and Portland Building—combined with Fountain Plaza, a mixed-use project with a Postmodern flavor, and Hugh Stubbins' modern satin-finish aluminum tower—"made the Portland civic center area one of the most attractive and varied in the country."

Portland was on the map and Graves, the Princeton academic had helped put it there. It is no wonder that Graves, considered by some to be the country's quintessential Postmodern architect, decided after studying the Portland vernacular for several weeks, that he would have to *intensify* patterns that *already* existed in the city, making what Jencks called "a unifying urban gesture." That gesture, of course, produced The Portland Building which eclectically borrowed (without copying) and juxtaposed different architectural themes from the past—each of which was admirably represented by other Portland buildings in the vicinity. The ambiguity of these

juxtaposed images, suggested Jencks, was almost "hallucinatory" but The Portland Building made us "look at our past with renewed interest and respect. The values made manifest in Graves' work . . . are public, shared ones: urban space, collective functions, measured dignity and local identity whether 'Portland' or 'France'."

If, as *New York Times* architecture critic Paul Goldberger suggested, Philip Johnson's AT&T Building in New York City had "the distinction of being among the most controversial buildings of the age," it had to share its laurels with the Portland Public Services Building. The temple-like design for the 15-story building won formal City Council approval 1 May 1980, ending a three-month controversy which sparked heated debate among local architects, critics and city officials. The polychrome scheme, chosen by Johnson and the jury from among others, was superior, and somewhat cheaper, than entries by Arthur Erickson and Romaldo Guirgola, both of which were also Postmodern, but in a more understated way. "The controversial plan was approved by a unanimous vote," wrote reporter Steve Jenning in the *Oregonian* on 1 May 1980, "with each council member congratulating both the citizen selection jury and the building's architect, Michael Graves."

Despite the competition's upbeat and hospitable finale, the road to approval of Graves's design was a stormy one. Spearheaded by Pietro Belluschi, a group of Portland architects launched a formidable attack against the proposed design. Belluschi, perhaps remembering Herbert Read's admonition that "in the back of every dying civilization sticks a bloody Doric column," delivered this March 12th address to the city council on behalf of the Portland Chapter of the AIA.

I am here to express the feelings of the vast majority of Portland architects about the recommendations of the jury for the Public Service Building competition.

I have personally agonized over assuming an adversary position in this interesting undertaking.

I usually welcome change and innovation, I also like the fact that a competition was held and carried through, if onesidedly. You have two solid reasons for voting as recommended.

The Michael Graves scheme is the cheaper and has the backing of a famous architect. The cost is obviously a very important consideration but it must not be the overriding one—a building such as this has a very very long future; it cannot be frivolous, it should represent the culture of our city at its best.

As to Philip Johnson, I have known him for thirty years through his many mutations and transfigurations. I worked along side him for fifteen years when the New York Lincoln Center was conceived and built. He is very witty and brilliant but he is by nature an iconoclast and, as the *New York Times* critic tells us, he loves forbidden toys.

Now in his maturity, he has become the high "guru" of a coterie of young gifted people who earnestly believe that visual chaos is the reality of today's world—by defintion, there is no longer any distinction between ugliness and beauty at least in the old sense; everything is permissable; innovation need not spring from any deep experience. Discipline, the back-bone of architecture as a civic art, is ridiculed. They have discovered that frivolous means get immediate attention, and that fashions need not last. They tell us that content and expression, function and form have no more fundamental a connection in architecture than in scene painting, dressmaking or hat design. So they demolish the hated glass box and erect the enlarged juke box or the oversized beribboned Christmas package, well knowing that on completion it will be out-of-date.

Ironically, Philip Johnson in his speech accepting the Gold Medal told us that we must respect the *Genius loci*; that if you were building in Virginia you would not think of paying no attention to Thomas Jefferson or in Chicago to Richardson. Well in Portland we have our own tradition. We strive for preservation, for continuity and for enduring values. So it happens that Michael Graves is an exceedingly talented young artist, a collage painter, the foremost representative of Johnson's own coterie. This is his first effort on this scale and it is indeed innovative, but as conceived it should be built somewhere else—perhaps in Atlantic City or Las Vegas—not in Portland. Or better yet he should live a little while among us and absorb the *genius* of our city, and then begin anew. Who knows, his understanding may bear wonderful fruits.

Pietro Belluschi
One Fairfield Street
Boston, Mass. 02116

STUDY FOR THE PORTLAND BUILDING
Michael Graves
1980

Many local architects, preservationists and critics concurred with Belluschi's admonition. No one doubted that Graves would produce a building with flash and dash. But unlike Belluschi's churches, private residences and skyline sculptures—most of which were exquisitely sensitive to regional and contextual factors—The Portland Building seemed to suffer from a peculiar sort of stasis—a failure to interact synergistically with neighboring buildings, its site and the region's climate.

While the multi-colored skin evoked a sense of history—and, perhaps, even ritual through its figurative elements—these sensations seemed to dissolve abruptly at the surface of the building, and failed to resonate throughout the structure as a whole. To pronounce The Portland Building, or any building, as Postmodern and, therefore, humanistic, simply because its skin had been gussied up with architectural elements that evoked and refigured grand styles of the past was to miss the point. As Belluschi emphasizes, "There are humanistic *experiences* that must be carried *through* a work of architecture . . . if you just take it as visual art, you get the Michael Graves, the intent of having something to shock, to have something different simply because that's the movement of art."

Robert Frasca, design principal at Zimmer Gunsul Frasca, steered a more moderate, optimistic course. Frasca proposed that the Graves design was a step toward crystallizing an architectural vocabulary that would be expressive of our own historical period. "Until very recently, contemporary architecture had not yet taken that last step toward inventing its own vocabulary of ornament and symbols," Frasca emphasized. "Graves, for example, is one architect who has tried to generate a new vocabulary. In the Portland Building, he begins with classical notions—the human body, and a lexicon of classical ornament—and elaborates them in a modern way. He couldn't afford to actually execute the details, so he did it with paint. That's why the building is flat and seems so crude—almost prehistoric, in fact." In Frasca's view, the building could be seen as the crude seed of a major new tradition. "Looking at it, one has the impression of seeing architecture regress. It's as though one compared one of the very first Greek temples to the Parthenon and discovered just how short and stubby those first columns used to be."

Not only was the intensity of public (and private) outcry against the proposed building unprecedented in Portland history, but never before had so many architectural heavyweights of international repute slugged out their differences using the city as their boxing ring. "Belluschi, a Late-Modernist who along with SOM had changed the face of *classical* Portland with his icy-cool boxes," wrote Charles Jencks in *Post-Modern Classicism*, "put himself in the *role* of the reactionary Beaux-Arts academic who, fifty-three years earlier, had teamed up with local interests to block Le Corbusier's winning scheme for the League of Nations in 1927." "The plans have not been drawn in Indian ink. I insist on their disqualification," were M. Lemaresquier's infamous remarks quoted repeatedly by Le Corbusier. In Jencks' view, "Belluschi's reactionary caricature seems destined to live along side the French academician."

The hulk-like, somewhat squat mass did, indeed, challenge architectural conventions and design philosophies that had been emerging since the introduction of the International Style in the 1930s. But it did more. The building focused national attention on the city itself. In his *New York Times* column of 10 October 1982, Goldberger wrote: "Although it may look strange . . . it is no exaggeration to say that, as far as the development of American architecture is concerned, it is the most im-portant public building to open thus far in this decade."

The building was not only important, but divisive. A more genteel debate would have transpired if architects and critics had taken the advice of Sir William Bragg. The British scientist once said, "We use the classical theory on Mondays, Wednesdays and Fridays, and the [modern] quantum theory on Tuesdays, Thursdays and Saturdays." Among architects, historians and critics, of both classical and modernist bent, who jockeyed for position vis-a-vis The Portland Building, few would heed Bragg's advice.

Instead, the Neo-Classicists and Modernists separated into opposing factions from the outset, a phenomenon that Goldberger advertised to the entire world: "The choice of Graves to design the Portland Building . . . was denounced as ridiculous by a figure as esteemed in American architecture as Pietro Belluschi and defended as a noble gesture by Philip Johnson, who had advised the city of Portland on its decision. The controversy between two of American architecture's most venerable practitioners—one saw Graves as a traitor to modern architecture; the other saw him as representing the best hope for the future—guaranteed that the building would become Portland's most famous work of contemporary architecture while it was still a set of elegantly colored drawings."

The city council gave its endorsement of the design in part due to Johnson's enthusiasm, but also because Mayor Frank Ivancie favored Graves's proposal. Moreover, the overall building design came out on top in an analysis conducted by Morse-Diesel project management company, which was hired by the city to rate all three proposals on practical aspects, such as mechanical systems, operating costs and efficiency of office design. Earl Bradfish, director of Portland's office of general services, emphasized that the Graves design "better met our specifications for space than others, was cheaper to build, and was more energy efficient."

The endorsements from high places, and the suggestion that such an unusual building might be more efficient than the modernist glass box, did little to silence Graves's critics. They journeyed from their glass and steel towers on the East Coast to praise or denounce America's most "fashionable" public building. Yale architectural historian Vincent Scully wrote that The Portland Building was "of Portland and for Portland, a victory of mind and spirit in this place . . . a totally unexpected cultural assurance . . . as one never expected to be in a modern office building." Others took exception with Scully's benediction. *Time* magazine's architecture critic, Wolf Von Eckhardt, produced what Goldberger called "one of the most violent denunciations of an American building ever written by an architecture critic." Von Eckardt pronounced the building an example of "pop surrealism," and found "dangerous" the prospect that other architects might pursue the direction set by Graves.

The Portland Building coaxed out a body of idiosyncratic criticism because, as Colquhoun and other critics emphasized, it was not amenable to the conventional analytic and descriptive approaches available within the existing architectural lexicon. "In his [Graves's] work, architectural elements (windows, walls, columns) are isolated and recombined in a way which allows new . . . metaphoric interpretations," wrote Colquhoun. "At the same time rhythms, symmetries, perspectives and diminutions are exploited in such a way which suggests the need for a descriptive vocabulary such as existed in the Beaux Arts tradition, and still exists in musical criticism, but which is generally *lacking* in modern architectural discourse."

In the spirit of academic freedom, the Princeton University professor of architecture addressed criticism directed at his work. He defended his own position from a number of vantage points. In a lecture that followed Belluschi's March 12th address (and official letter) to the city council, Graves pointed out that the Portland-based architect had forgotten to change his stationery when he wrote his remarks from "Boston, Mass." In a more serious vein, Graves argued at Portland's Swann Auditorium, that his design reflected a much deeper understanding of the Portland vernacular, its architectural history, and cast-iron classical tradition than previous architects who had disrupted its fabric with "Slick-Tech Jewels."

The "Late Modernist" sympathizers led by Belluschi and the "Early Postmodernist" faction which was inspired by Graves but which had the support of local architects Frasca, Willard Martin and Gary Reddick, jockeyed for position prior to the 2 April 1980 City Council session, at which time the building gained tentative approval. Meanwhile, the local press was deluged with commentaries from citizens who recognized that the building or, at least, its *concept*, would mark a turning point in the history of Portland architecture. Among these responses, a letter from David Rockwood appeared in the *Oregonian* of 17 March 1980. It not only summarized the important issues surrounding The Port-

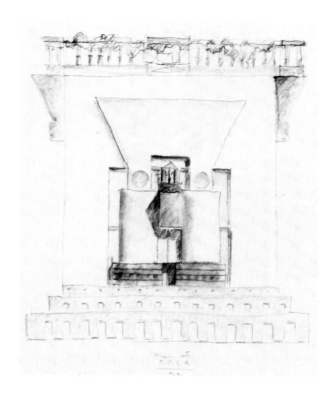

STUDY FOR THE PORTLAND BUILDING
Michael Graves
1980

land Building per se, but was a well-reasoned "White Paper" on the status of Portland architecture in the 1980s. For this reason, it is reprinted in its entirety.

To the Editor:

In following the current controversy over the Graves proposal for the Portland Public Service Building, I found myself asking some questions which I think must ultimately be answered if the issue is to be reasoned in rational terms.

1. Does the proposed building represent a true threat to the city in terms of its existing use and patterns and those projected for the future? If it is indeed a threat, is it more to the local architects than to those who will work and interact with the building?

2. If the building represents architecture as art, is it the place of government to support such a stance, and if the building meets its specific functional requirements does it ultimately matter?

3. Is the local architects' reaction one of fear (I don't understand current progressive architectural

thought and therefore I didn't like it), one of provincialism (It doesn't matter the quality of building we get as long as it helps to support the local architects) or perhaps one of jealousy (I wish my clients would let me do something creative).

4. Is the "Northwest Regional Style" real, or a myth supported by a sprinkling of quasi Sea Ranch houses which hide amongst the forested lots of the Portland West Hills, or did the style die after Portland's own Pietro Belluschi moved East to head the Department of Architecture of MIT? Do the numerous projects of SOM and ZGF which are quickly consuming and transforming our cityscape have more to do with the "Northwest Regional Style" or with toned commercialized versions of Chicago architect Mies van der Rohe?

5. If the issue is to use Portland architects for Portland buildings, how should we define Portland architects. Perhaps two years of residency is enough or should we require native status?

6. Does the Graves design address critical issues of urban design? Does it reinforce a traditional concept of urban space which defines the street and thus makes it a room, a place to be? Does it promote engagement, interaction and variety at the street level, i.e. make the street a lively supportive environment? Does the building respond on a variety of scales, an intimate scale up close with visual interest, and from further away does it promote an overall image of a unique object? Does it respond to its immediate context by alluding to specific or general themes and vocabularies of its immediate context, the courthouse and city hall, and larger context, the city? Is it an isolated element for use only by a select few or does it invite public participation? Does the building respond to people beyond a singular image, that is, does it provide a richness which can be interpreted in many ways to many people? Can a building in fact be like any truly great creative work, in which symbolism, foreshadowing, layers of meaning, and grammatical structure play a significant role?

7. Does an innovative work of architecture shock for long or does it like the Eiffel Tower or Center Georges Pompidou in Paris, become an exciting place, not merely a curiosity or tourist trap, but an amenity enjoyed by the city, a unique counterpoint to the normal everyday existence, and indeed a symbol of time and social condition in which it was built?

8. Are we to take the advice of the city's chosen advisor Philip Johnson, a man of distinguished talent and reputation, or withdraw into personal and preconceived ideas?

It is my hope that the courage which has been displayed by the city so far will remain steadfast. Philip Johnson said in Portland that the eyes of the architectural community of the United States and beyond are upon us. I hope we will not show ourselves to be compromising and take the easier and safer path. Portland has the potential to receive a building by one of the finest architects practicing today. Let us not squander this opportunity.

David Rockwood
Portland

The critical debate that surrounded the building before its construction, only intensified after Graves's deliciously colored paper model had been translated into a work of architecture. Officially christened on 1 October 1982, the building made it perfectly clear that Graves could build what he drew. Indeed, the painted surfaces of his building inspired a deep reverence for both classicism and cubism. Although the baby blue/burnt-brown/tan color scheme was provocative—flamboyant would not be an understatement—David Dunster astutely pointed out in *Architectural Monographs 5* that "To paint a surface of a building is always to lay some code over that building."

The City of Portland had commisisoned a work of architecture, not a color code. Yet apart from its purely architectural sources, most notably Le Corbusier, Graves's work had always been directly related to cubist painting. As architecture critic Colquhoun pointed out, "His work as a painter is closer to his architecture than that of Le Corbusier was to his. . . . Graves develops parallel themes in both painting and architecture, among which one finds the typically cubist notion of a world built out of fragments . . . according to the laws of pictorial construction. His buildings are, as it were, projections into *real* three-dimensional spaces of a shallow pictorial space."

Without question, strong pictorial instincts were expressed in The Portland Building, but a good painting did not necessarily a good building make. The first major-scale work of Graves's to be translated from paper to reality, the Portland Building was an architectural experiment in the supremacy of surface over form, paint over material, vocabulary over construction. By relying heavily on figurative and painterly devices, Graves drew criticism from architects who suggested that while he felt some nostalgia for the classical vocabulary, he did so without wishing to engage the mode of construction as an element which could be expressive in *itself*.

In much Postmodern architecture, elements, such as columns, that had previously existed in the *material* construction of a building, had paled into insignificance, and existed instead—in works such as those by Graves—as elements in the *intellectual* construction. Perhaps this was not all bad. Claude-Nicolas Ledoux, the fashionable, daring and extreme exponent of Neo-Classicism under Louis XVI, once said "art that lacks eloquence is like love without virility." There was no argument that Graves's Portland Building was eloquent—visually and intellectually. But when intellect and eloquence become the principal design generators in architecture, "the question then becomes," wrote Dunster about Graves, "to what extent is the [cherished] idea that a building be *united* at *every* level of its elements of plan, form, surface and detail now under attack?"

Not surprisingly, the articulate Princeton architect not only responded to, but, indeed, invited speculative discourse about his offering to Portland. "Maybe that's the point of modern work—the attendant critical debate, the idea behind it, rather than the work itself," he told Elizabeth Bunker, a Portland-based journalist who interviewed Graves. As any architect is well aware, a work of architecture—especially one that departs from tradition—will generate opinions that reflect best- and worst-case scenarios for its existence.

In the case of The Portland Building, the best-case scenario was readily apparent. At a distance, the building was prettier than a Belgian chocolate truffle. (Up close, it was in the municipal-swimming-pool genre, but that was the fault of inexpensive materials, not of Graves's vision.) And in much the same way that Henry Villard had solicited the help of the prestigious Boston firm of McKim, Mead and White in the early part of the century, Portland in 1980 had turned to a fashionable and reputable East Coast architecture firm. Portland's architectural landscape was begging for a touch of singularity, for an Eiffel Tower, a Marina City, a Space Needle—for a building that boasted a designer label.

STUDY FOR THE PORTLAND BUILDING
Michael Graves
1980

And it received something of equal and, perhaps, more important stature. The edifice was, after all, more than a conversation piece or 6.5 million ton novelty. Its neo-classical references made Portlanders swell with appreciation for the past, present and future, all of which coalesced and simultaneously annihilated each other, in the facade of the building. There was spectacle and mystery, the shock of the new.

Those who favored the design claimed that Portland had gained a building dedicated to humanism and art, that it rose self-assuredly above the collective human sludge, above twentieth-century philosophies of the absurd, above streets drenched in nihilism, hardened by organized murder, deafened by the noise of machines and blinded by the glitter of mass civilization. It was argued that the building was a bulwark against the fraudulent dreams promised by a world dominated, architecturally and otherwise, by the glass and steel faces of techno-fascism; that it was a welcome change from the banality of Portland's urban boulevards, overrun with undecorated concrete boxes, aluminum boxes, reflective boxes, partially reflective boxes and cracker boxes. Some, like Belluschi, have called it the world's almighty "jukebox." There was hope it might sing to the sky.

Although The Portland Building invoked anthropological and historical references, to many the interplay between human physiology and the structure, nevertheless, yielded a rather static experience. Despite the fact that Graves cited these figurative elements as evidence that the building merited the label of "humanistic architecture," the building was lambasted by a number of critics, locally and nationally, who commented that the overall design paid little respect to the building's future inhabitants. On this point, especially, Belluschi was quick to emphasize that the building designed by Graves, like any other work of architecture, had to go beyond the complexion of its surface in order to work successfully at the human level.

The skin of a building is of great importance, but historically, interior spaces have dictated whether a church or house elicited the requisite response, and, how well the architect had carried through the responsibility of making the person involved with the building happy or unhappy. "These are the quintessential elements of architecture," said Belluschi, "and this is why I resent, or have criticized, the Graves building. Because when you go inside, it has no respect whatever for the people who have to work in it. There is no sense of adventure as you enter, no inspiration."

"Graves reasoned that he was simply going to be more humanistic," explained Belluschi. "He wasn't wrong to appeal to these elements, since the Orbanco Building across the street is a deadly thing. It hasn't much of anything to offer besides an old idea whose time has passed. So there was a need for something. Graves took advantage of this void, exploited the desire of the man on the street for something more, but he couldn't deliver."

Those who spoke out on behalf of The Portland Building emphasized that its design and conception *grew* out of a sensitivity to context—to Portland's vernacular and historical buildings. This sensitivity was indeed apparent at one point during the building's construction. *Before* receiving its final coat of polychrome paint, the moody gray building was visually sympathetic with other government buildings in the area. One prominent local architect, Stanley Boles, suggested that the splash of polychrome robbed the building of its contextual poten-

tial and forced it, instead, to stand stubbornly aloof from its surroundings.

Although Goldberger pronounced The Portland Building "gracious and lively," he also noted in his *New York Times* review of 10 October 1982, that "The building pays only minor obeisance to its neighbors," while drawing attention to their difference from the existing buildings, did not ignore them. The Portland Building was, in the final analysis, more distinctive than contextual. Thus, it shared, ironically, with the Modern Movement, a penchant for creating architecture of a new order that stood in polemical contrast to the existing built environment.

In Portland contextualism and historicism had, after all, come of age. In a city with a rich tradition of architectural styles, a designer such as Graves—who to many was some sort of answer to the current trend back toward re-use of historical forms—seemed like the perfect choice for producing a respectable, lasting work of contextual architecture. In recent years, after all, local architects had—with increasing vengeance—expressed mounting concern for the way in which new buildings related to the existing built environment.

Several local architects had, by the early 1980s, already expressed a clear commitment to contextual design strategies. With its subtly rusticated exterior, extensive arcade and understated pre-cast concrete exterior, the Justice Center (1983, ZGF) paid homage to the architectural styles of Portland's government row. In a more pronounced historicist-cum-contextual vein, Willard Martin's (1984, Martin/Soderstrom/Matteson) Pioneer Courthouse Square used Romanesque columns, cast bronze pergolas and the original entrance arch from the old Portland Hotel to refer, somewhat whimsically, to classical pilasters in the adjacent American Bank Building (Northwestern Bank Bldg., 1914, A. E. Doyle) and to the city's rich tradition of cast-iron architecture.

In short, the climate in Portland was right for a devout historicist like Graves. His lyrical, iconoclastic designs—which provided enormous visual pleasure—seemed like they might be able to build on the themes and architectonic elements of Portland's older buildings, such as City Hall, and infuse them with new life. But for Graves, "context" was less a building, or a neighborhood, than an *interior* construct—memory, metaphysics and the cosmogony of western culture.

Writing about Graves's use of traditional and figurative elements, such as those which appear on The Portland Building, Colquhoun argued that "because these figures already exist in our memory, and because they

classicism that was being bandied about in academia's Postmodern think tanks, then Zimmer Gunsul Frasca's Justice Center would tap the rich vein of Portland's native Beaux-Arts sensibilities deposited during the city's Golden Age of Renaissance Revival. The firm's solution for accommodating a municipal police headquarters, county courthouse and detention center within a single structure would draw on an architectural vocabulary long familiar to the City of Portland's general public.

In the 1 December 1983 Paris edition of the *International Herald Tribune*, Carter B. Horsley summarized Portland's Postmodern face-off:

> The attention generated by the Graves project, which has no perimeter executive offices, has taken away some attention from the Justice Center directly across the park, a complex mixed-use building that houses a jail, courtrooms, the police department and retail space. From the travertine portal sculptures by Walter Dusenberry to the reflective-glass, convex central facade, the triangular building more than holds its own in comparison with the Graves Building. These are not timid, and they and the Fountain Plaza project define Portland more than its two major skyscrapers, the U.S. Bancorp Building by Skidmore, Owings & Merrill, just completed at the north end of the transit mall, and the older First Interstate Tower, designed by Charles Luckman.

In the process of modernizing and "clean lining" the formal historicist elements of their structure, Zimmer, Gunsul and Frasca peppered its skin with copious allusions to such downtown landmarks as Whidden and Lewis' City Hall, to A. E. Doyle's Multnomah County Public Library, American Bank Building and Public Services Building, and to Reid and Reid's Yeon Building. Like these towering predecessors, the Justice Center reiterated the structure of a magnified classical column. The front face of the massive octogonal building expressed the column's tripartite articulation. The street-level colonnade, flanked by two Egyptian-inspired obelisks, established a firm base from which the building's shaft rose a smooth 16 stories.

A colonnade spanning the recreation area on the tenth floor echoed the loggias that had become almost standard on the uppermost reaches of many Portland buildings erected during its Beaux-Arts period. The Yeon Building, the Northwestern National Bank and the Public Services Building all contained such colonnades. Interrupting the Modernist fenestration of the Justice Center, these columns made a unifying gesture with rooflines of Portland's pre–SOM "cloudscrapers," and supplied a stylistic rhythm that terminated in the gracefully curved moldings at the cornice line. Finally, the rusticated treatment at the base handsomely reinterpreted the horizontal emphasis Whidden and Lewis had given to the street level facade of City Hall.

The design team at Zimmer Gunsul Frasca had become increasingly preoccupied with decoration, form, detail, and with the entire range of issues that, since Bauhaus defeated the Beaux-Arts in the 1920s, had vanished from the curriculum of architecture schools. "When we were working on the coining at the base of the Justice Center, I was struggling to determine the size of the reveals," admitted Frasca. "No one in this office had any sense of how large they ought to be. To an architect practicing 50 to 70 years ago, this would have been second nature. We ended up going around to all the older buildings in the city and measuring the depth of the reveals on the old Portland Public Library and the City Hall. That was the only way we could enrich our vocabulary with elements and sensibilities our training had never given us. By going back to an *earlier* time, we didn't intend to be anachronistic. We merely wanted to regain the ground we had lost so we could start again at the point where our profession left off 40 or 50 years ago." From these investigations, the team hoped to "devise a vocabulary of architectural detail that is less derivative and more expressive of our own historical period."

Although the Justice Center did not generate the same degree of excitement that surrounded The Portland Building, it should have. *Architecture* magazine cited the building's public interior space "for its integration of ornament with architecture." In the February 1984 issue of the magazine, the editors wrote: "To communicate a feeling of permanence, the architect used honed precast concrete panels for the walls. In contrast are polished stainless steel for the railings and elevator doors, verde antique marble around the elevators and on other walls, and terrazzo floors with stainless steel strips, all crowned by a steel frame vaulted roof with mirrored glass. This vault runs the width of the lobby, terminating on a mirrored wall that further extends the volume." The large arched window dominating the space used a combination of beveled mirror glass and handblown French glass which, with their milky cast, diffused sunlight coming from the outside. Frasca likened the use of these precious materials against the background of precast concrete to "wearing a beautiful diamond broach on a gray flannel dress."

The project illustrated the enormous range of technical, philosophical and aesthetic questions that architects of jails and prisons are called upon to answer. Completed in 1983, the Justice Center typified the best of current correctional design. Visually, conceptually and structurally, the building was unlike anything that had ever been a part of Portland's urban landscape. In fact, the building was not even officially registered as a building. Instead, it was registered with the Federal Highway Administration, as Bridge number 16466. The new Interstate, I-205, had grazed a hair too close to Rocky Butte Jail for comfort. Consequently the Highway Administration was forced to pay for its construction under its "bridge" program.

The Justice Center generated considerable intrigue from the outset. The recreation area on the 10th floor commanded the city's most privileged view of The Portland Building. But whether to consider this part of the recreational program or the punitive process was a point of debate long after the building's completion. The building occupied a prime urban site one block from the Willamette River. It was big, luminous, elegant and had an understated Postmodern flair. Its public aspects—especially the crystal palace-like arcade and elliptical niche facing The Portland Building—expressed a unified image of civic dignity. Its highly refined precast concrete exterior exuded propriety, sterility and even-handedness. The beckoning concave glass dome suggested (at least from the outside) a spacious inner atrium dripping with sunlight. There was every indication the interior would be as vast and airy as a Bahai temple. No such luck. The exterior was a *trompe l'oeil*. Only 16 percent—or about one of every six—of the blue-tinted exterior glass panels actually transmitted light. The rest were decoys.

Jack Cornwall, project architect for the Justice Center, and associate partner of Zimmer Gunsul Frasca, summarized the design strategy when he commented: "Bob [Frasca] was very concerned that we not end up with some building that everybody could point to and say, 'That's the slammer.' That's why we worked so hard to avoid this problem and make it something else, give it some interest and a sense of the building as being something else than the jail."

Cornwall conducted a number of "arrest-to-freedom" tours of the facility during the last phase of its construction in 1983 one of which these authors attended. The architect emphasized the building "was not a *jail*, but a detention center," designed to be a pre-trial facility where inmates waiting to be sentenced would be housed. That was the directive given to Walker, McGough, Foltz, Lyerla, the Spokane-based architecture firm that designed the detention area in collaboration with the Zimmer partnership in Portland.

Although keeping people on the inside from getting to the outside was a new challenge for the Portland firm, the Zimmer team had gained some experience in designing structures intended to keep outsiders from getting inside. In 1979, the Zimmer partnership was selected to design the u.s. Embassy Addition in Vienna. The directive from the State Department (which for more than 25 years had been selecting distinguished American architects for u.s. embassies overseas) was to design the Vienna addition to withstand a full-scale terrorist attack.

Built originally in 1905 as a school for American diplomats, the existing building was ill-equipped to handle the onslaught of machine guns and explosives. Calling their remodeling project "bombproof Baroque," Gunsul and Frasca designed an entrance that incorporated concrete walls reinforced with steel plates, and laminated, bullet-proof glass. The original ornamented Baroque facade was then placed back in its original location. Although conceptually different, the Justice Center would also meld the richness of architectural ornamentation with the functional requirements of detention house security.

The Walker, McGough firm's national reputation in justice-facility architecture gave Cornwall the confidence to claim that Portland's Justice Center was "at the leading edge of 'justice architecture'. . . . The Federal Highway Administration was very specific that it would not pay for anything more than what mandated national standards required. The people at the Highway Department analyzed our architectural drawings very carefully and made sure that every cell had no more than 70 square feet . . . . Ours may be the only facility, before or after, that got built exactly to those space standards."

Being at the leading edge of incarceration design meant much more than complying with standards. It meant, among other things, Portland's first architectural structure with a split-personality. "So many people in the community will never see the inside of the building," explained the Portland architect. "I'm not being facetious. You've got to do something for the community. The building is downtown. You've got to enjoy it as a thing you walk past. There's got to be some delight there for the people who use it in an *external* sense."

The building had much to offer for the average passerby, who will never see the multifaceted, grisly labyrinth that constitutes the building's interior. He will never experience architecture at its coldest. He will never finger the unturnable doorknobs, which are there only for show; he will never know what it's like to be caged in the all-beige, windowless processing cells. He will gape with admiration at a light and airy building. The virginal purity of the precast concrete will pacify him. This is architecture as ablution, as exculpation, as psychic numbing. "It's the most beautiful concrete I've ever seen," said Cornwall, "and it got that way with a lot of fussing around."

The firm tried to reproduce the surface finish of Louise Davies Hall, a building that is part of San Francisco's Performing Arts complex. "We looked at the building in San Francisco and said, 'If we can achieve that, we think we can be satisfied.' We talked to the manufacturers of that precast concrete but they wouldn't tell us how they achieved their surface, so we really didn't learn anything except, 'Yes, it can be done'." Undaunted, they plugged ahead, and finally found a local contractor. "The precaster here started experimenting and things really started happening. I think it's better than the San Francisco product. We put a lot of hard work into that."

The Justice Center is architecture that cannot be judged by its cover. Its exterior public face and its interior private face were as antithetical as Dr. Jekyll and Mr. Hyde. If architecture could be duplicitous, even hypocritical, the Justice Center was a case in point.

The bone-white skin and copper-blue reflective glass made for a riveting combination. But style was not everything when it came to the business of securing prisoners. There were rivets and the nuts and bolts of keeping human beings confined in a space they preferred not to be in. That required ingenuity, so much ingenuity, in fact, that a prospering industry had developed around corrections architecture during the 1970s. It was called the "justice-industrial complex."

During the year 1982, state governments had spent $800 million on 90 prisons to be occupied by 1985. The projected total for state and federal commissions for correctional facilities over the next decade was nearly eight billion dollars. More facilities meant new architec-

tural designs and new strategies of incarceration based on technological innovation.

The most interesting, but least known, aspect of this architectural endeavor transpired at a little-publicized site beneath Portland's Marquam Bridge. Perched behind a bunker was the unambiguous building behind the building (e.g., the Justice Center) which housed a mock-up, two-cell jail at which destructive tests were performed to determine the security capabilities of the Justice Center detention cells. The exterior of this squat prototype was brutally minimal, consisting of cinderblock construction, separate ventilating units for each cell and metal doors. The interior was even more chilling: torch marks on the floors; burn marks on the wall; flaking paint from high-pressure water hoses.

The architectural experiment was a simple one: be bestial, wreak havoc, destroy, burn, smash and try to break out. The glass posed a special challenge. How long would it take to eat away at it with sledgehammers and cold chisels? Was the frame strong enough to hold it in? Among other people, the architects called on members of a local ex-convict's association to help ascertain the strength of the material. In one test, four men went at the security glass, made by Sierracin Corporation. Over and over again, they rammed the polycarbonate glass with a metal door, like a human-powered jackhammer. The frame holding the glass panel budged. The bolt heads sheared off. Since several more hours of ramming might have dislodged the frame, the architects redesigned the "stops." The architects were happy with the modification, which might even set an architectural precedent.

Filed under Job No. 6027 in the Zimmer Gunsul Frasca job log, these excerpts from the "Sierracin Glass Test" of 28 January 1981 provide a blow-by-blow behind-the-scenes look at justice architecture at its finest:

10:28:30 Duke Jennings started out testing the glass tapping lightly around the corners with an eye hook for approximately one minute.

10:35:00 Jennings started using a pipe wrench; put down immediately and returned to rebar.

10:36:30 Jennings started using a 12–16 oz. claw hammer working one particular spot with continuous blows, about one blow per second using two-handed blows; approximately one-quarter of the glass now cracked; surface area crazed.

10:37:10 Jennings switched to a sledge hammer with horizontal two-handed swings; large areas of the surface being broken away; the entire unit is still intact in the opening.

10:38:30 Jennings switched to claw hammer, then cold chisel and claw hammer; working on perimeter.

10:41:30 Jennings switched to pry bar and claw hammer in upper right hand corner; dropped crow bar for pry bar.

10:44:30 The test was stopped. The appearance of the glass: the entire length of the lower one-third of the surface was crazed and broken; still could see through upper two-thirds of the glass.

The architects and consultants seemed pleased with the destructive tests. They also experimented with the "eyebrows"—large, concrete slabs that would hang over the Sierracin panes in such a way that visibility into, and from, adjacent buildings would be compromised. "We rolled up and down in a cherry picker on the field outside the Marquam mock-up," explained Cornwall, "and jointly determined that this configuration gave the optimum in terms of views of people across the street as well as protecting the inmate from being looked on." The bottom line: no flashing.

Despite all the testing and innovation, there were still a few kinks to be worked out after the Center went into operation in January 1984. The real advances, however, were not in the decidedly *un*-jail like milieu, nor in the provision of television sets in the multi-purpose rooms, or banquettes, or the legal library. And while not yet commonplace, these standards of amenity culminated a trend in the 1960s and 1970s toward the eschewal of outward symbols and excessive rigors of incarceration. The real innovation of the Justice Center was the significant departure from the longstanding practice of restricting inmate mobility and a move toward increasing face-to-face contact between inmates and custody staff. Instead of immuring himself within a conventional control booth, shielded by steel and glass, guards assigned to each of the floor's three modules stand at an open desk, similar to a hospital nursing station.

There was a deceptive appearance of freedom in this corrections psychology. Of course, the open module is connected by video camera and electronic signaling devices to a well-secured central control post on each floor. The control post regulates the flow of inmate traffic using a state-of-the-art electronic detention system installed by G. B. Manchester, another member in good standing of the justice-industrial complex. Two back-up systems kick in should there be a power failure. Despite the high-tech security, architects who have specialized in building corrections facilities assert that in creating a less regimented, more domestic environment, they help to defuse tensions that trigger disturbances. Also basic to the Portland Justice Center, which is modeled, to a great extent, after the facility in Contra Costa County, California, is *flexibility*. By flexibility, corrections people mean a rigorous program for dividing inmates into manageable classification groups among a facility's housing modules.

Frasca, one of the principal designers of the Justice Building, described it as a "good building." The description was apt. The glassed-in portico protruding from the front of the building was a showpiece. The generous use of open space, stained glass, the exquisite columns, black marble and peach tones produced a pleasingly harmonious impression.

The authors finished their arrest-to-freedom tour of the Justice Center on an ironic note. The Zimmer Gunsul Frasca architect showed us the trial room and explained, "If you are free on probation, you simply go through this door and out to the lobby, where you can buy your first cigar at the variety stand." It was the wrong door. And so was the next one he tried. Call it architecture as metaphor. Call it a jail.

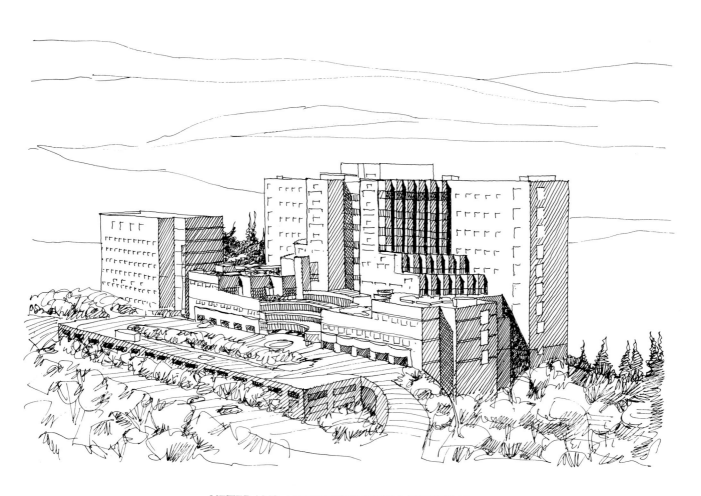

VETERANS ADMINISTRATION HOSPITAL
Skidmore, Owings and Merrill/Zimmer Gunsul Frasca
1984

FASHION IN CONTEXT

L IGHT TRAVELING through space is to architecture what the beat is to music—its primary pulse and driving force. A structure that intelligently apportions light through a three-dimensional space can possess all the power and magic of a perfect musical phrase. A monumental building can be as timeless and moving as the first four notes of Beethoven's *Ninth Symphony* or John Coltrane's "A Love Supreme."

Frank Lloyd Wright, a towering figure in twentieth-century architecture, once commented that to fully appreciate architecture, one "had to understand Beethoven." For Wright, oneness in diversity, depth in design and repose in the final expression of the whole were essential patterns shared by architecture and music. "So I am going to a delightful inspiring school of architecture when I listen to Beethoven's music," wrote the architect in his autobiography. "When I build I often hear this music and, yes, when Beethoven made music I am sure he sometime saw buildings, like mine in character? Whatever form they may have taken then—buildings."

"Planned progression, thematic evolution, the never-ending variety in differentiation of pattern, integral ornament always belonging naturally enough to the simplest pattern . . . upon which structure is based—Beethoven's rhythms are like that," Wright emphasized, "and likewise the work of the inspired architect."

Although architecture had not yet reached the zenith of its spatial and temporal complexity when the innovative designer made this comparison, the progression of architecture as seen through Wright's own work would show that what he suggested was not far off the mark. "His Romantic or anti-classical tendencies—call them what you will—reached an intensity of pure architectonic expression comparable to the musical intensity of the late quartets of Beethoven that Wright so much admired," wrote the distinguished historian Henry-Russell Hitchcock. "Falling Water, which might easily have been the swan song of Wright's career . . . proved but the opening *allegro* in a new period of innovation and experiment."

"Listen to the drum beat!" exclaimed Wright in his autobiographical essay called "Work Song." Indeed, he was so convinced of the importance of music to architecture that he required design students attending his Taliesin West workshops in Scottsdale, Arizona to gain at least some proficiency with a musical instrument. The eccentric architect even wrote the words to an architectural "work song" sung upon occasion in the Taliesin Fellowship by an a cappella choir. Written by the architect in 1896, and set to music by his wife Olgivanna Lloyd Wright in 1933, the lyrics adumbrated a controversy that would surface within architectural circles 50 years later: "I'll live as I'll work as I am! No work in fashion for sham . . . no deed in fashion for sham . . . I'll act as I'll die as I am! No slave of fashion or sham."

A work of architecture, like a sonata, is conceived, designed and, finally, "performed." Both architecture and music have evolved under the influence of continual experimentation in which historical antecedents have been either repudiated or refigured, depending upon the whims of fashion. In Portland, for example, architect Robert J. Frasca, chief designer for Zimmer Gunsul Frasca, has been credited with introducing a new—or, perhaps, re-introducing an old—architectural vocabulary into the city's landscape. It was a vocabulary that derived its inspiration from the "old that is good."

Buildings designed by the firm during the 1980s expressed an interest in once again presenting and refiguring classical elements and ornamentation commonly seen in Portland's finest Beaux-Arts-inspired buildings, including the Portland Art Museum, City Hall and the Multnomah Public Library. Attuned to the beat of history, Frasca characterized the relationship between music and architecture this way: "Architecture, like music, contributes to the richness that dignifies human experience. But change occurs slowly. When people first listened to Stravinsky's *The Rite of Spring*, they didn't accept it because it was different. The same may be happening now, to some extent, with the new vocabulary that has been introduced by the Post–modern movement."

Space is to architecture what sound is to music. As with a symphony, a building can be dense and episodic, or spatial and restrained. Pietro Belluschi's design for the Burke house (1949), for example, had much in common with the sparse, minimal and serene qualities of musical compositions by twentieth-century composers such as Erik Satie. Other Portland buildings were erected to the beat of a different drum. The Charles F. Berg building, for example, encapsulized the energy, flamboyance and tumultuousness of the American music in the 1920s. The theatrical passion and strangeness of its vibrant exterior were reminiscent of the quirky melodies and powerful rhythms of the Jazz Age.

For architects and critics practicing and writing in the twentieth century, it seemed natural to turn to music, which was paired with architecture because of a supposed kinship in abstraction and compositional methods. Writing in *The Beautiful Necessity*, architectural historian Claude Bragdon envisioned two distinct poles formed by music at one end, and architecture at the other. The remark that architecture is "frozen music," was, according to Bragdon, "a poetical statement of a philosophical truth, since that which in music is expressed by the harmonious intervals of time and pitch, successively, after the manner of time, may be translated into corresponding intervals of architectural void and solid, height and width." In Bragdon's view, music was dynamic, subjective and one-dimensional, while architecture was static, objective and three-dimensional.

Music was also used as a point of departure by other critics to explain why the public had, over the years, been interested in art forms such as painting, music and literature, but not architecture. According to Salvatore Vitale, one of the reasons for the public's lagging interest in the building arts had to do with their preference for artistic forms which unfolded over *time*, and which, presumably, could find adequate expression only in music and literary narrative. "To construct in space," wrote Vitale in *Is the Modern Spirit Anti-Architectural by Nature?*, "is the aim and end of architecture; but space is anti-spirit; it is pure extension, absolute, and complete realization, while spirit is pure and continuous tension, the everlasting condition of becoming. Thus, for modern thought, architecture seems hostile to the spirit. It is an inferior form of art that can acquire dignity only through its *spiritualization over time* (as in ruins, archeological remains, and ancient monuments) when it becomes a document of human life inserted in the course of history." For Vitale, then, in contrast to the temporal movement of a symphony, architecture was static and immobile, and did not lend itself to continual renovation and interpretation over time. To bolster his position, he quoted Foscolo's definition of architecture: "Most unfortunate of the arts, precisely because it is confined and constrained to remain exactly what it is."

In a later section, we shall have occasion to show how this perception of architecture as a non-temporal art form has been superseded. Portland's U.S. Bancorp Tower, designed by Skidmore, Owings and Merrill with consultation from Pietro Belluschi, would, despite its towering omnipresence, win over the "spirit" of Portland's architecture-viewing public. It would do so, because more than any building ever erected in the city, the pink skyscraper was an example of architecture that could respond to and reflect the fluctuations of both space *and* time. The building's ceaseless metamorphosis against the Oregon sky expressed temporal inflections created by the continuous rotation of the earth, the movement of the spectator and the flux of atmospheric elements (clouds, mist, et cetera) through space over time. Far from being static, this building argued convincingly that the element of time was indispensable to architecture.

Only with the spectator's movement over time—within and around a building—can molded space achieve the integrated reality that results from studying it from successive points of views. Bruno Zevi attempted to clarify the role of time in the experience of architecture when he wrote: "Whenever we speak of space in architecture, we refer to the idea of *space-time*, which has

been accepted by modern science, and which . . . has a specific application in the criticism of architecture."

If musical analogies could help clarify the emotional and compositional aspects of architecture, they could do little to illuminate its spatial essence. "To come alive, notes marked on the stave by Bach and Debussy wait to be played," wrote Zevi. Similarly, buildings wait, he suggested, "like characters in search of an author, for a modern criticism that will release and reveal them." In Zevi's view, a satisfactory history of architecture has not yet been written because critics are still not accustomed to thinking in terms of space. "To grasp space, to know how to *see* it, is the key to the understanding of a building," he wrote. Until one applies "this understanding as a central factor in the criticism of architecture, our history and thus, our enjoyment of architecture will remain haphazard."

The regulation of space in architecture has always been of paramount importance to Belluschi who remarked that "to observe architecture from the perspective of space" is an excellent guiding principle. "It is never free and pure, however," he explained. "All you can hope is that you will be able to discover a thread which is the result of having understood the climate, the traditions and habits of the people that live in it, and the human environment that is created by these forces. As a principle, if you discover the spatial thread running through, fine, but there are polluting factors and forces— things that have been done for other reasons."

To use the words of pioneering twentieth-century architect Mies van der Rohe: "Architecture is the will of an epoch translated into *space*." By the late 1970s, that "will," at least in Portland, had become increasingly restless, eclectic, atavistic—even, indulgent. The new fashion consciousness disseminated by Andy Warhol's *Interview* magazine and other literary outposts for the new chic had trickled up into the precious inner sanctum of Postmodern architectural design tanks, where ironic tricks, historical allusions and self-indulgent symbolism had become the main fare for a new generation of image-conscious architects. An increasing preoccupation with the composing of architectural form for its own sake, apart from the strict demands and requirements of physical construction, was hailed by many as a "baroque" flowering in the history of architecture.

By 1980, however, even with the full range of classical and modern vocabularies at their disposal, Portland architects (and their clients) would still be in a quandry as to what form the "quintessential" building should take.

It was obvious why. In a rapidly changing culture that could precipitously shift its aesthetic allegiances according to the whims of fashion, a building's stature could be weakened, or entirely lost, as the symbols of society changed over time. Architectural images powerful in one decade could become obscure, impotent or ambiguous in the next. They were signs that some in the profession were being seduced into a vast and exciting architectural extravaganza where almost anything was permissible: where style, glitz and flamboyance took precedence over process; where mold, mannerism and metaphor became more crucial for a building's marketing success than the integration of light, function and context into a unified architectural whole.

In the late 1970s, Portland architecture found itself in a full-blown identity crisis that no amount of Thorazine could put to rest. Over the span of a few years, buildings that exemplified a number of prevailing trends—including the "new eclecticism," the "computer aesthetic" and "romantic modernism"—were permanently affixed to Portland's architectural landscape. The completion of the U.S. Bancorp Tower, The Portland Building, and Pioneer Courthouse Square suggested that the unresolved, 5,000 year struggle between "less," "more" and "more or less," in architecture had come to a head on Portland's own architectural turf. In short, the city had become a microcosm for the schizophrenic state in which architecture across the country had found itself by 1980.

If architecture was undergoing an identity crisis,—and all signs pointed to this diagnosis—then Portland was in desperate need of psychoanalysis; or, as one architectural critic put it, "Portland needed to have its skyline 'shrunk'." It was as if he had taken Portland's pulse, when architect William Turnbull described the prevailing malaise within American architectural think tanks. Writing in the *Chicago Tribune Competition: Late Entries*, Turnbull observed: "Architecture in America is undergoing a profound change from the dichotomy between minimalists and inclusivists to a brave new world taking its inspiration from the historic past in both whole or in parts. This . . . comments on the hollowness of both the pragmatic minimalists who exclude people's aspirations from space and light as well as the historical inheritors of the Beaux-Arts who are busy introducing a neo-Edsel. Lasting architecture needs firmer roots and more freedom than the clipped lawns of the mind."

The clash between the historicists and neo-modernists would repeat itself in a number of design competitions which took place in the city during the early 1980s. In May 1980, the Portland City Council would choose among three very different designs submitted for the Portland Public Service Building, including the modernist glass box proposed by Arthur Erickson, the masterfully muted neo-classical design by Guirgola and BOOR/A, and the triumphant eye-popping, Play-Doh temple by Michael Graves. Only two months later, in July 1980, a distinguished jury assembled by the Portland Development Commission would have to select among five finalists for the Pioneer Courthouse Square competition. Again, the designs were sumptuous, but symptomatic of a deeply fissured vision. The proposals ran the gamut from the high-tech, crystal palace-like enclosures proposed by the Eisenman/Robertson team to the "wild and crazy" Postmodern Disneyland square submitted by Lawrence Halprin and Charles Moore. The winner, of course, was Willard Martin's (Martin/Soderstrom/Matteson) ultra-historicist design which, while winning a *Progressive Architecture* design citation, was criticized by one juror as a "very good example of the consequences of the current fashionable clichés failing to understand the fundamentals of urban design."

That the "clipped lawns" of America's finest architectural minds were engaged in a full-scale tête-á-tête was clear not only from jury debates in the Rose City, but from discussions at the American Institute of Architects Convention held in Dallas, Texas in 1978. At that meeting Philip Johnson who, along with John Burgee, would support Michael Graves' design for The Portland Building two years later, commented that architecture was "at the end of modernism as we have known it. . . . And [now] we have a new willingness to use history, to use symbols." Architect Cesar Pelli, a designer of cool, gleaming skyscrapers, took issue with Johnson's position. The reigning high-priest of techno-aesthetics, Pelli argued that "if the myth of technology is gone, that doesn't make the reality of it disappear. We must learn to use whatever appropriate technology exists." The standoff boiled down to a split between those designers who envisioned a contemporary architecture based upon the creation of pure space and form, and those who saw themselves making buildings filled with symbolism and historical allusion.

The fission was a very real one and its repercussions were felt acutely in Portland, where the city's two architectural mega-firms—SOM and Zimmer Gunsul Frasca—scrambled for position. To many architects, including Belluschi, it seemed that the emphasis on style, fashion and theories had shifted the focus in architecture away from fundamental design principles to more ephemeral concerns. Belluschi's involvement with myriad styles and compositional formats—ranging from the Italian Renaissance style of the Public Service Building to the Georgian-influenced Hamilton Corbett residence to the Modernistic Equitable Building—afforded him a unique perspective on the debate between Modernists and anti-Modernists. Having internalized *both* classical (Beaux-Arts) and Modern vocabularies in the course of his 60-year career, the Portland architect thus opined from his Olympian vantage point: "A structure gives a sense of satisfaction that is derived from the interplay of light and proportion, from the natural physiology of the human being, which recognizes intuitively when the fabricated environment is sympathetic with its own makeup. Architecture, then, penetrates into myriad dimensions, and goes beyond just saying that a form is Classical, International, or Modern, or Modernistic. Buildings travel to the spirit of things . . . but you need the satisfaction of the eye."

With the completion of The Portland Building in 1982 and Pioneer Courthouse Square in 1984, it was clear the worlds of architecture and fashion—to whose sensibilities architecture had looked with increasing frequency—had formed an unholy, yet temporarily stable alliance. Architecture seemed to have reached an impasse. Its turn toward assemblages of thought-out paradoxes, flamboyant coloration and whimsy was, as much as anything, an attempt to prop up a schism-riddled discipline. Unsure of their footing, architects of Postmodern vintage were becoming increasingly enamored of the past, which provided a security blanket in times riddled with internal dissension and confusion.

In Frank Lloyd Wright's prophetic work song of 1896, he admonished fellow architects to be wary of falling prey to "fashion or sham." Yet nearly a century later, fashion is precisely where architecture found its inspiration and a role model. In fact, architecture had been generating so much excitement and publicity, that its influence could not help but spill over into the world of fashion. Graves's design for The Portland Building appeared on paper shopping bags at I. Magnin's, and Meier and Frank followed suit with a cookie tin designed to the Building's specifications.

"Fashion pressed its nose to the windowpane," wrote *New Yorker* columnist Kennedy Fraser in "Architectural Fashion," "and saw architects moving freely in a bright and privileged world—long-established, powerful, public and masculine (to the point of being, especially with skyscrapers, notoriously phallic)." But while feminine fashion was looking to its big brother, architecture, with awe and envy, architects were looking right back at the world of fashion with an equally intense gleam in their eyes. "It is even tempting to see Philip Johnson's AT&T Building, with its neo-Chippendale twiddly bits," noted Fraser, "as some kind of giant late flowering of the historicism that the fashion world knows as 'thrift-shop chic,' and which it seems to be trying to leave behind."

The historicists, or neo-classicists, drew upon a vast repertoire of styles to create their structural theater. They were involved in a movement that had the potential for being submerged by fashion, a phenomenon Belluschi addressed when he said: "There is quite a difference between fashion and architecture. If you think of architecture as building, rather than as fashion, you are more apt to be right. There is enough challenge in carrying through a building, and more opportunity to do a work of art that lasts if you think of it as such. If the process is art, the building becomes a crystal, which is the result of all these forces—practical, human, and visual—having been given their proper place."

Fashion consciousness applied to Portland architecture of the 1980s meant leading it away from the austerity of orthodox Modernism—away, for example, from the Georgia Pacific (1971, Skidmore, Owings and Merrill) and Benj. Franklin (1976, Zimmer Gunsul Frasca) buildings—and toward designs that were more gutsy, symbolic and reliant on historical forms such as the Performing Arts Center, Pioneer Courthouse Square, The Portland Building and KOIN Center. "Architecture must be authentic," Belluschi emphasized, in an attempt to clear the air. "When you design a house, a church, or an office building, using inspiration that comes from having understood the problem," explained the architect, "that's authentic. When you think, on the other hand, 'Let's have a broken pediment here, or let's have a Greek temple,' authenticity is compromised." And then he cautioned: "You cannot fake being primitive. The moment you fake it you are no longer—you are just a phony."

But to many so-called Postmodernists, the past, itself, was authentic—and fashionable. It represented a world of paradisaical certainties. "Domestic architecture—as well as public building—has been self-conciously accepting the need to incorporate the past, in the form of memory-laden bric-a-brac," observed Fraser in 1982, one month after The Portland Building was completed.

"Still, it's one of the ironies of this process of refigurement, that just at a time when architecture seems to have taken on some of the traditional properties of fashion design—a taste for relatively rapid change and the construction of new collages for their own sake, for ornamental detail, and for publicity or promotion that seem almost as integral as the finished product—the world of clothing has been seeking out the very starkest austerity and visual purity that Post–modern architects are rejecting as sterile and inhuman."

During this (latest) epoch of "fashionable architecture," a number of buildings, both in Portland and in other American cities, were obsessively romantic and backward looking, finding inspiration in the ornate past, the very antithesis of Modernism and its emphasis on stark and simple forms. Fashionable architecture, however, had not been so bad for Portland. (Keeping up with fashion, after all, was, at least partially responsible for Portland's grand epoch of cast-iron and Richardsonian Romanesque architecture in the late nineteenth century, and, later, for the highly acclaimed Renaissance Revival buildings of the early 1900s.)

Whereas in other cities, "fashionable" architecture in the 1980s had come to mean "pastiche,"—polychrome collages and richly figurative facades—in Portland it had come to mean something different: promulgation, preservation and re-presentation of the city's rich architectural substrate in the form of new commercial skyscrapers and public projects. In December 1983 the Paris edition of the *Herald Tribune* summarized Portland's accomplishments this way:

Portland is a small, but mighty city that makes up for what it lacks in population, industry and size with an overabundance of amenities in urban design. While Portland was not the first city to build a major downtown transit mall or sponsor major architectural competitions for public projects, it has set the standard for the rest of the country in both areas.

The city's reputation for design quality and experimentation, highlighted by its selection of Michael Graves as designer of the Portland Public Service Building, is not new. The city has one of the nation's great city halls and an outstanding terra-cotta district of commercial and retail buildings, many of whose creamy-white, detailed facades with classical motifs are not yet landmarked.

By 1984, buildings designed by Zimmer Gunsul Frasca, the nation's 23rd largest architectural firm, had come to dominate the spatial essence of the city's skyline. Although the partnership had matured under the "spell" of Postmodernism, its design team had managed to steer an unusual and what might be called a "region-dependent" course between the over-mannered, symbolism of The Portland Building and the techno-aesthetic vision that New York architect Hugh Stubbins would bring to the city in the Pacwest Center.

In 1980, Frasca, the firm's design principal had called Postmodernism a "very positive trend, one toward permanence [and] quality." Resisting the vagaries of "kitsch," glitz and confectionary architecture, however, Frasca's team—which, until February 1982, had been spurred by Gary Larson, thought by many to be one of the firm's (and the region's) most shining designers—showing fierce independence and originality. They eschewed the hoopla and carte blanche polemic condoned by Postmodern architecture in favor of something which, indeed, seemed to be more lasting. While indisputably historicist in look and concept, the firm's buildings of the 1980s drew their inspiration primarily from regional factors and the city's architectural landscape.

This had not always been the case. During boom development years of the 1960s and 1970s, Zimmer Gunsul Frasca—which, accoridng to one local architect had been trying to "out-SOM SOM"—slathered the landscape with glass-and-steel high-rises in a watered-down Modernist idiom. "I want," said Frasca in a 1982 interview with *Willamette Week*, "to leave my thumbprint on the environment." To which Susan C. Orlean responded by writing:

A mighty thumbprint it will be. So much of the southern end of downtown Portland is Zimmer Gunsul Frasca's work that it's known as "Frascaland." There will be more: the firm, which was the architect in the aborted Cadillac Fairview project, is submitting another proposal for that same prominent chunk of downtown. The Veterans Administration hospital and the new light-rail stations are also its proposals. With all the work comes the attendant controversy. Other architects marvel at the firm's business acumen and quality work but rue its conservative design; those outside the profession keep worrying the old bones of Cadillac Fairview and complain about Zimmer

Gunsul Frasca's cold-blooded monuments to modernism. These buildings are cool and clean and open, with neither the whimsy and pomp of John Portman, nor the starch and austerity of Louis Kahn—just the plain, hard look of moderated Bauhaus.

Before the firm's shift to the massive, symmetrical ornamented forms of classical architecture, it had concentrated, during the 1960s and 1970s, on the abstract planar forms of the modern movement. The Evans Products Company (1975, Wolff, Zimmer, Gunsul, Frasca, Ritter), a multi-story office building sheathed in red Willamina brick, added warmth and stability to the Portland skyline. (It would be the city's last building to use Willamina brick. The company kilns shut down operations in 1974 after an illustrious 82-year history, during which time it had manufactured an estimated 280 million bricks.)

Less elegant than the Evans Products Company Building, but equally modernistic, was Crown Plaza (1971, Wolff, Zimmer, Gunsul, Frasca, Ritter), a two-block development in which an 11-story International Style office building was connected by way of two pedestrian bridges with a parking structure. Clean lines, simplicity, and an emphasis on repetitive structural elements to create a play of light and shadow characterized designs for the City of Portland Parking Structure (1975, Zimmer Gunsul Frasca/Deleuw, Cather and Company), the Esco headquarters office building (1967, Wolff and Zimmer), and the Operation Center of Tektronix, Inc. (1968, Zimmer Gunsul Frasca).

The austere rectilinearity that came into fashion with the Modern movement was highlighted in the firm's design for the Pacific Northwest Bell Fourth Avenue complex (1976, Gary Larsen of Zimmer Gunsul Frasca). The window mullions and general disposition of the cafeteria, as viewed from the adjacent park built over the computer center, recalled the pristine geometrics of Yeon's Shaw house and the Visitors Information Center. The design team led by Frasca showed great versatility. A nod to the stark curvilinear aesthetic of the Bauhaus was evident in two low-slung compositions for the Kaiser Foundation Health Plan clinics in Beaverton (1969) and on Interstate Avenue (1971). Perhaps their most successful offering in the modern idiom was the closely grouped cluster of buildings that comprised Portland Community College (1969, Zimmer Gunsul

Frasca). In its functionalism, response to program honesty in use of materials and use of glass, the complex could be seen as a tribute to the luminous architectural vision of Louis Kahn. Chiaroscuro depths, geometric abstractions and intersecting spatial planes were emphasized in order to create what Kahn, in referring to his own work, had once called a "treasury of shadow."

In earlier buildings, especially those designed in consultation with Belluschi, the firm had explored visual effects that could be achieved through a repetition of exposed structural elements. This program was expressed masterfully in the Oregon Historical Center (1964, Wolff and Zimmer, Pietro Belluschi design consultant), a five-story steel frame building faced with precast concrete. Reflecting an architectural program perhaps best described as "Neo-Brutalist," the exterior consisted of slabs of coarse aggregate and articulated window mullions which, in combination, created an effect that was more sculptural than mechanistic in character.

The expressive exposure of individual structural elements was integral to the design program, which derived its richness not from decoration but rather from the reverence with which the architects had treated the combination of concrete and glass. The exaggeratedly masculine lower levels of the Oregon Historical Center were balanced by the daintier fenestration of the upper floor, which was composed of vertical window slots. With its through-the-block lower walkway, museum exhibition spaces and upper level archives, the Center's plans emphasized the particularity of various internal functions, with overall organization tending towards an "additive compilation of contiguous spatial units, in some cases equal and modular, in others disparate both in size and shape." Unlike buildings the firm would design in the 1980s, such as the Institute for Advanced Biomedical Research (IABR), the Justice Center and KOIN Center—in which internal functions would be celebrated by their packaging into appropriate stylistic envelopes and spaces that became parts of a unified architectural collage—the Oregon Historical Center projected a single, unambiguously modern aesthetic.

A similar Neo-Brutalist formula was invoked in a number of buildings designed for the Portland State University campus, including Neuberger Hall (1967, Wolff, Zimmer, Gunsul, Frasca), the parking structure at 1872 S.W. Broadway (1965, 1967, Wolff and Zimmer) and the Gymnasium (1967, Wolff and Zimmer). Again, rough-

PORTLAND COMMUNITY COLLEGE
Zimmer Gunsul Frasca
1969

textured concrete walls—with an occasional smattering of brick—were used to achieve bold, repetitive sculptural patterns which expressed the building's structural underpinnings. Although less successful than the Oregon Historical Center in their execution of the Neo-Brutalist formula, the Portland State University buildings revealed a strong interest in ornamentation on the part of the firm's design team. In the University structures, as well as in other work of this period, the exterior geometries and volumetric manipulations gave rise to an architecture in which shadows replaced traditional ornamentation.

Ornamentation had not yet been revived in Portland in the 1960s, a period in which architects were still transfixed by Le Corbusier's incantatory proclamation that "architecture is the masterly, correct and magnifi-

cent play of masses brought together in light." By this time, the towering boxes were only beginning to dominate the urban core, relentlessly, like an incurable skin disease. Fortunately, in the 1960s Zimmer Gunsul Frasca had an opportunity to develop their ornamentation skills in concert with Belluschi, with whom the firm would join forces for a number of its early, and seminal, projects.

In 1965, the Zimmer firm had 25 employees and, as Orlean put it, "a nibble from Belluschi, whose relationship with Skidmore had soured when the firm decided his high profile didn't sit with its policy of faceless partnership." Belluschi had already obtained a commission to orchestrate a downtown office building for Equitable Savings, and after being approached by Wolff and Zimmer about the possibility of collaborating, he agreed. Described by Belluschi as "a tentative return to a more romantic architecture," the Equitable Building (1965, Pietro Belluschi with Wolff, Zimmer Associates) was a sensuous departure from the muscular concrete offerings the Zimmer firm would design in the years to come. In describing "Portland's first major structure in the new mode," George McMath wrote: "Belluschi again shows concern for the setting by establishing proportions and a scale that relates well with nearby City Hall, a statement that cannot be made of another neighbor, the monstrous First National Bank Tower to the east." Faced with precast quartz aggregate panels and detailed with Belluschi's old standbys, travertine and brick, the main structure was supported by free-standing columns rising above a stepped platform that looked like an ancient stylobate.

As principal designer for the 1969 addition to the Portland Art Association Museum Art School, Belluschi worked with Wolff, Zimmer and Associates to produce a building whose massing, general height and architectural characteristics were consistent with the first two phases of the Museum project. It was an important collaboration for two reasons. First, the addition rounded out an elegant complex of buildings. And second, the design team led by Frasca had its first opportunity to conceive a building that—both stylistically and structurally—referred directly to and established continuity with one of the city's cherished architectural monuments.

Again, in the boxy wing additions to the Oregon State Capital Building (1977), Frasca and Belluschi joined forces to extend the original design system to one of Oregon's finest buildings. The fenestration of the wing additions—although not identical to that in the existing structure—dramatically accented the original scheme. With Belluschi's input on these key projects, the firm gained experience designing buildings that "were of and for the city." Design programs for both the Museum and State Capital additions emphasized stylistic continuity, harmony in materials and contextual considerations. These were precisely the design generators who would figure so prominently in the firm's historicist buildings of the 1980s.

With large sections of Portland's downtown scooped out and readied for new development, the firm pinned down selected commissions with Belluschi, but secured also a number on its own based on its enlarging roster of projects. "We were constantly looking for ways to do better buildings," Zimmer said in 1982. "So when the late '60s and '70s came we were all dressed up and ready to go." Except for those buildings done in collaboration with Belluschi—which emphasized ornamentation and

historicization—projects designed by the firm during the 1960s and 1970s skillfully exploited the interplay of solids, voids and shadows, and had an unassuming modern character.

If historians go back in time, architects go back in space, which is what Zimmer Gunsul Frasca did to generate their design program for Portland General Electric's Willamette Center. Frasca, in particular, looked back to Paris of the nineteenth century, and New York of the twentieth, for models that might steer him to a good "space." "When we were commissioned to design the Willamette Center, we looked at successful solutions appropriate to our intention that other cities had elaborated," Frasca pointed out. "I researched the morphologies of European water cities for models. The opportunity to do three blocks in one stroke carried with it the responsibility of making 'place' on an urban scale. We studied the Place de la Concorde to learn what Haussmann had done in Paris to generate a dynamic setting for urban activity." Interestingly, the situation and specifications were analogous, since Haussmann had to gnaw out a big part of the city to make room for the Place de la Concorde. "He also began with a clean slate and then erected structures that would attract and collect energy from other parts of the city and spur further growth around them," Frasca emphasized. "For Hausmann, shops and arcades at street level were a particularly successful way of generating lively pedestrian traffic."

Frasca and his team took their cue from Haussmann's concepts. By placing retail stores along the street, they hoped to attract more people, not only to the Willamette Center, but to the waterfront as well. This is an old idea now (it eventually became part of the zoning code), but in 1974, when Portland planners were more interested in parking garages than shops, it was innovative. Almost as innovative—and controversial—as putting a retail floor into the Justice Center because the zoning code demanded it.

Relating the building to the river was another important consideration. "The solution, in this instance, was suggested by the outdoor skating rink at Rockefeller Center in New York City," noted Frasca. "An ice-skating rink in the middle of downtown would have been a perfect urban diversion. It would have made an ideal link between the casual, recreational mood of the waterfront and the 'big city' feel of the complex. What's more, it would have transformed the space into a small urban theater, where people could choose to be either spectators or participants. Unfortunately, the public utility commissioner was not receptive to the idea, and a carousel was used in the place of an ice rink."

The final design for the complex grew out of the spatial requirements of the program. The owners, PGE, specified an office building with small floors, a separate service building with larger floors, and a parking garage. They proposed putting the parking garage on the third block, but Frasca's group suggested they spend a little more money and put the parking underground. That would leave a block for facilities that would serve their own needs and that could be shared with the general public. "For instance, they were going to build an auditorium. So we said, 'Well, why don't you make the auditorium separate, so that on evenings and weekends Portlanders can use it.' They needed a cafeteria, so again we said, 'Why don't you put the cafeteria on the same block so that the general public could use it.' This is why the third block has always been referred to as the 'public' block'."

The Willamette Center was a radical departure for Portland and a pivotal project for the firm. It signaled a bold new approach to contextual urban planning that was at once responsive to the immediate physical setting and the natural environment, and capable of obeying the more ritualistic, cultural imperatives to which the firm had become increasingly sensitive (unfortunately, it also meant the demolition of some of Portland's finest cast-iron structures, including Warren Williams' Smith and Watson Building built in 1883).

The new space created by the three-block project responded to several dimensions—commercial, emotional and historical. The rationalist, rectilinear disposition of the on-site building, and continuous fenestration were overt allusions to the computer aesthetic in architecture that would come to Portland several years later in the form of the Pacwest Center. This futuristic projection was highlighted with particular panache in the high, lacy space-frame that connected the three buildings in a series of skywalks, reminiscent of a scaled down version of Fritz Lang's *Metropolis*. But the high-tech design was carried off with an ironic twist. By sheathing the structures in polished granite and reflective glass, the designers had literally given the buildings a "skin" that paid homage to the idea of a living, breathing, mutating city (Belluschi, incidentally, was a design consultant for the project). The materials were intentionally chosen for their ability to refract and absorb local light in a

number of ways in order to register different moods and complexions.

"We picked that particular gray shade of granite because it met the very strict and, almost contradictory, specifications we had in mind," emphasized Frasca. "It had to be both conspicuous and inconspicuous. At the time, we were very self-conscious about the size of the building and its impact on the skyline. We needed a non-aggressive color that would blend into the sky but, at the same time, we required something that would be vibrant . . . electric."

By 1982, the T square would shift dramatically. There were indications that the firm had broken new ground, that it had developed a new regional style in the area of commercial architecture. Something truly authentic seemed to be happening in the Portland skyline under the influence of the firm's design strategies. Led by Frasca, the design team used the eclectic, historicist impulse sanctioned by Postmodernism as a self-conscious program for exhuming, refiguring and re-presenting the city's ornamental and spatial riches. The objective, according to Frasca, was to build a contemporary architectural stratum that honored and resonated with the timeless contributions of Portland's architectural past while, at the same time, pointing a new direction for the future. (Belluschi, apparently, had fulfilled his role as Frasca's mentor).

If Graves's brand of Postmodernism was universal, metaphysical and pastiche-dependent, Zimmer Gunsul Frasca's home-grown variant had the distinction of being regional, pragmatic and *Portland-dependent*. Although the firm's work had the fashionable distinction of being Postmodern in character, its buildings were well-designed, sensitive to context and exquisitely crafted, demonstrating that lasting contributions could be produced, even within the general—and very trendy—framework of Postmodern architecture.

In short, the Zimmer firm did not sell out to the vagaries of mannerism and metaphor. And more importantly, its designs suggested that, indeed, it had required what Belluschi called "the genius of our city" to put Postmodernism in its best light. Put simply, *Portland*, not pastiche, had been very very good for Postmodern architecture. In fact, an entire architectural movement would play itself out in the city during a four-year span between 1982 and 1986. The Postmodern era made its debut in 1982 with The Portland Building. Its fluorescence would be heralded by the erection of the Justice Center a year later, and its "ruination" would be signaled by Pioneer Courthouse Square. By 1986, the revival of Postmodern architecture would begin to take form in the Performing Arts Center.

Zimmer Gunsul Frasca had always shown a knack for making the best of architectural trends, and for being able to move into a new design mode when the tides of fashion changed. Buildings of the 1960s had explored the Neo-Brutalism popularized by Le Corbusier and Louis Kahn; those of the 1970s expressed a staunch modernistic image, while projects built in the 1980s would be in step with Postmodernist theories erupting out of Princeton and New York. As the great architect Albert Kahn had pointed out, "architecture is 90 per cent business and 10 per cent art." And good business, at least in Portland, had always meant keeping up with the trends.

Belluschi, who had been a design consultant for the firm on several occasions, had once commented that "it is the discipline of the intellect and the respect for the means at hand . . . that keep the architect from straying too far into the shallow waters of mere fashion." And yet, Zimmer Gunsul Frasca attained stunning success designing within the context of prevailing architectural fashions. "What, exactly," it might be asked, "is so objectionable about fashion in architecture?" Perhaps, nothing. Writing in an essay titled, "In Defense of Artistic Fashion," critic Peter Schjeldahl made a strong case for its virtues:

> Enmity to artistic and intellectual fashion actually requires no rationale, because it is fueled by potent fears: fears of freedom and of the future. The freest of all our arenas for styles and ideas, fashion is a realm of seriously playful competition which scorns certainty in favor of whim, infatuation, wit, and fantasy—all the most volatile forms of imagination and desire. . . . Fashion also celebrates, by bracketing, the continuous arrival of the future . . . [and] spotlights the characteristic, unprecedented, unrepeatable aspects of an age. . . . Happily, we are never without it.

More fashionable than not, Portland could be seen, in a certain sense, as "Secessionist Vienna" coming back to haunt itself 100 years later. Self-conscious and experimental, Portland's architectural program of the 1980s expressed a vitality that had also characterized Viennese architecture during the late nineteenth and early twentieth century. Indeed, Portland's fin de siècle groping—this time it was twentieth century under fire—came with the requisite apocalyptic trimmings. In the case of Portland architecture, however, the search for a compelling vision, was based upon an *affirmation* of the past—of history with all its classical vocabulary—not its *rejection*, as had been the case in the Vienna of Otto Wagner and Josef Van Hoffman.

While architectural ideologues of both persuasions—Modernist and Postmodernist—flared their noses, a tectonic shift was rearranging the glass and stone edifices of Portland's architectural playground. The formal Romanesque elements of the Justice Center, the "streamlined" Gothic design of the KOIN Center and the proposed British Pacific Building—all designed by Zimmer Gunsul Frasca—were compelling testimonials to the new historicism. Moreover, these conspicuous quotation marks on the Portland skyline provoked the local branch of SOM into a serious examination of the architectural syntax that had served it so well for more than a quarter of a century.

This new epoch in Portland's architectural history may have culminated with the completion of The Portland Building, but was already being heralded by the quiet battle over design philosophies that had been waged for 10 years between Portland's two architectural giants—SOM and Zimmer Gunsul Frasca. Their gentlemanly competition for architectural supremacy was more than a matter of building commissions or structural domination over the skyline. It meant that Portland had, again, become a microcosm, as a result of the gradual change in architectural sensibilities—away from the austere, cool forms of the Modern movement to the historical eclecticism of Postmodernism—that was taking place on the international scale.

In the case of Portland architecture in the 1980s, then, the two prevailing architectural currents of the time—the ornamental historicist and the new romantic modernism (with its computer aesthetic leanings)—had not so much drifted together, as been forced into collision through competition. In many cases, the resultant buildings were oxymoronic, and reflected a combination of historicist yearnings and modernist leanings, all unresolved. Yet somehow, out of this body of architectural discourse, theorizing and speculation—in short, out of the confusion—there emerged a Portland skyscraper, the KOIN Center (part of Fountain Plaza), that suggested a fruitful merging of historicist and modernist sensibilities might be possible after all.

In an attempt, perhaps, to make restitution for the "cold-blooded monuments to modernism" generated by

MORRISON STREET PROJECT
ELS Design Group/Broome, Oringdulph, O'Toole, Rudolf and Associates
1986

his firm during the 1970s, Frasca said: "I think that architecture in general has, over the last 20 years, become lifeless and vapid and really buildings lost a great deal of individual identity. And this [KOIN Center] was really an attempt to restore some identity and some kind of degree of humanity to buildings. It's going to be a very nice building."

The breadth of Zimmer Gunsul Frasca's designs for Portland buildings erected between 1965 and 1984 was enough to give one pause. In the mid-1980s, the firm seemed to yearn for the vanished days when the "Mistress Art" gloried in the richness of her wardrobe, while only a decade earlier, it had preferred the architectural nude. In calling Portland's Modern period "lifeless and vapid," Frasca became a descendant of the anti-Modernists who

were bringing the world full circle, "from war cry, through description, to a nudging code word to imply dismissive ridicule of everything the Modern Movement stood for."

In *On The Rise, New York Times* critic Paul Goldberger would include the KOIN Center in a group of world-class buildings that, he felt, were strong testimonials to the successful merging of historicist and modernist impulses. Besides Portland's squat polychrome box designed by Michael Graves, which Goldberger wrote, was "surely not [Louis] Sullivan's 'proud and soaring' thing," the KOIN Center was the only Portland building that elicited the critic's exultation. "These two strains—the historicist and computer aesthetics—may yet join. There are hints of a connection in . . . Jahn's Chicago Board of Trade

KOIN CENTER
Zimmer Gunsul Frasca
1984

Addition . . . [and] can also be felt in Zimmer Gunsul Frasca Partnership's Fountain Plaza Project for Portland, Oregon, a tower of modern materials it is like Warren and Wetmore's Heckscher Building of 1925 on Fifth Avenue in New York, rendered cool and sleek . . . each of these designs does seem to emerge from a set of ideas that, while complex, come together to create a coherent and unified whole." The completion of the KOIN Center—with its fruitful melding of historicism and the computer aesthetic—signaled that Portland architecture was edging, slowly but with some trepidation, away from the glass boxes of Modernism. History met high-tech in the harsh angularity and sumptuous massing of the KOIN Center. Or, put another way, the software was Gothic and the hardware, state-of-the-art IBM.

Accolades for the KOIN Center trickled in from just about everywhere, even Seattle, Portland's architectural foe to the north. "A building is taking shape in Portland. It's not just another international style building. What is happening at Third and Columbia in downtown Portland is a fine demonstration of man's use of his inner resources," wrote Anthony Dodoye-Alali, arts editor for the *Seattle Daily Journal of Commerce*. "In just 29 levels the architects of Portland's Zimmer Gunsul Frasca Partnership have so arranged brick panels, limestone and glass that it will be impossible to take a glance . . . [at the KOIN Center] and not have a lasting imprint to beauty deep within your soul: It's architecture at the ultimate level."

In a time when unrestrained designers were feeling that architecture had to be crammed with images and historical allusions, often randomly flung together, the designs of Zimmer Gunsul Frasca were sedate, scholarly, scrupulously contextual and cautious. The Justice Center, the KOIN Center, and the proposed British Pacific Building suggested the emergence of a new regional style in commercial architecture. With their subtly mannered facades, two of these structures—the KOIN Center and the proposed British Pacific Building—were expressions of a decorative, sculptural architecture in which contrasting materials, rich in color and texture, were molded into a modified Gothic framework. The setback tower and faceted sides of the KOIN Center, rising sumptuously toward the blue crown, were reminiscent of the most romantic expressionist skyline view in New York of the 1930s. Using bits and pieces of Gothic and Classical and Moorish styles, the firm's designers indicated they could successfully knit surface and space together with a deliberateness and concentration that was breathtaking. The steel blue, illuminated crown of the KOIN Center, which

related in a somewhat clunky manner to the rest of the building, and the proposed glass dome for the British Pacific Building made clear the intent of returning expressive spatial elements to the skyline after 20 years of architectural nudity, glacial volumetrics (à la the Georgia Pacific Building) and the purging of ornamental details.

In 1928, Ely Jacques Kahn, one of New York's premier Art Deco architects, had dreamed of "a colored city, buildings in harmonious tones making great masses of beautiful patterns." The bell-shaped KOIN Center—whose massing bore an uncanny resemblance to the highly sculpted, setback buildings conceived in the 1920s by New York's visionary renderer Hugh Ferriss—would mark the beginning of Portland's answer to Kahn's dream. The building's geometric forms, as well as the refulgent steel blue pyramid at its apex, were reminiscent of theatrical devices and the sculptural programs of Manhattan's Art Deco skyscrapers.

New York was, indeed, on the mind of at least two Zimmer Gunsul Frasca architects involved in the Gothic Moderne design for the KOIN Center. "One of the things I think is very important in the design of cities years ago that we tend to forget about, was the skyline," commented Gregory S. Baldwin, one of the firm's partners. "When you think of Manhattan and all the things that happen at Wall Street, the skyline was the art, the thing that really identified parts of the city. And when you have a lot of buildings that have uniform parapets, you've completely lost that kind of character." To which Frasca added: "We felt that there are too many boxes for buildings in cities, and we have been responsible for some of them in Portland. But we felt because KOIN Center is a special building, it really demanded a unique image in the skyline."

Although clearly influenced by the ornamental historicism and symbolism promulgated by the high-gurus of Postmodern architecture, the Portland firm produced designs and used materials that maintained sensitivity to the architectural context of the city. The lightly rusticated exterior at ground level, torose molding, orange brick panels and limestone window frames of the KOIN Center resonated with corresponding formal elements (especially the entrance of the Portland Art Museum) that were part of the Beaux-Arts architectural stratum laid down during the successive reigns of Whidden and Lewis, Doyle and Belluschi. "We combined brick with limestone at the base so it became very traditional in terms of the vocabulary already present in the older part of the downtown," explained Frasca. "What we were trying to do is to bring that character from the older part of the downtown into this part, so that Portland wouldn't be characterized as kind of 1960's, 1970's in terms of materials, and then the 1920's and the 1930's sort of thing. We wanted to give some kind of continuity."

Thus, by the mid-1980s, as far as the Zimmer Gunsul Frasca design team was concerned, continuity was the name of the game. But when Frasca was asked whether the design for the tall rectangular windows delicately framed in limestone at the base of the KOIN Center had been consciously modeled on the strikingly similar arrangement gracing the Portland Art Museum, his response—"It was neither conscious nor unconscious"—did not leave the architectural critic much room to navigate. Was the architect invoking the existence of a mental realm even Sigmund Freud had failed to penetrate? Not quite. In a design statement published in the *Architectural Record* of November 1980, the architect's anthropomorphic analysis implied that the never-never land between conscious and unconscious resided not in the mind of the architect but in the building itself. "The forms [or architecture] were derived from the program, the neighbors, the streets and the sun," read Frasca's statement. "The KOIN building *wanted* to be small at the Forecourt Fountain, but 'big' behind that, and the scale of the elements reflects that. The footprint of apartments on top of the KOIN Tower *wanted* to be smaller than the offices below, which in turn *wanted* to be smaller than the 'street hugging' retail activity area."

Unlike the "pastiche" buildings—of which The Portland Building was a premier example—designed by Postmodernist architects from other cities, Zimmer Gunsul Frasca's entries in the new historicist vein eschewed ironic tricks and whimsy in favor of spatial integrity and calculated historical references to the city's architectural substrate. The contextual integrity and moderately mannered design of the KOIN Center and the monumental "Roman" interior space of the Justice Center demonstrated the Zimmer team had not only aligned itself with an architectual program that had captured "the spirit of the times," but that it had a strong commitment to what Frasca called, "making place" within Portland's unique urban fabric.

If the KOIN Center was an aspiring testimony to the revival of Gothic dynamism, then the Justice Center was Portland's most grandiose "Romanesque space." Situated on a prestige site near the Willamette River and a public park, the center was intended to eschew the appearance of the traditionally austere detention center

architecture. The entrance, alone, with its hourglass-fine precast concrete exterior, barrel vault skylight, terrazo floor, and two exterior sculptures—strongly reminiscent of sculptural monuments that sit at the foot of the stepped pyramid of King Zoser (Saqqara, Egypt)—had done much to "perfume the slammer." With its Art Deco pink and gray color scheme, monumental columns, black marble and glassed-in "arcade," the lobby expressed what Zevi called, "statically conceived Roman space": absolute autonomy with respect to neighboring spaces (especially the detention area) emphasized by thick dividing walls of exquisitely polished concrete; and a biaxial grandiosity on a monumental scale, essentially self-contained and indifferent to the spectator.

Like official, public buildings of ancient Rome between the first century B.C. and the second century A.D., the Justice Center was an affirmation of authority, or, to use the words of Zevi, "a symbol dominating the mass of citizens and announcing that the Empire *is*, that it embodies the force and meaning of their whole lives. The scale of Roman building is the scale of that mythos, later to become reality, still later nostalgia, and it neither is, nor was it intended to be, the scale of man." By invoking a Roman "spatial" theme for a building devoted to power and authority, the Zimmer partnership revealed its eclectic impulse for matching historically-generated spaces with their appropriate function (this spatio-functional correspondence would again be a guiding principle for the Institute for Advanced Biomedical Research building on Marquam Hill).

However fashionable it may have seemed, the design for the Justice Center lobby paid allegiance to classical forms. Writing in *Architecture and Space*, the Italian critic Zevi emphasized: "When academic eclectics draw upon Roman architecture, it is not for its elements of decoration, its facades or for the invaluable lessons of its domestic buildings. The 'Roman Style' is used for the interiors of great American banks, for the immense marble halls of railroad stations, for works which impress us with their size, but which do not move us with their inspiration, for structures which are almost always cold and where we do not feel at home." Perhaps unwittingly, Frasca acknowledged this "Roman connection" when he commented that the lobby would be "one of the public spaces in the city because we felt that the building ought to be in addition to a monument from the exterior—a very special space that belongs to everybody in the city. It's like railroad stations with great public spaces."

The Justice Center, after all, was not intended to be a

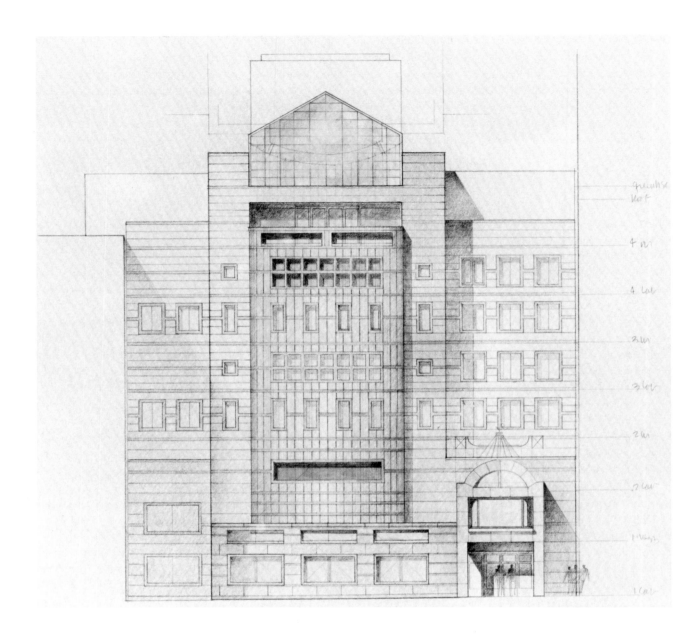

INSTITUTE FOR ADVANCED BIOMEDICAL RESEARCH
Zimmer Gunsul Frasca
1984

place where the public would want to tarry, as they might, let us say, in a Roman bath. To use Frasca's words, it was, nevertheless "a building that dignified human existence." In his view, architecture contributed "to the culture, tradition and history of life. Without it it would be like not having poetry, or music or painting or any of the other arts that show the evolution of culture and the meaning of civilization." To which he added: "I think that any society that neglects its architecture is really omitting one of the important ingredients demonstrating continuity of culture and tradition." To be sure, the awe-inspiring lobby of the Justice Center had established "continuity" with a long and celebrated academic tradition in the building arts. "Academicism has imitated Roman building," explained Zevi, "whenever it has had a program of architecture-as-symbol, expressive of vain

PROPOSAL FOR THE BRITISH PACIFIC BUILDING
Zimmer Gunsul Frasca
1983

attempts at imperial revival, at myths of military and political supremacy; the result has been buildings of static spaces, rapt in the bombast of megalomania and rhetoric."

Two models on display at the Zimmer Gunsul Frasca office—one of the Institute for Advanced Biomedical Research and the other of the British Pacific Building—reflected an intensifying interest in matching historically rooted spatial and ornamental sensibilities with their corresponding human functions.

The Institute for Advanced Biomedical Research (IABR) (scheduled for completion in 1986) exemplified a commitment to classical ideals endorsed by architectural theorists since Vitruvius. This view held that architectural forms and spaces should classify a mood or ambience appropriate to the function and meaning of the building. For the IABR, Zimmer Gunsul Frasca had taken this imperative one step further to create a structure resonating with historical and cultural messages. By in-

troducing a dramatic stylistic tension into the building's surface, the architects externalized the functions it was to accommodate and anchored each to a recognizable, historical form.

The terra cotta and glass facade, unmistakably Palladian in its inspiration, will enclose small reading lounges that recall the Oxbridge vision of scholarly interchange. From this space, one will move into a central core of research laboratories, housed in a section of the building designed in an unmistakably high-tech idiom. To effect the transition to existing structures, the design calls for transforming a nondescript parking lot into an enclosed garden, climaxed by a lattice-work gazebo designed by landscape architect Peter Walker. By providing a practical way in which human activity can segregate into two different spaces, each of which invokes its own spirit, the IABR building pushes the Postmodern designation beyond mere surface or figurative manipulation and into the realm of human activity. Historicism can be put to practice, which is key, and evolves beyond visual exercise.

Writing in the spring 1984 issue of *Architectural Technology*, Frasca explained how "aesthetic sensibilities applied to an evolving program can still produce classically good architecture."

Original architecture develops from unrelenting attention to technical and functional requirements, not from a stylistic predilection. The hair on my neck stands up when I hear "post–modern" applied to our work. The institute is not a look backward. It is as modern as a space ship, but it is conditioned by very personal sensibilities about what makes a splendid place to live and think.

In designing a medical research building the architect must provide two environments: flexible laboratories with complex electrical, air, plumbing and waste services; and meeting areas where researchers can talk with each other and with visitors in groups of varying sizes.

Shaped like a deodorant stick and festooned with fripperies of bygone architecture, perhaps the British Pacific Building would have best collected the multiple concerns that nourished Zimmer Gunsul Frasca's home-grown brand of Postmodernism. Projected to occupy a site at the foot of the Morrison Bridge, if erected as originally designed, the blue-green terra cotta-clad "gateway" structure would have realized Frasca's enduring dream: to create for Portland a comprehensible, integrated and enjoyable urban place filled with hidden presences, historical allusions and, most important, *energy*.

The proposed design for the building was reminiscent of New York's Buffalo City Hall, built in the 1930s. Dramatically sculpted, the Art Deco-inspired exterior suggested for the British Pacific Building made reference to the heroic visions of New York City's skyscraper architects of the late 1920s and early 1930s. Melding unabashedly the Gothicizing impulse of one age and the technological yearning of another, the British Pacific Building would have been a sensuous throwback to the pre-Crash years of economic optimism, to ornamental expressionism, to booming and seemingly inexhaustible opportunity and progress. This was a case in which architectural styling or, historicist allusion, would have taken on a subtle, but unmistakable twinge of boosterism.

Although rejected by the city's Design Review Board because it would have violated height restrictions established for the waterfront, the *design* for the British Pacific Building revealed a firm keenly attuned to both the city's existing architectural fabric and its increasing sophistication. More than any other of the building's features, its *base* and *crown* would have responded to the needs of an increasingly "Manhattanized" Portland public. At street level, the program called for an enclosed garden, while the apex would have been a non-functional, purely figurative glass dome. The garden ringing the base of the building—set off from the street with a wrought-iron fence—represented the architect's response to the growing popularity of al fresco dining and people watching. The hope was to return to the street its enormous *social* dimension and turn the urban "place" back into a stage set. The same theatricality informed the firm's decision to terminate the tower with an illuminated dome.

With the diaphanous dome suggested for its crown, the British Pacific Building, like the KOIN Center, promised to catapult Portland skyscraper architecture into a new "electrifying" epoch. Both towers mixed delicacy with strength, expressing at once the power of history and technology; in short, their designs honored application of graceful details to firm, potent and self-assured structures. But more importantly, both the KOIN Center and the British Pacific Building adhered to a half-century old philosophy promulgated by Art Deco architects of the 1920s. As Bletter explained in *Skyscraper Style*, "the Art Deco architect was not only concerned with giving the passerby and office worker an elevating experience by enhancing entrance area and lobby space with a profusion of ornament. He was equally concerned with having the building readable from a distance and with its general effect in the skyline, and therefore used unusual terminations at the top and ornament scaled to distance."

To the letter, these were the design generators that fired up Frasca's design team. "While relating to existing structures, a building has to be identifiable in the skyline to give it special place within the city," explained Frasca. As if he were paying tribute to the traditional Manhattan skyscraper of the 1920s, the architect stressed that "a well-designed building must project two visions—one from a distance and another at close range. The building has to work both ways. And each vision has to be different because a building has to look one way from a distance—strong and image-able—and another way close-up. And so the architect is solving both those problems, even though they co-exist in the same building."

Although the British Pacific Building was at variance with the downtown plan, which specified buildings with lower floor area ratios (FAR) along the waterfront, Frasca cited several compelling reasons to justify exceeding the height proscription: "The city has changed in the decade since the master plan for downtown was adopted. The light rail system was not anticipated 10 years ago, and now, putting density near mass transit is an important consideration. Moreover, by sticking slavishly to height restrictions, one will end up with a city that is monotonous, homogeneous, and mediocre." Moreover, Frasca emphasized that the exterior would be sculpted, "so that the image of the building against the skyline constantly changes depending on the light, atmospheric conditions, and the vantage point from which it's seen. From several locations, the building would appear much smaller than it actually is."

Although it seemed as if Portland architects, especially the Zimmer Gunsul Frasca partnership, had succeeded in taking the best of Postmodern values in architecture and applying them to the city's build environment, the national mood had changed significantly by 1984. The successful "regional" variant developed by the Zimmer partnership under the magic spell of Postmodernism, apparently, did not materialize elsewhere. Signs of a backlash were in the air.

Nearly four years after Belluschi delivered his City Council address, at which he criticized the Graves-Johnson-Burgee contingent for discovering "that fashions need not last," prestigious architecture magazines were also starting to look askance at Postmodern ornamentalism. James Stewart Polshek, jury chairman for the 31st annual *Progressive Architecture* Awards—which had given Portland's Performing Arts Center a Design Award—delivered Postmodernism one of its strongest public indictments when he said: "I read, in the projects we have seen, a very strong statement that we are moving away from producing architecture as pastiche, architecture as marketing, architecture as packaging, architecture as a kind of self-generating animus wherein the next project flows from the previous one by virtue of its abstract identification and its conscious loading with 'meaning,' meaning up until now being defined primarily by the architect with no relevance to those using the building."

With the completion of several buildings within a short span between 1982 and 1984, it was clear that architects commissioned for major projects in Portland had moved permanently away from the Modern Movement. Although by the early 1980s, they still did not always have a clear sense of where they were going, they seemed absolutely certain of what they were leaving behind. Buildings like the KOIN Center, the Justice Center and The Portland Building, as well as Pioneer Courthouse Square, did not in themselves crystallize a new direction, but they did a great deal to show how widespread the rejection of orthodox Modernism had become.

With Zimmer Gunsul Frasca "at the helm," Portland drew closer to fulfilling its destiny: becoming an architectural microcosm. Many local architectural firms— Broome, Oringdulph, O'Toole, Rudolph & Associates BOOR/A, Martin, Soderstrom and Matteson, WEGROUP, Sheldon, Eggleston, Reddick, Aanderud, Thompson and Vaivoda and others—became a linchpin between international trends and regional, contextual and historical forces. By 1984, the city's layered and eclectic architectural landscape would boast provocative stylistic juxtapositions that were uniquely its own: An impeccably preserved building in the High Renaissance Style (Portland City Hall, 1895) framed by a squat box that bristled with the polychrome flashiness of Postmodernism (The Portland Building, 1982); a perfectly proportioned structure in the handsome Roman Corinthian style (U.S. National Bank, 1917) set against a brilliantly coruscating skyscraper-sculpture (U.S. Bancorp Tower, 1983); an ivory-white Italian tower (First Congregational Church) with Arabic, Byzantine and Venetian elements framed by a pin-striped skyscraper (Pacwest Center) which combined the curvilinear starkness of the streamlined decade with the new "computer aesthetic"; an exquisite, earth-toned building in the Richardsonian Romanesque style (Plaza Hotel, 1894) knuckled against a cool glass-and-aluminum structure (Equitable Building, 1948) that had become a milestone in the International Style.

In 1922, Werner Hegemann and Elbert Peets had written that "the intelligent use, adaptation, and development of traditional forms makes constant demands on originality and good judgement." Put another way, the most enlightened architecture has always represented the search for a new synthesis based on technologic opportunities in the present grafted onto the "timeless" or continuing principles of classical composition.

Portland's architectural microcosm—with its diverse human, material and productive resources—made such a synthesis possible. Its tradition of historical preservation, technological innovation and experimentation with building styles fueled an architectural vitality that inevitably grows out of the explicitly represented dialogue between what is real in the *present* and what is imagined from the past—that is, the city's architectural grid. The juxtaposition, and ongoing expression of classical, vernacular and technological themes within the fabric of Portland's built environment set the stage for a synthesis between regional imperatives and a modern, pluralistic architectural tradition that would surface in the mid-1980s.

Throughout the history of Portland architecture in the twentieth century, the exploration of classical themes—whether it was in the work of A. E. Doyle, Pietro Belluschi or Zimmer Gunsul Frasca—did not thwart architecture's ability to come to terms with new modes of production or the new functional demands placed on it. "Rather, the use of known models and the mastery of classical grammar," wrote architect Robert Stern, in *Post–Modern Classicism*, "made it possible for architects to conceptualize some of the most functionally and technologically complex works ever built and also to make these works comprehensible to the public at large." Indeed, a number of Portland buildings exemplify this pluralist tradition in architecture: the willingness to combine natural, classical and vernacular forms with the techno-, or mechano-morphology of the times.

The conflation of classical vocabulary with the constructional processes characteristic of a specific time had produced some of the city's finest buildings. For example, the Blagen Block (1888) combined formal elements of a late Baroque Corinthian order with the cast-iron production process developed in the late nineteenth century. Similarly, Portland City Hall, designed by Whidden and Lewis in 1895, would wed the classical vocabulary of Roman styling with one of the state's earliest steel-frame skeleton structures. In 1932, Pietro Belluschi, who was then chief designer for A. E. Doyle and Associate, designed the Ayer Wing of the Portland Art Museum. One of his most admired buildings, the museum successfully combined the formal character of Roman architecture with a soaring skylight and other elements of modernistic architecture.

After a 50-year hiatus, during which time the International Style of the Modern movement prevailed and proclaimed the classical vocabulary of the past as irrelevant, the pluralist tradition would again take root in Portland architecture. The Justice Center, completed in 1984 (Zimmer Gunsul Frasca), combined elements of the formal Roman baroque vocabulary with innovative construction methods, including the latest methods in computerized incarceration and materials used for dentention-center architecture.

True to the Postmodernist credo, by 1984 Portland architecture stretched over history, celebrating at once the symbols and ornaments of the past and the techno-aesthetics of the present. Within a dense fabric, its buildings alternated between the historical forms of the past and the inchoate shapes of the future. The co-existence of myriad architectural strata created a vibrant field that was receptive to new and unprecedented structures, regardless of their stylistic orientation. Though based on diametrically opposed design philosophies, the Justice Center and Natural Gas Building (1983, Campbell, Yost and Grube), were, for example, nonetheless equally "claimed" by their urban environment. In the case of the Justice Center, a kinship with the city was coaxed out of the existing context by the fanciful ornamentation borne by the rusticated gray skin and formal arches. The Northwest Natural Gas Building, on the other hand, was "naturalized" into the urban fabric on the basis of a different process. Rather than projecting ornamental features into surrounding districts, it embraced everything within visual reach into its reflective shield. Emblazoned with its own silvery double of the White Stag sign, or tatooed with the pastel colors of the Old Town butterfly, or smudged with the lower-Manhattanite water tower, the hexagonal tower thrusted itself into the sky in a self-effacing and conciliatory gesture. Portland's architectural context permitted each building to slip into the temporal and spatial interstices of its respective setting.

By 1984, yet another architectural fashion—contextualism—had descended on Portland in full force. Fashionable or not, nothing could have been better for the budding microcosm. For a metropolis densely packed and richly layered with architectural styles and spaces, historic landmarks and exquisite building materials, contextualism was ideally suited for establishing continuity and defining symbols of permanence within Portland's urban fabric. At least conceptually, contextualism offered a framework within which contemporary architects could test Doyle's hypothesis that "there is little that is good that is not in some way based on something old that is good."

Ever since the mid-nineteenth century, Portland's

architectural jewels had been set together snugly, providing a source of stability and architectural continuity. By 1984, it had time for Portland architects to take full advantage of these spatial and stylistic reference points. Writing in the *New York Times* of 21 October 1982, Goldberger outlined a program for contextual architecture in terms that had special significance for two Portland projects—Pioneer Courthouse Square and the Performing Arts Center—already under construction during the mid-1980s:

> There is a word that has become very much the fashion in talking and writing about architecture lately, and it is "contextual." It is intended as a word of praise—good architecture, it is presumed, is "in context," which is to say it fits in with its surroundings. Bad architecture does not— it violates its surroundings, creating awkward and jarring physical connections to the buildings around it.
>
> The coming of contextualism, as this attitude is called when given its grandest appellation, to the lexicon of architectural criticism is a good thing. The values of contextual architecture are civilized and appropriate ones; *it should go without saying that we make better cities when each architect pays attention to what has come before and what sits on either side of whatever he is creating.*

The arrival of enlightened contextual architecture in Portland was celebrated by a *Progressive Architecture* Design Award—one of nine such awards among nine hundred entries—for the Portland Performing Arts Center, (ELS Design Group; Broome, Oringdulph, O'Toole, Rudolf and Associates, Barton Myers Associates). Presently under construction, the Performing Arts Center promises to offer a firm and distinguished architectural presence in downtown Portland. Writing in *Architecture California*, Donn Logan, of the California-based ELS group (a collaborator on the project), viewed the Performing Arts Center as an opportunity to create "a truly urban theater experience in the tradition of London and New York."

The charge given by the city in the initial brief to some 90 Performing Arts Center entrants was to design "a facility of international significance." Given the world-class stature to which the city aspired, little did the distinguished finalists, which included Philip Johnson and John Burgee, suspect that the winning scheme would be that which drew most literally on the historical and contextual parameters of the Portland site for its guiding inspiration.

Writing in *Architecture California*, Logan stressed the importance of integrating the winning Performing Arts Center design into Portland's existing architectural fabric: "The site and building program [for Performing Arts Center] are made to order for this approach. . . . Portland's . . . grid of small blocks with structures built tightly against the sidewalk convincingly validates the American tradition of town planning. . . . Existing buildings will remain on the two-block site. The new theaters will share their block with the Congregational Church, one of Portland's most important historic buildings. We intend to design [the] new complex to fit within the *context* of these existing buildings. The First Congregational Church in particular requires a formal response . . . we are attempting to emulate the church's basic geometry and organization."

Paying attention to what "sits on either side" of what is being created was an integral part of the design approach to the Performing Arts Center. The new theaters will open onto Main Street, which will form a major pedestrian street in Portland's downtown plan, as well as serving as an antechamber to the theater lobbies. At present, there are plans to cover the pedestrian arcade with an elaborate glass canopy supported on "wicket" frames. This flamboyant aspect of the design, however, came under some criticism at the *Progressive Architecture* review, and a revision is likely.

The Paramount Theater, a former grand movie house, was refurbished, given new stairs, elevators and theatrical rigging systems, while the exterior was restored to its original 1928 condition. As part of the Performing Arts Center, two new theaters—a 900-seat chamber designed like an intimate Edwardian theater and a 450-seat theater, orthogonally planned, with three levels and a movable orchestra floor—will be combined into a new building. This structure will use brick veneer construction, combining a buff brick similar to the Paramount's and a darker brick pattern with header bricks marking the tie positions. Dark basalt, the major ingredient of the adjacent First Congregational Church, will be used as string coursing.

Historical allusions will extend beyond local crystals, to architectural monuments of international significance. In the arrival area, the image of the proscenium opening of Milan's La Scala Opera House will convey a "theater lobby metaphor," allowing theater patrons entering through Main Street to become, for a brief moment, part

PROPOSED BROADWAY/MOYER BUILDING
Broome, Oringdulph, O'Toole, Rudolf and Associates
1984

PERFORMING ARTS CENTER
Barton Myers, BOOR/A, ELS Design Group
1986

of the spectacle as viewed from the lobby floor or box positions. The orientation of the new theater lobby is based on the view from the stage of the Teatro Scientifico Mantua, while the main arrival lobby will pay homage to the classical opera house. It is intended that this part of the complex will serve both as a traditional "grand lobby" as well as a fourth stage for informal performances. The 450-seat showcase theater is based on an early flexible courtyard theater parlor designed in 1926 by the Russian constructivist El Lissitzky. Finally, the 900-seat intermediate theater is based on the horseshoe plan of the Courtyard Theater in Nottingham, England.

The strong historical and contextual bent of the Performing Arts Center design underscored with particular eloquence the extent to which Portland's civic leaders and architects had abandoned the modernist mode in favor of an eclectic approach that could incorporate—figuratively and literally—design elements and materials of the past with those of a new structure. Architect Stanley Boles, director of the design group at Broome, Oringdulph, O'Toole, Rudolf and Associates, outlined the historical and contextual factors that influenced the final design: "The buildings that exerted the greatest design influence on the Performing Arts Center were the Paramount Theater, the Heathman Hotel and the First Congregational Church. We considered the construction of these three principal reference points; the masonry, the portals which signified entries into the building, the windows over the entries, and especially, the roof geometries of the First Congregational Church."

The Paramount Theater (1928, Rapp and Rapp), the First Congregational Church (1895, Henry J. Hefty) and the Heathman Hotel represented some of Portland's best known architectural landmarks. Not surprisingly, a unifying gesture that would integrate the architectural styles of these handsome structures into a single complex appealed to the jury which selected the ELS Group/BOOR/A design.

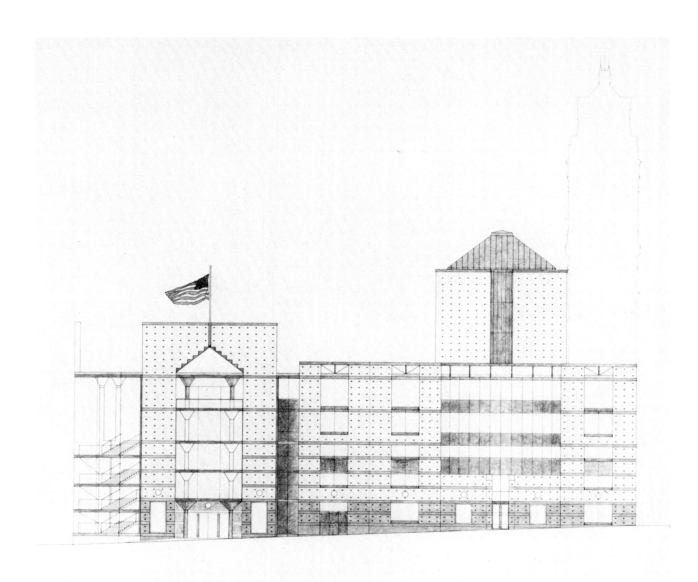

PERFORMING ARTS CENTER
Barton Myers, BOOR/A, ELS Design Group
1986

Boles emphasized that the exteriors of the new theater will use high-quality materials indigenous to Portland architecture. The diaper pattern brick work in the stone band coursing of the new masonry will be sympathetic to its context on either side, but is also derived from contemporary building techniques. The buff-colored brick on the existing Paramount will be mixed with darker bricks in patterns similar to those of the Paramount and the Heathman Hotel, creating an easy and articulate relationship between the Performing Arts Center and its older, distinguished neighbors.

It is interesting that the ELS Group/BOOR/A plan for the Performing Arts Center respected a number of explicitly stated design guidelines established for downtown Portland. Prepared by Michael Harrison under the auspices of the Portland Design Commission, *Downtown Design Guidelines* was published in January 1983. Guideline seven, called "unifying elements," provided a prescription for the design program used by the Performing Arts Center designers: "Similarity of materials, lighting standards, . . . and architectural materials form 'layers' of commonality that help establish the identity of an area, . . . strengthen the special identity of sub-areas of . . . downtown by respecting existing layers of similarity or by adding new layers that expand and enrich an area's character."

The exterior of the Performing Arts Center will use Flemish Bond, which will make reference to the checkerboard pattern created by string courses of dark basalt on the adjoining Congregational Church. Boles emphasized that while the color scheme and exterior grid bore some resemblance to the composition of Graves's Portland Building, this was accidental. "The brick color and grid were chosen based upon analogous features in the adjoining buildings, not for *philosophical* reasons that the base of a building should be brown, beige its flesh, and light blue its crown. . . . I think the Graves building could have been built anywhere . . . because he [Graves] has a strong, thought-out philosophical reason for doing things . . . no matter where a building is. He wouldn't alter his scheme in Des Moines . . . or if there were white buildings on either side . . . whereas our design philosophy would."

The ELS collaborator on the Performing Arts Center design, Logan made it clear that the design teams "wanted the theater buildings to be part of Portland's fabric, not a civic monument." Their approach coincided with this aim. The glass-covered arcade (which moves up and down according to the weather conditions), the illuminated stage house canopy (or "hoops"), and masonry responded not only to contextual and regional forces, but to Portland's historical fabric as well. "The illuminated canopy not only replicates corresponding "hoop" forms in the city's bridges," said Boles, "but it is a historical reference to the series of lighted arches that extended over Third Avenue in 1905, and which created a special district linked by a unified design feature. The use of portals that serve as 'bookends' for the arcade were inspired by temporary gateways once used to create a special convention district in Portland's downtown."

The contextual, and strongly historicist, program for the Performing Arts Center elicited praise from the *Progressive Architecture* jury which had given it a coveted

Design Award. Stuart Polshek, dean of the Columbia University Graduate School of Architecture and Planning, lauded the design for fulfilling the promise of a complex program he described this way: "The challenge was to create a center for the performing arts, unifying a 1920s motion picture theater on one block and a new building next to a historic church on the other, with a somewhat grungy part of town on one side and a great allee/park on the other." Polshek supported the project for solving "an uncommon problem wherein one creates a cultural center out of pieces both new and existing," but noted that "just because the architects are partly enclosing a street doesn't mean there should be a galleria." Another juror, Julia Thomas (who in her introductory remarks to the 31st Annual P/A Awards opined that, "We can find more excitement in American cooking and restaurants now than in architecture."), called the Center "a responsible piece of work, and a very difficult project."

The Performing Art Center will likely offer the city a distinguished architectural presence. And while it is still too early to tell, perhaps the finest example of contextual architecture is on its way to being completed. But the selection of this building's design was important for still another reason. Its unmistakable historical and contextual emphasis suggested a concrete and very interesting alternative both to the increasingly stale International Style championed by SOM and the more showy, provocative compositions that had come out of the Postmodern-leaning design group at Zimmer Gunsul Frasca.

As Boles explained, "I think we are in the midst of an exciting time. There is a vitality in Portland similar to that which existed in Seccesionist Vienna. By keeping your feet firmly on the ground you can go wherever you need to stylistically and with respect to design. You can put together and achieve exactly what you're after. There is a freedom that exists now—a fluidity between styles that is eclectic—and if you have a strong organizing idea and an aesthetic goal that you are after, you can achieve it by applying the most appropriate pieces from a whole range of idioms, whether it is high-tech or Romanesque."

The design for the new Performing Arts Center did more than steer a productive course between the two competing stylistic movements—the Modern and the Postmodern—that had divided the city into two camps. In some respects, it had pointed the way toward a viable *Modern* architecture that the city's architectural community seemed ready to embrace. "If one accepts the thesis that modern architecture appropriately represents the complex interaction between the often conflicting issues that characterize the Modern World," wrote architect Robert Stern, "then one must accept a hybrid or pluralist stance—in short, a humanist view of architecture." In Stern's view, pluralism is the characteristic state of the modern world. "In architecture," he continued, "it is represented by the interaction of three modes of representation—the *classical*, *vernacular*, and *production*. When architecture tips too far in the direction of one or another of these models . . . it runs the risk of becoming dry, dogmatic, dead, alienated."

The compositional approach to the Performing Arts Center was anything but dogmatic, and it did, indeed, reflect a *dialogue* among Stern's various modes. The classical paradigm was reflected in the building's exterior, which virtually reproduced the elements and proportions present in Italian gothic style of the church to which it will be joined. The vernacular mode, which according to Stern relies upon the "messy vitality of everyday life to supply forms that are culturally specific," is at work in the use of portals and in the "wild and crazy" illuminated hoops that are in keeping with the entertainment atmosphere of the Broadway district and, in particular, with its designation by the Design Commission as a Unique Sign District. Finally the production (or process) paradigm, which draws upon technological innovations of the present, is evident in the use of modular canopy structures, sliding glass curtain, movable floors and other high-tech embellishments.

In short, the Performing Arts Center is likely to be a Modern work. By responding to classical elements adjacent to its site, and, at the same time, addressing the vernacular sensibilities of the Broadway district, the Performing Arts Center will likely satisfy Stern's criteria for a pluralistic, modern work. And yet, the explicit dialogue between classical, vernacular and technological idioms was made possible because Portland was an architectural *microcosm*. Put another way, the design program for the Center was *specific* to Portland's urban, historical and architectural fabric; it was a singular, hybrid composition in which past, present and future melded into a confluent whole. This innovative Portland-dependent scheme, could not have been generated in another city. The Portland site and its adjacent buildings provided a unique combination of contextual, historical and formal constraints—and incentives—that permitted the final result to crystallize.

Within the tapestry of a city's architectural design, styles run along the surface, submerge themselves for an epoch or two, and then re-emerge, sometimes in unexpected places—The Portland Building, Pioneer Courthouse Square, Fountain Plaza, and most recently in the Performing Arts Center. These Portland projects, like many of those built by William Whidden and Albert E. Doyle, pursue an appropriate re-combination of modern and classic principles of the building arts. Through the development of a new typology, these buildings suggest how it is possible to build for a future that honors its past, while above all expressing the truth of the contemporary condition.

"For some years now, architects have been expressing a concern for the way in which a new building relates to its surroundings," wrote Paul Goldberger in the *New York Times* of 3 December 1981. "Whereas modern buildings once tended to be conceived as pure, abstract objects, independent of what was beside them," he continued, "there is now much more attention paid to the notion of fitting a building into its architectural context—trying, in other words, to make certain the building echoes many of the architectural themes of its neighbors."

Although Goldberger was referring to the School of Architecture designed by British architect James Stirling when he outlined this working hypothesis for contextualism, the same formula could also be applied to Portland's Pioneer Courthouse Square (1984, Willard Martin, Martin/Soderstrom/Matteson). Perhaps the most fantastical example of such architecture to be completed in the city, Pioneer Courthouse Square was as contextual as architecture could be. Peppered with whimsical twists and ironic allusions, the Square nevertheless responded to virtually every ornament and formal element appearing on the exterior faces of adjacent buildings.

"The gestation and birth of Portland's Pioneer Courthouse Square is a story rich in human endeavor," wrote chief designer Willard Martin, in the May 1983 *Architecture California*. "First came the dream, as in all great ventures, and the sharing of that dream by many people dedicated to the creation of a very special place for themselves and their children in the heart of the city." Martin emphasized that different points of view—with respect to style and concept—helped bring the dream to fruition, but not without "a family feud."

The family feud had come to a stiff boil as early as 1981, when Mayor Frank Ivancie attempted to end the project. Aligning himself with William Roberts (now

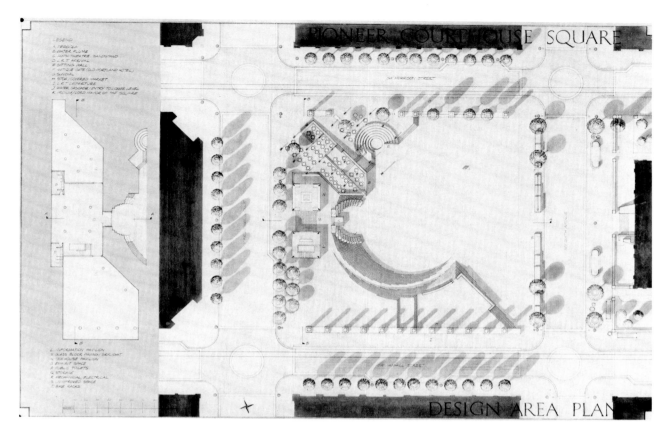

PIONEER COURTHOUSE SQUARE
Martin/Soderstrom/Matteson
1984

chairman of the Portland Development Commission, Roberts was then a member of a citizens' advisory board for the Square), Ivancie joined forces with influential citizens who adamantly opposed the concept of an open—rather than an enclosed—public square. Their opposition to the square was based on the fear that an "open" arrangement would attract transients into the area. In January of 1981, Ivancie declared the project dead.

Public response to the mayor's proclamation was one of indignation. "It would be a shock . . . to many Oregonians to learn that a few power brokers have declared that the result of a nationwide design rivalry is meaningless," offered former Governor Tom McCall, who was then a television commentator. Despite years of planning and public input, the project seemed doomed without the financial backing of the city's business pillars, led by the Association for Portland Progress. At least $2 million was required to complete the federal funding package, which included $3 million for acquisition of the land and

$4.3 million for construction of the square. With the project all but buried, city commissioners Charles Jordan and Mike Lindberg formed a citizens group that rallied on behalf of the faltering venture. Concentrating their resuscitation efforts on selling bricks in which contributors would have their names inscribed, they eventually succeeded in collecting enough riches to bring "Willard's Ruins" to fruition.

The site on which Pioneer Courthouse Square was constructed has played a pivotal role in the development of Portland architecture. In 1844, Asa Lovejoy and William Overton layed claim to a square mile of land for 25 cents, which included the present site, and which in turn they sold to shoemaker Elijah Hill for twenty-five dollars and "a pair of high boots." The parcel was sold to the city in 1856 for $1,000, and became the site of Portland's first schoolhouse. To commemorate Oregon's linkage to the Northern Pacific Railroad in 1883, Henry Villard hired New York's prestigious architectural firm of McKim, Mead and White to design the grand old Portland Hotel. Due to a recession, construction was at a standstill for several years, but the 17-story Queen Anne jewel was finally completed in 1890, under the design direction of Portland's premier architecture firm, Whidden and Lewis.

The pride and center of social activity in Portland for more than 50 years, the Portland Hotel was not only an architectural landmark, but developed a reputation for dining room service said to be "the slowest and most stately on the coast." The hotel was razed in 1951 and replaced with a two-story parking lot, which occupied the historic site for 30 years, until a comprehensive downtown plan was established in the early 1970s. The plan proposed that the site be dedicated as public space. The property was purchased by the city, and the Citizen's Advisory Committee recommended that an international design competition be held to determine the architectural future of Pioneer Courthouse Square.

The competition was announced early in 1980. The guidelines for the competition were developed by the Citizen's Advisory Committee in cooperation with local architectural and planning organizations, the Metropolitan Arts Commission, community groups and city agencies under the auspices of the Portland Development Commission.

From 750 responses initially logged, 162 submissions were received. The jury interviewed ten firms and selected five finalists who, they felt, would be most likely to produce "an elegant and inviting central attraction for the downtown, providing year-round day and evening public use." The five finalists asked to submit design concepts were: Eisenman/Robertson, New York; Geddes, Brecher, Qualls, Cunningham, Philadelphia; Lawrence Halprin and Charles Moore, San Francisco and Los Angeles; Machado/Silvetti/Schwartz/Silver, Boston; and a multi-disciplinary Portland team consisting of: architect Willard Martin (Martin/Soderstrom/Matteson), artist and photographer Robert Reynolds, sculptor Lee Kelly, writer Spencer Gill, landscape architect Douglas Macy and Terence O'Donnell of the Oregon Historical Society.

"Our design approach immediately took a strong and wonderfully human direction," wrote Martin, whose design was subsequently selected. Early programming sessions for the Martin team centered on two major areas of concern: the uses and activities that make public open spaces vital and interesting; and the most appropriate materials that would relate to the richness of surrounding buildings and streets. Review and recommendations of final submittals were made by a jury consisting of: M. Paul Friedberg FASLA, landscape architect; George A. McMath FAIA, of Allen, McMath and Hawkins, a firm specializing in historic preservation; Sumner M. Sharpe AICP, community development consultant; Donald J. Stastney AIA, AICP, professional advisor for the competition; and Pauline S. Anderson and John L. Rian.

In addition to the competition regulations and design program that evolved from jury discussions, several other considerations were introduced by the Portland Development Commission. It was specified that a "timelessness" to the design would be an attractive feature, and that, preferably, the final concept would not be of a specific period or architectural school of thought. Moreover, the jury felt that the "quality of the Northwest," including the casual lifestyle, an appreciation of the natural environment and "a concern for a delicate balance between man-made and natural artifacts in our urban centers" should all play a role in the final design.

These design generators provoked Martin to evaluate his "emotional responses to the nature of this place [Pioneer Courthouse Square], its people and [his] involvement here for over 20 years." Taking into account the full range of contextual constraints—climate, history and structures adjacent to the site—Martin conducted a rigorous investigation into shadow patterns, sunlight exposure and textural features impinging on the site from neighboring terra cotta-clad buildings by Portland's Beaux-Arts masters. "I felt the cold rain at 2 A.M. when there were no people," said Martin, "and noted reflections of artificial light on wet brick pavement." He turned, too, to international models that might suggest a direction: "I remembered the stoa of Attalus in Athens . . . I began to research ancient Greek villages and their public squares. The stoa and its use of shelter, edge definition and the marketplace became strong influences."

It was clear from Martin's "Pioneer Courthouse Square Design Statement" that he was after a spirit of exuberance. As architect and planner, he was interested in creating a novel spatial experience in the midst of an urban American square. It was people that Martin had on his mind when he wrote that the "world's great public squares are simple in concept . . . places to pass through or to linger in, to promenade or to sit, to wait for a friend, to sniff at flowers, to shop or eat. . . . Above all, places in which to gaze at the passing parade . . . ourselves. It is out of a desire for activities such as these that we have developed our design."

Other contextual factors that influenced the design

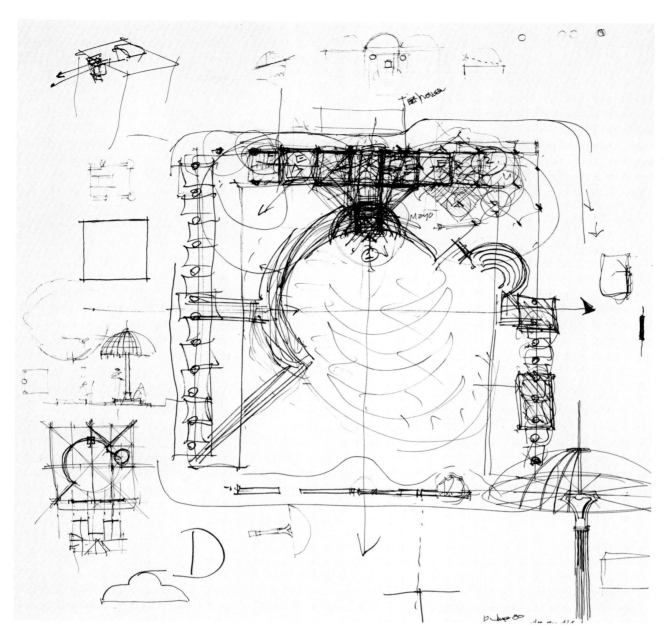

PRELIMINARY SKETCH FOR PIONEER COURTHOUSE SQUARE
Willard Martin
1984

were the projected light rail lines on two bordering streets, the brick paved transportation mall and the formal spatial elements of Pioneer Courthouse, the American Bank Building, Jackson Tower and the Meier and Frank Building. The functional symbolism generated by the context would prove to be the Square's most inviting and whimsical feature. From the southeast corner, one of two lines of 12 monumental terra cotta sheathed columns extended west. The level of their capitals addressed the building floor lines on the north (American Bank Building) and south (Jackson Tower) sides of the Square. But more than historic references, the stoa columns were also used to support large canopies for the protection of light rail passengers.

The design team not only introduced glazed terra cotta sheathing that would respond to magnificent buildings lining the Square, but they "reviewed and contemplated" Portland's rich tradition of cast iron architecture. Their contemplation suggested the tinted glass-covered pergola in the northwest corner of the square. Supported by cast bronze columns reminiscent of Portland's cast iron architecture, the pergola was latticed in bronze and crowned with arbors of climbing roses. Located to take advantage of the maximum sunlight exposure, the pergola housed a food service area with both enclosed and open-air seating. The intricate, subtle composition was full of wit and allusions to Portland's past.

Historic artifacts in the final composition included the wrought iron gate from the Portland Hotel, resurrected at its original site on the east side of the Square. Tiles salvaged the night before the hotel's demolition in 1951 covered the floor of the pergola, while an original door from the Pioneer Courthouse was used for the lower level entrance. One section of the Square contained "fallen" columns to provide seating, while other columns were replaced by trees. According to the architect, this was "a symbol association with classical ruins intimating the cycle of past, present, and future."

The final result, like the Graves building, generated a good deal of controversy. The cast-bronze pergola was criticized for its clunkiness, with one observer comparing the glass and metal assemblage to rock candy. While acknowledging that the product was "somewhat faddish," architect Richard Lakeman, praised Martin for his "brilliance," and declared that the Portland architect "had out-Gravesed Graves." Writing in *Willamette Week* on 2 April 1984, Keith Moerer offered this astute commentary:

Think of it this way: when the Statue of Liberty was first towed ashore, the average New Yorker sneered. And most of Paris grunted on first seeing the Eiffel Tower. Public art can usually be counted on to evoke a strong response; more often than not the reaction is closer to apoplexy than adoration.

The same can be said for civic architecture . . . in Pioneer Courthouse Square, Portland has a new civic symbol to mock or praise. Guaranteeing public complaint, it shares some of The Portland Building's postmodernist leanings. Designed by the architectural firm of Martin Soderstrom Matteson, it's a quirky mix of old and new.

The "Stoic" colmuns that line Yamhill and Morrison may have been inspired by the Greeks, but

their pinkish-cream color and their gold-rose capitals are touches of Graves-like whimsy. The purple-tiled peak of the square's waterfall, designed as a podium, looks as if it had been lifted from The Portland Building's east or west wall. Add to these the sloping, red-brick plaza; the glass-enclosed restaurant with cast-iron supports; and the ornamental grillwork recycled from the entrance of the old Portland Hotel, and you have a public space that . . . well, provokes a lot of comment.

Above all, Martin's interdisciplinary team created a novel spatial experience filled with historical references, time-honored symbolism and functional integrity. The composition invited the passerby to slip in and out of arcades of columns, in between fallen fragments sheathed in terra cotta and up and down red brick stairways, making it a participatory Square in the best sense. Boundlessly good-natured and humorous, in its orientation, the design team was cited by the jury for a concept that "provides . . . humor, without compromise of dignity and elegance," and was also complimented on the manner in which "adjacent buildings frame and create the edges of the space, with subtle but sensitive response to the Courthouse and local historical detail."

Along with the Piazza d'Italia (1979, August Perez and Associates/Charles W. Moore) situated at the edge of New Orleans's bustling business district, Portland's Pioneer Courthouse Square was one of the most innovative new urban plazas any American city had erected in years. Its idiosyncratic composition, in fact, had much in common with the Piazza d'Italia, which Goldberger called "a wild, mad vision." Attempting to place the Piazza's merging of classicism and modern urbanism in context, the critic wrote: "It comes as something of a shock. . . . as if the Roman Forum were re-erected in Las Vegas. One's first instinct is to say it is all a rather vulgar slap in the face of classicism—how could Corinthian columns painted yellow and lit up at night with neon be anything but vulgar?" In a show of confidence, however, Goldberger finally admitted—and his comments would apply equally well to Pioneer Courthouse Square—that the "place . . . [is] so utterly full of goodwill and eagerness to please, that you soon realize that it is not a mockery of classicism at all. It is a laughing, almost hysterically joyous embrace of the classical tradition."

For the designer of Portland's fantasy square, however, classical traditions were part of a larger human scheme. "The prevalent philosophy today respects historical precedent," explained Martin. "We did at the university but only because we were forced to do so, but we didn't like it." With Pioneer Courthouse Square, Martin's team seemed interested in creating a pastiche of visual and structural elements which, only after being processed by the sensory apparatus of the human machine interacting with the space, would somehow complete themselves and become emotionally provocative and spiritually fulfilling. "We can never lose sight of the most important criterion of all, and that is the human scale—the human response and the human emotion," explained Martin. "It all has to do with the human being, and any architect that tells you different is crazy, out of touch with humanity. . . . So I like the title 'a downtown living room for the people of Portland,' because that's really how I see it."

The design for the Pioneer Courthouse Square was embraced by *Progressive Architecture*, from which it received an Architectural Design Citation in 1981. Although the Portland jury had praised the Square's design for achieving "a graceful synthesis of classical allusions with more modern references," two of the jury members assembled by *Progressive Architecture* expressed reservations. Romaldo Guirgola, the distinguished architect who, perhaps, was still suffering the sting of having his design submission for the Portland Public Services Building rejected in favor of the Graves entry, commented that the Pioneer Square design was "very episodic . . . I have some doubt about the resulting character." Another jury member was less ambiguous in his dislike for the final result: "I don't like it; it's a very good example of the consequences of the current fashionable clichés failing to understand the fundamentals of urban design."

In response to the jury's criticism, Martin came to his own defense, explaining that "there are a lot of things going on in the Square. Guirgola called it 'episodic.' And it is. It was done deliberately. . . . Architectural episodes were established so that human episodes would take place within those architectural episodes." And then, on a more cosmic (and comic) note, the architect added: "If the Square really works, it's because the human psyche never changes . . . the ancient Romans were not that much different than we are. Nor were the Greeks. And the Star War people, if it lasts that long, will have the same wants and needs and delights and cares and interactions. I really believe that, basically, we're not going to

change that much. I don't think we're that different from Cro-Magnon man."

Offsetting the harsh opinion of "foreigners" on the jury, Frasca, also a jury member, emphasized that Pioneer Courthouse Square was potentially the most important urban space in Portland. "I believe it addresses most of the issues in terms of what space ought to do," he told the *Progressive Architecture* jury. "The streets have to go through; transit malls at either end are a fact. The design team has done a very good job of containing it at the edges and still letting people and activity be seen through it. You can argue about the geometry of the elements, but I think those problems are minor."

The geometric problems turned out to be minor in comparison to the funding problems that surfaced after the Martin design gained the jury's approval. According to Martin, "Lengthy council hearings and uncertainty about project funding presented a formidable obstacle." The principal designer cited "political forces and lack of downtown business support" as factors that in his words, "nearly sabotaged the entire effort." To draw attention to the project delay, Martin, along with local architects and volunteers, painted a stylized blueprint over the entire site. In the meanwhile, a group of Portland citizens, calling themselves The Friends of Pioneer Square, helped to mount a strong uprising of public support. Along with help from the media and several City Council members, the combined efforts gave the project the buttressing necessary for its ultimate success.

The Friends of Pioneer Square developed a marketing scheme in which citizens could "own a piece of the square" if they purchased an individual brick with their name stamped on it. A total of 50,000 bricks were sold, with a benefit of $750,000.

As the project neared completion in the early spring of 1984, it became clear that Pioneer Courthouse Square was one of the most idiosyncratic and innovative architectural works to grace the city's downtown. Although the protective canopies supported by the terra cotta columns are somewhat less "delicate" than conceived by the original design, the overall space is, as the Portland Development Commission proposed, "A place for the people in the heart of the City."

The adherence to contextual and historical concerns, however, did not infect all Portland architects with equal virulence. Caught between the late nineteenth-century architecture of Whidden and Lewis and the mid-twentieth-century boxes of Skidmore, Owings and Merrill, the optic of many Portland architects had slowly

PACWEST CENTER
Hugh Stubbins and Associates/BOOR/A
1984

fractured under the stress of two blindingly passionate back-to-back architectural movements of opposite persuasion—Classicism and Modernism. And by the mid-1980s, the history of Portland architecture would experience yet another fissure, one which would guarantee the wholesale deconstruction of the architect's lens into particles of hour-glass-fine sand. The new struggle,

brewing within architectural circles—and which would be played out on the Portland skyline—resulted in a bifurcation into two stylistic and academic camps: again, the historicists were pitted against the Modernists, with each faction, of course, proclaiming to champion the spirit of the times.

The ornamental-historicist school that had been

MACADAM PLACE
Thompson and Vaivoda
1983

ushered into vogue by Graves, Zimmer Gunsul Frasca and others invoked a theatrical approach to architecture. By refiguring Neoclassical, Gothic, Aztec and Egyptian architectural idioms, it was possible, claimed the historicists (or Postmodernists) for the contemporary architect to make theatrical the present. In this enterprise, functional forms of the present were transformed into theatrical sets which made allusions to different historical epochs, different stages of human development, different civilizational matrices.

In essence, the architect expanded the present moment into a mythological framework which emphasized the constants in human development, the constants in human experience and the constants of human organization in space. *New Yorker* fashion critic Kennedy Fraser explained the mythical-historical orientation as "a *fashion* for living out a ritualized experience. Its aim is the dandy old ideal of detachment, an ideal reinforced by the modern habit of passively watching a second world (more real and less so than the one we know directly) continuously rearrange itself in pictures on a screen."

In contrast to the ornamental historicists—and their first cousins, the contextualists—Modernists were not interested in making theatrical the present with borrowings from the architectural wardrobe of the past. Rather, the aim of this school was to mark the *specificity* and *differentness* of the present, to leave an architectural monument that would be distinctive of contemporary

sensibilities. Architect Bernardo Fort-Brescia, of the internationally acclaimed Arquitectonica group, explained that "good architecture is an architecture that represents its time . . . the real great buildings . . . are representing the moment in which they occur. Architecture should always be a statement of its time . . . it is this new *romantic* modernism we're trying to bring about."

Like their predecessors in the Bauhaus of the 1930s, the "romantic" Modernists of the 1980s saw the present as *interrupting*, rather than continuing a pattern of history. They were interested in creating an authentic history—and architectural vocabulary—that would serve as evidence of the specificity of the present moment. And in their search for a genuine ornamentation, only the sleek computer aesthetic seemed able to convince as a technological expression of the day. As Goldberger pointed out, this sensibility was "more a symbol of the romance of technology than it [was] a literal expression of the actual technology of building."

The computer aesthetic made a claim to timelessness founded on geometric absolutes. For the new Modernists, pure geometric forms—unadorned by historical ornament, or symbols—became undisputed champions for the regulation of visual space over time. Architects such as Vitruvius, Leonardo DaVinci and Le Corbusier, all developed this desire to use geometric, pure figures— especially the cube and sphere—as the basis of architectural expression. Moreover, this orientation toward the

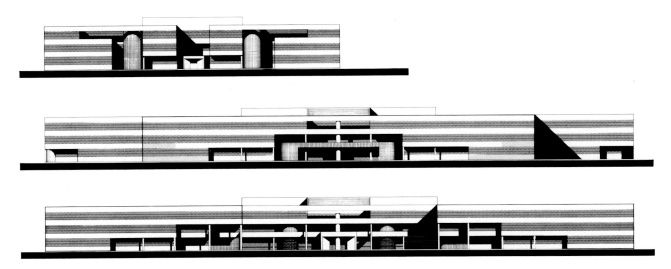

BUILDING FOR HIGH TECH COMPANY
Thompson and Vaivoda
1984

cube and sphere articulated, in concrete form, the agreement between geometry and the human impulse. These forms became a standard beyond which further simplification was impossible.

In Portland, the new Post–Miesian Modernism would highlight the computer aesthetic, geometric purity and rationalism. Grid-like designs would speak clearly to the forms, structural innovations and rituals of the computer age—efficiency, economization of force and energy, minimizing distraction. In this vein, Portland's Pacwest Center, Macadam Place and KOIN Center were monuments that—to varying degrees—carried the signature of the present moment. Crisp and geometric, these structures also revealed an immense finesse for bringing together the historicizing impulse of one current of our time and the technologic impulse of the present. In each building, however, a different historical vision was recapitulated.

In Portland, and elsewhere, being "modern" and capturing the spirit of the age had become synonymous with good architecture. Not surprisingly, there was little consensus on what this meant. Was the modern architect of the 1980s the enlightened historicist? The whimsical Postmodern Classicist? The devout contextualist? The champion of the computer aesthetic? Was he all of these? Or, none of these? Should the new Modernist look forward or backward for his inspiration? There seemed to be general agreement that good architecture was based on an understanding of the past, so that new buildings could be created that would not be a superficial

imitation in this or that style, but living successors in the true line of descent. Writing in *A Key To Modern Architecture*, F. R. S. Yorke and Colin Penn emphasized that "to build according to tradition is not to imitate in one period the obsolete work of a former time. It is to do as the architects of those periods did: to build for contemporary needs, getting the best out of the materials at hand. It is traditional to look forward, not to look back."

The Pacwest Center (1984, Hugh Stubbins and Associates/Skidmore, Owings and Merrill), criticized by some for being arrogantly disrespectful of the scale of buildings in the vicinity of City Hall, was a notable contribution to the cityscape. The sleek aluminum building was strongly reminiscent of the functional vernacular styles produced by "the streamlined decade" between 1930 and 1940, but it was also forward looking in its structural technology, use of materials and ground-level planning. Although it defied the vague trend toward historicist and contextual buildings, such as those designed by the local firm Zimmer Gunsul Frasca, the Pacwest Center was not daring by any means. It did, however, incorporate the best developments of the time in the skyscraper idiom.

Pacwest was a descendant of programs developed by America's great designers of the Depression—Raymond Loewy, Norman Bel Geddes, Henry Dreyfuss and others. Like the Airstream Clipper of 1936, the Greyhound "silversides" motorcoach (1940, Raymond Loewy) and the *20th Century Limited* train car (1938, Henry Dreyfuss), the Pacwest building was visually smooth and cool. And like

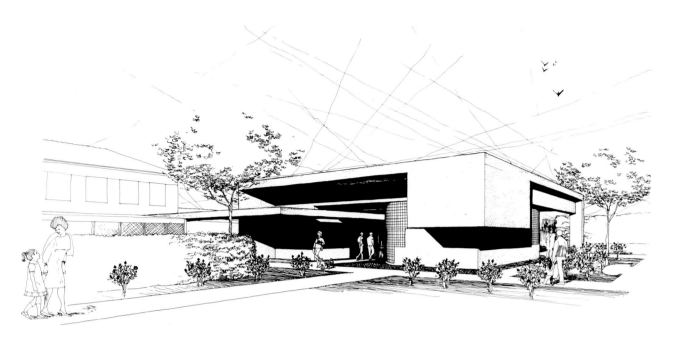

MORELAND CATTERY
Thompson and Vaivoda
1984

the skin of Belluschi's Commonwealth (Equitable) Building, the coolness was that of softly glowing aluminum and not of glass. (The building's contextual virtues, however, stopped here, since Belluschi's building was located in another section of downtown.) The building also offered an intriguing backdrop for City Hall and clearly outshined its cluttered and outdated neighbor, the First Interstate Tower (1972, Charles Luckman and Associates).

Although, to some extent, it collided with neighboring buildings, both stylistically and in scale, Stubbins's entry, in a fortuitous and unconventional way, made reference to Portland's rich tradition of Depression Modern architecture. Part soda-fountain, part domeliner and part Greyhound bus, Pacwest Center was a testimonial to the graceful curves and "cleanlined" simplicity of industrial buildings erected during the 1930s and 1940s. Stubbins's building reflected an infatuation with technology, shared by designers and architects of the 1930s. Steering America out of the Depression with their new aesthetic of functional dynamism, the industrial designers of the Streamlined Decade originated a new aesthetic of uncluttered sculptural forms that came to symbolize progress and the promise of a better future.

Before Pacwest, Stubbins had produced some of the best American buildings of the computer aesthetic to

date. Yet it is startling how much the design of his Pacwest building had in common with the *20th Century Limited*, a "stately but antiseptic" train designed in 1938 by Henry Dreyfuss for Penn Central Transportation Company. "It was Dreyfuss who used the word 'cleanlining' to describe his design strategy," wrote art historian Donald J. Bush in the *Streamlined Decade*, "and his work, like that of the other leading designers, was consistent with the machine aesthetic of purified, pristine forms that had developed in Europe—the *20th Century Limited* car may have appeared a bit inhospitable, but it had the virtue of simplicity and orderliness. There could be no hiding spilt coffee or ashes on those surfaces; one *knew* they were clean."

Like Dreyfuss's train car, the Pacwest Center—with its softly radiant aluminum facade—expressed a spit-shined antiseptic quality that, again, had become fashionable. Indeed, by the early 1980s this "Computer Moderne" aesthetic had been identified as an up-to-date style, and it had proved useful to financial institutions such as Pacific Western Bank wishing to project a new future-oriented image. Pacwest Center could best be described as a computer-influenced variant International Style, with much of that movement's starkness, severity and commitment to the processes and aesthetics of the

RESIDENCE

Robert L. Thompson

1984

machine age. "Where the work of Stijl and Bauhaus masters was uncompromising in its adherence to a canon of geometric functionalism," wrote Bush, "the Streamlined Moderne was less strident in voice and its forms were relieved by organic lines. It was marked by a combination of flat and curved walls, light in tone and silvery handrails of tubular metal . . . curved roof lines and rounded corners provided the same smooth, continuous visual experience afforded by the *DC-3* and the *Hiawatha*." Pacwest in a nutshell.

Despite its collision with neighboring buildings at the level of scale, Pacwest Center introduced a new stylistic orientation into the Portland skyline. It represented an architecture generally associated in the public mind with modernity. But not only the modernity of the streamlined decade—with the sweeping curves of the automobile and traincar—but the modernity of computer aesthetics. In describing Stubbins's contribution to the "quality of romanticism that ties all of the new skyscrapers of our time together," Goldberger wrote in *The Skyscraper*: "Hugh Stubbins' and Associates Citicorp Center . . . sleek aluminum tower . . . was a sign that at the end of the 1970's there were serious changes in the expectations of even the most conservative clients as to what a skyscraper should be . . . structure is entirely concealed in these cool buildings of the computer aesthetic, which do not even reveal floor divisions. They romanticize the idea of postmechanical technology, which is an altogether different matter than displaying the mechanical technology by which they were built."

The Pacwest Center, perhaps, more than any building ever built in the city, was "a machine for the living." Its high-tech exterior was Portland's finest contribution to

the new "computer aesthetic" in architecture. Alternating bands of anodized aluminum and darkly tinted glass spoke unambiguously to the forms and rituals of the computer age—efficiency, economy of force and energy, a minimum of distraction. This was a building whose interior delivered on the promises suggested by its shimmering surface.

Pacwest Center was Portland's premier example of the ultra-rational, modern vision in architecture. Corporate boardrooms seemed to give the building their approval. IBM and Amnet, two high-tech companies, chose the building as their home. A computerized elevator system, a high-tech lighting arrangement that combines specially tinted glass with "muted fluorescent lights, an extra few inches in floor height to reduce claustrophobia in the work space, all reflected architectural adaptations to the edgy temperament of modern man. Add to this a ground-level plaza configuration designed on principles generated by the "Project for Public Spaces" in New York and what leasing agent John Russell called the "most sophisticated communication system of any building west of the Mississippi," and you were talking high-tech, high function and high price— not to mention Hiawatha.

According to its silver-and-gold colored promotional material, Pacwest Center embraces "loving shapes" and projects "powerful softness." From afar, the building awakened our timeless fascination with trains, automobiles, airplanes and other things smooth, graceful and fluid. With Freudian symbolism and the computer on its side, how could it possibly go wrong?

It could not. Undaunted by the fashionability of Postmodern architecture, Stubbins had always been interested in designing buildings that would be "almost universally sensed and accepted, although," he confessed, "people may not know why." Aligning himself with Belluschi's position on fashion in architecture, Stubbins wrote that "in following fashion and in failing to analyze the enduring qualities of a building . . . the mode of the moment has almost encouraged the proliferation of cyclical, stylized clichés."

Although Pacwest Center and its neighbor, The Portland Building were both "children of the '80s," everything about these two structures suggested they had been built, if not on different planets, at least at different times. These differences reflected the philosophical perspectives of their authors: Graves, the historicist and maestro of high-symbolism, on the one hand, and Stubbins, the functionalist and virtuoso of high-integrity, on the other. The Pacwest Center had evolved out of a set of general guidelines Stubbins had published in 1979:

> I have a deep respect for function. The planning problems must be solved. The building must not only work for the user but also, if possible, be flexible for the future. Structure is of great importance. It should be forthright, logical, honest. It should have integrity, which does not mean that structure should necessarily be expressed. A building should express in some way its purpose as well as have unity in itself. It must be a whole thing, rather than a lot of pieces strung together. Integration within the environment is important, for, if we are to avoid the physical chaos with which we are now surrounded, we must respect to some extent the existing fabric, be it natural or man-made. In the long view, to be new and exciting may not be as important as to be courteous and restrained. But this does not mean that—within these parameters—we should not exploit fully the technology and materials we have at our command.

By 1985 the new romantic Modernists had made a strong imprint on Portland architecture. Much like the Pacwest Center, Macadam Place (1984, Thompson and Vaivoda), a cool and quietly gleaming three-story office building combined the ordered, self-assured geometry of the computer aesthetic with elements of Streamline Moderne: continuous black-opaque windows, white (almost luminous) pre-cast concrete and a lavish, over-scaled entrance way of translucent glass blocks that spanned the height of the building plus some. Clean and regimented as a computer chip, Macadam Place was

simple, modular and highly geometric. It expressed a clean-edged crispness rivaled, in this city, only by the Pacwest Center. The movement in the Macadam structure was all horizontal; the contrast between jet-black windows and bleach-white exterior walls gave the edifice a graphic majesty that was emblematic of its time.

The high-tech aesthetic championed by Thompson and Vaivoda was eagerly received in Portland, particularly by industries specializing in communications and computer-oriented products. Robert Thompson, the firm's chief designer, was a devout follower of the teachings of Le Corbusier, and, as late as 1984, he had remained relatively immune to the historicizing impulses of his contemporaries. Enamoured of the crystalline geometrics and chiaroscuro effects achieved by the early Modernists, Thompson would resuscitate the uncluttered Bauhausian aesthetic for Kruze Way Plaza (1984), the Moreland Cattery (1984) and a computer components manufacturing plant (1986).

Kruze Way Plaza consisted of two mirror-image, triangular buildings sheathed with alternating bands of anodized aluminum and opaque glass. With its rounded corners and silver-black color scheme, the building was strongly reminiscent of Stubbins's formula for Pacwest Center. Glass bricks and stark lines dominated the design for the Moreland Cattery, a building that reflected Thompson's interest in the 1930s residential architecture of Edward Durell Stone. With its flat overhanging roof, sharp angles and rounded glass brick bays, the Cattery— as well as the firm's Stoffer (1984) and Lindgren (1985) houses—expressed a commitment to re-present the modern forms of the late 1920s and early 1930s. Buildings by this partnership were a radical departure amidst the flurry of historicist buildings erected in Portland's downtown core during the early 1980s.

One could not help but admire the glittering transformation of Portland into a modern metropolis. Macadam Place, Pacwest Center and, to a lesser extent, KOIN Center, U.S. Bancorp Tower and the Veteran's Administration Hospital suggested that a new formal vocabulary had infiltrated the ranks of Portland's fecund architectural circles.

More than other buildings of the early 1980s, Macadam Place, KOIN Center and the U.S. Bancorp Tower exploited purely geometric forms in an attempt to produce an individualistic symbolism. The hope, of course, was twofold: First, that these broad geometric brushstrokes would have a clarifying and constructive influence on the direction Portland architecture might

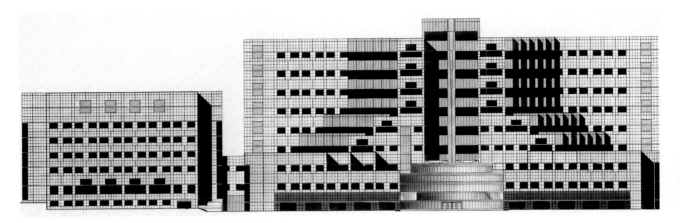

VETERAN'S ADMINISTRATION HOSPITAL
Skidmore, Owings and Merrill/Zimmer Gunsul Frasca
1984

take. And second, that the new computer-influenced aesthetic might generate a formal vocabulary, as rich and as capable of reorganization and resemanticization as the classical vocabulary elaborated by earlier architectural and historical periods. "All the things the architects of the Modern architecture period attempted to achieve have been achieved, and we need do nothing but select the ones we want," wrote Japanese architect Arata Isozaki. "But . . . we are in need of a new symbolic/formal structure that will generate a different meaning to help us make the right choice. The use of pure forms, displacement, . . . overscaling, oppositional use of materials . . . and accumulated quotations from the architecture of the past are all formal methods for the generation of new, independent semantic structures."

Breaking out of the morass of historicism, in which many Portland buildings of the 1980s were steeped, Macadam Place summarized the energy of the moment superbly—it was ordered, intense, controlled. In some respects, it was to the "Computer Modern" aesthetic of the 1980s, what Frank Lloyd Wright's Johnson Wax Administration Building was to the streamlined aesthetic of the 1930s. Although by no means a "major" commercial structure in terms of mass or volume, the building signaled the coming of a new synthesis. It was an edifice

at once flamboyant and restrained, whimsical and measured, technological and vernacular. More graphic than graceful, it borrowed a number of elements from the formal vocabulary of modern architecture: the expression of dry-method construction, metaphors born of gleaming glass and other elements that were the outcome of modern architecture's new technology and the novel expressive methods born of them.

Like Portland's streamlined Chase Bag, McCall Oil and Ball Bearing Company buildings—all of which reflected the graceful curvilinear aesthetic of the 1930s as well as an irrepressible infatuation with glass blocks—Macadam Place epitomized the craze for geometric purity and symmetry that by the 1980s had gripped a generation of young designers nursed on computer technology. Indeed, by the time Macadam Place and Pacwest Center were standing, a new direction had been forged. The romantic Modernist's instinct toward technological expression and the historicist's instinct for theatricality—in this case, it was the *regimented* theatricality of the computer age—seemed to have merged. These buildings spoke at once to history, technology and (contemporary) ritual; they were a hybrid composition that summarized the moment, by combining elements of the past with modern rituals and technologic capabilities.

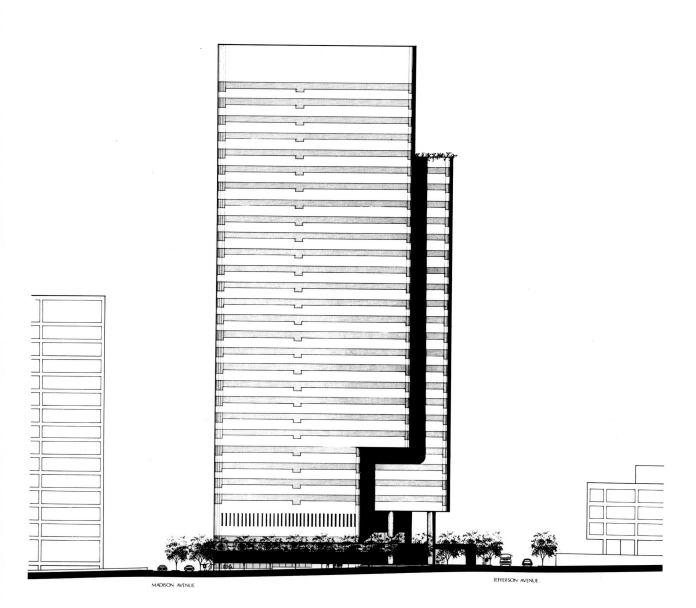

MADISON AVENUE

JEFFERSON AVENUE

PACWEST CENTER, SIXTH AVENUE ELEVATION
Hugh Stubbins and Associates/BOOR/A
1984

SEEING
THE LIGHT

ARCHITECTURE WITHOUT light is like desire denied fulfillment. "Vision finds itself in a purely theoretical relationship with objects," wrote Hegel, "through the intermediary of *light*, that immaterial matter which truly leaves objects their freedom, lighting and illuminating them without consuming them." Portland's most enlightened architects have not denied this detachment, nor have they celebrated it. Rather, they have explored the important and complex role light plays in bringing an architectural structure to completion.

Light alone can give architectural space its full value. Space without light is like an architect without a drawing pencil—lost, unfulfilled and wanting. The spatial essence of an architectural structure erupts with full force when light, shadow, color and texture convene in a three-dimensional arena fabricated by man. "Architecture . . . has the monopoly of space," wrote critic Geoffrey Scott in *The Architecture of Humanism*. "It can surround us with a void of three dimensions, and whatever delight may be derived from that is the gift of architecture alone . . . space affects us and can control our spirit; a large part of the pleasure we obtain from architecture—pleasure which seems *unaccountable* or for which we do not trouble to account—springs in reality from space."

And it springs from light. Anyone who has studied Portland's buildings with any degree of avidity understands there is something about the nature of solar illumination in the Willamette Valley that not only affects the mood of its inhabitants, but affects the way in which they perceive architecture. The region's crisp, active and blazing winter light, when it makes an appearance, offers little charity for mediocre buildings. Good architecture, on the other hand, can take on a magisterial, even monumental, quality under the influence of winter's forceful illumination. The KOIN Center (with its stepped-back, graphic tucks and creases), the Sixth Church of Christ Scientist (with its intricate brickwork and Aztec-like geometric forms) and the flush marble-skinned office buildings of Pietro Belluschi are outlined with great clarity and shadow detail under the scrutiny of winter's unmasking light. This is chiaroscuro at its finest.

The city's summer light imbues the architectural environment with an altogether different quality. The waning, red-tinged beams that usher in August evenings reflect Portland architecture in its best light, expressing a full range of chromatic values, and the continually changing relationships between architectonic forms and shadow depths. Mundane granite surfaces of Portland's "Government Row," the streamlined facades peppered with glass blocks in the Hollywood District and downtown buildings sheathed in terra cotta are ennobled by the passive, all-forgiving glow of early nocturne. The exquisitely painted stucco faces of the 7-Up Bottling Company, McCall Oil and Bearing Service buildings, as well as the pastel-colored stucco and fiberglass surfaces of Portland's Victorian jewels—the Blagen Block, the Willamette Block and New Market Theater, to mention only a few—are suffused with an ineffable glow thanks to the generosity of Portland's summer light.

Any description of Portland architecture would not be complete without addressing the region's mournful rain-sodden light. The moisture-soaked illumination of the Willamette Valley is, for the city's architecture, a great equalizer, removing blemishes, muting shadows and softening the complexion of buildings, like the gray, gauzey wash of a James Whistler painting. During protracted periods of shadowless days, architectural ornament, surface detail and the handsome rusticated exteriors of Portland's Beaux-Arts masterpieces—City Hall, the American Bank Building and the U.S. National Bank—are temporarily banished from sight, as if they had been forced into hibernation.

Light is an essential nutrient for any architectural structure. But never had the full potential of its nourishment been as fully realized in the history of Portland architecture as in the U.S. Bancorp Tower. The once revered Renaissance style of the U.S. National Bank, designed by A. E. Doyle, was put to rest as a corporate "architectural image," in 1983 when its Classical temple form was replaced by a symbolically more potent spatial configuration—a "sculptural skyscraper"—the U.S. Bancorp Tower.

Despite the transfer of symbolic importance (and the corporate boardroom) from one building to the other, each edifice represented a "timeless" architectural work. The enduring qualities of *both* buildings, however, had less to do with the *styles* in which they were built, than with their composition, the materials used in their construction and, most importantly, the way in which they interrupted urban space and interacted with the local light. Stylistic descriptions, alone, did not adequately explain the profound differences or similarities between one work and the other. The U.S. Bancorp Tower made clear that a critical architectural discourse had to include a vocabulary based on light, mass and space.

Italian critic Bruno Zevi stressed the importance of freeing modern architectural discourse from the shackles of a criticism based exclusively on style. In *Architecture as Space*, he wrote: "Today we can speak of non-limited space and of perspective of space, of pictorial qualifications of surfaces, of spatial infinity and of chromatic values, of atmospheric depth, of linear interweaving against a void, and of continually varying relationships between color planes and chiaroscuro depths, between wall masses and masses resolved in surfaces." According to Zevi, this effort toward critical precision based on light and space, meant searching for the individual life of each building, separating it from the common denominator of its "style" and promoting a more enlightened response to its aesthetic value.

Whatever the building or vantage point, it is through

U.S. BANCORP TOWER
Skidmore, Owings and Merrill/Pietro Belluschi (consulting architect)
1983

the perception of light and the negotiation of space that the human sensory machine digests and assimilates a work of architecture. The quality of light, however—its inflections and character—is never a universal constant, but rather, has a distinct regional flavor. Portland's most successful architects have been attuned to the important role that the region's light played in bringing their buildings to "completion." Kenneth Frampton, professor at Columbia University's School of Architecture, has suggested that the fundamental strategy of a critical regional architecture "is to find its governing inspiration in such things as the range and quality of local light." In an essay entitled, "Towards A Critical Regionalism: Six Points for an Architecture of Resistance," Frampton argued that a building's fenestration—its ability to modulate light between interior and exterior spaces across a structural membrane—has "the capacity to inscribe architecture with the character of a region, and hence express the *place* in which the work is situated." When architecture evolves under the impact of regionally and temporally inflected qualities of light, it gives rise to what the New York architect called a "place-conscious poetic—a form of filtration compounded out of an interaction between culture and nature, between art and light."

The regional residential architecture of John Yeon, John Storrs, Van Evra Bailey, Saul Zaik and Richard

303

Campbell, represented an enlightened response to local climatic conditions and human requirements. But when it came to art and light, Portland architect Pietro Belluschi was second to none in the magic department. Since 1925, Belluschi has been to Portland's three-dimensional world of architecture what photographer Ansel Adams had been to the two-dimensional world of photography—an arbitrator of light and shadow. If architecture had developed a "zone system," Belluschi, whose sensitivity to color, shadow and light developed in Italy during his youth, would have been its inventor. "I lived in Rome where I absorbed by osmosis everything that happened," he explained. "The counterpoint was coming to a very strange, frightening kind of country—the Pacific Northwest—which illuminated the differences between the environment in which I was born and Portland. But I never forgot, nor did I ever give up what I grew up with—the instinct for proportion, the use of materials with fine surfaces, the relationship of fenestration to masonry, and the importance of light."

Years of experimentation and designing within the physical constraints of the Pacific Northwest had viscerally imprinted the Italian-born architect with a talent for creating architectural "ornaments" based primarily on light, shadow, form and material. Along with this, came a special talent for arriving at simple, but timeless solutions for architectural problems. "There is the simplicity of the saint, and the simplicity of the fool," he said. "The simplicity of the saint is one that has rejected all transitory values and registers things with a great deal of clarity. The simplicity of a fool doesn't see or recognize, and therefore the simplicity of the saint is the one that takes time to discover, but is very satisfying because it is part of a philosophy that has rejected transitory values and trends."

As the architect suggests, Portland's celebrated, lasting buildings have always been expressions of material and the molding of space, both of which transcended any idea of their trends or fashion. Although architectural styles emblematic of a specific historical period may be associated with a building's "symbolic power" or "image," what is stylistically in vogue had little to do with whether a work of architecture would stand the test of time. In architecture, the test of time is best measured by *light*—specifically, by the character and impact of its through, and against, a three-dimensional form silently frozen in *space*.

That space—whose full potential is realized only after the introduction of light—should be the protagonist of architecture and is, after all, natural. In the mid-eighteenth century, two of Portland's first "urban planners," Asa Lovejoy and Francis Pettygrove superimposed a grid on the city of Portland, both men had become familiar with such layouts in the New England cities and towns from which they came.

Although economic and topographic constraints certainly played a role, the resulting urban matrix—which heightened the effect of ambient sunlight on the city's architectural spine—owed its distinctive geometry to their preliminary decision to plot the land into 200-by-200 foot blocks. These blocks were defined by streets and expansive north-south avenues, which strategically oriented the facades of downtown buildings toward the movement of the sun across the horizon. The aesthetic dividends anticipated by the Lovejoy-Pettygrove program were already being paid as early as 1870, dividends which, by allowing for an unusually high ratio of *open* to *built* space, made it a solar-sensitive urban plan. And they were still accruing, more than a century later. In 1983, Michael Harrison, director of the Portland Bureau of Planning, emphasized the importance of the city's original spatial layout when he wrote: "Portland's 200-foot block structure and frequent streets provide ready access to the open space, light and air that has helped give Portland its special quality."

Whether it is the elaborate cast iron brick and stucco Italianate facade of the Poppleton Building, the pressed brick and terra cotta walls, arched openings and Romanesque detailing of the Plaza Hotel, or the splendid rusticated stonework of the Durham and Bates Building (old Bank of California on s.w. Sixth and Stark), every architectural volume, every wall, cornice and detail—regardless of its style—constitutes a boundary, an interruption in the continuity of Portland's urban space. More specifically, all buildings—warehouses, skyscrapers, art museums, et cetera—function in creating two kinds of space: an *interior* space, completely defined by the structure itself, and an *exterior* space, which projects into the cityscape—into its streets, skyline, parks, gardens, squares and plazas.

An urban space embraces every pictorial surface, mass and color value in its vicinity. Portland's fractured, eclectic architectural fabric, excludes few elements from the spatial equation that characterizes any urban site. Bridges, neon signs, public art, obelisks, ash-covered mountain peaks and, most importantly, the facades of

Portland's buildings are all brought into play in the creation of architectural space. The final value of any architectural space depends upon the sum of all its components. Just as four exquisitely decorated walls do not, in themselves, create an aesthetically rich "space," so, a group of excellent buildings—especially if they have been constructed without sensitivity to pre-existing structures and the spaces which "project" from them—can define a poor urban space, and *vice versa*.

Over the years, Portland had become the repository of many satisfying, elevating urban-cum-architectural spaces. The most notable might include: the "Roman Renaissance corner" on s.w. Sixth and Stark; "terra cotta plaza" delineated by the north and south walls of Pioneer Courthouse Square; the "vernacular strips" of the Hollywood District; "neon alley" of the Broadway District; and the "cast iron spaces" that pepper the Skidmore/Old Town and Yamhill Historic Districts. Portland was unique among West Coast cities in the range of spatial values that its architectural fabric expressed. The preponderance of harmonious and, frequently, variegated but, nevertheless, stimulating urban spaces is best explained by sensitivity to context, space and light that was apparent in the design strategies that set the tone for the city's "spatial evolution."

Architect and historian George A. McMath addressed the spatial essence of "terra cotta plaza" when he commented on the light-colored facade chosen by A. E. Doyle for the Pacific Building (1926), one of the city's finest examples of the refined Italian Renaissance style: "The Portland Hotel and The Pioneer Courthouse were two relatively small gray buildings already surrounded by terra cotta elements of the Meier and Frank Store, the American Bank Building, and Jackson Tower." Arguing that Doyle may have been conscious of bringing Pioneer Square to its spatial destiny, McMath said: "The Pacific Building, which was built several years later, referred to these three existing buildings with respect to both height and color."

The messy vitality of architectural space in the Hollywood District, profusely peppered with Art Deco and Mission styles, grew less out of a single architect's vision than zoning laws. The large concentration of buildings—many reflecting the curvilinear-cum-glass-block aesthetic of the Depression Modern style popular in the 1930s—grew from the exclusion through zoning of stores from residential areas in the vicinity. This encouraged the development of continuous strips of stores along the extant trolley routes and the addition of new streets built especially for auto traffic.

By the late 1960s, establishing "spatial" unity had become part of a progressive self-conscious program developed by the Portland Design Commission for maintaining, enhancing and complementing the existing character of Portland's architectural fabric. These strategies eventually paved the way for a comprehensive design program for the city, a portion of which was published in *Downtown Design Guidelines* (1983) and read: "Historical links exist with the past in groups of buildings as well as individual structures, street character, and furnishing. Portland has a diversity composed of a wide variety . . . of styles of architecture, special features, and parks. Wide, sunny north-south avenues parallel the river reflecting the city's early development pattern. . . . This identity can be supported or denied by new development. Buildings which have no relationship to Portland, its setting or its past, buildings which could have been located in any modern city can disrupt Portland by creating *spaces* without identity."

Architectural "compatability," "harmony," "continuity," "unifying elements" and "the stage and its action" had become buzz phrases for the Portland Design Commission by the late 1970s. Their innovative formulations, along with those of the Portland Development Commission and the Historical Landmarks Commission, helped establish spatial and stylistic continuity in the city's urban core, especially within its historic districts. Ordinances, design competitions and planning concepts that originated in the city's political inner sanctum played an important role in shaping the city's overall architectural direction.

But the design guidelines, master plans and preservation programs, which had been implemented with the help of the city's political machinery since the late 1960s, could never, in themselves, have produced Portland's finest architectural specimens. Design commissions, juries and planning bureaus do not make architecture. They promote and regulate it. Architects alone make architecture. In Portland, the creation of dignified architectural spaces (Portland Art Museum), designs for monumental buildings (Masonic Temple) and elegant solutions that met stringent functional and aesthetic requirements Equitable (Commonwealth) Building were the result of personal, complex choices. Each reflected an architectural vision that was influenced by the aesthetic, political and economic currents of the time.

Great architecture is not the stuff of design commissions or planning bureaus, although clearly each of these may play a role in generating the final product. Architectural design—and its corollary, the creation of satisfying architectural space—originates in experience, both childhood and adult, academic and practical. It is derived from practical experimentation and meditation at the drafting table. Lasting work, or what Belluschi has called "authentic" architecture, results from understanding and anticipating the complex spatial relationships—interior and exterior—which a building will manifest after its two-dimensional drawing has been translated into a three-dimensional structure that is spotwelded to a plot of urban space.

A building has a greater chance for success if the architect can explore the spatial advantage points, color planes, chiaroscuro and chromatic values of the design within the province of his mind's eye, *before* the building is executed. "Architecture is the only art form that affords us the opportunity of being voyeurs who watch from the outside and also of being interior watchers," wrote architect John Hejduk, dean of the Cooper Union School of Architecture. "We can also observe the inside from the outside, the outside from the inside, and the inside from the inside. It is all made up of a series of inside fragments and outside fragments."

Combining and evaluating the myriad fragments that contribute to the success of an architectural work has always been a priority for Belluschi. During his career, Portland's maestro of space and light has produced designs based on a "sensitivity to certain forms" and spatial fragments—both interior and exterior. "In architecture, there is always infiltration, some pollution coming in," he explained. "But purely as a principle, space is a good place to begin. Whether it is a commercial building, a house, or a church, the process of taking into account all of the forces, intentions, and elements of the problem, and solving it with a free mind, makes the difference between architecture that appeals to the eye for the moment and something that is *timeless*."

As much as possible, Belluschi consciously devoted himself to an architecture that reflected an authentic impulse and to a process that was not conditioned by tastes, trends or other rear-window formulas. By relying on the most essential threads (line, shape, surface, color and light) and *removing* in turn, superfluous threads (imagery, symbol and ornament) which have come to be thought as usual in the recognition of buildings, Belluschi arrived at the essential subject of architecture—sculpt-

ing space. In the process, he became a master of mood and emotion, exploring a wide range of spatial values: The poignant silence created by the spatial confluency and understated materials of the Burke house (1949), the heavenly coruscations emitted by the copper-and-silver coated panes of the u.s. Bancorp Tower (1984, SOM, consultation by Belluschi), the spiritual serenity achieved in the Morninglight Chapel of the J. P. Finley and Son Mortuary (1937). Belluschi's architecture could evoke the full range of human impulses, from the primary to the cognitive.

Surface and color were the flesh and blood of many of his buildings and, perhaps, more than any other features, elevated his edifices to a high art. As an educator, practitioner and consultant in the architectural field, he had always been a virtuoso when designing the exterior skins and interior spaces of his structures. Whether it was the sublime wood-based glow that he used to fill the interior of the Cottage Grove Church, or the dramatic play of light against the cooper-and-silver plated glass panes he helped to assure in the u.s. Bancorp Tower, Belluschi was tapping a deeply personal boyhood vision nurtured by the action of light against exterior surfaces and interior spaces of buildings near Italy's Adriatic coast.

In cities like Tourastina, Belluschi's sensitive eye (the eye of a "dreamer" as he calls it) was imprinted on the understated, sun-drenched pigments of the local farmhouses, gardens, porticos and hillside churches. A respect for the visually catalytic experiences of his younger years erupted with unambiguous force when he reminisced about Rome, the city of his youth. "You are always aware of the *surfaces* of buildings in Italy, especially in Rome. The orange roof, for example, is a unifying element in the landscape of any Italian city. But equally important are the walls, which are painted in colors that range from ochre to Venetian red. And the sublime effect is achieved without heavy paint. Rather, a light water-based paint is used, so the surfaces have depth, and just glow."

That same ineffable, timeless glow has been the signature of many Belluschi buildings. Using primarily travertine, glass, wood and brick, Belluschi exercised his power to create environments and surfaces that harked back to subjective experiences in his childhood. "In a very sensitive age, whether you know or understand it, you develop a childhood sensitivity to your environment," he said. "You are a dreamer, you are poetic—and you *breathe* the colors and surfaces of buildings. You breathe the ochres, the venetian reds, and pastels—the earthy

U.S. BANCORP TOWER
Skidmore, Owings and Merrill/Pietro Belluschi (consulting architect)
1983

colors. These become an overpowering element in your eye, and you become so imbued with it that you see building and surface as one."

In both his private residences and commercial buildings, Belluschi expressed the sparsities of architecture. From his youth to the present moment, he has been entranced by the way light softly washes surfaces in gentle ways. The materiality of brick, glass, wood, alumi-num and marble has been celebrated and honored throughout his work. He developed a sixth sense for the way light and material both *affect* and effect space. But of all the Portland buildings in which Belluschi has had a significant consultative role, none expressed his mastery over the materiality of glass and granite, and his fascination with light more than the u.s. Bancorp Tower. De-signed by SOM under the direction of James Christenson, the building—although modern in orientation—was a successful departure from the boxy towers of steel and glass that had turned Portland's inner core into a tract for corporate behemoths.

It was called "The Rose Bank," "Big Pink," "The Pink Champagne Building," and many other names. But unlike the drab, static towers that had come out of the SOM design group in the 1970s, this gleaming descendant of Miesian Modernism bristled with authenticity and had a life of its own. It worked as a sculptural piece on the skyline. In a poll conducted by Alan Hayakawa and reported in the *Oregonian* of 18 December 1983, the U.S. Bancorp Tower was voted the best-liked building in Portland.

Light, sweet light, in combination with SOM and Belluschi's magic wand elevated this structure to a special position on the Portland skyline. The building *was* light in its most abstract sense. Light as time *and* space wrapped into one shining, wonderful-to-look-at package. Light transmitted, light reflected, light absorbed. Light pushing the plasticity of subjectivism to its transcendental limits. "The U.S. Bancorp Tower started me thinking about architecture as sculpture," said Belluschi. "But for sculptures of this magnitude to work, they require more than presence and strength. They must be receptive to the play of light, which does wonderful things. It creates shadows. And how you treat these shadows, their reflections, and their scale on the various materials determines whether or not you have *architecture*."

Like a lone rhinoceros, the tower stood proud and defiant, beckoning thousands of Portland residents each day to see its light—light in its most irreducible form, polarized and repolarized, light in full bloom, light silently spanking a parallelogram of granite and glass. "I realized the purity of the building's form could be achieved only if there existed a special relationship between the glass and granite," explained Belluschi. "The granite had to be polished so that the glass would reflect on it as much as the granite reflected on the glass. These were the elements I worked on in the Bank of America Building in San Francisco. That building was somewhat based on the same philosophy as that which I applied to Portland's U.S. Bancorp Building—to have a piece of sculpture in the skyline."

And sculpture it was. This gleaming testimony to corporate expansion towered over a part of town where clusters of people who skidded off the main track collect around heating vents and food lines. It was to Portland what the Eiffel Tower was to Paris, what the Washington Monument was to D.C., what the luminous monolith was to *2001: A Space Odyssey*.

The building's sheer bulk and conspicuousness made it Portland's ubiquitous edifice, whether one was driving in from the east on the Banfield Expressway, or from the west on Highway 26. Rising piously from an undistinguished urban plot on S.W. Fifth and Burnside, it was always in your field of view. It followed you around like a CIA agent, but was moodier and more protean. At sunset it glowed like a phosphorescent radium watch dial; at night its innards dissolved into charcoal nothingness, framed by a skein of white granite.

Despite its intrusive scale and lack of integration at street level, the building possessed virtues as a perpetual light machine, which made it the most talked-about edifice since The Portland Building. At a time when the static, flash imagery of Postmodernism had become the international currency of the architectural world, it was refreshing to see a challenge in the form of the U.S. Bancorp Tower. Especially in Portland, which had, for so long, been a proving ground for the modernist ideals of SOM. The result thus far had been a gargantuan laboratory with skyscraper boxes in every shape, size and color, most of them uninspiring. With the erection of The Portland Building, the limp orthodoxies of Modernism were supplanted by the pastiche pluralism of Postmodernism. The gleam and glitter of glass-and-steel edifices proved to many to be wasted edifices. Postmodernism was there to usher in the smell of newness, and figurative architecture catapulted American architecture into something it had not been previously— arty, intellectual and international.

When a building goes beyond providing shelter from the storm and becomes architecture, the direction it takes is anyone's guess. The architect can always fall back on formalized aesthetics, the thing of beauty as a joy forever. But this approach quickly results in chaos. "The best buildings and the most beautiful buildings are bogus gestures that make everything seem more chaotic," wrote architecture critic Herbert Muschamp in *File Under Architecture*, "by preventing us from fully accepting that and acting upon the fact that the old spaces are *dead*, that we no longer believe in the power of straight lines, fixed angles, corners or shapes, or *space packages of any kind* to have a significant effect on our experience." Nothing, he implies, can resuscitate architectural forms or phenomena whose time has passed, except in novel entertainment form.

Where did all this leave the u.s. Bancorp Tower? If you believe that good architecture shows what has never before been shown, it was in a very good place. Whether by accident or design, it was less a building than a large art installation. It never looked the same way twice and, more than any other structure in this city, struck all the chords of universal recognition. It was less a building than a perpetual motion machine at the disposal of individual consciousness.

Extending into an infinite number of spaces at once, the u.s. Bancorp Tower was a work in progress, a spatial projection of an event (the play of light on granite and glass) taking place in space-time. It created novel tensions between the traveler/spectator in motion and the position in which it was fixed. Time, motion and light constituted its structure, without ever providing a deterministic definition of the building in space.

The contrast between The Portland Building and the u.s. Bancorp Tower illuminated the issues separating the architectural determinists from the architectural potentialists. The neo-determinists, like Graves, used old elements in somewhat new, but nevertheless dogmatic, combinations, whereas the potentialists were interested in buildings that reflected fluid relationships and were more ambiguous. The debate between the determinists and potentialists, at least in the world of architecture, centered on the length and tightness of the leash by which architects held their structures. Graves's Portland Building, static and unyielding in most respects, was held on a taut leash, with the building's well-defined (albeit figurative) elements rooted in historical precepts and formalist traditions. It was qualitatively and fundamentally different from the u.s. Bancorp Tower, which was suspended by a long, loose cord. While making a nod to the Modernist sensibility, the tower was more concerned with the broad range of possibilities specified by the interaction of light, time and motion—or purely physical and mathematical, and, therefore, universal forces.

The u.s. Bancorp Tower was a success, in the true modernist sense. Maybe it was a mistake. Could anyone have envisioned such a play of light and color with glass and granite? If anyone could, it was the "light-thrower" himself, Belluschi. "The windows have a *threshold* value," the architect explained. "At a certain level of light, the panes reflect light. But just beneath this threshold value, the panes darken. It is a binary phenomenon—all or none. But the granite reflects light as well. Under some conditions the granite is darker than the glass, and in others vice versa. . . . there is a critical dialogue between the two surfaces."

The "simplicity of the saint" to use Belluschi's own phrase, transformed a building that might have been mundane and merely modern, into one that was magnificent and magisterial. "In the case of the u.s. Bancorp Building, my point was that unless we found a relationship between the reflectivity of the glass and granite, the building was not going to be successful," said Belluschi. "It would be just another building. But the threshold value is the clarity, a quality for which I feel completely responsible."

The Tower was a Modernist work, to be sure, but, with its ornamental touches—the stepped-back glass planes at the top and the stepped-back glass-granite motif recapitulated at the bottom—it made a quiet, subtle overture to the whimsical spirit of Postmodernists. And its grandiose, almost two-dimensional planarity demonstrated that it had not relinquished the progressive and utopian aspirations of dedicated, dyed-in-Brooks Brothers-wool Modernists.

Though most observers looked askance at the structure during its formative stages (many people still remember the billowing tarps, giving the appearance of a Cristo installation), most came to like the building with time. When the panes came, so did the sun—and the light. The luminosity of this structure had won over the optic nerves of both the lay public and the architectural experts. It was pronounced all sweetness and light. "As far as sculptures in the sky, I still believe that the skyscraper is the most American of all architectural forms," Belluschi confessed, "because they have been made possible by the technological advances which, whether you like it or not, are symbolic of our civilization."

In Belluschi's view it was still possible to have an authentic architecture in a technologic age, as long as the architect was freed from a set of prevailing intentions, tastes and trends, which led merely to replicate something that had already been done, "When designing a building, you begin by considering all of the forces, aesthetic and pragmatic. You analyze them with your brains so it will yield a satisfactory solution." So, like the u.s. Bancorp Tower, it can fill the skyline with the sound of music. "By virtue of the fact that you are trying to create a new part of *yourself*," Belluschi said, "the solution, if it is authentic, will *sing* like poetry, like the use of words."

Standing alone and virtually unencumbered by edifices of similar stature, the u.s. Bancorp Tower projected a singular, isolated presence on Portland's less-than-muscular skyline. It was a daring, flamboyant tribute to the new "machine" aesthetic; and the monolith transmitted this message to every nook and cranny of architectural space, close and far. Like an ectopic floater that stubbornly refuses to leave one's field of vision, the building was an architectural quotation mark for nearly everything in sight——for Romanesque warehouses and cast iron gems in Old Town, for boxy Miesian skyscrapers, for the Renaissance revival palaces of Albert E. Doyle and the Star Theatre and Caribou Clubs nothing seemed to escape its directive.

In one important respect, the u.s. Bancorp Tower violated the conceptual orientation of the Portland Design Commission, in that its design seemed to have "no relationship to Portland, its setting or its past . . . [and] could have been located in any modern city." A closer look, however, revealed that while the building received poor marks for "continuity" and "compatibility," it passed the light test with flying colors. Because of its strategic location on Portland's urban grid, the building was engaged in a constant dialogue with the region's climate——with its light, its rain and its cloud-dotted skies. The result was an architectural monument with lasting, "universal" values. Lovejoy and Pettygrove could not have asked for anything more. As the Swiss-born architect, Le Corbusier commented, "The masses do not want facts, reasoning, calculation, theorems . . . . They must have a spectacle." And in Portland, they had the u.s. Bancorp Tower.

AFTERWORD

A WEEKLY SERIES of articles on Portland's historic building that appeared in the *Oregonian* during the fall of 1898 began:

Standing in the middle of the block between Yamhill and Taylor on Fourth Street, facing the west, is a queer, old fashioned building with three dormer windows protruding from the roof, as though inquisitive to see all the strange new magic of the rushing world about it. Although a prim new front rises bravely from the sidewalk up to the antiquated roof, and although two leafy overtopping trees shade its telltale windows, the careful observer is sure to surmise that the old house belongs to a bygone day and generation. Such, indeed, is the case, for this is the old Crosby house, claimed by certain pioneers to be the oldest relic of those early days, when the log cabin of the man who tossed up a penny for the naming of Portland stood at the foot of Washington Street; when the tannery that stood on the grounds of the present Exposition building (site of present Stadium) was reached only by a laborious walk through the virgin forests; when Stephen Coffin's sawmill, that all the men in Oregon, summoned from the country round, could not lift into place, stood in a deep gulch at the foot of Jefferson Street; and when ox-paths and skid-roads among the giant fir trees and dismantled stumps took the place of streets.

These articles were the first popular writings on local historic architecture. Successive articles dealt with the "Old Portland Academy," "Old Ankeny House," "J. Failing's Original Store," "Occidental Hotel," "Old Willamette Theater," "Old Trinity Church" of 1854 and several others.

New buildings have long been a popular subject for newspapers and other publications. The *West Shore*, published between 1875 and 1891, was the principal journal of Northwest community development and today is still a major resource on regional architecture. But a certain time had to pass before our buildings warranted the label, "historic" or "old." At the time of the *Oregonian* series the Crosby house was 50 years old, a time span that is still a widely used standard for defining when a structure becomes "historic."

During the next half century, Portland's historic architecture received scant attention from local authors or the press—a few isolated articles on particular buildings appeared, but in no sense was there any systematic review of the period buildings. An exception in the larger context of Oregon was the work of architects such as Glenn Stanton and Walter Church in publicizing historic architecture in the early 1930s, and the Historic American Building Survey (HABS) of 1934–37.

HABS, led in Oregon by architect Jamieson Parker, was a joint program among the American Institute of Architects, the Library of Congress and the National Park Service. Architects were employed to record—through drawings, photographs and narrative descrip-

tions—the state's important historic architecture. The focus of Oregon's program was on the pioneer homes of the western valleys. While the architect/surveyors were all from the Portland area, none of the surveyed buildings were situated in Portland. Results of the HABS project were published in the *Oregon Historical Quarterly*.

The earliest book to deal with local architecture was *The Northwest Architecture of Pietro Belluschi*, edited by Jo Stubblebine. While not "historical" in the usual sense, this 1953 review of Belluschi's career covers the important 20-year period prior to his appointment as dean of the School of Architecture at MIT. This well-illustrated volume remains today the only book devoted to a single Oregon architect.

The first scholarly treatment of Portland and Oregon historic architecture appeared in 1956 with the *Oregon Historical Quarterly* publication of "Architecture in Oregon, 1845–1895" by Marion D. Ross, professor and architectural historian from the University of Oregon. The article was a comprehensive survey of Oregon's architectural development from the early pioneer structures to the sophisticated designs of Whidden and Lewis. "Architecture in Oregon" was the source of a growing interest in historic architecture and many consider it to be a seminal event in the State's historic preservation movement.

Later that year a series on historical buildings called "This Was Portland" by Louise Aaron began in the *Oregon Journal*. Perhaps prompted by the Ross monograph, Aaron's pieces dealt with prominent downtown landmarks, then (and now) still standing—New Market Theater, Pioneer Courthouse, Skidmore Fountain, Dekum Building, "Bishop's House" and many others. Ms. Aaron was perhaps the first to suggest that Portland government had a role in preserving our historic buildings when she concluded her 1956 article on the New Market Theater with the question: "Why not include such heritage from the past in city planning for the future?"

The national historic preservation movement gained official status in 1966 with passage of the Historic Preservation Act. A year later the first book on Portland's historic buildings, *A Century of Portland Architecture* by Thomas Vaughan and George McMath, was published by the Oregon Historical Society. Partially financed by a grant from the Department of Housing and Urban Development, *Century* was a tract for local preservation and was an important factor in the City Council adoption of the 1968 Historical Landmarks Ordinance. Photographs, and historical and topical narratives, addressed 68 buildings from the 1850s to Belluschi's Zion Lutheran Church of 1950. This book found an audience "ready and waiting" for local history. Early sales placed it on the local best-seller list where it stayed for many weeks. A second printing was issued in 1968 and today *Century* can occasionally be found in used book stores at three times the original selling price.

In fact, 1968 was a banner year for publications on Portland architecture and design, prompted no doubt by the national convention of the American Institute of Architects that met in our city. In addition to the second printing of *Century* there appeared the delightful *Portland Sketchbook* by Elizabeth Brewster, and the elegant Oregon Historical Society book on distinguished nineteenth century homes, *Nineteenth Street* by architect Richard Marlitt. For the 1968 AIA Convention, the Portland Chapter published *A Guide to Portland Architecture*, edited by Richard E. Ritz.

Historian/photographer Fred DeWolfe issued the first of three books, *Impressions of Portland* in 1970. Past and present views of buildings, people and urban scenes in a whimsical mix of historic pictures and current photos, many by the author, made for Christmas season best sellers. *Impressions* was followed by *Old Portland* in 1976, and in 1980 by *Portland Tradition in Buildings and People*.

Another national convention in Portland—the Annual Meeting of the National Trust for Historic Preservation of 1974—inspired the publication of two important works on Portland architecture. *How Do We Know It Is Us Without Our Past*, a line borrowed from John Steinbeck's "The Grapes of Wrath," was the title of a booklet put out by the Portland Historical Landmarks Commission. Prepared by the commission staff, headed by Leo Dean Williams, the slim volume, with beautiful and off-beat photography, high-style graphics and quotes from Henry David Thoreau, Alvin Toffler and a third grade student, presented the city's growing historic landmarks program. Written during the early days of "gender neutralization" it is believed to have coined the phrase "person hole cover."

Also published that year was the two volume anthology, *Space, Style and Structure: Building in Northwest America*, edited by Thomas Vaughan with Virginia Guest Ferriday, associate editor. Fourteen contributors authored nearly two-dozen essays on regional architecture and planning from prehistoric settlements to contemporary urban renewal in downtown Portland. This important contribution broke new ground in elucidating the importance of individual buildings within the larger context of urban and rural architecture in the Pacific Northwest. This eight pound tome was published within 12 months from the time authors were commissioned— no small feat when dealing with fourteen disparate egos.

The Bicentennial saw publication of the first Portland book on a specific building type, *The Grand Era of Cast-Iron Architecture in Portland*, written by architect William John Hawkins III. This thoroughly researched and finely illustrated book traces the cast-iron commercial period in downtown Portland from the mid-1850s to the last of the genre, Glisan's Building, completed in 1889. Hawkins's effort and his parallel organization of the Portland Friends of Cast Iron Architecture (PFCIA) were instrumental in creating public awareness of Portland's prime collection of cast-iron storefronts, believed to be the largest assemblage outside of New York City. As editor of the PFCIA *Newsletter*, Hawkins also contributed to our knowledge of Portland's nineteenth century architecture with his essays on prominent architects of the Victorian era, Warren H. Williams, Justus Krumbein and others.

The Oregon Historical Society's guide book, *Portland, A Historical Sketch and Guide* by Terence O'Donnell and Thomas Vaughan was published in 1976. Irish wit and wisdom abounds in this colorful retelling of Portland's early history and in the authors' personal views of the city's historic buildings and builders. Commenting on the Dekum: "This ornate old bastion was built by Frank Dekum, a Bavarian confectioner who was founder and president of the German Songbird Society, the group responsible for introducing into Portland gold finches, nightingales and other feathered creatures. Indeed there is much in Mr. Dekum's building which reflects this interest in both pastry and plumage." And later, "Among the more dramatic features are the entrances . . . the south entry on Third, its arch a massive blunted wedge supported by clustered pillars, the interior a bower carved in stone where griffins rear in battle." A revised edition of the *Guide* was issued by the Society in 1984.

A long awaited book, *Architecture Oregon Style*, was published in 1983 and written by Rosalind Clark for the city of Albany. Prompted by the plethora of conflicting style descriptors that began appearing in the historical surveys of the 1970s, Ms. Clark (with the able assistance of prominent historians, Marion Dean Ross, Phillip H. Dole and Elisabeth Walton Potter) catalogued and illustrated the architectural styles as they evolved in Oregon between 1840 and the 1950s. Many Portland examples are included. It was the hope of the author and her advisors that a common language of architectural styles would bring clarity and increased understanding of our architectural heritage.

Three additions to the literature on Portland's historic architecture appeared in 1984. *Landmarks, A Tradition of Portland Masonry Architecture*, was published by the Masonry and Ceramic Tile Institute of Oregon for the AIA Northwest Regional Convention. Detailed photos of brick, tile and terra cotta demonstrate the richness and versatility of masonry elements in our historic fabric. Local architects, historians and photographers contributed to the booklet and an instructive foreword was prepared by Michael Shellenbarger, associate professor of architecture at the University of Oregon.

A single building was the focus of *Portland's Historic New Market Theater*, written and published by William John Hawkins III. The author continued his exploration of cast-iron architecture and commemorated the 1984 rehabilitation of the city's "most colorful and venerable landmark." Hawkins traces the New Market's complex early history, its architects and builders, the brief life of the theater, and its evolution to the present. Of special interest is the historical reconstruction of the theater space on the upper floors which had been almost completely obliterated when the building was converted to a parking garage in 1913.

A careful analysis of contemporary writings during the theater's heyday, a study of period theater literature, small bits of physical evidence uncovered during restoration, and some conjecture, allowed the rendering of architectural drawings that show the early theater design. During the selective demolition prior to restoration, Hawkins notes, "Beneath later concrete floors were the remains of former walls. Blocked exterior doorway locations were revealed, and outlines of the former orchestra level were found at the sidewalls. Ticket stubs appeared from between floor joists, indicating that the contemporary newspaper accounts of the location of the ticket office had been accurate."

Last of the Handmade Buildings: Glazed Terra Cotta in Downtown Portland, by Virginia Guest Ferriday, considers a single historic building type somewhat in the manner of Hawkins's book on the city's cast-iron architecture, but is broader in scope and purpose. Portland's early twentieth-century terra cotta structures still form the essence of today's "Downtown," an area once described as, "one massive terra cotta pavilion." Ferriday covers the subject from the details of terra cotta manufacture and repair to the historical context of development, planning and construction methods that spawned such landmarks as the Meier and Frank Store, Journal Building, Benson Hotel and the Central Library. Part two of the well-illustrated text presents a comprehensive plan for preserving a downtown terra cotta district, and an outline of programs and techniques for the rehabilitation of this important historic resource.

The notion of "Renaissance Man"—and "Woman" —is epitomized in the approach of Gideon Bosker and Lena Lencek who bring us this book, *Frozen Music: A History of Portland Architecture*, the latest in writings on our city's heritage. It is most appropriate during this period of architectural ferment—if not chaos—that we are presented with a fresh overview of our past and present by generalists who are not burdened by the baggage of current architectural rhetoric. Bosker and Lencek, who regard architecture as a "cultural narrative," also bring views from other regions that allow them to see Portland with a clear vision uncluttered by insular bias.

They perceive in Portland, as some have only suspected, an "Architectural Microcosm" where fine examples of the last century's architectural patrimony have developed into a coherent continuum—Renaissance delight in the New Market Theater, robust "Romanesque" at the Dekum Building, Beaux-Arts splendor in the U.S. Bank, Charles F. Berg's with its elegant Art Deco facade, Belluschi's seminal Equitable Building, the unifying spine of the Transit Mall, to the Graves pastiche (which houses the planners who will shape our future). Whether focusing on the Beaux-Arts era or expanding our perception of the U.S. Bancorp Tower, the authors give us new, instructive ways of perceiving our built environment. To some, Pioneer Courthouse Square is a place to have lunch. To Bosker and Lencek it is a place to "experience the vacant stillness of ancient temples."

Previous histories of architectural development, elsewhere as well as in Portland, have generally paid little attention to the buildings of the 1930s and early 1940s, variously described as Art Deco, Moderne or Half-Modern. Most notably absent have been the industrial examples of the era that the authors have appropriately labeled "Mechano-Deco." Sleek manufacturing plants, streamlined gas stations and the brash symbolism of a "jug" restaurant are given their rightful place. So too are the unheralded architects such as Richard Sundeleaf who, few recall, received international acclaim for the design of the Jantzen plant in London.

Of special interest to architects as well as lay readers is the extensive use of architectural drawings to illustrate the text. Such renderings, most of them not previously published, often give rare insights into the design process. Gideon Bosker's elegant black and white pho-tographs of Portland's "high" and "low" architecture add a special bonus.

Frozen Music—an apt phrase borrowed from Goethe —is unique among publications on Portland architecture. In addition to a lively history and the reordering of architectural epochs, Bosker and Lencek find Portland at the forefront of architectural development. Their writing reveals for the first time the stylistic strategies and breakthroughs in visual aesthetics that give logic to the city's architectural past and form the basis for Portland's continued leadership as a great contemporary city.

George McMath
FAIA
Portland, Oregon

317

Bibliography

Abbott, Carl. *Portland: Planning, Politics, and Growth in a Twentieth Century City.* Lincoln: 1983.

Alebko, Michael. "Architecture Critic Feels portland Lacks Identity." *Oregonian.* 22 May 1979.

Allsop, Bruce. *Art and the Nature of Architecture.* London: Pitman, 1952.

————. *The Study of Architectural History.* New York: Praeger, 1970.

Architectural Record (April 1953).

Arnell, Peter and Ted Bickford, Eds. *Robert A. M. Stern 1968–1980 Toward a Modern Architecture After Modernism.* New York: Rizzoli, 1981.

Bailey, Van Evera. "In Portland Oregon." *Pencil Points* (February 1945).

Banham, Rayner. *Los Angeles: The Architecture of Four Ecologies.* London: Penguin, 1976.

————. *Theory and Design in the First Machine Age.* 2nd ed. New York: Praeger, 1967.

Barthelme, Donald. *Overnight to Many Distant Cities.* New York: G. P. Putnam's Sons, 1983.

Beiswenger, Mary. Letter to Van Evera Bailey. 11 March 1948. Private collection.

Belluschi, Pietro. Interview with authors. Portland, January 1984. Authors' collection.

————. Letter to Frank Lloyd Wright. 2 July 1931. Private collection.

————. "The Meaning of Regionalism in Architecture." *Architectural Record* (December, 1955).

Benevolo, Leonardo. *History of Modern Architecture: The Tradition of Modern Architecture.* Cambridge: MIT, 1977.

Benjamin, Walter. *Reflections.* New York: Harcourt Brace Jovanovich, 1978.

Bennett, Edward H. *The Greater Portland Plan.* Portland: n.p., 1912.

Boles, Stanley. Interview with authors. Portland, February 1984.

Bowes, William. "Tomorrow's Portland." *Portland Realtor* (4 June 1943).

————. "Tomorrow's Portland." *Portland Oregonian.* 12 February 1944.

————. "Tomorrow's Portland." *Portland Oregonian.* 17 June 1945.

————. "Tomorrow's Portland." *Portland Oregonian.* 3 August 1945.

————. "Tomorrow's Portland." *Portland Oregonian.* 3 November 1945.

————. William Bowes Papers (manuscript). Oregon Historical Society.

Bragdon, Claude. *Architecture and Democracy.* New York: Knopf, 1918.

————. *The Beautiful Necessity.* New York: Knopf, 1949.

Braybrooke, Susan, Ed. *Hugh Stubbins: The Design Experience.* New York: Wiley-Interscience, 1976.

"Brick Building Erected During 1868." *Portland Directory.* Portland: n.p., 1869.

Bush, Donald J. *The Streamlined Decade.* New York: Brazillier, 1975.

Cerwinske, Laura. *Tropical Deco: The Architecture and Design of Old Miami Beach.* New York: Rizzoli, 1981.

Cheney, Charles H. "The Work of Albert E. Doyle, Architect of Portland, Oregon." *Architect and Engineer* (July 1919).

Cheney, Sheldon. *Expression in Art*. New York: Liveright, 1934.

Christ, Yvan. *Projects et Divagations de Claude-Nicolas Ledoux, Architecte du Roi*. Paris: Editions du Minotaure, 1961.

Clark, Rosalind. *Oregon Style: Architecture from 1840 to the 1950s*. Portland: Professional Book Center, 1983.

Corbett, Harvey Wiley. "Design in Office Buildings." *Architectural Forum* (June 1930).

Crowd, Theresa. "Here's the Kitchen of Tomorrow." *Garden Magazine* (15 June 1972).

"David C. Lewis: Railway Exchange Building." National Register of Historic Places Inventory Nomination Form.

Dean, David. *Architecture of the 1930s*. New York: Rizzoli, 1983.

Dreyfuss, Henry. *Designing for People*. New York: Simon and Schuster, 1955.

Dunster, David, Ed. *Architectural Monographs 5: Michael Graves*. London: Academy Editions, 1979.

Eyre, Cynthia. "Our House is the Way We Live." *Better Homes and Gardens* (July 1954).

Fitch, James Marston. *American Building: The Forces That Shape It*. Boston: Houghton Mifflin, 1948.

Foster, Hal. *The Anti-Aesthetic: Essays on Post-Modern Culture*. Port Townsend, Wash.: Bay Press, 1983.

Frampton, Kenneth and Silvia Kolbowski, Eds. *Idea as Model. Catalogue 3*. New York: Rizzoli, 1981.

Frasca, Robert J. "Don't Call it Post-Modern." *Architectural Technology* (Spring, 1984).

————. Interview with authors. Portland, December 1983. Authors' collection.

Fraser, Kennedy. "Architectural Fashion—I." *New Yorker* (8 November 1982).

————. "Architectural Fashion—II." *New Yorker* (22 November 1982).

————. *The Fashionable Mind: Reflections on Fashion, 1970–1981*. New York: Knopf, 1981.

Frost, Susan E. "Turning a Dream into Skylines." *Oregon Business* (October 1983).

Gayle, Margot and Edmund V. Gillon, Jr. *Cast-Iron Architecture in New York*. New York: Dover, 1974.

Geddes, Norman Bel. *Horizons*. New York: Dover, 1977.

Goldberger, Paul. *On the Rise: Architecture and Design in a Postmodern Age*. New York: Times Books, 1983.

————. *The Skyscraper*. New York: Knopf, 1982.

Graves, Michael. Interview by Elizabeth Bunker, 1982. Typescript.

Greenough, Horatio. "American Architecture." In *Form and Function: Remarks on Art, Design and Architecture*. Edited by Harold Small. Berkeley and Los Angeles: California, 1966.

Greif, Martin. *Depression Modern: The Thirties Style in America*. New York: Universe Books, 1975.

Guth, Alexander G. "Small Buildings: The Automobile Service Station." *Architectural Forum* (July 1926).

Hamlin, Talbot Faulkner. *The Enjoyment of Architecture*. New York: Duffield, 1916.

Harris, Cyril M., Ed. *Illustrated Dictionary of Historic Architecture*. New York: Dover, 1977.

Harrison, Michael. *Downtown Design Guidelines. Portland, Oregon, January 1983*. Portland: City of Portland, Bureau of Planning, 1983.

Hawkins, William John, III. "Absolom B. Hallock, Architect, Engineer, Surveyor (1826–1892)," *Portland Friends of Cast-Iron Architecture Newsletter* (October 1981).

————. "E. M. Burton, Architect (1817–1887)." *Portland Friends of Cast-Iron Architecture Newsletter* (April 1982).

————. *The Grand Era of Cast-Iron Architecture in Portland*. Portland: Binford and Mort, 1976.

————. Interview with authors. January 1984. Authors' collection.

————. "Justus Krumbein, Architect (1847–1907)." *Portland Friends of Cast-Iron Architecture Newsletter* (June 1980).

—————. "Warren Heywood Williams, Architect (1844–1888)." *Portland Friends of Cast-Iron Architecture Newsletter*. (December 1980).

Heyer, Paul. *Architects on Architecture*. New York: Walther and Co., 1966.

Hirshorn, Paul and Steven Izenour. *White Towers*. Cambridge: MIT, 1979.

Hitchcock, Henry-Russell. *The Architecture of H. H. Richardson and His Times*. Cambridge: MIT, 1936.

—————. "An Eastern Critic Looks at Western Architecture." *California Arts and Architecture* (December 1940).

—————. *The Pelican History of Art: Architecture: Nineteenth and Twentieth Centuries*. Baltimore: Penguin, 1971.

—————. *The Rise of American Architecture*. New York: Praeger, 1970.

————— and Philip Johnson. *The International Style: Architecture Since 1922*. New York: W. W. Norton, 1932.

"A House Designed for Children." *American Home* (June 1951).

Huxtable, Ada Louise. "Architecture Critic Cites Change in Portland, Seattle, Vancouver." *Oregonian*, 12 July 1970.

—————. "Portland's 1st National Accused of Architectural Double Whammy." *Oregonian*, 2 July 1972.

Jencks, Charles. *Modern Movements in Architecture*. Garden City, N.Y.: Anchor Books, 1973.

—————, Ed. *Post-Modern Classicism*. London: Architectural Design, 1980.

Jennings, Frederick. "The Most Notable Buildings of a City—What are They?" *Architect and Engineer* (March 1919).

Kahn, Ely Jacques. "On the Use of Color." In *Ely Jacques Kahn*. By Arthur Tappan North. In Contemporary American Architects Series. New York: McGraw-Hill, 1931.

—————. "The Province of Decoration in Modern Design." *Creative Art* (December 1929).

Keene, Linda. "A Square History." *Willamette Week*. 9–15 March 1982.

Koolhaas, Rem. *Delirious New York: A Retroactive Manifesto for Manhattan*. New York: Oxford, 1978.

Kroly, Herbert. "New Dimensions in Architectural Effects." *Architectural Record* (January 1925).

Le Corbusier (Charles Edouard Jeanneret). *Aircraft*. New York: Studio Publications, 1935.

Lennard, Erica. *Classic Gardens*. New York: Lustrum, 1982.

Lisle, Forrest F., Jr. "Chicago's 'Century of Progress' Exposition: The Moderne as Democratic, Popular Culture." *Society of Architectural Historians Journal* (October 1972).

Lobell, John. *Between Silence and Light: Spirit in the Architecture of Louis I. Kahn*. Boulder: Shambhala, 1979.

Loewy, Raymond. *Industrial Design*. Woodstock, N.Y.: Overlook Press, 1979.

Lohr, Lenox R. *Fair Management: A Guide for Future Fairs. The Story of A Century of Progress Exposition*. Chicago: Cuneo Press, 1952.

Lowe, Lucy. "Service Stations as an Asset to the City." *American City* (August 1921).

Lowry, Bates. *Renaissance Architecture*. New York: Braziller, 1979.

McCaulrey, John W. "Ralph Waldo Emerson, 'Thoughts on Art' (1841)." In *American Art, 1700–1960: Sources and Documents*. Englewood Cliffs, N.J.: Prentice-Hall, 1965.

MacColl, E. Kimbark. *The Shaping of a City: Business and Politics in Portland, Oregon 1885 to 1915*. Portland: Georgian Press, 1976.

McMath, George. Interview with authors. Portland, January 1984. Authors' collection.

—————. "Morris H. Whitehouse: U.S. Courthouse." National Register of Historic Places Inventory Nomination Form.

Martin, Willard T. "Design Statement: Pioneer Courthouse Square." [Portland]: n.p., 1980.

—————. Interview with authors. Portland, January 1984. Authors' collection.

—————. "Pioneer Courthouse Square." *Architecture California* (May–June 1983).

Menten, Theodore. *The Art Deco Style in Household Objects, Architecture, Sculpture, Graphics, Jewelry*. New York: Dover, 1972.

Merry, Thomas B. "Portland: The Beautiful Metropolis of the Pacific Northwest." *Northwest Illustrated Monthly Magazine* (St. Paul, Minneapolis) (November 1885).

Millon, Henry A. *Baroque and Rococo Architecture.* New York: Braziller, 1965.

Mock, Elizabeth. "Built in USA Since 1932." In *The Museum of Modern Art, New York.* New York: Simon and Schuster, 1969.

Moerer, Keith. "A Square Design." *Willamette Week.* 2–8 April 1984.

Morin, Roi L. "Fred Fritsch of Portland: An Appreciation of a Rare Spirit in the Profession." *Pencil Points* (March 1936).

Moses, Robert. *Portland Improvement.* Portland: Journal Publishers, 1943.

Murray, Peter. *The Architecture of the Italian Renaissance.* New York: Schocken, 1968.

"New Airflow Chrysler." *Fortune* (March 1934).

"No Beams in the Roof." *House and Home* (May 1952).

O'Hara, John Michael. "William W. Piper." *Portland Friends of Cast-Iron Architecture Newsletter* (January 1983).

Orlean, Susan C. "The Town that Bob Built." *Willamette Week.* 9–15 March 1982.

Pare, Richard. *Photography and Architecture: 1839–1939.* Introduction by Phyllis Lambert. Montreal: Canadian Centre for Architecture, Callaway Editions, 1982.

Pevsner, Nikolaus, John Fleming and Hugh Honour. *A Dictionary of Architecture.* Woodstock, N.Y.: Overlook Press, 1976.

Peterson, Jon A. "The City Beautiful Movement: Forgotten Origins and Lost Meanings," *Journal of Urban History* 2 (August 1976).

"Pietro Belluschi Named to Receive AIA's Highest Honor." *AIA Journal* (February 1972).

Poe, Edgar Allan. *The Complete Tales of Edgar Allan Poe.* New York: Vintage, 1975.

Pugh, David. Interview with authors. Portland, December 1983. Authors' collection.

Richards, J. M. *An Introduction to Modern Architecture.* New York: Penguin, 1970.

Riseboro, Bill. *Modern Architecture and Design: An Alternative History.* Cambridge: MIT, 1983.

Robinson, Cervin and Rosemarie Haag Bletter. *Skyscraper Style: Art Deco New York.* New York: Oxford, 1975.

Rocchia, Andy. "New Library at Mt. Angel Abbey Wins Praise of N.Y. Times Critic." *Oregon Journal.* 5 June 1970.

Rosen, Laura. *Top of the City: New York's Hidden Rooftop World.* New York: Thames and Hudson, 1982.

Ross, Marion. "Architecture in Oregon, 1845–1895." *Oregon Historical Quarterly* (March 1956).

————. "A Century of Architecture in Oregon, 1859–1959." Portland, Women's Architectural League (AIA), 1959.

Rutherford, Janice. "Richardsonian Romanesque: Architecture in Portland, Oregon 1889–1895" (Seminar paper). Portland, 1980.

Scott, Geoffrey. *The Architecture of Humanism.* New York: Charles Scribner's Sons, 1925.

Schorske, Carl E. *Fin-de-Siecle Vienna: Politics and Culture.* New York: Vintage, 1981.

Schuelhadl, Peter. "In Defense of Artistic Fashion." *Vanity Fair* (April 1984).

"Standardized Service Stations Designed by Walter Dorwin Teague." *Architectural Record* (September 1937).

"Stretch Your Building Dollar by Finishing Your House Yourself." *House and Garden* (August 1952).

Stubblebine, Jo, Ed. *The Northwest Architecture of Pietro Belluschi.* New York: F. W. Dodge, 1953.

Teague, Walter Dorwin. *Design This Day: The Technique of Order in the Machine Age.* New York: Harcourt, Brace, 1940.

Tigerman, Stanley. *Chicago Tribune Tower Competition.* Vol. I. New York: Rizzoli, 1980.

————. *Late Entries to the Chicago Tribune Tower Competition.* Vol. II. New York: Rizzoli, 1980.

Turner, Judith. *Judith Turner Photographs Five Architects.* Introduction by John Hejduk. New York: Rizzoli, 1980.

"The Van Evera Bailey Beach House." *American Home* (February 1952).

Vaughan, Thomas and Virginia Guest Ferriday, Eds. *Space, Style and Structure: Building in Northwest America.* Portland: Oregon Historical Society, 1974.

Vaughan, Thomas and George McMath. *A Century of Portland Architecture.* Portland: Oregon Historical Society, 1967.

Venturi, Robert. *Learning from Las Vegas: the Forgotton Symbolism of Architectural Form.* Cambridge: MIT, 1972.

————— and Virginia Guest Ferriday, Eds. *Space, Style and Structure: Building in Northwest America.* Portland: Oregon Historical Society, 1974.

Venturi, Robert. *Learning from Las Vegas: the Forgotton Symbolism of Architectural Form.* Cambridge: MIT, 1972.

Vergo, Peter. *Art In Vienna: 1889–1918: Klimt, Kokoschka, Schiele and Their Contemporaries.* Ithaca: Cornell, 1975.

Vieyra, Daniel I. "Fill'er Up." In *An Architectural History of America's Gas Stations.* New York: Collier Macmillan, 1979.

Vitale, Salvatore. *L'Estetica dell'Architettura.* Bari: Laterza, 1928.

Waissenberger, Robert. *Vienna Secession.* New York: Rizzoli, 1977.

Williams, Richard Glenn. *Style and Vernacular: A Guide to the Architecture of Lane County, Oregon.* Portland: Western Imprints, 1983.

Woefflin, Heinrich. *Renaissance and Baroque.* Translated by Kathrin Simon with an introduction by Peter Murray. Ithaca: Cornell, 1979.

Wright, Frank Lloyd. *An Autobiography.* New York: Duell, Sloan and Pearce, 1943.

—————. Letter to Pietro Belluschi. 6 July 1931. Private collection.

Zevi, Bruno. *Architecture as Space.* Rev. Ed., New York: Horizon, 1974.

—————. "Quel palazzo e un juke-box," *L'Espresso.* 27 February 1983.

Index

Boldface numbers indicate illustrations.

AT&T Building, New York, 246, 265
Aaron, Louise: "This Was Portland" series, 314
Abbott, Carl, quoted, 182, 196, 209, 210, 219
Abington Building, 194
Abramovitz, Max, 51
Adams, Charles Francis, 105
Adler and Sullivan, 59
Aero Club of Oregon, 63
Ainge, P. T., 144, 152-54
Ainsworth, George J., 189
Ainsworth, John C., 183, 189
Ainsworth and Company, 189
Ainsworth Block, 7, 182, 189
Aladdin Theater, 149
Alcazar Service Station, 147
Alisky and Hegele Building, 191
Allen, Frank C., 194, 195, 210
Allen, McMath and Hawkins, 68, 88, 194, 196, 223, 288; historic preservation work, **189**, 199-205, 245; waterfront renewal project, 219
Allen, Russell W., 179
Allen and Lewis Block, 182, 190, 191
Alto, Aalvar, 93
Ambassador Apartments, 57
American Bank Building, 39, **71**, 72, **73**, 74, 252, 255, 289, 302, 305
American Can Company, 139, 141
American Institute of Architects, Oregon Chapter, 44, 96
American Institute of Architects, Portland Chapter, 200, 247
American Radiator Building, New York, 70
Ancient Order of United Workmen Temple, 29-30
Anderson, Pauline S., 288
Andrews, Wayne, 123
Ankeny, Alexander P., 187
Ankeny and Watson Building, 188
Ankeny Block, 186
Ankeny Park Comfort Station, 53
Ankeny Sewage Station, 152
Anshen and Allen, 208, **229**, 230
Aquatic Park Casino, see Maritime Museum
Arceneaux, Marc, quoted, 175-76
Architectural Iron Works, Boston, 183
Architectural Iron Works, New York, 184
Arlington Club (1891), 31
Arm and Hammer Baking Soda Company building, 154
Armory Building, **3**, 30
Arnold, W. H., house, 123
Art Deco style, 10, 62, 64-70, 135

Arthur Hotel, 60, 66
Associated "Flying A" service stations, 11, **137**, 142, 145
Association for Portland Progress, 281
Atwood, J. A.,Corp., 144
Auditorium and Music Hall, see Civic Auditorium
Auditorium Forecourt and Fountain, 84, 214, 216-17, 275
Aus Building, see Swetland Building
Austin, John C., Company, 10, 81, 136, 154-56

Bacon, Henry, 35, 36, 74, 84
Badger, Daniel D., 183, 184
Bagle and Downs Shopping Center, 181
Bailey, Van Evera, 89-91, 96, 99, **117**, **118**, **119**, **120**, **122**, **127**, **130**, 138, 179, 181, 303; house, 117, 120, 129-30; Neskowin beach house, 120-21; Portland architectural career, 116-31; quoted, 121
Baker, Fred C., 47, **60**, 74
Baldwin, George S., quoted, 274
Banham, Reyner, 124, 140
Bank of America Building, New York, 92
Bank of America Building, San Francisco, 308
Bank of British Columbia Building, 189
Bank of California Building, Portland (1924), **24**, 35, 40, 77, 79, 304
Bank of California Building, Portland (1969), 208, 224, **229**, 230
Bank of California Building, San Francisco, 74
Barbizon Plaza, New York, 172
Barcelona Pavilion, 178
Barthelme, Donald, 17
Bastian, Harry S., 123
Bates Motoramp Garage, 53, 178, 226
Battery King station (Associated Oil Company), **133**
Bauhaus school of architecture, 26, 47, 67, 100, 175, 211
Bearing Company Service Building, 175-76, **176**, 298
Beaux-Arts Atelier, 53, 202
Beaux-Arts movement, 40, 41, 44-45, 52-53, 87, 94-95
Becker, Ray F., Company, **137**, **138**, **140**, 141-44, 152
Behrens, Peter, 173
Beiswenger, Mary, 127-28
Beiswenger, Walter, 127-28
Bel Geddes, Norman, 142, 154, 294; quoted, 99-100, 135-36, 138
Bell, Sidney, house, 123
Belluschi, Pietro, 6, 7, 20, 40, **87**, **94**, **101**,

102, **103**, **104**, **107**, **110**, **111**, 237, 244, 249, 250, 274, 280, 295; association with Doyle, 77, 79-81, 87-88, 93, 94-95; consultant to SOM, 88, 203, **301**, **303**, 306, 307, **307**, 308, 309; consultant to Wolff, Zimmer, 267-69; correspondence with F. L. Wright, 14-15, 105-106; criticism of The Portland Building, 246-48, 252, 279; Portland architectural career, 13-15, 51, 87-112 passim, 121, 158, 170-71, 181, 193, 195-96, 210, 211, 314; quoted, 13-15, 79, 90-97 passim, 100, 265, 270, 304, 306; style, 55, 62, 88-112 passim, 121, 123, 126, 134, 138, 154, 159, 168, 170-71, 175, 262, 264-65, 302-309 passim; urban renewal area design consultant, 212
Belluschi, Skidmore, Owings and Merrill, 88
Belluschi house (Council Crest), 89, 91, 97, 123
Benington College Library, 111
Benjamin, Walter, quoted, 184
Benj. Franklin Plaza, 265
Bennes, John, house, 59
Bennes, John V., **49**, **50**, 58-60, 63-67 passim, 70, 144, 154
Bennes and Hendricks, 59, 60, 81, 157
Bennes and Herzog, 66, 152, **153**
Bennett, Edward H.: Great Portland Plan, 12, 37, 219
Benson, Simon, 49
Benson Hotel (1913), 39, 77, **80**, 230
Benson Polytechnic School, 56
Berg, Charles F., Building, 40-41, 67-69, **69**, 70, 81, 154, 168, 262
Bickel, Frederick, 192
Bickel Block, 190, 192, 198
Biddle, James, 196
Bidwell, Edmund, **147**, 151
Biomedical Research Center, see Institute for Advanced Biomedical Research
Bishop's House, 44, 190, 202
Blackstone Hotel, Chicago, 77
Blagen Block, 134, 202-203, 280, 302
Bletter, Rosemarie Haag, quoted, 65, 69-70, 278
Bliss and Faville, 74
Bluebird Theater, see Ideal Theater
Blue Cross Building, 212, 214
Board of Consulting Engineers, 152
Board of Trade Building, 59
Bogardus, James, 183, 184
Bohemian Restaurant, 10, 153
Boilermakers Union Building, 109, 158
Boise Cascade Building (1930s), 159
Boise Cascade Building (1968), 208, 212, 214

Boles, Stanley, 16, 252, 254, 283-84; quoted, 285
Boston Public Library, 24, 76
Bowes, William 197, 228
Boyd Coffee Company, 197
Bradfish, Earl, 248
Bradley, George C., house, 59
Bragdon, Claude, quoted, 262
Bragg, Sir William, quoted, 248
Brendt, Francis C., 39
Brewster, Elizabeth: *Portland Sketchbook*, 315
British Pacific Building (proposed), 237, 271, 274, 277, **277**, 278, 279
Broadway-Chambers Building, New York, 42
Broadway/Moyer Building (proposed), **282**
Broadway Theater, 79, 81, 94, 147
Brookman, Herman, 49, 50, **50**, 51, 70, 120, 144
Broome, Oringdulph, O'Toole, Rudolph and Associates (BOOR/A), 202, 223, 264, **272**, 279, **282**, **292**, **299**; Performing Arts Center, 34, 254, 281-283, **283**, 284, **284**
Brown, Richard, 116
Bruning, Herbert, house, Wilmette, Ill., 124
Bruno, Thaddeus B., house, 124, 125
Buffalo City Hall, 278
Bullier Building, 34, 66
Bunker, Elizabeth, 251
Bunshaft, Gordon, 211, 228
Burgee, John, 264, 279, 281
Burke house, 91, 97, 99, 100, 262, 306
Burnham, Daniel H., 34, 60
Burnham and Root, 39
Burton, Elwood M., 93, 134, 182, 185-87, 190-94 *passim*, 212
Bush, Donald J., quoted, 140, 296
Butcher, F. Claude, 154
Butler, Earl, house, Des Moines, 124

CH2M Hill, 218
C-W-S Grinding and Machine Works building, 157
Cadillac Fairview project, 266
Caine, Morton, 60
Calbag Metals Company building, 158
California Foundry, San Francisco, 184
California Ink Company building, 63
Calvary Presbyterian Church, 90
Camp, H. L., and Company, 147
Campbell, Richard, 90, 304
Campbell, Yost and Grube, 280
Campbell and Yost, 217
Canada Dry Ginger Ale Company building, 136, 139, 155, 156, **159**
Caplan Sport Shop, 154, **155**
Carlin, Jared, 240
Carson, Pirie and Scott Department Store, Chicago, 38
Carter, H. D., and Company, 48
Carter Building, 189
Cash, Earl, 151
Cast-iron architecture, 6-7, 134, 182-93 *passim*, 270, 315; restoration in Portland, 193-95,

197, 202, 202-205
Catholic Cathedral, 202
Central Block, 190
Central Lutheran Church, 92, 100, **101**, 102-104; proposed, **102**, **103**
Central Presbyterian Church, 144
Central School (1857-58), 185
Cerwinske, Laura, quoted, 66, 67
Chamberlin, William E., 22
Chambers, George, 39
Chase Bag Company building, 81, 136, 154, 155, 179, 298
Cheney, Charles H., quoted, 36, 37, 72, 74, 76, 77
Chicago Auditorium, 58
Chicago Board of Trade Building, 272
Chicago Exhibition of 1893, 58-59
Chicago Stock Exchange building, 59
Chicago Style, *see* Sullivan (Chicago) Style
Chicago Style Fast Foods buildings, *see* Hay's Electric Company building
Chicago Tribune Building, 51
Chinatown, 218, 221
Christensen, James, 223, 307
Chrysler Building, New York, 150
Church, Walter, **49**, **50**, 67, 314
Church and Dwight factory building, 154
Citizens Advisory Committee, 218, 288
City Beautiful movement, 144
City of Portland parking structure, 267
City planning, 12-13, 37, 40, 85, 196, 209, 218-23, 285-86, 304-306, 310; Portland downtown plan, 197, 218; *see also* Urban renewal
Civic Auditorium, 7, 28, 30, 59, 190, 216
Clark, Florence, 162-63
Clark, Frank, 162-63
Clark, Henry Paston, 21, 23
Clark, Rosalind: *Architecture Oregon Style*, 315-16
Clausen and Clausen, 139, 155
Clauss and Daub, 142
Cobbey, E. V., 230
Cobbs, F. J., house, 74
Coca-Cola Bottling Company building, Los Angeles, 125
Coca-Cola Bottling Company building, Portland, 10, 139, 159, **162**
Coe, Ralph T., quoted, 112, 116
Cohen, Stuart, quoted, 237
College Building, *see* Goodnough Building
Colquhoun, Alan, quoted, 245, 249, 250, 252-53
Columbia Gorge Hotel, 49
Columbia Neon, 149
Commodore Hotel, 70
Commonwealth Building, *see* Equitable Building (1948)
Concord Building, 26, 28, 58
Cooks' Building, 182, 191
Coolidge and Shattuck, 42, 76
Corbett, Emma R. (Mrs. Henry W.), 79
Corbett, Hamilton, house, 94, 265

Corbett, Harvey Wiley, quoted, 142, 226
Corbett, Henry J., 77
Corbett, Henry W., 22, 31, 170, 183; house, 90
Corbett Building (1870-1), 190-91
Corbett Building (1907), 28, 34, 59, **152**
Cordray's Musee and Theater, 28
Cormack, A. J., quoted, 167
Corno and Sons, **143**
Cornwall, Jack, quoted, 256-58
Cory, Walter M., 136, 139, 155, 156, **159**
Cosmopolitan Block, 182, 191, 198
Cotillion Hall, *see* Crystal Ballroom
Cottrell, George, house, 112, 115
Couch, John H., 183
Couch School, 56
Cramer, Arthur, 139, 158, **163**
Crisp, Gary, **143**
Croly, Herbert, 42; quoted, 36, 70
Crowd, Theresa, 130
Crowell, William H., 77, 195
Crown Plaza, 217, 267
Crutcher, Lewis, 196
Crystal Ballroom, 47-48, 166
Crystal Palace, London, 184

DMJM, 234
Danadjieva, Angela, 216
David's Mens Shop, **158**
Davis, H. W., 185
Davis Business Center, *see* Canada Dry Ginger Ale Company building
Dawson, Helen A., 130
Day, Clinton, 182, 189, 224
Dearborn, Phyl, 126
de Graaff, Jan, house, 121, 126
Dekum, Frank, 28
Dekum Block (1871-1954), 187
Dekum Building (1892), 7, 27-30, 192
DeLahunt, Marcus J., house, 59
Deleuw, Cather and Company, 267
Denny-Renton Clay and Coal Company, Seattle, 39
Depression Modern style, 10, 154, 157
Derran, Robert, 125
Deskey, Donald, 124
DeWolfe, Fred: *Impressions of Portland*, 315; *Old Portland*, 315; *Portland Tradition in Buildings and People*, 315
Director's Furniture Store, 174-75
Dixon, Thomas, house, 117, 121
Dodoye-Alali, Anthony, quoted, 274
Dole, Phillip H., 316
Dougan, Heims and Caine, 60, 63
Dougan, Luther Lee, 10, 60-64, 67, 134, 154
Dougan, Heims and Caine, **64**, 148
Downtown Waterfront Urban Renewal Area, 219-22; *see also* Portland Waterfront Renewal Plan
Doyle, A. E., and Associate, **8**, **9**, 13, **15**, 77, 79-81, 87-88, **89**, **90**, **93**, 95, **95**, **98**, 100, **108**, 113, 126, 166, 168, 170
Doyle, Albert E., 7-9, **13**, 22, 24, **32**, 34, 50-52, 57-58, 60, 63, **74**, **75**, **84**, 85-99 *passim*,

113, 116, 134, 145, 147, 160-62, 165, 170, 178, 189, 194-96, 210, 212, 224, 226, 230, 239, 244, 246, 252, 280, 302, 310; death, 77-81, 87, 95; importance in Portland architectural history, 6, 37, 43-44, 72, 81, 88, 96-97, 144, 255, 274, 286; Neahkahnie cottages, 97; Portland architectural career 20, 24, 31-32, 35-45 passim, 72-81; quoted, 17, 39, 81, 84, 85, 280

Doyle, A. E., and Paterson **14, 38**

Doyle, A. E., Paterson and Beach, **6, 12, 71, 73, 76, 78, 80**

Doyle, Sutton and Whitney, 7, 64

Dreyfuss, Henry, 294

Dunster, David, quoted, 250, 251

Durham and Bates Building, see Bank of California Building (1924)

Dusenberry, Walter, 246, 255

Dynagraphics, Inc., see General Electric Company building

ELS Design Group, **272,** 281, 283, **283,** 284, **284,** 285

Eastmoreland Golf Club, 49

Eastside Mortuary, **169,** 170, 172

Eastside Tire Shop, **136**

Edmundsen and Kochendorfer, 202

Eisenman, Peter, 254, 264

Eisenman/Robertson, 288

Electrical Products Company, San Francisco, 147, 149

Eliot, Lee S., 70

Elks Temple, **19,** 60, **60,** 61, 62, 94

Elmslie, George B., 59, 122-23

Emanuel Hospital, 53

Embassy Apartments, 58

Empire State Building, New York, 150

Endicott, Charles W., 230

Enke Dye Works building addition, 168

Envoy Apartments, 58

Equitable Center (1965), 211, 268-69

Equitable Building (1948), 6, 10, 20, 92, **111,** 168, 178, 237, 265, 279, 294, 305; Belluschi quoted on design concept, 109-10

Erfeldt, Arthur, 34

Erickson, Arthur, 246, 264

Erickson, August, 191

Ertz, Charles, 145-46

Ertz and Burns, 146

Esco Headquarters building, 267

Esmond Hotel, 190

Evans, Dudley, 41

Evans Products building, 217, 220, 267

Exchange Building, 28, see also Olds, Wortman and King Department Store

Eyre, David and Cynthia, house, 128

Failing, Henry, 22, 31, 79, 170

Failing, Josiah, 183

Failing Building (1886), 198-99

Failing Building (1900), 28

Failing Building (1907, 1913), 35

Fairbanks, Avard T., **72,** 74

Fairmont Hotel, San Francisco, 42

Farmers Insurance Building, 146

Farnham, Neil, 197, 198

Farnsworth house, 97

Farrier, Ralph E., 47-48

Farwest Assurance Building, see Stevens Building

Father's Restaurant, 157

Fechheimer and White Building, 191, 198

Federal Housing Act of 1949, 209

Federal Office Building, 200, 211, 220, 224, 234

Federal Public Housing Authority, 125

Federal Reserve Bank Building, **87,** 92, 100, 109, **110,** 154

Federated Metals Company building, Hammond, Ind., 154

Feig, Elmer E., 10, 58, 64, 66-67, 154

Feldman, Philip, house, 91

Ferriday, Virginia Guest, 315-16; Last of the Handmade Buildings: Glazed Terra Cotta in Downtown Portland, 316

Ferriss, Hugh, 274

Fifth and Oak Building, 223

Film Center building, New York, 172

Fine Arts Building, 46

Finley, J. P., and Son Mortuary, 92, 100, 158, 170, 306

First Baptist Church, 30

First Congregational Church, 34, 279, 281, 283, 285

First Farwest Building, 237

First Interstate Center, see First National Bank Tower

First National Bank Building (1882-1954), 189

First National Bank Building (1916), 42-43, 76

First National Bank Building, Eastside Branch, 144

First National Bank Building, Union Avenue Branch, 154, **156**

First National Bank Tower (1972), 81, 208, 224, 230, 232, 233, **233,** 234, 255, 269, 295

First Presbyterian Church, Portland (1864), 185

First Presbyterian Church, Portland (1890), 30

First Presbyterian Church of Cottage Grove, 92, 100-104, 306

First Presbyterian Church of Vancouver, 210

Fitch, James Martson, 129; quoted, 126

Fitch, Otis J., 122

Flanders, George H., 183

Flanders house, 192

Flatiron Building, New York, 60

Fletcher, William, 170, 171

Fliedner Building, 168

Fogg Museum, Cambridge, Mass., 14, 105

Ford Motor Company assembly plant, 138-39, 178

Forecourt Fountain, see Auditorium Forecourt and Fountain

Forestry Building, 31, **32,** 34, 36, 77, 115

Fort-Brescia, Bernardo, quoted, 293

Fouilhoux, J. Andre, 51, **52,** 53, 124

Foulkes, Edward D., 196

Fountain Plaza, see KOIN Center

Fox and Henderson, 184

Fox Theater, see Heilig Theater

Frampton, Kenneth, quoted, 303-304

Francis and Hopkins Motor Showroom, 175, 178, **179**

Frank, Lloyd, 70; estate, 144

Frank, Sigmund, 37-39, 41

Frankl, Paul, quoted, 10

Franklin High School, 56

Franz Building, 198

Frasca, Robert J., 7, 16, 88, 211, 246, 249, 254, 266-70 passim; quoted, 193, 262, 278, 291; quoted on British Pacific Building (proposed), 278-79; quoted on Justice Center, 255-56, 258, 276; quoted on KOIN Center, 269-72; quoted on Willamette Center, 269-70

Fraser, Kennedy, quoted, 265-66, 293

Freeways, 207-208, 222

Freiwald, Joshua, quoted, 217

Friedberg, Paul, 288

Friends of Pioneer Square, 291

Fritsch, Frederick A., 20, 44, 48-49, 63, 106, 136, 165, 178; architectural career, 51-56

Fritsch, Margaret Goodin, 55

Fruit and Flower Day Nursery, 53, 54, 106-107

Fuller Building, New York, 151

Fuller Company building, see Pacific Steel and Engineering Company building

Gaudi, Antonio, 114

Gayle, Margot, quoted, 184

Gaynor, John P., 190

Gebhard, David, quoted, 11

Geddes, Brecher, Qualls, Cunningham, 288

Gender Machine Works building, 156

General Electric Company building, 159, 166, 175, 176

Georgia Pacific Building, 208, 211, 220, 224, 230, 231, **231,** 232, 234, 265, 274

Gevurtz Building, see Failing Building (1907, 1913)

Gilbert, Cass, 13, 42, 81, 84, 93, 134

Gilbert, W. G., 188

Gilbert Building, 28, **29,** 201

Gill, J. K., Building, 53, 157

Gill, Spencer, 288

Gillion, Edmund V., quoted, 184

Gilman Block, 185

Gilmore Filling Station, **140**

Gladding, Charles A., 39

Gladding, McBean and Company, Lincoln, Calif., 7, 39-40, 74

Glass Block, 156-58

Glass House, 97

Glazer, Howard, quoted, 218, 219

Glisan, Rodney, Building, 192, 203

Goldberger, Paul, quoted, 42, 211, 226, 240, 246, 253, 272-74, 281, 286, 290, 293, 296; quoted on Portland architecture, 17, 222, 234, 237, 248, 249, 252

Golden Canopy Ballroom, Jantzen Beach, 164, 166

Goldschmidt, Neil, 219, 222
Goodnough Building, 29
Goodrich, B. F., Building, **149**, 151
Goodrich-Silverton, **149**, 151
Good Samaritan Hospital, **53**, **54**
Gordon, Walter, 196, 212
Gould, Aaron, 60
Governor Hotel, 39, 40, 45, **46**, 47
Grand Rapids Design Service, 40, 67, **69**, 70, 81
Grant High School, 45
Graves, Michael, 13, 81, 92, 93, 154, 166, 234, 245, 246, 266, 270, 279, 285, 290, 291, 297, 309; The Portland Building, 12, **16**, 39, 84, 237, **243**, 244-47, **247**, 248, 249, **249**, 250, 251, **251**, 252-54 *passim*, 264, 265, 285, 290, 309; quoted, 253, 254
Gray, John, 116; house, 128, 129
Green, Edith, 200
Green, Harry, 70
Greene, Charles K., 77-79, 95
Greene, Henry, 95
Greene and Greene, 91, 97
Green's Building, 190
Greif, Martin, 124; quoted, 154, 155, 157
Greyhound Bus Depot (1939), 46-47
Greyhound Terminal (1985), 221, **221**
Gropius, Walter, 95-96, 140, 141, 173, 210, 237, 238
Grout house, 45-46
Guardian Building, **151**, 152
Guild, Lurelle, 154
Guild Lake, 10, 31, 134, 139
Guild Theater, 62
Guirgola, Romaldo, 246, 264, 291
Gumbert Furriers, 10, 153
Guth, Alexander G., quoted, 142

Hagestead and Peace, 172
Hall, Clarence A., Design, 156
Hallock, Absalom B., 83, 184-85
Halprin, Lawrence, 13, 34, 84, 213-17, 264, 288
Halprin, Lawrence, and Associates, 214, **215**, 216, 222
Hamilton Building, 20, 24, 26-27, **27**, 28, 31, 44
Hamilton Hotel, 60
Harbor Drive, 81, 178, 182, 187, 195, 196-97; removal, 219
Harker Building, 197, 203
Harrison, Michael, 285, 304
Harrison, Wallace K., 51, 124, 226
Harrison Square, 212, 214
Harrison Street School, 185
Harvard University: Sever Hall, 30
Haseltine Building, 29
Haussmann, Eugene Georges, 223, 269
Hawkins, L. Leander, 189
Hawkins, William J., 189, 193-94
Hawkins, William John III, 90, 134, 192-94; *The Grand Era of Cast-Iron Architecture in Portland*, 315; historic preservation work, 190, 199; *Portland's Historic New Market*

Theater, 316; quoted on Portland cast-iron architecture, 182, 185, 188, 192, 198-99, 202, 203
Hawthorne Bridgehead district, 220
Hayakawa, Alan, 308
Hayes, Warren G., 30
Hay's Electric Company building, 156
Hayward and Bartlett, 190
Heathman Hotel, 283-84
Heckscher Building, New York, 274
Hefty, Henry J., 34, 283
Hegel, Georg Wilhelm Friedrich, quoted, 301
Hegemann, Werner, quoted, 279
Heiler, Joseph, **167**, **168**, 170-72
Heilig, Calvin, 148
Heilig Theater, 147-48
Heims, Bernard A., 60
Hejduk, John, quoted, 306
Henry Building, 39
Herbst, Renee, 152
Herzog, Harry A., 10, **49**, **50**, 51, 58, 64, **139**, **152**, 153, 154, **156**, **158**; Portland architectural career, 66-67, 70, 144, 152
Herzog and Barnes, **157**
Hess, Alan, quoted, 121
Heurn, Prosper, 190, 202
Hibernian Hall, 63
Higgins, Frank, 51
Hill, Elijah, 287
Hilton Hotel, 208, 211, 223-27, **227**, 228 *passim*, 230, 232
Hippodrome Theater, *see* Broadway Theater
Historic American Buildings Survey, Oregon, 314
Historic preservation and restoration, 17, 85, 142, 193-205, 220, 244, 281
Hitchcock, Henry-Russell, 103, 105, 115, 126; quoted, 11, 15, 97-99, 107-109, 112, 121-22, 211, 262
Hodge-Calef Building, 189
Hoffman, Lee, Jr., 125
Hoffman, Lee H., 116, 125; house, 126-27
Hoffman Construction Company, 126
Holbrook, Jeff, 198
Holloway, John, 202
Hollywood Auto Parts, *see* R.K.D. Brilliant Neon Company
Hollywood District, 134, 302, 305
Hollywood Movie Theater, 66
Holman Fuel Company building, 153
Holy Trinity Church, 101
Hood, Raymond, 51, 67, 70, 226
Hood and Howells, 51
Hood River Canning Company plant, 168
Hoover Dam, 137
Hope Abbey Mausoleum, Eugene, 153, 170
Horsley, Carter B., quoted, 246, 255
Hotel del Coronado, San Diego, 42
Hotel Ramapo, 34
Houghtaling, Chester A., 60, 70
Houghtaling and Dougan, **19**, 60, 62, 94
Houghton, E. W., 147-48
Housing Authority of Portland, 209

Hoving, Thomas D. F., 196
Howe, William, 55
Huber's Restaurant, 59
Huedepohl, Paul H., 164-65
Huntington, Wallace Kay, quoted, 31, 34, 114, 115, 168-69, 216
Hunt Transfer Company warehouse, 62
Huxley, Aldous, quoted, 10
Huxtable, Ada Louise, 81; quoted on Portland architecture, 6, 7, 15-17, 21, 84, 208-209, 214-15, 232, 234
Hyster Company, 159

Ideal Theater, 34
Imperial Hotel, *see* Plaza Hotel
Inland Steel Building, Chicago, 211
Institute for Advanced Biomedical Research, 7, 17, 240, 254, 267, 275, **276**, 277-78
International Business Machines Building, 159, **164**
International Harvester Servicenter, 178
International Style, 16, 63, 95-96, 99, 208-209, 211, 237-38
Ironclad Bank, Brooklyn, N.Y., 190
Irving Manor, 67
Isozaki, Arata, quoted, 298
Ivancie, Frank, 248, 286-87

Jack, Dave M., 77, 195
Jackson, C. S., house, 53
Jackson Tower, *see* Journal Building
Jacobberger and Smith, 63, 81
Jacobberger and Stanton, 101
Jacobs, Isaac, 31
Jacobs, Ralph, 31
Jacobs Building, *see* Gilbert Building
Jail facilities, 256-58
Jake's Crawfish Restaurant, 45
James, George V., house, 192
Jantzen, Carl, 162
Jantzen Beach Amusement Park, 164-66
Jantzen Knitting Mills buildings, 88, 136, 159, 167; administration building, 162, 168; warehouse, 166-67
Jeanne Manor, 10, 66
Jefferson High School, 49
Jencks, Charles, 17, 116, 245; quoted, 240, 246, 248
Jennings, Duke, 257-58
Jennings, Frederick, quoted, 56, 76, 77
Jennings, Steve, quoted, 246-47
Johnson, Philip, 92, 97, 246-50 *passim*, 254, 264, 265, 279, 281
Johnson and Johnson Industrial Tape Building, New Brunswick, N.J., 156
Johnson Wax Administration Building, 298
Johnston, Hollis, **11**, 154
Jolly Joan Restaurant, **160**
Jordan, A. H., 189
Jordan, Charles, 287
Jorgenson, Emil, 30
Jorgenson, Victor, house, 112, 114, 115
Joss house, 97

Journal Building, 42, **43**, **83**, 289, 305
Juilliard School of Music, New York, 92
Justice Center, 12, 17, 223, 240, 243, 244, **244**, 245, 246, 252, 255-58, **264**, 267-80 *passim*

Kahn, Albert, 51, 135, 136, 160, 173, 271
Kahn, Ely Jacques, 67, 172, 274
Kahn, Louis I., 267, 271; quoted, 3, 4, 9, 113
Kaiser Foundation Health Plan clinics, 267
Kamm, Jacob, 183, 192; house, 90
Kamm Block, 7, 182, 190, 192
Keally, Trowbridge and Livingston, 51
Keck, George Fred, 124
Keller, Ira, 209
Keller, Ira C., Fountain, 216
Kelly, Lee, 288
Kemery, William, 88
Kennedy School, 56
Kenwood, John, 209, 210, 212
Kerr, Albertina, Nursery, 201
KGW Broadcasting Station, 154
Kerr house, 89, 97
King Street Garden, 113
Kirk, Paul Hayden, 213
Kittredge, Jonathan, 184, 193-94
Knapp, J. A., 190
Knapp, R. B., house, 88, 192
Knickerbocker Trust Building, New York, 74
Knighton, William C., 39, 40, 45-47, **47**
Knighton and Root, 45
Knights of Columbus Club, *see* Aero Club of Oregon
Koch, Carl, and Associate, 111
Koch, Edward A., 175
Kohler, Frank, 152
Kohn, J., and Company building, 184
KOIN Center, 240, 246, 255, 267, 271-73, **273**, 274, 279, 286, 294, 297, 302
Koolhaas, Rem, quoted, 166, 226
Koren, Edward, 142
Kotchik, George, 210
Kraetsch and Kraetsch, 124
Kroner, Ernst, 63, **65**, 70
Krumbein, Justus, 6, 30, **85**, 93, 144, 182, 185, 188, 191-94, 198
Kruze Way Plaza, 297
Kubli-Howell Building, 156

Labbé Block, 191
Ladd, William S., 22, 170, 183
Ladd and Bush Bank Building, Salem, *see* United States National Bank, Salem
Ladd and Tilton Bank Building, 134, 189-90
Ladd Block, 190, 197
Ladd Building (1853), 183
Lafayette Apartments, 10, 62
Lakeman, Richard, 290
Landscaping, 31, 34, 35, 81, 93, 97-99, 112-14, 214, 216-17, 223, 277
Larson, Gary, 266, 267
Latrobe, Ferdinand C., quoted, 190-91
Laurelhurst Park, 35
Laurelhurst Theater, **146**, 149

Lavare, Gabriel, 141, 162, 168, 173
Lawrence, Ellis F., 10, 44, 89, 96, 152-53, 160, 166, 170, 200
Lawrence and Holford, 44, 63, 152, 153
Lazarus, Edgar M., 32-34, 44, 81
Leaburg Power Station, 153, 166
Leadbetter house, 88
LeCorbusier, Charles E. J., 192, 210, 237, 238, 244, 248, 250, 268, 271, 293-94, 297, 310; influence on Portland architects, 99, 100, 115, 141, 174; quoted, 124
Ledoux, Claude-Nicolas, quoted, 251
Lefaivre, Liliane, quoted, 90
Lemaresquier, M., 248
Leonard, H. R., 187
Lescaze, William, 55, 142
Lever House, New York, 211, 228, 238
Lewis, Cicero H., 183
Lewis, David C., 28, 32, 34, 36, 44, 58-59
Lewis, Ion, 20-24, 31-35, 85, 93
Lewis and Beckwith, 59
Lewis and Clark Centennial Exposition, 30-36 *passim*, 58-59, 62, 67, 81, 115, 193, 224
Lewis and Clark College, 70
Lewis Building, 59
Liberty Theater, **145**
Lincoln Center, New York, 247
Lincoln High School, 49
Lincoln Memorial Park Cemetery buildings, **167**, **168**, 170, 171
Lindberg, Mike, 287
Linde, Carl, 56-58
Lindgren house, 297
Lipman, Wolfe and Company Department Store, 37, 39, 41, 79
Lipman's Department Store (S. Lipman and Company), 187
Lisle, Forrest F., quoted, 135
Lissitzky, El, 283
Lister, Sid, 77, 81, 195
Little Chapel of the Chimes Mortuary, 163, 166, **170**, 172
Livingston and Blayney, 217, 219
Lloyd Center Union Station, *see* Rex Lee Auto Service
Lobell, John, quoted, 5
Loewy, Raymond, 142, 154, 176, 294
Logan, Donn, quoted, 281, 285
Logan, John, quoted, 13
Logus Block, 201
Lone Fir Cemetery, 169
Loos, Adolf, 35, 237
Love Building, 197
Lovejoy, Asa Lawrence, 40, 227, 287, 304, 310
Lovejoy Fountain, 214, 215, **215**, 216, 217
Lovell beach house, 124
Lovell house, Silverlake, Calif., 124
Loveness Guest House, Minn., 121
Lowengart and Company building, 60
Lownsdale Square, 220, 245
Luckman, Charles, and Associates, 81-84, 208, 230, 232, 233, **233**, 234, 255, 295
Lucky Stores supermarkets, 178

Lynch, Douglas, 119-21

Macadam Place, 157, **293**, 294, 297, 298
McBean, Peter McGill, 39
McCall, Tom, quoted, 287
McCall Oil Company building, 155, 157, 298
McCann Stone Company, 41
McCarthy, F. J., 126
McCaully, W. H., 141
McCaw, Martin and White, **3**, 28, 30, 31
McCaw, William F., 30, 93, 192
McCaw and Martin, 30, 192
McClelland and Jones, 152
MacColl, E. Kimbark, quoted, 191
McDonald's, **162**
McGoodwin, Dan, 196
Machado/Silvetti/Schwartz/Silver, 288
Mackenzie, Beverly Sundeleaf, house, 179
MacKenzie, K.A.J., house, 31
McKim, Charles Follen, 22, 26, 35, 244
McKim, Mead and White, 24, 44, 81, 154; influence on Doyle, 72, 74, 77, 91; Portland Hotel design, 13, 19, 21-23, 35, 38
McLoughlin Heights Shopping Center, 109, 181
McMath, George A., 40, 47, 79, 88, 193, 194-95, 226, 288, 314-15; account of historic preservation work, 196-205 *passim*; quoted, 24, 26, 28, 41, 42, 81, 91, 214, 228, 269, 305
Macy, Douglas, 288
Madeleine Church, 101
Madison Square Garden, New York, 35
Maegly, Aaron H., house, 59, 66
Maegly-Tichner Building, 34
Mail-Well Envelope Company building, 168
Mallet-Stevens, Robert, 124
Manchester, G. B., 258
Mande, Richard H., house, Mt. Kisco, N.Y., 124
Manhattan Apartments, 67
Mann Building, 201
Mansfield, George A., 70
Maritime Museum, San Francisco, 124
Marlitt, Richard: *Nineteenth Street*, 315
Marquam Grand Theater, 148
Marshall Field Building, Chicago, 26
Martin, Willard T., 16, 85, 249, 252, 264, 286-89, **289**, 290, 291; quoted, 286, 288, 291
Martin/Soderstrom/Matteson, 252, 264, 279, 286, **287**, 288, 290
Marylhurst College, 63
Masonic Hall (1871), 187
Masonic Temple (1907), 30, **56**, **58**
Masonic Temple (1924), 20, 53, 54, 63, 305
Masonry and Ceramic Tile Institute of Oregon: *Landmarks, A Tradition of Portland Masonry Architecture*, 316
Maybeck, Bernard, 91, 95
Mayer Building, 34
Mead Building, 39
Mechano Deco style, 135-36, 138, 140-41, 156

Medical Arts Building, 62
Medical Dental Building, 10, 62
Meier, Julius, 70
Meier, Richard, 81, 93
Meier and Frank Company, 200
Meier and Frank Department Store (1909), 17, 35, 37, 38, **38**, 39, 40, 195, 305
Meier and Frank Store (1897-1915), 31
Meier and Frank warehouse (1914), 167
Meier and Frank warehouse and delivery depot (1926), 53, 166
Memorial Coliseum, 224-25
Merchants' Hotel, 198-99
Merrill, John O., 211
Merry, Thomas B., quoted, 192
Metropolitan Arts Commission, 288
Midland Branch Library, 210
Mikado Block, 197, **199**
Miller, Edward A., 149
Miller Paint Company building (1884), **198**
Miller Paint Company building (1923), **147**, 151
Mills Building, San Francisco, 39
Milne Construction Company, 171
Mische, E. T., 34, 35
Mittlestadt, Edwin, house, 118-19, 128
Mobile Jiffy Lube and Gas, 142
Modernism, 237-39, 293-94
Moerer, Keith, quoted, 290
Monastes, David, 185
Montgomery Ward Company building, 139, 141
Moore, Charles W., 264, 288, 290
Moore house, 97
Mooser, William, Jr., 125
Moreland Apartments, 67
Moreland Cattery, **295**, 297
Moreland Theater, 149
Morgan Building, **151**
Morin, Roi, 68, **141**, **142**, 154
Morris, Benjamin Wistar III, 13, 40, 41, 81, 93
Morris, Hilda, 228
Morrison Bridgehead district, 220
Morrison Street Project, **272**
Moser, Kolo, 45
Moses, Robert: Harbor Drive plan, 81, 178; Portland improvement plan, 12-13, 220
Mt. Crest Abbey Mausoleum and Crematorium, Salem, 172
Mulkey Building, 47
Mullet, A. B., **201**
Multnomah Amateur Athletic Club, 49, 53
Multnomah Civic Stadium, 50
Multnomah County Central Library (1913), 76, **76**, 77, 201, 255, 262
Multnomah County Courthouse, 20, 44
Multnomah County Hospital, 53
Mumford, Louis, quoted, 208
Murgatroyd and Ogden, 172
Muschamp, Herbert, quoted, 308
Musick, Felicity, 77; quoted, 79
Myers, Barton, Associates, 281, **283**, **284**

Naito, Sam, 197-98

Naito, William, 197-98; house, 116, **117**, 118-19
Narramore, Floyd A., 56, 70
Nation, John, 185
National Historic Preservation Act, 196, 314
National Register of Historic Places, 47, 70, 114, 142, 196
National Trust for Historic Preservation, 196, 315
Neahkanie cottages, 72, 89, 91, 96, 97
Neahkanie Mountain highway, 113-14
Neighborhood House, 201
Neighbors of Woodcraft building, 53, 54, 57
Nelson Gallery of Art, Kansas City, 112-13, 116
Neon signs, 145-49
Nestor, John, 134, 185, 189-90, 224
Neutra, Richard, 121-22, 124, 126, 142
Newberry, Earl, 67-68
New Heathman Hotel, 225
New Market Annex, 26
New Market Theater and Block, 88, 134, 187-88, **204**; restoration, 203-205, 223, 245, 302, 316
New York World's Fair, 124, 135, 173
Nickel Star Theater, 148
Niemi, Karol, 157
Norman and Stanich, 197
North Park Blocks, 221, see also Park Blocks
Northwest Airlines, 109
Northwest Natural Gas Building, 280
Northwest Regional Style, 10, 23-24, 72, 89-91, 96-97, 109-10, 116, 179, 210
Northwestern National Bank Building, see American Bank Building

Odd Fellows Building (1925), 63, **65**
Odd Fellows Temple (1869), 185, 188, 191
O'Donnell, Terence, 288, 314
O'Hara, John Michael, 188
Olbrich, Josef Maria, 45
Old Church, 201
Olds, Wortman and King Department Store, 39; see also Exchange Building
Old Town, see Skidmore/Old Town Historic District
Olmsted, Frederick Law, 32, 35, 81
Olmsted, John C., 12, 35, 81
One Main Place, 234, **235**, 237
Ongford Apartments, 58
Ophthalmological Clinic and Research Center, 81
Orange Blossom Jug Restaurant, 11, 147
Orbanco Building, 211, 224, 234, **236**, 252
Oregon Art Tile Company, 152, **153**
Oregon Bank Building, see Spalding Building
Oregon Brass Works, 136, **151**, 152, **152**, 153
Oregon City Woolen Mills, 152
Oregon Centennial Exposition: House of Religious History, 210
Oregon Historical Center, 171, 211, 267-68
Oregon Hotel, see Benson Hotel
Oregonian Building (1891), 42, 82
Oregonian Building (1946), 42, 100, 109

Oregon Iron Works, 185
Oregon Museum of Science and Industry (OMSI), **165**
Oregon Pioneer Building, see Railway Exchange Building
Oregon Pioneer Savings and Loan Building, 42-43
Oregon Portland Cement Building, 163, 165, 168
Oregon State Capitol Building (1938), 51; wing additions (1977), 269
Oregon Steam Navigation Company building (block), 185, 186
Oregon Sign Company, 149
Oregon State University: Kidder Hall, 60
Oriental Community Center, 221
Orlean, Susan C., quoted, 266-68
Oswego Lake Country Club, 49
Overton, William, 287
Owings, Nathaniel, 211

Pacific Architectural League, 44
Pacific Building, 77, 79, **84**, 94, 305
Pacific First Federal Building, 224, 237, 239
Pacific Foundry, San Francisco, 184
Pacific Northwest Bell Building, 208, 230, 267
Pacific Power and Light Company, 79
Pacific States Engineering Corporation, 59
Pacific Steel and Engineering Company building, 157-58
Pacific Telephone and Telegraph Company building, 230
Pacific Western Bank Building, 295
Pacwest Center, 4, 12, 13, 25, 26, 81, 266, 270, 279, **292**, 294-98, **298**
Palace Hotel, San Francisco, 190
Pan Am Building, New York, 92
Panhellenic Hotel, New York, 51
Paramount Theater, **ix**, 147, 281, 283-84
Paris Exposition of 1925, 65-66
Park Blocks, 218; see also North Park Blocks
Parker, Jamieson, **61**, **63**, 70, 144, 314
Park Plaza Apartments, 63
Parkway Manor, 66
Parsonage, Salem, 200
Patterson, William B., 37
Paxton, Joseph, 184
Peabody and Stearns, 21
Pearne, Thomas H., quoted, 183
Pearne Building, 185, 203
Peets, Elbert, quoted, 279
Pelli, Cesar, quoted, 264
Pengh, Knighton and Howell, 47
Peninsula Park, 35
Penintentiary Building, Portland, 184
Penn, Colin, 294
Penny Saver Market, **147**
Perez, August, and Associates, 290
Performing Arts Center, 17, 34, 84, 237, 254, 265, 271, 281-283, **283**, 284, **284**, 285, 286
Petroleum Headquarters building, Bangkok, 239
Pettygrove, Francis, 40, 227, 304, 310
Pettygrove Park, 214, 216

Pfunder house, 88
Philadelphia Savings Fund Building, 55
Phillips, Truman, 158
Phillips Electronics Building, 157, **161**
Phoenix Iron Works, Portland, **186**
Phoenix Iron Works, San Francisco, 184, 194
Piazza d'Italia, New Orleans, 290
Pierce, J. Kingston, quoted, 120
Pink's, 157
Pintarich, Paul, quoted, 234
Pioneer Building, 59
Pioneer Courthouse, 32, 96, 185-86, **201**, 289,
   290, 305; restoration, 200-201
Pioneer Courthouse Square, 4, 22, 84, 85, 195,
   223, 237, 244, 265, 270-71, 279, 281, **287**,
   289, 304; construction, 287, 291; design,
   252, 254, 286-91
Piper, William W., 90, 93, 185-88, 194, 245
Piper and Burton, 134, 187, **204**
Pittock, Henry L., 22
Pittock Block, 39
Pittock Mansion, 196
Platt house, 97
Plaza Hotel, New York, 35
Plaza Hotel, Portland, 7, 28-30, 34, 279, 304
Polshek, James Stewart, quoted, 279, 285
"Pop" architecture, 10-11, 168
Poppleton Building, 203, 304
Portland Academy, 31
Portland Architectural Club, 44, 52
Portland Art Commission, 197
Portland Art Museum, 6, 55, 91, 92, 262, 274,
   275, 305; additions, 113, 211, 269; Ayer
   Wing, 13-15, **15**, 100, 104-108, **108**, 109,
   171, 280
Portland Atelier, 44, 96
Portland Bottling Company, 10, 139, 158-59,
   163, 302
The Portland Building (Portland Public Service
   Building), 12, **16**, 39, 81, 84, 166, 234, **243**,
   247, **249**, **251**, 256, 264, 270, 275, 279, 285,
   286, 308, 309; Belluschi criticism, 247-48;
   completion, 12, 250, 271; design
   controversy, 246-55, 264-66, 290, 291
Portland Center Apartments, **213**, 214
Portland Center Development Company, 212
Portland Central School (1872), 187-88
Portland City Club, 209
Portland City Hall, 7, 12, 20, **21**, 24, 25, **25**, 26,
   28, 44, 252, 255, 262, 269, 279, 280, 294,
   302
Portland City Jail, 187
Portland Civic Theater, **141**, **142**, 154
Portland Community College, 267, **268**
Portland Design Commission, 285, 286, 305,
   310
Portland Development Commission, 197, 209,
   214, 264, 287, 288, 291, 305
Portland Foundry, 185
Portland Friends of Cast-Iron Architecture,
   194, 315
Portland Garden Club building, 91
Portland Gas and Coke Company, 79
Portland General Electric Building, *see*

Willamette Center
Portland Historical Landmarks Commission,
   197, 220, 305, 315
Portland Hotel, 13, **14**, **22**, 35, 38, 42, 81, 84,
   147, 252, 290; construction, 19-23, 85, 188,
   193, 287-88; demolition, 178, 195-96, 200,
   288; recollections, 195
Portland Improvement Corporation, 218
Portland Medical Center, 168, **177**
Portland Memorial Cemetery, 170, **171**, **172**,
   172-73
Portland Memorial Coliseum, **225**
Portland Planning Commission: *Planning
   Guidelines/Portland Downtown Plan*, 218
Portland Plaza Condominum, 234-37
Portland Public Library (1891), **23**, 24, 31
Portland Public Library (1913), *see* Multnomah
   County Central Library
Portland Savings Bank, 191-92, 145
Portland State University: gymnasium, 267;
   library, 217; Neuberger Hall, 267; parking
   structure, 267; science building, 217; urban
   studies center, 218
Portland State University Urban Renewal
   Project, 209, 210, 217-18
Portland Transit Mall, 210, 220-24, **241**
Portland Union Stockyards, **36**
Portland Waterfront Renewal Plan, 210; *see
   also* Downtown Waterfront Urban Renewal
   Area
Portman, John, 267
Postal Building, 201
Postmodernism, 240, 245, 270
Potter, Elisabeth Walton, 316; *see also* Walton,
   Elisabeth
Powers Building, **181**, 202
Pries, G. G., 141
Princeton Building, *see* Elks Temple
Prudential Center, Boston, 234
Prudential Savings and Loan Building, 154
Public Building Authority, 125
Public Market, 153
Public Service Building, 7, 40, 77, 79, 81, 94,
   114, 134, 154, 255, 265
Pugh, David, quoted, 209, 212, 217, 220-26
   passim
Purcell, William Gray, 44, 59, 93, 122, 125;
   Palm Springs house, 123
Pythian Building, *see* Masonic Temple (1907)

R.K.D. Brilliant Neon Company, 151
Radditz, F. M., house, 118, **118**, **127**, 128
Radiator Building, Chicago, 51
Rading, Adolph, 124
"Radio City Hall of the West," Hollywood,
   155-56
Railway Exchange Building, 28, 59
Raleigh, Patrick, Building, 184
Ralston, William C., 190
Ramada Inn, 214-15
Ramsay Sign Company (Ramsay Neon), 146,
   149, 202
Rapp and Rapp, **ix**, 147, 283
Rasmussen Village Apartments, 70

Raven Creamery Building, **148**, 151
Read, Herbert, quoted, 247
Red Steer Cafe, **144**
Reddick, Gary, 249
Reed, Simeon G., 183
Reed College: Eliot Hall, 41, 74, 77
Reed College plan, **6**, **78**
Regent Apartments, 66, 67
Reid, James William, 42
Reid, Merrit, 41-42
Reid and Reid, 7, 42, **43**, 45, 81, **82**, **83**, 93,
   255
Reinhard and Hofmeister, 41
Reitz, Walter, 124
Renaissance Revival style, 24-26, 30-32, 35,
   72-77
Rex Lee Auto Service, 141
Reynolds, Robert, 288
Rian, John L., 288
Richards, J. M., quoted, 26
Richardson, Henry Hobson, 7, 21, 26, 91, 244
Richardson, Kenneth E., 196, 210
Richardson Romanesque style, 7, 26, 28-30
Richfield Oil Company building, Los Angeles, 70
Ringler Dancing Academy, 47
Riseboro, Bill, quoted, 210, 253
Ritz, Richard E.: *A Guide to Portland Architecture*,
   315
Riverview Cemetery, 169; caretaker's cottage,
   170; chapel, mausoleum and office, **107**,
   170-72; Hilltop Memorial, 171
Robert and Company, 159
Roberts, William, 286-87
Robie House, 35
Robinson, Cervin, quoted, 42, 67, 150
Robinson, H. L., Company, 149
Rockefeller Apartments, New York, 124
Rockefeller Center, New York, 41, 51, 150,
   217, 226, 270
Rockrise, George, 213
Rockwood, David, quoted, 249-50
Roebling Cable and Wire Rope Company
   building, 53, 136
Rogers, George, house, 123
Rosenberg, Louis C., 160
Roseway Theater, 148-49
Ross, Marion D., 28, 314, 316; quoted, 63
Rudat/Boutwell and Partners, 81, **207**, 208,
   214, 223

Safdie, Moshe, quoted, 254
St. Charles Hotel, 182, 185, 190
St. Mark's Episcopal Church, **63**, 144
St. Patrick's Church, 201
St. Thomas More Church, 92, 102-103
St. Vincent's Hospital, **85**
Salishan, 129
Salvation Army Building, 146
Sandberg, Grace, house, **122**, **130**
Sanderson, George A., 126; quoted, 125
San Francisco, 6, 36, 182, 184, 187, 219
San Francisco Gas and Electric Building, 76
San Francisco Performing Arts complex:
   Louise Davies Hall, 257

Sasaki, Walker and Associates, 217
Savier and Company building, 185, 186
Schacht, Emil, 32-34, 81
Schacht and Bergen, 34
Schindler, Rudolph, 124
Schjeldahl, Peter, quoted, 271
Schuette and Wheeler, 49
Scott, Geoffrey, quoted, 4, 302
Scott, Harvey W., quoted, 187
Scottish Rite Temple (proposed), **5**
Scully, Vincent, quoted, 248-49
Seagram Building, New York, 228
Seattle, Wash., 182
Selling Building, 39, 72, **152**
Service stations, 11, 141-45, 151
7-Up Bottling Company, *see* Portland Bottling
   Company
Sever Hall, Harvard University, 30
Seward Hotel, *see* Governor Hotel
Sexton, W. R., 51
Sharpe, Jesse R., house, 46
Sharpe, Sumner M., 288
Shaw, Lawrence, house, 112, 115, 267
Shaw, Steadman, house, **119, 120**
Shaw Surgical Supply Company building, 158
Sheldon, Eggleston, Reddick, Anderud (SERA),
   203, 223, 244, 279
Shellenbarger, Michael, 316
Shelton, Jesse M., 139, 159, **162**
Sherlock Building, 28, 29, 58
Shriner's Hospital, 53, **55**
Sierracin Corporation, 257
Simon Building, 198
Singer Building, New York, 35
Sixth Avenue and Washington Building, **139**
Sixth Church of Christ Scientist, **48**, 50, 302
Skidmore, Louis, 211
Skidmore, Owings and Merrill (SOM),
   Portland office, 6, 16, 26, 79, 93, 196, 208,
   209, **213**, **221**, **225**, **227**, **231**, **235**, **236**,
   241, 254, 255, 294, **298**, **301**, **303**, **307**;
   Belluschi association, 88, 100, 111, 210,
   263, 268, 306-308; decline, 239-40, 244,
   264-68 *passim*, 271, 285; International Style,
   40, 210-11, 213-14, 223-32, 234, 237, 250,
   291; urban planning, 210, 212, 221-23
Skidmore Fountain, 194, 205
Skidmore/Old Town Historic District, 193-99
   passim, 205, 218, 220, 224, 280, 305, 310
Skouras, Charles, 148
Smith, Burt, 115
Smith, C. E., **199**; house, 192
Smith, Claude, Building, 154
Smith, Herbert, 121
Smith, Irving G., 210
Smith, Norris Kelly, quoted, 93, 238
Smith and Watson Building, **188**, 270
Smith Brothers' Foundry and Iron Works
   (Smith and Watson), 185
Smiths' Block, 188, 197
Smithson, Robert, 114
South Auditorium Renewal Project, 209, 210,
   212-16, 220, 223; extension, 217

Sovereign Hotel, 57
Spalding Building, 42, 81, 84
Spreckles Building, San Francisco, 42
Stage Terminal, *see* Greyhound Bus Depot
Standard Insurance Building (Standard Plaza),
   10, 208, 211, 224-28, 232
Stanton, Glenn, 154, **155**, 314
State Office Building, 63
Steigerwald Dairy building, 146
Stern, Robert, quoted, 280, 286
Stevens, Wallace, quoted, 238
Stevens and Koon, 152
Stevens Building, 28, 34
Stewart, Allen and McMath, 196
Stewart, Donald J., 72, 84, 195
Stewart, Richardson, Allen and McMath, 196
Stewart and Richardson, 195, 210
Stirling, James, 286
Stoffer house, 297
Stokes, F. M., **150**, 152
Stokes, William R., 30
Stone, B. L., Building, 190
Stone, Edward Durell, 124, 297
Storrs, John, 90, 91, 99, 303
Streamline Moderne style, 10, 47, 109, 123-25,
   175, 295-96
Stubbins, Hugh, 13, 26, 93, 246, 266, **292**,
   295-97, **299**; quoted, 4, 296-97
Stubbins, Hugh, and Associates, 81, 294
Stubblebine, Jo: *The Northwest Architecture of
   Pietro Belluschi*, 314
Studio Building, 62
Sullivan, Louis H., 7, 27, 38-39, 58-60, 96, 122,
   123, 272
Sullivan (Chicago) Style, 7, 28, 35, 38, 39
Sundeleaf, Richard, 10, 88, 89, 96, 116, 124,
   134, 136, 138, 152, **164**, **165**, 170, **174**,
   176, **179**; architectural career, 158-79, 181;
   quoted, 160, 173, 174
Sundeleaf and Hagestad, **177**
Sunriver, 129
Sunshine Dairy building, 139, 155
Sutor, Jennings, house, 92, 93, 97-99, 123
Sutton, Whitney, Aandahl and Fritsch, 20, 53,
   53, **54**, 63, 81, 167, 178
Sutton and Whitney, **5**, **55**, **56**, **57**, **58**, 136,
   161
Swan, Kenneth, house, 89, 115
Sweeney Building, *see* Bishop's House
Swetland Building, 34

Taft Home for the Aged, *see* Hotel Ramapo
Talbot, David, 202
Taliesin West, 262
Tarlow's Building of the Hollywood Furniture
   Store, *see* Director's Furniture Store
Taylor, Hortense van Fridagh, 47
Taylor, James Knox, 32, **33**
Teague, Walter Dorwin, 9, 137, 142, 144;
   quoted, 137, 154
Tegan, Robert F., 47, 48
Tektronix Operation Center, 267

Temple Beth Israel, **49**, 50, **50**, 51, 70
Terminal Sales Building, 51, 77, 145
Terra cotta architecture, 7, 39-41, 288-90, 305,
   316
Terwilliger Boulevard, 35, 220
Teshnor Manor, 67
Texaco station, **138**
Third Church of Christ Scientist, 59
Thomas, John L., 185
Thomas, Julia, quoted, 285
Thomas and Mercier, **169**, 170, 172
Thomas and Thomas, 149
Thompson, Elizabeth, 129
Thompson, Robert, **296**, 297
Thompson, Robert R., 183
Thompson and Vaivoda, 157, 279, **293**, **294**,
   295, 297
Thompson-Reed Building, 186
Three Lions' Bakery, *see* Wegert's Pharmacy
Tilford Building, *see* Fine Arts Building
Todd, John W., house, 123
Tongue Point Naval Air Station, Astoria, Ore.,
   125-26
Tourtollette and Hummel, **17**, 54
Trinity Church, Boston, 30
Trinity Episcopal Church (1854), 185
Tucker-Maxon Oral School, 100, 111-12
Turnbull, James, 185
Turnbull, William, quoted, 264
200 Market Building, 81, **207**, 214, 223
Tzonis, Alex, quoted, 90

Union Pacific Building, **98**
Union Station, **96**, 220-21
Unitarian Society Church, **61**
United States Bancorp Tower, 100, 237, 255,
   263, 264, 279, 297, **301**, 302, **303**, 306, 307,
   307, 308-10
United States Courthouse, 51, 67, 68, **68**, 69,
   95, 154, 244
United States Customs House, 32, **33**, 34
United States Embassy, Vienna, 256
United States National Bank, 189
United States National Bank Building, Portland
   (1917), **13**, 20, **21**, 32, 37, 42-44, **72**, 74, **74**,
   75, 77, 279, 302
United States National Bank Building, Salem, 190
United States National Motor Bank, 224
Universal Plan Service, 155, 157, **161**
University Club, 49, 51, **52**, 53, 124
University of Oregon: Art Museum, 63, 153;
   Deady Hall, 188; Lawrence-designed
   buildings, 153
University of Oregon Medical School (Health
   Sciences University), 153
University of Oregon School of Architecture,
   10, 44, 52, 96, 141, 153, 160, 212
University of Portland: West Hall, 30
University Station Post Office, *see* Francis and
   Hopkins Motor Showroom
Urban Conservation Fund, 197, 220
Urban renewal, 197, 207-10, 212-20, 226, *see
   also* City planning

Van Alen, William, 67
Van Buren, E. W., house, 112, 115
van der Rohe, Ludwig Mies, 99, 109, 195, 209, 228, 237-38, 244; influence on Northwest Regional Style, 97, 115, 116, 210; influence on industrial architecture, 141, 178, 250; quoted, 4, 211, 263
van Fridagh, Paul, 47
Vanport, Ore., 182
Vaughan, Thomas, and George A. McMath: A Century of Portland Architecture, 314-15
Vaughan, Thomas, and Terence O'Donnell: Portland, A Historical Sketch and Guide, 314
Vaughan, Thomas, and Virginia Guest Ferriday: Space Style and Structure: Building in Northwest America, 315-16
Vaughan, Thomas, quoted, 24, 28, 42, 214
Vaughn Street Project, 209
Venturi, Robert, 238
Veterans Administration Hospital addition, 239, 254, **259**, **298**
Vigilance Hook and Ladder Company Number 1 building, 185
Villard, Henry, 13, 19-23, 81, 192, 193, 251, 287
Visitors Information Center, 10, 112, 114-16, 179, 224, 267
Vista House, 34
Vitale, Salvatore, quoted, 263
Volunteers of America Building, see Eastside Mortuary
Von Breton, Harriette, quoted, 11
Von Eckhardt, Wolf, quoted, 249
Von Hoffman, Josef, 157, 271
Von Svoboda, Alexander, 232

Waddle's Restaurant, 88, 109, 181
Wadhams and Company building, 152
Wagner, Otto, 45, 271
Waldo Block, **189**
Waldorf Astoria Hotel, New York, 150
Walker, McGough, Foltz, Lyerla, 256
Walker, Peter, 277
Walker and Gillette, 151
Walstrom, Ralph, 198
Walton, Elisabeth, quoted, 145; see also Potter, Elisabeth Walton
Warden, Carl, quoted, 175
Warner, Olin, 194
Warren and Wetmore, 274
Waterfront Esplanade, 220
Watzek, Aubrey, house, 6, 89, 91, 112-16

passim, 123, 126, 128
Waverley Country Club, 49
Waverly Baby Home, 54-55
Weatherly Building, 53
Webber, Fred T., 170, **171**, 172, **172**
Weber, Kem, 70, 124
WEGROUP, 208, 230, 279
Weiner Store, 179
Weinhard, Henry, Company, 145-46
Weisfield's, **157**
Wells Fargo Building, 7, 35, 40, 41, 81, 145
Wentz, Harry, 10, 90-91, 96, 97, 99, 112, 171
Werner, Carl, quoted, 164
Whidden, William M., 19-24, 34-35, 85, 93, 286
Whidden and Chamberlin, 36
Whidden and Lewis, 6, 7, 20, **21**, **22**, **23**, 24-25, **25**, 26-29, [29], 30, **32**, 33-45, passim, 51, 58, 59, 72-74, 81, 88-89, 94, 97, 134, 144, 210, 212, 244, 255, 274, 280, 288, 291; formation of partnership, 21-23; Lewis and Clark Centennial Exposition buildings, 31-32, 34
Whiskey Jug, see Orange Blossom Jug Restaurant
White, F. Manson, 6, 7, 28-30, 58, 93, 144
White, Stanford, 35
Whitehouse, Church, Newberry and Roehr, 63
Whitehouse, Morris H., 41, 44-45, **49**, **50**, 53, 63, 81, 89, 165, 245; architectural career, 48-51
Whitehouse and Associates, **48**, **68**, 95
Whitehouse and Church, 67, 70
Whitehouse and Fouilhoux, **52**, 124
White Stag neon sign, 146, 280
Whitney, Harrison, 44
Wilcox Building, 28, 34
Willamette Block, 202, 302
Willamette Center, 211, 269-70; Portland General Electric building, 220, 270
Willamette Iron Works, 185
Willcox, Walter R. B., 96, 141, 160
Williams, David Lockheed, 148
Williams, Hubert, 148-49
Williams, Leo Dean, 315
Williams, Stephen Hedders, 185, 191
Williams, Warren H., 6, 90, 93, 144, 145, 182, 185, 187, **188**, 191-98 passim, 224, 270
Williams and Company building, **150**, 152
Williamson, Cliff, Ltd., 167
Wilmsen, H. Robert, 230

Wilson Chambers Mortuary, see Little Chapel of the Chimes Mortuary
Wolff, George, 10, 138, 151, 158
Wolff, Zimmer, Gunsul and Frasca, 104, 197-99, 208, 211, 217, 267; waterfront renewal project, 219
Wolff, Zimmer, Gunsul, Frasca, Ritter, 267
Wolff, Zimmer and Associates, 269
Wolff and Phillips, 156, 158, 170, 172
Wolff and Zimmer, 267, 268
Wollflin, Heinrich, 115
Woodbury and Company warehouse, 88, 166, 173-74, **174**, 176, 178, 179
Woods, Lebbeus, quoted, 239
Woolworth Building, New York, 42
Works Projects Administration, 125
Wren, Sir Christopher, 238
Wright, Frank Lloyd, 59, 60, 95, 99, 114, 115, 121-26 passim, 142, 160, 195, 265, 298; correspondence with Belluschi, 14-15, **15**, 105-106; quoted, 15, 128, 261-62
Wright, Olgivanna Lloyd, 262
Wright, Russell, 154

Yamhill Historic District, 193, 194, 220, 244, 305
Yamhill Market, 194
Yeon, John, 10, 55, 89-91, 96, 97, 99, 121, 123, 126, 128, 134, 159, 175, 179, 224, 267, 303; architectural career, 112-16, 120; Neahkahnie highway design, 113-14
Yeon, John B., 34, 41, 113
Yeon, Mrs. John B., 113, 114
Yeon Building, 7, 41-42, 81, 84, 134, 255
Yorke, F.R.S., 294

Zaik, Saul, 90, 91, 99, 303
Zehntbauer, Carl, 162
Zehntbauer, Roy, 162
Zell, Martin, 70
Zell Brothers Jewelers building, 63, **64**
Zevi, Bruno, quoted, 91, 94, 99-103 passim, 263, 275-77, 302
Zig Zag Moderne style, 142-43, 171-72
Zimmer, Norman, quoted, 269
Zimmer Gunsul Frasca (ZGF), 6, 7, 16, 40, 88, 89, 93, 211, 239, 240, 248, 250, **259**, 262, 264-268, **268**, 269-273, **273**, 274-276, **276**, 277, **277**, 278-280 passim, 285, 293, 294, **298**; historic restoration work, 68, 201, 244; Justice Center, 187, 223, **244**, 246, 252, 254-58 passim, 264
Zion Lutheran Church, 92, 101-104, 158

Colophon

The typefaces for the text and titling of *Frozen Music*, mirror the vitality of Portland's architecture—the melding of modern and classical to create a pleasing whole. The clean, stream-lined curves of Futura, the display face, perfectly matches the graceful yet utilitarian architecture of recent times. Futura is a sans serif face (created by Paul Renner, a German designer, in the late 1920s) recognizable by its splayed M, a Q with a straight tail starting inside the bowl, and a lower case u with the same design as the uppercase.

The simple lines of Futura are balanced by the elegant beauty of Perpetua, the face used for text and captions. The most popular roman face produced by English type designer Eric Gill, Perpetua is characterized by small serifs, sharply cut and horizontal. Perpetua was first used in a printed translation of *The Passion of Perpetua and Felicity*. The roman face acquired the name Perpetua while the italic was given the name Felicity. G & S Typesetters of Austin, Texas set the text of *Frozen Music*. Display typesetting was provided by Paul O. Giesey/AdCrafters and the captions were supplied by Irish Setter, both Portland firms.

Dynagraphics, Inc. of Portland printed this volume on 80 lb. Condat Gloss. All color separations were supplied by Portland Prep Center, Inc. The binding is by Lincoln & Allen Company of Portland, Oregon. The watercolor cityscape featured on the dust jacket and title page was painted by Henk Pander, a Portland artist.

About the Authors

Gideon Bosker is the author of six books on a variety of subjects, a former syndicated columnist for Universal Press Syndicate and a screenwriter. As a photographer, he has had one-man exhibitions of architectural photographs at the Oregon Historical Society and the Architecture Gallery. Mr. Bosker's articles and photographs on architecture, fashion and the history of photography have appeared in a number of publications including *American Photographer*, *Vanity Fair*, *Interview*, *Willamette Week* and the *Oregonian*. He is currently contributing editor to *Arts + Architecture* magazine.

Lena Lencek, associate professor at Reed College, took her degrees in Slavic Languages and Literature from Barnard College and Harvard University, where she specialized in twentieth-century movements in literary modernism and avant-garde art. In 1982 she was decorated by the State Council of the National Republic of Bulgaria for her published translations of Bulgarian poetry. Other translations, articles, illustrations and photographs by Ms. Lencek have appeared in *Arts + Architecture, Willamette Week,* the *Oregonian* and the American and East European academic journals. She is on the editorial advisory board of *Arts + Architecture* magazine.

Pietro Belluschi has designed or been a design consultant for more than two thousand architectural works world-wide. A pioneer of the Northwest Regional style, he served as dean of the School of Architecture at MIT from 1950 to 1965. In 1974, Mr. Belluschi received the highly coveted AIA Gold Medal in architecture.

George A. McMath is the co-author of *A Century of Portland Architecture*. Senior partner in the firm Allen, McMath and Hawkins, Mr. McMath is one of Portland's most influential and widely published architectural historians. His award-winning firm has participated in the design of more than fifty of Portland's landmark preservation projects.